89443

RACE AND ETHNICITY

An Anthropological Focus
on the United States and the World

edited by

RAYMOND SCUPIN

Lindenwood University

Upper Saddle River, New Jersey 07458

Library of Congress Cataloging-in-Publication Data

Race and ethnicity: an anthropological focus on the United States and the world/edited
by Raymond Scupin.–1st ed.
    p. cm.
    Includes bibliographical references.
    ISBN 0–13–060689–8
    1. Ethnicity–United States.   2. United States–Race relations.   3. United States–Ethnic
relations.   4. Ethnicity.   5. Race relations.   6. Ethnic relations.   7.
Anthropology–Philosophy.   I. Scupin, Raymond.

E184.A1 R237 2003
305.8′00973–dc21   2001052359

AVP, Publisher: Nancy Roberts
Managing Editor: Sharon Chambliss
Project Manager: Joan Stone
Cover Director: Jayne Conte
Cover Design: Bruce Kenselaar

Cover Photo: Stephan Daigle/Stock Illustration
    Source, Inc.
Director of Marketing: Beth Mejia
Marketing Assistant: Anne Marie Fritzky
Prepress and Manufacturing Buyer: Ben Smith

This book was set in 10/12 Baskerville by ElectraGraphics
and was printed and bound by RR Donnelley & Sons Company.
The cover was printed by Phoenix Color Corp.
Credits appear on p. 471, which constitutes a continuation of the copyright page.

© 2003 by Pearson Education, Inc.
Upper Saddle River, New Jersey 07458

Printed in the United States of America

10   9   8   7   6   5   4   3   2   1

ISBN 0-13-060689-8

Pearson Education LTD., London
Pearson Education Australia PTY, Limited, Sydney
Pearson Education Singapore, Pte. Ltd
Pearson Education North Asia Ltd, Hong Kong
Pearson Education Canada, Ltd, Toronto
Pearson Educación de Mexico, S.A. de C.V.
Pearson Education–Japan, Tokyo
Pearson Education Malaysia, Pte. Ltd
Pearson Education, Upper Saddle River, New Jersey

CONTENTS

iii

PREFACE

Ethnic unrest and tension are prevalent in the contemporary world. Newspapers and television news are rife with stories about ethnic violence among the peoples of the former Soviet Union and Eastern Europe, Africa, Sri Lanka, India, Ireland, the Middle East, and the United States. Thus, as globalization rapidly expands and both undermines and strengthens ethnic and national identities, an understanding of race and of ethnicity issues becomes more pertinent.

This book is an introductory survey of the basic concepts and research in the field of anthropology on race and ethnicity in the United States and throughout the world. Anthropologists have been doing research on race and ethnicity for more than a hundred years and have developed a profound understanding of race and ethnicity issues. However, these anthropological insights have not been communicated widely. Race and ethnicity issues have had immense effects on both U.S. and global political trends and have created innumerable tensions and misunderstandings among different groups. An anthropological understanding of race and ethnicity has clarified some of these misconceptions and may help relieve some of these tensions.

One of the major objectives of anthropology is to comprehend both the differences and the similarities among different groups of humans throughout the world. A major lesson derived from anthropological research is that as different groups learn about each other's cultural values, norms, behaviors, goals, and aspirations, the less likely they are to maintain rigid stereotypes and misconceptions about one another. Thus, one of the practical results of anthropological research is a reduction in racism, ethnocentrism, and animosities and tensions. As students learn to discern what anthropologists have learned about race and ethnicity issues, they are more likely to be able to adjust and become more productive citizens in an increasing multicultural and globally integrated world. A comprehensive understanding of race and ethnicity issues is a fundamental aspect of a well-rounded liberal arts education.

This text is a collection of state-of-the-art but highly readable essays for undergraduate students. Part I deals with the basic concepts of race and ethnicity. Chapter 1 introduces the discipline of anthropology to students who may have never had a course in anthropology. Chapter 2 focuses on the concept of race, and what anthropologists have learned about "race" based on paleoanthropological, archaeological, population genetics, and other related research for the past hundred years or so. The concept of race has been subject to extensive investigations by both physical and cultural anthropologists, and these research findings need to be communicated to the student in a comprehensible manner. Chapter 3 is devoted to the history of "scientific" racialism and how it emerged as a means of promoting simplistic understandings of race and culture, which, in turn, have fostered forms of racism and misunderstandings throughout the world. One of the major lessons that has emerged from anthropological research, beginning with Franz Boas, is that culture is separate from biology or so-called "racial" characteristics. Students need to have a fundamental understanding of this important finding. Chapter 4 addresses the various features that are expressions of ethnicity or ethnic boundary markers, such as religion or linguistic differences. This chapter discusses concepts and theories of assimilation, pluralism, prejudice, discrimination, primordialist and circumstantialist approaches, nationalism and identity politics, and other basic concepts and theories for understanding race and ethnicity issues. Chapter 5 is an essay on the research of psychological anthropologists and others who have been investigating the universality or naturalism of ethnicity and ethnocentrism. This chapter is provocative and will result in a great deal of critical thinking for the undergraduate student.

Part II of the text addresses the patterns of race and ethnic relations in the United States based on anthropological research. An introductory essay, Chapter 6, delineates the basic patterns of race and ethnicity established by the Anglo and "white" ethnic groups based on immigration patterns and assimilation processes. This chapter includes some basic material highlighting the influence of WASP, or Anglo American, culture that established definitive contours of race and ethnic relations in the United States. Following are chapters (7–12) on American Indians, African Americans, Jewish Americans, Hispanic Americans/Latinos, Asian Americans, and Arab Americans, written by anthropologists who did ethnographic research among these ethnic groups. This part of the text fulfills the need to have a basic understanding of various ethnic groups in an increasingly multicultural U.S. society.

Part III is globally focused. Its chapters cover race and ethnic relations in Latin America and the Caribbean, Africa, the Middle East, Asia, the Pacific Islands, Europe, and Canada—all written by anthropologists who have ethnographic research experience in these different regions of the world. They draw on local-level ethnic processes to illustrate general macro-level tendencies. Chapter 13, on Latin America and the Caribbean, focuses on how colonialism has influenced ethnic relations among Indians, Spanish, Portuguese, and African peoples. The chapter (14) on Africa describes how different patterns of colonialism have affected race and ethnic relations in various regions of the continent. The chapter discusses apartheid in South Africa, as well as the tragic episodes of ethnic conflict and genocide in Rwanda. The Middle East is the subject of Chapter 15, which discusses the internal ethnic tensions and differences within Middle Eastern societies. Chapter 16, on Asia, includes discussions of race and ethnicity in South Asia (India and Sri Lanka), East Asia (China and Japan), and Southeast Asia (Thailand and Malaysia). The Pacific Islands chapter (17) discusses various patterns of colonialism and their consequences for ethnic relations throughout Oceania, including recent ethnic trends in Fiji and

Hawaii. Chapter 18, on Europe, includes a general discussion of nationalism and identity, as well as the ethnic conflicts in the Balkans and Ireland. Chapter 19 focuses on Canada and the French-Anglo conflict and how ethnic patterns differ from those in the United States. A final, brief chapter concentrates on the United States and other ethnic trends and tendencies that are influenced by globalization. In particular, this chapter critically examines the controversial thesis of Samuel Huntington's *Clash of Civilization* approach in understanding ethnic and cultural trends. The local-level ethnographic fieldwork that anthropologists have done on ethnic trends throughout the world tends to demonstrate that global theses such as those of Huntington and other political theorists are not adequate in explaining race and ethnic issues.

The editor would like to thank all of the contributors, who provided excellent chapters representing the most recent anthropological research on the various aspects of race and ethnicity. These contributors have also reviewed and suggested revisions for the chapters written by the editor. The editor, and the contributors, would also like to thank Bernard Bernier, University of Montreal; John J. Bukowczyk, Wayne State University; Martin Cohen, California State University, Fullerton; Pamela A. DeVoe, St. Louis Community College, Meramec; Francisco Gil-White, University of Pennsylvania; Dru Gladney, University of Hawaii, Manoa; Phillip Hamilton, Lindenwood University; Robert M. Hayden, University of Pittsburgh; Sharlotte Neely, Northern Kentucky University; Mary O'Connor, University of California, Santa Barbara; Susana Sawyer, University of California, Davis; Paul Shankman, University of Colorado, Boulder; Robert Sussman, Washington University; and William C. Young, American Anthropological Association, for reviewing the chapters.

We would also like to thank Sharon Chambliss, managing editor at Prentice Hall, for her organization and efforts during the manuscript review. Our thanks go to Nancy Roberts, Publisher for Social Science, for recommending this textbook for publication.

Ray Scupin

1

THE ANTHROPOLOGY OF RACE AND ETHNICITY

Raymond Scupin

Lindenwood University

In 1999, 21-year-old Benjamin Smith spent the July 4th weekend cruising in his car in Chicago and central Indiana areas shooting at African Americans, Orthodox Jews, and Asians. In this three-day shooting spree two were killed and nine were wounded before Smith shot and killed himself during a police chase. The African American killed was Rick Birdsong, a former basketball coach at Northwestern University. He was jogging with his children when he was shot in the back. Won Joined Soon, a Korean graduate student at Indiana University, was killed outside of a Korean church.

Benjamin Smith was a former member of the World Church of the Creator, which is currently led by Matt Hale of East Peoria, Illinois. Hale refers to himself as Pontifus Maximus and teaches that only white Anglo-Saxons are true human beings, descendants of Adam and Eve. Jews are believed to be illegitimate offspring of Eve and Satan, and African Americans and other people of color are descendants of inferior non-Adamite anthropoids called "mud people." The church believes that the United States should be "cleansed" of all Jews and nonwhites.

The church's Web site features a discussion of the mental inferiority of African Americans, with a reference to Canadian psychologist Philippe Rushton's "scientific" research confirming this view.

Although groups such as the World Church of the Creator are small, with only a few thousand members, their influence seems to be on the rise. For many years, most anthropologists and other social scientists believed that racism and ethnic conflict were going to decline. Unfortunately, however, more extremist racist and ethnic groups have emerged in many parts of the world within the past decade. For example, in the former East Germany there has been a rise of a neo-Nazi movement among German youth who resent the immigration of nonwhites into their society. Recently, ethnic extremism among the Hutu and Tutsi peoples in Central Africa has resulted in tragic genocidal policies. Conflicts among Serbs, Croatians, and Bosnians in Yugoslavia, Tamils and Sinhalese in Sri Lanka, Jews and Arabs in Israel, and so-called "white Europeans" and "people of color" in the United States are ongoing. Everywhere one looks ethnic conflicts seem to be

1

emerging worldwide. Although the causes of these conflicts are very complex, ethnic and race conflicts remain a continuing global problem in the twenty-first century.

Currently, we live in societies that are becoming more globalized, with more extensive contact among peoples of different ethnic backgrounds and cultures. Globalization refers to the expansion and interlinking of the world's economy through the spread of market capitalism, communications technology, and industrialization and their consequences. One of the results of globalization has been the transfer of capital, technology, labor, and media throughout the world. Global migration trends have been radically transformed since the 1950s. Immigration from Latin America and the Caribbean, Asia, Africa, and the Middle East—the so-called Third World—to the industrial societies of Europe, the United States, Australia, and Canada has increased substantially. For example, England and France have growing numbers of immigrants from their former colonies in Africa and Asia. Furthermore, the societies in the Third World are also being transformed by new trends in immigration. Refugees and migrants are becoming increasingly mobile throughout the world. Societies that may have been very homogeneous or ethnically similar in the past are now facing questions about their increasing multicultural and multiethnic differences.

As we will see in later chapters, U.S. society in the nineteenth and early twentieth centuries faced similar issues. Immigrants flowed into the United States from many areas of the world. Currently, the United States is again encountering the challenge of multiculturalism. For example, a typical elementary school in Los Angeles may have as many as 20 different native languages spoken by members of the school population. In 2000 California became the first U.S. state where the white ethnic population became a minority. Due to the increase of Hispanic and Asian populations, the white ethnic population was 49.9 percent. Event calendars in daily newspapers announce ethnic festivals in major U.S. cities that originated in many nations. All of these changes have resulted in some reservations regarding the new ethnic patterns and multiculturalism in the United States. In 1991, the distinguished historian Arthur Schlesinger wrote a book entitled *The Disuniting of America,* which argued that ethnic and racial separatism was the major obstacle for a truly integrated multicultural society in U.S. society. Schlesinger believes that extreme versions of multicultural education and what he terms the "cult of ethnicity" are tearing apart the U.S. social and political fabric. He suggests that the growing emphasis on multicultural heritage exalts racial and ethnic pride at the expense of social and political cohesion. On the other hand, other scholars, such as Nathan Glazer in his book *We Are All Multiculturalists Now,* argue that all children should be taught mutual tolerance and respect for all of the various ethnic groups in U.S. society.

As societies become more multicultural and multiethnic, they confront new challenges. In many circumstances, ethnic groups may be in competition with each other over political and economic resources. In other cases, they may be at odds over religious or other cultural differences. Conversely, some people are benefiting from the multicultural trends in their society by learning from one another's cultures, thereby discovering that multicultural environments can enrich one's experience and can be extremely rewarding.

In any case, many people are seeking answers to basic questions regarding these new changes in race and ethnic trends within their societies in the twenty-first century. What are the reasons for these continuing race and ethnic conflicts and problems? Do the claims of people like Matt Hale and the World Church about superior and inferior racial groups have any scientific validity? What are the significant distinctions among the races? What is the difference between race and ethnicity? What is the basis of one's ethnic identity? Why do some societies and countries have less race and ethnic conflict than others? Why has there been a recent increase in racial and ethnic conflict around the globe? Have these racial and ethnic conflicts always existed? Under what conditions do increases in race and ethnic conflict occur? Under what societal conditions do race and ethnic prejudice and discrimination develop? In what interracial and interethnic situations can race and ethnic prejudice be reduced? Under what conditions do different ethnic groups live peaceably together and benefit from each other's experience?

Anthropologists are currently engaged in major research efforts in an attempt to answer some of these questions. In fact, anthropology as a discipline has an intimate acquaintanceship with questions about race and ethnicity issues. Anthropology was the first field devoted to systematic scientific investigations into questions about race and ethnicity. These questions persist as one of the fundamental priorities within the research efforts of contemporary anthropologists.

This textbook will cover some of the most important research on race and ethnicity by anthropologists. But, first, we will discuss the interrelationship between these questions about race and ethnicity and the discipline of anthropology.

ANTHROPOLOGY: THE FOUR FIELDS AND RACE AND ETHNICITY ISSUES

The word *anthropology* stems from the Greek words *anthropo,* meaning "human beings" or "humankind," and *logia,* translated as "knowledge of" or "the study of." Thus, we can define anthropology as the systematic study of humankind. The field of anthropology emerged in Western society in an attempt to understand non-Western peoples. Europeans, including Christopher Columbus, had been exploring and colonizing the world since the fifteenth century. They had encounters with non-Western peoples in the Americas, Africa, the Middle East, and Asia. Various European travelers, missionaries, and government officials had described some of

these non-Western societies, cultures, and races. By the nineteenth century, anthropology had developed into the primary discipline and science for understanding these non-Western societies, races, and cultures. The major questions that these early nineteenth-century anthropologists grappled with had to do with the basic differences and similarities of human societies, cultures, and races throughout the world.

The predominant explanation that nineteenth-century anthropologists offered to explain the differences and similarities among human societies, cultures, and races became known as *unilineal evolution.* Charles Darwin had developed his theory regarding the evolution of life in 1859, with the publication of his book *The Origin of the Species.* Many anthropologists of the nineteenth century were influenced by Darwin's thesis, and attempted to apply these evolutionary concepts to the study of human societies, cultures, and races. These early anthropologists took the descriptions of early historians, archaeologists, classical scholars, travelers, missionaries, and colonial officials for their basic data. Based on these data, they proposed that all societies and cultures had developed from early, original "savage" stages through a stage of "barbarianism," and eventually some evolved into "civilized" stages. Thus, these early anthropologists developed models of the stages of humankind's universal history using the concept of unilineal evolution.[1] They constructed a model of a hierarchy of societies that could be ranked from savage to civilized based on differences in society, culture, technology, and race.

Since the nineteenth century, anthropology as a field has continued its research efforts of different societies, cultures, and "races." However, beginning in the twentieth century, many of the ideas of nineteenth-century theorists were thoroughly criticized and debunked through systematic and scientific research techniques. The efforts of nineteenth-century anthropologists need to be understood within their own historical setting. These early anthropologists did not have a very precise understanding of the concept of "culture," nor did they comprehend the roles of genetics and heredity. The development of a more thorough concept of culture and a scientific understanding of heredity and genetics did not develop until the twentieth century. Because of their limited understanding of culture and heredity, they labored under many misconceptions about non-Western societies, cultures, and races. One of the basic underlying assumptions was that their own society and culture were superior to those of any other. This is an example of what is known as *ethnocentrism*, the belief that one's own society and culture are superior to any other. In addition, during the nineteenth century most of these early anthropologists were convinced that their own so-called "race" was superior to that of any other "race." This is known as *racism*, the belief that there are distinctive biological "races" and that one can rank and categorize superior and inferior biological "races" within the human species.

It was only after twentieth-century anthropologists absorbed the new findings of genetics and heredity, developed a more sophisticated comprehension of the concept of culture, and had a better appreciation of concepts of "race" and "ethnicity" that these earlier views could be criticized exhaustively. One of the major anthropological projects that critiqued these early views was associated with the efforts of Franz Boas (1858–1942). Boas had been born, educated, and trained in physics in Germany. Later he became interested in geography and culture and did research among the Eskimo in the Canadian Arctic. Through these experiences he turned to the study of anthropology, immigrated to the United States, and taught for many years at Columbia University. While at Columbia, Boas and his students carried out extensive research in physical anthropology, archaeology, linguistics, and cultural anthropology (or ethnology), providing the contemporary foundations for the systematic investigation of such topics as race, culture, and ethnicity (Degler 1991; Stocking

1968). One of the primary aspects of research that Boas emphasized was the "fieldwork" experience in anthropology. Instead of speculating on various theories about the evolution of culture based on written materials, anthropologists had to go into the "field" and do empirical research among the people in different societies.

In the United States, Boas's research activities developed into what has become known as the "four-field approach" within anthropology. Most U.S. anthropology programs feature four subdisciplines, or subfields, that bridge the natural sciences, the social sciences, and the humanities. These four subdisciplines—physical anthropology, archaeology, linguistic anthropology, and ethnology—give anthropologists a broad, holistic approach to the study of humanity through space and time. In addition, all four of these fields have enabled contemporary anthropologists to contribute significantly toward the study of race and ethnicity. Though these four subfields demarcate the fields within which most anthropological research is conducted, we need to emphasize that within these four fields anthropologists draw on the findings of many other disciplines, such as biology, history, psychology, economics, sociology, and political science to examine race and ethnic relations. These four fields, however, offer anthropologists a unique perspective for assessing questions of race and ethnicity.

Physical Anthropology

Physical anthropology (or biological anthropology) is the branch of anthropology most closely related to the natural sciences. Physical anthropologists conduct research in two major areas: human evolution and human variation. The majority of physical anthropologists focus on human evolution. Some investigate fossils, the preserved remains of bones and living materials from earlier periods, to reconstruct the evolution and anatomical characteristics of early human ancestors. The study of human evolution through analysis of fossils is called *paleoanthropology* (the prefix *paleo* means "old" or "prehistoric"). Paleoanthropologists use a variety of sophisticated scientific techniques to date, classify, and compare fossil bones in order to determine the links between modern humans and their biological ancestors. For example, paleoanthropologists are studying the relationship of early populations of *Homo erectus* and Neandertals to determine their precise connections with modern humans.

As we will see in Chapter 2, on race, paleoanthropologists have been doing basic research on the evolution of physical characteristics of ancestral populations in all parts of the world. Paleoanthropologists have developed elaborate techniques to measure observable physical characteristics of humans based on their fossil remains, primarily fossil bones and teeth. Early paleoanthropologists tried to establish clear-cut criteria for distinguishing the evolution of various "races" in different regions of the world. However, modern paleoanthropologists have concluded that these early attempts were based on simplistic categories of racial differences. Today, paleoanthropologists have much more sophisticated methods and techniques for differentiating ancestral human populations, and they exercise extreme caution when evaluating the evolution of different races.

Another group of physical anthropologists focuses their research on the range of physical variation within and among different "modern" human populations. These physical anthropologists study human variation by measuring physical characteristics such as body size, by comparing blood types, and by examining differences in skin color or hair texture. *Human osteology* is the particular area of specialization within physical anthropology dealing with the comparative study of the human skeleton and teeth. Physical anthropologists are also interested in evaluating how disparate physical characteristics reflect evolutionary adaptations to different environmental conditions, thus shedding light on why human populations vary. Noting how specific physical traits have enabled these populations to adapt to different geographic environments, these anthropologists reveal how human populations have developed. Early physical anthropologists wanted to use biological attributes to classify various living populations throughout the world into distinctive "races." Eventually, however, physical anthropologists developed advanced research techniques and methods that led to the abandonment of simplistic constructions of "race" among human populations. As physical anthropologists have learned more about physical variation among human populations, they became more aware of how difficult it was to classify humans into distinguishable "racial" populations. They discovered that traditional biological characteristics such as skin color did not necessarily correlate with other physical characteristics that demarcate one "race" from another. In fact, the vast majority of anthropologists have rejected the concept of "race" as a useful scientific concept. Thus, today, physical anthropologists have learned to be extremely careful with their assessment procedures in attempting to study biological characteristics and classifications among human populations.

An increasingly important area of research for some physical anthropologists is genetics, the study of the biological "blueprints" that dictate the inheritance of physical characteristics. Research on genetics examines a wide variety of questions. It has, for example, been important in identifying the genetic sources of some diseases such as sickle cell anemia, cystic fibrosis, and Tay-Sachs disease. Genetics has also become an increasingly important complement to paleoanthropological research. Through the study of the genetic makeup of modern humans, geneticists have been working on calculating the genetic distance among modern humans, thus providing a possible means of inferring evolutionary relationships within the species. For example, genetic studies have been used to determine the physical and evolutionary connections between Native American Indians and Asian peoples.

Archaeology

Through *archaeology,* the branch of anthropology that seeks out and examines the artifacts of past societies, we learn much about the lifestyles, history, and evolution of those societies. *Artifacts,* the material remains of former societies, provide tangible clues to the lifestyle, environments, and political economies of extinct societies. Some archaeologists investigate past societies that did not have written documents through which to leave a record of their past. Known as *prehistoric archaeologists,* these researchers study the artifacts of groups such as Native Americans to understand how these people lived. Other archaeologists, called *classical archaeologists,* conduct research on ancient civilizations such as Egyptian, Greek, and Roman, in collaboration with historians and linguists. Another group of archaeologists, known as *historical archaeologists,* pursue research with historians and investigate the artifacts of societies of the more recent past. For example, many historical archaeologists are probing the remains of plantations in the southern United States to gain an understanding of the lifestyles of slaves and slave owners during the nineteenth century.

Only after intensive analysis do archaeologists cautiously interpret the data they have collected and begin to generalize about a past society. Unlike the glorified adventures of fictional archaeologists, the real-world field of archaeology thrives on the intellectually challenging adventure of careful, systematic, detail-oriented scientific research that enhances our understanding of past societies.

Modern archaeologists have developed a greater in-depth understanding of past societies in various parts of the world, and have shown how environmental circumstances and prehistoric or historic conditions have influenced the societal development of human populations in different regions. They have illuminated through careful research how nineteenth-century archaeologists were misled by their simplistic categorizations, and racist and ethnocentric beliefs, in assessing the societal developments of other cultures. Thus, recent archaeological research has refuted racist and ethnocentric views about non-European or non-Western societies.

Linguistic Anthropology

Linguistics, the study of language, has a long history that dovetails with the discipline of philosophy, but it is also one of the integral subfields of anthropology. *Linguistic anthropology* focuses on the relationship between language and culture, how language is used within society, and how the human brain acquires and uses language. Franz Boas was the founder of linguistic anthropology in North America, and his pioneering linguistic research revolutionized the study of language, culture, and ethnicity.

As do researchers in other fields within anthropology, linguistic anthropologists seek to discover the ways in which languages are different from each other as well as how they are similar. Two wide-ranging areas of research in linguistic anthropology are *structural linguistics* and *historical linguistics.* Structural linguistics explores how language works. Structural linguists compare grammatical patterns and other linguistic elements to learn how contemporary languages mirror and differ from one another. Structural linguistics has uncovered some intriguing relationships between language and thought patterns among different groups of people. Do people who speak different languages with different grammatical structures think and perceive the world differently from each other? For instance, do native Chinese speakers think or view the world and life experiences differently from native English speakers? This is just one of the questions that structural linguists attempt to answer. Such questions bear on the relationship among language, culture, and ethnicity.

Linguistic anthropologists also examine the connections between language and social behavior in different cultures. This specialty, called *sociolinguistics,* focuses on both how language is used to define social groups and how belonging to particular groups leads to specialized language use. For example, a number of linguists have been doing research on Ebonics, a distinctive variety of American English spoken by some African Americans. The term *Ebonics* is derived from the words "ebony" and "phonics," meaning "black speech sounds" (Rickford 1997). These linguistic anthropologists find that Ebonics is no more a lazy form of English than Italian is a lazy form of Latin. Instead, Ebonics is a different language with systematically ordered grammar and pronunciation usages. Linguistic research such as this has helped to undo racist and ethnocentric assumptions about various ethnic minorities.

Another area of research of interest to linguistic anthropologists is historical linguistics. *Historical linguistics* concentrates on the comparison and classification of different languages to discern their historical links. By examining and analyzing grammatical structures and sounds of languages, researchers are able to discover rules for how languages change over time, as well as which languages are related to each other historically. This type of historical linguistic research is particularly useful in tracing the migration routes of various groups through time, confirming archaeological and paleoanthropological data gathered independently. For example, historical linguistics has been used to confirm the migration of the Navajo Native American Indians from Canada down into the southwest region of the United States.

Ethnology

Ethnology, more popularly known as *cultural anthropology,* is the subfield of anthropology that examines contemporary societies. Contemporary ethnologists do fieldwork in all parts of the world, from the tropical rain forests of Africa and Latin America to the Arctic regions of Canada, from the deserts of the Middle East to the urban areas of China. Until recently, most ethnologists conducted research on non-Western or remote cultures in Africa, Asia, the Middle East, Latin America, and the Pacific Islands, and on the Native American populations in the United States. Today, however, many anthropologists are doing research on their own cultures in order to gain a better understanding of their institutions and cultural values. In fact, as will be seen in chapters in Part II, which focuses on the United States, ethnographers have been actively engaged in research on ethnic groups in the United States for decades.

Cultural anthropologists, or ethnologists, use a unique research strategy in conducting their fieldwork in different settings. Unlike the early nineteenth-century "armchair" anthropologists, contemporary ethnologists live for an extended amount of time within the societies that they study. The American Franz Boas and the Polish-born British Bronislaw Malinowski are two examples of those who used this important research strategy in twentieth-century anthropology. They knew that the early studies relied too heavily on superficial, nonquantifiable descriptions and comparisons from classical scholars, travelers, missionaries, and colonial government officials.

Boas and Malinowski promoted and institutionalized the practice of doing intensive fieldwork in the various societies around the world—a research strategy called *participant observation,* which involves learning the language and culture of the group being studied by participating in the group's daily activities. Through this intensive participation, the ethnologist becomes deeply familiar with the group and can understand and explain the society and culture of the group as an insider. Presently, many anthropologists use the term *etic* to refer to the description of the culture by the anthropologist, and *emic* to refer to the natives' point of view of their culture.[2]

The results of the fieldwork of the ethnologist are written up as an *ethnography,* a description of a society. The typical ethnography describes the environmental setting, economic patterns, social organization, political system, and religious rituals and beliefs of the society under study. However, some ethnographies concentrate on particular areas such as religious beliefs and practices, whereas others may focus on environmental conditions or political institutions. The description of a society is based on what anthropologists call *ethnographic data.* The gathering of ethnographic data in a systematic manner is the specific research goal of the ethnologist or cultural anthropologist. Some anthropologists use ethnographic data to do comparative cross-cultural studies of different societies. These comparative studies are extremely important in discovering both differences and similarities among people throughout the world—one of the major objectives of the anthropological project.

Most contemporary cultural anthropologists do their research in a much more different manner than Boas or Malinowski did in the beginning of the twentieth century. Today, in the twenty-first century, many of the so-called natives with whom ethnographers interact are combining their traditional understanding of their own culture with formal education, and some are even choosing to become anthropologists themselves. Thus, cultural anthropologists are becoming more like colleagues with the people they are studying, collaborating on research projects together. Instead of the "lone ranger" cultural anthropologist doing research alone on an island among isolated tribal populations, contemporary anthropologists are more likely to reside in urban areas and work with teams of people from the native population to comprehend the effects of globalization and related processes and change within local regions of the world. And, as we will see in this text, many present-day cultural anthropologists are working with ethnic groups within their own society and collaborating on research projects to gain insights into ethnic inter-action and cultural change within multicultural societies.

Most U.S. anthropologists are exposed to all four subfields of anthropology in their education. Because of all the research being done in these different fields, however, with more than three hundred journals and hundreds of books published every year dealing with anthropological research, no one individual can keep abreast of all the developments across the discipline's full spectrum. Consequently, anthropologists usually specialize in one of the four subfields. Though the four-field approach tends to be an ideal for anthropology in this age of proliferating information and research data, the research in these different disciplines has been important in establishing basic conclusions regarding race, culture, and ethnicity.

As emphasized earlier, anthropology does not limit itself to its own four subfields to realize its research agenda. Although it stands as a distinct discipline, anthropology is interdisciplinary and has strong links to other fields of study. Cultural anthropology, for instance, is closely related to the fields of history, cultural studies, and sociology. In the past, cultural anthropologists examined traditional, whereas sociologists focused on modern societies. Today cultural anthropologists and sociologists explore many of the same societies using similar research approaches. For example, both rely on statistical and nonstatistical data whenever appropriate in their studies of different types of societies. In later chapters, we will see how basic sociological research has informed ethnographic studies of ethnicity. A recent, allied field that has influenced anthropology is cultural studies, which combines a number of disciplines with the concept of culture to do research on a number of topics related to ethnic and race relations. Likewise, anthropology dovetails considerably with the field of history, which, like anthropology, encompasses a broad range of events. Studies of ethnicity could not be conducted without a comprehensive historical perspective. These fields, as well as others, which will become evident throughout this textbook, have contributed to the anthropological perspective on race and ethnic relations.

Through the four subfields and the interdisciplinary approach, anthropologists have emphasized both a *holistic* and a *global* perspective. The holistic and global perspectives enable anthropologists to consider the biological, environmental, psychological, economic, historical, social, and cultural conditions of humans at all times and in all places. Anthropologists do not limit themselves to understanding a particular ethnic group or set of societies but, rather, they attempt to demonstrate the interconnections among different societies. This combined holistic and global perspective is used throughout this text to demonstrate how different ethnic groups have developed unique interrelationships and patterns throughout the world.

In this age of rapid communication, worldwide travel, and increasing economic interconnections, young people preparing for careers in the twenty-first century must recognize and be able to deal with the cultural and ethnic differences that exist among peoples while at the same time also understanding the fundamental similarities that make us all distinctly human. In this age of cultural diversity and increasing internationalization, sustaining this dual perception, of underlying similar human characteristics and outward cultural differences, has both practical and moral benefits. Although nationalistic, ethnic, and racial bigotry are rife in many parts of the world, our continuing survival and successful adaptation depend on greater mutual understanding and cooperation. Anthropology promotes a cross-cultural perspective that allows us to see ourselves as part of one human family in the midst of tremendous diversity. Our society needs citizens that have skills in empathy, tolerance of others, and an understanding of a complex interlocking world. We need world citizens who can function in inescapably multicultural and multinational environments to work cooperatively and become productive citizens, as well as helping to solve humanity's pressing problems of bigotry, poverty, and violence.

NOTES

1. The British Edward B. Tylor (1832–1917) is one of the best known nineteenth-century anthropologists. Tylor's major anthropological and theoretical works are *Primitive Culture,* 2 vol. (volume 2 is titled *Religion in Primitive Culture,* part II of *Primitive Culture,* Harper Torchbooks, 1871/1958); *Researches into the Early History of Mankind and the Development of Civilization* (John Murray, 1881); and *Anthropology: An Introduction to the Study of Man* (D. Appleton, 1881/1898). The other well-known nineteenth-century anthropologist is the American Lewis Henry Morgan (1818–81). Morgan did an early anthropological work entitled *League of the Ho-De-No-Sau-Nee or Iroquois* (2 vols., New York), a detailed description of one group of Seneca Indians living in upstate New York. Morgan's later work included a cross-cultural analysis text called *Ancient Society* (1877), which had an enormous influence on nineteenth-century thought.

2. The terms *etic* and *emic* are derived from the words "phonetic" and "phonemic," as used in linguistics. Phonetics refers to the different types of sound units in languages. Thus, there is an International Phonetic Alphabet used to designate various sound units of languages throughout the world. In contrast, a phoneme is a sound unit that is understood to have a meaning within a particular language. Phonemics refers to the sound units understood by the native speaker of a specific language.

REFERENCES CITED

DEGLER, CARL N. 1991. *In Search of Human Nature: The Decline and the Revival of Darwinism in American Social Thought.* Oxford: Oxford University Press.

RICKFORD, JOHN R. 1997. Suite for ebony and phonics. *Discovery* 18(2):82–87.

STOCKING, JR., GEORGE W. 1982 [1968]. *Race, Culture, and Evolution: Essays in the History of Anthropology.* Chicago: University of Chicago Press.

2

THE CONCEPT OF RACE IN ANTHROPOLOGY

Scott MacEachern

Bowdoin College

Race is, first of all, a word, and like many words it has a variety of meanings. Some of these meanings occur frequently in everyday life, as we talk about "the human race" or about "race relations" in the United States. Other meanings are used in government offices and forms, as when Americans note which of a number of races they belong to for the census. Still other meanings of the term are more technical, when, for example, a biologist talks about different races of a particular species of plant or animal. The meanings attached to this word *race* are different in all of these contexts, sometimes drastically and sometimes much more subtly. In everyday usage, though, we continually blur the differences between these meanings and the ways that they are applied in different settings. This would be a recipe for confusion for any word, but, given the history of the term in the United States, the potentials for uncertainty and discord are especially great. *Race* is a loaded word, in part because different people use it in very different ways but assume that they are all talking about the same thing.

Anthropologists use the word *race* frequently as well. One of the most important tasks of anthropologists is to examine the biological and cultural variability that exists within the human species. We look at the customs and behaviors of societies in different parts of the world, seeking to find the common elements that define our shared humanity as well as the differences that lend variety to our lives. We study the biological characteristics of different human populations; our relations with our relatives, the apes and monkeys; and the evolutionary history of our species. We use archaeology to examine the prehistory of humanity, looking at the cultural processes (often too slow to be detected in a single human lifetime) that have resulted in modern human societies. We examine the central and often mysterious role that language plays in helping us define our worlds—and we seek to put all of this knowledge to use in the wider world around us.

One fundamental part of these studies of human diversity involves the examination of how we humans divide ourselves into subgroups both large and small. Every human occupies a position in a complex of groups with different sizes, constructions, and purposes. These groups can include families, bands, villages, religious organizations, fraternities, tribes, companies, and nations. We are a social species, and our membership in these different sorts of groups adds a vital structure to our lives, allowing us to learn how to be human and placing us in a dense web of relationships with family, workmates, friends, strangers, and enemies. Anthropologists study, among other things, how these groups are created by people, and the ways in which relations between individuals and the groups that they are a part of mutually interact in creating the social and cultural identities that allow us to make our way in the world. Questions of racial identification obviously can be important in these interactions, and are especially visible and significant in the multicultural societies that exist in so many parts of the world at the beginning of the twenty-first century. Given these investigations into the nature of human diversity and human groups, we could expect that anthropologists would have a lot to say about race as it applies to human beings. After all, we might argue that races are among the largest and most inclusive of such human groups, and many people seem to base expectations of other people's behavior on their racial identities.

The study of human races has been an important part of anthropology since its beginnings as a professional discipline in the nineteenth century. In the past physical anthropologists have studied the physical characteristics of members of different races; archaeologists and paleoanthropologists have studied human evolution with the goal of identifying the origins of these races; cultural anthropologists have studied the ways that people around the world use racial identifications to structure social interactions. There were even attempts in the past to associate racial identities with particular linguistic groups or language characteristics (but researchers gave up on that early in the twentieth century). Anthropologists certainly have had a lot to say about human races, and the results of their research sometimes reflect—and sometimes challenge—the various

meanings given to the word *race* by nonanthropologists in the United States.

This chapter will summarize some of the conclusions of anthropological research on human races: on their origins, on the ways in which people have been identified with different races, and on the roles that racial identifications can play in mediating interactions among individuals and groups. Such a summary is made more complicated by the fact that anthropologists working in the different subfields of the discipline have different conceptions of race and the meaning of racial identifications, and, like nonanthropologists, they sometimes use the term without specifying exactly what they mean. Among the questions that this chapter seeks to answer then, are What are anthropologists talking about when they talk about race, and are they always talking about the same thing? Are there common elements in all anthropological usages of the term *race,* or are these usages sometimes contradictory? Perhaps most important, what are human races, and how do they originate and function? This chapter will especially focus on the biological concepts associated with race, and particularly on the intersection between such concepts and cultural definitions of human races.

BIOLOGY AND CULTURE

Anthropologists consider the meaning of race with regard to humans in two different ways. For instance, physical anthropologists look at the biological characteristics of human populations in different areas of the world. They compare these populations to one another, with the goal of understanding the patterning of human biological variation. In the nineteenth century, anthropologists studied the bodily characteristics of humans: their skin color, the color and texture of their hair, the proportions of their limbs, the features of their faces and bodies, and the internal details of flesh and bone that make us both physically unique and similar to other people. In the twentieth century, studies of more subtle variation—of blood groups and antibody types and, most recently and most fundamentally, of genetic material—have added new levels of detail and complexity to that research. Physical anthropologists discuss, among other topics, the scales at which this human biological variability exists, from very localized communities to continental populations and beyond. We shall see that race for these anthropologists implies the existence of a number of elementary biological populations into which all humans can be sorted. This concept was a central part of studies of humanity from their beginning almost two centuries ago. The question before anthropologists in this case is: Do human biological races exist, and if so, what are their characteristics?

Other anthropologists, in their study of human cultures and behavior, look at race from an entirely different perspective. Their emphasis is not on the biological characteristics of human populations but, rather, on the ways in which people divide their social worlds into various groups of humans. Over the last five centuries, in Europe and North America these classifications often used language that focused on the physical and geographic differences among human populations. We all know the terms that were used—*black, white, Nordic, African,* and on and on. Similar terms are used in some other areas of the world as well, although often with different meanings attached to them. Cultural anthropologists have established that ingrained attitudes, general and scientific prejudices, and economic competition have often had far more to do with these racial definitions than have the real physical attributes or geographic origins of people. "Race" in these investigations by cultural anthropologists is conceived of as a cultural construction, not a biological fact. It is in reality a kind of ideology, a way of thinking about, speaking about, and organizing relations among and within human groups. This ideology of race may use the language of physical features when

discussing group differences, but biology and the biological characteristics of humans are not of fundamental importance in how these groups are defined. The question before anthropologists in this case is: How and why do people use cultural criteria to define human races, and how have these definitions changed over time?

These two ways of thinking about race are obviously dissimilar in many ways. If race is examined as a biological concept, then we must think about the physical features of humans—the external ones that we can see as well as our internal biological and genetic makeup. We would probably examine biological races by seeking to trace their evolutionary history, looking at their development over very long spans of time. Our data would be derived from genetics, from physical anthropology, and perhaps from archaeology. If race is examined as a cultural concept, then we must think about attitudes and cultural categories, ideas that exist within people's minds and that are acted upon in the real world. These attitudes and ideas can change very quickly indeed, so that we could probably trace the evolution of cultural categories of race over much shorter time periods—centuries or perhaps even decades. Our data would be derived mostly from cultural anthropology and historical research. An analysis of cultural categories of race would also shade into studies of ethnic relations, a topic discussed in later chapters.

It is especially important to remember that the objects of study—biologically defined races of humans and culturally defined racial categories of humans—are not the same in both of these cases. This means that the existence of one does not necessarily imply the existence of the other. Biological races might exist among humans without any cultural meanings being associated with them. If, for example, people were settled in one place and only saw neighbors who looked just like them, then quite likely their definitions of social groups would not include a racial component. This is a hard situation for us to imagine today, especially in cultures dominated by mass media and mass transportation and where we constantly see people from around the world. Similarly, people may use language that talks about physical features to categorize people into races, but that does not mean that membership in those races is necessarily based on those biological differences. We can see this in the United States by thinking about how many "whites" and "blacks" actually have skin that is white or black in color. The fact that people talk about "race relations" does not imply that those races are real biological units, any more than the fact that people tell ghost stories implies that ghosts are real supernatural phenomena.

For the most part, anthropologists examine race from one or the other of these two perspectives, and only rarely do they switch their points of view. Perhaps the most obvious exception involves forensic anthropologists, who study human skeletal remains in order to provide information for legal proceedings. This requires, first, that these anthropologists examine such skeletal remains carefully, gathering data on age at death, sex, stature, population affiliations, and a number of other possible characteristics of the individual who died. However, for that information to be used, they then have to translate the data that they have gathered into the racial categories that are used by the police, the legal system, and members of the general public. As we will see, this raises interesting questions about the relations between biological and cultural conceptions of race. In the rest of this chapter, I will examine some of the evidence for these different kinds of races, seeking to answer a number of the questions that have been posed earlier. As noted, particular attention will be paid here to biological concepts of race, as much of the evidence for race as a cultural concept is examined in later chapters.

BACKGROUND OF THE TERM

The precise origin of the word *race* is unknown, but it seems to derive via Italian from a Latin root, *ratio,* with a meaning similar to terms like "species" or "kind" (of thing) (Smedley 1999:37–41). In the sixteenth century, "race" was occasionally used in English to designate groups of humans marked by their common origins or by their shared characteristics, physical or otherwise. Over the next two hundred years, the word was increasingly used in English as a classificatory term, with a meaning akin to words like "group," "nation," "people," and so on. This very general meaning of the word persists today, although it is becoming obsolete. We still talk about "the human race," but in conversation rarely do speakers talk about "the Italian race" or "the Xhosa race." We almost never encounter people using terms like "the race of Campbells" or "the race of baseball players," although such uses were fairly common a century ago. Most usages of this generalized meaning of the term, which can take in all of humanity or the inhabitants of a single neighborhood, have disappeared. We will see, however, that it is still used in specific contexts in anthropology.

Over the last two centuries, a more restricted meaning of race has become common in English and other European languages. In this case, a race designates one of a number of fundamental divisions within the human species. These races are claimed to be ancient, stable, well-defined, and extraordinarily important population units. They are usually described in physical terms, although people have most often claimed that behavioral and cultural differences among races exist as well. (Such claims have been the basis for a great deal of popular racism and for the doctrines of scientific racism discussed in Chapter 3.) The number of races identified according to this meaning of the term has varied, but the landmasses of Europe, Africa, and Asia are usually identified as the homelands of three of these races, and people talk about "Europeans" (or "Caucasoids"), "Africans" (or "Negroids"), and "Asians" (or "Mongoloids") as if those three groups constituted fundamental units of humanity. Here is the meaning that people in North

America today most often associate with the word *race:* (a) human races are extraordinarily important; (b) they are based on physical differences; (c) they are ancient and (relatively) unchanging; and (d) they are easily distinguishable from one another.

Scientists, including anthropologists, contributed a great deal to the popularization of this notion of human races throughout the nineteenth and early twentieth centuries. They did so by furnishing what appeared to be objective support to these models of human division, but, as a variety of scholars have noted (Baker 1998; Barkan 1992; Hannaford 1996; Jahoda 1998; Smedley 1999), these researchers were themselves very much influenced by stereotypes of different groups and the relations among these groups that were pervasive in their own societies. They gathered a great deal of data on human physical diversity and on the cultures of societies around the world, but their interpretations were very much colored by their own prejudices.

The history of scientific racism is discussed in Chapter 3, but two things should be made clear at this point. First, we must remember that throughout much of the history of anthropological studies of human races, such studies were concerned with hierarchy and not only with classification. Scientists who were engaged in the comparison of human populations from different areas of the world were certainly trying to establish the criteria by which such populations could be distinguished from one another, but even well into the twentieth century they usually ranked these groups with reference to one another as well. Such rankings might be based on notions of intellectual superiority and inferiority, of savagery and civilization, or of greater and lesser degrees of evolution from some common ancestor, but they have almost always placed Europeans (and more usually upper- and middle-class European males) at the pinnacle of human development. Africans, Asians, Native Americans, and other peoples had to be content with lower positions, at varying distances from those "superior" specimens of humanity.

These researchers shared to varying degrees the pervasive prejudice against the populations that Europeans had encountered in other parts of the world, considering these other peoples to varying degrees either savage or degenerate. Many never had had any contact with the peoples they described in their writings, and when they did, these peoples were most often servants, slaves, or objects of curiosity. Perhaps the ultimate expression of these prejudices was the concept of *polygenesis,* widely accepted among scientists investigating human variation in the middle of the nineteenth century. The polygenetic model held that the different human races actually had originated and evolved separately from one another, that they were, in fact, separate species. Such a theory seems absurd today, with so much known about the evolution of human ancestors over the last 4 million years and with the concept of a species as a biological population that can interbreed accepted as commonplace. At a time when evolution was not well understood and when bigotry against non-Europeans was nearly universal, polygenesis seemed a reasonable theory of human origins and development.

These early studies also frequently mixed up physical, behavioral, and cultural characteristics when defining human races, just as nonscientists continue to do today. Linnaeus, for example, defined the different races not only by their physical features (skin and eye color, type of hair) and their temperaments (melancholy, lazy, timid) but also by the type of clothes they wore and the characteristics of their governments. This mixing of different kinds of characteristics in the definition of human races continued until at least the middle of the twentieth century among researchers on these topics, and it remains a fundamental element in scientific racism. It results in the construction of races that are not really biological units but, rather, expressions of a whole series of different kinds of influences and assumptions, on the part of both the populations involved and the researchers.

More seriously, it can cause people to mistake more or less transitory cultural influences, characteristics that exist because of the environment that people are brought up in, for permanent biological characteristics. We may, for example, laugh at Linnaeus for trying to define races based on whether people wear loose or tight clothing, but we run the same risk when, for example, we think of people of African descent as "natural athletes." A century ago, Africans and African Americans were excluded from many athletic competitions and considered incapable of playing many sports; today, the grandchildren and great-grandchildren of these people participate and excel in all sports. There is nothing "natural" in the cultural changes that have accompanied this transformation in athletic success. This confusion of different sorts of characteristics of human races causes a great deal of trouble, and we must try and keep biological and cultural influences quite separate when we evaluate whether such population units exist.

BIOLOGICAL RACES

Advocates of scientific racism sometimes claim that questioning the existence of human races is the same as denying the existence of physical variation among human beings. This is nonsense: everyone, including anthropologists, knows that such variation exists. I resemble my brothers and sister in some ways, but there are many physical features that distinguish us. Males and females, and old people and young people, differ physically in a variety of very significant characteristics. We can make a reasonable guess about whether someone we see in the street comes from Norway or Italy, or whether he or she is Moroccan or Senegalese (although there is often a good chance of making a mistake in such cases). We recognize that populations of Nuer from the Sudan are on average taller than

Mayan people from Guatemala. No one would argue that each of 6 billion human beings is a member of his or her own private race, or that I belong to a different race than does my daughter because I am forty and she is seven, or that six-footers belong to a different race than do people who are five feet tall. If the term *race* is to have any meaning at all within anthropology, it must involve something more exact than mere physical difference.

The primary questions remain, then: How do physical anthropologists define races, and what criteria have they used in defining them? How many human races have been defined, and on what bases? What are the origins of such human races, and what are the processes by which they acquired their modern characteristics? The answers to these questions depend very much on the definitions of race that researchers have used when investigating human biological diversity. There have been a variety of such definitions, reflecting the fact that races are not at all precisely defined within biology as a whole. The species is the fundamental unit of evolution, characterized by the ability of members of one species to successfully interbreed and thus to share genetic variations in a context of natural selection and adaptation. There are, however, no such clearly defined units below the level of the species, and both biologists and anthropologists must grapple with the question of how and when to usefully divide species up into subunits. Thus, Ernst Mayr (1963:453–460) notes that a whole variety of biological populations have been identified as races, and that these different kinds of populations actually vary considerably in their characteristics.

In practice, anthropological definitions of human races have paralleled the popular definitions of races. There have been approximately as many anthropological definitions of races as there have been physical anthropologists who have studied the question, but we can separate such definitions into three types, one of which is now entirely obsolete. Polygenicists thought of populations originating in different areas of the world—Africans, Europeans, Asians, and so on—as different *species* of humanity, each with their own origins, and with to some degree limited abilities to interbreed. Africans and Native American Indians were even at various times described as species intermediate between "real" humans and apes (Jahoda 1998:75–76). As already noted, this point of view stemmed in great part from the vicious bigotry toward these other populations that many Europeans and European Americans held in the nineteenth and twentieth centuries. It would be comforting if we could dismiss polygenesis as a fantasy of the nineteenth century, but the well-known British geneticist and racist Reginald Ruggles Gates was still claiming that Africans, Asians, and Europeans were different species in a book published just after World War II (Ruggles Gates 1948:366). Relicts of polygenesis are still to be found in the writings of racist organizations today, but no reputable anthropologist believes that polygenicist theories have any connection with reality at all.

Anthropologists in the twentieth century have conceived of human races in one of two different ways. In this chapter I will designate these as *typological* or as *population* models of human races, although other terms have often been used in these definitions. Some physical anthropologists have conceived of biological races as well-defined, stable *types*—real biological things in and of themselves, and thus worthy of study because of their inherent importance. We could also call this a *subspecies* model, because it implies the geographic separation, isolation, and differentiation that are sometimes used to define subspecies among animals (Futuyama 1986:107–109). Other physical anthropologists, in contrast, have conceived of races as simply expressions of difference in the physical features of different *populations* of people. In this case, any group of humans that can be differentiated from other groups based on some physical characteristic or characteristics can be considered a race.

A possible alternative term for this would be a *statistical* model of human races, because it depends critically on the statistical distribution of physical features within and between different human groupings.

There is no hard-and-fast distinction between these two concepts, since neither subspecies nor populations are fundamental biological units in the way that species are. The difference between them is one of degree, not of kind, with differing emphases on the evolutionary history, stability, and magnitude of change across the boundaries of the races that have been defined and with different ideas about the uses of the concept of race within physical anthropology. At the same time, typological and population models tend to yield different views of human biological variability, and they are subject to different sorts of criticisms. I shall now examine the background of these two definitions, and the implications that they hold for our conceptions of relations among human groups.

Races as Types

A race is a great division of mankind, the members of which, though individually varying, are characterized as a group by a certain combination of morphological and metrical features . . . which have been derived from their common descent.
Hooton [1946:446]

Many anthropologists throughout the nineteenth and into the mid-twentieth century have asserted that there exist (or existed in the past) a limited number of geographically distinct groupings of humans, each of which possess a more or less well-defined set of physical characteristics in common. They called these populations human races. These races are usually linked with a particular continental landmass, although their territories are not in fact contiguous with those landmasses. These researchers believed that these human races occupied these different parts of the world through very long periods of time, and that they evolved their unique physical characteristics as adaptations to the particular environments of these regions. Thus, "Negroids" evolved in sub-Saharan Africa, and a number of physical features—dark skin, everted lips, tightly curled hair, a long skull—are both characteristic of Negroid populations and adaptations to African environments. Similarly, "Caucasoids" (Europeans, but also people living in North Africa, the Middle East, and parts of Asia) evolved somewhere in Eurasia and a limited number of physical features—light skin, noneverted lips, straight or curly hair, a narrow nose—are both characteristic of Caucasoid populations and adaptations to the environments where the Caucasoid race evolved (wherever that might have been). The same would be the case for "Mongoloid" populations, supposedly associated with Asia and sometimes with the Americas. And so on for the variety of other human races that researchers have identified in different areas of the world.

There are two important characteristics of this typological model of human racial differentiation, and these two characteristics are closely related. In the first place, this model is *geographic.* Each race is closely associated with a particular region of the world, where it is supposed to have developed in relative isolation from other races and in adaptation to the particular environments of that region. Geographic isolation is often important in biological definitions of subspecies as developing species, populations of a single biological species that have been genetically isolated from one another by some geographic barrier that prevents interbreeding. This genetic isolation might eventually lead to the physical or behavioral divergence of the two subspecies into separate species. This has not, of course, happened with humans.

This typological model of human races also views such races as real biological *things.* As noted, these different fundamental types of humanity are held to have evolved over very long times in the geographic heartlands of each race. Thus, each race is relatively stable and

long-lived, with boundaries that were in ancient times comparatively easy to define (although they may have become blurred in recent times). Each race also has a set of distinctive and essential characteristics, physical adaptations to the particular environments of the regions where that race evolved. This set of characteristics is shared by the humans belonging to that race, although they may be expressed differently in each individual, and is a subset of the many thousands of distinctive features that go into defining every human on earth. The racial identity of every human is then supposed to be detectable through an examination of these characteristics. More generally, the different features of humans within one race are assumed to be covariant: we may think of a race as a well-defined group of people sharing a well-defined group of traits.

In the most extreme of these typological theories, race is conceived almost as a *substance,* a vital fluid that defines the essence of people and that intermixed determines the characteristics of any individual. Joseph Deniker writes of race as "once met with in a real union of individuals, now scattered in fragments of varying proportions among several ethnic groups, from which it can no longer be differentiated except through a process of delicate analysis" (1912:8). This view often led anthropologists to the conclusion that "pure races" had existed in the past, in those hypothetical ancient times when people were well behaved and stayed in one place, but that the migrations, conquests, and colonizations that we know of through recorded history had resulted in the disappearance of these pure races through admixture. Biological race in such cases is an almost purely abstract concept, inferred at secondhand through the observation of its blended traces in modern people. It has very little to do with the actual physical characteristics of humans.

Human races conceived of as subspecies would have a number of specific features, and we can look for those features as we try to decide whether these models are realistic. In the first place, the comparative isolation within which each human race developed would imply that the boundaries between those races will be relatively clear-cut, and generally will fall along the obstacles (deserts, oceans, mountain ranges) that separate them. It is, of course, possible that increased frequency of population movement in recent times has obscured such clear boundaries, although that is a possibility to be tested and not a proposition that can be assumed. In the second place, these races will be internally relatively homogeneous, at least in their essential characteristics, because these characteristics are supposed to be adaptive responses to the environmental conditions within which each race evolved. In the third place, we might expect that the repeated processes of isolation, adaptation, and differentiation that generate races would yield a fairly consistent hierarchy of such races through time. The idea of race as subspecies thus implies that races are relatively well-defined, stable entities and that definition and analysis of these human population units should be a straightforward process.

How well, then, do these implications match up against real human variability? We can draw upon data from archaeology, physical anthropology, geography, and genetics to look at this issue. What we find is just the opposite of this well-ordered model: populations identified as human races have been extremely variable, much disagreement about their characteristics exists, and even their associations with particular regions and environments are often quite weak.

Perhaps the most basic issue that we can examine is simply: How many human biological races are there supposed to be? Answers to this question have been very diverse, indeed. Many researchers have identified three primary human races—the Negroid, Caucasoid, and Mongoloid, as noted earlier, although sometimes using different and/or overlapping terms (see, for example, Bean 1926; Hooton 1946:569; von Eickstedt 1950:496). This parallels and seems to originate in the popular typologies of race that have been established in Europe and North America since the nineteenth century. As European and American knowledge of other parts of the world grew, other populations either were fit into one of these three categories or were established as independent races. Thus, a variety of aboriginal peoples living in South and Southeast Asia were lumped together as "Negritos" and either classified as part of the Negroid race (which assumes that they came there from Africa at some time in the past) or as a separate Negrito race. Australian Aboriginal people were frequently classified as a separate race ("Australoids"), sometimes alongside populations from New Guinea and sometimes not. Pacific Island groups were sometimes classified as "Mongoloids," sometimes as Australoids and sometimes as their own race.

Thus, anthropologists established a bewildering variety of classification systems that purported to divide humanity into races and subraces, major and minor races, and so on. Hooton (1946:575–650), for example, identified 3 "primary" and about 20 "secondary" races of different sorts. The geneticist William Boyd identified 6 races (1950), but increased this number to 13 some years later (1968). Keith (1948:235–244) identified two basic human groups, races in all but name. In 1950, three other well-known researchers (Coon et al. 1950) identified 30 human races. Coon (1965:7) later identified "five full-sized subspecies and two dwarfed subspecies" of modern humans, and called these "subspecies" races. Different researchers have at one point or another identified between two and two hundred of these "fundamental" human groups (Garn and Coon 1968:9). These more elaborate classifications very often conflict with one another in the number of races identified, in the characteristics of particular races, and/or in the racial affiliations of particular peoples.

Paralleling this question of race number is a question of geography: how well does the distribution of these groups called races correlate with real barriers to human interaction? The answer to this is, not very well at all. Perhaps the most striking example is on the continents of Europe and Asia, where the two races known as Mongoloid and Caucasoid are supposed to have evolved. The boundary between Europe and Asia is political rather than geograhic, as both continents are part of a single landmass, usually called Eurasia. No substantial barrier to human interaction exists between Europe and Asia, as we can see from the ancient presence in Central Asia of people speaking Tocharian languages related to Germanic (Adams 1984) and of Asian genetic contributions to populations in northwestern Europe (Zerjal et al. 1997). If "Caucasoids" and "Mongoloids" really evolved in isolation, what factors were enforcing that isolation?

The geographic origin of the "Negroid race" may seem to be more clear-cut: after all, Africa is a continent surrounded for the most part by oceans and seas. However, the barrier in this case cannot actually be those bodies of water, because northern Africa is inhabited by people traditionally referred to as "Caucasoids," but "Caucasoids" indigenous to Africa. These are primarily Berber-speaking peoples. The geographic factor enforcing isolation in the African case is supposed to have been the Sahara Desert, and "Negroids" are supposed to have evolved in the tropical lands south of the Sahara. Yet, even this is not as clear-cut as we might think, because the Sahara is not a permanent feature of the African landscape. Eighteen thousand years ago, it was larger and drier than it is now, but by nine thousand years ago the desert had disappeared, replaced by grasslands and inhabited by various groups of people. At that point, it was a fertile corridor between the Mediterranean and equatorial Africa, not a barrier to interaction. Furthermore, corridors have always existed along the Nile Valley (van Peer 1998) and across the Bab el Mandeb straits between Ethiopia and Arabia, and we know that these corridors have been in use for a very long time.

The isolation mechanisms associated with races in other areas of the world are equally obscure. We might think of Australian Aboriginal people as isolated on that island continent, but with the drastically lowered sea levels of the last Ice Age Australia and New Guinea were one landmass, called Sahul. This island continent was separated from mainland Asia by much smaller stretches of open water than is now the case, and Australia was settled by at least 35,000 years ago. Even after Australia and New Guinea were isolated from one another, there is some archaeological evidence for contacts between the two islands, and New Guinea itself had repeated contacts with Southeast Asia. The first unequivocal evidence of open-ocean voyaging, from about 25,000 years ago, comes from the Solomon Islands off the east coast of New Guinea (Wickler and Spriggs 1988). Such seafaring culminated in the expansion of Austronesian populations' occupation of islands as far apart as Madagascar and Hawaii over the last few thousand years. Farther to the north, peoples from Asia entered the Americas at some point during the last Ice Age. The processes by which the ancestors of Native Americans occupied the New World are not well understood, but there is some evidence for multiple immigrations into (and possibly out of) the continent over the last ten thousand years (Greenberg et al. 1986; Kozintsev et al. 1999; Starikovskaya et al. 1998). Alaska and Siberia are not, after all, very far apart.

In all of these cases, we could probably come up with some sort of speculations about ancient populations being isolated at particular times and evolving into the ancestors of modern races. However, such notions have to be tested, and so far no one has confirmed any such ideas about how races were formed. One of the reasons for this is that often it is very difficult to detect the racial affiliations of skeletons from archaeological sites, an issue that I will come back to later. When examination of skeletons more than a few thousand years old is undertaken, what we often see is that the characteristics of such skeletons do not fit *any* modern race, that they are in fact sometimes subtly and sometimes drastically dissimilar to the skeletons of modern peoples (see, for example, Henneberg 1988; Ozolins et al. 1997; Powell and Rose 1999). In some cases, these differences are probably due to factors like the introduction of agriculture, but in many other cases we have no idea of their origins. This uncertainty indicates that, skeletally at least, modern races are not basic subdivisions of humanity but rather transitory configurations of the human body in response to changing selection pressures, which can be environmental and/or cultural.

More generally, all the archaeological information we have points to one overriding fact: human beings are travelers, and we have been so for a long time. Our ancestors could not jump on an airplane and travel thousands of miles in a day, but over centuries and millennia they gradually changed their territories, they encountered new peoples, and sometimes they went on voyages of exploration and migration that covered substantial distances. Our ancestors moved around a lot, over longer distances than we may think, and they developed the technologies necessary for such movement further back in prehistory than we sometimes expect. The relevance of this fact to the development of human races is obvious: if people in prehistory were frequently on the move, then where would the isolation necessary for race development take place? We do know of a very few populations that seem to have been isolated for long periods of time. Tasmanian Aborigines seem to have been isolated on that island through most of the last ten thousand years, for example (Pardoe 1991), but such small groups are usually not considered separate races of humans. Some proponents of typological race models have recognized that the geographic isolation demanded by these models did not exist in the past (see, for example, Coon 1965:29–30) and thus invoke cultural barriers to such contact between human communities—an explanation even less convincing than that of geographic barriers.

This constant human movement has left its traces in one fundamental element of our physical beings: our genes. Humans are extremely homogeneous genetically, which is certainly due in great part to the constant interaction between communities both neighboring to and farther away from one another. All 6 billion of us, spread across the continents and islands of the entire world, contain within ourselves about the same genetic variation as do, for example, small populations of pygmy chimpanzees living over an area of a few hundred kilometers in Central Africa (Ruvolo et al. 1994:8902). Genetic diversity among human populations is very low indeed compared to that of other large mammal species that are spread over large areas of the world, or indeed compared to those found in very small areas (Templeton 1999:182). I have noted that the typological concept of race has often equated human races to human subspecies, but when we compare the genetic variability among human populations to that of accepted subspecies in other large mammal species, we see again that these subspecies are more different from one another than are the most distant of human groups.

These genetic studies have also substantiated earlier work on human populations, which indicated that the physical characteristics of racial groups are not covariant. Recall that if races originated in the adaptation of isolated human groups to particular environments, we would expect to see a set of characteristics shared by members of that particular race but considerably more rare outside of that group. These traits would derive from varying combinations of adaptations to those environments, descent from common ancestors and/or neutral mutations that appeared in the isolated racial group. Biologically, members of a particular race would, in that case, share a fairly well-defined bundle of physical traits, both externally visible and invisible. These might include combinations of traits for particular skin color, hair type, limb proportions, facial features, blood types, genetic markers, susceptibility to certain diseases, and so on. The boundaries of that race's territory would be comparatively abrupt, although possibly somewhat blurred by interactions and exchange of genetic material with neighboring communities of other races.

This is not what we see when we examine human groups. The various characteristics of human populations do not form such nicely defined sets, and characteristics that we think of as limited to one race are often far more widely shared. Thus, dark skin color is often taken as distinctive of "Negroid" peoples originating in Africa, but it is also found among "Caucasoid" populations in South Asia and "Mongoloid" and "Australoid" groups in the Pacific. Epicanthic folds, which give the eye shapes often associated with "Mongoloid" populations, are also found in some southern African groups. We think of reddish hair as a European physical trait, but it is also found among Aboriginal people in Australia. More broadly, we see an extraordinary variety in physical features among populations grouped together in particular races, and very significant similarities among neighboring populations across what are supposed to be racial boundaries.

As C. Loring Brace (2000) has noted, our perceptions of human racial variation are conditioned by how we see people in different parts of the world. In the modern age of mass media, we can view images of people from Stockholm, Lagos, and Bangkok, and we see that they tend to be physically very different. Centuries ago, European explorers and merchants sailed around the world, but the encounters they had with different populations were in many ways similar to our modern, electronic voyages; they simply took more time to move from port to port. However, the very fact that such voyages move from place to place means that travelers do not see the gradations of difference that separate these places. If a person could walk from Lagos to Stockholm, or to Bangkok, she would see a progressively shifting spectrum of physical char-

acteristics, reflecting the constant interactions between neighboring communities through many thousands of years. These interactions yield biological relationships among populations that are *clinal* (Livingstone 1962)—that is, there is a gradual transition in characteristics between the groups involved, not any sort of sudden boundary between them.

If our hypothetical traveler could look beneath the skin of the people she met, at their blood types, at the forms that their proteins take, and at their genetic material itself, the situation would become even more complex. Humans have historically grouped people into races on the basis of visible characteristics, but of course there is no reason to exclude these other, invisible but equally fundamental traits when we think about separating humans into groups. Human groups defined on the basis of these invisible traits in many cases do not, however, resemble races defined on the basis of external characteristics. Plots of the frequencies of blood types will in some cases group particular populations of Native American Indians with Australian Aborigines, and sub-Saharan Africans with Central Asians. Similar plots for particular variants of the Rh blood system will group Africans with Southeast Asians, Native American Indians being intermediate. The gene for lactose absorption links Europeans with African pastoral groups, and the hemoglobin S mutation is found in West and Central Africa, Saudi Arabia, and South Asia. The Lewis blood group variant LE*Le links North African and Aleutian populations (Cavalli-Sforza et al. 1994). Other examples of such connections and similarities across traditional racial boundaries are very common.

Perhaps the most striking example of this lack of fit between traditional race typologies and genetic data lies in the large-scale studies of genetic variation undertaken by the eminent geneticist Luigi Cavalli-Sforza and his collaborators in *The History and Geography of Human Genes*. Their studies involved gathering genetic data from a large number of human populations from different areas of the world and comparing the genetic samples to one another statistically. The trees of population relations that these analyses yield bear little resemblance to traditional typological models of human races. In some of these analyses, for example, Northeast Asian and Native American Indian populations fall more closely to Europeans than to Southeast Asians and Oceanians (Cavalli-Sforza et al. 1994:78). A situation where someone from northern China is genetically more similar to a Swede than to someone from southern China obviously does not provide much support for traditional concepts of race. Furthermore, the level of distinction at which humans are classified into different groups, racial or otherwise, is quite arbitrary (Cavalli-Sforza et al. 1994:19). We could, using exactly the same genetic data, claim that there are two, or three, or five, or nine, or twenty-one "races"—and none of those reconstructions would be more or less valid than any others. The authors of that study are not, needless to say, believers in the primordial reality of human races.

The conclusion seems obvious. Whatever races might be, they are not fundamental biological types of humanity. The clinal nature of human physical traits, the great genetic homogeneity of humans, and the archaeological evidence for ancient human population contacts do not reflect the existence of ancient population isolates over the periods when races were supposedly developing. The lack of covariation of human physical characteristics does not indicate long-term adaptation of such isolated racial groups to particular original environments. The scope of human physical variation is far too complex to be accommodated within simplistic typological models.

Races as Populations

A race is: a division of a species which differs from other divisions by the frequency with which certain hereditary traits appear among its members.
Brues [1977:1]

Typological models of race are still commonly accepted within the public sphere, but anthropologists have developed more sophisticated models of human biological variation. In some cases, however, the term *race* is still used for these systems. Such models define human races as groups of humans that can be distinguished from other groups based on the frequency of appearance of some heritable characteristic or characteristics as distinct biological populations. For example, high frequencies of red hair, fair skin, and freckles (if such exist) would allow anthropologists to define an "Irish race"; short stature, epicanthic folds, extreme hair curvature, and steatopygia would allow the definition of a "Khoisan race"; straight dark hair, dark eyes, epicanthic folds, and comparatively short arms and legs might allow the definition of an "Eskimo race." Examples abound. Furthermore, such features do not have to be externally visible. The elevated frequency of Tays-Sachs syndrome and Gaucher's disease among Ashkenazi Jewish populations (O'Brien 1999) or of the MNS*M, HLAB*18 and β^{39}-thalassemia alleles (Cavalli-Sforza 1994:274) among Sardinians would help define those populations as a "Jewish race" and a "Sardinian race," respectively. The suntans found among Australians of European descent are the result of particular behaviors, not heredity, and so we could not define an "Australian race" on that basis—at least not until such behaviors resulted in some selection for melanoma resistance on that continent.

This is a very different concept of human races than that of the typological models. It parallels some biological uses of the term. Ernst Mayr (1963:355), for example, defines "ecological races" as populations within a species that display evidence of adaptation to local habitats. "Evidence of adaptation" exists in the distinct morphological, physiological, and/or genetic characteristics of that population. This concept does not involve assumptions about the origins of races in isolated ancestral populations, or about the stability, age, and relative homogeneity of those groups. Stanley Garn (1971:6) notes that "a race is a race whether it goes back unchanged for six millennia or whether it resulted from admixture after 1850." Population models of racial variability locate the definition of races primarily in the perceptions and goals of the observer, and not in the detection of primordial human groups, whether "pure" or mixed with other populations through time. For this reason, the level of detail at which research is undertaken, and the choice of characteristics under study, can be varied almost indefinitely in these models. In general, advocates of population models of racial variation are less interested in erecting particular typologies of human races than they are in examining the processes by which human populations become different from or assimilated to one another.

The definition of human races in these models is to some degree *instrumental:* one defines races in order to do things. (Of course, people have often identified typological races in order to do things as well–to study human variability or to justify racism, for example–but the assumption in those cases was that the races under study were primordial.) Researchers examine human variability in order to investigate particular phylogenetic, biological, historical, or even medical problems. Why do Basque populations have very unusual Rh blood group distributions and somewhat unusual head shapes? What accounts for the elevated levels of Tays-Sachs syndrome among Ashkenazi Jews? Why do Inuit and Nilotic peoples have proportionally different limb lengths? What are the origins of high hypertension rates among African American men? The varying questions asked by researchers will drastically affect both the level of detail of the racial definition and the characteristics under examination.

Garn (1971:15–26) and Brues (1977:2), two of the most influential American advocates of population models of races, have both emphasized the hierarchical nature of their race definitions: researchers can define racial groupings at a variety of population levels, from the most general and widespread to the most specific and localized, depending on the objectives of their investigations. An anthropologist might in some cases study "Caucasoids" as a major race, in other research might subdivide that grouping and compare "European" and "South Asian" races, and in still other research might look within Europe at the differences between, perhaps, "Italian" and "Polish" races. Garn (1971) makes this hierarchy most explicit. He identifies nine "geographic races," including "Amerindian," "African," "Melanesian-Papuan," and "European," each of which is found over a significant area of the world. Within each geographic race is a number of "local races," including, for example, "Northwest European," "Northeast European," "Alpine," and "Mediterranean" groups within Europe. Garn claims that these local races are true units of evolutionary change, and that thousands of such races exist. Within each local race are again many "micro-races," which correspond essentially to any communities between which physical and/or genetic difference can be detected. There would, presumably, be tens or hundreds of thousands of such micro-races in the world today.

Population definitions of race escape many of the criticisms that can be directed at typological definitions. No assumptions are made about the primordial nature of human races, or about the degree of their isolation from one another, or about the limited set of essential characteristics that necessarily defines any particular race. Races are conceived of simply as the continuing results of population interaction, gene flow and interruption of gene flow, and adaptation, rather than as distillations of ancient racial essences. Disagreements between racial identifications made by different researchers become far less important if those identifications are made in order to further the purposes of particular research projects. At the same time, there are different problems associated with population models of race, and these need to be examined and evaluated. These have to do, first, with the structure of racial hierarchies themselves and, second, with the use of the term *race* to describe the population units defined in the research.

The relationships between different levels of the racial hierarchies constructed in population models are often not particularly clear. According to Garn's definitions, "local races" are the true units of evolutionary change, corresponding to endogamous human breeding populations. In that case, it becomes difficult to say exactly what kind of units "geographic races" and "micro-races" actually are. "Geographic races" correspond to the major continents and island chains (Garn 1971:18), and their distinctiveness is supposed to be caused by geographic barriers to gene flow between human communities. At the same time, the presence of four "geographic races" (the "Asian," "Polynesian," "Melanesian-Papuan," and "Micronesian") scattered across such island chains is itself evidence of the human ability to transcend such geographic barriers, and as we have seen, the potential for such barriers to isolate modern humans is often overstated. Garn's "geographic races," and similar distinctions in the work of other researchers, seem to be little more than relics of earlier typological classification systems. "Micro-races" would presumably be the result of restrictions in gene flow within "local races," which calls into question the status of the latter as fundamental evolutionary units.

The characteristics used to define races are also frequently difficult to determine. Population models of race tend to rely on a restricted list of traits for the definition of each racial unit, as typological models do. Again, the question arises: Why choose those particular traits instead of the many other traits that each of us humans possesses, and that might modify or erase the boundaries between different racial populations? To some degree, these traits can indeed be chosen according to the objectives of a particular research project—sickle-cell trait

when looking at adaptations to malaria, limb length when looking at cold adaptations, and so on—but the racial models advanced by Garn, Brues, and others are supposed to be general descriptions of human variability. There is little discussion in their work about the reasons for giving priority to some traits and not others when defining races, especially at large geographic scales. Garn (1971:169–178) gives examples of a variety of "large local races" that are defined according to a potpourri of physical, genetic, linguistic, religious, regional, and traditional criteria, but with no real indication of why combinations of these criteria usefully define these different populations. The availability of computer systems over the last forty years has allowed anthropologists to undertake complex statistical analyses of the geographic distribution of multiple human traits simultaneously, but these traits still have to be chosen by the investigator, and as we have seen with genetic studies, such statistical analyses can yield surprising results.

Definitions of "race" that merely call for the presence of some variation in trait frequencies also risk extending the concept to impossibly local levels. In principle, races would be identifiable in any case where any changes in gene flow have affected the genetic legacy of any group of people for any period of time. We could then easily conceive of a situation where people living in a particular district or neighborhood displayed very minor differences in trait frequencies, and so would be denominated as a separate "race." The detection of such subtle differences is also the basis of many folk typologies. These are informal classification systems used in various parts of the world to assign people to particular groups and to organize cultural expectations about how one acts toward such people and how they will act toward the observer. Thus, in the Cape Verde islands, off the west coast of Africa, a complex folk classification links particular islands and their traditions of European contact with particular physical and behavioral characteristics (L. De Andrade, personal communication, 2000). The people of Sao Vincente, for example, are believed to have dark skin, black and very straight hair, and sharp facial features as a result of the intermarriage of West Africans with people from Portugal and England, whereas people from Brava are ruddy-skinned and fair-haired because of French settlement on that island. At the most detailed levels of analysis, the boundary between "micro-races" and such folk typologies begins to blur: if "races" are to be defined on the basis of their purported detectability, then what weight must we give to the subtle blends of biological traits and learned behavior that Cape Verdean people use to partition their social worlds?

These anthropological models essentially define any distinct biological population, from continental to local scales, as races. The most important objection to this practice is one of meaning: this definition of "race" is so distant from common understandings and from earlier anthropological definitions of the term that it risks causing a great deal of confusion. Previous anthropological usage, and continuing popular usage in North America, involve typological definitions of "race" that are very different indeed from these definitions that designate any distinct human population as a separate race. Typological definitions identified a relatively small number of much larger racial groups, each of which is a fundamental human evolutionary unit, and this is reflected in use of the term by the general public as well. However, the idea that people living in a single neighborhood of a single town could be defined as a "race" implies that hundreds of thousands (or millions) of other "races" exist in the world today. Such lack of precision in meaning may be acceptable in general use, as when we talk about "the human race" at one extreme and, if we are so inclined, "the Bronx race" at the other. But even this usage is obsolescent, and the precision required of scientific research demands the use of correspondingly precise terminologies. From this point of view,

anthropologists probably should not use the term *race* as a synonym for biological populations.

INTERSECTIONS OF RACE, CULTURE, AND HISTORY

Biological variability among humans certainly exists, as anyone can see. Peoples in different areas of the world differ in myriad ways. Moreover, anthropologists and biologists can group humans into populations on the basis of a variety of physical and genetic features. On the other hand, no rule says that we have to call such populations "races," or that we have to use the term *race* at all in any biological sense. The history of science is full of terms that have become obsolete because the theories behind them were found not to correspond to reality. Three centuries ago, chemists wrote about "phlogiston," which was thought to be a kind of essence of fire, contained within all substances that burn and released upon combustion. Researchers eventually learned that no such substance existed, and they stopped using the term. A century ago, physicists used *ether* to denote a substance that permeated the entire universe and provided the medium through which light waves propagated. Researchers eventually learned that that this was an inaccurate conception of the properties of space, and they stopped using the term. Sentimental attachment to a term of long usage did not save either "phlogiston" or "ether," and so these terms were not re-used to describe the concepts that eventually replaced them. From a biological point of view, *race* appears to be another one of those terms whose time has passed, ripe for replacement by words that carry less, and less pernicious, historical baggage. Ashley Montagu (1969:xii) indeed called the race concept "the Phlogiston of our times."

If this is the case, then we might ask why the term *race* continues to be used by anthropologists. Anthropologists continue to talk about race because their study is human culture in general, and because in different areas of the world people talk in the language of physical characteristics and geographic origins when they are dividing up other humans into social groups. In the United States, this is done in the course of everyday social interaction, when terms like "black," "white," "Asian," and so on are used to describe a whole range of people who are, in most cases, Americans. Bureaucracies like the Census Bureau use a complex terminology (American Indian/Alaska Native, Asian, Black/African American, Native Hawaiian/Other Pacific Islander, White, Hispanic) that mixes ethnic affiliation, supposed physical characteristics and geography when defining race and ethnicity for governmental purposes—an ad hoc mishmash that certainly rivals the most obscure of academic racial classification systems.

Such classification is often not done according to criteria that we would recognize as valid today, or that have anything to do with real biological characteristics or human origins. Traditionally, racial identification throughout most of the United States was defined according to a hypodescent, or "one-drop" rule, where a mixed-race child was relegated to the racial group of the lower-status parent—in the American case, almost always an African or African American woman. Furthermore, the degree of racial admixture was more or less irrelevant; one drop of African blood was enough to identify a person as black. This arbitrary system, of course, had nothing to do with the way that biologists or anthropologists would actually characterize the ancestry and population affiliations of a human being. It was simply a way of conceptualizing and enforcing racial hierarchies in the United States, and the one-drop rule was a part of U.S. legal systems until the middle of the twentieth century. In parts of Central Africa, populations are referred to as being "black" or "white," exactly the terms used in North America. All of those people are Africans, however, coming from the same area of the continent. The distinction between them is made on religious

and cultural, not physical, grounds: people who are Muslim (or, increasingly, Christian) call themselves "whites" and call nonbelievers "blacks." This usage seems to go back to the period of European colonialism, but it has been entirely transformed to suit modern conditions. In some countries in South America, racial identity is based in part on socioeconomic status, and may vary from person to person depending on how well off they are (da Costa 1977:297–298).

Anthropologists study the ways in which these classification systems work within cultural systems, as we will see in other chapters in this book. The situation is even more complicated than this, however, because of the ways in which biological and cultural notions of race are intertwined even beyond explicit systems of classification. Anthropologists are no more immune to confusion about these questions than are other people. To illustrate the complexity of some of these issues, I now turn to some short examples of the difficulties that we may encounter in distinguishing biological and cultural concepts of race.

Race in Forensic Anthropology

Many of us have at one point or another watched television shows in which a forensic expert examined a human skeleton and was able to tell a great deal about the living individual from the characteristics of that skeleton: sex, age, stature, physical condition, sometimes even the person's occupation or the diseases and chronic conditions that he or she had endured during life. It is always an impressive exercise, an illustration of the power and sophistication of physical anthropological research. Very often, such analysis will also include determination of the race of that individual. Prominent forensic specialists, physical anthropologists who study human skeletal remains in order to provide information for legal proceedings, have affirmed the existence of human biological races and stated that the concept is fundamental to their research (see, for example, Gill 1990, 1998). Does this not speak powerfully for the existence of biological races among humans?

In fact, the circumstances in which race is identified in forensic research are rather complex. Forensic anthropologists, more than most other practitioners of anthropology, function in cooperation with nonspecialists in their discipline, in this case law enforcement officers, legal specialists, and members of juries. These latter people for the most part do not have a background in anthropology, and so their views of biological variation tend to be those of the North American public—they accept traditional racial divisions, and they hold typological views of race. Forensic anthropologists are thus faced with the necessity of reporting their results in terms that are meaningful to their (largely nonanthropological) audience, and they have adopted traditional race categories as the most effective way of doing that. As Gill (1990:viii) says, "Providing answers for the attribution of race solves cases just as much as providing a useful age bracket or living stature for the individual. Law enforcement agencies know this, and request simple, straight answers. Any anthropologist who contends that races do not exist and provides a vague answer as to ancestry of an unidentified skeleton, or launches into a discourse on 'ethnic groups,' will likely never be called upon again to assist in solving a case." A major reason for the use of racial categories by American forensic anthropologists is thus pragmatic: their target audience wants to hear about race.

Forensic anthropologists in other countries do not seem as fearful of talking about ethnic groups as the quote might suggest (see, for example, Evison 1999), and indeed even some American forensic anthropologists seem less than committed to the concept of race (Kennedy 1995). The author of a recent British work on the analysis of the human skeleton (Mays 1998) manages to go through the whole book without referring to race; he talks about human populations instead. More to the point, the races that forensic anthro-pologists are concerned with identifying appear to vary according to local demographic and social conditions. Thus, in the Southwestern United States a great deal of attention has been given to distinguishing the skeletons of Native American from those of people of European descent, whereas in the Southeast differentiation of Americans of African descent is at least as important. Among southwestern American samples that include people of European descent, Rhine (1990) makes a distinction between "Anglo" and "Hispanic" skeletons. That distinction might well be of importance to law enforcement and other government agencies in that area, concerned with the accurate identification of local people in terms that local people recognize, but no physical anthropologist would argue that "Anglo" and "Hispanic" are separate biological races in any conventional definition of the term.

Similarly, forensic anthropologists try to distinguish skeletons from Southeast Asian, East Indian, and Nubian populations, not because these groups are "races" but because modern North American urban populations include people from these groups (Brooks et al. 1990:45). In other cases, the variability in skeletons of particular races (Native American peoples, for example) has confounded attempts by forensic anthropologists to develop techniques for archaeological identification (Fisher and Gill 1990). In Britain, forensic anthropologists work at differentiating people of Western European descent from South Asians, whereas in France the forensic identification of peoples of Western European, North African, and Southeast Asian descent might attract comparable amounts of attention. In all of these areas, investigators are concerned that the increasing mobility and multiethnic backgrounds of peoples from all over the world will make their job more complex.

In these cases forensic anthropologists are examining the skeletal variability of different human populations. They investigate a variety of traits, recognizing that not all of these characteristics are distributed in the same way through the different populations under study, and that the reliability of their results may vary drastically depending on the relations between those populations and available comparative samples. These different identifications are not made because these groups are fundamental biological types of humans. They are made because human populations are physically variable in all kinds of detectable ways, because the remains that are found often reflect the makeup of local populations, and because both law enforcement agencies and communities at large need to know the identities of the dead. One might argue that forensic anthropologists should be trying to educate their clients about the complexities of human physical variation and the difficulties of grouping humans into well-defined populations, but they could (and do) as well argue that the necessity of providing well-understood information to everyone from local sheriffs to war-crimes tribunals takes precedence. Far from substantiating a view of human races as important biological groupings, as the claims of some researchers would imply (Gill 1998, 2000), the work of forensic anthropologists actually testifies to the complexity and range of variation in human populations—and to the important ways in which social classifications and social pressures can mold the outcomes of scientific inquiries.

Race and Running

The United States is a nation obsessed by sports, as well as by race, and it is no surprise that race relations in this country have often been played out in the arenas of amateur and professional athletics. International sport has equally acted as a field for competition among societies, nations, and political systems. (The inescapable metaphors testify to the ways in which sport pervades our everyday life.) Probably all of us can think of images and slogans that have brought race into athletics, and athletics into race: Jesse Owens at the Berlin Olympics in 1936, Jackie Robinson as the first black player in Major League Baseball, "white boys can't jump." In all of these cases, and many others, assumptions have been made about the physical and intellectual abilities of the athletes in competition and, by extension, about other members of the communities that they come from. Some of these—like the early twentieth-century idea that Jewish people are "natural" basketball players and boxers—are unfamiliar to us today, but others—the idea that blacks do not have the ability to play quarterback in football, for example—remain depressingly familiar.

A number of the beliefs underlying these assumptions will be examined in Chapter 3. A brief example, however, may serve to illustrate some of the complexities of untangling biology and culture. Jon Entine, in his recent book *Taboo* (2000), examines the relations between race and athletic success around the world today. The book is controversial: Entine takes the stance that race is a biological reality, that biological differences between races are reflected in differential success in particular sports, but that many Americans do not talk about these differences because they fear a slippery slope down to the vicious racism that has bedeviled so much of the history of the United States. The book is, in addition, a polemic; the author begins it convinced of the existence and importance of biological races, gives short shrift to any arguments made against the concept, and ends the book with, again, the conclusion that white men (and so, presumably, white boys) can't jump. At the same time, *Taboo* is very different from many of the earlier works written on the topic: Entine devotes a good deal of attention to the pernicious effects of traditional racist thought, in sports and in society in general. He also rejects the widespread assumption that athletic and intellectual ability are inversely related to one another—a destructive idea that has particularly followed people of African descent and which is directly related to earlier, hierarchical models of race differentiation.

The usage of race terminology in the book is, however, quite interesting. Entine writes about "black athletic superiority," but it seems that this superiority is actually a very complicated phenomenon. In the first place, it essentially encompasses two different sets of abilities. West Africans are good at sprinting and, it appears, at a variety of professional sports that use similar abilities, whereas East Africans are good at middle- and long-distance running. In many ways, these appear to call for rather different forms of musculature and cardiovascular development. Neither of those geographic terms is entirely accurate either, though. "West African" in this case encompasses not for the most part people from West Africa, but instead anyone born in the New World or Europe who is of African descent, on the (arguable) assumption that all of their enslaved ancestors came from West Africa. In this case, we might argue that a judicious mix of African and European ancestry seems to fit people best for sprinting, given the overrepresentation of African Americans in those events. Not only that, "West Africa" also encompasses countries like Namibia, which is in southern Africa; one might equally call Moroccan runners West Africans. (Namibia, in "West Africa," actually shares a border with the Republic of South Africa, which is—unsurprisingly—in southern Africa. All of the intervening countries of Central Africa appear to have been eliminated, perhaps because they do not seem to have produced many elite track and field athletes.) Namibian populations, environments, and economies are very different from those found in the countries of West Africa.

Similarly, most East Africans are not champion distance runners. Success at middle- and long-distance running is concentrated in two countries, Kenya and Ethiopia, and among particular ethnic groups. In Kenya, Kalenjin cattle pastoralist populations are especially well represented among elite distance runners, although Kikuyu, Kamba, and Kisii runners are also significant. Ethiopian runners have come from a variety of different populations, with, for example, a number of successful Amhara runners. Of these particular communities, the Kalenjin peoples, among whom distance-running success has been most marked, have only been considered a distinct ethnic group since the 1940s; before that, and still today, the term *Kalenjin* also refers to a group of related languages. (The distinction is important, equivalent to that between "the English" as a population and "English speakers" as a population. The fact that a Sri Lankan, a Nigerian, and a Scotsman all speak English does not mean that they are members of one ethnic group.)

Entine uses Kalenjin running success as a central argument for the existence of black athletic superiority, and thus for the reality of biological differences among racial groups as traditionally conceived of in North America. He argues that Kalenjin domination of distance running is so great that it cannot be completely explained by environmental factors: the availability of good coaches and good training, cultural practices that encourage young people to run a lot, the example of earlier runners, and so on. Instead, running success among Kalenjin speakers is supposed to be due to some genetic advantage, possibly related to selection for speed on foot when engaged in cattle raiding, or to the altitude at which Kalenjin people run. (Cultural factors can be kept in reserve, however; Entine uses such factors to help account for the lack of domination of women's distance running by Kenyans.)

These explanations seem, on the face of it, rather unlikely. There are a number of other groups of people in East Africa who engaged in cattle raiding but who have not generated champion runners. Kalenjin-speaking communities are known to have exchanged group members, through migration and intermarriage, with many surrounding, non-Kalenjin populations; we would expect this to disperse any "genes for running" over neighboring areas in Kenya, but so far this does not appear to have happened to any great extent. More than that, other Kenya peoples who have had success in international distance running–the Kikuyu and Kamba, for example–are Bantu-speaking farmers, not Kalenjin-speaking cattle pastoralists, and live some distance from the latter group. To the degree to which East African running success is concentrated among Kalenjin-speaking people, it is probably most realistic to think of it as the results of cultural factors. The specific biological adaptations that are supposed to contribute to "West African" sprinting success are never really addressed at all.

That being said, there is no reason to think that biological differences among populations could not contribute to success (or failure) in particular sports. At the margins, this is obvious: groups with a short average height, like Guatemalan Maya or Aka people from southern Cameroon, are much less likely to succeed as basketball players than are people from populations that are, on average, very tall, like the Dinka of Sudan. Manute Bol, former center for the Washington Bullets, is a Dinka, and stands 7' 7" tall. Anthropologists have documented a huge variety of physical differences among populations in different parts of the world, and it is quite likely that, for example, the height of Nilotic peoples like the Dinka or the oxygen-uptake capacities of some Tibetan populations would have implications for athletic success. The likelihood of more subtle effects may be even greater, especially given that extremely minor differences in performance can spell success or failure in elite athletics–but such effects must be demonstrated to exist, not merely assumed. It may be that at some point some such biological adaptations will be proven to have a genetic basis among Kalenjin people (Saltin 1996)–but this has not happened yet.

The question remains: What does all of this have to do with race? The scale of human groups under analysis shifts back and forth constantly in Entine's book, from black athletic superiority at the most general level, to West (in fact, mostly African American) and East African

abilities in a variety of sports, to the tremendous successes of Kalenjin runners. These are very different kinds of human groupings, yet all of this variability is supposed to be simply racial, and each level is supposed to imply the others. No one would seriously claim that the Kalenjin comprise a separate race from other East Africans, and the particular kinds of athletic success that Entine examines are in fact very unevenly distributed among populations of African descent, within and outside of the continent (Entine 2000, figure 4.1). A unitary black athletic superiority implies some unitary explanation for such superiority, but no such explanation is given, apart perhaps from some vague musings on the history of hunting and cattle herding on that continent–much of which is simply proof that the geneticists that Entine uses as sources are not very well-informed historians.

Success in particular athletic events is associated with fairly specific groups of people, and it appears to be traditional, typological views of race that lead Entine to generalize innate athleticism to all Africans and all people of African descent. Unfortunately, this view can lead to a lack of interest in the conscious commitment and planning that play a central role in so much of elite athletics. Chapter titles in *Taboo* like "Nature's Experiment: The 'Kenyan Miracle'" and "Winning the Genetic Lottery" illustrate this danger, with their implication–consciously made or not–that African athletic success is not due to the efforts of athletes themselves but to some unearned genetic legacy.

Anthropology and the Politics of Race

At the beginning of the twenty-first century, the concept of race retains its central place among American preoccupations, in society at large and in anthropology more particularly. Publication of controversial books like *The Bell Curve* (Herrnstein and Murray 1994) and *Race, Evolution, and Behavior* (Rushton 1995) has focused renewed attention on questions of race in America and fueled debates about the biological and cultural meanings of the word. These books attempt to resurrect the race hierarchies of the last century, primarily through varying claims that Africans and especially African Americans are, on average, less intelligent, more violent, and generally less civilized than people from Europe or Asia. At the same time, some anthropologists continue to argue that biological races are real and important entities, usually claiming that disbelief in the existence of such biological units amounts to nothing more than "political correctness." (Political correctness is never actually defined in such claims, and the exact meaning of the concept is usually somewhat unclear. However, one of two general meanings is usually implied: either an inappropriate interest in the experiences of women, people of color and the disadvantaged, or an inappropriate suspicion of the processes and objectivity of scientific research.)

Recently, a well-known anthropologist, Vincent Sarich, published an article entitled "In Defense of *The Bell Curve*," one that links these two threads of debate in ways that illustrate some of the complexities touched upon in this chapter. First, Sarich (1995:85) argues that races are real biological entities, designating them as "populations, or groups of populations, within a species, that are separated geographically from other such populations or groups of populations, and distinguishable from them on the basis of heritable features." He also emphasizes the lack of distinct boundaries among races and the multilevel nature of his race definition: the exact number of races to be defined depends on the level of detail with which individuals and populations are examined and the goals of the researcher in question. He further hypothesizes that the differentiation of modern human races has taken place relatively recently (in an evolutionary time frame), perhaps over the last 15,000 years. This is, of course, a quite conventional population definition of biological race, similar to those put forward by Garn and Brues.

It is at this point that the theme of Sarich's article changes substantially. The article is, after all, called "In Defense of *The Bell Curve*," and a population model of race does not of itself provide much support for typological models of racial hierarchy. Sarich claims that race formation needs only geographic separation plus time to occur—although population models of race do not imply geographic separation for the "substantial number" of races that Sarich thinks exist, and indeed it is difficult to find populations that have been geographically separated over a substantial part of the last 15,000 years. The rest of the article segues seamlessly into a discussion of race and the politics of race in an American context, but one that is dominated almost completely by very different concepts of racial variability. Black success in American professional basketball is brought forward as an example of the adaptive variability of human bipedalism between Africans and Europeans, and differences in brain size are claimed to probably be associated with racial differences in intelligence.

As noted earlier, most African populations do not produce professional basketball players, and the claimed correlations between brain size and intelligence are equally doubtful. As Jeremy Genovese (1999) has pointed out, Sarich overstates these latter correlations in a number of ways. A great deal of human variability in brain size relates to differences in body size: bigger people tend to have bigger brains. This does not, however, translate to differences in intelligence; if it did, women would, on average, be significantly less intelligent than men, since they have both smaller bodies and smaller brains. This is self-evidently untrue, nonsensical in fact. Modern humans function equally well culturally and socially over a significant spectrum of brain sizes—unsurprisingly, given the likely selection against lack of intelligence and sociability in human societies. This is not the place for a review of *The Bell Curve* and *Race, Evolution, and Behavior* (see Chapter 3), but we should note that both of these works exhibit important deficiencies in the ways that they control for the effects of low status and cultural bias in studying variations in human performance.

Most importantly for the purposes of this review, it is hard to see how the sorts of disparities in ability and intelligence that Sarich claims exist could have arisen without recourse to highly typological, differentiated racial groupings, evolving in relative isolation from one another over extended periods of time. This is especially the case given the differences in innate intelligence among racial groups claimed by Herrnstein and Murray (1994) and Rushton (1995). If brain size, intelligence, and athletic ability vary among modern human races according to the cultural and environmental backgrounds within which these races evolved (Sarich 1995:89), and if the difference in these factors is as great as Sarich and the authors of the book that he is defending claim, then presumably those races are supposed to have evolved in very different environments and in considerable isolation from one another.

This is, of course, a reversion to traditional, typological models of race, and so Sarich ends his essay with a very different definition than he used to begin it. Such a progression is almost inevitable. On the one hand, modern research has demonstrated that human biological variability is clinal and multivariate, with a substantial lack of concordance between a variety of genetic and physical characteristics. On the other hand, traditional concepts of race hierarchy in the United States require that races be relatively well differentiated from one another, so that they can be talked about, compared, and used as foundation for action essentially as monolithic, homogeneous things. Attempts to ground American popular views of race differences in biology—to naturalize them, in essence—are to a very great degree incompatible with any sort of understanding of how human populations vary. Reconciliation of these different viewpoints would seem to require the sort of gradual segue from anthropological to political arguments that Sarich makes. It is very

telling that Sarich's article involves an affirmation of the biological (and physical and even intellectual) importance of the race concept while at the same time apparently denying the social importance of racial identities in modern American society. "Race" persists, but to Sarich racism is not really important any more.

CONCLUSION

"Race" is a word, and it is a word that admits of a wide variety of meanings. The history of the United States of America has meant that some of these meanings of "race" are laden with an immense significance. This perhaps masks the fact that American definitions of race and American race relations are not necessarily universal—although the cultural, political, and economic power of the United States today means that social and cultural debates about race around the world are increasingly debated using American terms and understandings. The continuing American preoccupation with and debate about race and race relations is in some ways a testament to the ideals of the Republic, implying at least a theoretical commitment to the equality of all its citizens. Americans may disagree vigorously on whether such equality has been substantially attained—as a noncitizen, my outsider's perspective is that it has not—but there is broad agreement that the question itself is important. This has not been the case in all of the countries where important issues of race relations exist.

One central element in these debates involves decisions about when race is a useful and appropriate concept to be used in particular kinds of analyses and when it is not. To what degree can differences in educational attainment among different groups in the United States be ascribed to racial discrimination? Are there significant differences in the way elections are handled in predominantly black and predominantly white districts across the country, and is this due to these variations in population? Is race or socioeconomic status a better proxy for student needs in affirmative action programs? Active argument surrounds all of these issues, and hinges upon the meaning, scope, and utility of social concepts of race and upon the relations of those concepts to other ways of characterizing American society.

The same situation holds in anthropology: we can (and must) investigate the various dimensions of race, describing and critiquing the concept as we do so. This involves, among other things, examining whether biological race concepts are appropriate models for investigating variability among human beings. This has been one preoccupation of physical and biological anthropology for more than a century now, and it appears that the answer to this question is "No." The typological race models that had held sway in anthropology through most of the existence of the discipline are not good descriptions of how human biological variability works. The implications of population models, on the other hand, are so far removed from popular understandings of the term *race*—with hundreds of thousands or perhaps millions of "micro-races" around the globe—that use of the term in such cases does nothing more than risk needless confusion. Science is not an exercise in nostalgia: when a term progresses from being burnished by long use to being made obsolete by increasing knowledge, it needs to be discarded.

The concept of biological race concepts in anthropology is now at that point. This does not mean that anthropologists will stop studying human biological variability, either in individual or population terms. Such research will obviously continue, benefiting especially from the extraordinary advances in genetic research that have taken place over the last decade and that seem to accelerate every day. There is, however, no reason for such research to be hobbled by terminology that sows confusion rather than illuminating the real world. It is unlikely that people, in America and elsewhere, will stop using physical characteristics as representations for social difference. Such substitutions are very deeply ingrained within human societies, and they would not be easily given up. It remains, however, for both anthropologists and society in general to be continually conscious of the origins of such practices and of the nature of human biological and cultural variability.

REFERENCES CITED

ADAMS, D. 1984. Towards a history of PIE n-stems in Tocharian. *Journal of the American Oriental Society* 100:439–443.

BAKER, L. 1998. *From Savage to Negro: Anthropology and the Construction of Race, 1896–1954.* Berkeley: University of California Press.

BARKAN, E. 1992. *Retreat of Scientific Racism: Changing Concepts of Race in Britain and the United States between the World Wars.* Cambridge: Cambridge University Press.

BEAN, R. B. 1926. Human types. *Quarterly Review of Biology* 1:360–392.

BOYD, W. C. 1950. *Genetics and the Races of Man: An Introduction to Modern Physical Anthropology.* Boston: Little, Brown.

———. 1968. Genetics and the races of man. In *Readings on Race.* S. Garn, ed. Pp. 17–27. Springfield, IL: Charles C. Thomas.

BRACE, C. L. 2000. Does race exist? An antagonist's perspective. *Nova Online* (http://www.pbs.org/wgbh/nova/first/brace.html).

BROOKS, S., R. BROOKS, and D. FRANCE. 1990. Alveolar prognathism contour, an aspect of racial identification. In *Skeletal Attribution of Race,* G. Gill and S. Rhine, eds. Pp. 41–46. Maxwell Museum of Anthropology, Anthropological Papers 4. Albuquerque: University of New Mexico.

BRUES, A. 1977. *People and Races.* New York: Macmillan.

CAVALLI-SFORZA, L., P. MENOZZI, and A. PIAZZA. 1994. *The History and Geography of Human Genes.* Princeton, NJ: Princeton University Press.

COON, C. 1965. *The Living Races of Man.* New York: Knopf.

COON, C., S. GARN, and J. B. BIRDSELL. 1950. *Races.* Springfield, IL: Charles C. Thomas.

DA COSTA, E. 1977. Slave images and realities. *Proceedings of the New York Academy of Sciences* 292:293–310.

DENIKER, J. 1912. *The Races of Man: An Outline of Anthropology and Ethnography.* New York: Charles Scribner's Sons.

ENTINE, J. 2000. *Taboo: Why Black Athletes Dominate Sports and Why We Are Afraid to Talk about It.* New York: Public Affairs.

EVISON, M. 1999. Computerised 3-D facial mapping. Paper presented at the First International Conference on Forensic Human Identification, London, October 23–26.

FISHER, T., and G. GILL. 1990. Application of the Giles and Elliot discriminant function formulae to a cranial sample of northwestern Plains Indians. In *Skeletal Attribution of Race.* G. Gill and S. Rhine, eds. Pp. 59–64. Maxwell Museum of Anthropology, Anthropological Papers 4. Albuquerque: University of New Mexico.

FUTUYAMA, D. J. 1986. *Evolutionary Biology.* Sunderland, MA: Sinauer.

GARN, S. 1971. *Human Races.* 3rd edition. Springfield, IL: Charles C. Thomas.

GARN, S., and C. COON. 1968. On the number of races of mankind. In *Readings on Race.* S. Garn, ed. Pp. 9–16. Springfield, IL: Charles C. Thomas.

GENOVESE, J. 1999. The errors of the old physical anthropology. *The Race Gallery Online* (http://homepages. poptel.org.uk/racegallery/genovese.html).

GILL, G. 1990. Introduction. In *Skeletal Attribution of Race.* G. Gill and S. Rhine, eds. Pp. vii–xii. Maxwell Museum of Anthropology, Anthropological Papers 4. Albuquerque: University of New Mexico.

———. 1998. The beauty of race and races. *Anthropology Newsletter* 39(3):1, 4–5.

———. 2000. Does race exist? A proponent's perspective. *Nova Online* (http://www.pbs.org/wgbh/nova/first/gill.html).

GREENBERG, J., C. TURNER II, and S. ZEGURA. 1986. The settlement of the Americas: A comparison of the linguistic, dental, and genetic evidence. *Current Anthropology* 27:477–97.

HANNAFORD, I. 1996. *Race: The History of an Idea in the West.* Washington, DC: Woodrow Wilson Center Press.

HENNEBERG, M. 1988. Decrease of human skull size in the Holocene. *Human Biology* 60(3):395–405.

HERRNSTEIN, R., and C. MURRAY. 1994. *The Bell Curve: Intelligence and Class Structure in American Life.* New York: Free Press.

HOOTON, E. A. 1946. *Up from the Ape.* New York: Macmillan.

JAHODA, G. 1998. *Images of Savages: Ancient Roots of Modern Prejudice in Western Cultures.* London: Routledge.

KEITH, A. 1948. *A New Theory of Human Evolution.* London: Watts.

KENNEDY, K. R. 1995. But professor, why teach race identification if races don't exist? *Journal of Forensic Science* 40:797–800.

KOZINTSEV, A., A. GROMOV, and V. MOISEYEV. 1999. Collateral relatives of American Indians among the Bronze Age populations of Siberia? *American Journal of Physical Anthropology* 108(2):193–204.

LIVINGSTONE, F. B. 1962. On the non-existence of human races. *Current Anthropology* 3(3):279–281.

MAYR, E. 1963. *Animal Species and Evolution.* Cambridge, MA: Belknap Press.

MAYS, S. 1998. *The Archaeology of Human Bones.* London: Routledge.

MONTAGU, A. ED. 1969. *The Concept of Race.* London: Collier-Macmillan.

O'BRIEN, S. 1999. Ghetto legacy. In *The Biological Basis of Human Behavior: A Critical Review.* R. Sussman, ed. Pp. 59–62. Advances in Human Evolution Series. Upper Saddle River, NJ: Prentice Hall.

OZOLINS, E., V. H. STEFAN, M. RHOADS, and J. F. POWELL. 1997. Craniofacial morphometric similarities between modern and Late Pleistocene human populations. *American Journal of Physical Anthropology* 24 (Supp.):182–183.

PARDOE, C. 1991. Isolation and evolution in Tasmania. *Current Anthropology* 32(1):1–21.

POWELL, J., and J. ROSE. 1999. Report on the osteological assessment of the "Kennewick Man" skeleton (CENWW.97.Kennewick). In *Report on the Nondestructive Examination, Description, and Analysis of the Human Remains from Columbia Park, Kennewick, Washington* [October 1999] (http://www.cr.nps.gov/aad/kennewick/powell_rose.htm).

RHINE, S. 1990. Non-metric skull racing. In *Skeletal Attribution of Race.* G. Gill and S. Rhine, eds. Pp. 9–21. Maxwell Museum of Anthropology, Anthropological Papers 4. Albuquerque: University of New Mexico.

RUGGLES GATES, R. 1948. *Human Ancestry from a Genetical Point of View.* Cambridge, MA: Harvard University Press.

RUSHTON, P. 1995. *Race, Evolution, and Behavior: A Life History Perspective.* New Brunswick, NJ: Transaction.

RUVOLO, M., D. PAN, S. ZEHR, T. GOLDBERG, T. DISOTELL, and M. VON DORNUM. 1994. Gene trees and hominoid phylogeny. *Proceedings of the National Academy of Sciences of the USA* 91(19):8900–8904.

SALTIN, B. 1996. Exercise and the environment: Focus on altitude. *Research Quarterly for Exercise and Sport* 67(3):S1–S10.

SARICH, V. 1995. In defense of *The Bell Curve:* The reality of race and the importance of human difference. *Skeptic* 3(3):84–93.

SMEDLEY, A. 1999. *Race in North America: Origin and Evolution of a Worldview.* 2nd edition. Boulder, CO: Westview Press.

STARIKOVSKAYA Y., R. SUKERNIK, T. SCHURR, A. KOGELNIK, and D. WALLACE. 1998. MtDNA diversity in Chukchi and Siberian Eskimos: Implications for the genetic history of ancient Beringia and the peopling of the New World. *American Journal of Human Genetics* 63(5):1473–1491.

TEMPLETON, A. 1999. Human races: A genetic and evolutionary perspective. In *The Biological Basis of Human Behavior: A Critical Review.* R. Sussman, ed. Pp. 180–192. Advances in Human Evolution Series. Upper Saddle River, NJ: Prentice Hall.

VAN PEER, P. 1998. The Nile corridor and the out-of-Africa model. *Current Anthropology* 39:115–140.

VON EICKSTEDT, E. 1950. The science and history of the human races. In *This Is Race*. E. W. Counts, ed. Pp. 489–514. New York: Henry Schuman.

WICKLER, S., and M. SPRIGGS. 1988. Pleistocene occupation of the Solomons. *Antiquity* 62(237):703–707.

ZERJAL, T., B. DASHNYAM, A. PANDYA, M. KAYSER, L. ROEWER, F. SANTOS, and W. SCHIEFENHOVEL. 1997. Genetic relationships of Asians and northern Europeans, revealed by Y-chromosomal DNA analysis. *American Journal of Human Genetics* 60:1174–1183.

3

A HISTORY OF "SCIENTIFIC" RACIALISM

Leonard Lieberman

Central Michigan University

Have you heard statements like these?

- Blacks excel in athletics because of their race.
- The black race has lower intelligence.
- Intermarriage between blacks and whites results in degeneracy.
- The black race is closer to the apes.
- Proof of the superiority of whites is seen in their conquest of Africa, the Americas, and much of Asia.
- African cultures are simpler, therefore, inferior.

In the course of this chapter these misconceptions will be addressed. They are examples of widespread, everyday (folk) racialism. These and related stereotypes are directly or indirectly supported by "scientific" racialism.

SO WHAT IS "SCIENTIFIC" RACIALISM?

Embedded in this question are several others. What is science? What is race? What is racism? "Race" was fully discussed in Chapter 2. Briefly, it is the belief that the human species is divided into biological subdivisions thought to be easily identified by the similarity of their biological characteristics so that populations can easily be sorted into white, yellow, and black or Caucasoid, Mongoloid, and Negroid. However, anthropologists emphasize that humans vary biologically across geographic regions, and they do so in gradations (clines) that do not match the idea of separate populations with homogeneous biological features (Brace 1996).

Racialism is an ideology or doctrine, a set of beliefs (Todorov 1993). One dimension of racialism in Europe and the United States has been the ideology (beliefs) that Caucasians are biologically superior and that most people of color, especially blacks, have an inferior culture determined by their "race." *Racism* is the *practice* of discriminating against those alleged to be inferior, either intentionally or without awareness. Ideological racialism assumes a causal link between biological "race" characteristics and cultural behavior. Racialism received a powerful stimulus from nineteenth-century Darwinian theory in what came to be called *Social Darwinism*. It held that the superior biological "races" triumph over the inferior. The theory seemed to be confirmed by the European colonial conquest of the Western Hemisphere, Africa, and parts of Asia. The need to justify that conquest coincided with "scientific" racialism involving the use of apparently scientific techniques to measure brain sizes in an attempt to demonstrate hereditary superiority (Dennis 1996). Although racialism is ideology, and racism involves behavior, racialism's ideas are far from harmless. They seriously injure the populations they target by depriving them of self-respect, by defining them as the inferior "other," and by appearing to justify and encourage acts of racism.

In this chapter I will examine the extent of "scientific" racialism in only two disciplines: psychology and anthropology. However, there are, and have been, many varieties of "scientific" racialism in the many branches of biology and medicine. Why has "scientific" racialism been widely believed and so long-enduring? A first reason is because it presents a naturalistic explanation for its insistence that "races" differ in their behavior (Blakey 1998). In this case, naturalistic means that behavior is said to be determined by the inherited biology of each "race." Second, a biological explanation sounds more authoritative than do those based on social influences. Third, it explains social problems by reference to biological factors that seem to provide a persuasive causal explanation. Fourth, it is assumed that these biological functions cannot be significantly altered, avoiding the necessity of studying and considering changes in the environment, including social institutions and policy, thereby supporting the status quo (maintaining things as they are in a society). Fifth, they combine with, reinforce, and receive strength from the prevailing belief in the biological inferiority of people of color. A prime example of this last influence is, as stated earlier, Social Darwinism, originated by Herbert Spencer, in which he combined color prejudice with Darwin's theory of evolution by natural selection. Thus, "lesser races" (darker) were said to be less successful in the struggle for survival and doomed to extinction.

We have placed quotation marks around "scientific" in "scientific" racialism because in their writing and publication most of its practitioners use scientific concepts and measuring procedures but miss the essential character of science, which requires testing alternative concepts or hypotheses in a way in which they can be disproven if invalid.

On first encountering "scientific" racialism a person might ponder this question: If scientists were wrong in the past, how are we to know whether they are right or wrong now? Isn't it just one person's opinion against another? There are several guidelines to follow: First, what *evidence* does the author present? Evaluate that evidence, especially following the information presented later in this chapter. Second, what counterevidence does the author present against his or her own position? Third, does the author give an accurate and fair presentation of the evidence against racial hierarchies? Fourth, does the author really reply to that counterevidence? Fifth, does the author allow for significant and varying environmental interaction with heredity, or merely give it lip service?

ORIGINS OF RACE AND RACISM

Have the Ideas of "Race" and Racialism Always Been Present in Human Cultures?

Humans are a classifying species and they classify each other on the basis of whatever seems different. Ancient Egyptian wall paintings show individuals of different skin color. But we do not know if they conceptualized these as representing distinct and homogeneous "races," or merely differences in color and a few other traits. To ancient Athenians of 400 B.C.E., other people were automatically inferior by comparison to their own culture, a phenomenon that anthropologists refer to as *ethnocentrism*. But were these other people "races"? In translating from the ancient Greek, the noun *genos* is erroneously translated as "race," but the prime meaning of *genos* has to do with those who are bound together in families, clans, and tribes over generations (Hannaford 1996:220). The other peoples were designated *barbaros* or barbarians.

While the idea of "race" was not available to be used by the Athenians to create and justify a social hierarchy, there were other ways to achieve that end. As Plato told the story, Socrates, in the tale of the metals, advised that a stable society required three classes. Those whose souls corresponded with gold shall be the rulers, those corresponding to silver will be administrators and officials, and those corresponding to brass and iron shall be husbandmen (farmers, craftsmen). These will all be carefully taught that they "must keep to their proper place in society for when a man of brass or iron guards the State, it will be destroyed." The tale justifies a rank order on the basis of alleged biological inheritance (Gould 1996:51–52).

Socrates' tale omits slaves, one order of society lower than that of the husbandman. Aristotle justified slavery as necessary because he believed humans were innately unequal (Chase 1975). Ironically, many of these slaves were captured in warfare from other Mediterranean and Greek city-states and were not different in biological appearance from the Athenians. The significant difference between the conquered and the Athenians was that one group had power over the other; once enslaved, the "others" were defined as innately inferior and were required to dress and act in ways that reflected their lack of access to the dominant culture; therefore they were perceived as inferior to the classes above.

In medieval times, St. Thomas Aquinas synthesized the religious beliefs and traditions of the thirteenth century and justified the rank order in society as part of the divine plan. In the Christian tradition, the rank of slavery was justified by reference to the Bible and the story of Noah's son, Ham. Having seen his father naked in a drunken sleep, Ham was cursed and sent off in exile to become father of black people, who were seen as biblically justified servants of white men.

When Did "Race" and "Scientific" Racialism Originate?

The two ideas developed together. In the eighteenth century, a "scientific" concept of race and "scientific" racialism began to replace the medieval religious justifications of hierarchies. In 1758, Carolus Linnaeus, a Swedish scientist, developed a classification that placed *Homo sapiens* among the primates in the animal kingdom. *Homo sapiens* were divided into four varieties, or "races," different in biological traits, including skin color: white, red, yellow, and black; surprisingly, behavioral characteristics were included as part of each "race." Linnaeus described *Homo Europaeu* as gentle and governed by laws, *Homo Asiaticus* as haughty and governed by opinions, *Homo Americanus* as choleric (short-tempered) and regulated by customs, and *Homo Afer* as indolent and governed by caprice (whim). Thus Linnaeus presented a hierarchy ranging from superior laws to customs, to opinions, to the most inferior, caprice. The stature of Linnaeus as a botanist and taxonomist lent the aura of validity to his hierarchy. It was a taxonomy of superiority-inferiority that reflected the politically correct views of his time. It was a way of thinking that would prevail, with few exceptions, for the next three hundred years.

One such exception was Johann Blumenbach, a student of Linnaeus, who also classified humans into different races, but believed that "it is very clear they are all related, or only differ from each other in degree" (in Montagu 1942:15). Blumenbach saw the "Caucasoid race" as beautiful, naming it after crania from the Caucasus Mountains. He proposed five major races, the other four resulting from degeneration from the perfection of the Caucasoid (Spencer 1997:184). Blumenbach lived in an era of assumed European superiority and seemed unaware of the contradiction between his egalitarian belief and his idea of degeneration.

The nineteenth century saw the crystallizing of a core of racialist ideas that would persist into the twentieth. Prior to that century and in that century a number of scientists held blacks to be inferior to whites.[1] Charles Darwin (1809–82), who originated the idea of natural selection as the mechanism by which evolution occurred (1859), was skeptical of efforts to identify the number of races and denied that evolution had a progressive direction; yet he followed the thinking of his time by writing that women were in some respects like the lesser "races" of mankind. Lacking fossil evidence for evolution, he saw the lesser races as a stage linking humans and apes. While Darwin and many of the scientists of the time made contributions in their special areas, they also expressed the racialism of their day. They were operating from the European ethnocentric sense of superiority and the ideas that measurements led to knowledge and that "races" were biological realities. They did not seek to create racist inequalities, but in presenting a "scientific" explanation for them, they provided a set of ideas that justified and perpetuated those inequalities. To his credit, Darwin raised the question of whether the situation of the poor was due to nature or institutions: "If the misery of our poor be caused not by the laws of nature, but by our institutions, great is our sin (*Voyage of the Beagle,* quoted by Gould 1996). But this sentence did not appear in Darwin's major books. This, and the other voices of doubt about hereditary biological inferiority, constituted no more than a whisper.

Such quiet qualifications were drowned out by the impact of efforts to use measurements to prove racial inferiority. An influential example of this is in the work of Samuel G. Morton, who provided measurements to support the C>M>N (Caucasoid, Mongoloid, Negroid) hierarchy that many others espoused during the nineteenth century and into the next. Morton, a Philadelphia physician, collected and measured the volume of over 600 human skulls from around the world and produced the figures that he believed certified that "races" varied in the average cranial volume in a hierarchical pattern. Morton's works on "race" were *Crania Americana* (1839) and *Crania Aegyptiaca* (1849). He shared in the prevailing outlook that some "races" were superior and that the greatest among these was "Caucasoid," followed by the "Mongoloid" and then the "Negroid" (C>M>N).

Morton's numbers indicated that "Caucasians" had a mean brain size of 87 cubic inches, whereas "Mongolians" and American Indians measured 83 and 82 and "Ethiopians" 78. Stephen J. Gould (1981:54) explains the serious sampling errors that resulted in "Caucasoids" being ranked first. Only three Hindu skulls were admitted to Morton's "Caucasian" sample because, as Morton explicitly states, "the skulls of these people are probably smaller than those of any other existing nation" (1839:261). If more Hindu skulls had been used, the average cranial size for "Caucasoids" would have been lower. Morton's sample of Indians is also biased by overrepresentation of smaller Inca/Peruvian crania, whereas only three large-brained Iroquois skulls were included. Gould (1981:60) suggests that the difference in cranial size between "Caucasian" and "Ethiopian" is because half of Morton's "Caucasian" sample is male and probably only one-third the "Ethiopian" sample is male. Male cranial size is around 10 percent larger than that of females. Morton seemed unaware of this sampling error, since he explicitly described his procedure. It is indicative of the power of folk beliefs about blacks that they were placed last in hierarchies of the nineteenth century.

J. C. Nott and George Gliddon used Morton's data in their book, *Types of Mankind* (1854:454). Gliddon was an amateur Egyptologist who used Morton's method to support the claim that the pharaohs were "Caucasoids," the only race then thought to be capable of high civilization (Molnar 1992:16). Morton, Nott, and Gliddon came to be regarded as the nucleus of the American school of anthropology, noted for *polygenesis,* the idea that races had separate origins and that some were created inferior (Erickson 1997a:65). Nott and Gliddon presented Morton's research to the American South, hoping thereby to justify slavery (Brace 1997:865). Southerners accepted the skull measurements that seemed to prove black inferiority, but rejected the polygenic idea because it conflicted with the Genesis view of one and only one creation, that of Adam and Eve.

How and Why Did Racialism Originate?

The uniform support for the C>M>N hierarchy coincides with a century in which Europe had achieved dominance over most of the world's people with darker skin. From the 1830s on, the expansion of the power and territories of the United States was advocated as an expression of "manifest destiny." In the second half of the century, evolutionary ideas emerged and evolutionists would interpret the difference among "races" and their cultures as stages of evolution. Anthropology emerged in the nineteenth century as the study of evolution from primitive barbarism to advanced civilization. It was a point of view that assumed the superiority of Europe and the "Caucasoid" race. This paradigm of linked biological and cultural evolution supported the hierarchical ordering of the races in much of the nineteenth and early twentieth centuries.

Racialism, like the idea of races, can be traced to the attempt to justify European colonization of much of the world, the rise of European capitalism, and the slave trade (Dennis 1996:715). Colonization, although a highly varied process, in general involved entry of a militarily powerful society into the territory of a weaker one for purposes of forcefully extracting valuable resources. In order to justify the cruelties that were practiced, the colonized peoples were portrayed as inferior dark-skinned "races." Ethnocentrism laid the foundations for racialism by regarding people of different cultures as inferior, but racialism adds a seemingly persuasive biological dimension in which the "others" look different and therefore behave differently. We have seen that European and American scientists such as Linnaeus were building the idea of race in the eighteenth century, stimulated by the diversity of peoples in the New World. Scientists, scholars, and theologians were also confronted with explaining the origin of these "races." The only possible explanation in a pre-Darwinian era had to be consistent with the biblical teaching of creation by God. The two schools of thought that debated how this came about were monogenism and polygenism. Monogenists held that "races" were all part of one recently created species. As we discussed, Blumenbach (1795) held that racial differences arose because of degeneration from the original creation. The polygenists contended that the "races" were different species created at different times. The monogenic view was strongly supported by Catholic theologians and most scholars of the sixteenth and seventeenth centuries, the first two centuries of colonialism. The Catholic church and Queen Isabella of Spain insisted that all the peoples of the New World had souls that missionaries could save.

Polygenism became the predominant view in the first half of the nineteenth century, supported by a multitude of cranial measurements initiated by Morton, by Paul Broca in Paris, and by others in England and Germany (Erickson 1997b; Lieberman 2001). Polygenism and cranial measurements provided the scientific support for the alleged inferiority of the dark "races" that was intended to justify their exploitation, especially in the eighteenth and nineteenth centuries. Those who supported slavery and religiously held to monogenism could reject the idea of multiple creations but could take comfort in Morton's cranial measurements. For scientists, it would appear that polygenism was contradicted by Darwin's *Origin of Species,* published in 1859. But few scientists understood how Darwin's natural selection related to evolution, and polygenism remained an influential theory (Erickson 1997). In the first three decades of the twentieth century, in the context of the ideas of polygenism and racial hierarchy, IQ tests provided a new method of measuring individuals and comparing "races." Those decades from 1900 to 1930 were part of a terminal phase of colonialism in which 40 million Europeans came to the United States from 1880 to 1920. They encountered other Europeans already there, rather than Native Americans who could be shunted aside. After 1900, they were arriving when the idea of eugenics was developing across Europe and the United States.

The term *eugenics* was invented in the 1880s by Frances Galton,[2] a wealthy Englishman and a first cousin and contemporary of Charles Darwin, who assessed the number of great men in different "races" and concluded the British to be superior. Galton claimed that he was able to trace his ancestry (and Darwin's) back through 12 centuries of Norman dukes as well as Anglo-Saxon and French kings (Tucker 1994:39). Galton was much concerned that the better classes of society would decline in numbers and the lesser classes increase. He used the term *eugenics* to designate the science of improving the human species. In 1901, Galton's lecture to the British Anthropological Institute ignited interest and activity in England, the United States, and Germany. In Britain, prominent scientists and intellectuals, some of them socialists, who supported eugenics included Sir Ronald Fisher, J. B. S. Haldane, Julian Huxley, H. J. Muller, H. G. Wells, and George Bernard Shaw (Kevles 1985). The social movement that developed expressed fear of the expansion of the poor and the inferior "races," and zealously advocated sterilization (Tucker 1994).

Eugenicists came to focus upon hereditary social traits, and under the influence of the genetic principles of Mendel, rediscovered in 1900, assumed that these traits were controlled by one or two Mendelian factors (genes) operating in a simple dominant-recessive pattern. The social traits included pauperism, manic depression, scholastic ability, feeblemindedness,

epilepsy, and criminality (Allen 1999). These traits were attributed to the poor, blacks, and immigrants, making it possible to mobilize public interest in eugenics. Scientists and the public also supported eugenics because of the popularity of the social Darwinism of Herbert Spencer and the American sociologist William Sumner, with its emphasis on the survival of the fittest, those possessing superior qualities, which purportedly led to some races, nations, classes, and the male gender having more wealth, power, and status as a product of evolution. Therefore, attempts at social welfare for the poor were held to defy laws of nature and enable the unfit to multiply (van den Berghe 1996).

What Were the Social Consequences of Nineteenth-Century "Scientific" Racialism?

Over the first decades of the twentieth century prominent citizens became interested in eugenics and formed associations dedicated to improving their "race." Exhibits were displayed at county fairs. High school and college courses included eugenics as a topic. The pioneer scientist and eugenicist in the United States was Charles B. Davenport, a biologist, who organized the Eugenics Record Office (ERO) in Long Island in 1904. There he gathered family histories and trained eugenic fieldworkers. Davenport and Harry H. Laughlin, supervisor at the ERO, were especially interested in crime, tracing it primarily to inherited temperamental instability. Laughlin presented data showing that Negroes, Mexicans, and Puerto Ricans were overrepresented in prison populations, and he believed it was not because of slums or economic stress. Laughlin gave testimony for two days before the congressional committee that wrote the 1924 Johnson Act severely restricting immigration from southern and eastern Europe, including Catholics and Jews, most of whom were believed to be biologically inferior and prone to criminal behavior.

Eugenicists also urged sterilization of the unfit. Laughlin prepared a model sterilization law for introduction to various state legislatures. Laughlin and his coworkers argued for what they termed "progressive" legislation, and by 1935, thirty states had adopted similar legislation. Over 60,000 persons had been sterilized before the repeal of most of those laws in the 1970s (Allen 1999). The eugenic movement was international, with sterilization laws passed in Denmark (1929), Norway (1934), Sweden (1935), Finland (1935), Estonia (1936), and Iceland (1938), and in one Swiss canton (1928). Also included were Cuba, Czechoslovakia, Yugoslavia, Lithuania, Latvia, Hungary, and Turkey. In the first decades of the twentieth century various German sources praised the American sterilization laws and the immigration restriction law. Widely read were translations of American eugenic books such as Madison Grant's *Passing of the Great Race* (1916), as well as H. H. Goddard's (1912) study of the Kallikaks. Under the Nazis, Germany's eugenics law, modeled after those in the United States, used tubal ligation for women and vasectomy for men. In the first four years of the law over 50,000 persons were sterilized per year in Germany (Proctor 1988). In Germany, scientists in the universities and physicians strongly supported eugenics, as did scientists and physicians in other nations.

We have seen that the history of racism is not confined to any one nation. Eugenics was an international movement supported by scientists and essayists. The works of Morton, and then of Davenport, were read in France and Germany. Morton's procedures and conclusions, however erroneous, were widely cited as the alleged scientific foundation for proving that "races" were unequal. In *Essays on the Inequality of Human Races* (1854:111), Joseph-Arthur Comte de Gobineau presented a summary table of Morton's measurements to support his view that "Nordics" were superior to all other races, having created "high" civilizations (Molnar 1992:258). Gobineau has been nominated "grandfather" of academic racial-

ism for his work of 1853–55. He held that all high human achievements were the work of the Aryan superrace, who created the civilizations of the Hindus, Egyptians, Assyrians, Germans, Chinese, Mexicans, and Peruvians. According to Gobineau, the Aryan superrace declined because of interbreeding with other "races."

In turn, Gobineau's book influenced the opera composer Richard Wagner and his son-in-law, Stewart Chamberlain, whose "overtly violent Jew baiting" book in 1910 would in turn influence Kaiser Wilhelm II and then Adolf Hitler (Chase 1975:91). It is revealing to see these connections from "scientific" racialist research and writings to those like Gobineau and Chamberlain who popularized their work, to those who used these sources to support their view of racial superiority for Germans and inferiority for Jews, Gypsies, Poles, and blacks, and to justify the program of "race purification" by mass extermination in order to eliminate non-Aryans from the German gene pool.

Was Racialism in the Humanities and Sciences in the United States a Minority View?

By the end of the nineteenth century most of the world was under European control, and the acceptance of "scientific" racialism meant that few scientific or humanitarian objections were likely to be raised:

> In the United States during the latter portion of the 19th century the inequality of races was the predominant view of scientists and intellectuals. American thought from 1880 to 1920 "generally lacks any perception of the Negro as a human being with potentialities for improvement." Most of the people who wrote about Negroes were firmly in the grip of the idea that intelligence and temperament are racially determined and unalterable. [Gossett 1965:286].

In literary circles the list of those believing in the inequality of "races" included James Fenimore Cooper, Henry Adams, Frank Norris, Jack London, Owen Wister, and Henry James (Gossett 1965:198). In Europe a comparable group of writers included Rudyard Kipling and Sir Walter Scott, whose *Ivanhoe* converted a feudal class struggle into an affair of "self-conscious racial conflict" between Saxon and Norman (MacRae 1960:80). The majority of intellectuals and scientists had beliefs that helped give racism respectable veneer. But there were some intellectuals who did not support racism: George Washington Cable, Winslow Homer, Mark Twain, Stephen Crane, and J. S. Mill. Among scientists there were a few men who were generally not racist in their thinking. The list includes Adolf Bastian, Rudolph Virchow, William Ripley, Theodore Waitz, Friedrich Ratzel, Henry Rowe Schoolcraft, Lewis Henry Morgan, and John Wesley Powell (Gossett:245). They were forerunners of a reformed view of "race," generally believing that "races" differed only in minor respects (Lieberman 1968:134–135).

The nineteenth century also saw the emergence of a variety of fields of study organized in university departments, including sociology, psychology, and anthropology. With some exceptions, most of these social scientists shared with the literati and scientists the widespread idea of a racial hierarchy. As late as the 1920s, the sociologist Pitrim Sorokin (1889–1968) wrote that "perfect agreement of all these tests: the historico-cultural, the mental, the absence of geniuses . . . seems to indicate strongly . . . that the cause of such a difference in the Negro is due not only, and possibly not as much to environment, as to heredity" (1948:286).

"Scientific" racialism extended also to psychologists. G. Stanley Hall (1844–1924), a pioneer psychologist, held that primitive races were at earlier evolutionary stages (Gossett:154). Similar views were proposed by many anthropologists. Edward B. Tylor (1832–1917), considered one of the founders of anthropology, wrote in 1881:

> In comparing races, one of the first questions that occurs is whether people who differ so much intellectually as savage tribes and civilized nations, show any corresponding difference in their brain.

There is, in fact, a considerable difference. The most usual way of ascertaining the quantity of brain is to measure the capacity of the brain-case by filling skulls with shot or seed. Professor Flower gives as a mean estimate of the contents of skulls in cubic inches, Australian, seventy-nine; African, eighty-five; European, ninety-one. Eminent anatomists also think that the brain of the European is somewhat more complex in its convolutions than the brain of a Negro or a Hottentot. Thus, though these observations are far from perfect, they show a connexion between a more full and intricate system of brain-cells and fibres, and a higher intellectual power, in the races which have risen in the scale of civilization. [p. 60]

Tylor's statement illustrates the nature of "scientific" racialism: it assumes intellectual inferiority of tribes as compared to civilized nations; it draws upon measurements; and all this is related to the position of a "race" in the scale of civilization. This idea of unilineal evolution was interpreted to mean that peoples who supposedly had not evolved very far were doomed to extinction by the natural forces and power of the civilized nations. A similar view was expressed by Aleš Hrdlička (1869–1943), founder of the *American Journal of Physical Anthropology* and major advocate for the founding of the American Association of Physical Anthropologists: "We see that the higher civilized white man has already in some respects outdistanced others, that he is rapidly diversifying, and that all about us those who cannot keep the accelerated pace are being eliminated *by nature*" (Hrdlička 1915, emphasis added). Here Hrdlička clearly expresses Social Darwinism in which the superior races survive and the inferior are eliminated by nature.

A REVOLUTION IN SCIENCE

How Could an Accurate View Replace the "Scientific" Racialism That Prevailed in the Nineteenth Century?

The debate over the inequality of races was largely one-sided until the 1920s. The historian

Gossett writes that the stemming of the tide of inequality was the work of "one man, Franz Boas, who was an authority on several fields which had been the strongest sources of racism" (1965:429–430). Boas asked for proof that race determines mentality and temperament. From then on "it would be the racists who were increasingly on the defensive . . . it was clearly Boas who led the attack." In 1912, Boas published evidence demonstrating changes in head shape in children of Italian and Jewish immigrants. It weakened both the older concept of the fixity of race (Shapiro 1969:376) and the implication that mental ability was racially determined.

Boas was most influential through his leadership in cultural anthropology. According to Gossett, the ethnographic work his students began "had the utmost importance for race theory because the close and detailed knowledge of . . . primitive peoples showed how directly ideas and customs are interrelated and how fallacious is the idea that any society can be meaningfully interpreted in terms of its racial inheritance" (1965:416). Gossett holds that what was needed to break through the dominant misconceptions was a way to explain character as an outcome of institutions, history, and environment. Boas and his students did that by building the idea of culture, by developing the relativistic approach to cultural differences, and by insisting on masses of evidence.

Boas's influence on his students helps explain the spread of his views in anthropology. One of his most prominent students was Alfred Kroeber, whose 1917 article, "The Superorganic," was one of the influential statements calling for a sociocultural rather than a biological interpretation of human societies. Among the students of Boas were a number of women who became pioneer anthropologists and who combated racialism and racism through their teaching and research publications. They included Ruth Benedict, Katherine Dunham, Zora Neale Hurston, Margaret Mead, Elsie Clews Parsons, Ruth Underhill, and Gene Weltfish. Benedict's

Patterns of Culture (1934) was widely influential in popularizing the idea of culture, thereby providing a nonracial and nonracist explanation of human societies (Lieberman 1997).

Until about 1940, mainstream science was consistent about the reality of race and the inferiority of blacks. Almost all physical anthropologists utilized the typology of three major races and thereby indirectly gave support to the inferiority of the "other" species. There were two exceptions. One was, as discussed, the Boasian school, which had its beginning in those early decades. The second was "in the writings of those [African Americans] stereotyped by the sciences of the day" (Stepan and Gilman 1993:170). It is a measure of the power of "scientific" and everyday racialism that these authors are still too little known and seldom quoted. Among them was Frederick Douglass, a former slave, who in 1854 presented an audience with anatomical and cranial similarities of blacks and whites that outweighed the differences; therefore, he asserted that the Negro was entitled to full membership in the human species (Stepan and Gilman 1993:175).

W. E. B. Du Bois is another example of a neglected critic of racialism and racism. He was born in Massachusetts of African American and European American ancestry, and earned his Ph.D. from Harvard in 1895. In sociology Du Bois was the leading spokesman for liberal reform and against Social Darwinism, just as Franz Boas was in anthropology (Baker 1998:99). Early in his career, Du Bois argued that the color line of segregation in all walks of life prevented Negroes from progressing and that the inequality of the black "race" was due to the heritage of slavery, not biology (Baker 1998:111). He held that the color line was the central problem of the twentieth century.

Eventually, social scientists began to reassess their perspectives on "race," psychologists among them. Otto Klineberg (1935) was one psychologist who had contact with Boas and his students. He later gathered evidence in support of environmental influences through his work identifying the rising IQ scores of Negro children who had moved from southern to northern schools. In sociology the same trend occurred but under differing influences:

> Racial explanation disappears from serious sociology with the great generation of the early twentieth century: Pareto, Durkheim, Hobhouse and Max Weber made the issue of race irrelevant by the introduction of new canons of analysis and by their attempt to explain the social by the social. [MacRae 1960:445]

What numerous social scientists had done was to respond to racialism with a scientific rebuttal. Scientific antiracialism came to be the accepted position in the social sciences and among intellectuals. The idea was soon to spread and become a popular ideology partly replacing racialism and competing with it. But a set of ideas does not become an accepted ideology simply because it is soundly scientific. It spreads when cultural conditions are appropriate. The earlier ideas ran against the tide of social conditions supporting racialism. But in the 1940s, a social base for antiracialism was emerging.

Gossett comments: "We owe something to impersonal forces in the decline of [racialism], but the trouble with impersonal forces is that they can as easily work one way as another. We owe far more to the people and the organizations motivated by a concern for equality for all" (1965:445). Gossett's position seems to be that of the historian and humanist: people and ideas make history. The view that must be added is that individuals also can as easily work one way or another, who succeeds often depends on the influence of social and cultural conditions. Boas's ideas could spread only when the social structure was ready. Individual humans may make history, but they do not do so under circumstances of their own choosing.

In the early decades of the twentieth century, the forces for antiracialism began to develop in the United States through the emergence of the social sciences as organized disciplines and through their influence on education. To these must be added the transcendent influence of World War II. The propaganda developed during the war was based on the fact that Nazi Germany was totalitarian, racialist in ideology, and racist in practice. Since the enemy was racialist and racist, America had to proclaim itself antiracialist despite its history of slavery and continuing practice of segregation. The massive antiracialist propaganda and the racist policies of the enemy silenced the racialist groups in the United States that had been so vocal in the 1930s.

Beginning in 1942, anthropologist Ashley Montagu published the first of six editions of *Man's Most Dangerous Myth: The Fallacy of Race*. It reached a large popular audience with scientific evidence that the "race" concept was invalid and was inextricably tied to racialism and racism. Other scientists in the United States and in Great Britain began to see the need to combat racialism within science itself (Stepan 1982:160). The decline of racism among policymakers was clearly evident in the 1954 U.S. Supreme Court rejection of the established rationale of "separate but equal" and in the Court's mandating of desegregated schools. More than that, what the Court did was to accept the statements of social scientists concerning the belief that a number of alleged "racial" behaviors were not hereditary but were, in fact, a product of environment and learning (Barkan 1987:3).

In the 1950s scientists from several disciplines began to issue statements about "race" and racialism that marked the beginning of the end of "scientific" racism as the majority belief among scientists. Several statements on race were issued by the United Nations Education, Scientific, and Cultural Organization (UNESCO) and by professional organizations of scientists. Four statements were issued by UNESCO from 1950 to 1967, formulated by committees whose members were drawn from a number of scientific disciplines. The first statement, published in 1950, was "Statement by Experts on Race Problems" (Montagu 1972). It was five years after the end of the Second World War, and during the still-growing awareness of the 6 million Jews, Gypsies, and Poles killed in Nazi death camps and with the assumption that behavior is racially determined. One passage from the 1950 statement declares that:

> So far as temperament is concerned, there is no definite evidence that there exist inborn differences between human groups. There is evidence that whatever group differences of the kind there might be are greatly overridden by the individual differences, and by the differences springing from environmental factors. [quoted in Montagu 1972:10]

Similar statements appeared in the other three declarations.

THREE PEAKS OF IQ–"RACE" CONTROVERSY: THE IQ CENTURY

Why Is "Scientific" Racialism Reborn Again and Again?

Early in the twentieth century, at about the time that Boas and his colleagues were developing the concept of culture, a new way to measure intelligence was being introduced. This new method used pencil and paper tests to measure what has come to be called the *intelligence quotient,* or IQ. Three times in the twentieth century IQ test scores were used in an attempt to demonstrate racial inferiority. Stephen Jay Gould, a paleontologist and a specialist in the history of science, refers to these episodes as racial backlashes. Each was followed by research and debate among scientists disproving the racialist claims. Early in the century these episodes were reactions against the increasing numbers of immigrants. In the 1960s, the reactions followed claims for equal rights in the civil rights movement led by Martin Luther King, Jr. In the 1990s,

a third backlash criticized government social programs with emphasis on welfare.[3] These three episodes are examples of how racialist ideas are used to justify racism in practice. In the following section I will present the characteristics of "scientific" racialism in these three phases. I will follow each of these characteristics with examples of the evidence that contradicts and disproves the assumptions of race–IQ determinism.

The "Race" and IQ Tradition Begins

The nineteenth-century reliance on skull sizes was largely replaced when Alfred Binet (1903), a French psychologist, presented his method of mental testing involving analogies and reasoning skills. Before that, for three years beginning in 1898, Binet had measured the heads of students identified as the best and the worst. The differences he found were extremely small, and Binet wrote of resisting his own temptation to magnify those differences (Gould 1981:147). Binet had been commissioned by the Ministry of Public Education in France to develop a procedure for identifying pupils in need of special instruction. His test consisted of a diverse set of tasks relating to everyday problems requiring basic reasoning processes of logic and ordering, rather than skills learned through direct teaching such as reading. Binet avoided reducing intelligence down to a specific number suitable for linear ranking, and rejected distinguishing between acquired and genetic causes. His goal was not to label but to improve (Gould 1981).

In the first decade of the twentieth century our story shifts to Henry H. Goddard, who introduced the Binet IQ tests to the United States. Goddard was director of the New Jersey Institute for the Feebleminded. He had Binet's 1908 test translated into English, with minor adjustments. He tested it on 400 inmates and published the results in 1910. He also administered his test to 2,000 public school students in Vineland, New Jersey, and claimed to distinguish normal from feebleminded children. Later he assigned labels to mental age: including idiots through 2 years of age, imbeciles through 7 years, and morons through 12 years, and always with a hereditarian assumption. His books, *The Kallikak Family* (1912) and *Feeblemindedness: Its Causes and Consequences* (1914), claimed that inherited mental deficiency is the source of delinquency, crime, promiscuity, disease, drunkenness, illegitimacy, and pauperism. Goddard strongly supported eugenics, attributed inferiority to the "black race," and alleged that most social problems were caused by the feebleminded.

The IQ testing process took another step in 1913 when Goddard sent research assistants to Ellis Island. In two and a half months they were to identify the feebleminded (below age 12) by sight (Gould 1981:165). They tested 35 Jews, 22 Hungarians, 50 Italians, and 45 Russians. The results were frightening; some 83 percent of Jews were said to be feebleminded, as were 80 percent of Hungarians, 79 percent of Italians, and 87 percent of Russians. Gould explains that the tests were administered to "a group of frightened men and women who spoke no English and had just endured an oceanic voyage in steerage. Most are poor and have never gone to school; many have never held a pencil or pen in their hand" (p. 166). By 1928, Goddard later recanted his thinking to the extent that he acknowledged that only a small proportion of those who tested 12 years or less were feebleminded, and regardless of their mental age most could be trained to be useful citizens. Goddard concluded that feeblemindedness could be cured and that most of the feebleminded need not be institutionalized (1928:225).

Lewis M. Terman (1916), a professor of psychology at Stanford, would take IQ testing onto the national stage. He was not the first to utilize the Binet tests, but his predecessors had only translated the test or partly modified it. Terman undertook a thorough revision of the Binet tests. He was concerned with racial variations in intelligence:

> A low level of intelligence is very common among Spanish-Indian and Mexican families of the Southwest and also among Negroes. Their dullness

seems to be racial, or at least inherent in the family stocks from which they come. . . . The writer predicts that . . . there will be discovered enormously significant racial differences in general intelligence, differences which cannot be wiped out by any scheme of mental culture. . . . From a eugenic point of view they constitute a grave problem because of their unusually prolific breeding. [quoted by Lewontin et al. 1993/1984]86)

It was Robert M. Yerkes who initiated the testing of World War I army recruits. Yerkes, aware of preparations for the war, conceived of a grand foundation for a "scientific" psychology. He proposed that all recruits into the army be tested. As Colonel Yerkes, he would be commanding a select cadre of psychologists and would train those who would administer the tests to 1,750,000 recruits. Yerkes assembled the premier psychometricians to write the tests. And so Yerkes, Terman, Goddard, and their colleagues designed the largest program of mental measurement the world had seen.

The army made only casual use of the scores. Their impact arose from the attention given in the press to summary data, which reported three startling conclusions. First, the average mental age of white American adults stood just at 13, slightly above the level of "morons" (8 to 12 years). Second, the people of southern and eastern Europe were less intelligent than those of northwestern European nations. Third, the Negro scored at the lowest portion of the scale. Although thoroughly criticized by the journalist Walter Lippmann (1922), the new "scientific" racialism had been established and would reappear in both the United States and Great Britain.

The role played by Terman and Yerkes in the United States had its parallel in Great Britain in the work of Cyril Burt. Study of separated identical twins provided the evidence that Burt and others used to support their hereditarian beliefs. Since they were identical in their genes, the degree of twins' similarity in intelligence was presented as proof that IQ was highly heritable. Eventually Burt reported on 53 pairs of identical twins and correlated their IQ scores. He claimed

80 percent heritability for intelligence. His research was emulated by others, Burt's achievements praised, and he became Sir Cyril Burt. Burt's data were the keystone for the assertion that IQ was highly heritable, and was relied upon by later IQ researchers (Lewontin et al. 1993:155). However, studies by Burt finding high correlations of .94 for the IQ of identical twins in the same household did not allow for their very similar environments (Kamin 1974:38). Therefore, Burt used identical twins reared in separate households, and reported correlations of .77. These studies further supported the claim for high heritability, since the environments in the two households were said to be different. However, Kamin (1974) reanalyzed the data and found that the separate households were very similar, such as one twin reared by the mother, the other by her cousin in the same English village. Correlations of the IQ scores of separated twins were .5, indicating that both heredity and environment were important.

One discovery in particular brought Burt's research to public attention. Oliver Gillie, a journalist for the London *Sunday Times,* was unable to locate Burt's research coworkers, a Miss Conway and a Miss Howard. They had published papers in a journal Burt edited, but they had never been seen by any of Burt's other coworkers and could not be located. Gradually and grudgingly it was acknowledged that Burt had committed fraud. Yet his defenders said there was still much merit in his research. One reviewer of Burt's work concluded:

I do believe that Burt made things up about the twins, about factor analysis, and about the parent-child data used in his "social mobility" study. Having analyzed Burt's many publications, I find too many omissions in his references, too many inconsistencies among different articles, and definitely some clear contradictions between what he had written at one time, and what thirty years later he claimed to have written earlier—although he may not be unique in doing so. [Samelson 1992:231]

Can scientific conclusions sometimes be influenced by the social context? Comparison of the British and American hereditarians illustrates that these scientists may have been influenced by their own national cultures. The British strand of mental testing, pioneered by Burt and actively supported by others, focused attention on social class (the poor) and its relation to IQ and education. In the United States, the focus has had three concerns: race, immigrants, and the poor. Each nation has been obsessed with its own historical tensions. The British were justifying their class system. The Americans had to reconcile (or ignore) a history of slavery and discrimination, anti-immigrant feelings, and inequality between rich and poor with a tradition that proclaimed equality of opportunity. Furthermore, in the United States the three periods of controversy over race and IQ in the twentieth century occurred not merely because of developments in the discipline of psychology but because of the context of social events. The nineteenth century was the last opportunity to build empires. It was a time to defend subjugation of peoples with darker skins by supposedly superior races. If there had been no IQ tests, it is likely that some other scientific-appearing way of asserting biological differences would have been used. Of this, the nineteenth-century studies of cranial size contains abundant evidence.

The Second Phase of the IQ Century: The 1960s and 1970s

Beginning in the 1960s, a revival of "scientific" racialism began. For example, the journal *Mankind Quarterly* was sponsored by the Pioneer Fund, which supports and finances much "scientific" racialism. The historian who has thoroughly studied this phenomenon is Barry Mehler (1989; www.ferris.edu/isap). Mehler reports that the Pioneer Fund was endowed by Wickcliffe Draper, a textile manufacturer, and incorporated in 1937 by Harry Laughlin and

Frederick Osborne. The year before the journal's founding, Laughlin had received an honorary degree from Heidelberg University for his contributions to Nazi eugenics, and in 1937, Osborne wrote that the Nazi sterilization law was the most exciting experiment that had ever been tried.

The fund was based on the Nazi "breeding program," and its purposes were, first, to "encourage the propagation of those 'descended predominantly from white persons who settle in the original 13 states prior to the adoption of the Constitution of the United States and/or from related stocks, or to classes of children, the majority of whom are deemed to be so descended.' The second purpose was to support academic research and the dissemination of information about problems of heredity and eugenics and the problems of race betterment" (Mehler 1989:21). In short it was a program of positive and negative eugenics, increasing those descendants of colonial stock and providing information that would lead to reducing those not of that origin. Harry Laughlin, one of the founding directors of the Pioneer Fund, was influential with the congressional committee that passed the 1924 immigration law. A second director was Frederick Osborne, secretary of the American Eugenics Society and an admirer of the Nazi eugenic sterilization laws (Sedgwick 1994:234).

According to the grants the fund has awarded, it is interested in "limiting immigration, stopping busing, reversing integration, and ending affirmative action" (Sedgwick 1994:234). In other words, back to Jim Crow segregation plus even more limited immigration. Mehler (p. 21) reports on one of the fund's projects in 1937 in which plans were made for the distribution of two films to high schools, colleges, churches. The films were Nazi propaganda for eugenics showing luxury living for defectives, and poverty conditions for people of Aryan stock. In the years following the U.S. Supreme Court's *Brown* vs. *Board of Education* desegregation decision, the fund was allied with those opposed to that decision. Although the Pio-

neer Fund has relatively modest assets of $5 million it is able to grant about $1 million annually in income to scholars, including many who study IQ and its possible racialist implications (Mercer 1994:A28).

The reader should be reminded that I am looking at those periods during which considerable controversy developed. Published early in the 1960s was anthropologist Carleton Coon's *Origin of Races* (1962), which attempted to use fossils to support a racial hierarchy. He presented the idea that *Homo erectus* evolved into *Homo sapiens* five times as each of five "races" passed a threshold from one species into the other. Caucasoid was first at 250,000 years ago, Mongoloid passed over at 150,000, Australoid at 40,000, and African at 40,000 years ago. Of these transitions Coon wrote:

> It is fair inference . . . that the subspecies that crossed the evolutionary threshold into the category of *Homo sapiens* the earliest have evolved the most, and that the obvious correlation between the length of time a subspecies has been in the *sapiens* state and the levels of civilization attained by some of its populations may be related phenomenon (pp. ix–x). [If Africa was the cradle of mankind] it was only an indifferent kindergarten. Europe and Asia were our principal schools (p. 656).

Coon's views were met by vigorous critical opposition from anthropologists and book reviewers concerning his Eurocentric bias against Africans and his failure to explain societal differences using cultural and environmental history.

During the 1960s, the controversy was also ignited by an article by Arthur Jensen, with much advanced publicity, published in the 1969 *Harvard Educational Review* by the title "How Much Can We Boost IQ and Scholastic Achievement?" The article began with a statement that would infuriate the environmentally inclined: "Compensatory education has been tried and it apparently has failed." The paper that followed was 123 pages long and presented many of the elements of "scientific" racialism. There were no new breakthroughs, but it stimulated a large number of research studies that refuted its claims (Block and Dworkin 1976; Montagu 1975).

The Third Phase of the IQ Century

The third phase of the IQ century began with the publication of *The Bell Curve* in 1994, coauthored by psychologist Richard Herrnstein and political scientist Charles Murray. In brief, *The Bell Curve* claimed, as had earlier practitioners of "scientific" racism, that (1) IQ tests measure intelligence, an abstract mental property called "g" (p. 22); (2) IQ tests show a large gap between those at the bottom of society and those above; (3) similarly, there is a gap of 10 to 15 points between the African American race and whites (p. 276); (4) 40 to 80 percent of this gap is due to heredity (pp. 23, 298); (5) remedial environmental efforts, such as Head Start, can do little to improve IQs because heredity is so strong (p. 389); (6) poverty, crime, illegitimacy, and welfare dependancy are associated with low IQ (pp. 127, 235, 167, 191); and (7) we are moving toward a two-caste society with a cognitive elite upper level and an expanding cognitively deprived lower level (p. 509).

The argument in *The Bell Curve,* and in all the studies of "race" and IQ, are based on two false foundations. First, the race concept lacks supporting research because of the greater variation within traditional "races" than among them, as well as other evidence stated earlier. Second, as will be shown below, IQ tests really measure scholastic learning, not a hereditary essence in the brain. The general assumption that IQ tests measure an abstract ability called "g" led to the reductionist idea that intelligence was one uniform entity in the brain. This view has been successfully refuted by psychologist Howard Gardner (1985) using cross-cultural data, and the observation available to everyone that individuals vary in their aptitudes for mathematics, music, spatial perception, and interpersonal interpretation. Intelligence is a combination of many different mental potentials. IQ tests do not measure these multiple intelligences.

What IQ tests do measure is reflected in their predictive validity through correlations: .80 with scholastic achievement, .50 to .70 with occupational status, .35 with income, and .20 to .25 with actual performance on the job (Flynn 1980). Earlier I stated that IQ tests are said to measure what is called "g," which has to do with problem solving, abstract reasoning, generalizing from specifics, and perceiving abstract relationships. These skills are closely related to scholastic achievement, but because of low correlation with income and actual performance on the job, there are dimensions of important life chances poorly predicted by IQ tests.

In the context of evolutionary biology, we have evolved to manipulate and survive in a variety of changing situations, and test taking relates to that process only in the narrower scholastic sense measured by IQ tests devised for modern industrial society (Patterson 1995). An ethnic group may have a lower mean IQ score because the test reflects skills at participating in a society that prevents that ethnic group from the full participation that would equalize IQ scores (Chidley 1994). Examples are endless: Catholics in Northern Ireland score lower than Protestants; blacks in South Africa score lower than "colored" people (from India or mixed marriages), who score lower than whites under apartheid; blacks in the U.S. South score lower than blacks in the North; Jews entering Ellis Island in the early 1900s scored lower than Jews today. "George DeVos studied IQ scores of a Japanese minority caste, the Burakumin, thought traditionally to be 'unclean' because they worked as tanners. In Japan their test scores reflected their disadvantaged social-economic position, the gap between their scores and those of Japanese children was similar to the gap between Africans and whites in the U.S. But Burakumin children whose families migrated to the U.S. achieved scores identical to other Japanese-American children (5 to 11 points higher than average white scores)" (from Bates and Fratkin 1999:30, citing Goleman 1988). Put differently, "Racial differences in average IQ scores are simply one measure of the impact of racism and racial inequality" (Hudson 1995:6).

It is possible to test claims of Herrnstein and Murray and others that so-called races as biological entities differ significantly from each other in intelligence due to heredity. If the authors of *The Bell Curve* are correct, then African Americans who have more European and less African ancestry should have higher IQs. One study that directly tested this proposition was by psychologist Sandra Scarr (Scarr et al. 1977). Restated, the proposition was that the higher the proportion of European ancestry, the higher should be the IQ of African Americans. They gave an IQ test to a sample of 350 African American schoolchildren in the Philadelphia area. They estimated each person's degree of African and European ancestry from blood samples in which they could identify serum proteins indicating 12 hereditary traits that were more likely to have either African or European ancestry. These results were supported by degree of skin color and were similar for siblings. According to Scarr and Weinberg:

> The results were unequivocal. Blacks who had a large number of European ancestors did no better or worse on the tests than blacks of almost total African ancestry. These studies dispute the hypothesis that IQ differences between blacks and whites are in large part the result of genetic differences. [1978:32]

In the language of correlations, they found zero correlations between degrees of "race" and test scores. It is difficult to correlate "race" and "g," two phenomena that do not exist. Herrnstein and Murray do not refer to this study in the 552 pages of their main text, presenting only a brief footnote on page 729 (following appendix 7).

The claim made by Herrnstein and Murray in 1994 and Jensen in 1969 is that remedial environmental programs can do little because hered-

ity is so strong. I have already cited a crucial study that contradicts that biological determinism (Scarr et al. 1977). I have also cited comparative cultural studies showing the power of the environment. Illustration of the positive effects of an environmental program is provided by the Abecedarian project in North Carolina. Parents of the children in the project had low IQs and minimal family income. A large minority of the children were African Americans. The program provided enriched educational day care outside the home every weekday starting at three months of age until they entered public school. Children participated in baking projects requiring measuring amounts, group chats and games involving diverse experiences. By age three the toddlers averaged an IQ of 101, a huge 17 points over the control group. The results were lasting; a decade later, at age 15, children from the intervention group had maintained an average of 5 points over controls (97.7 vs. 92.6). The greatest improvements were shown by children of mothers with IQs below 70 (Wickelgren 1999). After the publication of *The Bell Curve,* the Science Directorate of the American Psychological Association issued a "media advisory" that "there is a wealth of research evidence showing that early educational interventions are effective in raising performance and achievement levels for disadvantaged groups" (Duster 1995:160).

According to *The Bell Curve,* those at the bottom of society are there because of low IQ, and since they have larger families, the intelligence of Americans overall will decline. The prediction was frequently made early in the century in reaction to the flood of European immigrants. That the United States would become a nation of imbeciles has been disproved by James Flynn (1987), who discovered that IQ tests move the norm to 100 every 15 to 25 years. The Wechsler test was first normed in 1953 and again in 1978. In 1981, a group of people took both tests and scored 7.5 points higher on the older test. Given the 25 years between the two standardizations the gain was 3 points per decade (Neisser

1998:12). This same rising curve has been found in 20 nations (Flynn 1984, 1987; Wickelgren 1999). At the same time the gap in scores between blacks and whites has narrowed, leaving a difference of only 7 IQ points on the Ravens Progressive Matrices Test (Nisbett 1995:50). These changes may be because the average number of years of schooling has increased from eight in the 1920s to over 13 in the 1990s. Also, more parents are better educated, and home environments are more enriched (Wickelgren 1999).

This rapid trend toward upward test scores cannot be explained by genetic evolution, which occurs over a much longer span of time. Rather, it is a powerful veto to the argument that "race" determines IQ. Environment is not a minor factor influencing IQ; it is a major factor enhancing the chances for success of individuals and groups. IQ is not a fixed or hereditary entity; it can change significantly over time. Remedial social programs are not unproductive; if the environment is enriched and sustained, performance increases proportionately. Insofar as IQ scores are important, their increase indicates that America is not dumbing down. With the publication of *The Bell Curve* in 1994, it appeared that "scientific" racialism had acquired a new focus of controversy. However, that controversy obscured the appearance in the 1980s of the more explicit and extreme voice of J. Philippe Rushton, to which we now turn.

What More Could Be Said about "Race" and IQ? The Excesses of J. Philippe Rushton

Rushton is a psychologist at Western Ontario University in Canada. He is dedicated to proving that there is a "racial" hierarchy that determines cultural differences in which blacks are inferior in almost every way. He draws upon scientific concepts and data in his attempt to support that racial hierarchy. He is unique in using both brain weight and/or cranial size and corre-

lating it with IQ scores. In other words, he uses data from the nineteenth and twentieth centuries that have been discredited as sources of information about intelligence of "races." He has modified the nineteenth-century hierarchy by moving "Mongoloids," or Asians, to the top, while "Negroids" stay on the bottom, and "Caucasoids" are in the middle but close to Mongoloids. Rushton's promotion of Asians to the top coincided with the enormous economic prosperity occurring in Asia beginning in the 1970s, an example of one more environmental influence on a supposedly gene-based theory (Lieberman 2001). Rushton's theory in diagram form appears in Figure 3-1.

Rushton places his explanation of racial and cultural differences in the context of Darwinian evolution. The three "races" evolve with "Mongoloids" in a *K* Pleistocene environment where they have clear expectations about the severe environment and must have few children and raise them with great parental care. "Negroids" are in an unpredictable less *K* and more *r*, African environment, and must have many offspring but giving less parental care. Greater cranial size and intelligence evolve among "Mongoloids"; they have higher cultural achievements, are more law-abiding and less permissive, and have the smallest penises; "Negroid" have a trade-off of less intelligence for larger phallic size. Rushton also described over two dozen cultural behaviors that are said to be genetically determined. These include intelligence level, number of offspring, law abidingness.[4] In each case "Mongoloids" have the best, "Caucasoids" are a close second, and "Negroids" the worst.

The flaws in Rushton's explanation are legion. The *r/K* concept originated with MacArthur and Wilson (1967) to explain differences between two species. Its application within the human species ignores the power of culture and environment to alter behavior. Rushton writes that the more *K* "races" have later ages of first pregnancy and lower intercourse frequencies, which should lead to smaller numbers of children. According to

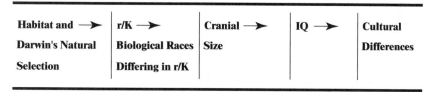

Figure 3-1

Rushton, then, the Hutterites of North America, like other persons of European descent, should have small families, but in fact they have one of the world's highest fertility rates (Potts and Silman 1979, cited by Weizmann et al. 1990). The idea of "racial" fertility rates being fixed by past evolution is also disproven by the sharp decline in total birth rates from 90 percent to 60 percent in two to three decades in Western Europe (Coale and Watkins 1986, cited by Weizmann et al. 1990). Finally, more rigorously designed studies have not supported the *r/K* model (Begon and Mortimer 1981).

"Race" is a pivotal concept for Rushton, yet most anthropologists have discarded the concept because there is more variation within "races" than among them, clear boundaries do not exist, "races" lack biological uniformity, and all of this stems from migration, the flow of genes through mating, and the operation of varying intensity of natural selection across geographic regions without respect to boundary lines. Yet Rushton uses the concept of "race" without precisely defining the term beyond referring briefly to skin color and a few facial features, and stating that they are biological and that the three "races" are in Asia, Africa, Europe, and the Near East. More abstractly, and without providing specifics for each population, he states that "races are recognized by a combination of geographic, educational, and morphological factors and gene frequencies of biochemical components."

Rushton asserts that "races" merge, that there are three major "races," and that there are varieties or minor races within them (1995:96). These assertions lump together within each "race" an enormous range of biological variation. Rushton justifies this by using what he calls the principle of aggregation. In other words, he claims that by combining and averaging the cranial sizes of many populations within each "race," any variations in the accuracy of particular research studies will be averaged out and that the resulting correlations will be higher as well. However, his low correlations do not support that claim. I also object to this procedure on the basis that before populations are aggregated and cranial measurements averaged, it should be demonstrated that they have similar biological characteristics that place them in that "race." Rushton "explains" variation in cultural achievement leading up to "civilization" with the claim that "Mongoloids" have the largest mean brain size and "Negroids" have the smallest, while "Caucasoids" are intermediate. I wish to place this brain-size explanation in several comparative contexts that demonstrate its scientific insignificance.

IQ in context 1: The normal range in cranial size from 1,000 to 2,000 cc. The question of which "race" has the largest cranial size and intelligence is devoid of merit because it rests on the invalid race concept, on aggregating diverse populations into the three race boxes, and on the dubious claims that IQ tests measure a hereditary essence in the brain. It is necessary to examine the mean measurements reported by Rushton (1995:130): M = 1,364 cc, C = 1,327, and N = 1,267. The range between these means is 97 cc. Figure 3-2 presents four contexts in which to interpret this range.

Normal cranial size for *Homo sapiens* varies from 1,000 to 2,000 cc. The range of normal

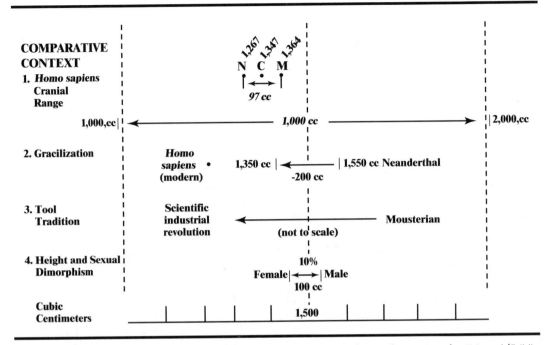

Figure 3-2. "Race" and Brain Size in Context: Rushton's aggregate of mean brain sizes for "Negroid" (N), "Caucasoid" (C), "Mongoloid" (M)

Note: Mean brain sizes based on data from a number of populations, aggregated by Rushton.
Source: From *Race, Evolution, and Behavior, Special Abridged Edition* (Transaction Press, 1999). Reprinted by permission of the author.

variation for modern *H. sapiens* is about 1,000 cc; therefore, a range of 97 cc between means is very small and cannot represent a casually significant difference. Normal human populations can appear anywhere along this continuum.

Contexts 2 and 3: Cultures change despite evolution of smaller brains. These concern the variation in cranial volume from Neandertal, at about 1,550 cc, to present-day *Homo sapiens* in Europe, at about 1,350 cc. The decrease was part of the skeleton becoming lighter, a process called gracilization, and marking the shift from Mesolithic (about 100,000 to 35,000 years ago) to modern *H. sapiens*. Despite this decrease in absolute cranial size, culture changed dramatically from the Mousterian to the period of the Neolithic, and then to the scientific and industrial

revolutions. If larger brains are smarter, as Rushton repeatedly tells us (often without correcting for body size or height), why did so many scientific and technological developments occur during the period when cranial head size had grown smaller by 100 cc—about the same amount that lies between the alleged means of Asians and Africans? Or can we assert that smaller brains are smarter? When challenged on these small differences in mean brain size, Rushton states that billions of neurons are involved in a 97-cc difference. There are also the multitude of dendrites connecting neurons. But the crucial point is that a greater number of neurons and dendrites can be packed into a smaller brain space. Holloway (1968) has reported that the packing distance between neurons decreases as the brain increases. It has also been demonstrated that women have 4,000 more neurons per cubic millimeter in their smaller cerebral cortex.

Context 4: Females have smaller brains but their IQ scores are not lower than those of males.   This represents height and sexual dimorphism. Brain weight varies significantly with body height. Females have about 10 percent smaller brains than men, an example of sexual dimorphism. Yet this difference disappears when corrected for height. Most importantly, no major sex differences exist in general mental ability, and mean IQ scores of males and females are very much the same (Jensen 1980, cited by Ankney 1992). Since the alleged difference in mean cranial size between blacks and whites is about the same as the average difference between sexes, we once again see that cranial size does not determine intelligence.

Where are the causal connections?   Rushton must demonstrate a causal relationship between brain size and intelligence to support his hierarchical view of human variation. In one sentence, Rushton and Ankney state that "only further research can determine if such correlations represent cause and effect," and they immediately go on to say that "it is clear that the direction of the brain size/cognitive ability relationship described by Paul Broca . . . , Francis Galton . . . and other nineteenth century visionaries is true" (1996:21). How strong is that relationship in terms of correlations? The coauthors assembled 47 studies correlating IQ scores with cranial or brain size. Using Rushton's principle of aggregation of scores, the range of correlations was .08 to .69, with a mean r of 0.24. The percent of variation "explained" is calculated by squaring the correlation: $.024^2 = .058$, or nearly 6 percent. Thus, 6 percent of the variance in brain size and IQ scores is "explained," leaving 94 percent unexplained. Although this 6 percent "explanation" may be statistically significant, it is substantively insignificant in the sense that it applies to a trivial portion of the *global* explana-

tion that Rushton proposes for differences in "race" behavior. A correlation between brain size and IQ does not, of course, demonstrate a causal connection, regardless of how high or low the correlation is and regardless of whether it is statistically significant or not.

At other times Rushton seems much less shy when relating correlations and environment and claiming a causal explanation based on genes:

> When there is a correlation between genetic and environmental effects it means that people are exposed to environments on the basis of their genetic propensities. [1995:66]

> That genes guide experience is shown in studies examining variables more often considered as environmental causes than as genetic outcomes. [1995:67]

> Thus, genes may have extended effects beyond the body in which they reside, biasing individuals toward the production of particular culture systems. [1995:67]

Rushton repeatedly uses data on cranial size, but fails to inform his reader that those sources reject his kind of conclusion and some provide a fundamentally different and strong nonracial explanation of the differences. In short, he misrepresents the sources that he uses. For example, he borrows cranial measurements from Kenneth Beals, Courtland Smith, and Stephen Dodd's 1984 study to aggregate data into the three "major races." Beals and coauthors found that correlations of brain size with "race" are weak because smaller crania are found in warmer climates regardless of "race." According to Carl Bergmann's rule, a more globular shape retains heat better in a cold climate (Beals et al 1984). In other words, cranial size varies with latitude and temperature. Beals et al. found that cranial size of North American blacks was similar to that of European Americans. Rushton obscured this relationship by aggregating data on African Americans from North America with data on Africans in hot climates. Clearly, it is not real populations that Rushton studies, but convenient fictional aggregates he calls "races."

In regard to brain weight, P. V. Tobias (1970) thoroughly analyzed 14 variables that must be controlled if measurements are to be accurate. Although Rushton cites Tobias, his report of brain-weight studies fails to indicate whether the original sources controlled for these 14 variables. Without these controls, the claims of brain size–IQ correlations must be rejected.

Another example concerns Rushton's report that black children are more precocious in their development than white (1988:1012), which he concludes demonstrates inferiority. One of his sources for precocious development is Daniel Freedman (cited five times on one page). Freedman, however, comments:

> Apparently one of the difficulties in the above findings involves the ill-intentioned hypothesis that human groups which exhibit motor precocity are "less sapient." . . . It is therefore important to report a recent study by Freedman and Strieby [unpublished data, 1973], using the Cambridge Neonatal Scales with 31 newborns of Punjabi extraction. The Punjabis are a Caucasian group of Northern India who have been highly successful economically in New Delhi, where the study was done. Our data indicate that this group is the most motorically precocious of any group yet seen, including Africans and Australian aboriginal newborns. . . . Thus, within the one race of Caucasians, differences wide enough to encompass the other groups have been found, and it would appear that motor precocity is related to localized adaptations rather than to broad phyletic trends. We hope these findings will help lay to rest unwarranted and mischievous speculation regarding the relative phyletic position of one or another group of mankind. [1974:170]

Again, Rushton does not inform the reader of research that contradicts his own racial hypothesis.

There is nothing to be gained by debating Rushton. He contends that opposition stems from "political correctness." The likely audience for pseudo-scientific racialism is not social scientists but policymakers and those either leaning toward ideas of racial inferiority or already committed to racialism and racism. Rushton thus joins that century-long network of race–IQ determinists for whom it matters little whether Europeans or Asians are on top. The major consequence of such "racial" hierarchies is to justify exploitation of those on the bottom. The further consequence is that such biodeterminism can be taken by policymakers to justify worldwide benign neglect of those living in poverty, including one in five of American children.

What about racialism in anthropology in the twentieth century? What I have said about IQ testing and race in the twentieth century mostly concerns the activities of psychologists. I have also noted that much of the fact-based criticism of these developments came from psychologists. A scientific discipline consists of many specializations and points of view. The primary responsibility for self-governance lies with individuals and with an association's committee on ethics. I would be remiss if I did not point to similar problems in anthropology.

In this regard I have already cited Tylor (1881), Morton (1839), Hrdlička (1915), and Coon (1962). Michael Blakey, a physical anthropologist, reviews the history of physical anthropology and concludes that the discipline has continually supported ideologies of human inequality. He writes:

> This history of anthropological racism is almost never mentioned in introductory texts of physical anthropology. More often, it is psychology that is pointed to as having a racist history through its biased use of IQ testing. One prominent physical anthropology text (Nelson and Jurmain 1991) gives Hrdlicka and Hooton their due as founders of the field but says nothing of their racist work. [1994:273]

A more recent and less obvious example of racism, albeit indirect, is research that pays "little attention" to the "biological and health effects of inequitable political and economic institutions," especially among people of color (Blakey, p. 275).

Still more recently Blakey (1998) has contributed a chapter to a collection of articles (Goodman and Leatherman 1998) that highlights this problem and calls it to the attention of physical anthropologists. It is too soon to assess the response.

Ethics and possible racialism and racism are also said to be involved in the Human Genome Diversity Project (HGDP), led by several physical anthropologists, which proposed collecting blood samples from 25 persons in several hundred, mostly indigenous societies, many on the verge of extinction. Patents had been sought for rare genetic sequences from the Hagahai, New Guinea hunters and gatherers, with a resistance to leukemia. The hope was that commercially and medically useful knowledge could be developed about the immune response to leukemia. In 1995, the U.S. government obtained a patent on a cell line developed from a Hagahai male. Millions of dollars have been spent to purchase other cell lines from various patent holders. Although HGDP, was not the sponsor of the blood drawn from the Hagahai, the event was used to draw attention to the HGDP, as did the assumption that indigenous peoples from around the world were to be similarly treated.

Nongovernment organizations began to protest the plan. Several anthropologists were critical of the HGDP (Goodman 1996; Lock 1997; Marks 1995), especially about the apparent lack of concern about why these indigenous people and other cultures were becoming extinct, and how they might be helped. The project was alleged to be a continuation of colonial exploitation of peoples of color and of the nineteenth-century idea of progressive evolution in which "primitive" peoples were placed at an early stage of evolution and therefore likely to become extinct. Further issues involved the doubt that local peoples would be effectively asked to give informed consent, and if they did, should they not receive some of the profit derived from their DNA? A proposed anthropological solution to some of these problems involves "collaboration," which would involve negotiating between the anthropologists and the people (Frankel and Herzog 1998). The negotiation would include "scope, design, goals, methods of implementation, and access to research results" (Cunningham 1998:227) and profits. Proponents believe such procedures will enhance the insight gained by the researcher. The proposal might also create a sense of shared purpose that would minimize exploitation. The HGDP is not racialist or racist in purpose, but the data collected by the enterprise may be interpreted in a racialist manner by those so inclined (Moore 1996:228).

At the time of this writing, there are controversies concerning issues of possible ethics and racialism in the work of anthropologists in the late nineteenth century and during the twentieth century. The people involved are almost always Third World and indigenous people of color in small, powerless societies such as Native Americans or those living in the Amazon River basin. For example, Allice Cunningham Fletcher's ethnography of Native Americans, the Omahas, in the 1880s salvaged disappearing knowledge of their language, music, tribal organization, and customs. She believed, as did most anthropologists of that time, the theory of evolution in stages from "savagery" to "barbarism" to "civilization." She did not believe the racialist idea that the Omaha were doomed to extinction but, rather, that they needed help to reach the next stage. Fletcher supported the Dawes Allotment Act of 1887, which called for federal allotments of tribal land to individuals in the hope that they would begin farming and complete their acculturation. It is described by David Hurst Thomas as "a monumental disaster for the American Indian" (2000:67). By 1933, two-thirds of their allotted land had been sold to whites (Temkin 1989). Fletcher is an example of some well-intentioned anthropologists who value indigenous cultures but are guided by ethnocentric theoretical assumptions and whose actions may unintentionally lead to racist consequences. On balance, it should also be stressed that many anthropologists were involved in antiracialism education and research in the late nineteenth and into the twentieth century (see Lieberman 1997).

A second issue concerns fieldwork in the twentieth century in which anthropologists were supported in part by various agencies of the U.S. government, and in return provided information to them. This included assistance to the military during the war in Southeast Asia. One anthropologist raises the issue that the American Anthropological Association inaction "sends the dangerous message to the under-developed world that the world's largest anthropological organization will take no action against anthropologists whose fieldwork is a front for espionage" (Price 2000:27). The association is addressing these and related issues.

A third issue is raised by Patrick Tierney (2000), an investigative journalist. Tierney charges that in research sponsored by the Atomic Energy Commission, medical geneticist James V. Neel was of a eugenicist orientation and contributed to a measles epidemic among the Yanomamo of Venezuela and Brazil by administering a problematic vaccine. Defenders of Neel state that Neel was opposed to eugenics, and that the measles virus had been brought to the Yanomamo by contact with missionaries. They further state that the vaccine does not and did not result in transmitting measles; rather it was approved by medical authorities and saved thousands of lives.

Napoleon Chagnon, a cultural anthropologist, assisted Neel by administering the vaccine. He also is said to have set up war dances for the camera that led to actual warfare, to have elicited sacred taboo names of deceased kin from competing villages, to have opposed government efforts to create a tribal reserve because of the violence between villages, and failure to obtain informed consent from the Yanomamo for his research. Further, he is said to have publicized a stereotype of the Yanomamo as a warlike people in his book (1968) *Yanomamo: The Fierce People.*

Chagnon's research was conducted at a time when the ethic of informed consent had not yet been fully developed. In later editions of his book (1977, 1983), following vigorous criticism from other anthropologists, Chagnon emphasized the basic humanity of the Yanomamo, and in the 1992 edition he did not use the subtitle *The Fierce People.* He also has observed that Yanomamo culture is possibly less violent than American culture (Bodley 1994:66). Other allegations about Chagnon remain to be evaluated. The American Anthropological Association is investigating the charges raised in Tierney's book and considering a revision of its code of ethics. One consideration to be addressed by the AAA committee concerns the sharing of profits from a book about the culture of small local society. Profit made without benefit to the local people is similar to colonial exploitation in which natural resources are taken without compensation.

The efforts of most cultural anthropologists add to knowledge about cultural diversity, and that they improve and maintain small endangered societies should be acknowledged. These efforts include the work of applied anthropologists, the Society for Applied Anthropology, and the organization Cultural Survival. These are developments in which data from research are used to offer workable solutions for problems confronting a society. Another primary role of cultural anthropologists is classroom teaching, and here the task is to explain why cultures differ. For centuries racialism has been used to explain cultural differences. In an earlier section we saw that anthropology helped provide a valid and persuasive rebuttal to racialism in the twentieth century. In the final section we will see that differences between cultures can be explained without racialism.

CONCLUSION

Yali's Question

In his 1999 condensation of his earlier book of 1995 Rushton has an added section entitled "Yali's Question and Marco's Answer." "Yali's

Question" appeared in a book by Jared Diamond (1997), a biologist. Yali is a public official in New Guinea who asks Diamond, "Why is it that you white people developed so much cargo and brought it to New Guinea, but we black people had little cargo of our own?" (p. 14). "Cargo" refers to all the manufactured products that Europeans brought to New Guinea. Yali had earlier been a leader in founding cargo cults. These cults viewed cargo as a product of the spiritual world and prayed that the spirits would bring cargo to the black people of New Guinea (Worsley 1957).

What would be Rushton's answer to Yali's question? Consider Rushton's racialist theory: "race" determines that blacks shall have the worst or least of everything, "orientals" the most, with whites a close second. Thus blacks will have the smallest brains, lowest intelligence scores, lowest cultural achievements, highest intercourse frequency and most sexually transmitted diseases, most aggressiveness and impulsivity, least marital stability and least law abidingness, least administrative capacity, and so on. (Rushton 1995:5). It is a truly comprehensive list in which blacks can do nothing right, according to Rushton. The one phrase, "cultural achievements," embraces a multitude of possible behaviors. So why those alleged differences? Rushton's answer to Yali is provided by Marco Polo, who after his time in China in the thirteenth century is alleged to have written: "Surely there is no more intelligent race on earth than the Chinese" (no source is given). The answer is consistent with Rushton's race–IQ determinism (see Table 3-1).

Jared Diamond (1997) gives a vastly different answer. He explains that the answer is not "race." He asks why the Aztecs did not bring guns, germs, and steel to Europe? If the Aztecs or the Africans had lived in the area of the Fertile Crescent then they would have invaded and conquered the rest of the world. Guns, germs, and steel were proximate causes, but the ultimate causes lie in a pattern of history in which

by chance most of those plants and large mammals that could be domesticated existed in the area of the Fertile Crescent of southwest Asia where the Tigris and Euphrates join.

Over thousands of years in the Fertile Crescent hunting and gathering was gradually replaced by farming. Harvests became abundant and farm animals provided plentiful protein, droppings for fertilizer, and power for plowing and transportation. Population grew, and small cities developed with stratified specializations in crafts, religion, and government. In such settings innovations were more likely, including writing. Centuries later there had accumulated the technological knowledge and power to conquer others. Germs to help conquer the Americas were present in the Europeans because they had acquired them through contact with their domesticated animals. They evolved resistance and developed immunity. The inhabitants of the New World had few animals, and did not develop the resistance needed and therefore suffered a massive loss of life after first contact with Europeans and their diseases such as smallpox. Diamond also adds that the processes of developing agriculture were easier in Eurasia because it is a continent along a horizontal axis in which the same latitudes allow for easy dispersal of plants and animals over wide geographic areas. By contrast, the Western Hemisphere and Africa are situated along a north to south axis that includes latitudes with very different climates that are barriers to plants and animals. In addition there were geographic barriers such as the Sahara Desert and tsetse flies in Africa, and in the Americas the greater distance, lack of animals for transportation, and the narrow isthmus of Panama with its tropical rain forest.

Diamond's explanation parallels what anthropologists have long argued: that the differences between cultures are not due to race but to geographic location and environmental resources (ecology), cultural history, and cultural contact. The nations and kingdoms of the Egyptians, Greeks, Romans, Spanish, British, Aztecs, Incas,

Table 3-1   Where Blacks, Whites, and Orientals Fall on Various Traits

Trait	Blacks	Whites	Orientals
Brain Size:			
Cranial capacity	1,287	1,347	1,384
Cortical neurons (millions)	13,185	13,865	13,787
Intelligence:			
IQ test scores	85	100	106
Cultural achievements	Low	High	High
Reproduction:			
2-egg twinning (per 1000 births)	16	8	4
Hormone levels	Higher	Intermediate	Lower
Sex characteristics	Larger	Intermediate	Smaller
Intercourse frequencies	Higher	Intermediate	Lower
Permissive attitudes	Higher	Intermediate	Lower
Sexually transmitted diseases	Higher	Intermediate	Lower
Personality:			
Aggressiveness	Higher	Intermediate	Lower
Cautiousness	Lower	Intermediate	Higher
Impulsivity	Higher	Intermediate	Lower
Self-concept	Higher	Intermediate	Lower
Sociability	Higher	Intermediate	Lower
Maturation:			
Gestation time	Shorter	Longer	Longer
Skeletal development	Earlier	Intermediate	Later
Motor development	Earlier	Intermediate	Later
Dental development	Earlier	Intermediate	Later
Age of first intercourse	Earlier	Intermediate	Later
Age of first pregnancy	Earlier	Intermediate	Later
Life-span	Shortest	Intermediate	Longest
Social organization:			
Marital stability	Lower	Intermediate	Higher
Law abidingness	Lower	Intermediate	Higher
Mental health	Low	Intermediate	Higher

Chart shows average for each race. There is variation within each race as well.

Source: J. P. Rushton, 1999. *Race, Evolution, and Behavior, Special Abridged Edition.* Brunswick, NJ: Transaction. Reprinted by permission of the author.

Chinese, Ghanaians, and Malians rose and fell independent of the "race" of their inhabitants. However, Yali's question about cargo is not fully answered. There is a gap in Diamond's explanation following the beginning of complex cities in the Fertile Crescent, and also following the time when European expansion began after Columbus's voyages of exploration and exploitation. The latter gap is the time in which European growth occurred in population, capitalism, science, and industrialization, accompanied and stimulated by the colonization and globalization of the rest of the world—all of which could have originated in Eurasia regardless of what "race" occupied Europe and the Fertile Crescent.

Rushton ignores how anthropologists have devoted themselves in the twentieth century to explaining differences among societies using historical, cultural, and ecologically based ethnographies. The many efforts by anthropologists of the Boasian school to end racialism and racism and develop the culture concept were summarized by Ruth Benedict and Gene Weltfish in 1943. Benedict stressed the plasticity of the human species, variation in ecological conditions, and information flow between societies. Conditions favorable to cultural change exist for a time in one place and then later in another. Nations and tribes cycle up and cycle down as conditions change, yet genes mutate at a much slower pace. Migration and interbreeding illustrate the futility of using the biological concept of "race" to explain human behavior. In addition to historical and ecological emphases, cultural anthropologists have taught that the concepts of ethnocentrism and the antidote of relativism are necessary to understand the working of any culture. It is often stated that African cultures were inferior because they were simpler, lacking the science and technology of Europe. Such comparisons ignore the complexity of religious beliefs, kinship systems, and knowledge of food sources and how to build their own houses and make their own clothing and tools in nonindustrial societies. Also neglected is the knowledge of the medicinal use of plants in their habitat. Explaining why populations differ cannot be done on the basis of IQ scores, but requires knowledge about the ecology, geography, demography, and history experienced by each society.

Final Questions

At the start of this chapter six common racialist statements were presented. Two of these have not yet been addressed. One has to do with the idea of blacks being closer to apes. Physical anthropology refutes that stereotype. Thick lips are cited, but apes have very thin lips. Many blacks have wide nostrils but whites have more body hair which is closer to apes. For every superficial similarity for whites there is one for blacks. The more fundamental fact is that all humans are about 5 million or 6 million years of evolution away from apes.

The second area concerns blacks in sports. Placing blacks closer to apes is done by arguing

that they excel in sports. It appears that for "scientific" racialism that whether blacks excel, or are said to be degenerate, marks them as inferior. In 1936, Montague Cobb, a physical anthropologist, wrote a rebuttal during the heated debate over Jesse Owens's triumph in the 1936 Olympics, a case of a black triumphing over German athletes despite Hitler's claim of racial superiority. Cobb tested the hypothesis that racial physical anatomy made for Owens's triumph. Cobb provided measurements and x-rays of Owens's legs and of several other black and white persons. These were submitted to another anatomist, who found no discernible difference. Cobb also compared average measurements and found them too small to make a difference (Cobb 1936:54; Rankin-Hill and Blakey 1994).

Finally, I wish to summarize the general characteristics of current "scientific" racialism (SR) as seen in the following practices. Not all apply to each practitioner to the same degree.

1. Unwarranted ranking: SR presents a racial hierarchy in which persons of African descent, or persons with darker skins, are placed at the bottom.
2. The outer form of science: SR employs the style and statistical techniques of science but seldom tests and improves propositions about the relationship between heredity and environment.
3. Biological determinism: SR allows that environment and heredity play a role, but at some point qualifies the role of environment so that environment is largely the result of genetic heredity. In measuring environment, SR uses weak measures, thereby limiting the influences of environment.
4. Unverified reification: All abstract thought creates names for phenomena that may or may not be real, but SR is based on the unverified assumption that "g" is the abstract core of intelligence in the brain, that it is real and has been identified by IQ tests.
5. Aggregation of populations: Assumes "races" are real biological subdivisions of the human species and that data on world populations can be aggregated, or lumped, into one of three major "races" without demonstrating the biological similarity of each constituent population. Alternatively, there is the assumption that specific populations can be classified as a "race" despite multiple ancestry.

6. Aggregation of complex phenomena: For example, law-abidingness is presented as if it were universally the same in all cultures despite the complexity and variation of laws over time and in different cultures.

7. Selective use of sources: SR borrows from scientists but quotes selectively and ignores the conclusions of those authors when they disagree with those of SR.

8. Discounting counterevidence: When SR cites evidence that contradicts its case that evidence is minimized, for example, by giving it little space or by placing it in a footnote.

9. Denial of racism: Since World War II, SR denies that it is practicing racism.

10. Funding from organizations like the Pioneer Fund and/or publication in *Mankind Quarterly* whose goals are the promotion of racial hierarchy.

11. Advocating reduction of social programs: SR denies the workability and cost-effectiveness of programs for raising IQ and reducing inequality because of the supposed high degree to which intelligence is limited by genes.

The best defense against "scientific" racialism is awareness of the counterevidence.

Until the mid-twentieth century "scientific" racialism in physical anthropology resembled that in psychology (see Coon 1962). These included (1) unwarranted ranking, (2) the outer form of science, (3) biological determinism, (4) unverified reification, and (5) aggregation of diverse populations into one of three races. There continues to be too little attention to environmental influences and how they affect population studies (exceptions are Blakey 1994, 1998; Goodman and Leatherman 1998; Armelagos and Goodman 1998). As Blakey has noted, little attention is paid to the history of "scientific" racialism in textbooks of physical anthropology which would serve as useful information, especially to students who might become professional anthropologists.

In cultural anthropology in the nineteenth and early twentieth centuries there is evidence of the first five characteristics listed in the preceding paragraph. In addition, there is the support of cultural anthropologists by British and American government agencies in exchange for information that might be used in controlling the populations studied. Increasingly in the late twentieth century it became clear that informed consent of the studied population was a necessary starting point.

Within the disciplines of psychology and anthropology, there are vigorous critics of past "scientific" racialism and of its twentieth-century manifestations. In both disciplines too little attention is paid to informing future scientists of that history and its present manifestations. In this history I have attempted to trace the consistent theme that the practitioners of "scientific" racialism present. Using the techniques but not the essence of science, they have claimed that there is a racial hierarchy in which blacks are always at the bottom. The consequences of such a contention is to justify the inferior and exploited position of people of color. I have presented the research of a number of those who developed such ideas over past centuries, as well as some of the counterevidence from almost a century of research and debate. The strongest evidence for an interaction of heredity and environment does not support the notion of biologically determined "race" differences in intelligence. The ultimate test for "race" differences in intelligence can only occur in a society where equal access to cultural resources is available to all. Yet it is precisely that access that is opposed, in one way or another, by "scientific" racialism. The differences among human populations and societies are best explained by examination of their different ecology, geography, demography, and contacts with other societies—in short, their different cultural histories.

NOTES

1. Among these seventeenth- and eighteenth-century scientists were (1) Franz Gall (1758–1828), a physician, studied the bumps on the human cranium and linked such bumps to intellect and morality, thereby reflecting and reinforcing the biological explanation of behavior. (2) Georges Cuvier (1769–1832), founder of paleontology, traced the "races" to Adam, and viewed blacks as the most inferior of all "races."

(3) Paul Broca (1824–80) specialized in neuroanatomy and physical anthropology. He developed many new tools for measuring the cranium, and asserted that mixed "races" were inferior in almost every way. (4) Ernst Haeckel (1834–1919), a specialist in embryology, enthusiastically adopted Darwin's ideas but differed from Darwin by viewing evolution as progressive, with inferior "races" eventually being eliminated, a view that would become state policy under Adolf Hitler in the 1940s. (5) Louis Agassiz (1835–1910), a zoologist, was an influential antievolutionist, and a strong supporter of the inferiority of blacks and the idea that the "races" had been created separately (polygenic) and were different species.

2. In *Hereditary Genius* (1869), Galton was among the first to apply to mental phenomena the principle of deviation from the average. He divided the normal curve of ability into classes A through C (although he did not have a procedure for assigning individuals to these categories (Tucker 1994). Galton also developed a calculus for the correlation coefficient, percentile ranking, regression to the mean, and the distinction between general mental ability (intelligence) and special abilities (particular aptitudes), and he advocated twin studies (Evans and Waites 1981:36). Galton was certainly not an egalitarian, and although he was opposed to hereditary aristocracy, he favored meritocracy based on purported mental abilities. "Galton achieved a synthesis of liberal individualism with Darwinism which offered a rationale for a class-stratified but socially mobile society" (Evans and Waites 1981:38). It was a line of reasoning still evident in the latter-day hereditarians, Jensen, Herrnstein and Murray, and others.

3. Stephen J. Gould interprets these phases in relation to their social context: the reasons for recurrence are sociopolitical, and not far to seek; resurgence in biological determinism correlates with episodes of political retrenchment, particularly with campaigns for reduced government spending on social programs, or at times of fear among ruling elites when disadvantaged groups sow serious social unrest or even threaten to usurp power. What argument against social change could be more chillingly effective than the claim that established orders, with some groups on top and others at the bottom, exist as an accurate reflection of the innate and unchangeable intellectual capacities of people so ranked (Gould 1996:28)?

4. In reporting that persons of African descent are the least law-abiding, Rushton uses Interpol data but does not explain how aggregating crime rates guarantees a precise comparison of something so complex, made up of different crimes and different measures of crime.

REFERENCES CITED

AGASSIZ, LOUIS. 1850. The diversity of origin of the human races. *Christian Examiner* 49:110–145.

ALLEN, GARLAND. 1989. Eugenics and American social history, 1880–1950. *Genome* 31:885–889.

___. 1999. Modern biological determinism. In *The Biological Basis of Human Behavior*. Robert W. Sussman, ed. Pp. 294–304. Upper Saddle River, NJ: Prentice Hall.

ANKNEY, C. DAVISON. 1992. Sex differences in relative brain size: The mismeasure of women, too? *Intelligence* 16:329–336.

ARMELAGOS, GEORGE J., and ALAN H. GOODMAN. 1998. Race, racism, and anthropology. In *Building a New Biocultural Synthesis*. Alan H. Goodman and Thomas L. Leatherman, eds. Pp. 359–377. Ann Arbor: University of Michigan Press.

BAKER, LEE D. 1998. *From Savage to Negro: Anthropology and the Construction of Race, 1896–1954*. Berkeley: University of California Press.

BARKAN, ELAZAR. 1987. From Race to Ethnicity: Changing Concepts of Race in England and the United States between the Two World Wars. Ph.D. dissertation, Brandeis University.

BATES, DANIEL G., and ELLIOT FRATKIN. 1999. *Cultural Anthropology*. 2nd edition. Boston: Allyn & Bacon.

BEALS, KENNETH L., COURTLAND L. SMITH, and STEPHEN M. DODD. 1984. Brain size, cranial morphology and time machines. *Current Anthropology* 25:301–315.

BEGON, M., and M. MORTIMER. 1981. *Population Ecology: A United Study of Animals and Plants*. Oxford: Blackwell Scientific Publications.

BENEDICT, RUTH. 1934. *Patterns of Culture*. Boston: Houghton Mifflin.

BENEDICT, RUTH, and GENE WELTFISH. 1943. *Race: Science and Politics*. New York: Viking Press.

BINET, ALFRED. 1903 [1973]. *Les Idées Modernes sur les Enfants*. Paris: Flammarion.

BLAKEY, MICHAEL. 1994. Passing the buck: Naturalism and individuals as anthropological expressions of Euro-American denial. In *Race*. Steven Gregory and Roger Sanjek, eds. Pp. 270–284. New Brunswick, NJ: Rutgers University Press.

___. 1996. Skull doctors revisited: Intrinsic social and political bias in the history of American physical anthropology. With special reference to the work of Aleš Hrdlička. In *Race and Other Misadventures: Essays in Honor of Ashley Montagu in His Ninetieth Year*. Larry Reynolds and Leonard Lieberman, eds. Pp. 64–95. Dix Hills, NY: General Hall.

___. 1998. Beyond European Enlightenment: Toward a critical and humanistic human biology. In *Building a New Biocultural Synthesis*. Alan H. Goodman and Thomas L. Leatherman, eds. Pp. 379–406. Ann Arbor: University of Michigan Press.

BLOCK, N. J., and GERALD DWORKIN, eds. 1976. *The IQ Controversy: Critical Readings*. New York: Random House.

BLUMENBACH, JOHANN FRIEDRICH. 1795. On the Natural Varieties of Mankind. Thomas Bedyshe, trans. New York: Bergman.

BOAS, FRANZ. 1912. *Report on Changes in the Bodily Form of Descendants of Immigrants*. New York: Columbia University Press.

___. 1940. *Race, Languages and Culture*. New York: Free Press.

BODLEY, JOHN H. 1994. *Cultural Anthropology: Tribes, States and the Global System*. Mountain View, CA: Mayfield.

BRACE, C. LORING. 1964. A nonracial approach towards the understanding of human diversity. In *The Concept of Race*. A. Montagu, ed. Pp. 103–152. New York: Free Press.

___. 1996. A four letter word called "race." In *Race and Other Misadventures: Essays in Honor of Ashley Montagu in His Nineteenth Year*. Larry Reynolds and Leonard Lieberman, eds. Pp. 106–141. Dix Hills, NY: General Hall.

___. 1997. Race. In *The History of Physical Anthropology*. Frank Spencer, ed. Pp. 861–867. New York: Garland.

BROCA, PAUL. 1861. Sur le volume et la forme du cerveau suevant les individus et suevant les race. *Bulletin Societé d'Anthropologie* (Paris) 2:139–207, 301–321, 441–446.

BRUES, ALICE. 1977. *Peoples and Race*. New York: Macmillan.

BURT, CYRIL. 1958. The inheritance of mental ability. *American Psychologist* 13:1–15.

CHAGNON, NAPOLEON. 1968. *Yanomamo: The Fierce People*. New York: Holt, Rinehart & Winston.

___. 1977. *Yanomamo: The Fierce People*. 2nd edition. New York: Holt, Rinehart & Winston.

___. 1983. *Yanomamo: The Fierce People*. 3rd edition. New York: Holt, Rinehart & Winston.

___. 1992. *Yanomamo*. New York: Holt, Rinehart & Winston.

CHAMBERLAIN, HOUSTON STEWART. 1910. *Foundations of the Nineteenth Century*. John Lees, trans. New York: H. Fertig.

CHASE, ALLAN. 1975. *The Legacy of Malthus: The Social Costs of the New Scientific Racism*. New York: Knopf.

CHIDLEY, JOE. 1994. The brain strain. *Maclean's* 107:72–73.

COALE, A. J., and S. C. WATKINS, eds. 1986. *The Decline of Fertility in Europe: The Revised Proceedings of a Conference on the Princeton European Fertility Project*. Princeton, NJ: Princeton University Press.

COBB, W. MONTAGUE. 1936. Race and runners. *Journal of Health and Physical Education* 7:3–7, 52–56.

COON, CARLETON. 1962. *The Origin of Races*. New York: Knopf.

CUNNINGHAM, HILARY. 1998. Colonial encounters in postcolonial contexts. *Critique of Anthropology* 18:205–233.

CUVIER, G. 1812. *Researches sur les Ossemens Fossiles*, vol. 1. Paris: Deterville.

DARWIN, CHARLES. 1859 [1968]. *The Origin of Species*. Harmondsworth: Penguin.

DAVENPORT, CHARLES B. 1911. *Heredity in Relation to Eugenics*. New York: Henry Holt.

DENNIS, RUTLEDGE M. 1996. Racism. In *The Social Science Encyclopedia*. Adam Kuper and Jessica Ruper, eds. Pp. 715–717. London: Routledge.

DIAMOND, JARED. 1997. *Genes, Germs, and Steel: The Fates of Human Societies*. New York: Norton.

DU BOIS, W. E. B. 1943. *Dusk of Dawn: An Essay Toward an Autobiography of a Race Concept*. New Brunswick, NJ: Transaction.

DUGDALE, RICHARD. 1970 [1916]. *The Jukes*. New York: Arno Press.

DUSTER, TROY. 1995. What's new in the IQ debate. *Black Scholar* 25:25–31.

ERICKSON, PAUL A. 1997a. American school of anthropology. In *The History of Physical Anthropology*. Frank Spencer, ed. Pp. 65–66. New York: Garland.

___. 1997b. Polygenism. In ibid., pp. 832–833.

ESTABROOK, ARTHUR H. 1916. *The Jukes in 1915*. Washington, DC.: Carnegie Institution.

EVANS, BRIAN, and BERNARD WAITES. 1981. *IQ and Mental Testing: An Unnatural Science and Its Social History*. Atlantic Highlands, NJ: Humanities Press.

FLYNN, JAMES R. 1980. *Race, IQ and Jensen*. London: Routledge and Kegan Paul.

___. 1984. The mean IQ of Americans: Massive gains, 1932 to 1978. *Psychological Bulletin* 95:29–51.

___. 1987. Massive IQ gains in 14 nations. What IQ tests really measure. *Psychological Bulletin* 101:171–191.

FRANKEL, MARK S., and ANTONIA HERZOG. 1998. The Human Genome Diversity Project, the model ethical protocol as a guide to researchers. Report of a symposium. Annual Meeting of the American Association for the Advancement of Science, Philadelphia.

FREEDMAN, DANIEL G. 1974. *Human Infancy: An Evolutionary Perspective*. Hillsdale, NJ: Erlbaum.

GALTON, F. 1869. *Hereditary Genius*. New York: Appleton.

GARDNER, HOWARD. 1985. *The Mind's New Science*. New York: Basic Books.

GOBINEAU, JOSEPH-ARTHUR. 1854. [1966]. *Essays on the Inequality of Human Races*. Adrian Collins, trans. Los Angeles: Noontide Press.

GODDARD, HENRY H. 1912. *The Kallikak Family: A Study of the Heredity of Feeble-Mindedness*. New York: Macmillan.

___. 1914. *Feeble-Mindedness: Its Causes and Consequences*. New York: Macmillan.

___. 1928. Feeble-Mindedness: A question of definition. *Journal of Psycho-Asthenics* 33:219–227.

GOLEMAN, D. 1988. An emerging theory on blacks' IQ scores. *New York Times,* Education Supplement, April 10: 22-24.

GOODMAN, ALAN. 1996. *Glorification of the Genes: Genetic Determinism and Racism in Science*. London: Intermediate Technological Publishers.

GOODMAN, ALAN H., and THOMAS L. Leatherman, eds. 1998. *Building a New Biocultural Synthesis*. Ann Arbor: University of Michigan Press.

GOSSETT, THOMAS F. 1965. *Race: The History of an Idea in America*. New York: Schocken Books.

GOULD, STEPHEN J. 1981. *The Mismeasure of Man*. New York: Norton.

___. 1996. *Mismeasure of Man*. Revised and expanded. New York: Norton.

GRADIN, GREG. 2000. Coming of age in Venezuela. *The Nation,* December 11.

GRANT, MADISON. 1916. *The Passing of the Great Race*. New York: Charles Scribner's Sons.

HANNAFORD, IVAN. 1996. *Race: The History of an Idea in the West*. Baltimore: Johns Hopkins University Press.

HERRNSTEIN, RICHARD J., and CHARLES MURRAY. 1994. *The Bell Curve, Intelligence and Class Structure in American Life*. New York: Free Press.

HOLLOWAY, RALPH L. 1968. Cranial capacity and the evolution of the human brain. In *Culture: Man's Adaptive Dimension*. Ashley Montagu, ed. Pp. 170–196. New York: Oxford University Press.

HRDLIČKA, ALEŠ. 1915. Evolution of man in the light of recent discoveries and its relation to medicine. Paper presented at joint meeting of Medical and Anthropological Societies, October 13, 1915. Washington, DC: National Anthropological Archives, National Museum of Natural History.

___. 1921. Lecture No. 27. Delivered at the American University, May 27, 1926. Washington, DC: National Anthropological Archives, National Museum of Natural History.

HUDSON, J. BLAINE. 1995. Scientific racism: The politics of tests, race, and genetics. *Black Scholar* 25:3–20.

JENSEN, ARTHUR R. 1980. *Bias in Mental Testing*. New York: Free Press.

KAMIN, LEON J. 1974. *The Science and Politics of IQ*. Potomac, MD: Erlbaum.

KLINEBERG, OTTO. 1935. *Negro Intelligence and Selective Migration*. Westport, CT: Greenwood.

KROEBER, ALFRED L. 1917. The superorganic. *American Anthropologist* 70:163–213.

KUZNICK, PETER J. 1987. *Beyond the Laboratory: Scientists as Political Activists in 1930s America*. Chicago: University of Chicago Press.

LEWONTIN, R. C., STEVEN ROSE, and LEON J. KAMIN. 1993[1984]. IQ: The rank ordering of the world. In *The "Racial" Economy of Science: Toward a Democratic Future*. Sandra Harding, ed. Pp. 142–160. Bloomington: Indiana University Press.

LIEBERMAN, LEONARD. 1968. The debate over race: A study in the sociology of knowledge. *Phylon* 39:127–141.

___. 1997. Gender and the deconstruction of the race concept. *American Anthropologist* 99:545–558.

___. 2001. How Caucasoids got such big crania and why they shrank: From Morton to Rushton. *Current Anthropology* 42:69–95.

LINNAEUS, CAROLUS. 1758. *Systema Naturae*. 10th ed. Stockholm.

LIPPMANN, WALTER. 1922a. The mental age of Americans, October 25. The mystery of the "A" men, November 1. The reliability of intelligence tests, November 8. The abuse of tests, November 5. Tests of hereditary intelligence, November 22. A future for the tests, November 29. *New Republic*. Reprinted in Block and Dworkin, ibid.

LIVINGSTONE, FRANK B. 1958. Anthropological implications of sickle cell gene distributions in West Africa. *American Anthropologist* 30:533–562.

___. 1962. On the non-existence of human races. *Current Anthropology* 3:279–281, 470.

LOCK, MARGARET. 1997. The Human Genome Diversity Project. *Social Science Medicine* 39:603–606.

MACARTHUR, R. H., and E. O. WILSON. 1967. *The Theory of Island Biogeography*. Princeton, NJ: Princeton University Press.

MACRAE, DUNCAN. 1960. Race and sociology in history and theory. In *Man, Race and Darwin*. Phillip Mason, ed. Pp. 76–86. London: Oxford University Press.

MARKS, JONATHAN. 1995. The Human Genome Diversity Project. *AAA Newsletter* 36:72.

___. 1997. Eugenics. In *History of Physical Anthropology*. Frank Spencer, ed. New York: Garland.

MEHLER, BARRY. 1989. Foundation for fascism: The new eugenics movement in the United States. *Patterns of Prejudice* 23:17–25.

MERCER, JOYE. 1994. A Fascination with Genetics. *Chronicle of Higher Education* 42:A28–29.

MOLNAR, STEPHEN. 1992. *Human Variation: Races, Topics, and Ethnic Groups*. 3rd edition. Englewood Cliffs, NJ: Prentice Hall.

___. 1998. *Human Variation: Races, Topics, and Ethnic Groups*. 4th edition. Upper Saddle River, NJ: Prentice Hall.

MONTAGU, ASHLEY. 1942. *Man's Most Dangerous Myth: The Fallacy of Race*. New York: Columbia University Press.

___. 1972. *Statement on Race*. 3rd edition. New York: Oxford University Press.

___. 1975. *Race and IQ*. New York: Oxford University Press.

___. 1997. *Man's Most Dangerous Myth: The Fallacy of Race*. 6th edition. New York: Columbia University Press.

MOORE, JOHN. 1994. Ethnogenetic theory. *Research Explorer* 10:10–23.

___. 1995. Putting anthropology back together again: The ethnogenetic critique of cladistic theory. *American Anthropologist* 96:925–948.

___. 1996. Is the Human Genome Project a Racist Enterprise? In *Race and Other Misadventures: Essays in Honor of Ashley Montagu in His Ninetieth Year*. Larry Reynolds and Leonard Lieberman, eds. Dix Hills, NY: General Hall.

MORTON, SAMUEL GEORGE. 1839. *Crania Americana*. Philadelphia: John Pennington.

___. 1849. *Crania Aegyptiaca*. Philadelphia: John Pennington.

NEISSER, UBRIC, ed. 1998. *The Rising Curve: Long-Term Gains in IQ and Related Measures*. Washington, DC: American Psychological Association.

NISBET, RICHARD. 1995. Race, IQ and scientism. In *The Bell Curve Wars: Race, Intelligence and the Future of America*. Steven Fraser, ed. Pp. 36–57. New York: Basic Books.

NOTT, J. C., and G. R. GLIDDON. 1854. *Types of Mankind*. Philadelphia: Lippincott, Grambo.

PATTERSON, ORLANDO. 1995. For whom the bell curves. In *The Bell Curve Wars: Race, Intelligence, and the Future of America*. Steven Fraser. ed. Pp. 187–213. New York: Basic Books.

POTTS, M., and P. SELMAN. 1979. *Society and Fertility*. Plymouth, UK: Macdonald and Evans.

PRICE, DAVID. 2000. Anthropologists as spies. *The Nation*, November 20: 24–27.

PROCTOR, ROBERT N. 1988. *Racial Hygiene, Medicine under the Nazis*. Cambridge, MA: Harvard University Press.

RANKIN-HILL, L. M., and M. L. BLAKEY. 1994. W. Montague Cobb (1903–1990): Physical anthropologist, anatomist, and activist. *American Anthropologist* 96:74–96.

RUSHTON, J. PHILIPPE. 1988. Race differences in behavior: A review and evolutionary analysis. *Personality and Individual Differences* 9:1009–1024.

___. 1995. *Race, Evolution, and Behavior: A Life History Perspective*. New Brunswick, NJ: Transaction.

___. 1999. *Race, Evolution, and Behavior*, special abridged edition. Brunswick, NJ: Transaction.

RUSHTON, J. PHILIPPE, and C. DAVISON ANKNEY. 1996. Brain size and cognitive ability: Correlations with age, sex, social class, and race. *Psychonomic Bulletin and Review* 3:21–36.

SAMELSON, FRANZ. 1979. Putting psychology on the map: Ideology and intelligence testing. In *Psychology in Social Context*. Allan R. Buss, ed. Pp. 103–168. New York: Irvington.

___. 1992. Rescuing the Reputation of Sir Cyril Burt. *Journal of the History of the Behavioral Sciences* 28:221–233.

SCARR, S., A. PAKSTIS, S. H. KATZ, and W. B. BARKER. 1977. The absence of a relationship between degree of white ancestry and intellectual skills within the black population. *Human Genetics* 39:69-86.

SCARR, S., and R. W. WEINBERG. 1978. Attitudes, interests, and IQ. *Human Nature* 1:29-36.

SEDGWICK, JOHN. 1994. The mentality bunker. *IQ* 64:228–236.

SHAPIRO, HARRY R. 1969. The history and development of physical anthropology. *American Anthropologist* 67:376.

SMEDLEY, AUDREY. 1993. *Race in North America: Origin and Evolution of a World View*. Boulder, CO: Westview Press.

___. 1999. *Race in North America: Origin and Evolution of a World View*. 2nd edition. Boulder, CO: Westview Press.

SOROKIN, PITRIM A. 1948. *Contemporary Sociological Theories*. New York: Harper & Row.

SPEARMAN, CHARLES. 1940. General intelligence objectively determined and measured. *American Journal of Psychology* 15:201–293.

SPENCER, FRANK. 1997. Johann Friedrich Blumenbach. In *History of Physical Anthropology*. Pp. 183–186. New York: Garland.

STEPAN, NANCY. 1982. *The Idea of Race in Science, Great Britain 1800–1960*. Hampton, CT: Shoestring Press.

STEPAN, NANCY, and SANDER L. GILMAN. 1993. Appropriating the idioms of science: The rejection of scientific racism. In *The "Racial" Economy of Science*. Sandra Harding, ed. Pp. 170–193. Bloomington: Indiana University Press.

TAYLOR, CAROL M. 1981. W. E. B. Du Bois's challenge to scientific racism. *Journal of Black Studies* 11:449–460.

TEMKIN, ANDREA S. 1989. Alice Cunningham Fletcher (1838–1923). In *Women Anthropologists*. Ute Gacs, Aisha Khan, Jerrie McIntyre, and Ruth Weinberg, eds. Urbana: University of Illinois Press.

TERMAN, L. M. 1916. *The Measurement of Intelligence*. Boston: Houghton Mifflin.

___. 1919. *The Intelligence of School Children*. Boston: Houghton Mifflin.

TERMAN, L. M., and MAUD A. MERRILL. 1937. *Measuring Intelligence: A Guide to the Administration of the New Revised Stanford-Binet Tests of Intelligence*. Boston: Houghton Mifflin.

THOMAS, DAVID HURST. 2000. *Skull Wars: Kennewick Man, Archaeology, and the Battle for Native American Identity*. New York: Basic Books.

THORNDIKE, E. L. 1940. *Human Nature and the Social Order*. New York: Macmillan.

TIERNEY, PATRICK. 2000. *Darkness in El Dorado: How Scientists and Journalists Devastated the Amazon*. New York: Norton.

TOBIAS, P. V. 1970. Brain-size, grey matter, and race—fact or fiction? *American Journal of Physical Anthropology* 32:3–26.

TODOROV, T. 1993. *On Human Diversity*. Cambridge, MA: Harvard University Press.

TUCKER, WILLIAM H. 1994. *The Science and Politics of Racial Research*. Urbana: University of Illinois Press.

TYLOR, EDWARD B. 1881. *Anthropology: An Introduction to the Study of Man and Civilization*. New York: Appleton.

VAN DEN BERGHE, PIERRE. 1996. Social Darwinism. In *The Social Science Encyclopedia*. Adam Kuper and Jessica Kuper, eds. Pp. 783–784. London: Routledge.

WARD, LESTER F. 1914. *Pure Sociology*. New York: Macmillan.

WEIZMANN, FREDRIC. 1990. Differential *K* theory and racial hierarchies. *Canadian Psychologist* 31:1–13.

WEIZMANN, FREDRIC, NEIL I. WIENER, DAVID L. WIESENTHAL, and MICHAEL ZIEGLER. 1996. Inventing racial psychologies: The (mis)uses of evolutionary theory. In *Race and Other Misadventures: Essays in Honor of Ashley Montagu in His Ninetieth Year*. Larry T. Reynolds and Leonard Lieberman, eds. Dix Hills, NY: General Hall.

WICKELGREN, INGRID. 1999. Nurture helps mold able minds. *Science* 283:1832–1834.

WORSLEY, PETER. 1957. *The Trumpet Shall Sound*. New York: Schocken Books.

4

ETHNICITY

Raymond Scupin

Lindenwood University

Ethnicity is based on a conception of a shared cultural heritage. An *ethnic group* is a collectivity of people who believe they share a common history, culture, or ancestry. However, the terms *ethnicity* and *ethnic group* have had a long history of misinterpretations in Western culture. For example, anthropologist David Maybury-Lewis has noted that "ethnicity has a will-o'-the-wisp quality that makes it extremely hard to analyze and not much easier to discuss" (1997:59). He goes on to say that everyone knows that ethnicity has something to do with a kind of fellow-feeling that binds people together and makes them feel distinct from others. Yet, it is difficult, if not impossible, he says, to say precisely what kind of feeling it is, and why and when people will be affected by it. Under some circumstances some people are willing to die on behalf of their ethnic group, whereas other people are not strongly preoccupied by their ethnicity in their everyday lives. In some circumstances, people will be classified as a particular ethnic group without feeling it or recognizing it themselves. Maybury-Lewis refers to the example of Native Americans, who were a diverse group of people

before receiving that ethnic label "Indians" from Europeans. Also, the criteria for distinguishing ethnic groups require a complex interpretive process. At times, an ethnic group may be distinguished by language, in other cases by religion, in still other situations by skin color or by a shared historical past. But it is also recognized that an ethnic group's shared past is open to reconstruction and reinterpretation in a variety of ways. This chapter will introduce the conceptions of ethnicity that have driven anthropological research and have led to a variety of insights into these complex questions.

As is evident in Chapters 1, 2, and 3, one of the fundamental misconceptions in early Western perspectives on race and culture, and in later "scientific" racist views, was the confusion between "race" and "culture." Purported racial characteristics, such as skin color or nose shape, were associated with particular "essences" that determined behavior and cultural attributes. These misunderstandings were also prevalent in the early usages of the word *ethnicity*. The Greek term *ethnos* (derived from *ethnikos*) was used to refer to non-Greeks, or to *other* peoples who shared some biological and cultural characteristics and a common way of life. The Greeks tended to refer to non-Greeks as peripheral, foreign barbarians, or *ethnea,* and referred to themselves as civilized peoples, *genos Hellenon* (Hutchinson and Smith 1996). Later, the word *ethnos,* as used in the Greek New Testament, was associated with non-Jewish and non-Christian peoples and nations that were referred to as pagans, heathens, and idolaters (Simpson and Weiner 1989). Eventually, in various European languages ethnic, ethnical, ethnicity, *ethnique,* and *ethnie* corresponded to an association with "race" (Simpson and Weiner 1989). As the field of anthropology, including the subdisciplines of cultural anthropology and ethnology, developed in the nineteenth century, the usage of ethnology or ethnicity also became associated with "race." Thus, ethnological studies focused on the scientific investigation of the different "races of mankind." Race, language, and religion were perceived as a fusion of physical and cultural traits by the Western scientists and anthropologists of the nineteenth century.

However, as emphasized in earlier chapters, one of the basic findings of the research of Franz Boas and later anthropologists is that the physical characteristics of a specific group of people are not associated with any particular behavior or culture or language. In other words, one's language or culture is not inherited through biological transmission or genetics. Boas stressed that culture was far more involved in explaining how people in different ethnic groups behaved than any biological factors. One acquires his or her language and culture through *enculturation,* by learning the language and various symbols, values, norms, and beliefs in the environment to which one is exposed. Since the 1960s, anthropologists and other social scientists have generally used the term *ethnicity* or *ethnic group* to refer to an individual's cultural heritage, separate from one's physical characteristics.

In the modern definition, we emphasize both the objective and subjective aspects of ethnicity.

The objective aspect is the observable culture and shared symbols of a particular group. It may involve a specific language or religious tradition that is maintained within the group, or it may be particular clothing, hairstyles, preferences in food, or other conspicuous characteristics. The subjective aspect involves the internal beliefs of the people regarding their shared ancestry. They may believe that their ethnic group has a shared origin, or family ancestry, or a common homeland. In some cases they may believe that their ethnicity has specific physical characteristics in common. This subjective aspect of ethnicity entails a "we-feeling" and a sense of community or oneness, or a distinction between one's own "in-group" versus an "out-group." It doesn't matter whether these beliefs are historically or scientifically accurate, genuine, or fictional. This subjective identification of individuals with an ideology of a (at least imagined) shared history, unique past, and symbolic attachment to a homeland are often the most important expressions of ethnicity (Smith 1986).

Thus, one's ethnicity is not innately determined by biology or purported racial characteristics. Despite early classifications of the European "race" or the English, German, French, or Polish "races," these differences among Europeans were not based on physical characteristics, but rather on linguistic and cultural variation. Likewise, there is no African "race." Rather, Africa is a continent of the world where hundreds of different ethnic groups reside that vary from region to region. The descendants of African slaves residing in the United States have a very different ethnicity than descendants of African slaves who live in the Caribbean. In Asia, the differences among the Chinese, Japanese, Koreans, Thais, Indonesians, Vietnamese, Cambodians, and Laotians are not based on racial differences but on ethnic differences. Though there may be some minor genetic differences among these populations, they are slight and do not result in distinctive "races." These ethnic groups have different languages, histories, and cultural traditions that create variation among them.

Since ethnicity is based on cultural characteristics, it is much more variable, modifiable, changeable, and, as we will see, more situational than an identity based on physical characteristics. But before we begin an analysis of ethnicity, we need to comprehend the importance of culture as it is employed by anthropologists to understand ethnic identity issues.

THE CONCEPT OF CULTURE

Culture is a fundamental concept within the discipline of anthropology. In everyday usage many Americans refer to culture as "high culture"– Shakespeare's works, Beethoven's symphonies, Michelangelo's sculptures, gourmet cooking, imported wines, and so on. Anthropologists, however, use the term in a much broader sense to refer to all of the learned and shared ideas and products of a society.[1] E. B. Tylor, a British anthropologist, proposed a definition of culture in the nineteenth century that includes much of human experience: "Culture . . . is that complex whole which includes knowledge, belief, arts, morals, law, custom, and any other capabilities and habits acquired by man[kind] as a member of society" (1871:1). This view suggests that culture includes tools, weapons, fire, agriculture, animal domestication, metallurgy, writing, the steam engine, glasses, airplanes, computers, penicillin, nuclear power, rock-and-roll, video games, designer jeans, religion, political systems, subsistence patterns, science, sports, and social organizations. In Tylor's view, culture includes all aspects of human activity, from the fine arts to popular entertainment, from everyday behavior to the development of sophisticated technology. It contains the plans, rules, techniques, designs, norms, and policies for living.

Nineteenth-century theorists such as Tylor linked biological traits with cultural characteristics. It was not until the twentieth century, when anthropologists such as Franz Boas began to use systematic scientific research techniques to demonstrate that there was no causal link between biological ancestry and possession of a particular culture, that scientists, including anthropologists, gained a better understanding of genetics, heredity, and the roles of environment and culture. Biological traits are passed to individuals through genes, whereas culture is transmitted to individuals through learning or what anthropologists refer to as *enculturation*. Most anthropologists today would accept a broad conception of culture as a shared way of life that includes values, beliefs, and norms transmitted within a particular society from generation to generation.

Notice that this definition includes the term *society*. In general, society refers to a particular group of humans within a specific territory. In particular, it refers to the patterns of relationships among the distinct social statuses and roles within this definite territory. In the past, anthropologists attempted to make a simple distinction between culture and society. Society was said to consist of the patterns of relationships among people within a specified territory, and culture was viewed as the by-products of those relationships. This view of society as distinguishable from culture was derived from ethnographic studies of small-scale societies. In such societies, people within a specific territory usually share a common culture. However, as we will see, in most countries where modern anthropologists conduct ethnographic research, societies are multicultural and multiethnic and consist of ethnic groups that maintain some commonalities in cultural tradition, but also may have very little commitment to many of these common aspects of the larger culture.

Symbols, Language, and Culture

The human capacity for culture is based in part on our linguistic and cognitive ability to *symbolize*. *Symbols* are abstract ideas that are embodied within language. *Language* is the standardized system of symbols that allows people to communicate with one another. Language ensures the continuity of a cultural heritage. As human children learn their language, symbols and culture are transmitted from generation to generation. One recognized aspect of language is that humans can speak using complicated phonological and syntactical and grammatical rules, without ever being conscious of those rules. Speakers and listeners of a particular language cannot consciously express those complicated rules. Obviously, some aspects of human culture are also unconscious. As humans learn their language, both consciously and unconsciously, they learn how to subsist, how to interact, how to govern their society, and what gods to worship. Culture is the transmission of learned knowledge. A group of people who share knowledge of this sort to a greater degree than they share it with others can be considered an ethnic group. Culture is the historical accumulation of learned symbolic knowledge that is shared by an ethnic group. This symbolic knowledge is transmitted through enculturation, and it can change rapidly from one generation to the next. Generally, however, most people go to great lengths to conserve their cultural and symbolic traditions. As we will see in later chapters, the persistence of cultural and symbolic traditions, the basis of ethnic identity, is as widespread as cultural and ethnic change.

We noted that culture consists of the shared practices and understandings within a society. To some degree, culture is based on shared meanings that are to some extent "public" and thus beyond the mind of any individual. Culture exists before the birth of an individual into the society, and it will continue (in some form) beyond the death of any particular individual. These publicly shared meanings provide designs or recipes for surviving and contributing to the society. On the other hand, culture exists within the mind of individuals. For example, a particular ethnic group learns the symbolic meanings of

their own group by observing practices and learning a language. However, the child is not just a passive receptor of that cultural knowledge; rather, the child uses that knowledge to make decisions and develop strategies for interacting with others. Cognitive anthropologists emphasize *schemas,* or cultural models that are internalized by individuals and influence decision making and behavior. Culture is acquired by and modeled as schema within individual minds, which can motivate, shape, and transform these symbols and meanings (D'Andrade and Strauss 1992; Quinn and Holland 1987).

In addition, culture has some influence on people's emotions. Cultural symbols, both implicit and explicit, can appeal to people in almost a physical way. People do not merely think about symbols, they feel and experience them emotionally. Anthropologists often discuss how culture and cultural symbols become *naturalized* within a particular society. The symbols become so natural to people that they cannot conceive of doing, feeling, or thinking in any other way. For some people, a particular ethnicity feels "biological" or "innate" or "natural." To be an Italian American, a Native American, an African American, an Igbo from Nigeria, a Fijian, or Irish may feel emotionally rooted within the self of an individual. On the other hand, depending on their experience, some people may not have deep emotional attachments to any specific ethnicity.

It is apparent that cultural understandings are not shared equally by all members of a society. Even in small-scale societies, culture is shared differently by males and females, rich and poor, young and old. Some individuals in these societies have a great deal of knowledge regarding agriculture, medical practices, or religious beliefs, while others have less. In a complex industrialized society such as the United States, culture consists of a tremendous amount of information and knowledge regarding technology and other aspects of society. Different people learn different aspects of this culture, such as repairing cars or television sets, understanding nuclear physics or federal tax regulations, or composing music. Hence, to some extent, culture varies from person to person, region to region, class to class, age to age grouping, and gender to gender. As will be discussed later in respect to ethnicity, anthropologists who conduct research on ethnic groups within multicultural and multiethnic societies find diverse configurations of shared culture and practices. There may be some overlap in shared practices and culture among these different ethnic groups, but there are various degrees of commitment to particular aspects of a "common" culture. In many cases, the so-called common culture may be contested and struggled against. The extent to which an individual or an ethnic group shares a particular culture is an empirical question that the anthropologist has to investigate.

The concept of culture has two dimensions that are sometimes distinguished by anthropologists: material and nonmaterial culture. *Material culture* consists of the physical products of human society (ranging from clothing styles to housing and building types to technologies of transportation). Material culture often constitutes important ethnic boundary markers, which are used to differentiate one group from another. Clothing styles are often used to demarcate one ethnic group from another. *Nonmaterial culture* refers to the intangible products of human society (symbols and language, values, beliefs, and norms). *Values* are the abstract standards by which members of an ethnic group define what is good or bad, holy or unholy, beautiful or ugly. They are assumptions that are shared within the ethnic group. Values are the abstract generalizations that underlie beliefs and practices. All ethnic groups have *beliefs,* which are cultural conventions that concern true or false assumptions, including specific descriptions of the nature of the universe and one's place in it.

When discussing culture, many anthropologists refer to the worldview of a particular ethnic group. A *worldview* consists of various beliefs about the nature of reality and provides a particular ethnic group with a more or less consistent orientation toward the world. Some beliefs may be combined into an ideology. An *ideology* consists of cultural symbols and beliefs that reflect and support the interests of specific ethnic groups or subgroups within an ethnic group. Particular ethnic groups promote ideologies for their own ends as a means of maintaining and justifying economic and political authority.

In some societies, especially complex societies with different ethnic groups, sociopolitical and ethnic configurations of power relations may produce *cultural hegemony,* or *ethnic hegemony,* the ideological control by one dominant ethnic group over beliefs and values. One ethnic group that has political power may impose its cultural beliefs on other subordinate ethnic groups. As we will see in later chapters, for a long historical period the dominant ethnic group in early U.S. history, white Anglo-Saxon Protestants, was able to impose its language, cultural beliefs, and practices on other ethnic groups in society. Likewise in Russian society, many ethnic minorities had to learn the culture and language of the dominant Russian majority. In many areas of the world, ethnic minorities were often forced to accept the ideologies of the politically dominant group.

Norms are an ethnic group's rules of right and wrong behavior. They are like the traffic regulations of behavior within an ethnic group. *Norms* are shared rules or guidelines that define how members of an ethnic group "ought" to behave under certain circumstances. Norms are generally connected to the values, beliefs, worldviews, and ideologies of an ethnic group. Some anthropologists use the term *ethos* to refer to the socially acceptable norms within an ethnic group. Norms guiding ordinary usages and conventions of everyday life are known as *folkways.* Thus, among different ethnic groups there are a variety of rules for greeting people, gift exchanges, table manners, and innumerable other social occasions. *Mores,* or morality norms, have much stronger sanctions than folkway or etiquette norms. Members of ethnic groups believe that their mores are crucial for the maintenance of a decent and orderly way of life. People who violate mores are usually severely punished, though punishment for the violation of mores varies from one ethnic group to another. It may take the form of ostracism, vicious gossip, public ridicule, exile, dismissal from one's job, physical beating, imprisonment, commitment to a mental hospital, or even execution.

When discussing values, beliefs, and norms, ethnologists often distinguish between ideal culture and real culture. *Ideal culture* consists of what people within an ethnic group say they do or should do, whereas *real culture* refers to their actual behaviors. Ethnologists have discovered that the ideal culture frequently contrasts with people's actual behavior. For instance, a Chinese anthropologist may learn that people in the United States cherish the value of equal opportunity, yet in observing U.S. culture, the anthropologist might encounter many cases in which people from different racial and ethnic backgrounds are treated in a highly unequal manner. This difference between ideal and real culture is an important distinction for anthropologists in assessing race and ethnic relations. Various patterns of prejudice and stereotypes regarding ethnic and race relations may not be expressed within the ideal culture, but may be an aspect of the real culture. Anthropologists find that there are differences between the ideal and real cultural practices of individuals in all societies.

The terms for nonmaterial culture, including values, beliefs, norms, ideologies, ethos, and worldviews, are used by many anthropologists in their research on ethnic groups. However, not all anthropologists agree with concise, clear-cut distinctions among these terms. Instead, these terms are based on the models that anthropologists build on when studying and interpreting other cultures. Terms such as values, beliefs, norms, or worldviews are used as heuristic devices and research aids to help explain behavior and understand the complex symbols shared by ethnic groups. Contemporary anthropologists recognize that these models are only partial solutions to explaining and understanding the empirical and existential realities of ethnicity and culture.

Additionally, anthropologists differ in respect to how culture should be understood and analyzed. They advance different methodological and analytical approaches that may result in variant understandings of the term *culture*. Some anthropologists view culture as an indirect reflection of the material aspects of a society. In other words, the environmental and technological factors within a society produce a specific form of culture. That is, culture is a by-product of the material conditions within a particular society (Harris 1979, 1999). These anthropologists maintain that certain types of economic, social, political, or other institutions develop in relation to specific ecological conditions and technological changes. Therefore "culture" is part of an adaptive mechanism that corresponds to the material conditions within the society. Thus, an ethnic group's culture and behavior are indirectly produced by the technological and ecological conditions that are available to the group. Other anthropologists emphasize how "culture" is an indirect reflection of the organization of political and economic interests within a society. In this view "culture" is used, shaped, modified, and changed to correspond to specific social, economic, or political interests of groups and individuals. Whether focusing on environmental or technological features, or economic and political phenomena, these anthropologists attempt to offer explanations for human behavior, ethnicity, and cultural characteristics.

Some anthropologists, however, refer to "culture" as a set of linguistic symbols that have to be treated and interpreted like a "text" (Geertz 1963) or "code" (Sahlins 1976). As these anthropologists conceptualize the cultural text or code, they focus on the highly symbolic and nonmaterial aspects of a society. They are not concerned with the question of why particular institutions or ethnic patterns develop but, rather, how to make sense of institutions and ethnicity in relation to specific cultural values, beliefs, norms, and practices. These symbolic anthropologists attempt to interpret the meaningfulness of cultural symbols within the ethnic groups that they study. In their view humans are meaning-seeking creatures that need to maintain an identity and purpose in their lives. These meaningful symbols or codes are shared by ethnic groups and provide coherent frameworks for interpreting the world. Anthropologists who rely on the symbolic approach tend to offer interpretations of culture and human behavior rather than explanations of these phenomena.[2]

As will be seen, anthropologists differ with each other on how culture and ethnicity ought to be understood based on whether they focus on material/political interests or symbolic-interpretive frameworks. The materialist perspective is viewed by some critics as overlooking the symbolic significance and meaning of culture for ethnic groups, and they argue that these important symbols and meanings cannot be reduced to adaptive mechanisms. These critics also express their skepticism about whether culture and ethnicity can be reduced to political dynamics and interests within a society. On the other hand, the symbolic approach is criticized for not grappling with the dimensions of power, politics, and material factors and the roles they play in ethnic relations.

Although recognizing that the differences and divisions in anthropology between those who prefer materialist or political explanations and those who prefer textual or symbolic interpretive understandings of culture have had their effects on analyzing ethnicity and ethnic relations, every society must confront the problem of adjusting to the practical circumstances of life. People need food, shelter, clothing, and the necessary technology and energy for survival. The material component of culture is related to a group's survival. There is also the nonmaterial aspect of culture: norms, values, beliefs, ideologies, and symbols. These cultural norms and symbols have emotional significance and are meaningful. Symbols may not be directly related to the practical circumstances of life; instead, they may indicate some aesthetic or moral values that are not directly related to the material conditions of society. Thus, most anthropologists admit that both the material and nonmaterial dimensions of culture are fundamentally important in comprehending ethnicity and ethnic relations.

THE CULTURAL SIGNIFICANCE OF RACE AS ETHNICITY

As we have emphasized, ethnicity is based on cultural characteristics, including language and other learned and shared values, beliefs, and norms. Our ethnicity is not transmitted to us biologically. And, as we have seen in the chapters on race and "scientific" racism, the notion of race as a biologically meaningful scientific concept is highly questionable. Anthropologists find, however, beliefs about "purported races" that are culturally constructed in many societies throughout the world. In other words, though the scientific meaning of a distinctive "race" or separate "races" is questionable, people in different societies have "folk categories" of "race" that are based on phenotypic differences, such as skin color, hair color and texture, nose shape, and other physical characteristics that become embedded within the culture.

These folk categories of race are perpetuated and become cultural models for how ethnic identities are understood by outsiders and sometimes by the people themselves. In some cases, physical traits become both objective and subjective ethnic boundary markers. They are used to designate the ethnic identity of individuals. And the people designated as belonging to a specific identity may come to believe that these physical traits are an aspect of their ethnicity. In many societies, these invented folk categories are extremely powerful and are used by government agencies to classify people according to highly arbitrary racial classifications. These racial classifications become culturally meaningful and become the basis for social interaction within many societies. Thus, "race," as well as language, religion, and beliefs about an ancestral homeland, is used to demarcate the boundaries of ethnic groups.

Since the nineteenth century in the United States a system termed the *hypodescent concept* of racial classification has been used in cases of racial mixture whereby the offspring of the parents have the race of the parent with the lowest racial status. Since black Americans were considered to be a lower-status "race," a person is considered black if he or she has a black ancestor anywhere in the family history. This is known as the "one-drop rule" of racial classification because it is based on the myth that one drop of "black blood" is sufficient to determine racial blackness. Thus, Americans with both white and black ancestry are usually classified as black and often encouraged to identify as black in personal and social contexts. In contrast, a person is classified as white if he or she has no black ancestry anywhere in the family history. This means that in order to be white, a person has to prove a negative, the absence of black ancestors. Other racial categories such as mulatto (half black and half white), quadroon (one-quarter black and three-quarters white), and octoroon (one-eighth black and seven-eighths white) were developed as an extension of the one-drop rule. Until the 1950s in Louisiana, it was illegal for a doctor to give a blood transfusion from a black person to a white person. Despite the fact that this notion of the one-drop rule is mythical and is based on false notions of "racial essences," these ideas still persist in some circles.

Anthropologist Virginia Dominguez (1986) did research on a legal case involving race classification used in Louisiana in the 1980s. In 1982–83, a Louisiana woman, Susie Guillory Phipps, contested the state's classification of her as a "black," and claimed that she had a white racial identity. She sued the Louisiana Bureau of Vital Records to change her racial classification from black to white. As a descendant of an eighteenth-century white plantation owner and a black slave, Phipps was designated "black" on her birth certificate. A 1970 state law declared anyone with at least one-thirty-second "Negro blood" to be black. This was a clear manifestation of the hypodescent rule or the one-drop rule. Phipps's attorney argued that the racial categories assigned on a birth certificate were unconstitutional, and that the one-thirty-second designation was inaccurate. The woman lost her case in Louisiana, and the court upheld the state law that quantified racial identity and classification. Eventually, the law was declared unconstitutional and was repealed. Nevertheless, the case illustrates how the concept of race is culturally constructed and employed for social, legal, and political purposes.

In contrast to the one-drop rule, Native American Indians in the United States are treated differently. Because Native Americans have entitlements based on legislation, the U.S. federal government has sometimes imposed blood quanta rules of at least 50 percent ancestry from a particular tribe in order to be classified as a Native American Indian. This has created considerable confusion both legally and socially for many Native American Indian peoples. The one-drop rule and blood quanta tests emphasize that the mythical ideas of racial essences are deeply embedded within the folk culture of U.S. society. Socially, legally, and politically these U.S. folk racial distinctions trump other ethnic cultural characteristics. A group's physical traits have become a significant impermeable boundary that separates European "white" Americans from people of color, including Native Americans, African Americans, Hispanic Americans, Asian Americans, and Arab Americans.

Similar folk conceptions are held about race in other societies. In Northern Ireland, some Protestants and Catholics believe that they can identify members of the other group based on physical differences, despite their obvious physical similarities. In South Africa, the government categorized different populations as "white," "coloured" (a mixture of different "races"), "Asian" (which includes Chinese and Indians but not Japanese, who were considered honorary "whites"), and "black." The South African government used this classification scheme based on highly arbitrary racial categories for social, legal, and political purposes. In Puerto Rico, an island colonized by the Spanish and later by the United States, racial classifications are used to categorize people by skin color. Puerto Ricans use *blanco* to refer to whites, *prieto* to refer to blacks, and *trigueño* to refer to tan-skinned people. In Brazil, a complex racial classification exists that uses different criteria with which to categorize people from those in the United States. An individual categorized as "black" in the United States might be categorized as "white" in Brazil (Harris 1964).

As we will see in later chapters, in countries such as China and Japan folk categories of race were historically important in classifying various peoples. Anthropologists have recognized that although these folk conceptions of race are based on subjective, arbitrary categories, they have a profound social and cultural significance in many societies. So, when assessing race and ethnicity issues, we find that folk beliefs about race are sometimes embedded within the ethnicity of a particular group of people.

ETHNICITY: MAJOR ANTHROPOLOGICAL PERSPECTIVES

Anthropologists have employed a number of different theoretical strategies to study ethnic groups and processes of ethnicity. One early model developed in the 1960s is known as the *primordialist model*. The primordialist model of ethnicity is associated with anthropologist Clifford Geertz, who suggested this view of ethnic identity in an essay entitled "The Integrative Revolution: Primordial Sentiments and Civil Politics in the New States" (1963). Geertz attempted to describe how many Third World countries were trying to build nations and integrate their political institutions based on a "civil order," a political system based on democratic representation processes rather than traditional ties of kinship or religion. However, as he indicates in the essay, this new civil order clashed with older traditional or "primordial" aspects of kinship, race, ethnicity, language, and religion.[3] Geertz states:

> By a primordial attachment is meant one that stems from the *"givens"*—or, more precisely, as culture is inevitably involved in such matters, the *assumed "givens"*—of social existence: immediate contiguity and kin connection mainly, but beyond them the givenness that stems from being born into a particular religious community, speaking a particular language, or even a dialect of a language, and following particular social practices. These congruities of blood, speech, custom, and so on, are seen to *have an ineffable, and at times overpowering, coerciveness in and of themselves.* One is bound to one's kinsman, one's neighbors, one's fellow believer, *ipso facto;* . . . in great part by virtue of some unaccountable absolute import attributed to the very tie itself. . . . But for virtually every person, in every society, at almost all times, some attachments seem to flow more from a sense of *natural*—some would say *spiritual* . . . affinity than from social interaction. [1963:259–260]

Geertz suggests that ethnic attachments based on assumed kinship and other social ties and religious traditions are deeply rooted within the individual through the enculturation process. He maintains that ethnic affiliation persists because it is fundamental to a person's identity. In this view, as people are enculturated into a particular ethnic group, they form deep emotional attachments to it. These emotional sentiments are sometimes evident through *ethnic boundary markers,* which distinguish one ethnic group from another. These ethnic boundary markers include religion, dress, language or dialect, and other visible symbols. But Geertz tends to focus on the intense internal aspects of ethnicity and the deep subjective "feeling of belonging" to a particular ethnic group. This is one of the strengths of the primordialist perspective on ethnicity. It emphasizes the meaning and significance that people invest in their ethnic attachments. Geertz emphasizes how the "assumed givens" are subjective perceptions of attributes such as blood ties and ancestry, which may or may not coincide with the actual circumstances of one's birth.[4] Geertz goes on to say that the primordial ties are experienced by the people of these new nations, and that despite the introduction of new forms of civil political institutions and ideologies, these ethnic attachments endure, and are at times obstacles as new nations attempt to integrate their societies based on a new civil political order. He suggests that there is a basic conflict between the modern state and one's personal identity based on these primordial ties.

Another proponent of the primordialist model is Joshua Fishman. In an essay entitled "Social Theory and Ethnography," Fishman describes how ethnicity is intuitively defined and experienced as part of an actor's "being" (as distinct from his "doing" and "knowing"). He says:

> Ethnicity has always been experienced as a kinship phenomenon, a continuity within the self and within those who share an intergenerational link to common ancestors. Ethnicity is partly experienced as being "bone of their bone, flesh of their flesh, and blood of their blood." The human body itself is viewed as an expression of ethnicity and ethnicity is commonly felt to be in the blood, bones, and flesh. It is crucial that we recognize ethnicity as a tangible, living reality that makes every human a link in an eternal bond from generation to generation—from past ancestors to those in the future. Ethnicity is experienced as a guarantor of eternity. [1980:84–97]

In his discussion, Fishman emphasizes the interrelationship between language, symbols, and ethnicity. He describes ethnicity as a *Weltan-*

schauung (worldview) that provides explanations for origins and other meaningful questions. As Fishman describes, the "blood, bones, and flesh" of ethnicity become symbolic metaphors in the language of the ethnic groups. They are not based on scientifically based biological realities but on symbolic metaphors that are deeply rooted both consciously and unconsciously within the emotions of individuals. Fishman indicates that the language of ethnicity is the language of kinship. Kinship is the basis of one's felt bond to one's own kind. It is the basis of one's solidarity with others in times of stress. It is the basis of one's right to rely upon them in times of need; it is the basis of one's dependency, sociability, and intimacy with others as a matter of course. Various songs, chants, sayings, prayers, rites, jokes, and riddles are aspects of the language of ethnic expression and identification. They are symbols of ancestral patrimony that Fishman refers to as the "corpus mysticum."

For example, a small ethnic group known as the Old Order Amish maintain very strong ethnic boundary markers in U.S. society (Hostetler 1980; Kephart and Zellner 1994). They emphasize their ethnic difference through language by speaking a German dialect among themselves. The Amish dress in a traditional manner similar to the cultural codes of the 1600s. Men wear hats and long beards, women wear long hair, which is always covered by a hat in public. Based on their interpretation of the Bible, the Amish strive to maintain a conservative, traditional way of life that does not allow the adoption of modern technology such as electricity, automobiles, and television. They do not allow their children to be educated beyond the eighth grade so that they are not exposed to modern U.S. culture. The Amish have a deeply emotional attachment to their ethnicity and culture. These primordial sentiments are deeply rooted within Amish culture and are evident in the *ethnic boundary markers*—language, dress, a traditional style of life—that distinguish them from other North Americans.

One of the criticisms of the primordialist model of ethnicity is that it appears to be based on what Geertz refers to as "ineffable" givens or spiritual traditions, or what Fishman refers to as "mystical" concepts. Some anthropologists have suggested that Geertz reduced primordial attachments to innate, fixed, unchangeable, unmodifiable, and unanalyzable characteristics (Eller and Coughlan 1993). It is not surprising that most of the anthropologists who have utilized the primordialist approach tend to be symbolic anthropologists who interpret culture as a "text" or "code." These texts or codes are deeply rooted within the emotional characteristics of the individual through enculturation. However, Geertz does emphasize how historical and political processes play a role in exacerbating or reducing primordial ethnic tensions. He says that as newly modernizing states attempt to repress ethnic attachments and construct new arrangements based on a somewhat alien order, people risk losing their personal identity, and in many cases end up being dominated by some other rival ethnic group (1963:258–259). Thus, to some extent, these primordial identities or "assumed givens" are produced by concrete historical processes that vary from person to person, from time to time, and from society to society. Also, as Geertz points out, individuals differ in respect to how much attention they pay to these primordial attachments.

The Circumstantialist Model

Another model of ethnicity began to surface within anthropology during the 1960s based on research within multiethnic societies. Michael Moerman, in a classic essay entitled "Who Are the Lue?" (1965), had intimated that ethnicity was more problematic than anthropologists had assumed. The Lue were a group of people in northern Thailand who lived among other ethnic groups, and Moerman was attempting to describe their ethnicity. But when he asked them to identify their cultural traits, such as language, culture, political organization, and religion, he found that they often mentioned cultural traits that they shared with other ethnic groups in the region. In addition, individuals differed with respect to the cultural traits that they listed as criteria for their ethnic group.

Moerman concluded that being "Lue" was not based on any objectively identifiable traits but, rather, stemmed from a completely subjectively defined and variable identity. In fact, he states that the Lue cannot define themselves ethnically without referring to other ethnic groups. The Lue did not make up a discretely bounded ethnic community but, rather, a more diffuse and situationally defined community. Instead of clear-cut objective categories, Moerman points to a more *emic* ("the native's point of view") understanding of their ethnic boundaries. In other words, anthropologists cannot use a "cookie-cutter" notion of culture, or a coherent-bounded homogeneous unit, to analyze ethnic groups. Ethnic groups in multicultural societies are not simplistic, easily identifiable culture units. Instead, they are overlapping groups that encompass other ethnic groups.

These problematic issues were clarified with the publication of anthropologist Fredrik Barth's *Ethnic Groups and Boundaries* (1969). In a number of case studies in this book Barth noted the fluidity of ethnic relations in different types of multiethnic societies. Although ethnic groups maintain boundaries such as language to mark their identity, people may modify and shift their language and ethnic identity in different types of social interaction. He criticized a view of culture based on earlier anthropological research in small-scale societies that tended to treat ethnic groups as having discrete, impermeable boundaries. Barth emphasized the interaction between ethnic groups and how people identify with different elements of their own ethnicity and express or repress those elements and characteristics in different circumstances for economic, political, or other practical interests. This model is sometimes referred to as an *instrumentalist* approach to ethnicity but has become known widely in anthropology as the *circumstantialist* model of ethnicity.

In the circumstantialist approach, Barth emphasizes how ethnic boundary markers, such as language, clothing, and other cultural traits, are not based on deeply rooted, enduring aspects of ethnicity. Ethnic boundaries are continually being revised, negotiated, and redefined according to the practical interests of the actors. Ethnic boundaries are generated by the varying contexts and circumstances in which people find themselves. For example, in the United States, people of German descent may refer to themselves as "German Americans" to distinguish themselves from "Irish Americans" or "Italian Americans." Should they happen to be among Europeans, however, these same people might refer to themselves simply as "Americans." The circumstantialist model explains how people draw on their ethnic identity for specific economic, social, and political purposes. People strategically use their ethnic affiliations as the basis for collective political mobilization or to enhance their economic interests. Barth showed how some people modify and change their ethnic identity when it is perceived to be advantageous for their own interests. They may emphasize the ethnic or racial identities of others or establish boundaries between themselves and others in order to interact with others for political or economic purposes. Thus, in Barth's view, ethnicity is not fixed and unchanging but is, instead, fluid and contingent, as people strategically use, define, and redefine their ethnicity to respond to their immediate basic needs.

Anthropologist Abner Cohen's approach to ethnicity is an example of the circumstantialist view. Cohen views ethnic collectivities as types of political organizations that are mobilized for different purposes. He notes that ethnic group organizations have two distinctive dimensions. They provide a symbolic meaningful framework for people, but they also have potential as political networks and associations. The symbolic framework offers people answers to the basic questions of life concerning ancestral origins and destiny, whereas the political aspect furnishes people with organizations to accomplish practical goals.

In a classic ethnography in West Africa, in the country of Nigeria, Cohen analyzed the relationship among various ethnic groups. He focused on the interrelationship between the people known as the Hausa and the Yoruba in Ibadan, a city dominated by the Yoruba. Cohen (1969, 1974) described how ethnic distinctions between the Hausa and Yoruba became the basis of political and economic competition over various resources. Hausa migrants had entered the city and became very successful in monopolizing the cattle trade in a short period of time. Cohen used the term *retribalization* to refer to the Hausa strategy of using ethnic affiliations as an informal network for economic and political purposes. The Hausa drew on their shared culture and ethnicity, including their Islamic religious tradition, to strengthen their group solidarity and political networks. These networks were, in turn, used to extend and coordinate Hausa cattle-trading activities in Ibadan. Cohen demonstrated how ethnic processes and the meaningful cultural symbols used by ethnic groups can mobilize political and economic behavior. Ethnicity, in Cohen's view, is an idiom and mechanism for producing political alignments, which are strategically used for practical ends. Thus, ethnic continuity or revival can be found in almost all societies, both developed and undeveloped.

Cohen's ethnography illustrates how individuals within ethnic groups that adapt to specific types of economic and political circumstances in a multiethnic society may emphasize their shared identity as a means of enhancing cooperation with other members of the group. Throughout the world individuals migrating to different areas often use ethnic ties as a means of social adjustment. Individuals may pursue political interests through ethnic allegiances. In numerous situations people may manipulate ethnic traditions and symbols to their advantage.

This circumstantialist view of ethnicity also asserts that ethnicity will be displayed to a different degree by various ethnic groups. Ethnic traits will vary from one historical time to another, and group identity may shift from one generation to another. Ethnic groups are not stable collective entities. They may appear and vanish within or less than a generation. Ethnic groups will come into being during different historical periods. *Ethnogenesis* refers to the origins of an ethnic group. Ethnogenesis has taken place throughout the world in many different historical circumstances. For example, the Amish ethnicity described earlier originated in Switzerland during the sixteenth century. The Amish descend from a group of Anabaptists who split off with their own leadership during the Protestant Reformation. After this split, the Amish began to define themselves as different from other Anabaptists, Protestants, and Catholics, and they faced a great deal of persecution from the religious authorities (Kephart and Zellner 1994). This new definition of themselves resulted in ethnogenesis. Eventually, the Amish fled to the United States in the 1700s, settling first in Lancaster, Pennsylvania. From there, they have grown in size, and live in 20 different states. The Amish population is more than 100,000 today. There are no longer any Amish in Europe. Ethnogenesis is a continual, ongoing sociocultural and political process that began in prehistory and continues today for many people.

There have been many criticisms of the instrumental or circumstantialist view of ethnicity. The strength of this approach is to demonstrate how fluid and contingent ethnic boundaries and the cultural criteria defining them are supposed to be. These theorists emphasize how ethnicity is not "static," but a highly dynamic aspect of human behavior. Most of the anthropologists who employ this circumstantialist approach tend to view "culture" as an indirect reflection of politics, economics, and other materialist factors. Ethnicity is a process that is activated and cultivated for strategic purposes in different contexts. The major criticism of this circumstantialist view, however, is that at times ethnicity does appear to endure and persist despite changes in historical, economic, and political change. Critics suggest that the circumstantialist view does not account for the fact that ethnicity is not highly mutable or changeable for some people. Some groups are not as able to free themselves from their ethnic attachments as others. Under some conditions, groups cannot jettison, negotiate, or manipulate their ethnic identity to pursue particular interests. Another criticism suggests that the circumstantialist view assumes that the individual is a completely "autonomous," "rational," "calculating" actor in social interaction. This assumption has been questioned by many anthropologists, who emphasize that "culture" plays a much more important part in human decision making and strategic interaction than the circumstantialist theorists admit.

As a result of the criticisms of both the primordialist and circumstantialist models, most contemporary anthropologists have drawn from both perspectives to explain or interpret ethnicity. Both models have elucidated the nuances of ethnic identity throughout the world. The primordialist model has been extremely useful in substantiating the persistence of ethnicity, whereas the circumstantialist model has helped demonstrate how ethnic identity can be altered and constructed in various economic and political conditions. Presently, many contemporary anthropologists occupy a middle ground between these positions as they pay close attention to the detailed manner in which ethnicity may be both primordial and manipulable. As seen in the example of the Amish in U.S. society, both the primordial and circumstantialist views were useful in explaining and understanding different aspects of ethnicity.

Anthropologists today investigate how societal conditions may impinge on how people define themselves ethnically. What are the ethnic categories that have enduring meaningfulness and purpose for people, and under what circumstances are those categories asserted, negotiated, reaffirmed, or repressed? Also, to what extent and to what ends are the elements of ethnicity "invented" and "imagined" by ethnic groups? Anthropologists have to provide a detailed understanding of the ethnogenesis of a particular ethnic group. How does an ethnic group come to construct a shared sense of identity? What are the particulars of this ethnic identity? Is most of the ethnicity tied to religion? Or is it based on common ancestors or shared myths of common history and territory? Furthermore, anthropologists find it necessary to understand the global and local economic and political dynamics and processes that affect ethnic relations in continually changing societies. Globalization, government policies, the labor market, urbanization, and other aspects of the political economy have a profound influence on how ethnicity is expressed in different societies.

PATTERNS OF ETHNIC RELATIONS

Pluralism

To analyze ethnic relations within a single nation, the concept of the plural society was elaborated by the late anthropologist M. G. Smith. In his book *Pluralism in Africa* (1969), edited with the late anthropologist Leo Kuper, Smith describes a plural society as one in which different groups are internally distinguished from each other by institutional and cultural differences. Instead of one overarching homogeneous identical system of institutions shared within a society, a plural society consists of ethnic groups that differ in social organization, beliefs, norms, and ideals. Building on this framework, anthropologists have utilized the phrase *cultural pluralism* to describe how various ethnic groups maintain diverse cultures within one society. The example of the Amish in U.S. society would exemplify cultural pluralism. In contrast, *institutional pluralism* is the phrase used to

refer to how different ethnic groups may have a similar culture but maintain separate institutions, including schools, churches, businesses, and other organizations, within a society. These ethnic groups may share the same language, dietary practices, and subscribe to the same values and beliefs, but they have minimal social interaction with other ethnic groups. In the United States the Mormon religious community exemplifies this type of institutional pluralism.

Smith and Kuper classify different forms of plural societies based on the political order and legal institutions (1969). In some forms of plural societies, ethnic groups are not only divided culturally and structurally but are also organized in highly unequal political relationships. They term such societies as "radically plural" societies. In these radically plural societies a minority ethnic group rules other ethnic groups through coercion. The state or government rules as an agent to protect the interests of the dominant ethnic group. The subordinate ethnic groups are treated as "subjects" rather than "citizens." This results in an ethnic hierarchy with the dominant ethnic group in control of the political, economic, and prestigious social positions within the society. Some radically plural societies evolved in early ancient agricultural civilizations. However, Smith and Kuper note how these forms of radically plural societies developed in more recent times with European colonialism in many parts of Latin America, the Caribbean, Africa, the Middle East, and Asia. These radically plural societies had a European elite that ruled through the control of the political economy and the legal institutions within these colonized regions. Typically, these inegalitarian plural societies usually result in divisive ethnic conflict and strained ethnic relationships.

Other forms of plural societies, sometimes referred to as *consociational plural societies,* are based on more egalitarian relationships among ethnic groups. In these plural societies, the government protects the structural and cultural differences among the ethnic groups. These ethnic groups are formally recognized by the state and legal institutions to allocate political rights and economic opportunities proportionally. Each ethnic group has a great deal of political autonomy, and, in theory, there is no politically dominant ethnic group. In Europe, Switzerland is often cited as an example of a plural society where different ethnic groups have distinctive cultures but have parity or equality with each other. Switzerland consists of French, Italian, German, and Romansh ethnic groups, and they all have relatively similar political and economic opportunities. Another European country, Belgium, is also known as an egalitarian plural society in which the population is divided into two major ethnic groups: the Dutch-speaking Flemish and the French-speaking Walloons. In such plural societies ethnic groups have the legal and political right to maintain their own language, educational systems, and culture. A balance of power is often reached among the different ethnic groups according to a political formula that grants each group a proportional representation of the multiethnic population. As expected, cultural pluralism endures and remains stable in these ethnically egalitarian societies, resulting in relatively amicable relationships.

Many plural societies today fall between the inegalitarian radically plural and egalitarian consociational forms. Following decolonization in most of the countries of Latin America, Africa, the Middle East, and Asia, the radically plural forms of society were dislodged. The European elites were replaced by indigenous elites in these postcolonial societies. However, as will be seen in later chapters, these societies remained pluralistic, as they were composed of many different ethnic groups. In some cases, the indigenous elites represented one particular ethnic group and perpetuated a continuation of radically plural politics. In other situations, new indigenous-based governments developed policies to manage competition and rivalry among different ethnic groups. This resulted, under some conditions, to another form and pattern of interethnic relations known as assimilation.

Assimilation

Another pattern of ethnic relations and interaction within many societies described by anthropologists is often referred to as assimilation. *Assimilation* is a process of ethnic boundary reduction that may come about when two or more ethnic groups come into contact with each other. One or more ethnic groups adopt the culture, values, beliefs, and norms of another ethnic group. The process of assimilation results in the similarity of culture and homogeneity among ethnic groups. As would be expected, assimilation occurs more easily when the physical and cultural characteristics of the different ethnic groups are more similar from the beginnings of contact.

Pierre van den Berghe has indicated a number of general factors that favor assimilation (1981). He notes that when ethnic groups are very different physically and culturally from one another, assimilation takes place at a slower pace, if at all. Also, if ethnic groups are dispersed within a territory they tend to assimilate more quickly. For example, if ethnic groups are residing in different cities or rural areas throughout a particular country, they would assimilate at a rapid pace. A corollary of this is that if a specific ethnic group is located within a specified region with ties to the territory, the pace of assimilation would be very slow. In addition, if the ethnic group is a small minority and dependent on a larger ethnic population for vital economic resources, assimilation is likely to be rapid. Also, low-status groups usually assimilate more readily than do high-status groups, and immigrants are more likely to assimilate than the native resident population, because of economic and political pressures.

Anthropologists have been engaged in research to determine whether these general factors are valid in different societal and cultural contexts. But in order to refine their research, they distinguish different forms of assimilation: cultural assimilation, structural assimilation, and biological assimilation.

Cultural assimilation involves one ethnic group's adoption of the cultural traits, including language, religion, clothing styles, diet, and other norms, values, and beliefs, of another group. Anthropologists such as Robert Redfield and Melville Herskovits in the 1930s used the term *acculturation* to refer to the tendency of distinct cultural groups to borrow words, technology, clothing styles, foods, values, norms, and behavior from each other (1936). Generally, cultural assimilation and acculturation have slightly different meanings to anthropologists. Cultural assimilation involves a subordinate ethnic minority adopting some of the culture of another ethnic group, whereas acculturation refers to the overall adjustment and adaptation of the group to the dominant ethnic group. Obviously, the process of cultural assimilation or acculturation has been going on since the earliest days of humanity and continues today.

As groups came in contact with one another, they borrowed from each other's cultures. Anthropologists, however, find that cultural assimilation and acculturation can be a very complex process for many ethnic groups. These processes may vary, depending on government policies and other societal conditions. For example, some cultural assimilation may be voluntary, wherein a particular ethnic group may choose to embrace the culture of another group. Many ethnic groups who immigrate into a particular society adopt the culture of the ethnically dominant group to secure their political rights and economic prospects. In some societies, government and educational policies may encourage groups to assimilate the culture of the dominant ethnic group. During different historical periods, the policies of many governments, such as the U.S., French, Mexican, Nigerian, Israeli, and Chinese, have promoted cultural assimilation on a voluntary basis within their societies.

Conversely, under some historical conditions, governments may require nonvoluntary or *forced cultural assimilation*. This is where the government forces ethnic groups to take on the culture of the dominant ethnic group of the society. Sometimes, anthropologists refer to forced cultural assimilation as *ethnocide,* which implies the killing of the "culture" of a particular ethnic group. Ethnocide demands an ethnic group to abandon their language, religion, and other cultural norms, values, and beliefs and to adopt the culture of the dominant group. This process of ethnocide developed in various ancient agricultural civilizations such as Egypt, India, China, Rome, and the Aztec. As these agricultural civilizations expanded and conquered territories and other ethnic groups, at times they forced these other ethnic groups to assimilate and adopt the culture of the dominant ethnic group. This pattern of induced ethnocide was also prevalent during more modern forms of colonialism. For example, as Europeans colonized areas of Latin America, or as the Japanese colonized areas in Asia such as Taiwan, or as the United States colonized the region of North America, indigenous peoples were often forced to assimilate. This type of forced assimilation is usually extremely difficult for individuals. They have to forsake their own language and cultural traits to become a part of a different, often antagonistic set of values and beliefs. As will be seen in later chapters, forced cultural assimilation, or ethnocide, continues to influence many contemporary patterns of ethnic relations.

Structural assimilation, or *integration,* is the process by which ethnic groups not only adopt the culture of another ethnic group but also become participants within the basic institutions in the society. In other words, an ethnic group increases their social interaction with members of the other ethnic group within neighborhoods, schools, businesses, clubs, churches, and other organizations within the society. It would also include intermarriage among the different ethnic groups. The degree of structural assimilation within the society depends on the accessibility for ethnic groups to "integrate" within a particular society. In some societies there may be obstacles for structural assimilation for specific ethnic groups. Racism, ethnocentrism, prejudice, and discrimination may play a role in the access of some groups to structural assimilation. Despite the cultural assimilation of some ethnic groups, there may not be opportunities for structural assimilation for these groups. In other cases, ethnic groups may become both culturally and structurally assimilated, which entails the complete eradication of their status as "another" ethnic group. At that point, in some circumstances, whatever minority status they may have had is completely eliminated.

One pattern of assimilation identified by researchers on ethnic relations has been referred to as *segmented assimilation* (Portes and Zhou 1994). Segmented assimilation combines some elements of assimilationist and pluralist tendencies in ethnic relations. In most cases of cultural assimilation, ethnic minorities adopt much of the culture of the dominant ethnic group. In some situations, however, some of these ethnic minorities are believed to be so different from the dominant ethnic group that their structural assimilation is obstructed. Physical characteristics, language, or religion may inhibit some groups from being completely assimilated within the society. Consequently, the children of these ethnic minorities may be encouraged to retain some of their ethnic group's culture while at the same time to adopt the majority ethnic group's culture in a piecemeal fashion. Under some conditions, an ethnic minority group may become economically successful but intentionally try to conserve some of their basic cultural traditions, thus advocating assimilationist and pluralist strategies.

Biological assimilation refers to the process of intermarriage and reproduction among different ethnic groups resulting in a new ethnic group. This is also known as *amalgamation,* or the biological merging of formerly distinct ethnic groups. The process of biological assimilation has been taking place for thousands of years as different groups began intermarrying and reproducing with each other. Usually intermarriage among ethnic groups occurs after a great deal of cultural and structural assimilation following extensive interethnic contact. Thus, usually ethnic boundaries have been extensively reduced, if not eliminated, when intermarriage takes place. The degree of biological assimilation may range from a society where there are no longer any cultural and biological distinctions among the population to societies where new forms of ethnicity develop. Historically, in the United States intermarriage among different European Americans (descendants of English, Irish, Germans, Italians, Polish, etc.) has reduced most meaningful ethnic boundaries. On the other hand, as will be seen in the chapter on Latin America and the Caribbean, new forms of ethnicity emerged as intermarriage took place among Europeans, native populations, and African slaves.

Contemporary anthropologists who study ethnicity have become extremely cautious about utilizing the concepts of pluralism and assimilation in making generalizations about different types of ethnic relations. They find that these models may simplify or exaggerate tendencies found in different societies. One way they have tried to overcome the simplicity of these models is to differentiate between group and individual behavioral tendencies. Thus, in some cases, pluralist or assimilationist patterns may not affect whole ethnic groups within a society; rather, some individuals may define their ethnic identity in pluralistic terms, or adopt the culture of the dominant ethnic group, or intermarry within another ethnic group. In these situations, one will have difficulty specifying the pluralistic or assimilationist trends for the entire society and different ethnic groups. Anthropologists have learned to distinguish between group and individual levels of behavior in assessing pluralist and assimilationist patterns. The patterns of pluralism and assimilation are to be understood as models that allow anthropologists to focus on the outcome of processes that effect ethnic relations.

Three other patterns of ethnic interaction have been identified by anthropologists and other social scientists. One is *segregation,* or the physical and social separation of categories of people. Segregation was the policy of many southern states in the United States following the abolition of slavery until the civil rights movements of the 1950s and 1960s. Jim Crow laws were developed which resulted in the creation of separate facilities and institutions for African Americans and white Americans. There were segregated schools, restaurants, drinking fountains, rest rooms, parks, neighborhoods, and other areas. Until recently, the South African government had developed similar laws to segregate the "races" and ethnic groups within its legal constitution.

Another pattern of ethnic interaction is *ethnic cleansing,* the attempt to remove an ethnic group from its location and territory within a society. Recently, the Serbs have attempted to bring about ethnic cleansing and remove ethnic groups such as the Bosnians from the country of Yugoslavia. In East Africa, the former ruler Idi Amin expelled East Indian immigrants from Uganda for economic and political reasons. Following the Vietnam War in 1975 the Vietnamese government encouraged the migration of more than 1 million ethnic Chinese from their country. These people were abruptly eliminated as an ethnic minority, despite the fact that many had assimilated into Vietnamese society. In the past, the U.S. government removed Native American Indians from their territories, a process of ethnic cleansing that resulted in reservation life for these ethnic groups.

Finally, the third pattern of ethnic interaction is known as *genocide,* the systematic attempt to kill and eliminate a particular ethnic group. Genocide may overlap with ethnic cleansing. In both the cases of the U.S. government and Native American Indians and the Serbs and the Bosnians, removal policies were often combined

with more deadly policies of genocide. When the British colonized the area of Australia, native populations such as the Tasmanians were exterminated. There were 5,000 Tasmanians in 1800, but as a result of being attacked by the British, the last full-blooded Tasmanian died in 1876. In the settling of South Africa by the Dutch, indigenous populations such as the Hottentots were systematically killed off. In the twentieth century, the most horrific forms of genocide befell European Jews and other ethnic groups under Adolf Hitler's reign of terror. The Nazi party murdered over 6 million Jews and millions of others of different ethnic groups, including European Gypsies. In Cambodia, the Communist ruler Pol Pot killed as many as 2 million people (one-fourth of the population) in what has become known as the "killing fields." Ethnic minorities such as people with Chinese ancestry or Muslims were favored targets in this genocidal campaign (Kiernan 1988). In 1994, in the country of Rwanda in Central Africa, the majority ethnic group (the Hutus) slaughtered some half-million ethnic Tutsis within a few weeks. Though genocidal policies have been condemned by recognized moral standards throughout the world, they have occurred time and again in human history.

ETHNICITY AND NATIONALISM

Another important aspect of ethnic relations examined by anthropologists is how nationalism influences ethnicity, and how ethnicity has an impact on nationalism. *Nationalism* is a set of symbols and beliefs providing the sense of belonging to a single political community. *Nationalism* involves a strong sense of loyalty, ideological commitment, and feelings of identification with a distinctive sovereign nation-state or country. A *nation-state* is a centralized political entity, exercising the legal authority to collect taxes, rule over a specific territory, and employ military force. The "classical" form of nationalism is a relatively new development, emerging in eighteenth- and nineteenth-century Europe and areas influenced by Europe. Before the development of this classical form of nationalism, the primary focus of loyalty was to the local community, a particular ruler, ethnicity, religion, and the family (Anderson 1991; Gellner 1983). For example, in the agricultural states of Europe, most peasants rarely identified with the entire population within a specific territory. However, as industrialization uprooted many peoples from their traditional communities, and peasants moved from rural areas to large cities for employment, new forms of loyalty were demanded.

In industrializing states, with increases in literacy and mass education, nationalism became a unifying force of political expression. Print technology was particularly important because it helped to create what political scientist Benedict Anderson (1991) refers to as "imagined communities," an allegiance to a nation-state that is often far removed from everyday family or local concerns. As a literate populace began to read about their history and culture in their own language, they embarked on a new self-identification. In most cases, a particular language had to be legitimized by the government to serve as the basis of nationality. But eventually people began to express a source of pride in and loyalty to these newly defined countries. Anderson, though, is not suggesting that nationalism is just "invented," but holds that people who begin to define themselves as members of a nation will never know most of their fellow members, meet them, or even hear of them. He notes that the fact that people are willing to give up their lives for their nation or country means that nationalism has a powerful influence on people's emotions and sentiments.

Unlike nation-states, ethnic communities are as old as human prehistory, and ethnicity did not disappear with the development of nationalism. Some theorists argue that there is no radical break between the prenation ethnic communities and the evolution of nation-states. For example, Anthony Smith proposes that most nations were fundamental continuities of earlier ethnic communities or revitalized ethnic communities (1981). He endorses the view that early ethnic communities used their myths of common ancestry, religion, and other cultural symbols to unify themselves and develop their nation-states around ethnicity. When one examines the development of classical nationalism in Europe (England, France, Germany), Asia (Japan, China, Korea), or other areas of the world, ethnicity does appear to play a significant role in the development of this form of classical nationalism.

Anthropologists Clifford Geertz (1963) and the late Ernest Gellner (1991) have distinguished two forms of nation-states in the contemporary world that draw on different forms of nationalism: civic and ethnic. Civic polities or nation-states attempt to unify a population on "universalistic criteria," regardless of their ethnicity, race, language, religion. These civic polities try to gain allegiance and loyalty through a political creed that gives people equal political and social rights based on their individual choice. This political creed is usually a constitution or other political and legal documents that offer universal justice and equality to all of its citizens. In contrast, ethnic polities maintain that a citizen's allegiance and loyalty are based on their ethnicity into which they have been born or assigned to by the nation-state. In other words, their national loyalty overlaps considerably with their ethnicity and "particularistic features," which are transmitted and inherited through their cultural and symbolic traditions. As we will see in later chapters, as many parts of the world have become more ethnically diverse through globalization processes, many ethnically based polities are attempting to transform their states into civic polities. Nation-making based on a political creed rather than ethnicity is a major phenomenon in many multiethnic societies.

Conversely, globalization has also resulted in the fragmentation of nation-states into smaller ethnic groups, which combine ethnicity and nationalism. In some cases, these ethnic groups may be minorities who perceive the "universalistic criteria" or the political creed–based political, legal, and social rights of civic polities as a *particularistic* expression of a dominant ethnic group. They view the imposition of language, culture, and the political creed of the dominant ethnic group as a form of cultural hegemony. To contest and resist this cultural hegemony, these ethnic groups may want to secede and develop their own ethnically based nation-states. Such ethnic secessionist developments are often called *ethnonationalist* movements. One question that arises is how can these ethnic groups be nationalistic, when they really do not have their own nation-state? It would appear that these ethnonationalist movements are slightly different than the classical forms of nationalism. In some cases, the sentiments and emotions of nationalism may be "prior" to the actual formation of a nation-state. Obviously, these nationalist sentiments are indirectly influenced by the cultural milieu of nationalism expressed by the countries in which these ethnic groups are minorities. In Canada, for example, the Native American Indian peoples refer to themselves as "First Nations." Subsequently, as a way of expressing its sympathy with Native American Indian nationalist sentiments, the Canadian government uses the term "First Nation" as a label for Native American Indian communities. Many other indigenous people and ethnic minorities have expressed their identity in nationalistic terms, without actually having an existing nation-state.

Many ethnonationalist movements emerged in areas of the world that were once colonized by Europeans. Ethnonationalist movements played a role in the struggle against European colonialism. Leaders such as Mohandas Gandhi in India, Jomo Kenyatta in East Africa, and Simon Bolívar in Latin America mobilized new forms of ethnonationalism in order to free themselves from European colonialism. After independence,

these new postcolonial societies had to form nation-states that incorporated disparate ethnic communities and cultures. In some instances, during the colonial period some ethnic groups had prospered more than others, and this often resulted in postcolonial states in which ethnic and cultural hegemony was prescribed by the dominant ethnic group. As yet, many of these postcolonial states have a very weakly developed sense of nationalism because ethnic minorities perceive their own local interests and culture as being undermined by the dominant ethnic group.

Another variation on the postcolonial ethnonationalist movements occurred with the downfall of the former Soviet Union and its satellite countries in Eastern Europe. Various ethnic minorities, such as the Latvians, Estonians, Lithuanians, Belorussians, Ukrainians, Georgians, Turkmens, Uzbeks, Tajiks, and others, began to stress their ethnic identities and regional nationalism as the Soviet Empire began to collapse in the late 1980s. Historically, the Soviet Union was administered by 15 Soviet Socialist Republics that contained Autonomous Republics that were defined by ethnic groups or nationalities. However, under the orthodox Marxist ideology that provided the foundations for Soviet political policies, ethnic groups, or "ethnos," were supposed to "wither away" and be replaced by a Soviet "super-ethnicity." This was an attempt by the Soviet political elite to use its own version of nationalism, based on a political creed, to produce a civil polity (Banks 1996; Gellner 1988). In reality, none of these autonomous regions were allowed political rights, and they were strictly controlled by Soviet authorities in Moscow. Members of ethnic groups were subject to deportation or exile, and their boundaries were manipulated by the Soviet state.

In most cases, contrary to Marxist dogma, the various ethnic minorities did not abandon their cultural, linguistic, and religious traditions as expected. As the Soviet system began to disintegrate, a variety of ethnonationalist movements developed throughout the empire. In the aftermath of the dissolution of the Soviet Union, these ethnonationalist aspirations resulted in myriad newly independent countries. In Eastern Europe, as the communists lost their authority over Hungary, Czechoslovakia, Bulgaria, Romania, Poland, Yugoslavia, and East Germany, ethnonationalist movements materialized, which have had major consequences for these regions. For example, deep tensions between the ethnic Czechs and Slovaks led to the division of the former Czechoslovakia. Much more tragic results transpired in Yugoslavia, which will be discussed later in this text.

In general, globalization processes have been a major factor in the appearance of ethnonationalist movements (Friedman 1994). At times, regional and ethnic identities are intensified in a response to and as a defense against the growing impact of the wider world on their lives. Globalization processes usually result in the production of uniform forms of culture and identity that are imposed on local regions and ethnic groups. The communications media, including television, film, and the Internet, are diffusing particular forms of culture as globalization has an impact on all areas of the world. Some theorists have referred to this globalization process as the "McWorld tendency"–the proliferation of McDonalds, MacIntosh computers, and Mickey Mouse throughout the world (Barber and Schulz 1996). One response to these globalizing trends is a reassertion and revitalization of one's own ethnic and local identity leading to ethnonationalist movements. Many ethnic groups view these globalizing trends as a menacing process that tends to obliterate their own cultural traditions. Today, as a result, ethnonationalist movements include Scottish and Welsh nationalism in the United Kingdom, Catalan and Basque nationalism in Spain, Igbo nationalism in Nigeria, Kurdish nationalism in the Middle East, Quebecois nationalism in Canada, Sikh nationalism in India, and Native Hawaiian nationalism in the United States. These and many others will be discussed in later chapters.

CONCLUSION

Anthropological research on ethnicity has established that ethnicity is not simply an "innately based" propensity for human beings to bond together (Maybury-Lewis 1997). Instead, ethnicity is altered, modified, and asserted in differing historical, social, political, and cultural contexts. The centrality of culture, consisting of symbols, language, values, beliefs, worldviews, myths, ideologies, and norms, has enabled anthropologists to understand and explain ethnic processes in many different societies. Anthropologists examine questions such as why and under what conditions ethnic groups develop cordial and peaceable relationships, and when and how ethnic conflict erupts.

One of the problems that anthropological studies of ethnicity have highlighted is that of stereotyping, or making generalizations about various ethnic groups. This problem is frequently referred to as essentialism. *Essentialism* is the tendency to reify a "culture" or an "ethnicity" as a separate totalistic entity and emphasize the boundedness and immutability of this entity. This was a deficiency of most early anthropological research on ethnicity. Early anthropologists overemphasized the boundedness of a particular ethnic group and its specific distinctiveness. Thus, various peoples were categorized as Germans, Irish, Italians, British, Hispanics, Chinese, and so on. Anthropologists today view this as an abuse of the concept of culture. It reduces the complex behavior of people to the embodied creators and bearers of stereotyped ethnic traditions. This essentialist strategy usually exaggerated the internal homogeneity of the particular ethnic group and its manifest culture (Turner 1993). Contemporary anthropologists have been extremely wary of any totalistic generalizations about "races" or "ethnic groups." To combat these essentialist notions, anthropologists have to do deep, rich, fine-grained investigative research to illuminate the external and internal relations in ethnic processes.

This problem of essentialism is not just a challenge for anthropologists; it is a challenge for everyone. All humans classify the world and the people within the world into general categories. These general categories result in simplistic stereotypes and folk beliefs about "races" and "ethnic groups." These racial and ethnic mental images and stereotypes can become the foundations for *prejudice,* arbitrary beliefs and feelings toward an entire group of people. In some cases, essentialism also results in *discrimination,* the active denial of members of "racial" or "ethnic groups" the opportunity to enjoy equal access to human rights. Serious forms of prejudice and discrimination can create violence directed at an individual, or in extreme cases the annihilation of an entire group of people. Essentialism can be overcome by recognizing the complexities of ethnicity and realizing that these stereotypes and generalizations about "races" and "ethnic groups" do not stand up when subjected to empirical studies, critical thought, and analysis. The various studies by anthropologists, taken up in subsequent chapters, will enable you to perceive the inadequacies of essentialism and the dangers of stereotyping ethnic processes and interactions.

NOTES

1. There were different understandings of the term *culture* in various European societies. In the nineteenth century the French term *culture* was identified with "civilization," and represented the culmination of a progressive evolution of French civilization. The German word *kultur* was used by nineteenth-century intellectuals to refer to a romantic, emotional passionate feeling about one's language and nationality (Herder 1800). Like the French usage of *culture,* the British in the nineteenth century used culture to refer to civilization, and usually to indicate a superior form of European "British" civilization (Arnold 1873).

2. Some anthropologists attempt to mediate between the more material perspectives on human behavior and culture and the symbolic interpretive approach. For example, Dan

Sperber (1996) advocates a theoretical program that begins with interpretation of symbolic representations, but suggests that anthropologists can complement this interpretive approach with explanations of human behavior and culture. In a book illustrating complementary approaches between the explanatory and interpretive approaches, James Peacock uses metaphors from photography (1986). Peacock refers to the anthropological lens that consists of "harsh light" and "soft focus." The "harsh light" concerns the basic realities of the human condition, including biological realities, whereas "soft focus" is the attempt to interpret the symbolic interconnections of human affairs.

3. The primordial tradition of ethnicity is an outgrowth of earlier sociological theories such as the distinction between *Gemeinschaft* and *Gesellschaft* developed by such German theorists as Ferdinand Toennies (1963). Geertz's perspective on ethnicity drew on the ideas of sociologist Edward Shils (1957).

4. Another version of the primordialist perspective is that of Pierre Van den Berghe, who takes a sociobiological view of ethnicity. In his book *The Ethnic Phenomenon* (1981), Van den Berghe suggests that family and kinship relations are the biological basis of ethnicity, and that humans are naturally motivated to aid in the reproduction of their own ethnic group. He believes that these biological ties are deep-seated and genetically based. Ultimately, these primordially based biological ties result in ethnic and racial competition throughout the world among different ethnic groups, resulting in slavery, colonialism, warfare, and the like. This biological version of primordialism has been criticized by many anthropologists, sociologists, and sociobiologists who refer to this view as "pop sociobiology." The most extensive review and critique of Van den Berghe's view is by anthropologist Richard Thompson in his *Theories of Ethnicity* (1989), chapter 2.

REFERENCES CITED

ANDERSON, BENEDICT. 1991 [1983]. *Imagined Communities: Reflections on the Origins and Spread of Nationalism.* 2nd edition. London: Verso.

ARNOLD, MATTHEW. 1873. *Literature and Dogma.* London: Macmillan.

BANKS, MARCUS. 1996. *Ethnicity: Anthropological Constructions.* London: Routledge.

BARBER, BENJAMIN, and ANDREA SCHULZ, eds. 1996. *Jihad vs. McWorld: How Globalism and Tribalism Are Reshaping the World.* New York: Ballantine.

BARTH, FREDRIK, ed. 1998 [1969]. *Ethnic Groups and Boundaries: The Social Organization of Culture Difference.* Prospect Heights, IL: Waveland Press.

COHEN, ABNER. 1969. *Custom and Politics in Urban Africa.* London: Routledge.

____. 1974. *Two-Dimensional Man.* London: Tavistock.

D'ANDRADE, ROY, and CLAUDIA STRAUSS, eds. 1992. *Human Motives and Cultural Models.* New York: Cambridge University Press.

DOMINGUEZ, VIRGINIA R. 1986. *White by Definition: Social Classification in Creole Louisiana.* New Brunswick, NJ: Rutgers University Press.

ELLER, JACK, and REED COUGHLAN. 1993. The poverty of primordialism: The demystification of ethnic attachments. *Ethnic and Racial Studies* 16(2):183–202.

ERIKSEN, THOMAS HYLLAND. 1993. *Ethnicity and Nationalism: Anthropological Perspectives.* London: Pluto Press.

FISHMAN, JOSHUA. 1980. Social theory and ethnography. In *Ethnic Diversity and Conflict in Eastern Europe.* Peter Sugar, ed. Pp. 84–97. Santa Barbara, CA: ABC-Clio.

FRIEDMAN, JONATHAN. 1994. *Cultural Identity and Global Process.* London: Sage.

GEERTZ, CLIFFORD. 1963 [1973]. The integrative revolution: Primordial sentiments and civil politics in the new states. In *The Interpretation of Cultures.* Clifford Geertz, ed. Pp. 255–310. New York: Basic Books.

GELLNER, ERNEST. 1983. *Nations and Nationalism.* Oxford: Oxford University Press.

GELLNER, ERNEST, ed. 1988 [1977]. *State and Society in Soviet Thought.* Oxford: Blackwell.

HARRIS, MARVIN. 1964. *Patterns of Race in the Americas.* New York: Norton.

___. 1979. *Cultural Materialism: The Struggle for a Science of Culture.* New York: Random House.

___. 1999. *Theories of Culture in Postmodern Times.* Walnut Creek, CA: Altamira Press.

HERDER, JOHANN GOTTFRIED. 1967 [1800]. *Outlines of a Philosophy of the History of Man.* T. O. Churchill, trans. London: Luke Hansard.

HOSTETLER, JOHN A. 1980. *Amish Society.* 3rd edition. Baltimore: Johns Hopkins University Press.

HUTCHINSON, JOHN, and ANTHONY D. SMITH, eds. 1996. *Ethnicity.* Oxford: Oxford: University Press.

KEPHART, WILLIAM M., and WILLIAM ZELLNER. 1994. *Extraordinary Groups: The Sociology of Unconventional Life Styles.* 4th edition. New York: St. Martin's.

KIERNAN, BEN. 1988. Orphans of genocide: The Cham Muslims of Kampuchea under Pol Pot. *Bulletin of Concerned Asian Scholars* 20(4):2–33.

KUPER, LEO, and M. G. SMITH, eds. 1969. *Pluralism in Africa.* Los Angeles: University of California Press.

MAYBURY-LEWIS, DAVID. 1997. *Indigenous Peoples, Ethnic Groups, and the State.* Boston: Allyn & Bacon.

MOERMAN, MICHAEL. 1965. Who are the Lue? Ethnic identification in a complex civilization. *American Anthropologist* 67:1215–1229.

PEACOCK, JAMES L. 1986. *The Anthropological Lens: Harsh Light, Soft Focus.* Cambridge: Cambridge University Press.

PORTES, ALEJANDRO, and MIN ZHOU. 1994. The new second generation: Segmented assimilation and its variants. *Annals of the American Academy of Political and Social Science* 530:74–96.

QUINN, NAOMI, and DOROTHY HOLLAND, eds. 1987. *Cultural Models in Language and Thought.* Cambridge: Cambridge University Press.

REDFIELD, ROBERT, and MELVILLE HERSKOVITS. 1936. Memorandum on the study of acculturation. *American Anthropologist* 38:149–152.

SAHLINS, MARSHALL. 1976. *Culture and Practical Reason.* Chicago: University of Chicago Press.

SHILS, EDWARD. 1957. Primordial, personal, sacred and civil ties. *British Journal of Sociology* 7:113–145.

SIMPSON, J. A., and E. S. C. WEINER. 1989. *Ethnic.* vol. 5. *Oxford English Dictionary.* 2nd edition. Oxford: Clarendon Press.

SMITH, ANTHONY. 1981. *The Ethnic Revival in the Modern World.* Cambridge: Cambridge University Press.

___. 1986. *The Ethnic Origins of Nations.* Oxford: Blackwell.

SPERBER, DAN. 1996. *Explaining Culture: A Naturalistic Approach.* Oxford: Blackwell.

THOMPSON, RICHARD H. 1989. *Theories of Ethnicity: A Critical Appraisal.* New York: Greenwood Press.

TOENNIES, FERDINAND. 1963 [1887]. *Community and Society (Gemeinschaft and Gesellschaft).* New York: Harper & Row.

TURNER, TERENCE. 1993. Anthropology and multiculturalism: What is anthropology that multiculturalists should be mindful of it? *Cultural Anthropology* 8(4):411–429.

TYLOR, EDWARD. 1958 [1871]. *Primitive Cultures.* 2 vols. London: Torchbooks.

VAN DEN BERGHE, PIERRE L. 1981. *The Ethnic Phenomenon.* New York: Elsevier.

5 ETHNICITY AND ETHNOCENTRISM: ARE THEY NATURAL?

Donald E. Brown

University of California, Santa Barbara

Ethnocentrism—a preference for one's own kind and their ways—is a pervasive, and often profoundly unfortunate, feature of present-day life. But it is nothing new, and there is little reason to think that it flourishes more today than in the historic past. Ethnocentrism is such a robust phenomenon that it was recognized as a human universal well over 2,000 years ago. The ancient Greek historian and traveler Herodotus tells the story of King Darius noting the mutual horror expressed by certain Greeks and Indians when they were called before the king and told how each treated the bodies of their deceased fathers. Herodotus concluded that all peoples were "convinced that their own usages far surpass those of all others" (*Persian Wars,* Book III, 38).

The universality of ethnocentrism remains almost entirely unquestioned to this day.[1]

Note: Earlier versions of this chapter were given at Arizona State University, at the University of Michigan, at a 1996 conference in Stockholm on Human Behavior and Evolutionary Biology sponsored by the Royal Swedish Academy of Sciences, and at the 68th annual meeting of the Southwestern Anthropological Association (Brown 1997). The author received valuable comments from attendees at all those occasions, as well as from Francisco Gil-White and Raymond Scupin on this version.

William Graham Sumner (1906), who coined the term *ethnocentrism,* assigned it a highly important role in shaping both the relationships between peoples and many of the internal dynamics of their societies. Sumner argued, for example, that ethnocentrism served to strengthen respect for a society's customs and usages, and that conflict with outsiders would typically result in a strengthening of this tendency. Sumner, like Herodotus, put stress on the preference for the ways or customs of one's own kind. But it is important to note that the preference for one's own kind—one's own people—is as much a part of ethnocentrism as the preference for their ways or customs.

Equally important is that from Sumner's writing onward "ethnocentrism" has been something of a misnomer, as it has not been confined to ethnic settings:

> Ethnocentrism is by no means confined to tribes and nations. It manifests itself in social groups of all kinds—families, . . . local communities, classes, castes, sects, races, etc.—and assumes such diverse and developed forms as nationalism, patriotism and chauvinism, family pride, class consciousness,

sectionalism, religious intolerance and race prejudice. [Sumner 1906:613]

Although Sumner envisaged ethnocentrism
as having evolved in the context of intersocietal
relations among hunters and gatherers, he was
very much concerned with its manifestations, by
extension, in all sorts of intergroup settings
within modern societies and among the nation-
states of the modern world (where he saw it as
giving rise sometimes to dire consequences).
Thus Sumner also coined the terms *in-group* or
we-group and *out-group* or *others-group* as settings
for a generic ethnocentrism that occurs even in
nonethnic settings. The phrase *in-group bias* has
come to designate this generic phenomenon, and
studies of the various components of ethnocentrism have often been conducted in these more
generic settings. In many contexts, in-group bias
and ethnocentrism are simply synonyms. Some
of the illustrations given in this chapter are from
the generic settings.[2]

Twenty-five years after Sumner's writings, an
influential encyclopedia entry on ethnocentrism
(Murdock 1931) expanded both on its complexity
and the extent to which its basic elements are not
confined to ethnic contexts. Much later, in an
exhaustive survey of the concept of ethnocentrism,
Le Vine and Campbell (1971) formulated what
they called the "the universal syndrome of ethnocentrism," a set of features that either define ethnocentrism or are closely related to it in all societies.

A revised version of the syndrome will be
presented here, but two qualifications should be
noted first. One is that toward the end of the
description of the syndrome a few features will
be included that are not universal in the usual
sense of that term. The reasons for their inclusion will be explained at that time. The other is
that, for reasons that will be given later, the existence of its universal syndrome suggests the
possibility that ethnocentrism—and ethnicity,
too—might be fundamentally natural rather than
cultural. This possibility and its implications will
be discussed after the syndrome is described.

The list of elements in the syndrome begins
at the very basic level of group formation, which
includes, but is not confined to, ethnic settings.[3,4]

THE ETHNOCENTRIC SYNDROME

1. *Group thinking, collective thinking (the reification
or entification of collectivities when physically all we have
is individuals).* In the United States one talks
and thinks about blacks, Asian Americans, Anglos, and many, many more groups and categories (that even include such entities as General
Motors, or Amazon.com, or California, or the
United Kingdom) as though they were entities
or actors in our social order. Similarly, in
Rwanda one might hear that "both the Tutsi and
Hutu look down on the Twa" or in Malaysia
that "the Chinese control the economy." The
extent to which the members of any imagined
entity of this sort really do act in concert or get
treated as a unit is highly variable. Nonetheless,
peoples everywhere assume that individuals do
coalesce into social entities (some of the general
issues are summarized in Brown 1976; see also
item 30 below).

2. *Individuals identifying with collectivities, and
assuming such identifications on the part of others.*
Asian Americans or Native Americans, Germans
or Russians, Hutu or Tutsi, along with many
other human groupings—ethnic and nonethnic—
are, in important senses, only imaginary entities,
made real ("entified") by the individuals who
share in the imagination and act accordingly.

3. *Division into in-group and out-group members,
we-they, we-others.* Whereas "we" can be an
ethny,[5] a race, or a nationality, it can also be a
family, a group of friends, a village, a nation, or
myriad other entities.

4. *Endowing collectivities with continuity/perpetuity,
so that past actions are relevant to the present.* Americans have no difficulty in imagining that Native
Americans regret "their" losses to settlers, mostly
of European origin, who founded, peopled, and

expanded the United States. And yet the regret is felt now, while the loss occurred generations ago, to persons long deceased. Similarly, the modern state of Israel was founded by persons many of whose ancestors had not lived in Israel for many, many generations but who had millennia-old claims upon the land. In all such cases living individuals identify with and are identified by others as having a tie with long-deceased members of a category or group of people that persists as an actor among the social entities of human imagination.

5. *In-group badging.*   Whether it is a distinct language or dialect, a tribal hairstyle, a taste in food or music, the business suit, the jargon of a profession or occupation, or a multitude of other such patterns, people everywhere have characteristics that mark who is in their group and by which they are set off from outsiders.

6. *Stranger-recognition mechanisms.*   By failing to exhibit the appropriate in-group "badges"—for example, by having a different accent or language, different means of deporting oneself, different tastes and habits—individuals are identified as being strangers, not members of one's in-group(s).

7. *Marked sensitivity to out-group markers.*   Not only do humans notice differences of accent, gait, and the like, but they are very sensitive to them—seemingly without any special instruction. It appears to be the case that humans cannot train themselves not to notice accents different from their own.

8. *(Relative) peace (cooperation) inside, conflict (non-cooperation) outside.*   Within any particular group there is greater willingness to cooperate and to resolve conflict than there is with strangers or outsiders.

9. *Greater empathy with members of the in-group.* Humans are more concerned with what happens to their fellows, the persons of their kind, than with what happens to strangers. This pattern is found even among those societies with universal-istic ethics. Thus Christians are generally more concerned with the welfare of other Christians than with non-Christians. The saying that "charity begins at home" expresses this idea. "Germany for Germans" is the slogan for those opposed to current immigration trends in Germany.

10. *Lack of empathy, or a heightened threshold for empathy, for outsiders.*   From chuckles over the misfortunes of rivals, or the ready thought that "they had it coming to them," this is very much a part of everyday life. In extreme forms it is pleasure in out-group misfortunes, even of the most tragic sort. In his seminal work on the (ethnically) plural society, J. S. Furnivall (1956:150, 306, 308) identified the absence or weakness of a "common social will" as one of its distinctive features. That absence resulted from the diminished concern the members of each ethnic segment of the society had for the welfare of their fellow humans in the other segments. (See also item 28 below.)

11. *Mistrust of those in the out-group.*   This is one of the most frequently reported elements in the syndrome. In its stronger forms it becomes fear or even a sort of paranoia. Among the numerous examples is the suspicion among some African Americans that AIDS is a disease designed by white scientists to wipe them out, or the fear of villagers in various places that outsiders will kidnap their children to harvest their organs for transplants. In an early twentieth-century collection of stereotypical sayings about the members of various castes in India, which were and are envisaged by many Hindus as distinct races (Béteille 1967), mistrust was one of the commonest themes. Among the saying about Brahmans, for example, was "Trust a pariah [outcaste] in ten things, a Brahman in none" (Risley 1915:306).

12. *Assuming the worst of out-group members; giving the benefit of a doubt to in-group members.*   In spite of the commonplace belief that there are two sides to every story, humans much more readily accept the stories told by those in their in-group and are much more likely to doubt the stories told by those in out-groups.

13. *The out-group's saints/heroes are the in-group's devils.* In part, this is perhaps an exaggerated form of the preceding item. Examples can be read in our newspapers on almost any day, as in the vilification of Saddam Hussein, Fidel Castro, and many others who, to many of their countrymen, are heroes. As one writer to a newspaper put it, "The Palestinian terrorists . . . are considered heroes by the Palestinians; we think of them as criminals."

14. *Ethical dualism.* As in our own society, it is almost always wrong to kill within the group—for that is murder—but glory may be achieved by killing out-group members, even in great numbers. (If not glory, then greater or lesser degrees of indifference.) Similar attitudes and practices prevail with respect to lying to or stealing from out-group members. Sasanka Perera captures the issues in the attitudes of many Buddhist Sinhalese of Sri Lanka:

> Here we are faced with a contradiction in terms of Buddhist ethics and common sense: it is barbaric for Tamil militants to kill defenseless Sinhalese civilians, but it is not barbaric for the military to massacre Tamil civilians in the guise of anti-terrorist operations. The [Sinhalese] head of the household who recounted the many massacres of Sinhalese peasants was genuinely grieving and angry about the incidents. He made the following statement in the same conversation:
>
> > "One of my friends in the army told me that when they move through a village in the north not even a cat is left alive. That is the way these Tamils should be treated. They are getting too big for their boots." [1991:94–95]

15. *Loss/absence of objectivity.* While this is fundamental to ethnocentrism or in-group bias, it probably takes various distinct forms. It is acknowledged in phrases like "truth is the first casualty of war." It drives home the point that ethnocentrism is a state of mind, in its extreme forms almost like an altered state of consciousness, in that the ethnocentric mind processes everyday information in a distinctly distorted manner. This feature deserves further discussion.

The cognitive distortions that result from in-group bias are so obvious that already in the fourteenth century the Arab historian ibn Khaldun identified a form of this bias as the first among his reasons for why falsehoods are so common in the historical record:

> If the soul is infected with partisanship for a particular opinion or sect, it accepts without a moment's hesitation the information that is agreeable to it. Prejudice and partisanship obscure the critical faculty and preclude critical investigation. The result is that falsehoods are accepted and transmitted. [1958:71]

However, as perceptive as ibn Khaldun's observation is, it understates the problem. It is not only in the transmission of information that bias occurs; it occurs, too, in the perceptions of eyewitnesses. Two extraordinary studies are particularly revelatory of the phenomenon. The first study (Hastorf and Cantril 1954) revealed the sharply divergent perceptions reported by the supporters of Princeton and Dartmouth at an unusually rough football game. It was the last game of the season for both teams. Princeton was unbeaten and its star player had just appeared on the cover of *Time* magazine. The game took a nasty turn early on, and many penalties were called. Princeton's star was removed from the game with a broken nose and mild concussion, and a Dartmouth player suffered a broken leg. Reports and analyses in the press conflicted wildly.

Hastorf and Cantril conducted a follow-up study, in which some of their subjects were eyewitnesses to the game and others only saw a movie of the game. Disagreements about what happened in the game, and how to characterize those happenings, were substantial. Even on more objective matters—such as the number of infractions and characterizations of their severity—supporters of the two sides who viewed the same movie differed sharply. Hastorf and Cantril concluded that "the 'same' sensory impingements emanating from the football field, transmitted through the visual mechanism to the brain, . . . gave rise to different experiences in different people" (1954:132).

The second study, and one more directly related to ethnicity, demonstrated the same phenomenon but under more controlled conditions in which supporters of Israel and of the Palestinian Arabs watched the same television news reports of the 1982 Beirut massacre, and then judged the extent to which the news reports were biased (Vallone et al. 1985). The partisans of *each* side found that the reports were so (intentionally!) biased against their side that they felt that neutral observers seeing the same news reports would come away with a more unfavorable view of their side. On a seemingly objective task—counting the negative and positive statements about Israel in the reports—the supporters of each side arrived at sharply contrasting numbers.

The authors of the study concluded that basic cognitive and perceptual mechanisms seemed to be involved, so that the disagreements between the two sets of partisans were not just over evaluation of what they had seen but over the very *content* of what was seen. A particularly depressing finding of the study was that those subjects who judged themselves to be more knowledgeable about Near Eastern affairs tended to arrive at the stronger perceptions of bias against their side. So, too, did those who judged themselves most emotionally involved in the issues.

The authors noted that what they examined experimentally is in fact an everyday observation: that partisans regularly find strong support for their positions in what neutrals see as ambiguous. What should be stressed is that the observers on both sides in cases like this very often consider their assessments to have been "obvious," which is evidence that their minds have tricked them, so to say, and that they are not intentionally trying to deceive.

The implications of these findings for ethnic relations are sobering indeed. They suggest, for example, that even mutually fair treatment may be perceived—by each party to a conflict or competition—as systematically biased against them.

16. *Certitude, moral certitude.* The normal skepticism that we might exercise in our everyday affairs is regularly suspended when judgments cross the boundary between in-group and out-group. The judgments we make about our heroes and their devils, who is the victim, who the most unfair, and so on appear to be "obviously" true.

17. *Degrading or dehumanizing the out-group.* Outsiders are often seen as deficient in morality, decency, or intelligence, with the extreme lying in a denial of the humanity of the out-group. Certain untouchable, outcaste groups among the Japanese (described in De Vos and Wagatsuma 1967) were so despised that they were referred to with an extended hand, thumb folded under the palm, with the four fingers hanging down like the legs of an animal—to symbolize their animality. In Ruanda, Tutsi and Hutu alike referred "half-jokingly" to the very small minority of pygmoid Twa among them as "more akin to monkeys than to human beings" (Maquet 1961:10).

18. *In-group pride.* The emotional side of ethnocentrism must not be ignored (see, e.g., Scheff 1994). Building pride in an organized group—whether an army, a school, a nationality, or an ethnic or racial group—is a serious business everywhere. Ethnic pride and shame are significant concerns in present-day polyethnic states, where perceptions of shame often easily lead to rage. Humans can be very sensitive to possible insult, as when individuals find jokes about their ethny less funny than others do or when, in very recent years, citizens of Mexican American heritage in California—perhaps by assuming the worst intentions—perceive a slander against themselves from opponents of illegal immigration.

19. *Discrimination.* This term refers to the very wide range of *actions* taken on the basis of ethnocentrism, as when persons of a particular race or national origin are not allowed to hold certain occupations or live in certain areas, or are denied education, or are denied voting rights—to give but a few examples from modern societies.

20. *Stereotyping.* This consists of two elements: simplification, such that a few traits come to stand for the full complexity that collections of individuals everywhere possess; and the generalization of those few traits to all members of the category being stereotyped (i.e., ignoring the individuality of out-group members). Stereotypes are attached to all sorts of groups, and in some cases provide the ideological underpinning for social order. Thus stereotypes between northerners and southerners are as vigorous in Italy (Romanucci-Ross 1975) as in the United States; and stereotypes are a central feature of the caste system of Hindu India (see, e.g., Sinha and Sinha 1967).

21. *Ignoring or downplaying others in myth-history while focusing on the in-group.* In modern societies, such as the United States, this tendency is now countered by attempts to produce more "inclusive" histories. In many other societies, out-groups are just not mentioned. In the myth-histories of yet other societies, out-groups are singled out for vilification, as was the case for Jews in many European images of the past.

22. *Judging others in the in-group's terms.* Familiar examples abound, as when the haves and the have-nots, or men and women, or capitalists and socialists each employ their own perspectives, values, and insights to assess those whose experiences have been so different. Interethnically, this item in the syndrome may be an inevitable effect of linguistic and cultural differences, which pose further difficulties in grasping other peoples' perspectives and worldviews. The relativistic attitude and the development of the intellectual tools required to grasp other people's perspectives have been rare accomplishments in human history.

23. *Scapegoating, and a generalized tone of praise and blame in discussions of intergroup relations.* Scapegoating consists of blaming the out-group

for one's problems. A familiar example is the blame put on Jews in Nazi Germany. In a striking example from Sri Lanka, Perera found a consensus even among high school teachers that "all our problems are the result of terrorism by Tamil guerrillas and the separatist demand by the Tamil United Liberation Front" (1991:152).

24. *Endogamy.* Probably most individuals everywhere tend to marry within their own ethny, and among many peoples it is a conscious or cultural preference. But it may also be an accidental tendency resulting from such underlying factors as a general tendency to marry persons nearby or to more easily establish amicable relations with persons of similar culture and language. Moreover, there are clear exceptions to endogamy, as when individuals in relatively small minority groups, scattered throughout a larger population, find themselves more frequently marrying outside their group—as is true today among Japanese Americans and Jewish Americans. Yet even in these cases the tendency toward endogamy may still result in statistically disproportionate tendencies to marry one's own kind.[6]

25. *Intensification of ethnocentric tendencies in times of internal crises.* During economic downturns, for example, existing tensions between groups intensify. One manifestation is the rise and fall of hostility to immigrants in U.S. history: when times are good, immigrants are more welcome; when times are bad, they are less welcome. (On the other hand, it should be noted that existing tensions within a society may be muted to meet with greater unanimity an external crisis, for example, conflict with parties who are even more outsiders.)

26. *Some sort of vicious cycle or "feeling trap."* An example of a feeling trap occurs when one is embarrassed, notes that others have sensed the embarrassment, and then feels all the more embarrassed; the others note the deeper confusion, which is yet further embarrassing, and on and on (Scheff and Retzinger 1991:104). The sociologist Thomas Scheff (1994) has argued that feeling traps of spiraling shame and rage figure importantly in ethnocentrism and large-scale intergroup violence. The phrase "cycle of violence," often applied to situations such as that between Palestinians and Jews in Israel, or between the Tamils and Sinhalese in Sri Lanka (Tambiah 1986), refers to conditions that are at least partly set or kept in motion by feeling traps.

27. *Sensitivity to out-group coalitional tendencies.* This is not documented in all societies but in enough to suggest that it is probably a near universal. It is often expressed as a dislike of clannishness. The Sinhalese of Sri Lanka, for example, have "the strong impression that the Tamils are 'clannish,' 'communal-minded,' and motivated to form strong networks to protect and promote their interests" (Tambiah 1986:105). Perera quotes a Sinhalese college student claiming that the Tamils "always stick together" (1991:97).

28. *Ignoring the concerns of subordinate out-groups.* This trait logically follows, and is an implication of, item 10 above. But as familiar as it may be in modern settings, it applies only in plural societies. Hence it is a "conditional universal": given a specified condition (in this case the condition is ethnic plurality), it always appears.

29. *Ghettoization, niche-exploiting.* This is another conditional universal, occurring regularly in the context of plural societies. It is strongly related to ethnicity alone and not to the broad range of possible in-groups. It refers to the tendency of members of specific ethnies to be confined to particular locations and/or particular occupations, professions, or other economic specializations. Where it is imposed upon groups, ghettoization seems the better term. Where it is more a matter of choice, niche-exploiting seems appropriate. Many cases may, of course, straddle the boundary.

Among the numerous striking examples are the sudden dominance of immigrant Cambodians in doughnut retail shops in California (Akst 1993) and the dominance of Koreans in shops in African American inner-city neighborhoods, a pattern that developed initially from Korean domination of the wig industry that sprang up to provide Afro wigs (Yoon 1991:165–169). In the old capital of Brunei (a Malay sultanate in northwest Borneo), its various wards were economically specialized, and each ward claimed a distinctive origin, virtually a distinct ethnic identity (Brown 1976:157–158). South of Brunei, in Kuching, Sarawak (now a part of Malaysia), the various Chinese subethnies (Cantonese, Hokkien, etc.) specialized in and sometimes monopolized one or another occupation or craft (Brown 1976:152–157). The caste system of Hindu India, in which each caste was associated with particular occupations, is among the many other examples.

30. *The essentialization of ethnies.* This item might more properly be called a hypothesized innate universal. What is meant by this is that the members of particular ethnies are conceived as having an inner essence that makes them what they are. Because they are "essentialized," ethnies are perceived as distinct human "kinds," analogous to species (Gil-White 2001; Hirschfeld 1996). In the modern world, the essentialization of ethnies is more unambiguous in racial than in ethnic classifications, but there is little doubt that throughout the world a great many peoples conceive of what we would call ethnic differences as very much like racial differences. The essentialization of ethnies sets them apart from most of the other human categories and groups referred to in item 1.

DISCUSSION

Although the list of elements in the universal syndrome of ethnocentrism raises numerous issues, only two will be addressed here. One is a cautionary statement concerning the sorts of refinements the list requires. The other is the large issue of whether the syndrome is natural or cultural, and what the implications of this would be.

Clearly, the list needs more specification of the kinds and ranges of conditions that elicit each item and the ranges or variant forms that responses take. For example, in item 7, I noted that detecting accents is obligate; one cannot turn off that feature of the mind. By contrast, stereotyping, discriminating, and other elements of the syndrome are more optional or open-ended in nature and more variable in their range of intensity (even though they occur in all societies and probably in all individuals). More needs to be said (or known) about the conditions that elicit those responses.

Another refinement concerns ordering the items in relation to each other. Some may be core features, some more peripheral; some may be preconditions to others, and surely there are other forms of interaction between the items. It is tempting to think, for example, that identification of an individual as either a member of the in-group or out-group (by noting badges or their absence) in some fundamental sense "frames" the subsequent processing of information on him or her and thus switches one's mind-set and behaviors between those designed for the in-group and those designed for out-groups. A *frame,* which is a term derived from cognitive science, must be built into any computational system (as in a computer or a mind) to guide the processing of what would otherwise be overly cumbersome masses of informational input.

A recent study gives intriguing clues about how such a framing process works (Warnecke et al. 1992). In this study American subjects watched (without accompanying audio) unidentified televised leaders from France, Germany, and the United States. The subjects felt more negatively toward the foreigners, but this effect disappeared when the images were accompanied by audio. Apparently, the subjects detected differences in facial expressions and deportment in the foreign leaders and thus saw them as strangers, perhaps not to be trusted. But when sound was added, the foreigners, though still different, could be identified as friendly—the allies of Americans—and the wariness or mistrust of strangers declined. Thus the different sets of badges or markers to be scanned triggered two different frames: one for strangers, another for allies.

In spite of the tasks that remain to refine the description of the ethnocentric syndrome, enough is already known to emphatically raise the question of whether it—including ethnicity itself—is natural, whether it is a feature (or set of features) of human nature. This possibility is suggested by the universality and complexity of the syndrome and by other evidence, too. Let us explore some of the issues.

To begin, why does a universal syndrome suggest nature instead of culture? Much of the explanation can be found in conventional anthropological thought. Cultural anthropologists have often assumed that if a phenomenon is universal—that is, is found among all peoples, past as well as present—then there is some likelihood that in some direct manner it must reflect human nature rather than environmental circumstances.[7] This is because our humanity goes with us everywhere, whereas most environmental influences on human life—whether physical or sociocultural—vary considerably from place to place and time to time. That the ethnocentric syndrome is complex, as well as universal, even more strongly suggests that human nature is involved, since its complexity makes ethnocentrism even less likely to have developed everywhere in the same form either by accident or through the usually highly variable forms of cultural development.

Beyond its universality, the principal lines of evidence that ethnocentrism, including ethnicity, is natural consist of signs of psychological preparedness in humans. "Preparedness" refers to a capacity to learn something relatively easily. For example, humans are innately prepared to learn language (Pinker 1994) but not to memorize strings of random numbers (computers are roughly the opposite). Often, preparedness manifests itself in a particular period of maturation of the individual, called a "critical" or "sensitive period" (see Seligman and Hager 1972 for a general review of these matters).

In a recent work, *Race in the Making,* Lawrence Hirschfeld (1996) provides highly relevant evidence for preparedness. Although an anthropologist, his work is rooted in experimental psychology and an approach to discovering features of human nature by exploring child development to determine whether the mind seems specially prepared to think about particular topics in particular ways. Hirschfeld found that very young children acquire racial conceptions so easily and, in the earliest ages, in theory-like forms sufficiently unlikely to have been learned from their elders, that one must conclude that the human mind is innately prepared to think about "human kinds."[8] "Theory-like" means that children have certain assumptions or expectations about human kinds. The *specific* kinds— Swede, American, Navajo, Yanomamo, Malay, Chicano, Korean, black, white, and so on—that we classify under the heading of "ethnic" or "racial" kinds are *not* given in nature and, typically, are appropriately analyzed in terms of social, cultural, political, economic, and historical factors.

Hirschfeld's findings suggest that humans have a functionally specialized mental faculty—a "mental module"[9]—for thinking about human kinds. The specific set of ethnic or racial categories found among particular peoples results from an *interaction* between this module and its propensities, on the one hand, and the specific social, cultural, political, economic, and historical setting of those peoples, on the other. This formulation goes a long way toward resolving the uncertainty among social scientists as to whether ethnicity, including racial thinking, is a product of time and place or is something "primordial." In very important senses it is both (see also Gil-White 1999).

It is important to stress that Hirschfeld is *not* arguing that specifically *racial* thinking is natural in the sense that it is an evolved characteristic, an adaptation. On the contrary, it is an "effect," which is a by-product of one or more other adaptations.[10] As Hirschfeld (1996:13) correctly

notes, whatever the reality of racial differences they would have been difficult to observe in the environments in which humans evolved: during nearly all of human evolution, humans did not have the ability to travel the distances required for anything approaching common observation of racial differences.[11] And unless the differences were recurrently observed, there would be little likelihood of any evolutionary adaptation to them. Thus Hirschfeld argues that racial thinking "parasitizes" our adaptation to think about, perceive, and pay attention to human kinds.

What Hirschfeld means by this is, first, that the human mind is functionally specialized (and presumably adapted) to readily distinguish children from adults or male from female, and to be attuned to the differences between peoples. Such differences might include the different styles in which people in different societies dress, ornament, and deport themselves, but might also include reputed differences that are not readily observed. Second, this specialization to detect different human kinds works just as well—and hence is parasitized—to detect racial differences. It is as if the racial differences so readily observed in the modern world mimic the cultural differences that humans had observed for tens of thousands of years.[12]

Note that some evidence concerning the theory-like way that humans innately think about human kinds suggests that it is quite close to racial thinking as indicated in item 30 of the ethnocentric syndrome. According to Hirschfeld's findings, humans tend to naturalize human kinds—that is, to consider them as "naturally" occurring and possessing an inner *essence* that distinguishes them from other kinds (see also Gil-White 2001). Racial thinking is one means of doing this. That human kinds are natural is the "theory" (or default assumption, so to say) that human minds tend to impose upon their perceptions of human kinds.

As Hirschfeld summarizes the evidence, humans are psychologically prepared to perceive and reason about human kinds, which include what he calls "ethnoraces" (1996:20–21). What this term indicates, apparently, is the tendency of the human mind to impose upon ethnies a "theory" that treats them much like races.

The other line of evidence for preparedness is related to in-group bias and is shown by an extensive body of data that refers to what are called "minimal-group" studies. These consist of attempts to discover how little it takes to make individuals think in terms of we–they and to prefer the we. *Very* little is required:

> In numerous experiments by Henri Tajfel and other social psychologists, people are divided into two groups, actually at random but ostensibly by some trivial criterion such as whether they underestimate or overestimate the number of dots on a screen or whether they prefer the paintings of Klee or Kandinsky. The people in each group instantly dislike and think worse of the people in the other group, and act to withhold rewards from them even if doing so is costly to their own group. This instant ethnocentrism can be evoked even if the experimenter drops the charade with the dots or paintings and divides people into groups by flipping a coin before their eyes! The behavioral consequences are by no means minor. In a classic experiment, the social psychologist Muzafir Sherif carefully selected a group of well-adjusted, middle-class American boys for a summer camp, and randomly divided them into two groups which then competed in sports and skits. Within days the groups were brutalizing and raiding each other with sticks, bats, and rocks in socks, forcing the experimenters to intervene for the boys' safety. [Pinker 1997:513–514, with references on 586; for a lengthier summary, see Rabbie 1992; for a caveat, see Mummendey et al. 1992]

Not only does in-group bias appear to be something for which we humans are strongly prepared, there is even reason to think that this preparedness has truly ancient roots. Since coalitional behavior occurs among chimpanzees (Waal 1982) and other species (Harcourt and Waal 1992), it is entirely possible—indeed, likely—that in-group bias in some form predates the formation of ethnies, which are uniquely human.

In sum, there is indeed evidence beyond its universality to suggest that ethnicity/ethnocentrism is natural. Although evidence on behalf of this proposition falls short of a conclusive demonstration that it is in fact correct, it is sufficient to justify continued research and thinking to explore the issues further.

Such research and thinking is two-pronged. On the one hand, research must look toward the ancient past and ask how ethnocentrism evolved, how it came to be what it is.[13] In the course of answering this question, the phenomenon will be better understood, we will have greater insight into ourselves, and—one hopes—be better able to control our lives.

On the other hand, research issues lie in tracing the workings of ethnocentrism—and all its components, including ethnicity itself—in our present-day or historically recorded lives.[14] Here the literature and the opportunities for observation and experimentation are vast, because the issues are so large and so pervasive. But large as the issues are they will be better understood if the underlying psychodynamics—the way the human mind produces and reacts to ethnocentrism and ethnicity—are well understood. The ethnocentric syndrome is both a central part of those dynamics and a manifestation of them.

In pursuing both lines of research, and in thinking through their implications, it certainly must be borne in mind that *natural* does not mean *good* (which is the "naturalistic fallacy"). Anger, the flu, headaches, lightning, hurricanes, and innumerable other phenomena are natural, yet they inflict hardship, pain, and suffering upon us. So, too, with ethnocentrism.

Perhaps it goes without saying that we must also bear in mind that if ethnocentrism is in any way natural it is nonetheless changeable. Some parts, such as detecting accents, may not readily change. Similarly, one should probably not hope that stereotyping will easily disappear from our lives. But stereotypes can and do change and *can* be changed. In very large measure the social sciences, certainly anthropology, have taken as a central mission the task of understanding ethnocentrism so that it can better be ameliorated if not eliminated. Much of the methodology of anthropology, for example, is specifically designed to circumvent the effects of in-group bias and thus allow more objective analyses of the situation of ourselves and others in the world. An objective understanding is a crucial step toward control.

The clearer our understanding of ethnocentrism, the more enabled we will be to curb its excesses. There is no shortage of materials to study, and ample reason to give the subject high priority.

NOTES

1. Certain exceptions or qualifications should be noted. For example, Swartz (1961) cites Pacific Islanders, who considered their society or culture inferior to that of the United States. However, Swartz noted that the Islanders did not cease to consider themselves superior to neighboring peoples. And he explained the apparent exception away by arguing that the Islanders considered themselves and Americans to be essentially the same people. Sometimes individuals find the exotic attractive, and the evidence is overwhelming that many individuals voluntarily leave their own societies to become members of others. The latter does not entail an immediate and full defection from one's ethnic affiliation, but it often leads in that direction. Limited as these exceptions may be, they should figure into any careful understanding of ethnocentrism.
2. One should not conclude, however, that in-group bias is aroused with equal ease or intensity in all contexts. Hirschfeld (1996:61) notes that humans find ethnicity or race more salient and/or easier to think about than class, and he suggests that class often transmutes itself into race (imagined "race," of course) because the latter is so much easier to think about. A corollary of this, I would suggest, is that where class (or any other analogous social structural principle) comes to resemble ethnicity—as when it results in distinct accents, apparel, or deportment—it becomes more salient, more meaningful to people.
3. Although it has its origin in Le Vine and Campbell's (1971) list, the list given here has been considerably revised in the light of further research, and is subject to further refinement. Some elements could probably be combined; others could probably be split up. Given further evidence, some items may be dropped from the list and others added.
4. As used here, "syndrome" denotes an objectively observed set of co-occurring traits, not necessarily negative or abnormal. This is not to deny, of course, that in many contexts ethnocentrism does have negative consequences.
5. The term is van den Berghe's (1987), and it has the advantage of referring both to an ethnic group and an ethnic category. Generally in the social sciences a "group" has some degree of organization as a unit, while a "category" does not. It is unfortunate that the term *ethnic group* tends, misleadingly, to be used for both of these conditions.

6. Gil-White (2001) considers endogamy to be one of the necessary and sufficient conditions of an ethny; that is, an ethny will be perceived as such to the extent that it is perceived as biologically self-reproducing, like a species.
7. Nonetheless, *cultural* universals do exist. Generally they are very ancient and very useful—like the use of fire or cooking food—or they are in some way reflections or responses to universal conditions; kinship terminologies are an example (Brown 1991).
8. For Hirschfeld, human kinds include, of course, ethnic and racial kinds ("ethnoraces"), but also occupational kinds, kin, the two sexes, and unspecified other kinds. (But cf. Gil-White [2001], who argues for a more specific adaptation for thinking about ethnicity, per se.)
9. See discussions of mental modularity in Barkow et al. (1992) and Hirschfeld and Gelman (1994).
10. That human ears can hold up glasses is an effect or by-product of the adaptive design of the outer ear, which functions to channel sound waves to the eardrum.
11. Very recent paleontological findings indicating that Neandertals and *Homo sapiens* overlapped in time and space (or, much earlier, that differing species of hominids may also have coexisted) might force a rethinking of this statement.
12. As Hirschfeld notes, "Costume, clothing, and ornaments were surely the most marked physical differences that our ancestral populations encountered" to distinguish human kinds (1996:107). Interestingly, Hirschfeld found that the present-day markers of occupation, just like racial differences, seem to trigger human-kinds thinking in children, so that they imagine occupations to be similar to races. Equally interesting is that although children exhibit a considerable interest in human kinds, they are not quick to learn how to identify persons by race. Children may, for example, absorb racial stereotypes without realizing that their very playmates are of the race or races being stereotyped (Hirschfeld 1996).
13. The literature on this matter is relatively small but still too large, speculative, and contentious to be summarized here. See, for example, van den Berghe (1987), Reynolds et al. (1987), and Gil-White (2001). For theoretical guidance on the evolution of human nature, see Barkow et al. (1992).
14. For the role of history in discovering human nature and tracing its effects, see Brown (1999).

REFERENCES CITED

AKST, DANIEL. 1993. Cruller fates. *Los Angeles Times,* March 9: D1, D6.

BARKOW, JEROME H., LEDA COSMIDES, and JOHN TOOBY, eds. 1992. *The Adapted Mind: Evolutionary Psychology and the Generation of Culture.* New York: Oxford University Press.

BÉTEILLE, ANDRÉ. 1967. Race and descent as social categories in India. *Daedalus* 96:444–463.

BROWN, D. E. 1976. *Principles of Social Structure: Southeast Asia.* London: Duckworth.

——. 1991. *Human Universals.* New York/Philadelphia: McGraw-Hill/Temple University Press.

___. 1997. Are ethnicity and ethnocentrism natural? *Southwestern Anthropological Association Newsletter* 38(1):1, 4, 6, 9–10, 16–17, 19.

___. 1999. Human nature and history. *History and Theory* 38:138–157.

DE VOS, GEORGE, and HIROSHI WAGATSUMA, eds. 1967. *Japan's Invisible Race: Caste in Culture and Personality.* Berkeley: University of California Press.

FURNIVALL, J. S. 1956. *Colonial Policy and Practice: A Comparative Study of Burma and Netherlands India.* New York: New York University Press.

GIL-WHITE, FRANCISCO. 1999. How thick is blood? The plot thickens . . . : If ethnic actors are primordialists, what remains of the circumstantialist/primordialist controversy? *Ethnic and Racial Studies* 22(5):789–820.

___. 2001. Are ethnic groups biological "species" to the human brain? Essentialism in our cognition of some social categories. *Current Anthropology* 42(4):515–554.

HARCOURT, ALEXANDER H., and FRANS B. M. DE WAAL, eds. 1992. *Coalitions and Alliances in Humans and Other Animals.* Oxford: Oxford University Press.

HASTORF, ALBERT H., and HADLEY CANTRIL. 1954. They saw a game: A case study. *Journal of Abnormal and Social Psychology* 49:129–134.

HERODOTUS. 5th century B.C. *The Persian Wars.* Various editions.

HIRSCHFELD, LAWRENCE A. 1996. *Race in the Making: Cognition, Culture, and the Child's Construction of Human Kinds.* Cambridge, MA: MIT Press.

HIRSCHFELD, LAWRENCE A., and SUSAN GELMAN, eds. 1994. *Mapping the Mind: Domain Specificity in Cognition and Culture.* Cambridge: Cambridge University Press.

IBN KHALDUN. 1958. *The Muqaddimah: An Introduction to History,* vol. I. Franz Rosenthal, trans. Princeton, NJ: Princeton University Press.

LE VINE, ROBERT A., and DONALD T. CAMPBELL. 1971. *Ethnocentrism: Theories of Conflict, Ethnic Attitudes, and Group Behavior.* New York: Wiley.

MAQUET, JACQUES J. 1961. *The Premise of Inequality in Ruanda: A Study of Political Relations in a Central African Kingdom.* London: Oxford University Press.

MUMMENDEY, AMÉLIE, et al. 1992. Categorization is not enough: Intergroup discrimination in negative outcome allocation. *Journal of Experimental Social Psychology* 28:125–144.

MURDOCK, GEORGE PETER. 1931. Ethnocentrism, vol. 5, pp. 613–614. In *Encyclopaedia of the Social Sciences.* New York: Macmillan.

PERERA, SASANKA. 1991. Teaching and learning hatred: The role of education and socialization in Sri Lankan ethnic conflict. Ph.D. dissertation, University of California, Santa Barbara.

PINKER, STEVEN. 1994. *The Language Instinct: How the Mind Creates Language.* New York: Morrow.

___. 1997. *How the Mind Works.* New York: Norton.

RABBIE, JACOB. 1992. The effects of intragroup cooperation and intergroup competition on in-group cohesion and out-group hostility. In *Coalitions and Alliances in Humans and Other Animals.* Alexander H. Harcourt and Frans B. M. de Waal, eds. Pp. 175–205. Oxford: Oxford University Press.

REYNOLDS, VERNON, VINCENT FALGER, and IAN VINE, eds. 1987. *The Sociobiology of Ethnocentrism: Evolutionary Dimensions of Xenophobia, Discrimination, Racism and Nationalism.* London: Croom Helm.

RISLEY, HERBERT. 1915. *The People of India.* London: W. Thacker & Co. (See Appendix I, "Caste in Proverbs and Popular Sayings.")

ROMANUCCI-ROSS, LOLA. 1975. Italian ethnic identity and its transformations. In *Ethnic Identity: Cultural Continuities and Change.* George De Vos and Lola Romanucci-Ross, eds. Pp. 198–226. Chicago: University of Chicago Press.

SCHEFF, THOMAS J. 1994. *Bloody Revenge: Emotions, Nationalism, and War.* Boulder, CO: Westview Press.

SCHEFF, THOMAS J., and SUZANNE M. RETZINGER. 1991. *Emotions and Violence: Shame and Rage in Destructive Conflicts.* Lexington, MA: Lexington Books.

SELIGMAN, MARTIN E. P., and JOANNE L. HAGER. 1972. *Biological Boundaries of Learning.* New York: Appleton-Century-Crofts.

SINHA, GOPAL SHARAN, and RAMESH CHANDRA SINHA. 1967. Exploration in caste stereotypes. *Social Forces* 46:42–47.

SUMNER, WILLIAM GRAHAM. 1906. *Folkways: A Study of the Sociological Importance of Usages, Manners, Customs, Mores, and Morals.* Boston: Ginn.

SWARTZ, M. J. 1961. Negative ethnocentrism. *Journal of Conflict Resolution* 5(1):75–81.

TAMBIAH, S. J. 1986. *Sri Lanka: Ethnic Fratricide and the Dismantling of Democracy.* Chicago: University of Chicago Press.

VALLONE, ROBERT P., LEE ROSS, and MARK R. LEPPER. 1985. The hostile media phenomenon: Biased perception and perceptions of media bias in coverage of the Beirut massacre. *Journal of Personality and Social Psychology* 49:577–585.

VAN DEN BERGHE, PIERRE. 1987. *The Ethnic Phenomenon.* New York: Praeger.

WAAL, FRANS DE. 1982. *Chimpanzee Politics: Power & Sex among Apes.* New York: Harper & Row.

WARNECKE, A. MICHAEL, ROGER D. MASTERS, and GUIDO KEMPTER. 1992. The roots of nationalism: Nonverbal behavior and xenophobia. *Ethology and Sociobiology* 13:267–282.

YOON, IN-JIN. 1991. Self-employment in business: Chinese-, Japanese-, Korean-American, black, and white. Ph.D. dissertation, University of Chicago.

6

U.S. ETHNIC RELATIONS: ANGLOS AND THE "WHITE ETHNICS"

Raymond Scupin

Lindenwood University

The purpose of this chapter is to set the stage for an understanding of race and ethnic issues in U.S. society. Subsequent chapters discuss Native American Indians, African Americans, Hispanic Americans, Jewish Americans, Asian Americans, and Arab Americans. These more specialized chapters were written by anthropologists who concentrate on the study of different ethnic groups in the United States. In order to form some basis for understanding these various ethnic groups, we need some background on the establishment of patterns of ethnicity and race relations by the European settlers in America. We begin the chapter with an overview of the early English settlers, the so-called WASP ethnic group, which provided the basic cultural heritage for U.S. society. In addition, we examine the patterns of non-WASP immigration from Europe in the nineteenth century and the consequences of this immigration for U.S. society. In order to grasp the complexities of this process, we focus on the early trends of immigration from northwest Europe by examining the experience of the German and Irish ethnic immigrants. To investigate later trends of immigration

from southern and eastern Europe in the nineteenth century, we concentrate on the experience of the Italian and Polish ethnic groups. Finally, we address the various policies of assimilation and pluralism in U.S. society and how these so-called "white ethnics" have influenced these policies.

WASP DOMINANCE

The early European colonization of what was to become the United States begins with the so-called WASP, or white Anglo-Saxon Protestants. In actuality, the term *Anglo-Saxon* is a bit of a misnomer. The phrase is derived from the northern European ethnic groups, the Saxons and Angles, who invaded England during the fourth and sixth centuries A.D., displacing other ethnic groups such as the Celts and Romans, who had come from Europe in earlier centuries. Eventually, the Normans invaded England from France to intermingle with these other ethnic groups. Thus, the English settlers who came to settle the New England colonies were a product of a long history of the merging of different ethnic cultures. The acronym WASP was not actually popularized until the publication of a book in 1964 called *The Protestant Establishment* by sociologist E. Digby Baltzell (Christopher 1989). The term *WASP* has come to denote a northern European ethnic group with a particular cultural and institutional complex that dominated U.S. society for generations. The British settlers were able to overcome their rivals, the French, Spanish, and Dutch in colonial America, and were free to develop their own form of culture. With the exception of Native American Indians and enslaved African Americans, four out of five colonial settlers in America were British Protestant. Smaller groups of settlers, including Scots and Welsh, as well as Scotch-Irish (Protestants from Northern Ireland), Dutch, Germans, and Scandinavians, were present in early America. Yet, by the end of the seventeenth century, these early non-Anglo settlers assimilated, culturally and structurally, becoming part of the core WASP ethnic group that became dominant.

WASP ethnicity became preeminent in the United States through the establishment of its language, symbols, and culture. The English language was the fundamental underpinning of the cultural legacy that was bestowed by the WASPs on American society. It became the acceptable written and spoken language for the building of the nation-state and country, and it represented the standard for creating ethnic identity in colonial America. English was the institutional language of education and religion among the WASPs. Prior to the American Revolution, education was private and only accessible to affluent WASP citizens. The educational system was founded largely on the tenets of primarily Anglican and Calvinist-Puritan forms of the English Protestant traditions. Later, groups of Baptists and Methodists (and smaller groups of Lutherans and Quakers) influenced WASP religious culture. The cultural values of these religious traditions were transmitted through the English language. English language facility was

necessary for any type of education in early American society. Other early immigrant groups such as the Germans, Scandinavians, and Dutch were expected to readily adopt the English language or suffer the consequences if they did not.

Xenophobic attitudes (fears of foreigners) were expressed by some of the early English settlers when faced with ethnic groups who did not speak English. For example, Benjamin Franklin was extremely wary of German immigrants who were coming into America speaking another language and maintaining another culture. He said: "Should the Palatine Boors [Germans] be suffered to swarm into our settlements and by herding together establish their language and manners to the exclusion of ours? Why should Pennsylvania, founded by the English, become a colony of aliens who will shortly be so numerous as to Germanize us instead of our Anglifying them, and [who] will never adopt our Language or Customs" (Christopher 1989; Kamphoefner 1996:152). From the early establishment of WASP culture, the expectation held that any subsequent ethnic groups that came to America would have to learn the English language. This was the first stage of what has sometimes been referred to as "Anglo-conformity."

Along with the English language, the WASPs brought their basic fabric of the economic, legal, and political institutional framework for U.S. society. One of the primary reasons for colonization of North America by the British was to extract raw materials and to produce new markets for England. The English Crown chartered companies and granted territory for these companies to develop commercial capitalism in America. The ideals of commercial capitalism, including the right to own private property, were brought to America by the English settlers. The initiatives for taking land from Native American Indians, for developing European forms of agriculture including the importation of slaves, and for sending raw materials across the Atlantic were all aspects of the market-oriented capitalism that was transported from England to America.

Following the American Revolution, this market-oriented capitalism became the cornerstone of the expansion of the Industrial Revolution in the United States. As the principal ethnic group that was engaged in the development of commercial capitalism and the industrial revolution, the WASPs were able to dominate and manage the major economic capitalist institutions within U.S. society.

Both the legal and political institutions of what was to become U.S. society emerged as a combination of early British and eighteenth-century French philosophy. The substance of the early laws enacted by the WASPs in the colonies was English in origin. Rights of property holders, contracts, equality before the law, and representative government had been institutionalized by the British government and were espoused by English philosophers such as John Locke (1632–1704). The English colonists' conceptions of a decentralized form of political process based on town meetings and participatory democracy were developed in early America. Broader philosophical and political beliefs that expressed ideals of equality, freedom, justice, individual rights, anti-aristocratic values, and checks and balances among separate divisions of government authority were adopted by leaders such as Thomas Jefferson and Benjamin Franklin from such French philosophers as Montesquieu (1689–1755) and Jean-Jacques Rousseau (1712–78). These cultural ideals became the basis of the American Revolution and the fashioning of the new nation-state. Constitutional government and abstract principles of equality, justice, freedom, and political autonomy were promoted through this political creed and cultural ideals.

One of the questions that arises when discussing U.S. history after the American Revolution is to what extent the political leaders were intent on fashioning a nation-state that was based on Anglo ethnicity or whether they were trying to develop a civic polity based on a more universal basis. On the one hand, in *The Federalist Papers* (1787–88), the political documents that provided the foundation for the U.S. Constitution, John Jay describes the American people as "descended from the same ancestors, speaking the same language, professing the same religion, attached to the same principles of government, very similar in their manners and customs. Surely, a band of brethren so united should never be split into a number of unsocial, jealous, and alien sovereignties" (cited in Walzer 1997). Thomas Jefferson developed an obsessive interest in beliefs of the superiority of the Anglo-Saxon race, and actually tried to learn the ancient language itself (Smedley 1999). These beliefs suggest that an "Anglo-WASP" ethnicity should (would) be the basis for the new American nation.

Conversely, it would appear that as the revolutionaries were forging a new nation-state, a number of the leaders were also fashioning the notion of a new form of identity for the nation, an "American" identity and nationality. With the Revolution, many U.S. citizens developed "Anglophobia" and hostility toward the British. In order to distinguish themselves from their European predecessors, including their British ancestors, some of the early leaders emphasized "American ideals," which were embodied in the political documents of the Revolution. It appears that some were trying to establish a civic polity rather than an ethnically based polity (Gleason 1980). In this view, ideally, to become an American, individuals did not have to be of any particular national or ethnic background. All they had to do was to subscribe to the political and cultural ideals of liberty, equality, and constitutional government. However, the *ideal culture* of the United States differed substantially from the *real culture*. For example, many of the revolutionary leaders perpetuated the slavery of Africans and the appropriation of land from Native Americans. It appeared that "whiteness" was the primary criterion for distinguishing different identities. European descent and "whiteness" were inextricably linked to create a divide among different groups of Americans. Thus, despite the attempt to be as inclusive as possible, the "American identity," which referred to all "men" or "mankind" in the various political documents, remained fairly exclusive. So, the question as to what extent the new "American identity" converged with or diverged from an Anglo-WASP identity has remained significant for many people throughout different periods of U.S. history.

NEW ETHNIC CHALLENGES FOR U.S. SOCIETY

It is necessary to reiterate one of the themes of this textbook at this juncture. The WASP or Anglo ethnic group, like any other ethnic group, exhibited a great deal of internal diversity and variation regarding socioeconomic status and cultural traditions. For example, in his book, *Albion's Seed: Four British Folkways in America* (1989), David Hackett Fischer identifies four distinct peoples that represent British culture in early America: the English Puritans of New England, the southern planter culture of Virginia, the Quakers of Pennsylvania, and others who settled in the backcountry of Appalachia. However, as the economic and political institutions developed along with the Industrial Revolution in the United States, only a comparatively small number of persons within these different Anglo populations became part of the dominant elite. This political and economic elite, however, was able to maintain its political hegemony over other ethnic groups for a substantial period of U.S. history.

No one can question the reality that the language, cultural values, and practices of the descendants of the English settlers disproportionately influenced the institutional framework of the United States for generations. As we will see, in respect to later-arriving ethnic minorities, the WASP elite controlled the playing field for assimilation into U.S. society. Because they did not have many non-Anglo ethnic groups with economic or political power to compete with for resources or power, the WASPs had definite advantages in establishing their dominance. Historically, the significant rules for cultural and structural assimilation were established by the WASPs through immigration policies, laws regarding segregation or integration, removal policies, voting restrictions, and a number of other measures aimed at ethnic minorities. Most sociologists and historians agree that the descendants of this WASP ethnic group still maintain an enormous and disproportionate amount of economic and political influence in U.S. society. For example, Arthur Schlesinger states: "For better or worse, the white Anglo-Saxon Protestant tradition was for two centuries, and in crucial respects still is, the dominant influence on American culture and society. This tradition provided the standard to which other immigrant nationalities were expected to conform, the matrix into which they would be assimilated" (1992:28).

The nineteenth century, however, was to see an enormous number of non-Anglos flowing in from other parts of the world who would begin to challenge Anglo dominance. More than 30 million non-Anglo European immigrants would come to the United States in the nineteenth century. Typically, sociologists and historians classify this immigration from Europe in the nineteenth century into two distinctive historical periods. The period from 1820 to 1880 is the first era of non-Anglo immigration and is sometimes called the "Old Immigration" period. The period from 1880 to 1920 is referred to as the "New Immigration."[1] The Old Immigration period is associated with immigrants from northwest Europe, including the Irish, Germans, and Scandinavians from Norway and Sweden. The New Immigration era is identified with southern and eastern European immigrants, including Italian, Polish, Greek, Russian, and Jewish groups. All of these European populations were considerably different ethnically from the WASPs. Many were non-Protestant, maintaining either Catholic or Jewish religious traditions. In addition, especially in respect to those ethnic groups from southern and eastern Europe, these people had different languages that were historically far removed from the developments of the English language. To illustrate the patterns of ethnicity in the United States, we will focus on the German and Irish immigrants to examine the early period of European immigration from northwest Europe. Later we will focus on the Italian and Polish immigrants to illuminate how U.S. society regarding these people from southern and eastern Europe.

GERMAN AMERICANS

Since the seventeenth century, approximately 7 million people born in the area now known as Germany settled in North America. Currently, more Americans trace their ancestry to Germany than any other country. Although it is difficult to assess these numbers precisely, some 50 million to 60 million Americans are descendants of Germans (Adams 1993).[2] One group of the earliest German immigrants arrived in 1683 in Philadelphia and settled nearby in an area that became known as Germantown. These immigrants were mostly religious Quakers and Mennonites, and Pennsylvania provided a tolerant atmosphere for them. In the first American census of 1790, the population of the city of Germantown was 225,000, about a third of the citizens in Pennsylvania. Most of these Germantown residents were weavers, merchants, or artisans. Other early German immigrants settled in the English colonies of New York, New Jersey, Maryland, Virginia, and South Carolina. The population of Germans in the colonies at the time of the American Revolution was approximately 9 percent of the total. These early German settlers came to America primarily in search of a better standard of living and to escape the extremes of the class structures, which limited economic opportunities in Ger-

man society. Political and religious freedom and the threat of military induction motivated others to immigrate from Germany. Many early German settlers were "chain migrants" who followed relatives and friends into the colonies (Adams 1993; Kamphoefner 1987). These friends and relatives helped provide aid and comfort for these new immigrants. Early German immigrants were very diverse, divided by class, education, religion, and dialect. Most of the residents of Germantown anglicized their names, quickly learned English, and began to intermarry outside of their group. On the other hand, some of the German settlers were threatened by the WASP ethnic dominance, and were fearful of language loss and culture (Conzen 1980).

Later, in the nineteenth century, largely because of failed political reforms and revolutions, crop failures, and the lack of economic opportunities in Germany, German immigrants flowed into the United States. These German immigrants represented different religious traditions—Protestant, Catholic, and Jewish. (See Chapter 9 on Jewish Americans.) Some of these migrants came as "indentured servants." As indentured servants, they signed a contract with a ship's captain who had the right to sell the passenger, along with his family, into a form of servitude for three to four years in order to pay their passage (Adams 1993). More than 220,000 Germans arrived in the year 1854.

Up until the twentieth century, when Germany was able to industrialize enough to absorb its rural population into its labor force, German immigrants continued to choose the United States for settlement. Over 5 million German immigrants came to the United States in the nineteenth century (see Table 6-1). Unlike earlier German immigrants, who began to assimilate swiftly, generally the migrants of the nineteenth century began to move to areas where there were substantial German settlements. Many of the Germans with rural backgrounds sought out reasonably priced farmland

Table 6-1 Germans in the U.S. population, 1850–1970

Year	Number	Percent of Foreign-Born
1850	583,774	26.0
1860	1,276,075	30.8
1870	1,690,533	30.4
1880	1,966,742	29.4
1890	2,784,894	30.1
1900	2,663,418	25.8
1910	2,311,237	17.1
1920	1,686,108	12.1
1930	1,608,814	11.3
1940	1,237,772	10.7
1950	991,321	9.5
1960	989,815	10.2
1970	832,965	8.7

Source: U.S. Bureau of the Census, *Historical Statistics of the United States, Colonial Times to 1970* (Washington, DC, 1975), Series C, pp. 195–227, 286–295.

in areas where German schools and German-language churches already existed (Adams 1993; Kamphoefner 1987). Those from the same villages in Germany would follow each other into rural America. The chain migration continued to form significant German communities throughout the Mid-Atlantic states. Most of the rurally based German populace settled along the waterways of the Great Lakes or the Ohio, Missouri, and Mississippi rivers.

Many of the German immigrants entering the United States were urban-based people skilled in crafts, trades, or professional occupations. The booming cities of Cincinnati, St. Louis, Chicago, Pittsburgh, Milwaukee, Indianapolis, and Louisville, located along waterways or railways, were attractive sites for Germans with urban skills. Breweries, bakeries, distilleries, flour millers, tailor shops, print shops, surveying businesses, and plumbing stores were established by these immigrants. A number of well-educated immigrants who had fled Germany for political reasons became important political activists and officials within the U.S. government. Thus, nineteenth-century German American ethnic communities included both skilled and unskilled laborers. Because of their numbers and the occupational diversity of their population, German

Americans could develop extremely self-sufficient communities. By 1900, one-third of Wisconsin's population was German, and Minnesota and Illinois had more than one-fifth from Germany (Adams 1993).

As the numbers of immigrants from Germany increased, rather than assimilate quickly into U.S. society, many attempted to retain their ethnic identity, including their language, culture, and religious traditions. As in other areas of Europe, the Industrial Revolution in Germany engendered nationalist movements. These nationalist movements began to draw together disparate peoples throughout Germany into a perceived unified ethnicity and identity, and these movements affected the migrants entering the United States as well. Many of these German immigrants wanted to conserve their ethnic and nationalist identity within the United States. Aside from German-language schools and churches, they began to establish ethnically based organizations such as music societies, theater clubs, beer halls, lodges, and political clubs. In particular, the institution known as the *Turnvereings* ("Turner Clubs"), which emphasized physical body-building through gymnastics and calisthenics, as well as German nationalistic, intellectual, and artistic culture, were sites for emphasizing ethnic expression and Germanness. The Turner Clubs provided German-language instruction and adult classes in German history, politics, and philosophy. Through these organizations and institutions, as well as the private schools and churches within specific neighborhoods, various "Little Germanies" emerged throughout major cities such as St. Louis, Cincinnati, and Milwaukee. The endeavor to preserve German culture in the United States even led to a proposal to establish an exclusive German state in the Union (Adams 1993; Cornell and Hartmann 1998).

The German language was prevalent in the schools and churches within the German American communities throughout most of the nineteenth century. German was spoken by about 9 million people in the United States as late as 1910 (Adams 1993). Most of the private schools in the German American neighborhoods taught exclusively in German, and for some time states like Pennsylvania and Ohio allowed German as an alternate language to English in the public schools. German Americans struggled politically with the public school systems to allow for bilingual education so that children would not forget their native tongue. German-language books, magazines, and newspapers were published and circulated widely within these communities. By the late nineteenth century, the largest non-English-speaking ethnic group were the Germans, who chose to differentiate themselves ethnically from the WASP majority by maintaining their language and culture. To a great extent, the Germans and non-Germans maintained separate communities, which were institutionally apart, the hallmark of what is known as a plural society.

As seen earlier in the remarks of Benjamin Franklin, some of the WASPs were concerned about ethnic Germanness and its impact on U.S. society. Eventually, in the 1850s, these latent xenophobic feelings led to an open nativistic political movement aimed at Germans and other immigrants. A political party known as the Know-Nothings developed. The Know-Nothing program aimed to elect only WASPs to political office, to fight against Roman Catholicism, and to restrict citizenship and voting rights to immigrants who had resided in the United States 21 years instead of the 5 years required by law. (They were known as Know-Nothings because party members were instructed to divulge nothing about their political program and to say they knew nothing about it.) However, it was not until World War I and then World War II that extensive anti-German prejudice emerged within U.S. society. As the United States entered World War I against Germany and Italy, the ethnic German American status became endangered. The excessive nationalistic tendencies in World War I Europe were countered by an intensive

"Anglo American nationalism" in the United States. During the war, U.S. newspapers were filled with anti-German hysteria. Numerous political cartoons characterized the German American community as a perceived threat to U.S. society. The German language was no longer taught in public schools, and public libraries removed German-language books and magazines from their shelves. Wartime hysteria even led to the banning of the use of the German translation of the Bible in Lutheran churches. As a reaction to these anti-German sentiments, rapid cultural assimilation began to dominate within the German American communities. For example, German surnames and German business names were Anglicized.

World War II and the horrors of Nazism sealed the fate of ethnic Germanness in U.S. society. The aftermath of the wars resulted in most German Americans adopting and assimilating to Anglo culture as quickly as possible. Typically, the use of the German language was thoroughly abandoned in advertising and in the teaching of history and religion. German parents no longer taught their children German. In addition, there was a high rate of intermarriage among German Americans and other ethnic groups. Most German Americans had been successful in adjusting economically, socially, and politically in American society. Large numbers of them had achieved equality with WASPs in terms of education, income, and occupation. And, in reality, ethnic German culture had a major impact on the culture of the WASPs. The national diet, work habits, intellectual culture, educational system, and political and religious traditions were influenced widely by German cultural traditions. But, following the world wars, ethnic Germans did not want to forsake their overall success in the United States by emphasizing their Germanness. They did not want to be a target of persecution, discrimination, and prejudice. Consequently, cultural and structural assimilation became their predominant ethnic strategy. Only small groups such as the Old Order Amish (see Chapter 4) and other smaller religious communities retained the German language and culture in order to preserve a separate ethnic identity.

IRISH AMERICANS

Immigrants from Ireland began to enter colonial America during the 1600s. Most of these early immigrants were the so-called Scotch-Irish who had earlier immigrated to northern Ireland from England after England conquered Ireland in the twelfth century. Most of the Scotch-Irish were Protestants, of the Anglican or Calvinist (Presbyterian) religious traditions, along with smaller numbers of Methodists, Baptists, and Quakers. However, about one-third of these early immigrants were Irish from southern Ireland, who had been Catholic but most of whom converted to Protestantism. Since there were few Catholic institutions such as churches and priests at the time in colonial America, most early Irish immigrants became Baptists or other kinds of Protestants (Byron 1999). It is estimated that some 40 percent of George Washington's revolutionary army were Irish (Christopher 1989). An Irishman, John Barry (1745–1803), became the "father of the United States Navy" (Blessing 1980). At the end of the American Revolution, the Irish made up about 10 percent of the U.S. population.

The major influx of Irish immigrants into the United States, however, came during the nineteenth century. Over 4 million Irish settled in the United States during the 1800s (see Table 6-2). Today, some 40 million Americans trace their ancestry to Ireland. A variety of factors led to the flood of Irish immigrants in the 1800s. Like Germany, Ireland lacked a sufficient industrial base to absorb the increasing population of rural laborers. As a result of British policies in Ireland, there were enormous numbers of rural Irish who were landless or who held marginally small landholdings. The constant pressure of popula-

Table 6-2   Irish immigration to the United States, 1820–1975

Years	Number of Immigrants
1820–30	54,338
1831–40	207,381
1841–50	780,719
1851–60	914,119
1861–70	435,778
1871–80	436,871
1881–90	655,482
1891–1900	388,416
1901–10	339,065
1911–20	146,181
1921–30	220,591
1931–40	13,167
1941–50	26,967
1951–60	57,332
1961–70	37,461

Source: U.S. Immigration and Naturalization Service, *Annual Report, 1975* (Washington, DC, 1976), pp. 62–64.

tion on the resources of the Emerald Isle resulted in heavy emigration. And most importantly, the well-known Great Famine of the 1840s was a traumatic ecological and economic disaster that resulted in large-scale immigration. Most of the rural Irish subsisted on the potato crop. In 1845, a fungal potato blight resulted in 80 percent of the harvest being destroyed. Approximately 90,000 people starved to death because of nutritional deficiencies and other related physical problems (Blessing 1980; Byron 1999). The potato famine resulted in at least a million Irish immigrating to the United States between 1847 and 1854. The severe persecution of the poor Irish by British landlords and political authorities in southern Ireland was another significant factor in driving immigration. An intensive ethnonationalist movement based on Irish Catholic ethnicity had developed in Ireland, and a number of politically active Irish were attempting to revolt against the British authorities. One response of the British authorities was to promote immigration as a solution to the "Irish troubles" (Miller 1985). Thus, both economic and political factors "pushed" Irish immigration and led to the arrival of many Irish to U.S. shores in the mid-nineteenth century.

The Irish immigrants in the United States represented diverse peoples from different regions of Ireland. Like the German immigrants, many of the Irish came as chain migrants who relied on networks of relatives and friends to help them settle. In particular, kinship networks and people sharing a surname aided each other in the settlement process. Also, many employers sent money to Ireland to pay the passage of the cheap labor they wanted. There were rural laborers and also urban workers from cities like Dublin, Belfast, and Cork. Some people from the middle stratum of Irish society could pay their own passage and had education, skills, and capital to make a start in the United States. Others, fewer in number, were from more remote and distressed famine areas of Ireland. They were the poorest immigrants and lacked education, skills, and capital. Many of them had to come as indentured servants. The better-off immigrants spoke English (and many may have resided in Britain for some time before moving to the United States), while fewer in number, the poorest rural Irish from remote areas spoke only Irish (Gaelic, the ancient Celtic language of Ireland), while many other Irish were bilingual. On the whole, the majority of the Irish were English-speaking immigrants, albeit, there were a number of Anglo-Irish dialects that were (and still are) often identified as the "brogue" (Byron 1999). And though the vast majority of these Irish immigrants were Catholics, smaller numbers were Protestants.

As the Irish Catholics settled in the United States, they adapted within many different types of occupations, skilled and professional. Many of the immigrants with education, capital, and skills were able to establish their own businesses in the booming economies of nineteenth-century America. Some of them became the leaders of major enterprises. Other white-collar workers were clerks, clergy, or teachers. However, the many Irish who came with little education and capital were forced to take the lowest-paying jobs in factories, mines, mills, construction, and other unskilled occupations. For example, large numbers of Irish workers were involved in the construction of the Erie Canal in New York State. Later, Irish labor was used to build the intercontinental railroad across the country. Others worked in foundries, railway locomotive factories and repair shops, furniture factories, boat-building shops, breweries, and other unskilled industries. Many of the Irish women began to work as domestic servants for WASP households, or in the textile mills and factories in eastern cities such as New York and Boston. In large cities like New York and Boston the Irish crowded into tenements, at times 20 or more families within a house. The press referred to these Irish tenements as "human rookeries." The availability of both Irish skilled and unskilled labor was instrumental in transforming the United States into a powerful industrial economy.

As Irish (and German) immigration increased in the nineteenth century, xenophobic sentiments (fears of foreigners) helped usher in nativistic movements among the WASP. In particular, Roman Catholicism, associated with the Irish, was perceived to be untrustworthy. Anti-Catholicism had originated in Europe and was brought to colonial America by the early WASP immigrants. Part of this anti-Catholic sentiment was the fear of the Pope taking control of various institutions and religious traditions. But the cry against "popery" and Catholicism increased as Irish immigrants flooded into the United States. As mentioned earlier, the Know-Nothing Party, the nativist political organization, was directed at prohibiting non-WASP and Catholics from participating in American social and political life. Much of the party's activity was aimed at the Irish, who were unwelcome because they were non-WASP and Roman Catholic. The Irish Catholics were beginning to bring their priests, religious institutions, and schools with them to America, and this reawakened old European religious hatreds. Like the Germans, the Irish Catholics reestablished these institutions as a means of retaining their Irish Catholic ethnicity. They formed societies such as the Hibernians, an organization linked to the Catholic Church, which promoted Irish ethnicity. But these activities resulted in the Irish feeling the sting of prejudice and discrimination from the WASP majority.

Other conceptions of Irish Catholic immigrants began to circulate among many WASPs. The Irish Catholics were perceived to be a "separate race" and were purported to have a distinctive biology that made them different from the WASPs. This construction of "race" was associated with prevalent stereotypes and generalizations about the Irish Catholics. Of course, this was at the time when "race" was confused with "ethnicity." The Irish "race" was perceived by the WASPs as undesirables who were immoral, unintelligent, uncouth, dirty, lazy, ignorant, temperamental, hostile, and addicted to alcohol. Some of these stereotypes and prejudices held by the WASPs had emerged in England and were imported into America. But in America these racially based stereotypes became vicious caricatures that were used to discriminate against the Irish. Underlying these stereotypes were the anti-Catholic prejudices, the extreme poverty associated with Irish immigrants, and their willingness to work for lower wages than other Americans. This resulted in some WASP employers blatantly refusing to hire the Irish. In cities such as Boston and New York, there were signs in storefronts, housing complexes, and factories saying, "No Irish Need Apply."

Unlike the German Americans, many of the Irish resisted their secondary status in WASP America by utilizing economic and political strategies. For example, many of the Irish involved themselves in early labor organizations to challenge their employers. The Irish workers frequently found themselves in bad working conditions and shameless exploitation. In addition, they faced the nativist WASP Americans who resented them because of their competition in the labor market. Wages were extremely low, ranging from 82¢ to $1.25 per day, and some of the Irish workers were paid in whiskey or "credit" in company stores, which charged high prices. To counter these conditions, Irish workers began to organize themselves. In the anthracite coal mines of Pennsylvania, the Irish formed the Molly Maguires, an organized union group that fought for better working conditions. The Mollies had actually started in Ireland but was transported to the United States (Kenny 1998). They used strikes and sometimes threats of violence, and actual violence, arson, and sabotage in order to struggle against coal company bosses who wanted to squelch their union. It is generally acknowledged that the Molly Maguires' struggle was the embryo of the organized labor movement in the United States. Irish workers continued their organized labor activities and eventually came to dominate many local unions. George Meany (1894–1979), a grandson of an Irish refugee from the Great Famine, became president of a major American union, the AFL-CIO. This union activity enabled the Irish to overcome some of the discrimination directed at them, and thereby become more economically successful in U.S. society.

Another means of success for the Irish in the United States was the employment of political strategies. The historical experience in Ireland and the struggle with the British pre-adapted the Irish for American politics. In the large cities, the Irish were adept at learning the political game that developed in nineteenth-century America. In particular, the Irish became associated with the Democratic Party in U.S. politics. Big-city political machines were often created and controlled by the Irish immigrants. Through the political process the large numbers of immigrants were able to elect their own Irish representatives. As soon as new immigrants landed in New York or Boston, they were drilled by Irish voters and representatives about the political issues that affected them. Irish ethnic unity was cultivated by anti-WASP attitudes. The Irish political ward bosses frequently provided government jobs for their own group, and city contracts were given to Irish-owned private businesses. These political machines also furnished needed services such as better housing, food, coal, and other amenities to poor immigrants. The infamous Tammany Hall political machine in New York City in the early 1800s was controlled by Irish political bosses. Though there were many political scandals that developed based on graft and corruption at this time in U.S. society, these Irish-dominated political machines created opportunities for the Irish in the large cities to move upward to challenge the WASP political hierarchy. Overall, this tradition of Irish American politics and its affiliation with the Democratic Party left a legacy that eventually resulted in the accomplishments of the descendants of the Irish such as the Kennedy family in Massachusetts.

Anthropologist Reginald Byron's (1999) in-depth ethnographic and historical study of the Irish in Albany, New York, suggests that the experience of the Irish in the cities of New York and Boston do not tell the complete story of the Irish in the United States.[3] Indeed, only about 10 to 15 percent of the Irish stayed in the large cities. Most of them settled in small cities, towns, villages, and rural communities throughout the United States. In order to gain an understanding of the more typical Irish American experience, Byron concentrates his ethnographic work on Albany, a town where many Irish immigrants settled. His ethnographic study on what it means to be Irish in the United States reveals complex phenomena that counter any simplifications or generalizations. He suggests that many of the generalities about the Irish American are based on the historian's interpretations of newspapers, church records, government reports, and other documents that are associated with the Irish in the large cities. By focusing his ethnographic study on a medium-sized city with a substantial Irish immigrant population, Byron was able to investigate another side of the Irish

American experience. Instead of finding people who were clinging to a "primordial" ethnic identity in distinctive neighborhoods, like the portrayal of the Irish in Boston or New York, he discovered that the descendants of the Irish immigrants in Albany have a highly abbreviated "Irishness." They have very vague recollections of their ancestral history, and overall, Irish ethnic identity does not have much resonance beyond participating in the St. Patrick's Day parade.

ITALIAN AMERICANS

During the second major period of immigration (the so-called "New Immigration," 1880–1920), many southern and eastern European ethnic groups entered the United States: Greeks, Italians, Serbians, Hungarians, Bulgarians, Russians, Ukrainians, and Poles. The United States was undergoing an unprecedented economic and industrial transformation that demanded large reservoirs of labor. Industrial expansion in the garment industries, food processing, mining, construction, and other manufacturing and services offered opportunities for people in southern and eastern Europe. Approximately two-thirds of the foreign-born population that came into the United States during this period were from these regions. Unlike the northern European groups, such as the German, Dutch, and Irish, these new immigrants had languages and cultures that were far and away much different from those of earlier immigrants.

A small number of northern Italians had settled in colonial America during the seventeenth century. Later, during the mid-1800s, other northern Italians came to California for the gold rush, and stayed to work as merchants, grape growers, wine makers, storekeepers, and truck farmers. But most of the Italians, over 4 million, primarily from southern Italy, came to the United States between 1880 and 1920 (see Table 6-3). Some of these southern Italians only stayed

Table 6-3 Italian Immigration to the United States, 1820–1970

Years	Number of Immigrants
1820–30	439
1831–40	2,253
1841–50	1,870
1851–60	9,231
1861–70	11,725
1871–80	55,759
1881–90	307,309
1891–1900	651,893
1901–10	2,045,877
1911–20	1,109,524
1921–30	455,315
1931–40	68,028
1941–50	57,661
1951–60	185,491
1961–70	214,111

Source: U.S. Bureau of the Census, *Historical Statistics of the United States: Colonial Times to 1970* (Washington, DC, 1975), pp. 1, 105–106.

for a short time before returning home; however, the vast majority remained. Presently, over 15 million Americans trace their ancestry to Italy. In the nineteenth century, regions like Naples and Sicily in southern Italy were the most undeveloped parts of the country. An oppressive feudal agricultural system dominated by absentee landlords, and discrimination in trade, industry, and education by northern Italians drove emigration from southern Italy. Although some southern Italians immigrated to North Africa and South America to work in agriculture, the wages and opportunities of the U.S. industrial economy were strong attractions for these people. In contrast to the northern Italians, these new immigrants tended to be poor, uneducated, and less skilled. Thus, most of them entered the labor force at the lowest end of the unskilled jobs (Lopreato 1970).

In the nineteenth century, Italy itself was in the process of creating its own nationalism out of its many different ethnic groups. It was the American experience that helped forge ties of ethnic identity among Italians. As these different ethnic groups from Italy arrived they were classified by the U.S. government officials as "Ital-

ian." And, as 90 percent of these "Italians" settled in urban areas, and founded communities, they came to recognize their similarity of tastes and preferences for food, dress, and other cultural traditions. Different ethnic groups such as Neapolitans and Sicilians came together to assist one another in their settlements in the U.S. urban environments. Many of the early immigrants had come through a form of indentured labor known as the "padrone system." A *padrone*, or boss, would recruit laborers in Italy, pay for their passage to the United States, and arrange work for them, mostly in construction. Other padrones recruited immigrant labor at the port of entry. The worker was obligated to pay a commission to the padrone for his services. Other Italian immigrants came through "chain migration," relying on kinship networks. As Roman Catholics, they used church organizations and other voluntary mutual aid societies to help them adapt to the new conditions in the United States. Because of these ties, eventually, these immigrants began to perceive themselves as having a common identity as "Italian Americans" (Alba 1985). This new identity created the foundation for the "Little Italys" in urban areas such as New York, Boston, Chicago, and St. Louis.

By the twentieth century, Italian Americans had adapted to a variety of professions, trades, and occupations in U.S. society. Many of the unskilled laborers had started as stone workers, cement workers, dock workers, luggage makers, and railroad workers. A number of Italian Americans had established major businesses such as the Planter Peanut Company, cigar companies, real estate and building companies, and banks. Italian women were working in the garment industries, as well as in candy, paper, and cigar companies within the larger cities such as New York and Chicago (Nelli 1980). Like the Irish, many Italians organized and joined unions to help them to move ahead economically in the United States. The founder of the amalgamated Clothing Workers of America, a labor union representing garment workers in Chicago, was an Italian American. Eventually, both Italian men and women joined unions to improve working conditions for their communities.

Italians also used the political process and the big-city political machines to gain advantages in the United States. In the Italian wards, the political bosses tended to be of Irish ethnicity. The Irish political bosses hired Italian men to organize the voters and lead their communities to the polls. The Italians provided votes that retained ward bosses and political machines in operation in exchange for jobs and contracts for Italian American businesses. Numerous Italian Americans sought public employment within the cities for a steady income and job security. As the Irish had developed connections within the Democratic Party and controlled the political machines, so the Italian Americans became associated with the same political party. In some instances, a few Italian Americans anglicized their names and ran for political office. For example, Paolo Antonio Vaccarelli, born in Naples, took the name Paul Kelly and became an influential politician in the Democratic political machine in New York (Nelli 1980).

As Italians were adjusting to U.S. society, Italian-language newspapers and the Roman Catholic Church served as integral aspects of their ethnicity and culture. The Italian-language newspapers provided a mechanism for communication in the neighborhoods for the first generation of immigrants. They allowed these immigrants to voice their grievances and complaints about the new society in which they found themselves. It also enabled Italians to maintain their ethnic cohesiveness in the early years of immigration. Like the political machines, the Roman Catholic Church in the United States was controlled and staffed by the Irish. Italian Catholicism was culturally different from that of the Irish austere form of Catholicism. The Italian Catholics emphasized the images, processions, colorful festivals, and other rituals that were not part of the Irish tradition (Nelli 1980). Therefore, many of the first-generation Italians felt alienated from the Church. Eventually, the Church in the United States began to develop "national parishes" to serve the needs of the Italian and other non-English-speaking immigrants. These national parishes were another means of consolidating an Italian ethnicity for the peoples from different locales in this first-generation of immigrants.

Italian Americans confronted a number of problems that were similar to, but different from, those of other earlier immigrants. Like the Irish, the Italians were categorized by many WASPs as a different "race" that was inferior intellectually and morally to that of the Anglo-Saxons. But this construction of an "Italian race" was even more severely restrictive than that applied to the Irish. An "Anglo-Saxon based racialism," which was linked to "scientific racism" in the 1880s and 1890s, grew in the United States as a reaction to the immigration of southern and eastern European peoples (see Chapter 3). The "Italian race," as well as other Mediterranean and eastern European "races," were classified as inferior, in contrast to the northern European "races." IQ tests and literacy tests were given to these early Italian Americans, and as expected, they scored lower than the "average" American. These IQ and literacy tests were purported scientific proof of these new immigrants' inferior intellect (Kamin 1974). These racist beliefs were promoted by the media and other "scientific" works of the time. Anglo-Saxon Americans were warned not to intermarry with Italians because it would cause the degeneration of the "race." The "Italian race" was identified with such characteristics as jealousy, overly-emotional, rough, mean, dirty, lazy, and other negativities.

Anti-Catholic prejudices and other stereotypes were also directed toward the early Italian immigrants, as many WASPs saw these immigrants bringing in non-Protestant beliefs and traditions. These anti-Catholic sentiments developed into stereotypes about how Italians (or the more pejorative labels of "wops" or "dagos") were superstitious, ignorant, and could not become Americanized. Since the Russian Revolution developed during this period of massive immigration, working-class Italians, especially those involved with unions, were sometimes identified with radical revolutionary movements.[4] In addition, along with Italian immigration, the organized criminal system known as the "Mafia" was modified and adapted to America by some Sicilians. Although until the time of prohibition, most of the crime syndicates in the United States were controlled by the Irish, Jews, and other groups, in the minds and stereotypes of many Americans, the Italian Mafia was associated with most organized crime. Crime was a means of upward mobility for many new immigrants in U.S. society, including the Italians. However, despite the fact that very few Italians in the United States have been associated with the Mafia, the stereotype endures. The film and television industries continue to perpetuate and reinforce these stereotypes.

Most of the sociological evidence suggests that in spite of the problems that Italian Americans had in adjusting to U.S. society, by the second and third generations, assimilation, both culturally and structurally, had taken place. Sociologist Herbert Gans (1982) wrote a classic study of the Italian Americans in Boston's West End. He found that by the second generation, Italian Americans had no strong loyalty to their traditional culture or language. The children of the first generation began to learn English and abandoned Italian. The children did not read the Italian newspapers that their parents had relied upon for their ethnic identity, and they no longer spoke Italian with each other. Although they tended to follow the food preferences of their parents, Gans found that there was very little visible about traditional ethnicity for these second-generation Italian Americans. And, as many of the third generation of Italian Americans have continued to move upward from the working class into the middle class in U.S. soci-

ety, their ethnic status as Italian Americans has dissolved. For the most part, friendship, work connections, and interests are not based on Italian American ethnicity but on educational and class-based preferences (Alba 1995; Waters 1990).

POLISH AMERICANS

Like many others from Europe, people from Poland were pushed and pulled by economic, political, and religious factors that influenced their decision to emigrate. Poland, a Roman Catholic nation founded by the Western Slavs in the tenth century A.D., became a large empire in the sixteenth century. At that time Poland was a large agricultural civilization known as the granary of Europe, and it was the most powerful country in Europe. The 1500s were known as the "Golden Century" to Polish historians (Bukowczyk 1987). In the 1600s, other countries, such as Sweden to the north, launched a series of invasions into Poland, and gradually, the Polish state began to decline. The Polish empire was surrounded by the newly centralized states of Prussia (later Germany), Russia, and Austria in Eastern Europe. Internal economic and political weaknesses led to the partitioning of Poland by these stronger states in the eighteenth century. Russia seized the largest part of Poland, and Prussia and Austria divided up the rest until after World War I. The Poles, most of whom were peasant laborers on outmoded feudal estates, were at the mercy of these invading empires. Although Polish resistance leaders attempted to challenge these larger empires, Poland as a country disappeared from the map of Europe. During the partitioning, these larger empires attempted to suppress the language and cultural heritage of the Polish people. Various insurrections and uprisings by Polish nationalist and religious leaders in the foreign-occupied Polish partitions were crushed by these large powerful empires.

Poland, like most other European states, consisted of a feudal agrarian economy during the period of partition. During the nineteenth century, however, while it was under the control of these other empires, early stages of industrialization, commercialization, and mechanization of agriculture were transforming the feudal economy. Rural peasants were displaced from their traditional livelihood as serfs on the feudal estates and became a large surplus class of impoverished, landless peoples (Bukowczyk 1987). Some of this displaced labor moved into the cities and industrializing centers in different areas of Europe, but many of the Polish peasants (together with some members of the Polish middle class and intelligentsia) began to seek a new way of life in the United States. Letters from relatives and friends in America advertised high wages and employment opportunities there. In addition, class, political, and religious oppression from the occupying rulers propelled Polish emigration. Poles with sufficient funds could buy transatlantic tickets, and others depended on their relatives to provide kinship connections in the process of chain migration for their resettlement in the United States.

Small numbers of Polish immigrants arrived in the eighteenth and early nineteenth centuries and settled in farming communities in the midwestern and southern regions of the United States. The major migration of Poles took place between 1890 and 1920, when approximately 2 million moved to the United States. Although about three of every ten migrants returned to Poland, about 9 million Americans trace their descent to Polish ancestry. Many of the early Polish immigrants came through Ellis Island in New York harbor and were interrogated by U.S. immigration officials. Like the Italian immigrants, many were approached by labor recruiters, who would take them by train or rail to their new destinations (Bukowczyk 1987). Many went to coal-mining towns like Scranton, Wilkes-Barre, Windber, and Hazelton in Pennsylvania, or to steel manufacturing cities such as Pittsburgh and Cleveland. Midwestern cities like Toledo, Milwaukee, Minneapolis, St. Louis, Chicago, and Detroit attracted Poles who were seeking work in the mills, slaughterhouses, foundries, refineries, and factories. In 1920, Chicago had 400,000 Poles, New York 200,000, Pittsburgh 200,000, Buffalo 100,000, Milwaukee 100,000, and Detroit 100,000 (Greene 1980). Within these towns and cities, Polish immigrants founded neighborhoods and communities known individually and collectively as "Polonia" (Latin for Poland).

One of the first studies of the Polish immigrant communities in the United States was carried out by sociologists William Thomas and Florian Znaniecki in the 1910s. In their five-volume work called *The Polish Peasant in Europe and America*, they used quantitative data, newspapers, books, letters, autobiographies, and extensive interviews to provide insight into Polonia communities. They conducted research in Poland in order to gain background on the conditions and factors that had an effect on these immigrants. This cross-national research enabled them to understand that the Polish immigrants were not just replicating an ethnic identity that was found in Poland but were constructing a new Polish American ethnic identity in the United States. This new identity was formed by a combination of elements and experiences in Poland and the new environment and conditions within the United States. The researchers concluded that the Polish American ethnic communities suffered from "social disorganization," and were in a state of decline. They predicted the dissolution of Polish American ethnicity very quickly in U.S. society. Contemporary scholars, however, have debunked their portrayal of this ethnic dissolution and find that they failed to take into account the signs of Polish culture in America (Lopata 1994; Pula 1995).

Like the Italian immigrants, the Poles drew on their connections with relatives, voluntary organizations, small businesses, Polish-language newspapers, and, most importantly, the Catholic

Church to develop their ethnic communities in Polonia. Voluntary organizations were developed by both men and women to serve the community. Similar to the German American Turner Clubs, the Poles established the "Polish Falcons," a nationalist organization that promoted the culture and traditions of Poland, and other large fraternal associations like the Polish National Alliance and the Polish Women's Alliance. Mutual funds were established in the neighborhoods and churches to aid families through crises, such as sickness, accident, or death. Eventually, these evolved into extensive insurance businesses to serve the Polonia communities. Building and loan associations were set up to help each other to buy homes and businesses, and bakeries, butcher shops, saloons, restaurants, print shops, funeral parlors, and other businesses were started. These businesses promoted their own enterprises within the Polonia communities through slogans such as "Buy Polish" or "Patronize Your Own" (Bukowczyk 1987). As these businesses flourished, they gave money to Polish charities to help the poor, jobless, or other indigent community members. The Polish-language newspapers flourished and featured news stories on politics in Poland, as well as problems that the Polish encountered in America. Chicago's *Gazeta Polska* ("Polish Gazette"), Buffalo's *Polak w Ameryce* ("Pole in America"), and other influential newspapers served to reinforce ties of Polish American ethnicity (Pula 1995).

The most important institution that maintained Polish American ethnicity was the Roman Catholic Church. Similar to that of Italian Americans, the experience of Polish Americans with the Catholic Church was difficult at first. In partitioned Poland, the Church was administered by the Polish clergy and was the basis of their nationalism and ethnicity. However, in the United States the Church was controlled primarily by a German and Irish hierarchy. The Polish immigrants' religious traditions, which focused on a variety of rituals and the venera-

tion of symbols such as the "Black Madonna," the Blessed Virgin Mary who protected Poland, differed from American forms. At first, the Poles (like the Italians) were treated as second-class citizens by Church authorities. In the German-dominated churches, the Poles had to sit in segregated pews. Eventually, as Polish immigration increased, the American Catholic bishops saw that they needed to do something to retain the loyalty of the Polish community. Some of the immigrants had begun to build their own independent churches outside of the Catholic hierarchy. Therefore, ethnically based Roman Catholic parishes were established for the Polish communities to ensure their loyalty and to protect them from the independent churches or Protestant denominations. Polish American churches were developed along with parochial schools, which enrolled about two-thirds of the children of Polonia (Bukowczyk 1987; Pula 1995). The Church was the fundamental institution that transmitted the language, culture, and ethnicity of the Polish American communities.

With unprecedented immigration from southern and eastern Europe in the first two decades of the twentieth century into the United States, the Poles were subjected to severe discrimination and prejudice from many Americans. As we saw earlier, nativistic movements and the beliefs of the superiority of the WASPs and anti-Catholicism were developing at this time. The Poles were considered to be of the "Slavic race" and supposedly inferior to the "Anglo-Saxon race." Like the Italians, the Poles were given IQ tests when they entered the United States through Ellis Island, which were used to "assert" their supposed mental inferiority. The nativist movement ideology proposed that Polish immigrants were diluting the superior Anglo American racial stock (see Chapter 3). The Poles were viewed as "noisome and repulsive," "the beaten members of beaten breeds" (Bukowczyk 1987). Also, according to the nativist, like other eastern Europeans, many of the working-class Polish immigrants were associated with the Bolshevik revolution in Russia and other radical social movements. It was believed that these working-class Poles were going to create revolutions and disrupt U.S. society.

Despite the racial prejudice and discrimination they faced, the Polish American communities were able to adjust to their circumstances through organized efforts in economic and political activities. For example, working-class Poles became very active in union organization and participation. Poles working in the coal mines of eastern Pennsylvania organized unions. In Milwaukee, Polish men and women organized unions to fight sweatshop conditions in the textile factories. Thousands of Polish workers participated in the sit-down strikes at the Hamtramck Dodge plant in Detroit, which eventually led to the increase in strength of the United Automobile Workers union. Solid union towns in Pittsburgh, Chicago, and Detroit were developed by working-class Polish Americans.

In politics, like other immigrants, many Polish Americans began to become involved in the Democratic Party. Unlike the Irish, generally the Poles did not run for office themselves, but they enthusiastically supported Democratic candidates, and they participated in machine politics in cities such as Chicago. Like other ethnics, the Polonia communities were rewarded with a considerable share of patronage, jobs, and a sense of control over their neighborhoods. Eventually, because of their links with the Democratic Party, the Poles turned out majority votes within their communities for Al Smith, the first Roman Catholic to run for president, and later Franklin D. Roosevelt. Both union and political activities provided the foundations for improvement in living standards and upward mobility for Polish Americans.

The second and third generation of Polish Americans began to assimilate culturally and structurally into U.S. society. Despite a resurgence of Polish American ethnicity during World War II, when the Nazis invaded Poland the new younger generation of Polish Americans began to lose the "Polish" side of their identity. The younger generation began to move into white-collar and skilled occupations and moved out of the older urban Polonia communities, going to the suburban regions that developed after World War II. Intermarriage between Polish Americans and other ethnic groups led to persistent patterns of assimilation. Urban renewal in the major cities destroyed the housing and residential areas of Polonia communities throughout the United States. Reindustrialization and the shutdown of steel and auto plants led to the demise of many working-class jobs for Polish Americans. These economic and demographic changes resulted in the erosion of most of the urban Polish communities. By the 1970s, the Polish parish churches and parochial schools began to use English in sermons and education and reached out to recruit other ethnic groups (Pula 1995). Polish-language newspapers began to have English sections. Although this represented the final blow to the coherent Polonia urban communities in the United States, and in due time they resembled "deserted cities," eventually the Polish American community began to reorganize itself, based on new professional networks and organizations. Instead of an urban-based ethnic form of "Polonia," these new Polish organizations represent nationally based professional associations with their own Polish language newspapers and foundations.

THE MELTING POT: ASSIMILATION OR PLURALISM?

As we discussed, U.S. society was challenged dramatically by the massive immigration of non-Anglo populations in the nineteenth and early twentieth centuries. Questions were raised about whether German, Irish, Italian, and Polish immigrants could really become "Americans." Nativistic groups such as the American Protective Association directed prejudice and discrimination toward these immigrants. Prejudice against Catholicism and other ethnic traits, including language and purported "race," eventually resulted in restrictive immigration policies. In 1921, legislation was passed to limit the number of immigrants from southern and eastern Europe to 155,000, while permitting about 200,000 from northwestern Europe. In 1924, further legislation limited the annual number of immigrants to 164,667. This 1924 legislation stated that the number of visas allocated for each European nation should correlate to 2 percent of that nation's immigrants already residing in the United States as of 1890 (Adams 1993). With these new quota laws, the unlimited immigration for most Europeans, the age of the open doors, had come to an end. During this same period, state and local authorities began to restrict the use of languages other than English in schools and to require all teachers to be U.S. citizens. Government policies tried to promote the use of the public school system to "Americanize" and assimilate the various non-Anglo immigrants.

One of the popular manifestations of these policies of assimilation was the concept of "the melting pot," which became the popular symbol of ethnic interaction in the United States during the early twentieth century. The term *melting pot* was associated with a play by a Jewish immigrant Israel Zangwill called *The Melting Pot,* which had a long run in New York in 1909. Zangwill's play focused on the life of a Jewish immigrant who believed that the Old World nationalities and languages ought to be forgotten in the United States and that all ethnic elements should fuse together in the creation of a new and superior American nationality and ethnicity (Gleason 1980). This was not a new idea, but it was popularized at the time as a response to anti-immigration and antiforeign attitudes of the nativist movements. The melting pot ideal implied that the new "American" ethnicity would represent only the best qualities and attributes of the different cultures contributing to U.S. society. It became a plea for toleration of the different immigrants as they poured into American society. It was assumed that the American ideals of equality and opportunity for material improvement would automatically transform foreigners into Americans. It also suggested that the Anglo or WASP ethnicity was itself being transformed into a more comprehensive global type of an "American" ethnic identity.

Despite the tolerant tone, universal appeal, and openness of the metaphor of the melting pot, it was still an emphasis on assimilation. The belief that immigrants must shed their ethnic identity and Americanize and adopt a "Yankee" ethnic identity was at the heart of this concept. As we have seen, for one reason or another, most of the descendants of the Germans, Irish, Italians, and Poles began to adopt the English language and American culture surrounding them. World Wars I and II compelled German Americans to abandon their language and traditions very rapidly. The second generation of Irish, Italians, and Poles also tended to assimilate into the Anglo American culture of the majority. Economic, social, and political benefits accrued to these "white ethnics" upon assimilation. Economically, union participation for working-class immigrants tied different ethnic groups together. As the United Mine Workers, the United Automobile Workers, and the CIO unions emerged, there were separate groups of Irish workers, Italian workers, and Polish workers. Ultimately, these working-class ethnics recognized that they were *all* workers, regardless of their ethnicity, fighting for better working conditions and human rights. To pursue the American Dream, the "white ethnics" assimilated culturally and structurally into the fabric of U.S. society. As older ethnic neighborhoods and communities began to decline, most of the "white ethnics" abandoned their traditional languages and cultures. The metaphor of the melting pot appeared to have some validity, at least for most of these "white ethnics."

Along with this assimilationist trend in U.S. society, the crystallization of the race concept of "whiteness" was reinforced. Eventually, the people who came from Ireland, Germany, Italy, Poland, and other European countries became "white Caucasians," in contrast to other ethnic minorities (Jacobson 1998). For many Americans, "whiteness" became a new socially constructed category of race that differentiated these Europeans from non-Europeans in the United States. Native American Indians, African Americans, Hispanic Americans, and Asian Americans were nonwhites, and thereby excluded from the institutional benefits and privileges of the people with white identities. Although there were some who still referred to the Anglo-WASP racial category, the enlarged category of a "white identity" assigned to Europeans tended to become part of the racial consciousness of U.S. society.

Cultural Pluralism

Beginning in the late 1950s and 1960s, the Melting Pot metaphor was being challenged by many non-European ethnic groups. As we will see in later chapters, African Americans, Hispanic Americans, Native American Indians, Asian Americans, and other non-European ethnic groups demanded equal rights and opportunities for their communities. Non-European ethnic groups asserted that because of their skin color and other cultural elements, they were not as "meltable" as the European ethnic groups. Some civil rights leaders such as Martin Luther King, Jr., rejected the assimilationist policies of U.S. society and called for a "plural" society, where different ethnic groups could retain their culture and heritage, but have equal rights and opportunities like other Americans. The demand for cultural pluralism became a dominant trend within ethnic relations in the 1960s in U.S. society.[5] Various non-European ethnic groups emphasized a pride in their own unique history, experience, and culture. "Black Power"

among African Americans, "Brown Power" among Hispanic Americans, and "Red Power" among Native American Indians became the rallying anthems for cultural pluralism in America. Rather than emphasizing the melting pot as an ideal, these groups suggested that the United States should be a "salad bowl" or, better yet, a "stir fry," which implied that each group could maintain its own distinctive culture and ethnicity (ingredients) and still contribute to U.S. society.

The developments of the civil rights movement in the 1960s, and the call for cultural pluralism, resulted in a heightened sense of ethnic awareness for many Americans. Many of the third- and fourth-generation "white ethnics" were influenced by these new ethnic trends. Sociologists Nathan Glazer and Daniel Moynihan, in *Beyond the Melting Pot* (1963), emphasized that many of the immigrants such as the Italians and Irish had not really assimilated into the melting pot but rather had transformed their ethnicity. They argued that as these "white ethnics" had moved out of their former ethnic neighborhoods they now articulated and revitalized new forms of ethnicity based on their traditional attachments with each other. They emphasized that these ethnic identities were not "survivals" from the age of mass immigration but were newfound social identities. Later, in 1972, another book, *Rise of the Unmeltable Ethnics,* by Michael Novak, a descendant of Slovak immigrants, reinforced similar themes. It appeared that there was an ethnic resurgence for the "white ethnics." The first generation of these groups had maintained their culture, the second generation had become assimilated, and then in the 1960s and 1970s, the third and fourth generations were beginning to reassert their hyphenated ethnic identity. Bumper stickers and political slogans emphasizing "Italian American Power," "Polish Americans Are Beautiful," and ethnic festivals such as Octoberfest for German Americans were proliferating throughout U.S. society.

One of the questions regarding this ethnic

resurgence for anthropologists and other social scientists is the degree to which ethnic resurgence among the "white ethnics" was based on the "primordial attachments" that people feel toward their history, culture, and language, or whether this revitalization was merely a "circumstantial" or situational adjustment to the civil rights and cultural pluralist movements of non-European ethnic groups. A number of sociologists, such as Herbert Gans, Richard Alba, Mary Waters, and Stanley Lieberson, have investigated this issue.[6] For example, Gans, in his study on Italian Americans, introduces the concept of "symbolic ethnicity." Symbolic ethnicity refers to a type of ethnicity that is individualistic in nature and does not have any real cost for individuals. Gans suggests that among the middle-class third and fourth generations of the "white ethnics," symbolic ethnicity developed as a means of individual satisfaction. These identity needs are met by visiting an ethnic restaurant, participating in an ethnic festival, or having pride in an ethnic politician, artist, or entertainer. Sociologists agree that white Americans have a great deal of individual choice in terms of their ethnic identities. Individuals within one family may choose to identify with their hyphenated ethnicity, or choose to be just "white" or "American," or choose to switch back and forth in different social contexts and situations. As Mary Waters emphasizes, "The option of choosing among different ethnicities in their family backgrounds exists because the degree of discrimination and social distance attached to specific European backgrounds has diminished over time" (1998:404).

Sociologists, however, also agree that these particular forms of symbolic ethnicity do not exist at present for African Americans, Hispanic Americans, Asian Americans, Native American Indians, or other non-European ethnic groups. As we will see in later chapters in this section of the textbook, the non-European racial and ethnic minorities have had a much different experience in U.S. society.

MULTICULTURALISM IN U.S. SOCIETY

In the 1950s during the cold war, the United States opened its doors to political refugees from Communist countries, such as Hungary and Cuba. Later, during the civil rights movement, and because of the demands for more cultural pluralism in the United States, a new immigration law in 1965 opened the doors again to other areas of the world. During the past forty years there has been a significant growth in the population of peoples of non-European ancestry. A decline in the birth rate of the majority of the white population of European descent, coupled with new trends in immigration and higher birth rates of ethnic minorities, is changing the ethnic landscape of U.S. society.

As indicated in Figure 6-1, recent immigration from Europe to the United States represents a tiny fraction compared with that from Latin America and Asia. The ethnic diversity of non-European immigrants is remarkable. Among the Asians are Filipinos, Koreans, Chinese, Japanese, Vietnamese, Laotians, Cambodians, Thais, Indians, and Pakistanis. From South and Central America are people from El Salvador, Guatemala, Mexico, and other countries. And from the Middle East and Africa have come Palestinians, Iraqis, Iranians, Lebanese, Syrians, Israelis, Nigerians, and Egyptians. Like the nineteenth-century immigrants from Europe, the majority of these immigrants have come to the United States seeking economic opportunities, political freedom, and improved social conditions. The United States has truly become much more of a multicultural society. A movement known as *multiculturalism* developed as an extension of the demand for cultural pluralism in U.S. society. As a result of this multiculturalist movement, federal, state, and local governments have encouraged the development of educational programs to prepare people to live in this new type of society.

Multiculturalism led to revisions of the

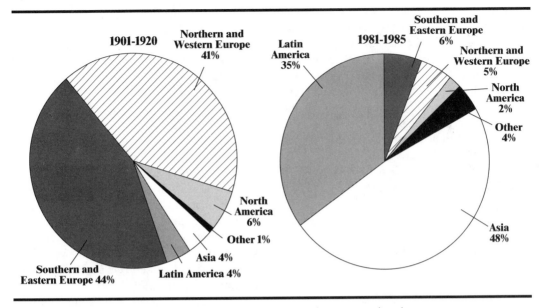

Figure 6-1.   Legal Immigrants Admitted to the United States by Region of Birth
Sources: From "Immigration to the U.S.: The Unfinished Story" by Leon F. Bauvier and Robert W. Gardner. Copyright © 1986 by the Population Reference Bureau. Reprinted by permission; and U.S. Census Bureau, *Statistical Abstract of the United States, 1998.*

curricula in educational programs throughout the United States. Instead of focusing narrowly on a Eurocentric or an Anglo-centric version of history, texts were revised to include discussions of non-European ethnic groups and their contributions to U.S. history. Bilingual education was developed to extend equal education to those students not proficient in English. The ongoing multicultural movement emphasizes that there is no one model type of "American." Cultural pluralism is endorsed fully, and the multiculturalist movement tends to suggest that there are no significant costs for retaining one's ethnic heritage. The movement for multiculturalism views cultural and ethnic differences as positive. It downplays any kind of competition or conflict among ethnic groups. Rather, the emphasis is on encouraging tolerance and cooperation among different ethnic groups. The hope is that as students become more ethnically literate, and more educated about ethnic groups, they will be able to appreciate and tolerate other people from different ethnic backgrounds. In addition, they will be able to make personal decisions, which would affect public policy promoting a more harmonious form of ethnic and race relations in the United States.

Although the goals and objectives of the multiculturalist movement are laudatory, some anthropologists have expressed reservations about this development. Terence Turner argues that the multiculturalist movement has become a form of identity politics, which is fraught with both theoretical and practical dangers (1993). He suggests that multiculturalism risks reducing race and ethnic groups and cultures to essentialist, stereotypical constructions and images. Cultures are not just collections of facts, vocabularies, assorted histories, and other elements. When these elements are taken out of their original cultural context and then reassembled into packaged curricula for educational programs, they are unlikely to reflect the complexities, nuances, inequalities, pride, and difficulties of race and ethnic groups. Multiculturalism can result in extreme revisionist forms of history and identity politics that do not have any critical basis.

Turner differentiates two forms of multiculturalism, *difference multiculturalism* and *critical multiculturalism.* Difference multiculturalism tends to become obsessed with "otherness" and ethnic identity, and it gives license to separatist tendencies and balkanization. This fixation on ethnic difference and identity politics tends to inhibit social relationships among groups. On the other hand, Turner emphasizes, "Critical multiculturalism seeks to use cultural diversity as a basis for challenging, revising, and relativizing basic notions and principles common to dominant and minority cultures alike, so as to construct a more vital, open, and democratic common culture" (1993:413). He proposes that anthropologists adopt this critical form of multiculturalism, which can only be done by extensive ethnographic studies to recognize the complexities of cultures, races, and ethnic groups. This textbook is devoted to this critical form of multiculturalism, which results in a deeper understanding of race and ethnic relations.

descendant of the Irish immigrants of the nineteenth century. His family settled in Albany, New York. However, Byron moved to England as a graduate student in anthropology, and then moved to Northern Ireland, where he teaches at Queens University in Belfast in the department of social anthropology. He began to do his ethnographic project on Irish America in 1991 and continued his work on this project along with some research assistants through 1997.

4. The most well-known linkage between Italian Americans and radical politics was the Sacco and Vanzetti trial in 1927. Nicola Sacco and Bartolomeo Vanzetti, two Italian immigrants, were allegedly involved in an armed robbery in Massachusetts. Despite contradictory evidence and eyewitnesses who attested to their innocence, these individuals were found guilty. Following a number of appeals, Sacco and Vanzetti were executed. Supposedly, the two immigrants were members of an anarchist group. Anti-immigration and anti-union attitudes were elements that played a role in the trial. In 1977, after a review of the trial and evidence, the state of Massachusetts declared the trial unfair (Monroe 2000).

5. Cultural pluralism had been advocated earlier in the twentieth century by people like Horace Kallen. Kallen had argued against the "melting pot," viewing it as an extension of Anglo-Saxon ethnic hegemony. His views, however, were confused and undeveloped and never reached a substantial audience within U.S. society (Gleason 1980).

6. The sociological literature on the "white ethnic" revival is enormous. Some of the most important references include Mary Waters, *Ethnic Options: Choosing Identities in America* (Berkeley: University of California Press, 1990); Richard D. Alba, *Ethnic Identity: The Transformation of White America* (New Haven, CT: Yale University Press, 1990); and Stanley Lieberson and Mary Waters, *From Many Strands: Ethnic and Racial Groups in Contemporary America* (New York: Russell Sage Foundation, 1988).

NOTES

1. In actuality, this division between the Old Immigration period and the New Immigration period is artificial. For example, substantial numbers of Germans were coming from Europe in the 1880s (see Table 6-1). However, this divide between northwest European immigrants versus southern and eastern European immigrants is useful as a historical narrative device for describing the different streams of Europeans.

2. The statistics for current numbers of ethnic groups in U.S. society have been drawn from the U.S. census. In the 1990 census figures, reported in the *Statistical Abstract of the United States, 1995,* the number of people identifying themselves as having German ancestry was 57,947,374. However, these figures are only rough approximations of ethnicity. Many of these people claim a mixed ethnicity, that is, they may claim themselves as German and English, or German and Irish, or a mixture of different ethnicities. This needs to be understood with respect to all of the various white ethnic groups in the United States

3. Reginald Byron is a fourth-generation American and a

REFERENCES CITED

ADAMS, WILLI PAUL. 1993. *The German Americans: An Ethnic Experience.* L. J. Rippley and Eberhard Reichmann, trans. Indianapolis: Indiana University–Purdue University at Indianapolis.

ALBA, RICHARD. 1985. *Italian Americans: Into the Twilight of Ethnicity.* Englewood Cliffs, NJ: Prentice Hall.

___. 1995. Assimilation's quiet tide. *The Public Interest* (Spring):3–18.

BLESSING, PATRICK J. 1980. Irish. In *Harvard Encyclopedia of American Ethnic Groups.* Stephan Thernstrom, ed. Pp. 524–545. Cambridge, MA: Harvard University Press.

BUKOWCZYK, JOHN J. 1987. *And My Children Did Not Know Me: A History of the Polish-Americans.* Bloomington: Indiana University Press.

BYRON, REGINALD. 1999. *Irish America.* Oxford: Clarendon Press.

CHRISTOPHER, ROBERT C. 1989. *Crashing the Gates: The De-*

Wasping of America's Power Elite. New York: Simon & Schuster.

CONZEN, KATHLEEN NEILS. 1980. Germans. In *Harvard Encyclopedia of American Ethnic Groups*. Stephan Thernstrom, ed. Pp. 405–425. Cambridge, MA: Harvard University Press.

CORNELL, STEPHAN, and DOUGLAS HARTMANN. 1998. *Ethnicity and Race: Making Identities in a Changing World*. Thousand Oaks, CA: Pine Forge Press.

FISCHER, DAVID HACKETT. 1989. *Albion's Seed: Four British Folkways in America*. Oxford: Oxford University Press.

GANS, HERBERT. 1982 [1962]. *The Urban Villagers: Group and Class in the Life of Italian Americans*. New York: Free Press.

GLAZER, NATHAN, and DANIEL MOYNIHAN. 1963. *Beyond the Melting Pot: The Negroes, Puerto Ricans, Jews, Italians, and Irish of New York City*. Cambridge, MA: MIT Press.

GLEASON, PHILIP. 1980. American identity and Americanization. In *Harvard Encyclopedia of American Ethnic Groups*. Stephan Thernstrom, ed. Pp. 31–59. Cambridge, MA: Harvard University Press.

GREENE, VICTOR. 1980. Poles. In *Harvard Encyclopedia of American Ethnic Groups*. Stephan Thernstrom, ed. Pp. 787–803. Cambridge, MA: Harvard University Press.

JACOBSON, MATTHEW FRYE. 1998. *Whiteness of Different Color: European Immigrants and the Alchemy of Race*. Cambridge, MA: Harvard University Press.

KAMIN, LEON. 1974. *The Science and Politics of I.Q.* New York: Wiley.

KAMPHOEFNER, WALTER D. 1987. *The Westfalians: From Germany to Missouri*. Princeton, NJ: Princeton University Press.

___. 1996. German Americans: Paradoxes of a "model minority." In *Origins and Destinies: Immigration, Race and Ethnicity in America*. Sylvia Padraza and Ruben Rumbant, eds. Pp. 152–160. New York: Wadsworth.

KENNY, KEVIN. 1998. *Making Sense of the Molly Maguires*. Oxford: Oxford University Press.

LOPATA, HELENA ZNANIECKA. 1994. *Polish Americans*. Second Revised Edition. New Brunswick, NJ: Transaction.

LOPREATO, JOSEPH. 1970. *Italian Americans*. New York: Random House.

MILLER, KERBY. 1985. *Emigrants and Exiles: Ireland and the Irish Exodus to North America*. New York: Oxford University Press.

MONROE, JUDY. 2000. *The Sacco and Vanzetti Controversial Murder Trial: A Headline Court Case*. New York: Enslow.

NELLI, HUMBERT S. 1980. Italians. In *Harvard Encyclopedia of American Ethnic Groups*. Stephan Thernstrom, ed. Pp. 545–560. Cambridge, MA: Harvard University Press.

NOVAK, MICHAEL. 1972. *The Rise of the Unmeltable Ethnics: Politics and Culture in the Seventies*. New York: Macmillan.

PULA, JAMES S. 1995. *Polish Americans: An Ethnic Community*. New York: Twayne.

SCHLESINGER, ARTHUR M., JR. 1992. *The Disuniting of America: Reflections on a Multicultural Society*. New York: Norton.

SMEDLEY, AUDREY. 1999. *Race in North America: Origin and Evolution of a Worldview*. Boulder, CO: Westview Press.

THOMAS, WILLIAM I., and FLORIAN ZNANIECKI. 1918. *The Polish Peasant in Europe and America*. New York: Knopf.

TURNER, TERENCE. 1993. Anthropology and multiculturalism: What is anthropology that multiculturalists should be mindful of it? *Cultural Anthropology* 8(4):411–429.

U.S. Bureau of the Census. 1995. *Statistical Abstract of the United States, 1995*. Washington, DC: U.S. Government Printing Office.

WALZER, MICHAEL. 1997. *On Toleration*. New Haven, CT: Yale University Press.

WATERS, MARY. 1990. *Ethnic Options: Choosing Identities in America*. Berkeley: University of California Press.

___. 1998. Optional ethnicities: For whites only? In *Race, Class and Gender: An Anthology*. M. L. Andersen and Patricia Hill Collins, eds. Pp. 403–412. Belmont, CA: Wadsworth.

7 AMERICAN INDIANS

Rachel A. Bonney

University of North Carolina at Charlotte

One can make the case that the Native people of the United States are perhaps the most studied and least understood of all those who make up the tapestry of American life."

[Hirschfelder and de Montaño 1991:ix]

American Indians can be distinguished from other American ethnic groups in several ways: they have been in America longer than any other ethnic group; they are the only ethnic groups whose ancestors did not emigrate to North America voluntarily—and as the descendants of once independent nations, they are the only ethnic groups to have treaty rights; and, as a group, they are so diverse that they are not one single ethnic group as much as a number of distinct groups. Technically, until the "discovery" of the "New World" by Europeans, "American Indians" did not exist; more than 500 distinct named tribal entities inhabited North America. Columbus, thinking he had found the East Indies, erroneously termed the peoples he encountered "Indians," a categorization that has had repercussions throughout history as first Europeans and then Euro-Americans treated "Indians" as a single cultural unit with a common language and culture. Nothing could be farther from the truth. American Indians were and continue to be distinct cultural, political, and ethnic groups, despite efforts to assimilate them into the mainstream of American culture.

Contemporary definitions of "Indians" are imprecise. The federal government has no legal or consistent definition of Indian established by either Congress or the courts, although to be eligible for federal services, individuals must be members of federally recognized tribes or groups. Eligibility to receive federal services from the Bureau of Indian Affairs requires a "blood quantum," while census figures are based on self-ascription or identification. "Recognized" or "acknowledged" Indians usually have reservations—lands reserved or set aside for exclusive Indian use and held in trust by the federal government—where government agencies provide educational, health, economic, and social services to registered tribal members. Each tribe has its own criteria for membership, usually based on a "blood quantum" of varying degrees of ancestry. Indians lacking federal recognition may have state recognition and/or state reservations, but they do not receive services or financial assistance from the federal government through the Bureau of Indian Affairs; also, they are ineligible for a variety of federal programs and may not have gaming operations in their communities. Unofficial criteria of Indianness include genetic characteristics or physical appearance, membership in specific families, participation in viable Indian cultural systems, belief and participation in a native religion, speaking a native language, and living on a reservation or in an Indian community or enclave—resulting in more diversity among Indians than most non-Indians realize.

This chapter will examine the American Indians as peoples who have maintained cultural and, sometimes, linguistic integrity and a sense of Indian identity, despite pressures for assimilation. Fredrik Barth, in the Introduction to *Ethnic Groups and Boundaries* (1969), examined the persistence of ethnic groups in larger societies through "boundary-maintaining mechanisms" that separate ethnic groups from each other as well as from the dominant society: overt signs or signals—language, style of clothing, house form—or general lifestyle and basic value orientations. Boundary maintenance is based on identity systems and personal affiliation with certain shared symbols: artifacts, words, role behaviors, or ritual acts, as well as commonly shared cultural traditions and historical events. In "Persistent Cultural Systems" (1971), Edward H. Spicer (1971:795) focused on the "oppositional process" as a primary boundary-maintaining mechanism in the historical continuity of ethnic groups that have been absorbed into larger political entities—as, for example, African nations incorporated into the British Empire or Indian tribes under the jurisdiction of the United States. Despite changed political systems, these groups have persisted because of collective identity systems grounded in shared symbols—flags, leaders, a series of past (historical) events. One common feature Spicer identified in the ten cases of persistent cultural systems he investigated was "a continued conflict between these peoples and the controllers of the surrounding state apparatus" (1971:797); he saw this continued opposition as the "essential factor in the formation and development of the persistent identity system" maintained through linguistic communication, shared moral values, and a political organization to achieve group objectives.

For over 400 years Indians have survived as distinct ethnic groups, despite efforts to annihilate them, assimilate them, or legislate them out of existence. They must operate in a variety of arenas and interact with a wide range of persons while retaining their sense of Indianness. Their separate and collective experiences have strengthened an identity that has persisted and maintained the boundaries separating them from other ethnic groups and from the dominant society, although tribal identities may be superseded by a situational "Indian" identity. To understand who the American Indians are today, one must understand where they started and what experiences they have undergone. The following cultural descriptions are, of necessity, brief. For more detailed discussions of tribal cultures, see Hodge (1981), Hudson (1976), Josephy (1991), and Kehoe (1992).

PREHISTORY

Long before the arrival of the first Europeans in the "New World," the Americas were inhabited by populations of Asian or Mongoloid ancestry which had migrated into the Americas by way of a land bridge connecting North America and Siberia at the Bering Straits some 30,000 years ago during the Pleistocene (glacial) age. Small nomadic bands hunted Pleistocene megafauna such as bison and mammoth using stone-tipped spears. With the recession of the glaciers at the end of the Pleistocene, the resulting climatic shifts created a variety of ecological zones in

North America, triggering changes in human subsistence and lifestyles as populations adapted to new flora and fauna, which, in turn, created the diversity of cultural types encountered by the Europeans.

During the Archaic period, beginning about 7000 or 8000 B.C., hunting was supplemented by increased reliance on wild plant foods that were ground into meal. Ground stone axes and adzes in the East indicate a shift to a forested environment, and the *atlatl*, or spear-thrower, improved hunting efficiency. In the Great Basin, Plateau, and Plains, the Archaic persisted to historic times; in the Southwest, it was replaced by the Anasazi, Mogollon, and Hohokam traditions, (A.D. 1–1541), and in the East by the Woodland tradition (1000 B.C.–A.D. 700). In both areas these cultures were transitional between hunting-gathering and farming economies. Domestication of plants (corn, beans, squash) provided the food surplus that permitted sedentary village settlement patterns; technological innovations included bows and arrows tipped with small stemmed or triangular points, tapered axes or celts, stone pipes, basketry, and ceramics.

The cultural traditions encountered by the Europeans were the Mississippian (A.D. 500–1600) in the Southeast, the Anasazi on the Colorado Plateau (A.D. 1 to modern times), and the Hohokam in the Sonoran Desert (A.D. 900–1450) in the Southwest, all with similarities to Mesoamerican civilizations. All were characterized by a farming economy supporting town life, complex political and religious organization, and elaborate material cultures with distinctive ceramic styles. The largest urban center was the Mississippian site of Cahokia, near East St. Louis on the Mississippi River; the Anasazi perhaps are best known for the "cliff dwellings" of Mesa Verde and large fortified towns such as Pueblo Bonito in New Mexico's Chaco Canyon; the best-preserved Hohokam site is Casa Grande in Arizona. For more complete descriptions of North American prehistory, see Fagan (1999).

THE AMERICAN INDIANS AT FIRST CONTACT

Although Columbus mistakenly identified the first natives he encountered as "Indians," the North America population consisted of distinct cultural groups in what anthropologists call "culture areas," geographic areas characterized by distinctive cultural types: the Northeastern and Southeastern Woodlands, the Great Plains, the Southwest, the Northwest Coast, the Great Basin-Plateau, California, the Subarctic, and the Arctic. Cultural descriptions of these areas usually are based on the "precontact" cultures immediately prior to or at the time of the arrival of the first Europeans.

Despite the diversity of precontact cultures, similarities existed. Kinship was important in economic, political, religious, and social life; family heads represented their kinsmen on village or tribal councils or acted as judges to settle disputes. Spirituality was reflected in the integration of religion, ritual, and supernatural beliefs into all aspects of daily life. Many beliefs revolved around nature and natural phenomena and the belief that humans are part of the natural scheme of life. The importance of religion and ritual also is reflected in mythology, art forms, dance, music, and, in some cases, games.

The Southeast

The rich fertile soils, long growing season, and heavy precipitation evenly distributed throughout the year made the Southeastern Woodlands—southern Virginia to the Gulf of Mexico, the Atlantic coast to eastern Texas—attractive to both pre-Columbian and European farmers. The area was dominated by the Five Civilized Tribes—the Cherokee, Choctaw, Chickasaw, Creek, and Seminole (a Creek offshoot). Some are gone—the Timucua and Calusa and Natchez—and others survive as small remnant populations—the Catawba, Caddo, and Chitimacha, for example.

Southeastern culture in the sixteenth century was based on the Mississippian pattern. Sedentary farmers lived in fortified towns on watercourses near cities or ceremonial centers such as Cahokia and Etowah, and supported complex sociopolitical and religious organization. Fortified towns were supported by crops grown in fields located around the houses or outside the palisade. Chiefs' houses, council houses, and ceremonial grounds were built on earth mounds facing central plazas. Towns, some belonging to confederations, could be ceremonial centers where political and ceremonial leaders lived and ritual and political activities were held.

The basis of the farming economy was corn, beans, and squash, although tobacco, sunflowers, and gourds also were raised. Although men assisted in clearing and harvesting of fields, farming was the women's responsibility. Cultivated foods were supplemented by wild foods gathered by the women and by meat provided by male hunting and fishing. With the exception of the priest-chiefs, full-time specialists were unknown.

The important social unit, the matrilineal family, determined descent and inheritance; membership in matrilineal clans, named after animals or plants, cross-cut town lines and determined social position, political roles, place of residence, and choice of marriage partners. A town's peace chief, whose position was based on his clan affiliation, was assisted in decision making and sometimes dispute settlement by a war chief and an all-male council. Towns often were allied in confederacies for mutual aid and defense; warfare was frequent, ritualized, and a source of male prestige.

Religion played an integral part in virtually all aspects of life, from individual prayers to the spirits of animals killed in the hunt to elaborate group rituals, such as the annual "Green Corn" (or "busk") ceremonies. The latter was both a harvest or first fruits ceremony and a new year renewal of the world and of life involving a ritual cleansing and purification, a time when

houses were cleaned out, utensils were replaced, new fires were started from the central sacred fire, all offenses but murder were forgiven, and individuals were cleansed internally (taking an emetic known as the "black drink") and externally (sweat baths). Prayers, singing, dancing, and feasting were all part of the ritual, which lasted several days.

The Northeastern Woodlands

The environmental diversity of the Northern Woodlands (extending from the Atlantic Ocean to the Mississippi River and from the Ohio River north to western Ontario and Manitoba) is reflected in its cultural diversity: north-central tribes relied on wild rice as their staple food, coastal hunting-and-gathering tribes also farmed, and the Iroquois and the Huron supplemented farming with hunting and gathering.

The Iroquois. The Iroquois, an intrusive linguistic wedge extending north into an otherwise all-Algonkian-speaking area along the eastern Lower Great Lakes, were culturally like their southern relatives. A matrilineal farming people living in palisaded villages of approximately 50 longhouses, they were united in a political confederation of five separate tribes (six with the addition of the Tuscarora in 1760) known as the League of the Ho-de-no-sau-nee, or "Longhouse People": the Seneca, Cayuga, Onondaga, Oneida, and Mohawk. Originally established for mutual protection by culture heroes Deganawidah and Hiawatha, the confederacy expanded through force and cajolery, incorporating smaller tribes into the alliance; the "protected" or "conquered" smaller tribes were denied the rights and privileges accorded to the five founding tribes.

The distinctive Iroquois democratic political structure grew out of their kinship system. A League council of 50 sachems (peace chiefs elected by the women of their clans to lifelong positions; hereditary in certain matrilineal clans) handled only external relations with other tribes and, later, with the Europeans; it had no voice in local town or tribal matters. The sachems' votes represented the opinions and wishes of their tribes/clans, which could remove them from office for unsatisfactory performance of duties.

In historic times, the French, who did not understand the Iroquois political system, preferred to deal with the "Pine Tree Chiefs," men, usually war chiefs, and sometimes women, rewarded for meritorious service by the tribal and League councils. The numbers of these non-transferable and nonhereditary titles increased during times of war, and over time the title did become hereditary; today, individuals with the greatest amount of power tend to be descendants of famous Pine Tree Chiefs.

Algonkians. Northeastern Algonkian-speaking tribes in New England's North Atlantic slope, a zone transitional between farming/hunting and fishing, were marginal maize farmers; in the subarctic areas south of Hudson Bay, hunting and fishing supported small tribes spread over large territories; and in the Upper Great Lakes wild rice supplemented hunting and fishing. Despite regional or tribal variations, all the northeastern Algonkian groups were hunters of big game and smaller fur-bearing animals; men also fished, and women gathered wild plant foods in season.

Their dependence on food collecting in a boreal environment of scarce resources necessitated a lifestyle of independence and autonomy, isolation, nomadism or seminomadism, and seasonal shifting of bands. Households, scattered and isolated during the winter, came together in summer villages for communal subsistence activities, games, and ceremonies. Recognized band territories could be subdivided into smaller family units. Ojibwa men had clearly marked hunting territories that even wives and children were forbidden to use without permission. Winter fishing grounds were owned individually,

summer fishing grounds were communal property, and game was regarded as private property to be turned over to the women for distribution. The division of labor was gender-based: men hunted and went to battle, and women did everything else, including collecting maple sugar from individually owned sugar maple trees (women owned the vats and the sap, which they collected and boiled cooperatively).

Life and activities corresponded to the shifting seasons. The Ojibwa spring began in March at the maple syrup camps and ended in May, when 3 to 15 related families moved to the summer villages. Summer activities—berrying, fishing, and trapping small game—lasted until the August move to the wild rice beds for the communal wild rice harvest. By November, the wild rice beds were abandoned as the groups broke up into small family units to winter in the deeper and more protected areas of the forests.

The pattern of shifting settlement affected social organization. The largest units, patrilineal bands rarely numbering more than 200 persons, were groups of nuclear families. No overall political or tribal organization existed, and bands never came together to take tribal actions. The headman, spokesman for the band, held his position by virtue of his skill and prestige as a hunter. Since political control was in the hands of a council of elders, he had little real authority.

Algonkians tended to emphasize individual achievements and dependence on one's own survival skills over collective and group concerns. Male success in life depended upon lifelong supernatural aid obtained through the vision quest at puberty. Young men spent four or five days in isolation, without food or water, praying and sometimes inflicting wounds to bring the visions that put them in contact with their supernatural guardian spirits. Leadership of war parties also depended on visions, and visions brought supernatural powers that could be used for curing illness caused by evil spirits or sorcery. Control of supernatural powers was regarded as personal property, and possession of such power was a source of influence and prestige.

The Great Plains

For most modern-day Americans, "Indians" lived on the Plains, wore warbonnets, rode horses, lived in tipis, and hunted buffalo. Since the Plains Indians have been depicted most frequently (often inaccurately) in Hollywood and TV westerns, because they were among the last to succumb to white political domination, and because Buffalo Bill Cody's Wild West Shows put Plains Indians on display, such a stereotype is not surprising. However, the Plains culture was a historical development made possible by the introduction of the horse and the gun, and the "typical" Plains tribes (Cheyenne, Comanche, Kiowa, and Dakota or Sioux) were comparative newcomers to the Plains. In precontact times, small foraging bands roamed the High Plains, and sedentary farmers lived along the major rivers.

The large, treeless, subhumid or semiarid Plains extend from the Rockies to the Mississippi River and from Alberta and Saskatchewan south almost to the Rio Grande and Mexican border. The hot summers and cold winters of this harsh climate are intensified by relentless wind. Native grasses supported large herds of bison, pronghorn antelope, and other nomadic herd animals, and deer, elk, and small animals could be found in the well-forested river valleys.

Classic/Nomadic Buffalo Hunters. The introduction of horses and guns into the Plains coincided with white expansion in the East, displacing and forcing tribes onto the Plains. The nomadic hunting, gathering, and pastoral culture that emerged was necessitated by the reliance on nomadic herd animals for food and was facilitated by the use of the horse in hunting

and moving material possessions (by means of the *travois,* a hoop with a rawhide net attached to two tipi poles dragged behind the horse).

Although elk, antelope, and smaller animals were hunted, the bison, or American buffalo, was the primary source of food, shelter (tipi covers), sleeping robes, tools (made from bones and horns), and cooking containers (made from the stomachs). Human settlement followed the bisons' movements: small herds of the winter months, when forage was scarce, came together in immense herds in the late summer. Small groups hunted during the winter, but the most important economic event was the communal cooperative summer bison hunt, when the entire tribe gathered to try to kill enough animals to provide food to last all winter. Everyone participated in the hunt, including women and children, and before the hunt military societies maintained rigid control over all hunters; anyone trying to hunt prematurely was punished severely. The remainder of the summer was spent curing the meat for use in the winter and participating in communal rituals such as the Sun Dance.

Most nomadic Plains tribes traced descent bilaterally, and most had bilateral kin groups responsible for social control within the band, groups of related families or bands that camped together in the protected river bottoms during the winter. The larger social and political unit, the tribe, came together in the summer for the communal hunt, rituals, and political gatherings. Both men and women also belonged to voluntary associations connected to warfare, the men's military fraternities and the women's auxiliaries.

Warfare was the mechanism by which men earned honor and prestige in an otherwise egalitarian society. Warfare was both defensive—defense of camps under attack or pursuit of small enemy parties that had driven off horses or taken scalps—and offensive, to redress a wrong or for booty. New war parties were formed each time they went to war, under the leadership of proven warriors whose visions promised success. Men achieved status and prestige through war honors earned by counting coup, taking something (guns, scalps, horses, lives) from the enemy. Coup was counted by touching a portion of the enemy's body with the hand or with a coup stick, actions honored because of the danger overcome by the warrior or because of the conditions under which it was accomplished. Coup, graded according to the order in which it was counted or the degree of danger involved, encouraged hand-to-hand combat in front of witnesses. War honors also included capturing a gun, weapon, shield, or horse belonging to an enemy, and leading war parties. A man's claim to war honors was validated by his comrades in victory celebrations, often dramatic reenactments of battles. For each war honor performed, a man also earned the feathers that could be made into his warbonnet by the members of his military society. Thus the warbonnets, worn only on ceremonial occasions, were a kind of honorary degree indicating a man's status as warrior and bestowed by his comrades.

The guardian spirits that brought hunters and warriors success were acquired through the vision quest. Men unsuccessful in this quest could assume the alternative role of *berdache*, or "man-woman." The berdache wore women's clothing, performed women's tasks, and was believed to possess strong supernatural powers to aid young men in courtship or bring good fortune to war parties.

One common communal ceremony of the Plains was the Sun Dance, held annually midsummer as a world renewal ceremony to ensure the perpetuation of the supernatural world. Men pledged to participate in the piercing of the ceremony—attaching themselves to thongs fastened to a pole by a skewer piercing the pectoral muscles and dancing around the pole for 24 hours or until they went into a trance. Women, having

proved their ability to bear pain in childbirth, did not have to participate in the ceremony.

Sedentary Plains Tribes. Located along the alluvial floodplains of the Missouri River drainage were the sedentary farming tribes: Mandan and Hidatsa of North Dakota (who merged their villages in 1835); the Arikara on the Missouri River in the Dakotas; the Omaha, on the west side of the Missouri River in Nebraska; the Iowa on the eastern side of the Missouri River; the Oto, Kansa, and Missouri; and the southernmost tribes, the Osage and the Wichita.

The sedentary tribes, whose origins can be traced to the prehistoric Upper Republican culture, lived in semisubterranean earth lodges in villages on terraces above streams. Stockades protected villages from marauding nomadic tribes, and most towns had enormous ceremonial lodges for winter and communal events. Between 70 and 80 percent of their food came from farming, but the diet was supplemented by the communal bison hunt held every summer, an event in which all able-bodied people participated.

Descent was unilineal, patrilineal among the southern tribes (Omaha, Ponca, Iowa, and Missouri) and matrilineal in the north (Mandan, Hidatsa, Arikara); lineages were strong corporate landowning units. Military fraternities also were found among the sedentary Plains tribes, but, unlike those of the nomadic tribes, they were age-graded, so that a group of males progressed from one level to the next, purchasing the paraphernalia associated with each grade from the group preceding them.

Religion focused on farming, maize cultivation, and weather control and incorporated such Southwestern elements as shrines, sand paintings, clowns, and certain deities. The preeminent supernatural beings were the Sun, related to the eagle, whose feathers were sacred ritual objects, and the Moon, a female deity associated with fertility and maize. Unique to this area, and found primarily among the Pawnee, was the morning star ceremony in which a female virgin was sacrificed to Venus each year.

The Southwest

As both a geographic and culture area, the Southwest—present-day Arizona, New Mexico, southwestern Colorado, southern Utah, eastern Texas, and northwestern Sonora—is far more heterogeneous than any other area of North America. The major unifying feature of the area is its aridity. The mesas and mountain ranges of the Colorado Plateau in the north, with elevations of 5,000 feet to 11,000 feet, are drained by the Colorado River system. A climatic drying cycle, compounded by overgrazing by livestock, has caused the thick grasslands of the past to be replaced by scrub vegetation mixed with piñon, mesquite, and cactus. The Colorado Plateau ends abruptly in the Mogollon Rim, a sharp escarpment dropping 1,000 feet to the Sonoran Desert of southwestern Arizona and northern Sonora. Here the basin and range topography is drained by the Gila and Salt River systems, and desert vegetation mixes with a variety of trees wherever water is found.

The plant and animal life of the Southwestern desert were sufficient to support hunting and gathering economies, while floodwater farming, irrigation, and drought-resistant varieties of corn made farming possible along the rivers. Subsistence for most societies was farming, ranging from the irrigation farming of the Eastern Pueblos on the Rio Grande and the Pima along the Salt and Gila Rivers to the floodwater farming of the Tohono O'odham to their west to the dry farming of the Hopi and Zuni on the Colorado Plateau. While the Navajo and Apache, newcomers to the Southwest, also farmed, the Apaches were primarily hunters and gatherers, and the Navajo became pastoralists with the Spanish introduction of sheep and goats after 1540. The Colorado River tribes also farmed, and all tribes in the Southwest supplemented their farming with hunting and gathering, some placing more reliance on food collecting than others.

Anasazi/Pueblo.   The Spanish called the descendants of the Anasazi the Pueblo because they lived in *pueblos*, the Spanish word for *towns*. Anthropological distinctions between Eastern and Western Pueblos are based on differences in kinship, political and ritual organizations, languages, and farming technologies. The small Eastern pueblos, along the Rio Grande from Albuquerque north through Santa Fe to the Colorado border, have been occupied since at least 1700. The Western Pueblos are the Hopi on Black Mesa in north-central Arizona; the Zuni, located 30 miles south of Gallup, New Mexico; and the Laguna and Acoma in north-central New Mexico.

Pueblo villages were permanent compact clusters of multistoried, terraced houses inhabited by multiple families. Each village also had underground ceremonial structures, *kivas*, which also served as men's clubhouses in the west. Spanish-introduced crops of wheat, alfalfa, and fruit trees were added to aboriginal crops of maize, beans, squash, cotton, and tobacco. Because the Western Pueblos relied on rainfall to water their drought-resistant varieties of crops, their religious rituals stressed weather control more than those of the Eastern Pueblos, who were able to irrigate their fields. Villages or clans owned the land, which was worked by the men, who also hunted, built the houses, and wove the fabrics for their clothing.

Among the Western Pueblos kinship was based on exogamous matrilineal clans; the bilateral extended family was the primary social unit among the Eastern Pueblos. Villages in both the east and west were autonomous. The Western Pueblo village chief came from a specific clan and held his position for life; a council composed of clan or association heads assisted with his political and ceremonial responsibilities. Eastern Pueblo political organization also dealt with both religious and secular issues but was based on a dual organization: political and ceremonial responsibilities alternated between two chiefs who were equal in status and authority.

Religion and ritual permeated all aspects of Pueblo life, which they saw as interrelated, balanced, and based on interdependent and reciprocal relationships between humans and nature. Disruption of the equilibrium by human thoughts, words, and deeds caused illness, disasters, and drought, but it could be restored and maintained through ceremony. Western Pueblo ritual focus was on weather control, manifested in the Kachina cult, whose masked dancers impersonated the kachina spirits who brought the rains. Eastern Pueblo religion was centered on both weather control and on health. In both the Eastern and Western Pueblos, "clowns" maintained social control during the public dances. Ritual concerns also included warfare (Eastern war associations), control of flora and fauna (hunt and clown associations), and village harmony.

Southern Athabascans. Relative latecomers to the Southwest, the similarities of the Athabascan-speaking Navajo and Apache indicate their common origins. Both moved into the Southwest from the Subarctic about 800 years ago, the Navajo settling along the San Juan drainage on the Colorado Plateau as neighbors of the Pueblos, and the Apache moving to the Mogollon Rim. Initially, both groups were nomadic hunters and gatherers, but the Navajo borrowed farming (and other cultural elements) from the Pueblos and, later, horses, sheep, and goats from the Spanish. They became seminomadic pastoralists dependent on livestock for food, clothing, and cash. Weaving, also learned from the Pueblos, became a source of cash income in historic times as Navajo women became as well known for their woven rugs and saddle blankets as the men were for their silver and turquoise jewelry. The Apache relied on hunting and gathering and later raiding (primarily Piman groups in the Sonoran Desert) for subsistence, supplemented by some farming done by the women.

Both the Navajo and Apache had matrilineal clans and matrilocal residence. The largest political unit was the band; neither had a tribalwide political structure until the twentieth century. The Navajo "outfit" was an extended kinship unit headed by an older man, a *Nataani* or "peace chief," responsible for maintaining diplomatic external relations. Apache bands were broken into family groups or outfits led by headmen chosen by the entire group for their wisdom and generosity.

The focus of religious ceremonies was health and curing to restore the harmony or balance of good and evil in the universe. Both groups had female puberty rituals, held shortly after a girl's first menses. Rituals in both tribes often involved masked dancers who impersonated the Holy People (the Navajo *Yeibechei* and the Apache *Ghaan* or Mountain Spirits). The primary deity for both tribes was Changing Woman, who gave birth to the War Twins (fathered by the Sun), Child of the Waters and Monster Slayer. Also significant were the Sun, First Man and First Woman, and a number of animal spirits.

The Pimans. Culturally, the Sonoran Desert was dominated by the Piman-speaking Pima and Tohono O'odham (Papago), believed to be descendants of the prehistoric Hohokam tradition, with its Mesoamerican traits of ball courts, temple mounds, ceramic styles, and irrigation. Pima (O'odham) settlements were located along Sonoran rivers from the Gila in Arizona to the Altar in Mexico, while the Tohono O'odham inhabited the more arid country west of the Pima.

Both the Pima and Tohono O'odham were farmers, depending on maize, beans, and pumpkins. Pima irrigation of their fields with waters from the Salt and Gila rivers made permanent village life possible. The Tohono O'odham relied on flooding from the summer rains to water their fields, located on the floodplains of dry washes and impermanent streams; summer camps were located near their fields, their winter camps near permanent sources of water. Although both Pima and Tohono O'odham women gathered wild plant foods to supplement the diet, food collection was more important to the Tohono O'odham. All parts of a variety of cactus were used, but the fruits of the prickly pear, called "tunas," and the saguaro cactus were of particular importance. Saguaro fruits were made into a fermented wine consumed ceremonially to usher in the new year and to ensure the coming of the late summer rains. Men hunted deer, antelope, and jackrabbits communally during the winter, an activity less important to the Pima, who usually had a food surplus, than to the Tohono O'odham, whose professional deer hunters were exempt from farming responsibilities.

Villages usually were made up of patrilineal extended families or clans presided over by headmen and councils. Originally both tribes had dual headmen to oversee peace and war, as well as a moral leader known as the "Keeper of the Smoke." Continual Apache raids on Pima villages eventually made war leaders more powerful. Lifelong leadership positions were based on charisma among the Tohono O'odham and were hereditary in the patrilineal line among the Pima. All decisions of the village council, composed of all the adult men, had to be unanimous or consensual.

Of the religious ceremonies focused on crops and rain, the July saguaro (rain) ceremony was the most important. The harvest ceremony, held about November every four years, was essentially a world-renewal ceremony. Rituals, including hunting ceremonies, girls' puberty rituals, and purification rituals for warriors (requiring 16 days of isolation outside the village) involved recitation of the accounts of *Iotoy,* "Elder Brother" (a helpful supernatural being who had

killed the monsters in the mythical past), songs, and offerings. Shamans, whose powers came from dreams, directed rituals to diagnose and cure diseases caused by witchcraft. "Curing singers" acquired their powers in dreams from the animal spirits that caused the diseases. Shamans who lost too many patients were suspected of witchcraft—using their supernatural powers to cause sickness and death—and were clubbed to death.

Rancherias. The farming village settlement pattern of tribes along the Colorado River (Hualapai, Yavapai, Havasupai, Mojave, and Quechan/Yuma) gives them the name *rancheria* people. All practiced a mixed economy of hunting, gathering, fishing, and farming, depending on location and water supply. Most were patrilineal, and the Mojave and Yuma also had totemic patrilineal clans. The responsibilities of political leaders, whose positions were hereditary in certain families or clans, revolved around warfare, mediation of disputes, organization of communal hunts, and the care of the sick and elderly. Tribal councils composed of headmen from villages or clusters of villages and war leaders whose positions were based on their reputations as warriors and on having had special dreams were found in some tribes.

The rancheria peoples believed they had little control over the supernatural. Dreams were important sources of knowledge and ritual competence, and ritual leaders were usually shamans who had acquired their powers through a vision experience, sometimes expedited by the use of jimson weed *(datura)*. Shamans cured illness caused by witchcraft, violation of taboos, or contact with enemies. The Keruk was a major annual communal ritual to commemorate the dead. All tribes had a girls' puberty ritual.

California–Great Basin–Plateau

Three culture areas that had similar subsistence activities were California, the Great Basin or desert country, and the Plateau. In all three areas subsistence was based on food collection–gathering, marginal hunting, and fishing–and their material cultures and social structures reflected this subsistence orientation.

The Great Basin. The combination of semidesert and true desert of the Great Basin, part of Utah and Nevada between the Wasatch and the Sierra Nevada mountain ranges and the Snake River in Idaho and the Colorado River and Grand Canyon, is caused by low precipitation and high evaporation rates, creating an arid climate with high daytime temperatures and rapid nighttime cooling. Although much of the vegetation, adapted to minimal water requirements, can be eaten by humans as seeds, fruits, or bulbs, it does not support large game animals. The principal large game was a scattered, sparse, and unreliable food source, necessitating reliance on smaller animals and a variety of plant foods. The basic food in the higher elevations was piñon nuts; roots, bulbs, and deer were more abundant in the piñon-juniper belt. At elevations over 8,000 feet, mountain sheep were hunted for food.

Population density along the Snake and Colorado Rivers and in the piñon-fir-aspen zones of the lower slopes of the Sierras varied with the food supply and the ecology of the area. These tribes relied on the rich and nourishing piñon nut and almost 100 other kinds of plants. Rabbits and antelope, though hunted, were less important than all the other animal foods combined, including rodents, reptiles, and insects. Whenever antelope and rabbits were sufficiently plentiful, communal hunts were organized under the control and direction of the shaman.

The scattered and sparse availability of food resulted in a nomadic settlement pattern of small groups roaming over large territories according to season. Poorly built temporary shelters consisted of arbors or windbreaks in warm weather; caves and rock shelters also were utilized whenever possible. Sweat houses were used for sweat

baths and as meeting places for the men. The material culture of the Basin tribes was meager, limited to what could be carried from camp to camp.

With a gender-based division of labor, men hunted, a time-consuming, arduous, and often unrewarding task, and women gathered wild plant foods, prepared the food, cared for the children, did camp chores, and wove fabric for clothing. Children assisted the parent of their sex and assumed adult roles at an early age.

The primary social unit of the Great Basin, the family–a man, his wife or wives, their children, and often several other relatives–moved wherever food was available. Individual families might camp alone for several days at a time, and families came together for collective or communal hunts directed by the "rabbit boss," an experienced older man, and in years of good piñon harvests. Marital rather than political ties linked different groups. Infrequent warfare was usually sporadic feuds caused by suspected witchcraft or disputes over women.

Individualistic supernatural beliefs focused on supernatural powers that came from dreams and vision experiences, welcome but not deliberately sought. Shamans who acquired supernatural powers through visions earned prestige and honor as curers but also were feared lest they use their supernatural powers to harm through witchcraft.

The Plateau. The Plateau, more a geographic than a culture area in eastern Washington, Oregon, and western Idaho, ranges from sagebrush and juniper flats to meadows and prairies to volcanic wastelands, rugged canyons, and heavily forested mountains. The Rocky Mountains protect the region from the harsh winter storms of the Plains, contributing to the area's mild climate. Rainfall amounts vary; the south is warm and arid, and the north is cool and humid with more than 25 inches of annual precipitation. The Fraser and Columbia Rivers provided both a reliable and easily accessible food supply and avenues of communication and transportation.

The cultural diversity of the area reflects environmental and cultural influences, the latter from tribes in neighboring culture areas. Marginal Northwest Coast traits are seen in northern tribes (Lillooets and Klikitats); Plains influences among the Kutenais, Flatheads, and Nez Percé; and California elements in tribes in the central portion of the area. Tribes uninfluenced by outside areas fit more closely with the food-collecting patterns already described.

Fish, particularly salmon, were a source of protein for tribes along the Fraser and Columbia Rivers and their tributaries; bulbs were important to the Nez Percé. Despite the variety of game animals on the Plateau, their numbers were not great enough for them to be a major source of food. Some large animals were hunted communally under the direction of qualified leaders.

Small semipermanent villages located along the rivers and streams of the salmon runs ranged in size from hamlets of five families to villages with populations up to 400 in areas where fishing was particularly good. The larger circular semisubterranean earth lodges usually were multiple family dwellings. Although the autonomous villages controlled nearby fishing stations, berry patches, and camas meadows, this control was not exclusive. Villages were free to make use of resources near other villages, and residents were free to move from one permanent village to another. The village headman's primary duties were to maintain internal peace and to settle disputes, sometimes assisted by subchiefs and councils. No overall tribal organization existed, although neighboring villages shared kinship ties from frequent intermarriage, a common language and culture, and met for social and ceremonial activities. Disputes were settled without violence or warfare, although sporadic small-scale raids sometimes occurred.

Nuclear families or several related nuclear families made up the households. Bilateral descent emphasized the patrilineal line. Women were important in all aspects of life, including political and religious, and they also had puberty rituals. The male ritual tended to be longer and more vigorous than that of the females and culminated in a mandatory vision quest.

Religious focus was individual. The world was believed to be filled with a variety of spirits and supernatural forces that could be either helpful or dangerous; vision quests by both sexes revealed a guardian spirit(s) that guaranteed success in life. Those with particularly strong guardian spirits were likely to become shamans, each directing activities related to his animal guardian. Shamans also cured illness attributed to witchcraft or soul loss.

California. Most of the present state of California, from the western slopes of the Sierra Nevada to the Pacific Ocean and from the deserts of southern California to the area of Mount Shasta, is isolated from the rest of North America by rugged mountain ranges. Dominated by the vast interior valley drained by the San Joaquin and Sacramento River systems, the diverse region of narrow coastal plains, warm interior valleys, and mountain systems stretches for almost a thousand miles along the Pacific. The diversity in natural resources is reflected in the diversity of tribes, languages, and subsistence modes, although most groups depended on acorns as their staple food. Regional variations included the southern Mojave and Yuma farmers, similar to their Southwestern neighbors, and the northern Yurok and Hupa, with their Northwest Coast traits.

In addition to acorns, California tribes depended on a variety of foods: shellfish, saltwater fish, and salmon, while groups near inland lakes relied heavily on fish and waterfowl. The maritime hunters of Santa Monica Bay and along the channel islands took advantage of stranded whales and used Northwest Coast–style plank canoes to fish and to hunt sea lions and sea otters. The abundant and regular food supply made permanent village life possible. Single or extended families lived in circular or oval houses and used temporary brush shelters away from the villages. All villages had semisubterranean sweat lodges used daily by the men, and larger villages had large circular dance lodges.

The patrilineal or bilateral nuclear family was the basic social and economic unit of California societies. No overall tribal organization existed; the primary territorial units were primary villages with several lesser settlements, occupied continuously over several generations. Boundaries of village-owned territories of approximately 100 to 150 miles were known and respected. Political leadership was in the hands of councils made up of all the adult males of the local community. Hereditary headmen were more ceremonial than political; they were respected and wealthier than others in the village but had little authority, other than settling disputes.

Warfare was usually infrequent, motivated by unauthorized trespass on a village's territory or to avenge a death attributed to enemy warfare. Individuals of skill and courage led war parties in surprise attacks and brief skirmishes. Scalps were taken, and captured women and children usually were adopted into the tribe.

Annual and semiannual ceremonies helped to ensure the continuity of the food supply and to ward off disasters. The Kuksu cults of the interior valley were secret societies into which all men were initiated during the male puberty ritual. In curing ceremonies, shamans cured diseases caused by foreign objects shot into a victim's body by dancing, singing, and smoking, followed by the removal of the foreign object by sucking it from the patient's body.

The Northwest Coast

The heterogeneous environment of the Northwest Coast, a narrow coastal strip extending 1,500 miles from northern California to southeastern Alaska between the mountains and the Pacific Ocean, shifts gradually from a maritime boreal zone in the north (where the cultures were the most highly developed) to the marginal areas of northern California. Although Northwest Coast tribes were hunters and gatherers, the richness of natural resources and the resulting food surpluses made possible cultural patterns normally associated with farming economies: village life, elaborate material cultures, and social stratification.

The moderate climate and heavy rainfall of the Northwest Coast produce a heavy temperate rain forest, abundant and diverse shrubs and bushes for a range of edible berries and roots, and a plentiful animal life. Most food came from the Pacific Ocean and the rivers flowing into it. Fish, particularly salmon, were an important part of the tribes' diet, but the coastal waters also were rich in shellfish and marine mammals, such as seals, sea lions, porpoises, sea otters, and whales.

Settlements scattered along narrow coastal beaches, usually near the mouths of rivers, in coves, on islands, and in river valleys, were made up of large, rectangular red cedar plank houses—multiple family dwellings—with gabled roofs. Round or oval doors in the gabled end faced the sea and beach. A series of steps or benches led down to fire pits in the center of the house; family sleeping compartments, sometimes miniature duplications of the house itself, were located along the outer walls of the house.

The food surplus supported a complex social organization and an elaborate material culture. Autonomous local groups were based on kinship ties, each with its own chiefs, ceremonies and ceremonial rites, and crests. Local groups were drawn together into economic cooperation and temporary military alliances by combinations of extended unilineal kingroups, called moieties, and clans and the related mutual obligations and reciprocal duties. No overall political linkages existed, however.

The stratified Northwest Coast society was not a typical class system of nobles, commoners, and slaves. Two classes existed, "freemen" and "slaves." The class of "freemen" was a ranking of social positions, nobles (whose parents had given a potlatch) and commoners (whose parents had not). High-status individuals were granted greater deference and more prerogatives and rights than those of lower status, but no formal dividing line separated high-ranked individuals from those of low rank, other than the potlatch. Upward and downward mobility also was common, a result of the potlatch. Because the class of "slaves" was not involved directly in the potlatch cycle, they did not belong to the class system characterized by upward and downward mobility.

Persons born to their ranks did not automatically assume them; claims to high status had to be validated through *potlatches*, ceremonies in which valuable material goods—food, blankets, and copper (shieldlike sheets of hammered native copper)—were given away. Funeral potlatches validated the inheritance of one's status; house-building potlatches validated a man's status as "house chief"; mourning potlatches were held at the death of a chief; and vengeance potlatches redressed grievances. In order to hold high status, one's parents had to have hosted a potlatch. Potlatches reinforced group solidarity and cohesiveness: all members of the kinship group participated by helping collect the goods for distribution and by dancing and singing during the celebrations, and all benefited in sharing the prestige accrued from the display and dispersal of their wealth, for the honors and titles were bestowed on family members who had contributed. Potlatches also provided an economically important means for redistribution of economic goods throughout the society.

Northwest Coast art was distinctive and is well known, particularly woodworking, wood carving, and basket-making. Wood-carving skills are evident in ceremonial masks, many of which had movable parts; in sculptured food dishes and bowls; and in red cedar boxes, containers, and canoes. Huge oceangoing canoes used in hunting and warfare, sometimes more than 50 feet long and 7 to 8 feet wide, were decorated with carved or painted family crests. The best known art form is probably the totem poles, which have come to be almost as symbolic (or stereotypic) of American Indians as are the Plains Indians' tipis and warbonnets. Totem poles were narrative family histories, originally erected at or near the graves of persons to be honored and commemorated. During the nineteenth century these poles were greatly elaborated as corner and doorposts in houses and as mortuary poles and became symbols of status and privilege.

The distinctive decorative arts are characterized by highly conventionalized and stylized heraldic art showing ancestry and glorifying individual and family status. Animals were the most common motif in the two-dimensional caricature-like representations, identifiable by ears and distinctive attributes: the killer whale's exaggerated blowhole and dorsal fin, the beaver's tail and teeth, the bear's claws and canine teeth, and the shark's dorsal fin and teeth. This art differs from European art in its emphasis on symmetry, splitting and spreading animals out in ways that are strange to outsiders, and in filling all blank spaces with interlocked and intertwined figures. Decorative arts could be found on the painted exterior walls of houses, carved doors and corner posts of houses, on canoes, boxes, and eating utensils, and on ceremonial objects.

The Subarctic

A wide belt of coniferous forest extending across North America from central Alaska and the Canadian Rockies to Hudson Bay, Labrador, and Newfoundland, the Subarctic is rugged and wild. Mountains, streams, lakes, and large expanses of muskeg and spruce stands are interspersed with balsam fir and deciduous trees. In the past, wildlife included large herds of caribou—the primary game animal—and musk ox, many smaller mammals, fish in the glacial lakes and rivers, and waterfowl and birds.

Because of the remoteness of the area and the early decimation of the tribes and cultures, Subarctic cultures have not been well studied or described. Local adaptations to environmental conditions accounted for regional cultural variations. Two linguistic groups predominated: the small, constantly shifting Athabascans—the Koyukons, Hares, Slaves, Yellowknives, and Beavers—in the west, and a small number of Algonkian speakers in the east—the Naskapi, Montaignais, Cree, and Ojibwa-Ottawa.

Subarctic subsistence was based on nomadic hunting and fishing; hunting small mammals and birds and gathering berries and other wild plants were of secondary economic importance. On the tundra, the large barren ground, caribou was the primary animal hunted; other groups fished and hunted animals such as moose. Athabascan groups along western streams took advantage of the annual salmon runs; because of the richness of this food supply and the Athabascans' proximity to the Northwest Coast, their culture was more elaborate than those of other Subarctic tribes. The one universal of Subarctic subsistence was that it was precarious, and during historic times periods of starvation seem to have been common.

Material culture was limited by and adapted to the environment. Snowshoes and toboggans were Subarctic inventions to facilitate travel during the winter; in the summer, transportation was usually by bark canoes on the lakes and streams. The most common type of dwelling was the conical tipi, its framework covered with brush or bark or with hides. Some groups, such as the Slave, made small gabled earth-covered log houses for winter stays of fairly long duration.

The nomadic lifestyle contributed to the simple and largely unstructured social organization known as "composite bands," amorphous and leaderless groups of often unrelated families. Nuclear or extended families hunted and camped together; bands were formed when they were joined by other, similar family groups. Membership in the ephemeral bands was fluid; headmen were skilled hunters who sometimes possessed special supernatural powers but had no real authority. No political units existed beyond the band, although bands might speak the same language or similar dialects, share a common culture and lifestyle, and occupy adjoining territories.

Puberty for boys was marked by a vision quest, a period of fasting and isolation to acquire "power" or "medicine." Because menstruating women were considered dangerous—they could deprive men of their strength and supernatural powers—and a source of potential contamination, they were isolated and had to observe taboos and restrictions, particularly in relation to men. Both senilicide (killing of the elderly) and cannibalism appear to have existed during times of starvation, more commonly among the Algonkians and the Cree than others. Because of the social stigma attached to cannibalism, individuals who craved human flesh were considered to be possessed by the cannibalistic supernatural monster Windigo or Witiko spirit.

The Athabascans attributed illness and death to sorcery or other supernatural causes, and ghosts and death were so feared that lodges in which people died were abandoned and the dead were buried immediately. Algonkians expressed grief through self-mutilation and held annual feasts for the dead. Supernatural beliefs and rituals appear to have been individualistic—informal, unstructured vision quests seeking the guardian spirits, who were more important than a creator god, to help in times of crises and for protection from harmful spirits. Other beliefs and rituals centered around the hunt. The belief that animals allowed themselves to be caught and killed meant that violation of the taboos or inappropriate behavior could offend the spirits of the animals, who would withhold themselves from the hunters.

Shamans were men who possessed special supernatural powers and who could deal with the supernatural world to determine the cause and cure of illness and, in some groups, to determine why game was scarce or absent and to foretell the future. Shamanistic rituals were held to prevent illness and to ward off disease-causing evil spirits. Although shamans could use their powers for witchcraft, generally they believed that sorcery was caused by witches outside one's own social group.

The Arctic

A vast, treeless arctic desert stretching across northern North America, from Siberia to Greenland, from the rocky islands and flat barren lands of the Canadian Arctic Plains and Alaska to the cold glacial fjords of Greenland, the Arctic is characterized by a range of topography and land form, climate, vegetation, and fish and game. The Arctic is a desert of cold with surprisingly little precipitation, as little as 4 inches of snow annually. Freshwater sources include streams (which freeze in the winter), brackish stagnant water that collects in shallow depressions of the tundra bottomlands, and the summits of ocean ice along the winter shore. This seemingly inhospitable tundra supported an aboriginal population of approximately 100,000 people calling themselves Inuit ("humans" or "men") or Yuit. Physically, culturally, and linguistically, they were different from the populations to the south, who called them Eskimo ("raw meat eaters").

Arctic life was affected by the two seasons, summer light and winter darkness. During the short summers, from June to Fall, temperatures rise above freezing and the sun shines for 24 hours; water travel is facilitated by the melting of streams, and the breakup of ocean ice opens expanses of sea for hunting walrus and whales. Swampy conditions created by the melting of the tundra to the permafrost level make land travel difficult. The first severe freeze, in November,

marks the onset of winter, which lasts until the spring equinox. Temperatures are cold, averaging 30 degrees below zero (Fahrenheit) on the coast and 65 degrees below zero in the interior, and the wind chill of the cold, gale-force winds lowers coastal temperatures dramatically. During the long, dark winters, the people returned to permanent villages and campsites with the food collected during the summer; summer tents were replaced by winter houses, and boats were exchanged for travel by dogsleds.

While all native Arctic dialects are mutually intelligible, no tribal units were recognized. The Copper Eskimo, the Greenland Eskimo, the Caribou Eskimo, the Netsilik and Ingulik Eskimo of the central Arctic refer to geographic rather than political groups. Some scholars base their division of the eastern and western Inuit on how they exploited sea mammals, but essentially Arctic culture was characterized by a common shared base of hunting with similar tools and weapons.

Arctic natives relied almost entirely on animals for their food. The seal, found in all areas of the Arctic, was the primary source of food, clothing, and oil for cooking and lighting. Whales and walrus were hunted in Pacific waters; the pelts of polar bears were particularly prized; caribou were hunted; and wolves, wolverines, and fox were hunted for their pelts. Fish and birds were of secondary importance in the Inuit diet.

Summer camps were moved frequently in search of game, but winter base camps were fairly permanent. The stereotypical igloos, or snow houses, were used when hunting seals away from the winter base camps, but they were not the primary winter habitation except in the Canadian Arctic, where nomadism was common even during the winter. Winter houses in the east were made of sod and stone, and in the west of sod; summer shelters were easily transported tents.

Hunting techniques varied according to region and the type of animal being hunted. Seal hunting tended to be individual endeavors or the efforts of fathers and sons, and large game—whale or caribou—was hunted in cooperative groups in which each hunter had an assigned task. Large-game hunting involved careful adherence to ritual to ensure successful hunts and to avoid insulting the spirits of the animals.

Arctic transportation was distinctive. During the winter, dogs hitched in fanwise traces pulled sleds with wooden or bone runners, and in the summer travel was usually by water in lightweight boats with wooden or bone frames covered with skins. The kayak was used by single hunters, using double-bladed paddles, seated in the middle of the vessel and protected by skin coverings that laced around the hunter's waist. The larger umiak was used for whale hunting and for transporting freight and families from one camp to another.

Social structure revolved around the economic and subsistence activities of the household, a kinship unit consisting of a nuclear family and additional relatives led by the head of the family. Marriage ties were economically and socially important, reflecting the cooperative relationship between men and women necessary for both survival and for prestige and status. Preferred marriage partners were those with whom no kinship bonds of support, assistance, or mutual aid already existed. Legally, marriage was defined as continuous cohabitation, but marriages were considered stable and binding only when children were born. Ties between nonkin were established through economic and social partnerships involving friendship, hospitality, and social interaction, consummated by wife-lending or reciprocal wife exchange (such exchanges were not viewed as adultery).

Religious beliefs centered around the special relations between humans and animals, reflected in food taboos, songs, and charms. Animals had to be cajoled, coerced, or placated into letting themselves be caught. Fresh water had to be offered to all sea animals, which allowed themselves to be caught because they were thirsty. Special care had to be taken with bones and waste so as not to offend the animals' spirits, which were released at death. Offended spirits could communicate with other spirits, and all animals then would withhold themselves from humans, causing starvation. Some religious rituals or festivals involved masked impersonations of animals and animal spirits; through dancing, singing, and drumming hunters attempted to exercise some control over the animal spirits. Animals also were the source of the mana-like power of successful hunters, lovers, and shamans. Shamans' spirit helpers usually were associated with land animals; brown bear, wolf, and fox power were highly valued, bear power because it was valuable in curing.

HISTORIC RELATIONSHIPS

Although a number of European nations explored the "New World" in the fourteenth through the sixteenth centuries, American Indian cultures were affected most by the French, Spanish, and English. Of these, the fledgling American nation based its practices on established English policies. European attitudes and treatment of the natives depended on their reasons for coming to the New World at a time when European politics were in turmoil. With the Spanish expulsion of the Moors from Spain and the imposition of the Inquisition, the Spanish Crown had to fulfill its promise to provide land to the men who had fought the Moors. Northern Europe was in the midst of social reform, the beginning of industrialism, the rise of the middle classes and decline of the landed aristocracy, and the Protestant Reformation. France, involved in the Huguenot wars, sought trade routes to the Orient, while in England, after Oliver Cromwell's "Roundheads" (Puritans) gained and then lost power, a number of them fled first to Holland and then to the New World, seeking religious freedom. The changes in the sociocultural environment resulting from the European presence in the Americas also led to changes in the Indian cultures.

Early European Contacts and Policies

Initially, neither the French nor the Spanish came to the New World as colonists. While the Spanish came for gold, to save souls, and for land for the veterans of the Holy Wars, the French sought the Northwest Passage or northern waterway to the Orient and commerce in the fur trade. Because neither included women or children in their expeditions, both not only permitted but encouraged intermarriage between Indian women and European men. The French, who respected Indian customs, also tried to learn the native languages. Both regarded the Indians as human beings, albeit innocent, who were capable and deserving of civilization, which, to them, was conversion to Christianity. Both groups needed peaceful contacts with the Indians (the French need for tribal alliances to facilitate the fur trade led to an avoidance of tribal displacements or annihilations as they moved to the interior of the continent). The Spanish *encomienda* system, which gave Spanish landowners the right to the labor of the natives living on their land grants and which became a form of slavery in some areas, was the result of the need for Indian laborers in the mines and on the estates.

The English goal, however, was settlement—establishing homes in the New World where they could own land and raise families. Indians were seen as inferior heathens with whom intermarriage was sinful and for whom conversion to Christianity was inappropriate. English colonial policy was based on commerce. Because the Protestant English colonists did not consider hard work degrading, they had no need for serfs or slaves, and no legal mechanisms were developed to exploit Indian labor. Most conflicts were over land caused by different value systems and perceptions: to the English, land was a com-

modity to be owned, purchased, and fenced off; to the Indians, land was something shared and used but not owned.

By the time of the American Revolution, the English had established a number of policies that the Americans adopted and that are still in place today. Compensable Indian title to the land, an important principle underlying the Indian Claims Commission cases of the mid-twentieth century, was established in colonial America in the early seventeenth century with laws requiring whites to *buy* Indian lands. This concept had no legal precedents in British law; the colonists used the Bible as their authority. The policy of "reserving" protected lands (reservations) for the Indians also was established in the colonial period, and by the 1750s most New England legislatures had established guardianship over Indians and their lands. "Plantations," or Indian communities, in Massachusetts, for example, were governed by three guardians who had the power to allot land, to rent or lease remaining lands to "suitable" non-Indian persons, to prevent trespass on Indian lands, and to approve sales or leases of land between Indians, all basic tenets of later reservation policy.

Colonial governments controlled Indian trade, requiring licenses for traders going into Indian Country (lands west of the frontier); prohibited the sale of alcohol and firearms to Indians; made the Indians "protected" wards of the federal government; negotiated treaties; and appointed superintendents to regulate trade and negotiate acquisitions of Indian land. A boundary drawn in the Proclamation of 1763 between Indian Country and the colonies, west of the Appalachians from the tidelands of eastern Florida into Canada, was the basis of twentieth-century suits of tribes seeking compensation for lands lost to whites through the Indian Claims Court. Eligibility depended on location west of that boundary line; most tribes to the east were considered to have lost their lands prior to the establishment of the United States.

Early American Policies

The American Revolution marked a turning point in Indian-white relations and in Indian cultures: Indian power and independence were undermined by alliances with the European powers who lost the battles for white supremacy in the New World. The French defeat in the French and Indian War left Indians in the interior with no European ally to protect them from English advances. Which side Indian nations had taken in the American Revolution also affected how they were treated in the following years.

Indian affairs were of concern to white Americans, and in 1775 the Second Continental Congress established an Indian Department and appointed commissioners to deal with Indian nations. The policy of the Continental Congress was to treat Indians as dependent internal nations with whom legal treaties concerning land use were made. The seeds of paternalism can be seen in the policy prohibiting Indians in Indian Country from selling land without congressional consent. The Constitution of the United States granted Congress plenary, or supreme, power over Indian affairs in trade, treaty, warfare, and welfare and the power to take Indian land for public purposes as long as just compensation was paid. While a number of American policies were intended to further Indian assimilation, many, in fact, intensified Indian isolation and strengthened ethnic ties and identities.

Following the Revolution, the main American concern was economic—getting Indian trade. The Indian Trade and Intercourse Act was passed in 1790, and between 1790 and 1834 all Indian legislation came under this heading, including licensing of traders in Indian Country; requiring treaties to purchase Indian land; determining the penalties for murder of Indians by non-Indians in Indian Country; appointing agents in Indian Country; defining Indian Country; and prohibiting the sale of alcohol to Indians. Much legislation dealt with land issues, which continued to be the primary source of conflict between Indians and whites. As settlers pushed into Indian Country, the question became one of accommodation or extinction of the Indian peoples. Treaties established boundaries in the belief that Indians would be absorbed slowly into American society and would be willing to sell their lands; when this did not happen, pressures were applied to Indian tribes to cede their lands and move west to Indian Territory (present-day Oklahoma). In 1875, for example, the Shawnee cession of a small amount of land in Pennsylvania was supposed to guarantee their protection; between the Revolutionary and Civil wars, 11 treaties of cession were signed in exchange for protection by the government.

The Indian Removal Act. Despite treaties of cession and appropriation of federal monies to pay southeastern tribes to move to Indian Territory and the newly acquired Louisiana Purchase, Indians were reluctant to leave their homelands. White pressure to remove Indians from the East led to the passage of the Indian Removal Act on May 20, 1830, setting up districts in Indian Territory to accept the eastern tribes. Indians could choose to be under federal jurisdiction or have title to the land and be free of the U.S. government. One-half million dollars was appropriated in compensation for improvements on their land, to support them for one year, and to protect them.

Despite Indian resistance to removal, the process could not be stopped, and during the 1830s and 1840s most Indians east of the Mississippi were moved to Oklahoma, overseen in part by the government agency responsible for Indian Affairs created in 1834 and placed in the War Department. At the same time Congress redefined Indian Country and trader policy and established the basic structure of Indian administration. General superintendents were appointed for designated areas of Indian Country, with subagencies and agents responsible to the superintendents. The position of Indian Commissioner was authorized by Congress in 1832, and in 1849 control over Indian Affairs was shifted from the War Department to the Department of the Interior.

During the 1850s and 1860s, the attention of the federal government was on the South and the Civil War, but after the war, attention shifted to the West (Plains) and the Southwest (acquired through the Gadsden Purchase in 1853), where continued pressures for Indian lands and Indian military reactions led to the Indian Wars of the 1860s and 1870s. Defeated Indians were forced onto reservations in an effort to eradicate Indian cultures and assimilate them into American culture: nomadic hunters and gatherers were taught to farm; traditional ritual practices of most tribes were prohibited; polygynous marriages were prohibited; and schools were established or children were removed from reservation communities, sometimes forcibly, to attend all-Indian boarding schools in the East, where they would learn white ways. Children often were not allowed to go home for visits lest they "backslide."

Exploitation of Indians by agents, politicians, missionaries, and military personnel was typical of this period. Missionary and military pressures led to congressional investigations of Indian affairs in 1865. In response to an 1867 report, which described drastic population decline, violation of reservation boundaries, intolerable reservation conditions, and rampant disease and starvation, proposals suggested turning Indian matters over to missionaries, relocating Indians in the Dakotas and Oklahoma, and dividing the Rockies into districts. By 1873, reservations had been divided among missionary groups, whose presence did lead to some improvement, although exploitation of the Indians continued.

Dawes Severalty Act. During the 1870s, settlers pushing into "protected" Indian lands and, violating reservation boundaries, pressured

for termination of Indian title. As the government's long-range goal always had been assimilation of the Indians, a policy of "allotment"—the individualization of Indian lands—seemed a practical way to accomplish both purposes. Communal ownership and civilization were considered incompatible. Indians farming individually owned plots of land would become self-sufficient and independent of the federal government's support; they would own their land and be able to sell it—to non-Indians—if they wished.[1]

Despite the fact that Indians usually lost fee simple lands, in the 1860s efforts to pass allotment legislation began. Advocates of allotment claimed that Indian tribes threatened with extinction would become self-supporting and would be protected from the loss of reservation lands; domination by certain families would be avoided, and allotment ultimately would lead to assimilation. Opponents to allotment argued that allotment would lead to the alienation of Indian lands, that tribes to be allotted had a non-agricultural orientation, and that the concept of land as private property was alien to Indians.

Allotment bills introduced in 1878 and 1880 failed; the Indian Homestead Act of 1884 gave Indians restricted title to land that could not be sold for 25 years and could not be taxed. Allotment proponents won with the passage of the General Allotment Act in 1887 (Dawes Severalty Act), which required all tribal lands to be surveyed and divided among members according to the formula of the Omaha Treaty of 1854: 80 acres to single persons, 160 acres to married couples, and 320 acres to families of five or more. A provision to sell surplus lands at public auctions was not mandatory but usually was invoked. Lands would be held in trust for 25 years, after which trust patents would be issued and the Indians would become U.S. citizens under state jurisdiction. The Curtis Act of 1898 extended allotment to the Five Civilized Tribes of Oklahoma, effectively ending their tribal government and education systems, and in 1906 the Burke Act waived the 25-year waiting period for issuance of fee simple title, depending on the competency of the Indian owner.

The most significant long-range result of allotment, which ended in the 1930s, was the loss of approximately 100 million acres of land, most through the sale of surplus lands on large reservations owned by small tribes. "Checkerboarding," when Indians and non-Indians own adjoining tracts of land, made development of allotments and governing of Indian lands impossible, and factionalism, lack of political unity, and little or no social or economic progress resulted. Traditional settlement patterns and social organization were disrupted among some tribes, such as the Pima of Arizona, when individuals left traditional agricultural villages to live on their allotments. Disputes over political rights led to factionalism between the Quinault and other tribes given land on the Quinault reservation. Leasing of lands owned by a number of heirs has to be handled by the Bureau of Indian Affairs, since non-Indians found it easier to deal with one agency than a number of landowners. Ultimately, allotment increased rather than decreased Indian dependency.

Indian Responses to European and American Contacts. Indian tribes were autonomous sovereign nations in control of their own territories and destinies when the Europeans arrived in the fifteenth century. Intertribal contacts were based on economic trade networks or military or political alliances. Initially, some tribes that shared cultural traditions and, sometimes, language reacted to the European presence by strengthening intertribal alliances—the New England Algonkian confederacies: the Abenaki, Wampanoag, Delaware, and Massachusetts confederacies (Underhill 1953:80–81). Several Caddoan confederacies were located in what is now Texas, Louisiana, and Oklahoma (Swanton 1952), but among the better known alliances are the Powhatan Confederacy (Lurie 1971) in tidewater Virginia (perhaps best known for Powhatan's daughter Pocahontas), the Creek

Confederacy of Muskogean speakers incipient in the Southeast at the time of Hernando de Soto's arrival (Swanton 1928, 1952), and the Iroquois Confederacy of the Lower Great Lakes region (Wallace 1970). The only early western alliance led the Pueblo Revolt of 1680 in New Mexico, when autonomous Pueblo villages allied themselves temporarily to drive out the Spanish, if only for a brief time. Such alliances intensified with increased European threats to Indian lands and sovereignty. Indian political and military organization remained strong, their cultures continued to be based on traditional social and belief systems, and they believed themselves, if not superior to, at least equal to the whites and able to deal with them on even terms.

Indian perceptions of their situation changed over time. Increased white settlements encroached on their territory; treaties were violated; efforts of Christian missionaries and white educators intensified; and the ravages of illness and warfare caused the decline in Indian populations. No longer could they vanquish the whites through military force and political unity alone; supernatural assistance was necessary and took the form of revitalization movements (Wallace 1956)—efforts to restore balance in the face of cultural loss resulting from intense acculturation. Nativistic or millenarian movements attempted to return to a "golden age" of past culture, often through a cataclysmic event brought about by supernatural intervention. Such movements were revolutionary and openly hostile to whites:

> The religious trend reflects the yearnings of the Indians for the recovery of their own culture, which was rapidly declining. Such movements . . . sought to salvage and renovate a culture already in crisis by rejecting the white man and his civilization. This trend is retrospective; for in these movements it is the past that offers the way to salvation. [Lanternari 1963:114–115].

Approximately 20 such nativistic or messianic movements appeared in the United States prior to 1890 (Barber 1941:475–476). Their doctrines were similar, attributing the problems and suffering of the Indians to the coming of the whites and to the Indians' rejection of traditional ways and acceptance of white customs. If the Indians returned to their traditional or aboriginal ways of life, rejected foreign traits and customs, and participated in special ritual practices, the Great Spirit and his emissary would intervene to transform the world into a utopian paradise of eternal happiness and no sickness or death. The essentially peaceful doctrines excluded whites and those Indians who had taken up the white way of life.

During the eighteenth century, just before the forced removal of some northeastern Algonkians from their homelands, several messianic movements provided mythical justification for and reinforcement of military confederacies. The first was the 1760s "conspiracy" of the Ottawa chief Pontiac, based on the teachings of the Delaware Prophet (Hunter 1971; Spicer 1969); the second appeared about 40 years later among the Shawnee, led by Tecumseh and his prophet brother, Tenskwatawa (Eggleston 1878; Mooney 1896; Spicer 1969). The military alliances of Pontiac and Tecumseh tried to drive the English from their lands; both efforts failed. In the Pacific Northwest, the "Dream" religion of the prophet Smohalla provided the justification for the 1877 Nez Percé "uprising" led by Chief Joseph. All these movements were nativistic, advocating a return to the old ways, yet also representing a syncretism of both traditional Indian religions and Christianity. However, the nativistic emphasis on a return to the old ways meant that they could use only native weapons such as bows and arrows, no European firearms, which contributed to their failure; the numbers of Europeans moving into Indian territories continued to increase.

The most widespread messianic movement among western tribes was the Ghost Dance religion of the 1870s and 1890s. The 1890 movement grew out of the earlier 1870 movement, led by the Paiute prophet Wodziwob (Lanternari 1963:131). By the 1870s, the peaceful hunting and gathering Paiutes were losing their hunting grounds to white ranches and were forced to take whatever wage work they could find in the white settlements (Spicer 1969:90). Wodziwob taught that a major cataclysm would shake the world and swallow the whites, but the whites' buildings, goods, and tools would remain behind for the use of the Indians and their dead ancestors, who would return in a railroad train. With the establishment of this heavenly era, the Great Spirit would come to live among them, and they would live in prosperity and immunity to sickness and death (Wax 1971:138). The early movement died out, to be revived about 20 years later by the prophet Wovoka at a time when all western Indians faced drastically altered conditions: restrictive reservation life, military defeat, extinction of the buffalo, and increased dependence on the Bureau of Indian Affairs for food and clothing (Spicer 1969:91). Faced with the threat of starvation and the loss of the old way of life, the message of Wovoka provided hope for salvation and a restoration of the old ways (Barber 1941:476).

In a vision in 1890, during a solar eclipse, in which he believed he died, Wovoka was taken to the "other world" where he saw God and the old people who had died long ago and where he was given God's message and dance to take back to his people. By dancing at intervals for five consecutive days, they could hasten the return of the old ways and the elimination of the whites: "The time will come when the whole Indian race, living and dead, will be reunited upon a regenerated earth, to live a life of aboriginal happiness forever free from death, disease, and misery" (Mooney 1896:19). The fact that there was no place for whites in the utopian world probably contributed to the widespread popularity of the movement. Whites and all things that served a temporary purpose would be removed by supernatural means; Indians only had to observe certain rituals and behaviors. Wovoka's teachings included ritual, a mythology, and a moral code that involved changes in Plains behavior patterns unacceptable to the whites. Although Wovoka stressed peaceful coexistence with whites and obedience to authority until the millennium arrived, as Spicer points out, "It was nevertheless a teaching opposed to the acceptance of White values and way of life. It rested on the belief that Indian ways were good and could be restored" (1969:90).

The original date for the millennium was the spring of 1891; when it failed to materialize, advanced dates were set, until finally the date was left open for sometime in the unknown future. The Ghost Dance spread rapidly among western, particularly Plains, tribes and Sitting Bull introduced it to the Dakota, who gave it a more warlike interpretation. The Indian agent on the Pine Ridge reservation, who did not understand the significance of the Ghost Dance and feared it was an uprising, banned the dance, and asked for—and received—additional soldiers. Confiscation of Indian guns left them with no means for hunting, threatening them with starvation and leading to the "uprising" at Wounded Knee in 1890, precipitated by the murder of Sitting Bull as he was being taken into custody. Some of Sitting Bull's followers joined the band of Big Foot as they were going to a Ghost Dance celebration. All 300 men, women, and children were massacred by white soldiers, who left the bodies to freeze where they lay. The religion spread to other tribes both east and west of the Rockies, with less tragic results; ultimately, it withered away when the expected millennium failed to materialize.

Not all revitalization movements stressed a return to the old ways; several were "adaptive," combining elements of native concepts with Christianity and stressing accommodation to and acceptance of the changed conditions under which they lived. Although these religions were messianic in origin, because they stressed adaptation rather than a millennium, several of them emerged as fully fledged religions and continue to function in supratribal contexts.

The earliest adaptive movement was the Handsome Lake religion of the Seneca, which developed at the same time that the Shawnee Prophet and Tecumseh were advocating a return to the old ways. Handsome Lake's teachings spread to all the Six Nations and became the religion known as the Long House religion, which still functions on the Six Nations Reserve in Canada. After the Revolution, the unity of the Iroquois League was broken, and its members suffered destruction, illness, population decline, alcoholism, and social pathology. Wallace (1970:194–201) refers to the conditions on the Seneca reservation after the Revolution as "slum conditions." Added to disease, population decline, and starvation during the harsh winters was the American policy of waging "total war" against the Iroquois, which included destruction of complete settlements and the loss of confidence in their ability to survive as a people.

Handsome Lake (Ganeodiyo), half-brother of Seneca chief Cornplanter, was an alcoholic who suffered from ill health, which culminated in a trance in June 1799, during which he was believed to have died. During his vision he was visited by four supernatural beings who gave him the *Gaiwiio*, or "Good Message," from the Creator. Three more visions gave him his gospel of three interrelated themes: the imminent destruction of the world by a great fire that would destroy the wicked; sin, the most serious of which was the failure to believe in the Good Message; and salvation through belief in the Good Message and adherence to its teachings and practices. Subsequent visions gave Handsome Lake a social or moral code that stressed temperance, peace, retention of tribal lands, selective acculturation, and domestic morality in daily life. Handsome Lake's teachings represented an adaptive syncretistic movement that utilized elements of both traditional Iroquois culture and Quaker elements of white culture, creating a new social system and a new religion that was adopted by all the Iroquois. After Handsome Lake's death, the Good Message was written down in the Code, which continues to be recited to the adherents of the religion and is still practiced by the tradition-oriented Iroquois on the Six Nations Reserve.

Another syncretism of native and Christian (Roman Catholic) elements was the Indian "Shaker" religion of the Pacific Northwest, so-called because of the bodily shaking of the head and arms during worship. Like Handsome Lake, the prophet John Slocum, a Squaxin Indian from the Puget Sound area, had turned to alcohol and gambling as an escape from reservation conditions in the late nineteenth century.

At the same time that the Ghost Dance was spreading through the western Plains, another religious movement was beginning. Although messianic, it also stressed adaptation to the changed cultural conditions of the Plains tribes and eventually evolved into a fully established religion, the American Indian Church, which involves the ingestion of peyote as a sacrament.

The small cactus peyote grows in the Rio Grande valley of Texas and farther south into Mexico. Ingestion results in sensory alterations, such as sensations of levitation, visions of brilliantly colored images, and enhanced perception of sounds and shapes to the point of hallucinations, with occasional nausea as the only negative side effect. The button is neither deleterious nor habit-forming (LaBarre 1959:7). The use of peyote by American Indians has been recorded among the Aztecs but is probably older. Before its introduction into the Plains area, peyote was used by tribes of northwestern Mexico; the Huichol and Tarahumara used it in a first-fruits ceremony in conjunction with shamanism. Its ritual use spread north to the Mescalero Apache in the 1870s where it was incorporated into the individualistic Apache search for power through visions. By the mid-1870s, peyote had reached the southern Plains Comanche and Kiowa, where it emerged as a collective syncretistic cult utilizing the therapeutic properties of peyote but stressing "the problems engendered by the relationship between the Indians and the whites" (Bee 1965:23). By the 1880s, the religion had begun its rapid diffusion throughout the Plains and eastern areas, where the degraded and deprived conditions of Indians made it a hope of adjustment to and acceptance of their changed circumstances.

The man credited with being the founder and chief promoter of the peyote religion was John Wilson, an Anadarko, Oklahoma, native of mixed Delaware, Caddo, and French ancestry (Hertzberg 1971:243–245; Lanternari 1963:69–72). Introduced to peyote in 1890 while attending a Ghost Dance at Darlington, Oklahoma, Wilson went into seclusion to study its effects on him and to analyze the revelations he experienced. During his visions, Wilson was taken to heaven, where he saw representations of different events in the life of Christ and the home of traditional Delaware beings; he also saw the "Peyote Road," a road leading from the open grave of Christ to the moon over which Christ had walked in order to reach his Father. By following the Peyote Road in their lives, believers could increase their knowledge until they reached the end of the journey—death—bringing them into the presence of Peyote and Christ. At the same time, Wilson received a body of moral and religious teachings, details of the ceremonial procedures to be followed, detailed instructions on the construction of the Peyote altar (crescent moon), paraphernalia to be used in the rituals, and the songs to be sung during the rituals (Aberle 1965:12–13; Lanternari 1963:69–71). Because Indians were not responsible for Christ's crucifixion, they did not need the Bible to receive God's truth but would receive it directly from the Peyote Spirit. The fact that peyotism was exclusively for Indians was an important factor in Indian opposition to whites and white policies (Lanternari 1963:71). The moral code was supported by supernatural sanctions. Those who followed the Peyote Road would find tranquillity in life and material goods and bliss in the next life; those who lapsed morally would suffer in the peyote meetings, both spiritually and physically, in the form of nausea (Aberle 1965:13).

As the religion spread, prophets appeared in other tribes, and the doctrine underwent modification in keeping with individual tribal traditions. Between 1900 and 1910, the religion had spread throughout the Plains, the Southwest, and the northern Woodland tribes. By 1918, when the peyote religion was incorporated as the American Indian Church, there were approximately 12,000 members. Today those numbers are greatly increased. Although the peyote religion originated in the Plains and contains many elements of Plains traditions, its spread can be attributed to a number of factors: it is a compromise between the old and the new; it is an "Indian" religion expressing the concept of brotherhood; the prohibition of alcohol cured many Indians of alcoholism; peyote was regarded as a panacea or "cure-all" for many things (one purpose of peyote meetings was curing); the hallucinatory vision experienced by eating peyote was in keeping with the Plains tradition of vision quests for spirit helpers (Hertzberg 1971:280–282).

TWENTIETH-CENTURY POLICIES

Twentieth-century federal Indian policy has fluctuated from efforts to assimilate Indian tribes to programs stressing Indian self-determination and some degree of autonomy. The lack of consistency in policy has contributed to a continuing sense of tribal and supratribal or "Indian" ethnic identity. In the early twentieth century, the disorganization in Indian communities could be attributed to such federal policies as allotment, forced school attendance, mandatory adherence to federal regulations, and prohibition of tribal ceremonies (Pueblos who held Kachina ceremonies were tried by a Court of Religious Offenses). The corruption, mismanagement, and prejudice typical of the Bureau of Indian Affairs, and Indian reactions to the loss of civil rights, prompted investigations by the government and private organizations. The 1922 Red Cross investigations of reservation health conditions and health care delivery revealed shocking conditions: death rates double those of the rest of the country and excessively high rates of diseases such as trachoma and tuberculosis. Additional investigations were triggered by the failed Indian Omnibus Bill in 1923, which focused on individualization of all remaining tribal lands and the withdrawal of all federal responsibility from Indian reservations. In 1924, legislation gave full citizenship to all Indians born in the United States, although some civil rights were withheld (Arizona Indians were denied the right to vote until 1948).

The Indian Reorganization Act.   The Roosevelt administration of the 1930s has been referred to as the "New Deal" for Indians. Directed by Commissioner of Indian Affairs John Collier, new policies and "new deals" resulted in legislation affecting education and tribal government. The 1934 Johnson-O'Malley Act allowed the federal government to contract with individual states to provide services to Indians, such as education (federal funds were given to individual school districts to take over Indian education), social welfare, health, and agricultural assistance. The most significant and far-reaching legislation of this era was the Indian Reorganization Act (Wheeler-Howard Bill), also passed in 1934, which was designed to stop the alienation (loss) of Indian lands, to authorize tribal organization, and to develop modern business opportunities, credit, and scholarships. Eventually all provisions of the act were extended to all tribes, including those in Alaska and Oklahoma.

The Indian Claims Commission.   In 1946, Congress created the Indian Claims Commission, which permitted Indian tribes to sue the federal government for a series of grievances, most of which concerned lands and treaty violations.

Tribes had five years to file their claims, and over a period of 10 to 15 years more than 800 separate causes of action were filed with about $400 million awarded in settlement. The government saw the court-type proceedings as final justification for withdrawal from "the Indian business" and termination of tribes.

Relocation. Included in the government's efforts to "get out of the Indian business" was the Voluntary Relocation Program, intended to ease economic pressures and unemployment on reservations (created by returning World War II veterans and defense workers) by relocating Indians and their families in major urban centers. After initial assistance in finding housing and jobs and providing financial assistance until the first paycheck, the Indians were on their own. Later, vocational training and social and welfare services were added to the program. Although relocation was not part of the termination policy, the two programs were linked in the minds of the Indian people.

Termination. U.S. government policy has always encouraged Indians to assimilate into the dominant society. Eventually long-lasting hostilities and resentments led the government to realize that assimilation could not be legislated, and the Indian Reorganization Act was passed in hopes that Indians could be assimilated by letting them use their own cultures as springboards and bases of integration into the dominant society. The 1940s and 1950s saw an emphasis on policies intended to end the federal government's responsibilities to Indian tribes through "termination," a policy that can be interpreted several ways. One branch of the federal government can turn its responsibilities over to another (transfer of the Bureau of Indian Affairs Division of Health to the U.S. Public Health Service); the Bureau of Indian Affairs may relinquish certain responsibilities to tribes; the Bureau may withdraw certain services usually provided to tribes; or states may be given authority to extend civil and criminal laws to reservations (Public Law 280), depriving the tribes of the powers of self-government. What usually is meant, though, is legislation severing the historic relationships between the federal government and the tribes, abolishing tribal governments, and placing tribal affairs and resources under state control.

The termination act, House Concurrent Resolution No. 108, was passed in 1953 for the "rapid freeing" of Indians from federal support and dependency. Each tribe to be terminated required special legislation. The first to be terminated were the Menominee of Wisconsin in 1954, and others followed: the Klamath in Oregon, smaller Oregon tribes, a mixed-blood Ute settlement, small Paiute bands in Utah, the Wyandotte, Peoria, Ottawa, California rancherias, the Catawba (South Carolina), and the Alabama-Coushatta of Texas. Termination was not a success. Conversion of the 234,000-acre Menominee reservation into a county meant that the Indians were responsible for road maintenance, utilities, sewer and water plants, and schools. Children were bused to white community schools, the Public Health Service hospital was closed, and all roads and utilities had to be improved to meet state standards. Because their one economic endeavor, a local sawmill operation, could not support the community and its people, the Menominee were forced to convert part of their land and lake area into a resort community, which was sold to whites. Still they were unable to meet all state requirements, and a grass-roots effort, supported by the state government and congressional representatives, actively sought restoration to tribal and reservation status. The Menominee Restoration Act was signed into law in October 1973, a landmark event reversing the termination policy that had been promoted so enthusiastically 20 years earlier. In 1992, the Catawba of South Carolina also were restored to federally recognized status.

Other legislation in the 1950s was intended to promote termination: Public Law 280 transferred civil jurisdiction to Minnesota, Nebraska,

Oregon, Wisconsin, and California; the Indian Health Service Branch was transferred to the U.S. Public Health Service in 1954; and 1953 legislation allowed state laws and tribal organizations to regulate the sale of liquor on reservations in conformity with state law.

Tribal Development. Although Congress did not recognize the failure of termination officially until 1973, the procedure ended as an official policy between 1960 and 1966 under Commissioner of Indian Affairs Phileo Nash, an anthropologist whose policies stressed economic and political development, relocation, education, and on-the-job training programs; many of these programs have been carried out by his successors, most of whom have been Indians. Tribal development focused on enhancing existing resources, tourism, and industry, and by 1965 approximately 56 industrial plants were located on or near reservations. Tourism was promoted among the North Carolina Cherokee and the White Mountain Apaches of Arizona, and mineral and timber operations have been significant among the Navajo, Laguna Pueblo, Klamath, and Red Lake Chippewa. Tribal farming and ranching and arts and crafts have been promoted among some tribes, and during the 1990s gaming became an important source of revenue for a number of tribes.

Late Twentieth-Century Legislation/Policy. During the administration of Lyndon Johnson, federal policy shifted from termination, officially repealed in 1988, to self-determination, a policy that has continued to the present, particularly evident in such late twentieth-century legislation as the Indian Self-Determination and Education Assistance Act (1975), which permitted tribes to administer their own federal programs if they desired. The American Indian Religious Freedom Act of 1978 was intended to provide constitutional protection of religious freedom under the First Amendment. But because the legislation failed to give Indians rights that could be enforced legally, this act is regarded as a policy statement. Passage of the Indian Child Welfare Act in 1978 ended the practice of placing Indian children in non-Indian homes for foster care, or adoption. In 1982, the Indian Tribal Governmental Status Act permitted tribal governments to issue bonds, and the 1990 American Indian Language Act reversed policies suppressing and exterminating Indian languages and cultures (Hirschfelder and de Montaño 1992).

Some legislation involved the settlement of land claims against the government: the Alaska Native Claims Settlement Act, passed in 1971 and amended in 1988; and the 1978 Maine Indian Claims Settlement Act, which also confirmed the recognition of the Passamaquoddy, Penobscot, and Houlton Band of Maliseet. Several tribes that were terminated in the 1950s were restored to federally recognized status. In 1983, the U.S. Seventh District Court of Appeals recognized the hunting, fishing, trapping, and gathering rights of the Lac Courte Oreilles Band of Chippewa Indians (Wisconsin), guaranteed in treaties in 1837, 1842, and 1854. Other acts restored sacred lands, objects, or treaty rights to tribes: in 1970, Blue Lake was returned the Taos Pueblo; Mount Adams was returned to the Yakima of Washington in 1972; and in 1974, treaty-guaranteed fishing rights were returned to 14 tribes in Washington, including the right to fish in off-reservation waters. In 1991, after passage of legislation in 1989 creating the Museum of the American Indian as part of the Smithsonian Institution (which also required the Smithsonian to return human remains to tribes requesting them), sacred objects taken from the Omaha in 1898 were returned by the Smithsonian and by the Peabody Museum of Harvard University, and the Smithsonian returned the skeletal remains of 756 Kodiak Islanders for reburial.

Of particular importance to a number of tribes were the 1988 Indian Gaming Regulatory Act and the Native American Indian Graves Protection and Repatriation Act (NAGPRA) passed in 1990. The Gaming Act created opportunities for economic development by permitting gaming on reservations of federally recognized tribes, especially important after budget cuts reduced tribal revenues. More than 50 tribes have compacts with states for one of three kinds of gaming: class I–social games with prizes of minimal value; class II–Bingo and similar kinds of gaming; and class III–dog and horse racing and casino-style games. The largest Indian gaming operation in the United States is the Mashuntucket Pequots' Foxwoods High Stakes Bingo and Casino in Ledyard, Connecticut. Under NAGPRA, museums or agencies receiving federal funding are required to inventory collections of Indian human remains, mortuary objects, sacred items, and materials of "cultural patrimony" and to return them to tribes requesting them (which had to prove tribal ownership). As tribes have reclaimed items of "cultural patrimony," a number of tribal museums have been developed to house them.

Not all legislation has had positive results. The Indian Arts and Crafts Act of 1992 was intended to protect American Indian arts from forgeries by requiring anyone selling arts and crafts as "Indian" to be on a tribal roll or "certified" as an Indian by some tribe. Many recognized Indian artists, particularly in Oklahoma, no longer can sell their art as "Indian" because they are not on a tribal roll; penalties are severe–fines of up to $1 million and 15 years imprisonment.

Some of the policies of the latter part of the twentieth century have their roots in the activism of the late 1960s and early 1970s (Bonney 1975; Day 1972; Steiner 1968). Beginning in 1958, armed Lumbees in Robeson County, North Carolina, broke up a Ku Klux Klan rally. In 1961, Indian leaders at the American Indian Chicago Conference, organized by anthropologist Sol Tax, created a "Declaration of Indian Purpose," a statement of Indian intent to retain spiritual and cultural values and to promote self-determination. A group of Indian college students, uninvited and excluded from the conference proceedings and frustrated with Bureau of Indian Affairs policies and the caution of the "Uncle Tomahawks" (tribal councils and other Indian leaders), met and formed the National Indian Youth Council at the Gallup Intertribal Ceremonial in 1961. Their policy of "red nationalism" and their tactics of direct action and civil disobedience emulated the sit-ins of the black civil rights movement, as did Iroquois Wallace "Mad Bear" Anderson, who took over the Six Nations' council house to protest the construction of a dam on the Tuscarora Reserve. Using revolution to accomplish their goals, they initiated a series of "fish-ins" protesting the violation of treaties signed by several Washington tribes that had ceded tribal lands in exchange for the right to fish in traditional, off-reservation fishing grounds.

The success of the Washington fish-ins and the sympathy of the dominant society set the stage for other "red power" actions (associated with Indian militants). The Mohawk demanded, and won, free admission to the 1964 New York World Fair in Flushing Meadows, New York, on the basis of their treaty of cession of that land in 1684; Isleta Pueblo in New Mexico evicted a Catholic priest in 1965 for interfering with and ridiculing traditional Pueblo practices; the Mohawk blocked the International Bridge between New York and Canada under the leadership of "Mad Bear" Anderson in 1965; and in 1967, Red Lake Chippewa Tribal Chairman Roger Jourdain protested a General Electric advertisement in *The Saturday Evening Post* saying, "When you decide to shoot wild Indians, you can't afford to miss." The Passamaquoddy in Maine stopped logging operations of the Georgia Pacific Company in 1968, and in 1969 set up a roadblock on U.S. Highway 1 protesting the state legislature's failure to provide funds for child welfare; the Quinault tribe closed 25 miles of their beaches in Washington to whites in protest of abuses of beach-use privileges; and the Fort Yuma Quechan seized Bureau of Reclamations equipment to regain lands.

Attention in the 1960s was focused on the seizure of the former federal penitentiary Alcatraz, in California, by a group of Indian students calling themselves Indians of All Tribes, under the 1868 Fort Laramie Sioux Treaty, which called for surplus federal lands to be returned to the Indians. They intended to create an Indian Cultural Center, Institute of American Indian Studies, research center, medical center, and a museum. The occupation ended in 1971 with the removal of the 15 Indians remaining on "the Rock" by armed federal marshals.

The American Indian Movement (AIM), founded in 1968 in Minneapolis, Minnesota, by young urban Ojibwa and Sioux, probably is the best-known red power organization. Initial concerns focused on local issues—discrimination against and harassment of Indian peoples and negative stereotypes. By 1970, however, membership had become national, drawing primarily from urban and disenfranchised rural communities, and the issues of Indian sovereignty and broken treaties became the focal point of AIM's efforts. The group's tactic of direct confrontation was first seen in sit-ins at Mount Rushmore in 1971 and 1972 and the seizure of the Chippewa Dam at Winter, Wisconsin, by the Lac Courte Oreilles Chippewa Band. National attention was drawn to AIM with the "Trail of Broken Treaties" and the occupation of the Bureau of Indian Affairs building in Washington, D.C., in November 1972, and with the 77-day occupation of the Pine Ridge Sioux community of Wounded Knee, South Dakota.

Wounded Knee was an expression of AIM's concern over Indian sovereignty and the validity of traditional forms of tribal government rather than those imposed by the Indian Reorganization Act. Originally, AIM members were invited to an open meeting at Wounded Knee to discuss tribal government and the Bureau by the Pine Ridge Civil Rights Organization, Sioux traditionalists who rejected official tribal government and protested the administration of tribal chairman Richard Wilson. Within hours, the village was barricaded by police roadblocks and cordons, but the seizure and occupation of the village by AIM was triggered by a beating of AIM leader Russell Means and AIM's desire to fight for the rights of all Indians. Wounded Knee, the site of a massacre in 1890, became the symbol of white injustice to Indians. After a 77-day siege, AIM leaders and federal officials signed an agreement to end the occupation; Wounded Knee defendants were indicted on a number of felony charges, and most defendants, tried in Sioux Falls, South Dakota, were convicted. The trials of seven AIM leaders, indicted on 11 charges, were held in Federal District Court in St. Paul, Minnesota, beginning in January 1974. AIM leaders Russell Means, Dennis Banks, and Clyde Bellecourt were acquitted. Since that time, AIM has concentrated on legal actions, including efforts to gain freedom for Leonard Peltier, convicted of the murder of two FBI agents in a shoot-out with Indians on the Pine Ridge Sioux reservation in 1975.

AMERICAN INDIANS TODAY

As we move into the twenty-first century, Indian ethnic identity appears to be stronger than ever, usually focused on specific tribal identities reinforced by legislation, shared historical events and relationships, and participation in both traditional and pan-Indian organizations and activities. The definition of "Indian" is not precise. Dictionary definitions usually refer to aboriginal inhabitants of the New World based on European explorers' beliefs that they had found Asia or the Indies; census definitions tend to be based on self-ascription rather than biological or genetic determination. Persons who are less than one-fourth "Indian"—the usual "blood" requirement—must be accepted as "Indians" by the community. Mixed stock refers to the non-Indian parent as white; mixed Indian and black generally are considered black unless Indian characteristics predominate or they are accepted as Indians by the Indian community.

Eligibility for Bureau of Indian Affairs services requires residence within or adjacent to reservations or trust or restricted lands receiving *direct* Bureau services. Membership in federally recognized tribes—those with reservations and receiving federal services—requires one-fourth degree of Indian ancestry. Tribal rules for inclusion on tribal rolls vary, from one-sixteenth degree of Indian ancestry among the Cherokee to tribes requiring one Indian parent (one-half degree). Most "recognized" or "federal" Indians are in the West, where first European contacts were sporadic and later in time than those in the East, where they were able to maintain their territorial base and their languages. Acculturation and cultural borrowing were selective, usually connected to material culture and economy. Recognized Indians receive federal services through the Bureau of Indian Affairs, the branch of government within the Department of the Interior responsible for carrying out federal programs authorized by Congress, acting as trustee for Indian lands and resources, and creating a climate in which Indian groups can operate by and for themselves. The commissioner of Indian Affairs, a presidential political appointment confirmed by the Senate, oversees all Bureau functions, including education, welfare programs, employment, tribal development, and financial assistance.

During the nineteenth century Indian education was in the hands of missionary groups that received federal money to run the Indian schools with the long-range goal of assimilation. The first off-reservation government-run Indian schools were opened, reinforcing policies of allotment and assimilation; the military academy atmosphere of Carlisle Institute in Pennsylvania served as a model for Indian education of the time. From 1890 to the 1930s, on-reservation boarding and day schools continued to strive for assimilation, hiring non-Indian teachers who conducted all classes in English. The National Study of Indian Education (1955), under the direction of Estelle Fuchs and Robert Havighurst, investigated conditions in seven cate-

gories of Indian schools and resulted in the passage of the Indian Education Act of 1972. This act was not only to improve educational opportunities and programs on reservations but to make federal money available for special programs for nonreservation and "unrecognized" Indian children in public school systems, as well as for adult education in both on- and off-reservation communities.

The latter part of the twentieth century saw an increase in Indian control over the education of their children through Indian-controlled school boards (the Navajo Nation's Rough Rock Demonstration School teaches a curriculum chosen by the community in both English and Navajo), the growth of a number of Indian magnet schools that focus on multicultural education, and of tribal colleges, such as Navajo Community College and Sint'e Gleska University at Rosebud, South Dakota. These schools stress native values and ways of learning rather than the competition and individualism of the public school systems.

Members of recognized tribes also receive medical care through the Indian Health Service, which was transferred to the U.S. Public Health Service in the 1950s. Reservations clinics, health stations, or hospitals provide medical care to reservation Indians that is unavailable to urban Indians. Although health care has improved since the 1960s, Indian life expectancy tends to be below the national average. While they no longer suffer from some of the epidemics of the past (influenza, measles, whooping cough, diphtheria, and tuberculosis, one of the major killers), Indian health problems reflect social and economic conditions, especially alcohol and drug abuse. Primary causes of death include heart disease and cancer (both have increased since the 1960s), diabetes, influenza, pneumonia, and cirrhosis (high in the past and remaining high), as well as accidents (often related to alcohol), suicide, and homicide. The incidence of disease depends on environmental conditions, economic status, educational level, and traditional attitudes, all of which contribute to practices related to nutrition, cleanliness, health consciousness, and the availability of and demand for medical services. Medical facilities are not available to geographically isolated communities, few medical care providers are Indian, speak Indian languages, or understand Indian cultures and values. Most doctors stay for only a brief time, so there is little continuity. Also, Western medicine is not the holistic medicine to which Indians are accustomed.

"Unrecognized" Indians include those who relinquished their rights to government services and their reservations, such as urban Indians, and terminated Indians, but the term usually refers to tribes, primarily along the eastern seaboard, who have never been under Bureau control but who have maintained Indian and tribal identities and, sometimes, ceremonies. Among such groups are the Lumbee, Coharie, Haliwa, and Tuscarora of North Carolina, the Narragansett of New England, small enclaves in Virginia, and the Houma of Louisiana. Early European contact led to loss of land, intermarriage, acculturation, mixed ancestry, and rural enclavement as they sought to retain their Indian identity. Many of their ancestors fought in the Revolution and are referred to in the 1790 census as "free persons of color," distinguishing them from black slaves. Until the 1830s they could own property, vote, serve in the militia, and, in the South, own slaves. But then they were disenfranchised. Denied the right to self-government, and segregated and discriminated against as "colored," and despite the loss of cultures, languages, religions, and social organizations, they retained a sense of "Indian" identity, separate from blacks and whites. For many, one of the primary boundary-maintaining mechanisms was education: denied the right to attend white schools and the right to "Indian" schools, they were forced to send their children to black ("colored") schools. Opposed to ascription of a "colored" identity, they chose not to send their children to public school and attempted to open

"Indian" schools. The University of North Carolina at Pembroke began as the Lumbee Indian Normal School in 1887.

Many of the unrecognized groups have sought or are seeking recognition or acknowledgment through the Bureau of Indian Affairs. Between 1830 and 1970, recognition required the tribe to have existed as a "distinct political community"—a social group distinct from non-Indians—and that the federal government had taken actions acknowledging the political relationship with and responsibility for the tribe (Roth 2001).

Many of the unrecognized Indians in urban areas had left the reservations to improve their economic situations. As early as 1928, Indians were recognized as living in urban areas and were covered in a special chapter of the Meriam Report. Many of these early migrants to urban centers were assimilated into the dominant society as they internalized its values. Their descendants often do not identify themselves as "Indians," nor are they considered such by reservation Indians. The first government effort to relocate Indians in urban areas occurred after World War II when about 75,000 Navajos and Hopis who had served in the armed forces or had been employed in off-reservation war industries returned to their reservations and were unable to find jobs.

In 1952, the program, now called the Voluntary Relocation Program, was expanded to include other tribes. Intended to teach Indians to be self-sufficient in urban areas, the program provided a range of services for relocatees and their families, including selection of the relocation point, finding temporary and permanent housing for the applicant and his family, financial assistance for transportation and subsistence en route to the destination and until the relocatee received his first paycheck, and follow-up services to relocatees and their families. Major relocation points included Chicago, Los Angeles, Denver, San Francisco, St. Louis, Oakland, and Dallas.

Though the program ended in 1980, the number of Indians living in urban centers in some cases exceeds that of Indians on reservations; more than 50 percent of the total Indian population today is urban. Adjustment to urban life was difficult for a tradition- and kin-oriented people, and problems such as returning to home communities (and losing jobs) and alcohol abuse were pervasive in some urban communities (Graves 1970; Price 1968). Urban Indian centers were established to provide services—economic, social, educational, and recreational—to relocated Indians. Powwows became an important feature of many urban Indian centers as a way of allowing Indians to express and reaffirm their ethnic identity.

Originally the word *powwow* was used to refer to New England Algonkian community gatherings for political deliberations and feasting around large fires (Wissler 1954:62–63). Today it refers to secular intertribal gatherings found across the country, ranging from large intertribal ceremonies, sometimes organized by chambers of commerce as tourist attractions (the Gallup, New Mexico, Intertribal Ceremonial) or by mixed Indian and non-Indian committees (All American Indian Days at Sheridan, Wyoming), to small annual reservation or community social events held in the summer and urban center powwows. The latter may be held monthly throughout the year, though they tend to be more common during the winter months when there are no reservation powwows to attend.

Modern powwows evolved out of the early Plains reservation culture as Indians attempted to reorganize and stabilize community life by providing opportunities for socializing and singing and dancing in the old "Indian" style—reasserting their Indianness—as well as escaping temporarily from acculturation pressures. The modern focus on such Plains traits as singing, dancing, and regalia is a result of the Wild West and Indian medicine shows, which usually featured Plains Indians. Powwows focus on competitive dancing, the primary form being the "war dance," an amalgamation of northern and southern tribal styles (Powers 1968). Underlying the "fast" or "fancy" war dance, performed by young men, with its fancy footwork, abrupt posture changes, and quick spins and dips, is an older form dating to the 1870s, referred to as the "classic" style and usually danced by older men. Dance styles continually evolve and spread throughout Indian Country, including the newer "jingle dancing" from the northern Plains and the women's shawl dance, which involves intricate footwork similar to that of the men's fast war dance.

Although there are regional variations, certain features are central to powwows: dancers, regalia, singers and drummers, competitions (a way to win honor and recognition), dances honoring veterans and other individuals, giveaways, tipi encampments, feasting, and social dances in which everyone may participate. Although non-Indians may participate in powwows if they are dressed in the appropriate regalia, powwows are primarily an Indian activity.

CONCLUSIONS

Instead of being assimilated into the mainstream of U.S. culture, today the American Indians seem to be in a strong position of ethnic survival, their ethnic identity strengthened by the very policies intended to assimilate them by placing them in positions where they were forced to resist and to oppose the federal government and its policies. Reservation and removal policies reinforced geographic isolation, and their status as wards of a paternalistic government enhanced social isolation and dependency, further separating them from the mainstream of American culture. The lack of consistency in federal policy has increased their resistance to assimilation, and recent legislation only reinforces their separate ethnic identity. The Indian Arts and Crafts Bill, NAGPRA, Indian gaming—all make Indian identity something to be desired, whether on a tribal (federally recognized) or individual level.

Despite different tribal backgrounds, most American Indians share common historical experiences that bind them together in a shared identity of "Indian," a situational supratribal identity that supersedes tribal identities. Milton Gordon, in *Assimilation in American Life* (1964), referred to identity systems as a series of concentric rings around a person's "core" identity. For Indians, this can be a layered identity encompassing core identity to kinship to tribal to Indian to American. Within the tribal community, identity is based on kinship connections; in a supratribal situation, identity may be tribal, but in the larger outside world, where tribal distinctions are not recognized by the general public, an Indian identity is assumed—always a distinct identity separate from mainstream America. For many the important part of that identity is "Indian"; one AIM leader said he preferred to be called an "Indian American" than an "American Indian." The important part of his identity was the Indian component, not the American.

Ethnic awareness and pride are expressed in the revival of traditional arts and crafts, participation in supratribal events such as powwows or in "Indian" religions, such as the American Indian Church, and identification with "Indian" symbols. This awareness and pride are evident in the increased efforts of a number of eastern tribes to gain acknowledgment. As tribal or ethnic groups, American Indians have resisted assimilation for four hundred years, and, though statistically a small percentage of the overall population, they remain strong—at least two hundred distinct ethnic groups.

NOTE

1. Indian lands are held in three types of title: *fee simple* (the full range of landownership giving individuals full title to the land, which can be sold or willed to others); *trust* (the land is held in trust for the Indians, who use it in perpetuity and must be compensated if it is taken away; lands cannot be taxed, sold, mortgaged, or leased without government consent); and *restricted* (may be subject to taxation but cannot be sold or leased without federal permission). Although individual Indians own land in all three classes, most prefer trust status, which provides the most protection.

REFERENCES CITED

ABERLE, DAVID. 1965. "The peyote religion among the Navajo. *Viking Fund Publications in Anthropology*, no. 42.

BARBER, BERNARD. 1941. Acculturation and messianic movements. *American Sociological Review* 6:662–667. Reprinted in William A. Lessa and Evon Z. Vogt, eds., *Reader in Comparative Religion*. Pp. 474–477. Evanston, IL: Row, Peterson, 1958.

BARTH, FREDRIK. 1969. *Ethnic Groups and Boundaries: The Social Organization of Culture Difference*. Boston: Little, Brown.

BEE, ROBERT L. 1965. Peyotism in North American Indian groups. *Transactions of the Kansas Academy of Science* 68(1):13–61.

BONNEY, RACHEL A. 1975. "Forms of supratribal Indian interaction in the United States." Ph.D. dissertation, University of Arizona, Tucson.

DAY, ROBERT C. 1972. The emergence of activism as a social movement. In *American Indians Today: Sociological Perspectives*, Howard M. Bahr, Bruce A. Chardwick, and Robert C. Day, eds. Pp. 506–532. New York: Harper & Row.

EGGLESTON, EDWARD. 1878. *Tecumseh and the Shawnee Prophet*. New York: Dodd, Mead.

FAGAN, BRIAN M. 1999. *Ancient North America: The Archaeology of a Continent*. 3rd edition. New York: Thames and Hudson.

GARBARINO, MERWYN S. 1976. *American Indian Heritage*. Boston: Little, Brown.

GORDON, MILTON M. 1964. *Assimilation in American Life: The Role of Race, Religion, and National Origins*. New York: Oxford University Press.

GRAVES, THEODORE D. 1970. The personal adjustment of Navajo Indian migrants to Denver, Colorado. *American Anthropologist* 72(1):35–54.

HERTZBERG, HAZEL. 1971. *The Search for an American Indian Identity: Modern Pan-Indian Movements*. Syracuse, NY: Syracuse University Press.

HIRSCHFELDER, ARLENE, and MARTHA KREIPE DE MONTAÑO. 1992. *The American Indian Almanac: A Portrait of Native America Today*. New York: Macmillan.

HODGE, WILLIAM H. 1981. *The First Americans: Then and Now*. New York.: Holt, Rinehart, & Winston.

HUDSON, CHARLES E. 1976. *The Southeastern Indians*. Knoxville: University of Tennessee Press.

HUNTER, CHARLES E. 1971. The Delaware nativist revival

of the mid-eighteenth century." *Ethnohistory* 18(1):39–49.

JOSEPHY, ALVIN M., JR. 1991. *The Indian Heritage of America.* Boston: Houghton Mifflin.

KEHOE, ALICE B. 1992. *North American Indians: A Comprehensive Account.* 2nd edition. Englewood Cliffs, NJ: Prentice Hall.

LABARRE, WESTON. 1959. The peyote cult. *Yale University Publications in Anthropology,* no. 16. New Haven, CT: Yale University Press.

LANTERNARI, VITTORIO. 1963. *The Religions of the Oppressed: A Study of Modern Messianic Cults.* New York: Knopf.

LURIE, NANCY O. 1971. Indian cultural adjustment to European civilization. In *The American Indian: Past and Present.* Roger L. Nichols and George R. Adams, eds. Pp. 42–60. Waltham, MA: Xerox College Publishing.

MOONEY, JAMES. 1896. The Ghost Dance religion and the Sioux outbreak of 1890. *14th Annual Report, Bureau of American Ethnology.* Pp. 666–667. Washington, DC. Abridged edition, Anthony F. C. Wallace, ed. Chicago: University of Chicago Press, 1965.

POWERS, WILLIAM K. 1968. Diffusion of the Plains war dance. *Powwow Trails* 5(6):68–72.

PRICE, JOHN A. 1968. The migration and adaptation of American Indians to Los Angeles. *Human Organization* 27(2):168–175.

ROTH, GEORGE. 2001. Law and the Southeastern Indians. In *Anthropologists and Indians in the New South.* Rachel A. Bonney and J. Anthony Paredes, eds. Tuscaloosa: University of Alabama Press.

SLOTKIN, J. S. 1955. The Peyote way. *Tomorrow* 4(3):64–70. Reprinted in William A. Lessa and Evon Z. Vogt, eds., *Reader in Comparative Religion.* Pp. 482–486. Evanston, IL: Row, Peterson, 1958.

SPICER, EDWARD H. 1969. *A Short History of the Indians of the United States.* New York: Van Nostrand Reinhold.

___. 1971. Persistent cultural systems. *Science* 174:795–800.

STEINER, STAN. 1968. *The New Indians.* New York: Harper & Row.

SWANTON, JOHN R. 1928. Social organization and social usages of the Indians of the Creek Confederacy. *Bureau of American Ethnology Annual Report 42.* Pp. 23–472. Washington, DC: Smithsonian Institution.

___. 1952. The Indian tribes of North America. *Bureau of American Ethnology Bulletin 145.* Washington, DC: Smithsonian Institution.

UNDERHILL, RUTH. 1953. *Red Man's America.* Chicago: University of Chicago Press.

WALLACE, ANTHONY F .C. 1956. Revitalization movements. *American Anthropologist* 58:264–281.

___. 1970. *The Death and Rebirth of the Seneca.* New York: Knopf.

WAX, MURRAY L. 1971. *Indian Americans: Unity and Diversity.* Englewood Cliffs, NJ: Prentice Hall.

WISSLER, CLARK. 1954. *Indians of the United States: Four Centuries of Their History and Culture.* Garden City, NY: Doubleday.

8

AFRICAN AMERICANS

Susan Love Brown

Florida Atlantic University

This chapter will explore the development of African American culture within the context of American history. African Americans constitute about 13 percent of the population of the United States, or about 34.5 million people, making them the largest minority group in the country as the twenty-first century began. Contrary to general perceptions fostered by the media, most African Americans are working class and middle class; however, around 27 percent of all African Americans do live below the poverty level (U.S. Census Bureau 1999).

People of African descent have been involved in the discovery, peopling, and building of civilization in North America for as long as Europeans, and although most of them are the descendants of slaves and have suffered many indignities in the course of their history, they have also left a legacy of fighting for civil rights and achievements in all areas of life. African Americans have been major contributors to American culture through their labor, language, and artistic creations, all of which had roots in African culture. However, because of the particular power of racism in North America, African

Americans have often been misrepresented and misunderstood (see Smedley 1999).

African American ethnicity involves a great deal of diversity, for people of African descent continue to immigrate to the United States from countries in Africa, the West Indies, and South America. And from the beginning, African Americans have interacted with people from Spain, England, Holland, and France, as well as many Native American groups, and in doing so have created new cultural features. If we look at the beliefs, values, and norms that broadly define African American culture, we find that the focus is on the importance of family, the centrality of religious beliefs, and the struggle for freedom. However, these and other African American cultural assumptions have been fashioned by particular physical environments, social circumstance, and experiences.

African Americans were the only people brought to the North American continent unwillingly in large numbers, subsequently enslaved for two hundred years, and then subjected to a state-imposed system of racial apartheid that effectively deprived them of all their civil liberties and set up a racial caste system that still affects American society today. These circumstances must be taken into consideration in any attempt to understand African American ethnicity.

THE GREAT DEBATE OVER THE PAST OF AFRICAN AMERICANS

For a long time people did not recognize any contributions from African culture at all, either to African American culture specifically or to American culture generally. In fact, African Americans were considered an inferior caste, not simply because they were slaves from "uncivilized" societies, but because whites and some blacks believed they had been deprived of any culture of their own and had had to adopt an ill-fitting European culture, making them less than adequate as people. This, however, turned out to be a false assumption.

Melville Herskovits, an anthropologist and a student of Franz Boas, referred to these beliefs as "the myth of the Negro past," embodying five points that seemed to support the case for Negro inferiority:

1. Blacks were childlike and adaptable to many situations, including slavery.
2. Those Africans enslaved were the less intelligent members of the community—those unclever enough to get caught.
3. The regional diversity of slaves meant that there was no common cultural background among them.
4. Any residual African traits would have been so inferior that the slaves would have given them up in favor of superior European customs.
5. "The Negro is thus a man without a past."[1]

Herskovits set out to systematically disprove these contentions by bringing to bear his knowledge of African culture and its retention by people of African descent in the United States. The claims of Herskovits brought him into direct opposition to sociologist E. Franklin Frazier, who, following an assimilationist model, contended that hardly any African culture remained, a condition that strongly disadvantaged blacks in the United States. For example, in his *The Negro Family in the United States,* originally published in 1939, Frazier wrote:

> Probably never before in history has a people been so nearly completely stripped of its social heritage as the Negroes who were brought to America. Other conquered races have continued to worship their household gods within the intimate circle of their kinsmen. But American slavery destroyed household gods and dissolved the bonds of sympathy and affection between men of the same blood and household. Old men and women might have brooded over memories of their African homeland, but they could not change the world about them. Through force of circumstances, they had to acquire a new language, adopt new habits of labor, and take over, however imperfectly, the folkways of the American environment. Their children, who knew only the American environment, soon forgot the few memories that had been passed on to them and developed motivations and modes of behavior in harmony with the New World. . . . But, of the habits and customs as well as the hopes and fears that characterized the life of their forebearers in Africa, nothing remains. [1966:15]

Frazier's erroneous conclusions were a consequence of not understanding the nature of culture and its durability (see Strauss and Quinn 1997) and his lack of familiarity with the depth of African culture and the way in which culture is transmitted. In *The Myth of the Negro Past,* originally published in 1941, Herskovits presented detailed evidence demonstrating the presence of African cultural features among Americans of African descent, including retentions in music, dancing, and religious beliefs and practices. For example, West African cultures contributed musical elements that resulted in the creation of jazz, an African American musical form (Maultsby 1990), and the East African bardic tradition became the origin of the blues (Ottenheimer 1992).

Herskovits was not the only scholar to take issue with the myth. African American scholars, such as Carter G. Woodson and W. E. B. Du Bois, wrote books challenging the myth. Woodson, who was the first descendant of a slave to receive a Ph.D. in 1912 and also the founder of the Association for the Study of Negro Life and History and the originator of Black History Week (the precursor of Black History Month), wrote in *The African Background Outlined:*

> This elementary treatment of the African background of the Negro, together with brief outlines for the study of the race in the modern world, is intended to stimulate greater interest in this field. Hitherto most Europeans and practically all Americans have regarded the Negro merely as an undesirable—an undeveloped person constituting a problem in not being able to keep pace with others. The facts herein presented will show that the Negro has achieved much in various spheres, and to know the possibilities of the race a scientific appraisal of its past is necessary. The author considers the Negro as human—responding very much as others do to the same stimuli, advancing when free to go forward and lagging behind when hindered by obstacles not encountered by others. [1936:v]

W. E. B. Du Bois, the first African American to receive a Ph.D., wrote *Black Folk: Then and Now* in 1939 in which he also attempted to give depth to African and African American history. All three of these scholars spoke of the African cultural heritage of African Americans at a time when such a heritage was denied.

Herskovits, who had done fieldwork in Africa, the Caribbean, and the United States, was in a position to have seen the cultural similarities among peoples of African descent in Africa and the Americas, and was able to establish that African culture had not been lost, although it had been many times transformed. In North America, where Africans were in the minority (unlike many Caribbean societies), it often appeared that African culture had disappeared and been replaced by European culture. But it is wise to remember that even European cultures were transformed in the new environment (for example, see Sobel 1987).

Today, we would not assume that a people moving from one area to another as adults had lost their culture. It is not easy to divest a people of their culture, which is largely unconscious and very persistent and tends to reassert itself in form if not in content (Strauss and Quinn 1997). In fact, many elements of African cultures have worked their way into mainstream American culture but go largely unnoticed (Philips 1990; Thompson 1990). Nor would we assume that cultures remain unchanged in new environments. Just as Europeans became various kinds of Americans, so did African Americans. To what degree aspects of African culture have been retained, either in form or substance, is a matter for empirical study. But what is certain is that people from Africa forged and continued to forge new cultures in America (Mintz and Price 1976). It is these diverse cultures, bound together by the common experience of slavery and the struggle for freedom, that defines African American ethnicity.

This chapter will explore the development of African American culture within the American racial context and the diversity within that experience. We can think of the formation of African American culture as the result of a three-step process that involved (1) the adaptation of Africans from different groups to each other, (2) the adaptation of African cultural understandings to a new environment, and (3) the interaction of these understandings with those of other groups in North America, including Europeans and Native Americans. These factors varied greatly across geography and time, which makes African American culture exceedingly diverse.

Like that of most American ethnic groups, the story of African Americans begins elsewhere. We, therefore, begin in Africa, the point of origin of all human life and peoples, examining the specific areas from which most Africans came. Since it is not possible to give a full accounting in the space allowed, we will broadly sketch the origins of Africans coming to North America.

THE AFRICAN ROOTS OF AFRICAN AMERICAN CULTURE

From the beginning of the slave trade to the end, approximately 10 million to 12 million men, women, and children were taken from the continent of Africa to the Americas. Of these, approximately a half-million ended up on the North American continent in what was to become the United States. The most immediate history and culture can be traced primarily to West Africa and Central Africa with minor populations from East Africa as well. Joseph Holloway notes that "although the West Africans arrived in North America in greater numbers, the Bantu of Central Africa had the largest homogeneous culture among the imported Africans and the strongest impact on the development of African-American culture" (1990:1–2).

Slaves destined for the new world came from settlements near the Atlantic coast of Africa, primarily from areas today known as Guinea-Bissau, Gambia, Senegal, Sierra Leone, Liberia, Ivory Coast, Ghana, Togo, Benin, and Nigeria in West Africa and from the Congo and Angola in Central Africa. It is important to remember that each of these areas encompassed multiple ethnic groups; however, many of these groups had some common cultural features, so that in spite of the diversity of African slaves, they also had a common cultural background.

Africans emphasized the extended family based on lineage systems in which either the father's line (patrilineal) or mother's line (matrilineal) was recognized, along with the preeminence of the mother-child bond and sibling bonds. Women often ruled beside men as queen mothers in West African societies and were skilled farmers. They also ran West African local markets, while men handled long-distance trade. Thus, African women were full participants in

economic life. Africans had well-developed oral and storytelling traditions different from those of Europeans, and these would form the basis of a new folklore in North America. African education emphasized the use of memory, and Africans had developed sophisticated political and religious systems, as well as elaborate musical traditions and instruments.

The people of West Africa and Central Africa were experienced farmers and cattle herders. In fact, Leonard Liggio (1976) has argued that African slaves were sought specifically for their agricultural expertise. Africans brought to America included those skilled at iron smelting (blacksmithing) and textile manufacture (for example, cotton). There were also skilled artisans who worked in gold and silver and carvers of wood, who participated in elaborate markets on a regular basis. The peoples of sub-Saharan Africa had long engaged in trade and cultural exchange with those from North Africa, the Middle East, Europe, and Asia. They were not the primitive peoples that many early scholars portrayed. In fact, Africans had been present in Europe, especially Spain, for a long time when colonization of the Americas began.

PEOPLE OF AFRICAN DESCENT IN THE COLONIES

Africans accompanied various European expeditions to the New World, coming initially from Europe. For example, in 1492 Pedro Alonzo Nino, believed to have been of African descent, accompanied Christopher Columbus on his first voyage to the Americas, as did Juan las Canarias, who traveled on the *Santa Maria*. Balboa, during his discovery of the Pacific, had 30 men of African descent with him. Another black, Estevanico, explored the southwestern part of the North American continent from Mexico to Arizona in 1538. Thus, people of African descent were always present (albeit sometimes in small numbers) as both slave and free persons (see Deagan and MacMahon 1995:9; Mabunda 1997:3; Singleton and Bograd 1995:5).

Slavery had existed in Spain and Portugal long before exploration of the Americas began, but it did not generate the kind of racism that was to arise in North America (see Smedley 1999). The decision to import slave labor to the New World came at the impetus of Bartolomé de Las Casas, who felt sorry for the Native American populations devastated because of their lack of immunity to Old World diseases. He recommended to Charles V, king of Spain, that Africans be used as slaves. Africans had been exposed to the same diseases as Europeans and were experienced farmers. Thus, African populations became the basis for the plantation agriculture that flourished in North and South America and the Caribbean.

In 1526, the first Africans who arrived on the shores of what was to become the United States were brought by Spanish explorers to settle the area. According to Deagan and MacMahon (1995:16), they accompanied Vásquez de Allyón to what today is Georgia. The one hundred black laborers rebelled and many joined Native Americans, abandoning the unsuccessful attempt to colonize North America. In 1528, Esteban, "gunbearer, scout, slave and soldier," made his way to Florida but died ten years later in the southwest of the North American continent. At least three Africans accompanied Coronado to the New World in 1540, one of whom was a free person who acted as an interpreter (Deagan and MacMahon 1995:12). Blacks from the West Indies, South America, and Africa peopled Spanish Florida, where the oldest North American city, St. Augustine, was home to both slaves and free blacks. Kathleen Deagan and Darcie MacMahon estimate that they accounted for 10 percent of the population there (1995:16). Indeed, the first legally established African American town, Fort Mosé, was founded in 1738 in Florida.

In 1619, the Dutch brought 20 indentured servants of African descent to Jamestown, Virginia. Although indenture is a temporary state of servitude, it represented the beginnings of the slave trade in what was to become the United States. Most scholars agree that slavery came gradually upon the colonies as more and more restrictions were visited upon black indentured servants, separating them from their white counterparts, lengthening their terms of service, and extending the conditions to their offspring.

SLAVE AND FREE: THE FORMATION OF AFRICAN AMERICAN CULTURE, 1619–1863

Slavery was practiced throughout the colonies before the American Revolution, even in the North, largely due to a shortage of white laborers. Slaves were imported into the New England colonies throughout the seventeenth century by English settlers, but the first colony to legalize slavery was Massachusetts in 1641. Maryland passed a law in 1663 making all imported Africans slaves. In 1670, Virginia passed a law denying the right to vote to freed slaves and indentured servants and designated all imported persons permanent slaves (Mabunda 1997:4, 5; Quarles 1964:33–38; Singleton and Bograd 1995:7–8).

In spite of the presence of slavery in all of the colonies, there were those who disapproved of the institution. The first antislavery resolution in North America was signed in 1688 by Mennonites in Germantown, Pennsylvania. The Quakers, another religious sect in Pennsylvania, also objected to slavery and threatened to expel any of their members who were found importing slaves. In fact, Pennsylvania actually moved to forbid slavery in that colony but was prevented from doing so by the English government (Mabunda 1997:5).

By 1700, about 28,000 slaves were in the colonies, about 5,000 in the North and 23,000 in the South, and many colonies had passed fugitive slave laws and other laws, more clearly defining the role of slaves in society. New York had more slaves than any other colony but South Carolina, and slaves were responsible for building much of New York City. African Americans recovered from a burial ground uncovered in the late twentieth century and studied by biological anthropologist Michael Blakey and his team at Howard University, revealed much about the status of those blacks. Likewise, it has come to light recently that blacks, both slave and free, participated in the design of the District of Columbia (Washington, DC) and even the building of the Capitol. By 1714, the number of slaves in the colonies had multiplied to 59,000, growing to around 263,000 in 1754. This growth was spurred by the development of tobacco and rice agriculture and the continuing need for laborers. At the beginning of the Revolutionary War, more than half the slaves in the colonies were located in Virginia.

There were also eighteenth-century slave rebellions, and these led to repressive laws that affected both slaves and free people of color. For example, in 1723 Virginia denied free blacks the right to vote or carry weapons, and in 1740 South Carolina passed codes that prevented African Americans from owning and raising livestock. On the other hand, colonies also enacted laws to protect slaves from ill treatment. There were even attempts at emancipation in the South as, for instance, when Thomas Jefferson attempted to enact a law for the emancipation of slaves in 1769 in the Virginia House of Burgesses.

In 1775, on the eve of the American Revolution, the Continental Congress barred blacks from participating in the army at the same time that the first abolitionist society was founded. On the other hand, Lord Dunmore, the royal governor of Virginia, offered freedom to those slaves who fought for the English, forcing General George Washington to change his mind and recruit blacks for service on his side (Mabunda 1997:6–7). Thus, before the American Revolution, the institution of slavery was still in its founding stages and attitudes toward blacks were ambivalent, even in the North.

In spite of their lofty ideals founded on individual liberty, the men who wrote the Constitution founding the United States of America did not resolve the contradiction that slavery presented them. Instead, they allowed the institution to prevail, setting up the conditions for a century of racial strife, including a devastating civil war and a racial ideology set deeply into American culture (see Smedley 1999). With the invention of the cotton gin in 1793 and the growing market for cotton, the economic incentive to maintain the institution of slavery was redoubled.

By 1804, all of the northern states had taken steps to eliminate slavery, and it remained a thriving legal entity only in the southern states (Nash 1983). By 1807, the slave trade had been prohibited in the United States, although not slavery itself, and much illegal importation of slaves took place. Benjamin Quarles estimated that as many as 5,000 slaves per year were illegally imported (1964:64). From this point on, the North and South would take divergent paths with regard to African Americans, but the ongoing racial ideology in the South would affect the general reception of African Americans within U.S. society as a whole.

The defense of slavery and of the white, southern way of life became the basis of American racism and the foundation for "the myth of the Negro past." As Audrey Smedley (1999) has pointed out, the racial caste system first characterized by slavery and then by racial segregation laws was unique to North America. Southern whites developed an elaborate justification for the institution, reinforced by federal, state, and local law. Slavery was an inhumane and immoral system that contradicted the very basis upon which the United States of America had been founded, but its edicts became deeply ingrained in the American consciousness as a consequence, and many persist to this day.

Even so, it is useful in understanding African

American culture if we look at enslaved blacks as real people with everyday lives, as members of families, as laborers and producers, as people with creative faculties like any other people, and as problem solvers. While slavery generally left little latitude for blacks, it nevertheless offered some choice in its varied environments and conditions, and blacks often created more choice than circumstances seemed to allow. Thus, slaves exercised a certain amount of self-determination and were active agents in their own lives.

For example, in the North before the Revolutionary War many slaves were skilled craftsmen, often acquiring the ability to read and write in order to work as clerks or in the printing industry. And Quakers, through the administration of religious education, constituted a major source of learning for blacks. Reading and writing were considered prerequisites to freedom. Rhode Island, which had more slaves than any other New England colony, required the children of slaves to learn to read and write (Quarles 1964:41–43). In the South, blacks constituted about 80 percent of the skilled labor and even developed a "vernacular architecture" based on designs from Africa and used in various plantation buildings, including smokehouses, icehouses, and other structures such as shotgun houses (Deetz 1996:212–252; Jones 1985: 200–207).

Living conditions for slaves varied according to crops and locations and the attitudes of the slave owners. Contrary to popular belief, plantation slavery was not typical in North America. According to Philip D. Curtin, the American South came to plantation life only in the eighteenth century and varied considerably from its Caribbean counterparts (see also Morgan 1998; Singleton 1985). Whereas the lucrative sugar plantations of the Caribbean had majorities that were black (both slave and free), southern plantations (with the exception of South Carolina) had majorities that were white who worked side by side with blacks. Curtin also noted that "even

in the 1850s, when slavery reached its fullest development, fewer than half of the slaves belonged to planters who owned 30 or more" (1990:108).

Slavery in the American South differed from slave systems in other parts of the New World in that slaves experienced a natural increase rather than the frequent deaths known elsewhere, due largely to a healthier physical environment with fewer epidemic diseases and "a more even sex ratio in the slave population at an early date, which, in turn, may reflect the greater variety of tasks and smaller size of the American slave plantation" (Curtin 1990:109). Slavery required fairly close contact between owners and slaves, and most slaveowners on small farms or large plantations knew the names of all their slaves. Eugene D. Genovese, speaking of the kind of life lived on small farms, noted:

> Farms of ten slaves or less did not develop an extensive division of labor. The white farmer and his wife divided chores, but the extent of specialization among the slaves rarely went beyond the assignment of one or two women to house work, and even they had to work in the fields when needed. A common effort by master and slave at work together produced an easy familiarity, reinforced by living arrangements. The mistress or perhaps a female slave cooked for all at the same time and in the same way. Only segregation at table drew a caste line. The slaves either slept in one small house with the master's family or in a cabin that faced on the same yard. Slave and free, black and white, lived close to one another, and their relationship led to a widespread reputation for "better treatment." [1974:8–9]

Slaves who lived on larger plantations were part of a paternalistic world in which the slave owner ruled over them, his wife, and his children and any other dependents. According to Genovese, most slaves lived on farms (small or large) with the owner in residence, and "no more than one-third and possibly only one-fourth of the rural slaves worked under overseers, and many of these either worked under an overseer and a resident planter simultaneously or under an overseer who was a relative of the planter" (1974:13).

Many scholars believe that slavery constituted the beginning of the disruption of the black family and the pathology that followed it. But there is ample evidence that both the meaning of family to African Americans and the actual facts concerning black families during slavery were greatly misunderstood. In his book, *The Black Family in Slavery and Freedom*, Herbert G. Gutman presents evidence that, in spite of the nature of slavery and the power of the owners over the fate of slaves and their family members, slaves were family oriented, and some scholars "underestimated the adaptive capacities of the enslaved and those born to them and to their children" (1976:xxi). Gutman found evidence that two-parent households and enduring unions characterized black families even in slavery and directly following emancipation.

Although it was true that children were often sold away from parents and spouses from one another, the importance of family to slaves manifested itself in efforts taken to keep track of family members and to find them following the war.

In the United States, a highly graded system based on color never developed as it did in the Caribbean and South America, largely because Americans practiced what is called *hypodescent*, a form of racism in which the race of the child is determined by the lower caste parent (see Chapter 4). Because of laws and customs that declared as Negro any person with African heritage, no formal mulatto class developed as it did, for example, in Haiti. Although color consciousness did develop among American blacks, and slaveowners were more likely to free their own children, this system tended to create a solidarity among all people of African descent in the United States.

Nor did slavery manage to deprive Africans of their deep spirituality. According to W. E. B. Du Bois,

In Africa the Negro had learned that there is in Heaven the God that made everything; but, diverging from the Europeanized creed of the Orient, the Negro believed that this God after creating things went so far off and became so unmindful of man that there was no necessity for man to concern himself about his divinity. What man needed to do, as the African understood it, was to appease the spirits of the millions of things organic and inorganic in which the spirit of this divinity is manifested. Such Christianity as the Negro conceived in his beginning in America was influenced by this African animism. [1970:358]

Slaves, in their roles as forced laborers, were nevertheless productive members of society, and often accomplished feats barely acknowledged. Let us use the example of the rice cultivators of South Carolina, descendants of peoples from Sierra Leone, a country on the west coast of Africa known for its rice cultivation techniques. South Carolina had a slave population larger than that of any other state, and blacks outnumbered whites two to one. Although slaveowners originally preferred Africans from the Congo and Angola, "in 1739, when African-born Angolans rose up against Carolina masters, slaves from this region were no longer so desirable" (Creel 1990:69). Instead, Africans from West Africa, namely, present-day Sierra Leone and Liberia—peoples called the Gola and Kissi, among others—were preferred. On the coast of South Carolina, because of its isolation and because of the cultural similarity and numbers, Africans retained much of their culture, which they adapted to the new environment.

According to Margaret Creel, "Africans from Upper Guinea (Gola, Vai, Mende, Kissi, Kpelle, and so on) shared a common socioreligious bond that provided a certain cultural uniformity through mandatory secret societies. Names related to these societies appear in Gullah Creole" (p. 70). These slaves created a whole new language based on their African languages, which became known as Gullah Creole. This language is still spoken by some African Americans today and is related to the Krio language of Sierra Leone (Asante 1990).

These slaves, who cultivated rice and indigo, had done so in their native lands. Archaeologists who have studied the landscape of South Carolina coastal areas have discovered that the slaves engaged in massive work projects, moving earth in order to prepare the land for rice cultivation, actually moved as much earth as the slaves who built the pyramids of Egypt thousands of years before. In the course of transforming the face of the South Carolina and Georgia seacoast, they also created a distinctly African American culture, manifested in their own language, their own approach to religion, and their own attitudes toward life (Creel 1990:69–97).

It is worth noting that not all slaves were agricultural laborers or lived on plantations. Many lived in urban areas. For example, Loren Schweninger points out that many slaves worked in coastal areas "employed as shipwrights, ropemakers, and coopers," and others were "gold beaters, silversmiths, and cabinetmakers" (1990:80). Female slaves often resumed their role as market women, acquiring "control over much of the marketing network, selling slave-grown produce along the docks or through the streets of port cities" (ibid.). Urban opportunities for labor sometimes provided slaves with the means of obtaining their freedom, working for hire to pay their masters in return for their emancipation.

There was always a population of free blacks in the United States. In 1790, there were 59,557 free blacks (about 7.9 percent of the black population). In 1860, on the eve of the Civil War, there were 488,070 free blacks (11 percent of all blacks), more than half of whom lived in the South (Quarles 1964:83). The origin of free blacks was as varied as that of slaves, but they tended to live in urban areas. They were the descendants of indentured servants, runaways, those who had been freed after military service

in the Revolutionary War, those who came from new territories, those who purchased their own freedom through their labor, and those freed by owners (especially those who were the children of unions between slaves and slaveowners). Quarles points out that by 1850 "the proportion of mulattos was 581 to every 1,000 blacks in the free Negro group, whereas it was only 83 mulattos to every 1,000 blacks in the slave population" (p. 84).

In the North, free blacks had fewer constraints because of antislavery sentiments, although they still were often subject to racial discrimination. Black males could vote in Massachusetts, Maine, New Hampshire, and Vermont, and even in New York if they owned $250 worth of property (an unlikely occurrence). In a number of states—California, Illinois, Indiana, Iowa, Ohio—blacks could not testify against whites. And in some cases, blacks could not serve on juries. As a rule, blacks were restricted to menial jobs, even when they had the qualifications for skilled labor, and blacks were not admitted to labor unions, because they were seen as competitors for jobs, especially as white immigrants increased in number (Quarles 1964:92–93).

In the North, free blacks founded the first independent black churches: the St. Thomas Protestant Episcopal Church, by Absalom Jones, and the Bethel African Methodist Episcopal Church, by Richard Allen. Both denominations founded in 1794 in Philadelphia spread throughout the North (Quarles 1964:99–100). These congregations played an important role in unifying African Americans and providing centers for social life. Blacks also founded mutual aid societies and library companies, and joined abolitionist societies.

Free blacks in the South had special problems, because they represented a threat to the institution of slavery and often faced restrictive legislation that curtailed their rights. Free blacks were always required to prove their free status, usually by producing papers to that effect, and they seldom enjoyed the right to vote, hold office, testify in court, bear firearms, or assemble freely. They could, however, make contracts and acquire property (Quarles 1964:86–89).

Thus, African American culture was forged in both slavery and freedom, in rural and urban areas, in the North and the South, by both women and men, and within the context of an active spirituality and a continuing support of family.

While many scholars concede too quickly that blacks who lived in close proximity to whites retained less of their African culture than those who did not, they also fail to see culture as flowing in both directions or to see European culture changing as well in a new environment. Although it is generally agreed that African culture was more widely diffused among blacks in North America than elsewhere in the Western Hemisphere, this also resulted in this culture permeating the white community. "Cultural traits of African origin can be found in the white community, as well as the black, and in new forms that have continued to evolve in the United States—forms as various as jazz, southern cooking, and expected behavior in church" (Curtin 1990:110).

Early on, the diffusion of African cultural features into the general American culture was invisible, so that today many Americans are unaware that the banjo, many folk songs, certain foods and style of preparation (okra, black-eyed peas, fish stews, deep fat frying, etc.), many words *(okay, tote)*, and even cattle herding techniques used by cowboys in the West originated in African cultures (Philips 1990:225–239; see also Morgan 1998 and Sobel 1987).

Anthropologists have known for some time that *acculturation*—the forceful imposition of the culture of a dominant group on a subordinate group—is a tenuous process and a two-way street. That is, a subordinate group will only accept from a dominant culture that which interfaces with its own culture in some meaningful

way, that a subordinate group often accepts the dominant culture by using it in a superficial way to disguise its own cultural features, and that the dominant culture at some point begins to absorb features of the subordinate culture through prolonged contact and interaction. John Philips concludes that "when social scientists and historians begin to investigate systematically the survival of African culture among European-Americans they will discover that as much African culture survives now among whites as among blacks in the United States" (p. 227).

RESISTANCE TO SLAVERY

While most states had a variety of laws designed to limit the ill treatment of slaves by their masters and overseers, slaves had no real legal recourse in the American South under slavery. Slaves were vulnerable to the whims of their masters, although in extreme cases masters could be punished for the mistreatment of slaves. But slaves did not enjoy their bondage. The stories, songs, and hymns of African Americans embody a passionate desire for freedom, an abiding and pervasive theme. Thus, the history of slavery is also the history of resistance to slavery and outright rebellion. Although in many respects blacks in North America had a more difficult time than their counterparts in the West Indies and South America with their black majorities and large maroon communities, slaveowners recognized the constant possibility of rebellion, feared it, and took steps to prevent it.

Resistance to slavery began in Africa and continued during the "Middle Passage"—the name given to the trip from Africa to the Americas—and continued once blacks were settled into their new lives. Throughout the course of slavery in North America, slaves engaged in various forms of resistance, including rebellions and escape. And although many southern whites from colonial days to the days of Jim Crow tried to convince themselves that blacks were content with their lives, their actions to prevent blacks from escaping those lives speak to the opposite reality.

Everyday resistance to slavery took the form of working more slowly and mishandling or destroying the master's property by breaking things or setting fires, pretending to be sick, self-mutilation, and mocking slaveowners in stories or songs (Quarles 1964:75–76). At times, slaves attempted to harm their owners through poisonings or beatings and other acts of "open defiance." According to John Hope Franklin and Loren Schweninger, "Nearly every year, in virtually every state in the South, slaves were indicted for killing their owners" (1999:78).

Throughout the eighteenth century, slaves revolted in different parts of the colonies. As early as 1712 in New York City, a slave revolt ended in the execution of 21 slaves, who had killed at least 9 whites (Mabunda 1997:5). In 1739, in South Carolina, several slave revolts took the lives of at least 81 whites and the lives of even more blacks. The Revolutionary War was itself a stimulus to black rebellion. Blacks had a vested interest in liberty, and Crispus Attucks was one of the first to fall in the battles that led to the struggle with England for independence.

In 1800, a slave named Gabriel Prosser conspired to lead a slave attack on Richmond, Virginia. The plan did not succeed, and the insurrectionists were captured and hanged. In 1822, in Charleston, South Carolina, Denmark Vesey planned a revolt that also failed, but the extensiveness of the conspiracy led to the establishment of laws that limited the mobility of both free blacks and slaves. In the end, Vesey and 36 co-conspirators were hanged, but 130 blacks and 4 whites were also arrested.

In this same year, blacks from the United States founded the African nation of Liberia. Repatriation of blacks to Africa was a constant theme among both blacks and whites, who saw it as a solution to the problem of slavery. Thomas Jefferson considered it a viable alternative to blacks and whites living together. Believing that blacks and whites were too different to live together, Jefferson believed that all parties would best be served if blacks simply left America. The American Society for Colonizing the Free People of Color of the United States (referred to as the American Colonization Society) was founded in 1816 mostly by slaveholders to remove free blacks (whose freedom they considered a threat to their ownership of slaves) from the United States. Liberia also became a repository for Africans from liberated slave ships and freed slaves. The federal government supplied some of the money for this venture, and the capital of Liberia, Monrovia, was actually named after American President James Monroe. Liberia became an independent nation in 1847.

Because southern whites feared the influence of free people of African descent, both for the effect they might have on slaves and for the possibility of miscegenation, many of them supported this effort. However, in the long run, the movement removed relatively few blacks from the United States—around 15,000 in all, a number in any case offset by the continuing smuggling in of new slaves to the United States. Furthermore, the American Colonization Society was not popular in the Deep South, where black slave labor was in high demand. Nevertheless, return to Africa was a continuing, if unsuccessful, alternative to slavery into the early twentieth century.

The most famous slave revolt in the history of the United States was the Nat Turner Rebellion in 1831 in Southhampton County, Virginia. Turner, a preacher, led a group of slaves in rebellion. They killed 60 whites. Turner was hanged after being caught, leaving behind his famous *Confessions*. Southern whites responded to these rebellions by passing laws forbidding the education of blacks, forcing free blacks to leave the state, and limiting emancipation. In the long run, while slave rebellions occurred, they did not succeed in freeing the slaves. Nor did the growing protests of whites in the North and the abolitionist movements in which both whites and blacks participated.

Protests against slavery went as far back as the 1688 declaration signed by Mennonites in Germantown, Pennsylvania (Mabunda 1997:5). These protests spread to the Quaker population and gradually picked up adherents throughout the eighteenth century, taking the form of anti-slavery societies and participation in the Underground Railroad, the name given to the series of groups of people who hid runaway slaves.

The New England Anti-Slavery Society was founded in 1832 by whites meeting at the African Baptist Church in Boston. Blacks and whites together established the American Anti-Slavery Society in 1833 in Philadelphia. Besides publishing antislavery tracts and sponsoring lectures, these societies also sometimes purchased the freedom of slaves. Presumably, their agitation had a certain effectiveness, especially in the wake of the British emancipation of all slaves in 1834, because President Andrew Jackson tried to prohibit the mailing of their tracts to the southern states. Congress also attempted to silence the abolitionists by disallowing the consideration of any legislation pertaining to antislavery. In 1839 in Warsaw, New York, the Liberty Party, an antislavery political organization, was founded and began to encourage boycotts of southern products (Mabunda 1997:14).

Fugitive slave laws had been on the books in some states since the seventeenth century, testifying to the fact that escape was a problem from the beginning of the slave trade. Slaves ran away because of harsh punishments and poor treatment, because their family members had been sold away, or because they simply had the desire for freedom. While some women plotted their escapes, the majority of runaways were male. Frederick Douglass, an escaped slave who fled North and then to England, was an active abolitionist, returning to the United States once his freedom had been purchased by his fellow abolitionists. Douglass escaped to the North from Maryland by borrowing the papers of a free black sailor and using them to take a train north. Harriet Tubman, the most famous "conductor" on the Underground Railroad, known to her people as "Moses," was herself a runaway slave.

But other slaves were too far south to head toward "the Promised Land" in the North, and many opted to get lost in a nearby city or to flee to the West or even further south. Some blacks went to Florida and lived among the Native Americans there, the Seminole, and became known as the Black Seminoles.[2] Some of these were former members of the Spanish military who remained behind and settled among the Seminole, while others were escaped slaves from South Carolina and Georgia. Others were actually slaves purchased by the Seminole (Lower Creeks) from the English. These slaves lived a much different life from their counterparts in other states, because the Seminole gave them tools and land and corn to plant. The slaves gave some of their crops to their masters and kept the rest. As the word of these conditions spread, slaves sought out the Seminole, who let them live in their own villages and carry weapons. According to Kenneth W. Porter (1996:6), there was "basically no personal inequality between the two groups," and blacks served as interpreters of English, Spanish, and Muskogean and became advisers, eventually intermarrying with the Seminole.

AFRICAN AMERICANS AND RECONSTRUCTION, 1863–77

Inevitably, the contradiction that slavery constituted in a nation founded on the principle of individual liberty and the economic and political conflicts between North and South led to violence, when the Confederacy attacked Fort Sumter in 1861, and the Civil War began. African Americans fought on both sides, with both slaves and free blacks recruited for the Confederate army. There were 4,441,830 slaves in the United States when the Civil War began. In 1863, Abraham Lincoln signed the Emancipation Proclamation, freeing all slaves in the Confederacy, but with no effect on slaves in those southern states that had not seceded or were under Union control (Delaware, West Virginia, Kentucky, Maryland, Tennessee, Louisiana, and Missouri). Nevertheless, the proclamation was inspirational, and many African American communities would hold emancipation celebrations.

Eventually, with the passage of the Thirteenth Amendment to the Constitution of the United States, adopted on December 18, 1865, slavery was abolished in the entire country. The Fourteenth Amendment, adopted on July 28, 1868, made all people born or naturalized in the United States citizens. The Fifteenth Amendment, adopted on March 30, 1870, guaranteed every citizen the vote regardless of race and previous status as a slave. However, it was black men who achieved the full status, while black women, along with white women in most states, though citizens, were still prevented from voting. Thus, following the Civil War, blacks gained equal status with whites in the eyes of the law for the first time in history, although exercising those rights would take a monumental struggle that would last well into the middle of the twentieth century, another hundred years.

Following the Civil War, various measures were taken to bring the Confederate states back into the Union. The attempt on the part of those in southern states to enact "black codes" to control the newly freed black population resulted in federal military occupation of the South largely for the purpose of drafting new state laws that recognized the rights of blacks. This period, from 1863 to 1877, was called Reconstruction.[3] It was a traumatic time for the United States, a time in which former slaves exercised their power as citizens but also had to face what W. E. B.

Du Bois called "a reign of terror" in the form of the newly organized Ku Klux Klan, which used violence to keep newly freed blacks in their "proper place" as people subservient to whites (1970:209).

Although the experience was different in each of the southern states, the period was characterized by race riots in which whites assaulted blacks, who had little or no protection from either local law enforcement officials (who were often involved themselves) or the Union troops stationed in the states. It also exposed the effects of class difference between middle class, educated blacks and those rural, often newly freed blacks. Nevertheless, African Americans made strides during this period.

The black leadership that developed during Reconstruction rose from the ranks of the black middle class, mostly men who had been free before the Civil War. According to Du Bois, these politicians accomplished three goals: (1) they established democratic government in the South following the war; (2) they established free public schools, thus affording education to those who had previously gone without it; and (3) they introduced a variety of social legislation that stayed on the books into the twentieth century (p. 210).

As part of Reconstruction in the South, state and local governments began to include African Americans as well as whites, yielding a democratic system for the first time. Many southern blacks were elected to political office during this period, and their efforts changed the face of the South. For example, between 1867 and 1876, 487 men were elected to state office in South Carolina, half of whom were black (Holt 1977:1). The first black to serve in the U.S. Senate was Hiram Revels of Mississippi in 1870. Blacks held offices as governor (Louisiana), lieutenant governor (Louisiana, Mississippi, and South Carolina), treasurer (Louisiana and South Carolina), superintendent of education (Arkansas, Florida, Louisiana, and Mississippi), and secretary of state (Florida, Mississippi, and South Carolina) during Reconstruction (Foner 1988:353). In addition, many blacks became policemen and even chiefs of police in municipalities across the South, and they also served in a number of other offices, such as magistrates and jury members (Foner 1988:362–363).

The struggle for education in the postwar South was notable as well. Because there had been no universal system of education for blacks or whites prior to the Civil War, the beginnings of universal education began after the war with efforts to set up a total public school system in the South as a basis for an egalitarian society (Foner 1988:366). Blacks were eager for education, and former slaves pushed for "universal, state-supported public education," in direct opposition to the planter elite who believed that education was not the business of the state (Anderson 1988:4).

African Americans also wanted to control their own schools, and the

> values of self-help and self-determination underlay the ex-slaves educational movement. To be sure, they accepted support from northern missionary societies, the Freedmen's Bureau, and some southern whites, but their own action—class self-activity informed by an ethnic of mutuality—was the primary force that brought schools to the children of freed men and women. [Anderson 1988:5]

Blacks resisted control of their educational institutions by others and had gone a long way toward establishing schools, even before missionaries came down from the North.

James D. Anderson tells of a case in Louisiana in which a well-established school system, supported by federal money and property taxes, was shut down by officials of the Freedman's Bureau. The freed slaves whose children attended these schools immediately offered to pay the entire tax burden in order to have the schools re-opened. Anderson attributes the establishment of universal education largely to the efforts of freed slaves: "Ex-slaves used their

resources first in a grass-roots movement to build, fund, and staff schools as a practical right; then they joined with Republicans to incorporate the idea into southern state constitutional law. With these actions they revolutionized the South's position regarding the role of universal public education in society" (1988:19–20).

During this time, we can see the rise of sharecropping as a way of life for many African Americans in the South. This system, which involved renting land from an owner, farming the land, and sharing the results with the owner, eventually developed into a "system of tenantry" in which former plantations in 40–80-acre pieces were parceled out. This system ultimately sustained the control of the white owners and placed black farmers under their economic control by establishing indebtedness that could never be paid off (Du Bois 1970:211–212).

Part of the failure of Reconstruction to realize total liberties for African Americans lay in the pervasive racial model that dominated American culture in both the North and the South. The lack of enthusiasm for bringing blacks into the fold of American citizenship ultimately led to failure in the South. Free blacks in the North had faced special problems with discrimination with the sudden influx of European immigrants, who competed with them for jobs and other resources. Many of these immigrants received special help from the government in the form of land grants in new territories that blacks did not share. White control of legislatures meant the continuing threat of disenfranchisement for blacks even in their own towns. Southern whites, who had created a unique and pervasive caste system based on race, tried to restore the order to their racial hierarchy by using city ordinances, state statutes, and federal court decisions to limit the freedom of African Americans and confine them to the lower economic level. The end of Reconstruction and the withdrawal of federal troops from the South introduced a new era in the struggle of African Americans to exercise the equal rights and citizenship they had been granted in the Constitution. The new era, coming gradually, was known as Jim Crow.

THE JIM CROW ERA: RACIAL APARTHEID IN THE AMERICAN SOUTH

Any gains that African Americans made during Reconstruction were short-lived. Little by little southern states began to disenfranchise blacks legally by passing state statutes and local ordinances that prevented blacks from voting, denied them easy access to education, limited their participation in business, and restricted their movement and safety within southern society as a whole. Racial segregation in the South was an attempt to reestablish white control by reinventing the social caste system that had prevailed during slavery. Although the laws that established legal segregation were only gradually enacted, they were finally in place by the first half of the twentieth century.

Segregation constituted a major impediment to the realization of true American citizenship that other peoples came to take for granted. It introduced a whole host of evils and troubles for blacks: the attenuation of political power, lack of or inferior education, limitations on the creation of black businesses, and stifling of meaningful employment and competition. This era would lead directly to many of the problems in the black community identified by social scientists later in the twentieth century.

It is important to realize that racial discrimination had been a part of American life in both the North and the South from the beginning. In spite of the fact that northern communities had abolished slavery, the political and economic aspects of many of them were segregated, although sometimes casually so. The same was true in the South following the Civil War. A variety of practices on the part of private businesses continued racial discrimination. Hotels, restaurants, stores, and theaters often excluded blacks altogether or created separate or special accommodations for them. Railroads were also segregated. The difference between North and South, then, was relative but significant in terms of the economic opportunities provided in the industrial North compared to the rural South.

Blacks were affected by the reform movements that seized the United States in response to its rapid urbanization and industrialization in the nineteenth century. However, they were often forced to the periphery of these great issues due to the racial discrimination in labor unions and other key institutions that were the focus of reforms, or they were used as obstacles (as strikebreakers, for example) that management could call upon to frustrate the demands of white workers. Thus, blacks were in a political, economic, and educational no-man's-land in both the North and the South. But since the majority of them were located in the South, the system of legal segregation affected them more.

Nevertheless, the system of racial segregation did not eclipse the freedom of African Americans all at once. Some believe that the rise of poor whites to economic power and the competition over resources were responsible for the institution of segregation laws (Cashman 1991:7). It at once allowed poor whites to prove their superiority and at the same time to quash economic competition. But this racial caste system was not new, merely a transformation of the old set of relationships from slave days into a new set—this time equally supported by the government through an extensive network of laws. Blacks had to develop their own institutions—churches, schools, businesses, burial societies, social clubs—in order to survive, and these became an important locus of solidarity within African American communities. However, black institutional development was always limited by the laws that privileged white citizens over blacks in every phase of life.

The gradual achievement of segregation took between thirty and fifty years after the Civil War:

Thus South Carolina segregated the races in successive stages, beginning with trains (1898) and moving to streetcars (1905), train depots and restaurants (1906), textile plants (1915 and 1916), circuses (1917), pool halls (1924), and beaches and recreation centers (1934). Georgia began with railroads and prisons (1891) and moved to sleeping cars (1899) and, finally pool halls (1925), but refused to segregate places of public accommodation until 1954. . . . Mississippi was the first state effectively to disfranchise African-American citizens by a constitutional convention in 1890. It was followed by South Carolina in 1895, Louisiana in 1898, North Carolina (by amendment in 1900), Alabama in 1901, Virginia in 1901 and 1902, Georgia (by amendment) in 1908, and the new state of Oklahoma in 1910. Four more states achieved the same ends without amending their constitutions: Tennessee, Florida, Arkansas, and Texas. [Cashman 1991:7]

Southern states used poll taxes, literacy requirements, grandfather clauses, and gerrymandering to prevent African Americans from registering to vote. Thus, the black vote diminished as the nineteenth turned into the twentieth century. Without recourse to political power, blacks were vulnerable on every front.

A series of U.S. Supreme Court cases solidified the actions of the states. In 1896, the case of *Plessy v. Ferguson* upheld the right of Louisiana to provide "separate but equal" accommodations for whites and blacks on public transportation. In 1898, the case of *Williams v. Mississippi* upheld literacy tests for voters. The loss of civil rights that occurred during this period would have a number of effects: (1) it led to the formation of many black institutions, solidifying the centrality of the church in African American life; (2) it led to the formation of national rights organizations and the rise of a new black nationalism; (3) it led eventually to the modern civil rights movement that dismantled this system.

As the nineteenth century came to a close and the twentieth century opened, two views of what course blacks should take came forth from two different men: one was a former slave, Booker T. Washington, who grew up in the South; the other was the first African American to earn a doctoral degree from Harvard University, W. E. B. Du Bois, who grew up in the North. Their opposing views would define different courses of action for African Americans for decades to come and in many ways dramatized the different environments of the North and the South but also the schizophrenic nature of racial oppression.

Booker T. Washington, born into slavery in 1856 in Virginia, advanced what came to be known as "gradualism." Washington was a graduate of Hampton Institute in Virginia, and he started the Normal and Industrial Institute for Negroes in 1881 in Tuskegee, Alabama. He wrote his autobiography, *Up from Slavery*, and founded the National Negro Business League, which encouraged entrepreneurial activity among African Americans. At the Cotton States and International Exposition in Atlanta, Georgia, on September 18, 1895, Washington gave a talk that came to be known as the "Atlanta Compromise." In his speech, Washington emphasized the importance of increasing economic opportunities for blacks through training in industrial skills rather than through social equality. "In all things social we can be as separate as the fingers, yet one as the hand in all things essential to mutual progress" (cited in Cashman 1991: 13–14).

In assuring whites that African Americans were not going to push for immediate social equality but work hard to better their lot, he removed some of the threat that blacks presented. Washington was successful in courting white philanthropists and getting them to support his various educational enterprises, and he was even invited to the White House by President Theodore Roosevelt. Having grown up in the South and understanding firsthand the violence possible against blacks by whites, Washington took a pragmatic approach to black progress (Cashman 1991:16).

William Edward Burghardt Du Bois, born in 1868 in Massachusetts, was a graduate of Fisk University and Harvard. A sociologist, Du Bois published *The Souls of Black Folk* in 1903, and his perspective was that of a northerner. While Du Bois was in favor of black laborers developing skills, he saw Washington's objectives as missing the point that white capital used "race prejudice and rivalry" within industry and white labor movements. Du Bois thought that education based on specific skills was pointless in view of developing "mass production" that would make them "obsolete in a generation or even in a day" (Du Bois 1970:213–214).

Blacks were usually left out of the union and populist movements of the day, so Du Bois did not hold out much hope for the Washington approach and disliked the seeming acceptance of racial inferiority in the equivocation about social equality. Du Bois advocated a broader educational program for African Americans, and he himself taught at the university level, eventually ending up at Atlanta University. He authored a number of significant works in the field of sociology, but *The Souls of Black Folk* remains the classic among his efforts.

In 1905, Du Bois was among a group of blacks and whites concerned about racial justice, who embarked upon a new approach at the Niagara Conference, which eventually led to the formation of the National Association for the Advancement of Colored People (NAACP) in 1910. This organization would be at the forefront of the civil rights movement, becoming known for its legal approach to the eradication of black inequality. For example, it was the NAACP that filed suit against election officials in Oklahoma who instituted a grandfather clause—one that stated that you could not vote unless your grandfather had voted in a previous election, which eliminated most blacks from the electoral process. In *Guinn v. United States* in 1915, the Supreme Court declared this tactic unconstitutional (Cashman 1991:22–23).

Du Bois believed that socialism was the answer to racial discrimination in the United States, a view that the majority of blacks never really agreed with. Eventually, Du Bois became disillusioned with American socialists, who failed to condemn both lynching and segregation. In his later years, Du Bois left the United States and moved to Africa, away from the racism that had plagued him throughout his life.

In 1911, the Urban League was founded in New York. Its main objective was to address social welfare issues. As more and more blacks migrated to the major cities of the North, its focus on the problems of poverty and ultimately institutional discrimination accounted for its longevity. Like the NAACP, the Urban League made slow progress but some inroads against the problems of urban blacks, which would become much more important later in the twentieth century when the modern civil rights movement, begun as a protest against legalized segregation, called attention to the plight of blacks in northern and western urban areas as well.

Meanwhile, in the United States generally and the South particularly, violence was getting out of hand. In 1892 alone, 235 lynchings occurred. Between 1882 and 1927, almost 5,000 persons were lynched, 3,500 of whom were African Americans (Du Bois 1970:214). Lynchings usually occurred because of alleged crimes by blacks against whites. Well into the twentieth century (between 1900 and 1960) 196 whites and 1,796 blacks were lynched, and the perpetrators of those killings were rarely, if ever, prosecuted. Southern whites defended lynching as a form of social control "as an indirect act of self-defence against the Negro criminal as a race" (Winfield H. Collins, cited in Cashman 1991:34). Southerners fought attempts to enact federal legislation against lynching, and lynchings were often social events in which whole families witnessed the violence as a form of entertainment, thus reinforcing the erroneous racial biases reinforced by the poor economic conditions that plagued the South—economic conditions generated by the interests of elite landowners who controlled political and economic power in the South.

Thirty Years of Lynching, 1889–1918 was published by the NAACP as part of a larger project seeking a federal antilynching law. Although southern senators managed to keep antilynching legislation from passing, the publicity created by the NAACP embarrassed the region, and eventually the number of lynchings decreased as southerners began to consider their actions more carefully and police themselves (Cashman 1991:34–35).

An equally difficult problem was posed by the rise of the Ku Klux Klan once again. Originally, the Klan was formed by elite southerners and manned by those who were disenfranchised after the Civil War because they had been officers in the Confederate army or complicit in the war in some other way. Under the pretense of protecting themselves and their society from dishonest and criminalistic former slaves, they used direct violence to terrorize former slaves and to keep them from exercising their right to vote. The reinstitution of the Klan in the twentieth century (1915 to 1944) found it largely changed in composition, no longer dominated by elite southern whites (many of whom joined White Citizens Councils). It consisted of those who felt displaced because of economic depressions, competition over resources due to immigration, and other social dislocations occurring during the period. While a central motive of the Klan was to keep blacks in line, it also discriminated against Jews, Catholics, and foreigners generally. The Klan decreased in influence and effectiveness as many of the country's problems were solved by economic improvements, assimilation, and by legal suits. But strains of the Klan persist even to this day.

The gradual divestment of rights that African Americans had gained directly after the Civil War, the increasing violence used by whites to force blacks to conform to a social order in which they were the low caste, and the rise of repressive systems of labor in the form of sharecropping to replace slave labor, combined with changes in the world at large—and especially labor shortages in the urban North caused by growing businesses and the curtailment of immigration—led to a massive movement of African American people that became known as the Great Migration.

THE NEW CENTURY AND THE GREAT MIGRATION OF AFRICAN AMERICANS, 1910–40s

The twentieth century began with the consolidation of racial attitudes in the United States as well as concerted efforts to oppose those attitudes. In the early decades of the twentieth century, anthropology became an organized discipline within academia, and Franz Boas became one of its key figures. The work of Gregor Mendel in genetics had been rediscovered in 1900, and this led not only to scientific advancements but to the rise of scientific racism in the form of the eugenics movement, which sought to improve humanity through genetic selection, and these presuppositions were imbued with deeply ingrained social attitudes toward race.

Because Boas recognized that many of the traits assumed to be biological were learned (and that there was a general confusion about the relationship among race, language, and culture), he found it necessary to separate the edicts of the physical anthropology of the time from the study of culture, thus becoming the founder of American cultural anthropology. But, more importantly, Boas and his students were true public intellectuals. They carried out a concerted effort to educate the general public, both through their scientific studies and their writings in the popular newspapers and magazines of the day. Boas corresponded with Booker T. Washington and also knew W. E. B. Du Bois, who eventually invited him to give the graduation address at Atlanta University, during which Boas expounded on the marvels of African civilization, which were then generally unknown. But such enlightenment and such efforts to redirect the attention of scholars from race to culture did not bear fruit for a long time. Although Boas and his students provided the scientific underpinnings for the assumption of human equality, they were acting against the culturally ingrained attitudes toward race that had been two hundred years in the making.

A decade into the twentieth century, a great migration of African Americans took place, beginning prior to World War I, when the need for workers stimulated the recruitment of African Americans from the southern states, and continuing well into the 1940s. In 1900, there were approximately 8,834,000 African Americans in the United States, constituting 11.6 percent of the total population, most of whom lived in the southern states. The movement out of the South to the urban areas of the North changed the composition of the country's population and set the historical background for future problems for blacks living in cities across America (see Henri 1976; Lemann 1991; Marks 1989; Trotter 1991).

Although there are many theories that attempt to explain this phenomenon, it is clear that many blacks stood to benefit from higher wages and better jobs in the industrial North. "Emigrant agents," better known as labor recruiters, went south expressly for the purpose of urging blacks to move north. Their inducements included information on available employment in distant places, financial assistance in moving through the provision of train tickets, and even payment of debts. But blacks didn't need to be too deeply induced, because picking up and leaving was "a form of political protest," emigrant agents provided a means of escaping natural disasters that would have otherwise left many African Americans destitute, and the ability to absent themselves from the scene encouraged whites to treat them better (Bernstein 1998:782–783).

In fact, as David Bernstein points out, southern whites attempted to control the black labor force by interfering with developing labor mar-

kets after the Civil War. The agents who came south to steal away the members of this labor force constituted a threat to southerners and their way of life. Therefore, the planters used licensing laws and other devices to penalize the agents (Bernstein 1998:785). Not only does this indicate the degree to which government action was involved with the repression of civil rights, according to Bernstein, but it indicates how deeply committed to a racial caste system southern whites were, and how willing they were to use their political power to maintain it (p. 785).

However, whites did respond to the great migration of blacks away from the South by engaging in some reforms, such as providing better schools for black children. As James Anderson notes, "Public elementary schools became available to the majority of southern black children during the first third of the twentieth century, long after common schools had become universal for other American schoolchildren" (1988:148). Slaves had made the first push for universal education, while the second push came as an attempt to induce blacks to remain in the South. At the turn of the century, in the 16 southern states, out of a total of 1,120,683 black children, aged 5 to 9 years old, only 246,273, or 22 percent, attended elementary school (compared to 37 percent of white children). For children 10 to 14 years of age, the percentage attending school was 52 percent, compared to 76 percent of white children (Anderson 1988:151).

By 1940, 66 percent of black children aged 5 to 9 attended school (compared to 65 percent of white children), and 90 percent of black children aged 10 to 14 attended school (compared to 91 percent of white children) (p. 182). Thus the impetus to improve black education that came from the migration of blacks from the South resulted in universal education for African Americans. While it was true that much of that education was in a segregated environment—a problem that would be addressed in the second half of the century–it was, nevertheless, an improvement.

In spite of efforts to keep blacks in the South, their "escape" was made easier by the existence of railroads. "In sum, the South lost 323,000 African-Americans in the 1910s and 615,000 in the 1920s–about 8.2 per cent of its African-American population" (Cashman 1991:26). The twentieth century would see some of the worst repression, and some of the greatest successes, for African Americans in the history of the country. The New York City African American community of Harlem and the city of Chicago became focal points for African American struggles and achievement (see Henri 1976; Lemann 1991; Marks 1989; Trotter 1991).

In 1914, a Jamaican-born printer named Marcus Moziah Garvey founded the Universal Negro Improvement and Conservation Association (UNIA) in Harlem for the purpose of bringing together peoples of African descent. In 1921, the UNIA had more than a million members. While black leaders such as Du Bois advocated integration of blacks into U.S. society, Garvey encouraged separatism, and his movement became one of the earliest expressions of black nationalism in the new century. Defined by Wilson Jeremiah Moses as "the effort of African Americans to create a sovereign nation-state and formulate an ideological basis for a concept of national culture" (1996:2), nationalistic feelings among blacks can be traced as far back as the American Revolution.

Garvey's organization set up the Black Star Steamship Line with an eye toward repatriating blacks to Africa. "It also petitioned the League of Nations to transfer the former German colonies in Africa, South West Africa and German East Africa, held as mandates by South Africa and Britain, respectively, to Garvey's control. In 1922 Garvey designated himself president of a new African republic" (Cashman 1991:38). Garvey's contemptuous attitude toward many African American leaders led him into many ideological disputes. Garvey and Du Bois came to

verbal and written blows over ideology, and in the end the UNIA itself was plagued with the problem of integrationism versus separatism, which eventually led to the killing of a former member of Garvey's camp and the indictment of Garvey himself for mail fraud in 1923. He was later deported from the United States. But the amount of support he gained from blacks in New York was indicative of the desire of those same blacks to find a solution to their many problems and made his movement the most successful black nationalist movement in history to that time (Moses 1996:241).

Harlem was also the site of the Harlem Renaissance, an efflorescence of black culture that emerged in the 1920s. The Renaissance was the product of the Great Migration and its effects on prosperity in Harlem. Such writers as Claude McKay, Zora Neale Hurston, Langston Hughes, Jean Toomer, Countee Cullen, Nella Larsen, Alain Locke, Jessie Redmond Fauset, and James Weldon Johnson made their names during this era. Many of these writers published their poems and fiction in *Crisis*, the magazine of the NAACP, and other, similar publications. Their books were published by mainstream publishers and read by whites as well as blacks. At the same time, black artists, musicians, and performers were busy creating new art forms, and their work was in much demand. Thus, the Great Migration shifted populations from rural areas to urban areas and brought together a critical mass of black talent such as had never been seen before. Although much of the achievement of the Harlem Renaissance was eclipsed by the Great Depression that began in 1929, it stands out as a period of extreme creativity and cultural success in African American history.

Those who remained in the South had to live in a racially divided society in which they had very little political power. In her ethnographic study, *After Freedom: A Cultural Study in the Deep South* originally published in 1939, anthropologist Hortense Powdermaker captured the lives and interactions of blacks and whites in a

Mississippi town she called Cottonville, a commercial hub of a cotton-farming community.

She found a town in which virtually all of the whites belonged to families that had been in the South "for three generations," and they were all born in the town in which they lived. They were divided into an upper class of plantation owners; a middle class of small farmers and those who actually managed the plantations, craftsmen, and merchants; and poor whites. The white section of town was beautifully landscaped and with no hint of "slums," because all of the poor white people lived outside of town, as did the large landowners (1993:14).

Blacks were located literally "across the tracks" from the white part of town or nearby the farms on which they worked. Their neighborhood did not display a uniform level of economic well-being, but "runs the gamut of possibilities from comfort and poverty" (p. 12). Blacks patronized mostly white businesses, the exception being a black-owned grocery store, restaurant, doctor, and dentist. Many of the blacks moved between the country and the town.

Powdermaker describes a situation in which the physical separation of blacks and whites symbolized the social separation of the two groups. And while whites had negative stereotyped ideas about blacks, most of them thought themselves virtuous in their treatment of blacks; poor whites, however, resented blacks, who competed with them for employment. On the other hand, blacks were not allowed to ride in the best cars in trains or eat in white restaurants; and they were called by their first names or "Aunty" or "Uncle" while being required to address whites as "Mr." or "Mrs." Powdermaker also found that when whites talked among themselves, they almost always referred to blacks as "niggers" or "darkies." There was a taboo against blacks and whites eating together. Blacks were required to enter white homes through the back door (pp. 43–55).

Beyond these social constraints, African Americans in Cottonville also suffered from political and economic constraints, sometimes due to the uncertainty surrounding single-crop agriculture but also because of the pure lack of power. In Cottonville, only 39 percent of the full owners of farms were black (181 blacks to 467 whites), 30 percent of the part owners, and 2 percent of the managers, but 81 percent of the tenant farmers were black. "One fear of the Whites has always been that their labor supply would be taken from them. In the boom years there was intense feeling against northern agents who came to entice Negro workers up north, and every effort was made to oppose them" (p. 81).

Thus, Powdermaker substantiated through fieldwork in 1931 the reality of the fear of black migration, as well as the reasons why blacks might want to leave. Given these facts, the continuing migration of blacks to the North between the world wars is no surprise.

In 1945, St. Clair Drake and Horace R. Cayton published a landmark study of African Americans, *Black Metropolis: A Study of Negro Life in a Northern City*. This study is special because it attempts to look at an African American community as a whole. Not only does it capture the history of African Americans in the city of Chicago but also the diversity and complexity of their culture. The authors combined sociological and anthropological techniques in collecting the data for their study, and the book stands as one of the most comprehensive treatments of a black community. In a city founded in 1790 by a man of African descent, Jean Baptiste du Sable, the struggle of African Americans is rendered in microcosm, capturing the escape to freedom and the assumption of employment with economic possibilities and political participation, along with the blatant racism that resulted in riots, discrimination, and a vicious policy of housing segregation. The black community in Chicago was second in population only to that of Harlem.

In 1890, the population of Chicago consisted of 58 percent native whites, 41 percent foreign-born whites, and 1.3 percent African Americans.

By 1944, the composition of Chicago's population was 73 percent native whites, 17 percent foreign-born whites, and 9 percent African Americans. In terms of actual population, in 1900 out of a total population of 1,698,575 people, 1,081,720 were native whites, 586,705 were foreign-born whites, and 30,150 were blacks. By 1944, out of a total population of 3,600,000, native-born whites were 2,642,000, foreign-born whites 621,000, and blacks 337,000 (Drake and Cayton 1945:8–9).

As African Americans arrived in greater and greater numbers in Chicago, they found their way to the center of the city–"poverty clusters near the center of the city" (p. 13). Foreign-born whites tended to move into colonies of like people, and as people became assimilated to American culture, they gradually moved toward the outer parts of the city. As immigrants moved into Chicago, they took on the unskilled jobs, allowing the native-born whites to move up to more skilled (and more highly paid) employment. In the meantime, their children became better educated than their parents and moved out of the poorest neighborhoods, becoming part of the native-white groups. However, "Negroes have replaced immigrants as the primary source of unskilled and menial labor," since World War I, constituting "the bottom of the social and economic pyramid and have inherited the slums" (p. 18).

Because of its centrality to the Midwest and its farm equipment and meat-packing industries, Chicago became a center of management-labor disputes, subject to violent outbreaks as the stresses, both economic and social, grew from time to time. Recurrent riots over labor practices and racism became part and parcel of Chicago's character as a city. Nevertheless, Chicago became a "refuge" for blacks escaping from the South before the Civil War where, after the passage of fugitive slave acts, they were protected by resident blacks, who formed a Liberty Association expressly to fight off the slave catchers and local magistrates who often kidnapped members of the free black population. It was also a destination after the war for those who wished to escape the increasingly repressive political and economic environment in southern states in hopes of freedom and a living wage (p. 34).

Any economic progress that blacks made in Chicago after the migration was eventually cut short by the Great Depression in 1929, but between "1930 and 1940 the Negro population increased by more than 43,000. With the collapse of cotton tenancy in the South, and because of discrimination in the dispensing of relief and emergency employment, thousands of Negroes set out for Chicago" (p. 88). This exacerbated an already difficult economic situation in which "four out of every ten persons on relief were Negroes" (ibid.) and increased the tension between blacks and whites in Chicago.

"The Great Migration created the 'Negro Problem,'" said Drake and Cayton (p. 733), bringing into direct contact whites with blacks and into specific relief the racial problems endemic to American culture. This problem would be addressed directly following World War II.

WORLD WAR II AND THE RISE OF AMERICAN POWER AND AFFLUENCE

World War II brought about many changes in U.S. society that laid the foundation and cleared away some obstacles for the start of the modern civil rights movement that began in the 1950s. First of all, World War II brought American hypocrisy to the foreground. While fighting against Hitler and the racism of the Nazi regime in Germany, the United States did so with a segregated army and with rights for blacks sharply curtailed by legal segregation and institutional racism at home.

A. Philip Randolph (1889–1979) decided that a "march on Washington" to protest the discriminatory treatment of blacks in defense industries would be a good idea. He and other leaders (among them Walter White, Mary McLeod Bethune, and Lester Grange of the Urban League) planned a march for July 1, 1941. However, because the march threatened President Franklin D. Roosevelt's own political agenda, Roosevelt took steps to prevent it by issuing an executive order that desegregated all training programs and defense industries on June 18, 1941. He also created the Fair Employment Practices Committee (FEPC) to enforce his order, but the organization lasted only for the duration of the war (Cashman 1991:73–74). With the increase in jobs brought about by the war industries, black migration to the North began again.

African Americans had participated in all of America's wars, and World War II was no exception. More than a million blacks joined the segregated armed forces where they continued to be subjected to unequal treatment and menial jobs. "Experiments," such as training almost one thousand black pilots at Tuskegee, Alabama (later called the Tuskegee Airmen), for service in the army air force, provided evidence of black competence, but it was not until 1948 under President Harry Truman that the armed services were finally desegregated.

Following the war, the United States embarked on an unprecedented economic boom as it began its move to the status of world power, and its economy became a corporate one. The middle class grew from 13 percent to 46 percent of the population, due to government incentives, which offered education and housing to former GIs. As Americans became economically better off, so did African Americans, but not to the extent that they wished. For example, unemployment among whites in 1950 was 4.9 percent; it was 9.0 percent among blacks. The following year, unemployment had fallen to 5.3 percent among blacks and 3.1 percent among whites. However, whites still made more than twice as much as nonwhites: in 1950, whites had a median income of $7,057, whereas nonwhites

had a median income of $3,828 (Cashman 1991:104, 109).

When black veterans returned home, open hostilities toward them from whites who feared the push for equality called attention to the fact that racial problems persisted. President Truman issued executive orders to eliminate racial discrimination in civil service hiring and in the military. Black migration to northern cities put pressure on politicians to respond to the growing number of votes coming from the black community. But the South was changing too, becoming more urbanized and more industrialized. Merchants in large southern cities often depended on black consumers for their profits.

The African American community was poised for the push that would succeed in desegregating the South and bringing the rights of American citizenship, including the right to vote, finally into their grasp. The push would begin in the South where the violation of these rights was most egregious and the opposition to the violation most dangerous. However, the repercussions of these early struggles would be felt in African American communities all over the country. Each area had its own special problems to solve, but in every case African Americans drew on their own cultural understandings in deciding just how this battle had to be fought in their own backyards. And as they went about their protests, using their nonviolent strategies, millions of Americans watched on television as southern whites did become violent.

THE RISE OF THE MODERN CIVIL RIGHTS MOVEMENT

The NAACP had been sporadically successful in prosecuting cases of discrimination here and there before the war, signaling a change in the attitude of the U.S. Supreme Court, which in the past had upheld many laws imposing legal segregation or abridging the voting rights of blacks. NAACP lawyers decided to make an even more extensive bid against segregation by continuing to employ a legal strategy of bringing suits in court, getting a positive decision from the Supreme Court, and then acting on that positive outcome to bring about change. When the moment came, blacks would call upon the institutions established under segregation, their solidarity, and their emotional resources to guide them.

In 1954, the Supreme Court, by a unanimous vote in *Brown v. Board of Education of Topeka, Kansas*, found that separate educational facilities were inherently unequal. This case was one of many that had been filed by Thurgood Marshall, head of the NAACP Legal Defense Fund. Eighty percent of southern whites polled were against school desegregation, and it was not supported by President Dwight D. Eisenhower or Congress. Many forms of obstruction were employed to prevent blacks from acting on the Court's decision, and the NAACP itself was the subject of skillful political maneuverings on the part of southern politicians who passed laws requiring the organization to disclose its membership (a very unsafe thing in many southern towns), prevented municipal or state employees from belonging, and engaged in acts of violence.

Most people date the formal beginning of the modern civil rights movement to the day when Rosa Parks, a seamstress in Montgomery, Alabama, refused to yield her seat on the bus to allow a white person to sit down on December 1, 1955 and was arrested. This case is particularly instructive, because it illustrates the way in which African Americans drew on their cultural and social strengths in order to participate in a contest that they would ultimately win, but not without great cost.

The city of Montgomery had at one time been the capital of the Confederacy, but its segregated bus system was different from most segregated systems in the South, including other parts of Alabama. Ralph Abernathy, in his autobiography, *And the Walls Came Tumbling Down*, explained:

Throughout most of the South, the law prescribed that blacks begin seating from the rear forward and whites from the front backward. Under this arrangement, on a predominantly black route our people might well occupy all the seats on the bus or, if there were a few whites aboard, almost all. On the other hand, on a predominantly white route, blacks might be found only on the back row. The boundary would be established by the proportion of blacks to whites and by who got on first. This method was used in several Alabama cities, including Mobile.

In Montgomery, however, the first ten seats were reserved for whites only—whether or not there were any white riders on the bus. This meant that blacks could not sit in the three-seat benches in the front that faced each other or in the four first-row seats. So Mrs. Parks was acting within the law when she sat down in an outside seat in the eleventh row, with a black man to her right (next to the window) and two black women across the aisle. [1989:133]

The arrest of Rosa Parks became the deciding factor in the decision of African Americans in Montgomery to launch their bus boycott. Blacks had had problems with bus seating for years, and in this instance bus drivers had police powers and could forcibly remove blacks from the buses. Many black men chose to walk rather than suffer the humiliation of getting on the front of the bus to pay their fare and then walking to the back of the bus to get on, especially since blacks who had paid were sometimes left standing outside as the bus pulled away. Other people had been arrested not long before the Parks incident, but Rosa Parks was an upstanding member of the community around whom everyone could rally (see Abernathy 1989:131–134; Robinson 1987:19–22).

It was the Women's Political Council (WPC) that served as the liaison between the black community and the city officials when it came to complaints about the treatment of blacks on the buses (Robinson 1987:23). This organization had already mapped out its plans for integration in Montgomery, although it did not do so openly. Its chapters, which covered all parts of the city, also constituted an efficient means of communicating information about the boycott to all parties. Jo Ann Gibson Robinson, its president at the time of the boycott, had already met with the mayor and other city officials, and WPC members regularly attended city meetings until the boycott began. Other black organizations were also in place to help deal with complaints and other political issues that affected blacks and had met with bus company officials before to discuss problems. The 68 black organizations in the community meant that a network of both communication and action was in place when the decision to engage in a boycott was reached (pp. 27–39).

The plans for a bus boycott came to fruition on December 5, 1955, the Monday for which Rosa Parks's trial was set. Initially, the boycott was to last only one day. Robinson drafted the notice of the boycott and ran it off on the mimeograph machine at her college, making thousands of copies with the help of her students. The network of organizations aided in the distribution of the notices to all parts of the community. Because African Americans constituted three-quarters of the customers who rode the bus, a successful boycott would get the attention of the bus company (pp. 45–47).

Because the ministers were the leaders of the community and the churches were natural meeting places, and because the issue was an important one, the ministers rallied together "for the first time in the history of Montgomery," regardless of their denominations or the kinds of congregations they had. On the Friday evening before the boycott, a meeting was called at the Dexter Avenue Baptist Church (the church at which Martin Luther King, Jr., had just become pastor) at which all community leaders—ministers, presidents of organizations, and others—were present. They decided to call for a mass meeting at the Holt Street Baptist Church for Monday night.

Although members of the white community had found out about the boycott, and police officers accompanied the buses on Monday, the boycott was a total success. Black riders walked to work or took black taxicabs for a reduced rate. White passengers had also avoided the buses, some out of support for the boycott. Rosa Parks was tried and found guilty and fined. That afternoon Ralph Abernathy and Martin Luther King, Jr., gathered with other ministers to form the Montgomery Improvement Association. King was elected president. It was that evening at the Holt Street Baptist Church that King introduced the principles of nonviolent protest—an old strategy of earlier civil rights actions.

The boycott began as a one-day event for the purpose of gaining better treatment for blacks on the buses. However, due to the failure of city officials to yield on any points, blacks decided to continue the boycott and to push for total desegregation of the bus system. Whites formed White Citizens Councils and enlisted the aid of the chief of police. Houses and churches of blacks were bombed, and other acts of intimidation practiced. The movement, however, did not flag. With nightly church rallies, the boycott was maintained until 1957, when the federal courts declared segregated seating unconstitutional. The African Americans of Montgomery, Alabama—ordinary women and men—had succeeded in their attempt to desegregate buses by calling upon their institutions, their discipline in applying nonviolence, and their fortitude in maintaining their resolve in the face of overt violence on the part of both private individuals and government officials. The boycott had lasted a total of 381 days.

The bus boycott ignited a number of other movements throughout the South and set the civil rights movement into full sway. The Civil Rights Act of 1957 created the infrastructure in the Department of Justice to handle civil rights issues and prohibited interference with voting, allowing the attorney general to handle such actions in district courts (Cashman 1991:136).

Martin Luther King, Jr., rose to national prominence as a result of his leadership during the boycott, and he and Ralph Abernathy, along with others, formed the Southern Christian Leadership Conference (SCLC) to encourage the continuation of activism. There followed a number of protests in various southern cities with different degrees of results. Americans watched on television as African Americans, practicing nonviolence, were confronted by jeering crowds of angry whites during attempts to desegregate Central High School in Little Rock, Arkansas, and as policemen arrested protesters in Birmingham, Alabama, intimidating them with dogs and water hoses.

Of particular significance was the beginning of student protest in the form of sit-ins at lunch counters in segregated restaurants. Four students from North Carolina Agricultural and Technical College were refused service at a Woolworth's lunch counter in Greensboro, North Carolina, on February 1, 1960, setting off spontaneous lunch counter sit-ins across the South. This led to the formation of SNCC, the Student Nonviolent Coordinating Committee, the brainchild of Ella Baker, a former executive director of SCLC, who wanted to make sure that sit-ins were coordinated and their participants trained in nonviolent protest. SCLC held a conference at Shaw University during an April weekend in 1960 for student leaders of sit-ins and northern whites who had begun to lend their support to the movement (Stoper 1989:6–7).

Because lunch counters had been successfully desegregated the previous summer, in May 1961, SNCC members began their attempts to desegregate interstate transportation by taking "freedom rides" on interstate buses. Those riding from Washington, DC, to Louisiana were attacked in Birmingham and arrested in Florida. In 1964, SNCC sponsored a "Freedom Summer" during which 700 students from the North went to Mississippi. Three of those participants were murdered (Stoper 1989:13). But 1964 also saw civil rights activist Fannie Lou Hamer of Mississippi challenge the right of white Democratic delegates to seats at the Democratic convention. Although Hamer's contingent was not seated, segregated delegations became unacceptable after that year.

The previous year had seen four momentous events: the murder of NAACP officer Medgar Evers on June 12, 1963; the gathering of 250,000 people at the March on Washington where Martin Luther King, Jr., delivered his famous "I Have a Dream" speech (on August 28, 1963); the bombing on September 15, 1963, of a Birmingham, Alabama, black church in which four young girls attending Sunday school were killed; and the assassination of President John Fitzgerald Kennedy on November 22, 1963, in Dallas, Texas.

An ever growing amount of federal legislation and executive orders led to the effective end of legal segregation in the South. In 1962, President Kennedy had issued an executive order ending segregation in federally assisted housing. The Civil Rights Act of 1964, passed during the administration of President Lyndon Johnson and supported by 152 Democrats and 138 Republicans, prohibited discrimination in public accommodations, businesses, and trade unions. The 1965 Voting Rights Act allowed federal agents to register blacks denied this right.

The civil rights movement begun in Montgomery, led by ministers, and participated in by the rank and file dealt with the problem of segregation in the South. The movement captured the attention of blacks all over the United States, especially those in urban areas who faced different kinds of problems that required different tactics. Some of these blacks did not think of integration as an appropriate goal, and some sought a separate nation altogether. Following in a tradition of black nationalism that stemmed from revolutionary days, a group that had been around for many decades, the Nation of Islam, produced a leader who captured the imaginations of the impoverished in northern ghettos. His name was Malcolm X.

BLACK NATIONALISM: MALCOLM X AND THE NATION OF ISLAM

Black nationalism, the idea of a separate black state, had been a strain of thought among African Americans from the revolutionary era onward (Moses 1996). The Nation of Islam was a religious movement that had started in 1931 in Detroit, Michigan, primarily among poor and unemployed blacks, probably in response to the Great Depression. Its founder, W. D. Fard, originally called it the Temple of Islam. By the time the modern civil rights movement began, the Nation was led by Elijah Muhammed (1897–1975), who held that leadership for 41 years until his death. Openly nationalistic and hostile to whites, the Nation of Islam had between 65,000 and 100,000 members by 1960 (Cashman 1991:171). In 1960, Elijah Muhammad made the call for a separate black nation, rejecting the goal of integration that so many American blacks believed in.

However, it was Malcolm X, a charismatic minister, who succeeded in attracting more young adherents to the Nation of Islam. Under his guidance, the Nation gave a sense of dignity and purpose to thousands of disenchanted black youths in urban areas. Malcolm X was an articulate speaker, and he did not back down or comfort those who wanted a softer approach to the problems of racism. Because of differences with Elijah Muhammad, Malcolm X left the Nation of Islam in March 1964. After traveling to Mecca and meeting Muslims of many different races, he created the Organization of African Unity. While still adhering to a philosophy of black nationalism, Malcolm X had changed his perspective from one of fighting racism to one of fighting oppression generally on a worldwide basis. Before he could implement his ideas, he was assassinated on February 21, 1965.

The Nation of Islam had been successful in getting young people off drugs, establishing a network of businesses, and generally making its members better off. After Elijah Muhammad died in 1975, his son, Wallace Deen Muhammad, sought to "seek integration into the American system" by shifting the group to Sunni Islam; establishing a new organization, World Community of Al-Islam in the West; admitting whites; and becoming known as Bilalians. In 1977, Louis Farrakhan and other members of Elijah Muhammad's organization re-established the Nation of Islam (Cashman 1991:178; Walker 1999:119–120). Farrakhan was instrumental in bringing about the "Million Man March" on Washington in 1995, but his racism and anti-Semitism, as well as the initial exclusion of women, brought him a good deal of criticism.

THE RISE OF BLACK POWER AND THE END OF THE CIVIL RIGHTS MOVEMENT

As the 1960s wore on and more and more strides toward ending legal segregation were made, the nature of the civil rights movement began to change. In many ways, the rise of the black power movement was the product of generational differences as well as ideological shifts. Not content to practice the nonviolence that had become part and parcel of black protest, younger members of the civil rights movement promoted militancy and even violence in the pursuit of black goals. And because of the increasing violence against blacks in general, black political figures, and the growing threat to young black men of the military draft, it was harder and harder to justify nonviolence as a strategy. Riots across the United States broke the decorum established by the nonviolent protests in the South. Young people in Los Angeles, Detroit, Philadelphia, and New York did not have the patience of their elders who had dismantled legal segregation in the South.

Led by Stokely Carmichael, chairman of SNCC, the Student Nonviolent Coordinating

Committee shifted from its nonviolent, integrationist stance to one of black separatism, effectively destroying the organization by splitting its membership. According to Carmichael, black power was "a call for black people in this country to unite, to recognize their heritage, to build a sense of community" (cited in Cashman 1991:199). Black power protests drew upon different kinds of people than those who had started the movement; they were from the North and West, concerned with the plight of blacks in cities, and were not religious leaders. For example, in 1966, Huey P. Newton and Bobby Seale founded the Black Panther Party in Oakland, California, and openly challenged the authority of the state and police, adopting a radical agenda and openly carrying firearms.

The decade of the 1960s ended with the assassinations of Martin Luther King, Jr. (April 4, 1968), in Memphis, Tennessee, and Robert Kennedy (June 5, 1968) in Los Angeles, California. Although blacks would continue to take advantage of affirmative action and civil rights legislation enacted during the Johnson administration, the formal civil rights movement had clearly come to an end, partially eclipsed by the conflict in Vietnam. War protests began to replace civil rights protests, especially when young men were drafted in great numbers. Black men served disproportionately in this conflict and died disproportionately as well. The 1970s brought the end of the war in Vietnam and the beginning of economic recession in the United States. In the decades approaching the end of the twentieth century the problems confronting African Americans were largely social and economic, but as a group they had made more progress than ever before.

ECONOMIC DOWNTURNS AND THE RISE OF THE UNDERCLASS

Throughout the decades following the civil rights movement, a growing number of African Americans began to make impressive intellectual and cultural contributions. Spurred on by their success in dismantling segregation and identifying problems in the urban North, they continued to identify problems and work toward solutions. However, a new set of problems began to emerge, tied particularly to the economic shifts within the nation and the world.

African Americans as a group had always achieved economic success at a lesser rate than Americans as a whole. However, in the 1970s, social scientists began to realize that a great disparity had emerged between middle-class blacks and those at the very bottom of the economic ladder, the underclass. In a series of studies published as three books, William Junius Wilson, a Chicago sociologist, described dramatic changes that had taken place within the African American population. In *The Declining Significance of Race* (1980), Wilson pointed out that middle-class blacks had been able to take advantage of new opportunities arising out of the increased prosperity following World War II and the elimination of many of the racial obstacles that had previously stymied their progress. However, those without the necessary education and skills actually became worse off. At the very bottom of the lower class was an underclass, the subject of Wilson's second book, *The Truly Disadvantaged* (1987).

According to Wilson, the underclass reached a state of crisis in the 1970s that had not before been known among ghetto-bound poor people. This crisis took the form of what he called "social dislocation"—that is, the increase in "inner-city joblessness, teenage pregnancies, out-of-wedlock births, female-headed families, welfare dependency and serious crime" had reached "catastrophic proportions" (1987:3). The loss of middle-class and working-class families from the neighborhoods resulted in a destabilizing of ghetto communities and the erosion of patterns of mainstream behavior. Wilson also argued that racism in the standard sense couldn't explain the situation. Rather, the historical effects of racism and their institutionalized expression in labor markets were to blame and perhaps constituted an ongoing problem (1987:7–12).

Wilson tied the plight of the underclass to the continuous migration of blacks to cities just as the labor market was changing, so that relocation of many industries outside city centers, along with a general shift to service industries, constituted a major economic disadvantage to those blacks with the fewest skills and mobility. Because more blacks were always arriving, there was always a critical level of poor blacks (1987:142). The ensuing joblessness had a profound effect on family structure that Wilson says led to the particular inner-city pathologies he identified.

In his third book on the topic, *When Work Disappears*, Wilson reinforced the idea that it is the severity of unemployment that leads to the problems of the inner-city underclass: "As the population drops and the proportion of nonworking adults rises, basic neighborhood institutions are more difficult to maintain: stores, banks, credit institutions, restaurants, dry cleaners, gas stations, medical doctors, and so on lose regular and potential patrons" (1997:44). Thus, neighborhoods deteriorated more and more, and blacks who might have shared the same values as other Americans found it impossible to implement them in such dire circumstances.

FAMILY, RELIGION, AND THE AFRICAN AMERICAN EXPERIENCE AT THE TWENTY-FIRST CENTURY

The identification of a black underclass fed into an ongoing American myth about the pathology of the black family—myths reinforced by social scientific studies such as Gunnar Myrdal's *An American Dilemma* (1944), which concluded that African American culture was *"a distorted development, or a pathological condition, of the general American culture"* (p. 928, emphasis in original) or that

"peculiarities in the Negro community may be characterized as social pathology," or that "the average Negro family is more disorganized than the white family" (pp. 929, 931); or such as *The Negro Family*, by Daniel Patrick Moynihan, which states that "at the heart of the deterioration of the fabric of Negro society is the deterioration of the Negro family" (1965:5). Although both reports, among others, were meant to spur action on behalf of African Americans, the assimilationist assumptions, also inherent in the earlier work of E. Franklin Frazier (1966), came close to declaring that any forms of family not exactly like the "typical" American family were inherently pathological and that female-headed households so prevalent in the black community were inherently pathological. And while truly disintegrating families characterized only a small percentage of all African American families, this image came to stand for the whole, once again invalidating the lives and culture of the group.

However, as Robert Staples has pointed out, changes in the American family generally have followed the same pattern as African American families in terms of single-parent households and out-of-wedlock pregnancies. For example, in 1992, 25 percent of all white mothers were not married, 30 percent of all families were presided over by single parents in 1991, and 30 percent of all households were made up of single people (1999:286). In other words, the constitution of the American family generally has undergone changes that were once considered pathological among African Americans but that seem to reflect lifestyle shifts and structural changes in the dominant society.

Although family has always been a central value of African Americans, the form of the family in the black community did not always conform to the larger society's idea of the isolated nuclear family headed by a male with a stay-at-home mother. Rather, African Americans tended to place emphasis on extended family relationships, parent-child bonds, sibling bonds, and kin networks—facts substantiated by a number of studies (see Cheatham and Stewart 1990; Collins 1991; Martin and Martin 1978; Shimkin et al. 1978; Stack 1974; Staples 1999)—and African American women tend to be employed outside the home. The fate of the black family in the twenty-first century will most likely depend on the social and economic climate of the country as a whole.

However, an enduring characteristic of African Americans has been their deep religious conviction. In the last decade of the twentieth century, pollsters George Gallup and Jim Castelli not only declared the United States the most religious of developed countries, but African Americans as the most religious Americans and some of "the most religious people in the world" (1989:122). Gallup and Castelli also report that 77 percent of all African Americans are Protestants, 11 percent are Catholic, and 10 percent have no affiliation. More than half of all African Americans are Baptists. "They account for 29 percent of all Baptists" (1989:124). Thus, a deep spirituality, taking many forms, constitutes an abiding continuity with the past.

End-of-century developments, such as the rise of black feminism, the rise of Afrocentrism, and the coming into prominence of black intellectuals, indicate that African Americans continue to act as agents of change and contributors to culture within the United States.

NOTES

1. African Americans have been called many things over the years. First, they were referred to as Africans, then Blacks, Negroes, colored, blacks, Afro-Americans, and finally African Americans. Although African American is my term of choice and the appropriate contemporary usage, I will occasionally quote from works of an earlier era in which other names are used. I will also use black interchangeably with African American for the sake of brevity and variety.
2. The name *Seminole* means "seceders," those Native Americans originally known as the Lower Creeks, who separated from other Lower Creeks by moving into Florida in the 1700s (Porter 1996:5).
3. Reconstruction is a complex and controversial subject among historians, and I cannot do justice to it here. For more elaborate treatment of this period and of the role of African

Americans, see Anderson (1988), Foner (1988), Gutman (1976), Holt (1977), Schweninger (1990), and Shenton (1963)—to name only a few.

REFERENCES CITED

ABERNATHY, RALPH DAVID. 1989. *And the Walls Came Tumbling Down: An Autobiography*. New York: Harper & Row.

ANDERSON, JAMES D. 1988. *The Education of Blacks in the South, 1860–1935*. Chapel Hill: University of North Carolina Press.

ASANTE, MOLEFI KETE. 1990. African elements in African-American English. In *Africanisms in American Culture*. Joseph E. Holloway, ed. Pp. 19–33. Bloomington: Indiana University Press.

BERNSTEIN, DAVID E. 1998. The law and economics of post–Civil War restriction on interstate migration by African Americans. *Texas Law Review* 76(4):781–847.

CASHMAN, SEAN DENNIS. 1991. *African-Americans and the Quest for Civil Rights, 1900–1990*. New York: New York University Press.

CHEATHAM, HAROLD E., and JAMES B. STEWART, eds. 1990. *Black Families: Interdisciplinary Perspectives*. New Brunswick, NJ: Transaction.

COLLINS, PATRICIA HILL. 1991. *Black Feminist Thought: Knowledge, Consciousness, and the Politics of Empowerment*. New York: Routledge.

CREEL, MARGARET WASHINGTON. 1990. Gullah attitudes toward life and death. In *Africanisms in American Culture*. Joseph E. Holloway, ed. Pp. 69–97. Bloomington: Indiana University Press.

CURTIN, PHILIP D. 1969. *The Atlantic Slave Trade: A Census*. Madison: University of Wisconsin Press.

——. 1990. *The Rise and Fall of the Plantation Complex: Essays in Atlantic History*. Cambridge: Cambridge University Press.

DEAGAN, KATHLEEN, and DARCIE MacMAHON. 1995. *Fort Mose: Colonial America's Black Fortress of Freedom*. Gainesville: University Press of Florida/Florida Museum of Natural History.

DEETZ, JAMES. 1996. *In Small Things Forgotten: An Archaeology of Early American Life*. Expanded and Revised. New York: Anchor/Doubleday.

DRAKE, ST. CLAIR, and HORACE R. CAYTON. 1945. *Black Metropolis: A Study of Negro Life in a Northern City*. New York: Harcourt, Brace and Company.

DU BOIS, W. E. BURGHARDT. 1970. *Black Folk Then and Now: An Essay in the History and Sociology of the Negro Race*. New York: Octagon Books.

FONER, ERIC. 1988. *Reconstruction: America's Unfinished Revolution 1863–1877*. New York: Harper & Row.

FRANKLIN, JOHN HOPE, and LOREN SCHWENINGER. 1999. *Runaway Slaves: Rebels on the Plantation*. New York: Oxford University Press.

FRAZIER, E. FRANKLIN. 1966. *The Negro Family in the United States*. Revised and Abridged. Chicago: University of Chicago Press.

GALLUP, GEORGE, and JIM CASTELLI. 1989. *The People's Religion: American Faith in the 90's*. New York: Macmillan.

GENOVESE, EUGENE D. 1974. *Roll, Jordan, Roll: The World the Slaves Made*. New York: Pantheon.

GUTMAN, HERBERT G. 1976. *The Black Family in Slavery and Freedom, 1750–1925*. New York: Vintage.

HENRI, FLORETTE, 1976. *Black Migration: Movement North 1900–1920*. Garden City, NY: Anchor Books.

HERSKOVITS, MELVILLE J. 1990 [1941]. *The Myth of the Negro Past*. Boston: Beacon Press.

HOLLOWAY, JOSEPH E. 1990. The origins of African American culture. In *Africanisms in American Culture*. Joseph E. Holloway, ed. Pp. 1–18. Bloomington: Indiana University Press.

HOLT, THOMAS. 1977. *Black Over White: Negro Political Leadership in South Carolina during Reconstruction*. Urbana: University of Illinois Press.

JONES, STEVEN L. 1985. The African-American tradition in architecture. In *The Archaeology of Slavery and Plantation Life*. Theresa A. Singleton, ed. Pp. 195–213. San Diego: Academic Press.

LEMANN, NICHOLAS. 1991. *The Promised Land: The Great Black Migration and How It Changed America*. New York: Vintage.

LIGGIO, LEONARD P. 1976. English origins of early American racism. *Radical History Review* 3(1):1–36.

MABUNDA, L. MPHO. 1997. *The African American Almanac*. 7th edition. Detroit: Gale.

MARKS, CAROLE. 1989. *Farewell—We're Good and Gone: The Great Black Migration*. Bloomington: Indiana University Press.

MARTIN, ELMER P., and JOANNE MITCHELL MARTIN. 1978. *The Black Extended Family*. Chicago: University of Chicago Press.

MAULTSBY, PORTIA K. 1990. Africanisms in African-American music. In *Africanisms in American Culture*. Joseph E. Holloway, ed. Pp. 185–210. Bloomington: Indiana University Press.

MINTZ, SIDNEY W., and RICHARD PRICE. 1976. *The Birth of African-American Culture: An Anthropological Perspective*. Boston: Beacon Press.

MORGAN, PHILIP D. 1998. *Slave Counterpoint: Black Culture in the Eighteenth-Century Chesapeake and Lowcountry*. Chapel Hill: University of North Carolina Press.

MOSES, WILSON JEREMIAH. 1996. *Classical Black Nationalism: From the American Revolution to Marcus Garvey*. New York: New York University Press.

MOYNIHAN, DANIEL PATRICK. 1965. *The Negro Family: The Case for National Action*. Washington, DC: Office of Policy Planning and Research, U.S. Department of Labor.

MYRDAL, GUNNAR. 1944. *An American Dilemma: The Negro Problem and Modern Democracy*. New York: Harper & Bros.

NASH, GARY B. 1983. Forging freedom: The emancipation experience in the northern seaport cities, 1775–1820. In *Slavery and Freedom in the Age of the American Revolution*. Ira Berlin and Ronald Hoffman, eds. Pp. 3–48. Charlottesville: University Press of Virginia/United States Capitol Historical Society.

National Research Council. 1989. *A Common Destiny: Blacks and American Society*. Committee on the Status of Black Americans, Commission on Behavioral and Social Sciences and Education. Washington, DC: National Academy Press.

NORTON, MARY BETH, HERBERT G. GUTMAN, and IRA BERLIN. 1983. The Afro-American family in the age of revolution. In *Slavery and Freedom in the Age of the American Revolution*. Ira Berlin and Ronald Hoffman, eds. Pp. 175–191. Charlottesville: University Press of Virginia/United States Capitol Historical Society.

OTTENHEIMER, HARRIET. 1992. Comoro crossroads: African bardic traditions and the origins of the blues. *Human Mosaic* 26(2):32–38.

PHILIPS, JOHN EDWARD. 1990. The African heritage of white America. In *Africanisms in American Culture*. Joseph E. Holloway, ed. Pp. 225–239. Bloomington: Indiana University Press.

PORTER, KENNETH W. 1996. *The Black Seminoles: History of a Freedom-Loving People*. Revised and edited by Alcione M. Amos and Thomas P. Senter. Gainesville: University Press of Florida.

POWDERMAKER, HORTENSE. 1993. *After Freedom: A Cultural Study in the Deep South*. Madison: University of Wisconsin.

QUARLES, BENJAMIN. 1964. *The Negro in the Making of America*. New York: Collier.

ROBINSON, JO ANN GIBSON. 1987. *The Montgomery Bus Boycott and the Women Who Started It*. Knoxville: University of Tennessee Press.

SCHWENINGER, LOREN. 1990. *Black Property Owners in the South 1790–1915*. Urbana: University of Illinois Press.

SHENTON, JAMES PATRICK, ed. 1963. *The Reconstruction: A Documentary History of the South after the War: 1865–1877*. New York: Capricorn Books.

SHIMKIN, DEMITRI B., EDITH M. SHIMKIN, and DENNIS A. FRATE. 1978. *The Extended Family in Black Societies*. The Hague: Mouton.

SINGLETON, THERESA A., ed. 1985. *The Archaeology of Slavery and Plantation Life*. San Diego: Academic Press.

SINGLETON, THERESA A., and MARK D. BOGRAD. 1995. *Archaeology of the African Diaspora in the Americas*. Guides to the Archaeological Literature of Immigrant Experience in America, No. 2. Tucson: Society for Historical Archaeology.

SMEDLEY, AUDREY. 1999. *Race in North America: Origin and Evolution of a Worldview*. 2nd edition. Boulder, CO: Westview Press.

SOBEL, MECHAL. 1987. *The World They Made Together: Black and White Values in Eighteenth-Century Virginia.* Princeton, NJ: Princeton University Press.

STACK, CAROL B. 1974. *All Our Kin: Strategies for Survival in a Black Community.* New York: Harper Torchbooks.

STAPLES, ROBERT. 1999. *The Black Family: Essays and Studies.* Belmont, CA: Wadsworth.

STOPER, EMILY. 1989. *The Student Nonviolent Coordinating Committee: The Growth of Radicalism in a Civil Rights Organization.* Brooklyn, NY: Carlson.

STRAUSS, CLAUDIA, and NAOMI QUINN. 1997. *A Cognitive Theory of Cultural Meaning.* Cambridge: Cambridge University Press.

THOMPSON, ROBERT FARRIS. 1990. Kongo influences on African-American artistic culture. In *Africanisms in American Culture.* Joseph E. Holloway, ed. Pp. 148–184. Bloomington: Indiana University Press.

TROTTER, JOE WILLIAM, ed. 1991. *The Great Migration in Historical Perspective: New Dimensions of Race, Class, and Gender.* Bloomington: Indiana University Press.

U.S. Census Bureau. 1999. *Statistical Abstract of the United States, the National Data Book. 119th edition* (October 1999). Washington, DC: Economics and Statistics Administration, U.S. Department of Commerce.

WALKER, DENNIS. 1999. America's Western system and Black Muslim protest. *Eastern Anthropologist* 52(2):119–143.

WILSON, WILLIAM JUNIUS. 1980. *The Declining Significance of Race: Blacks and Changing American Institutions.* 2nd edition. Chicago: University of Chicago Press.

——. 1987. *The Truly Disadvantaged: The Inner City, the Underclass, and Public Policy.* Chicago: University of Chicago Press.

——. 1997. *When Work Disappears: The World of the New Urban Poor.* New York: Knopf.

WOODSON, CARTER G. 1936. *The African Background Outlined.* No publisher listed.

9 JEWISH AMERICANS

Jack Glazier

Oberlin College

Even before the founding of the United States, Jews were living in North America. The first Jewish residents of the New World were Spanish speakers, and, indeed, Columbus's crew on his first voyage to the Western Hemisphere in all likelihood included a few Sephardic Jews (Jews of Spanish origin). Sephardim were the predominant Jewish group in the colonial era and in the early years of American independence. Although tracing their origins to Spain, many arrived in the New World by way of Holland and England, where their forbears settled following the Jewish expulsion from Spain in 1492. Since the 1970s, a large immigration of Jews from the former Soviet Union, as well as a smaller number of arrivals from Asia and the Middle East, has added to the diverse mix of Jewish Americans. During the intervening centuries, Jews from many places, but especially Germany, Russia, Poland, and other countries of Central and Eastern Europe, settled in the United States. Jewish ethnicity represents a dynamic phenomenon, changing its character with each Jewish immigrant accretion and alter-

ing again as each immigrant stream adjusted to life in the new country.

Across the diverse spectrum of Jewish immigrant groups to the United States, few people returned to the places of their birth. The precarious status of Jews in their European countries of origin explains to a considerable extent the low rates of Jewish reverse migration. As a case in point, Eastern European Jews, known as Ashkenazic Jews, were for centuries a particularly visible minority without civil rights, and therefore vulnerable to official and unofficial discrimination. They were subject to anti-Semitic decrees and policies restricting them to particular locales and limiting their ability to earn a living. The anti-Semitic climate also encouraged periodic mob attacks against Jewish life and property. By the 1880s, these factors set in motion a large Jewish immigration to the United States that continued until the mid-1920s. During those four decades, approximately 2.5 million Jews from Eastern Europe settled in the United States (Goldscheider and Zuckerman 1984:162).

The circumstances of Jewish life in Eastern

191

Europe did not encourage the kinds of nationalistic or political ties to the old country that the descendants of Polish, Serbian, Greek, Hungarian, or other Eastern and Central European immigrants embrace. Despite some strong cultural attachments to their communities of origin, Jewish immigrants cast their lot irrevocably with America. Their one-way immigration pattern also typified the experience of Jewish immigrants during the American colonial period, the movement of German-speaking Jews in the mid-nineteenth century, the arrival of Sephardic Jews from the Balkans in the early twentieth century, and, most recently, the immigration of Russian Jews over the last three decades.

The Jewish population of the United States numbers approximately 5.9 million people (Kosmin and Scheckner 1995:171). This population is fairly stable, with births and deaths nearly balanced. Some increase in the Jewish population in the 1990s is accountable by immigration, predominantly from the former Soviet Union. Without the addition of immigrants, Jewish American demographic trends are toward zero or even negative population growth. In addition, strong tendencies within Jewish communities to assimilate into American society diminish, but do not obliterate, the distinctiveness of Jewish Americans.

Religiously endogamous for most of their history—that is, a community that emphasized marriage within the group—Jews of America are now marrying exogamously (outside of the group) in record numbers, and there is no indication that these figures will decline. Reporting on marriages between 1985 and 1990, a large national survey found that approximately 52 percent of Jewish Americans were marrying non-Jewish people (Kosmin et al. 1991:14). The majority of the children of these unions in all probability will maintain only the weakest bonds to Jewish life. These factors, as well as other assimilative tendencies that diminish the religious and ethnic distinctiveness of Jewish communities, raise questions about the Jewish future in the United

States. Seymour Lipset and Earl Rabb observe that "current evidence suggests that group identity and cohesiveness are severely eroding for the large majority" (1995:47).

Throughout the twentieth century, when some 40 million newcomers arrived in the United States, immigrants actively struggled to synthesize new identities out of diverse cultural elements of the old and new countries. How could it be otherwise? The decision to emigrate, and especially, to settle permanently in a new country, is momentous. One enters a novel social and linguistic world. Familiar patterns of life and networks of social and economic support can be found only among other immigrants from one's homeland. Additionally, immigrant communities have received as much criticism as praise from the host society. Such processes can only bring turmoil in a person's self-concept and sense of tradition as he or she tries to negotiate a psychological and social place in the new society.

Ethnic culture, therefore, changes in accord with the strategies an immigrant group utilizes to adapt themselves to vastly new circumstances. These strategies, in turn, depend on how the host society views the persistence of immigrant cultures in its midst. Until the 1960s, American society took a dim view of ethnic communities seeking to maintain their cultural traditions and, instead, exhorted them to conform to the cultural mainstream, as the "melting pot" metaphor suggests. Relatedly, the prior experience of co-ethnics or coreligionists in the new country also influences accommodation strategies. The millions of Jewish immigrants arriving in the four decades after 1881 had before them relatively successful models of assimilation; these were the German American Jews, who had immigrated in the mid-nineteenth century. Their ideology of cultural assimilation into American society as well as their economic achievements accorded well with American values and set the stage for the next wave of Jewish immigrants.

Jewish immigrants as a whole identified

closely with the new country, and hence the stakes were extraordinarily high in their effort to reach some accommodation and a reformulated identity. There was simply no going back. By contrast, some immigrant groups of the time—Italians for example—included many people who were "birds of passage," that is, temporary sojourners planning ultimately to return to the old country. Less consumed by identity conflicts, they were also impervious to pressures to learn English or to adopt American cultural patterns. The "birds of passage" aimed to work for awhile and then return to Europe with money far beyond their potential earnings in Italy. In some years, the Italian rate of return was over 50 percent, while the Jewish return averaged about 8 percent (Glazier 1998:83).

Although there was not a single mode of Jewish immigrant adjustment to America a century ago, one way dominated. I refer here to *assimilation*, a process fully in keeping with the mainstream discourse about how to be an American. In the course of the immigrant experience, identities were largely reformulated in a complex process that alienated many of the newcomers, and especially their children, from old country traditions. The immigrants were, after all, faced with two mutually exclusive but very uneven choices—to be culturally different or to be equal. To remain different was to spurn the widely endorsed process of assimilation, or Americanization, as it was sometimes designated; immigrants would thereby lose the respect of their American neighbors and forgo the possibility of social and economic mobility. During the years of immigration, there was little discussion of how the country at large might adjust to the newcomers. Rather, the adjustment was conceived in the popular view as a one-way street bearing only immigrant traffic en route to assimilation. Still, assimilation is not a simple process; it has affected Judaism and Jewish culture somewhat differently

The public discourse exhorted the immigrants to throw off ethnic practices in favor of conformity to more "American" styles. Such conformity occurred in many ways, large and small, including a turning away from ethnic vernaculars in favor of English and spurning ethnic-sounding names in favor of names that would not betray one's cultural origins. Jewish name-changing abounded among ordinary people and celebrities alike, including popular actors and entertainers such as John Garfield (Julius Garfinkel), Tony Curtis (Bernie Schwartz), Doris Day (Doris Kapplehoff), Kirk Douglas (Issur Danielovitch), and Bob Dylan (Robert Zimmerman). Of course these patterns were not limited to Jewish immigrants and their children; all Eastern and Southern European immigrant groups were subject to the same pressures toward Anglo conformity.

Along with other ethnic groups, Jewish immigrants had great difficulty sustaining themselves in a manner approximating their life in the old country. Moreover, repudiating cultural assimilation was unpatriotic. Until the 1960s, many Americans believed that a healthy, functioning democracy required cultural homogeneity, and hence the commitment of immigrants to the United States was in part measured by their progress in learning English and adopting American values and behaviors.

Jewish immigrants and others certainly experienced enormous prejudice and bigotry in the early 1900s. Often cast in racial terms, anti-Jewish and anti-immigrant sentiment in some ways paralleled the racism suffered by African Americans. Yet without the visible marker of skin color, the European immigrants endured the most overt and destructive forms of bigotry for only a generation, and it did not impede economic mobility over the long term. In effect, Jews, along with other European groups, "became white" (Brodkin 1998).

Collectively, Jewish Americans, whatever their immigrant origins, have achieved extraordinary success by virtually any measure. But that record is by no means universal among Jewish Americans. National statistics on Jewish success obscure the Jewish poor, who can usually avoid public relief and welfare rolls. Jewish communal organizations care for the poor across the country and, because they are private, manage to keep Jewish dependency from public view. Nevertheless, pockets of Jewish poverty occur, particularly among the elderly (Myerhoff 1979). But many Jewish immigrants from the former Soviet Union also require the assistance of Jewish organizations as well as the federal supports available to refugees. A recent estimate indicates that one-quarter of the Jewish population of New York City is near or below the poverty level (*Cleveland Plain Dealer* 2000).

Conventionally, social scientists utilize data on income, occupation, and education as indices of class. Among all ethnic groups in the United States, Jews have reached some of the highest rankings. Family incomes are far above the American average, and Jewish representation in the professions, business, and the arts is well in excess of their numbers in the general population. Strong values on learning and scholarship combined with economic success have enabled the majority of Jewish Americans to send their children to college. Jewish Americans have thus attained a remarkably high educational level. They hold a wide range of elected and appointed political offices at the federal, state, and local levels; judicial posts, including U.S. Supreme Court judgeships; and advisory positions at the highest echelons of government.

These patterns clearly indicate that widespread anti-Semitism withered over the course of the twentieth century. Virulent anti-Semitism is now the province of only the most fringe elements of American society; no one can inject any form of anti-Semitism into the public discourse without the severest opprobrium and condemnation. Jewish Americans have indeed achieved equality in American life, and, as they have done so, cultural differences between themselves and their fellow citizens have atrophied.

The force of assimilation has resulted in the cultural convergence of several different streams of Jewish immigration. Although of diverse European origin, the Jewish American population has grown more uniform through its upward economic and social mobility and its entry into the American cultural mainstream. What were once cultural or ethnic differences among several Jewish immigrant groups—German and Eastern European Ashkenazic Jews and Sephardic Jews from the Balkans—have attenuated in the course of two generations. Now, the grandchildren of the Jewish immigrants arriving from Russia in 1910 and the grandchildren of Jewish immigrants arriving from Serbia at the same period share more in common culturally than they do with their respective grandparents. While ethnicity is not obliterated by the openness and opportunities of American society, it has certainly been fundamentally transformed in the experience of Jews and other European-derived groups.

RELIGION, RACE, ETHNICITY

Whereas Judaism constitutes a universally recognized world religion, the status of Jews as an ethnic category apart from their religious affiliation has been much less apparent. In the matter of "race," the same confusion consistently attaching to that term points up the error of considering Jews as a distinct biological group. Many years ago, Franz Boas, the most influential American anthropologist of the twentieth century, exposed the fallacies of the race concept. Writing in 1938, he observed that

> The term race, as applied to human types, is vague. It can have a biological significance only when a race represents a uniform, closely inbred group, in which all family lines are alike—as in pure breeds of domesticated animals. These conditions are never realized in human types and impossible in large populations. [1938:227]

He also pointed out the inadequacy of race as a scientific tool for understanding culture, or shared and learned human behaviors. Yet the resurgence in recent years of racialized explanations of culture in the face of definitive evidence to the contrary gives Boas's viewpoint great contemporary relevance. His caution about race applies no less to Jews than to others. The Jewish people do not collectively constitute a "uniform, closely inbred group."

Boas also strenuously argued that no necessary or causal relationship linked biology and culture. The twentieth century bore grim witness to the baleful consequences of asserting such connections. Prior to the realization of its worst manifestations, Boas exposed the fallacy of Nazi racial ideology, explaining that in the Nazi view, "every person is supposed to have a definite, unalterable character according to his racial descent and this determines his political and social status" (1938:226). Likewise, he also criticized the attribution of many negative qualities to black people, whose actions were erroneously portrayed as "racially determined, unescapable [sic] qualities" (p. 22). Consequently, false assumptions about unalterable patterns of behavior stemming from biology have profoundly impeded the life chances of African Americans. When clothed in the language of science, such racial explanations of human behavior have been particularly pernicious, for they have provided the authority and rationale for justifying the suppression or even the killing of minority populations. Race is more properly regarded as a social and political invention, rather than an objective biological category. Cultural learning, not genetics or race, is the wellspring of human thought and behavior.

Unlike the explanatory dead end of race, the concept of "ethnicity" advances our understanding of the shape and diversity of cultural experience. Anthropologists regard ethnicity as a set of cultural features marking a distinctive community of descent, that is, a community of common cultural origin that continues through many generations. The cultural features that define an ethnic group are manifold and include shared language and religion. These, in turn, stem from a mutual history. Additionally, people of a single ethnic group have in common a broad range of cultural practices and beliefs that mark the group as distinct and delineate the group's social and cultural boundaries. These shared cultural features include dress, food, music and dance, humor, ceremonies, family dynamics, folklore, and a host of other traits. The cultural markers of an ethnic group represent the outward symbols of personal and collective identity and at the same time enable outsiders to distinguish it from other ethnic groups.

Individuals acquire the behavioral features characteristic of their ethnic groups through enculturation, or socialization, from earliest childhood. Ethnic affiliation is thus very much a matter of birth rather than choice. Yet a word of caution is necessary: one is born into an ethnic group, but ethnicity is acquired through the medium of culture rather than biology, no matter how deeply rooted, primordial, or "natural" ethnic patterns of behavior may appear. It is, therefore, erroneous to "racialize" ethnicity.

In considering Jewish ethnicity, the first task is to differentiate it from Judaism as a religion. The set of rituals, practices, beliefs, and sacred symbols constituting Judaism can be compared to those of Catholicism, Protestantism, Islam, and other world religions. But, in addition, Jewish ethnic affiliation is comparable to Polish, Italian, or Irish ethnic identity, apart from the Catholicism that these three groups share. The distinction between the religious and ethnic, or cultural, dimensions of the Jewish experience helps to make intelligible the segmentation characterizing the lives of many Jewish Americans. However paradoxical, they may identify closely with the distinctive cultural characteristics of their communities and forthrightly affirm a Jewish identity while also insisting that they are agnostics or even atheists.

To sort through the religious as opposed to the ethnic dimension of Jewish life, the anthropological distinction between the Great Tradition and the Little Tradition is particularly helpful (Redfield 1956). The *Great Tradition* refers to the sectors of culture that are codified or systematized by a literate elite. They are the authorities on the "official" version of the religion. In Judaism, the Great Tradition includes a body of sacred texts, prayers, liturgy, rituals, and a cycle of holy day observances determined by a lunar calendar. The Hebrew language serves as the medium of religious practice. Transcending place and time, these features with some variation define Jewish religious life throughout the world, although particular Jewish communities may otherwise differ culturally and linguistically. The rituals for any particular Jewish observance will thus be similar across the spectrum of the world's Jewish communities.

Until the eighteenth century, the range of variation in rabbinic understandings and interpretations of the Great Tradition was limited by the prevailing orthodoxy of Jewish communities and their religious leadership. Controversial tendencies toward liberalization in belief and practice then emerged. Some communities abandoned the dietary laws or utilized languages other than Hebrew in the religious service. Support of tradition or a move toward change or innovation hinged on whether one believed that customary beliefs must adjust to the realities of a modern scientific world.

Complementing the Great Tradition is the *Little Tradition*, where ethnic features of community life independent of religion are paramount. The Little Tradition springs from the experience of daily living. It includes an entire cultural complex of activities and outlooks within a community. The languages of the Little Tradition, as well as the cultural practices, vary considerably in the Jewish communities in North America, South America, Europe, and Asia. The Little Tradition varies much more than the Great Tradition. In effect, it is appropriate to identify several Little Traditions, or ethnicities, within Judaism

The intensity or significance of ethnic affilia-tion can vary over time. In keeping with its place as a cultural phenomenon, ethnicity is always fluid, changing gradually or, sometimes, dramatically, as exemplified by the Jews of America. Change in ethnic consciousness is particularly apparent in regard to the idea of the melting pot.

Prior to the 1960s, for example, many native-born Americans embraced the melting pot metaphor. That is, old bonds, loyalties, and cultural patterns were to be left behind in the old country in favor of a new, American identity. In this view, the distinctions and boundaries among various ethnic groupings would dissolve as the children of immigrants would come to share more with each other than they did with their immigrant parents and grandparents. They would simply be "Americans" rather than German-Americans, Italian-Americans, Polish-Americans, or some other hyphenated identity. The process of "melting" began among the immigrants and accelerated in the second generation as ethnic groups rejected hyphenated identities. They sought instead to enter the mainstream only as "Americans" without a qualifying designation.

A telling illustration of the hold that the melting pot metaphor had on the American imagination is its literalization at the Ford Motor Company. Between 1914 and 1921, Ford offered its workers a profit-sharing plan if they would join the Ford English School, "to impress these men that they are, or should be, Americans, and that their former racial, national and linguistic differences are to be forgotten." As described by the historian Lawrence Levine,

> Commencement exercises were held in a large hall. On the stage in front of a model of an immigrant ship stood a huge pot, seven and a half feet high and fifteen feet in diameter. The graduating members of the class, dressed in clothes representative of the nations from which they had come and carrying the types of luggage they had brought with them when they first arrived in the United States, marched down the gangplank from the ship and disappeared into the pot. Six of their teachers then stirred the pot with ten-foot-long

ladles. When the pot began to "boil over," the workers emerged, . . . dressed in their best American clothes and waving American flags. [1996:111]

While the Ford English School commencement was unusually heavy-handed in conveying its cultural message, melting pot values in one form or another were ubiquitous in American society.

The power of the melting pot metaphor has greatly diminished in recent decades, and various Americans of European origin are now seeking to rediscover their immigrant and ethnic roots. Jewish Americans, as well as other groups, realize that the changes wrought in their ethnic communities over the course of the twentieth century have been extraordinary; various projects in cultural reclamation attest to the strong contemporary interest in asserting and demonstrating an ethnic heritage.

SEPHARDIC JEWS IN THE COLONIAL ERA

Until the eighteenth century, most of the early Jewish settlements in North America were composed of Sephardim—descendants of the Jews of Spain. Under the Spanish Inquisition, the latter had suffered expulsion from their homeland, beginning in the year of Columbus's westward voyage. Later, Jewish expulsions also occurred in Portugal. After 1492, Spanish Jewish refugees managed to find safe haven in a few places, including the Ottoman Empire, Holland, and the settlements in the Americas. The first documented arrival of Sephardic Jews in colonial America occurred in 1654, when 23 Jews arrived in New York following their banishment from Brazil. Dutch settlements in Brazil had provided a relatively safe haven for Jews, but the Portuguese conquest of these settlements imperiled the Jewish settlers. Mostly merchants and tradesmen, Sephardic Jews in the early days of the United States very successfully accommodated themselves to their new communities. In Spain, they were a generally prosperous, cosmopolitan minority, respected by their neighbors and unconfined to ghettos or other restricted areas. They mingled easily with the Christian majority in a social pattern that would eventually be duplicated in America. By the early nineteenth century, many Sephardic Jews had converted to Christianity or else married Christians in such large proportions that their descendants were eventually absorbed into the majority population.

GERMAN JEWS

Beginning in the late 1700s, other European Jews immigrated to America and eventually outnumbered the Sephardic settlers. Known collectively as Ashkenazic Jews, they originated in Central Europe and the German states, where Jews had lived since Roman times. After the First Crusade, anti-Jewish sentiment increased. The Jews then endured centuries of subjugation and periodic violence. By the 1300s, some Jews moved eastward into Poland and other parts of Central Europe. These Yiddish-speaking communities were the forbears of the wave of Jewish immigrants who began arriving in the United States in the 1880s.

The civil status of Jews in the German states and in parts of Western Europe greatly improved by the early nineteenth century after they were granted citizenship. Jews gained many of the social and political rights enjoyed by the Christian majority. They were thus able to participate in the Christian world on a more equal footing than at any time in the past. As a consequence of greater contact beyond the Jewish community, the process of linguistic and cultural assimilation gained momentum. Jewish communities came to utilize German more than Yiddish as other social differences between Jews and their neighbors eroded. At the same time, currents of religious change brought about a liberalization of Jewish belief and practice in some communities.

By the 1820s, economic decline and periodic outbreaks of anti-Semitism spurred many Jews in Central Europe, including the German states and Austria-Hungary, to seek refuge and commercial opportunities in the United States. This process continued over the next thirty years, increasing the Jewish population of the United States from roughly 1,200 in the late eighteenth century to approximately 50,000 in 1850 (Goldscheider and Zuckerman 1984:158). The German-speaking Jews were part of a much larger German immigration arriving over the course of several decades but particularly during the 1830s and 1840s.

Although German Jewish immigrants plied several trades, they were mostly merchants and itinerant peddlers. Quickly distributing themselves throughout the country, they took advantage of the opportunities for trade and commerce created by the movement westward. They were eager to make a new life where Jewishness would not narrow their opportunities. Settling in towns and cities, they also ventured into frontier settlements as shopkeepers or itinerant peddlers. Many contemporary American Jewish communities thus trace their origins to these German Jewish merchants. Until the 1880s, German Jews defined the ethnic and religious character of American Jewish life.

With little reservation German Jews in America embraced assimilation and Reform Judaism, a very liberal version of their faith that accorded well with their goal of blending into the new country. Reform Judaism rejected many traditional beliefs and practices that were believed to be unenlightened and irrational in a scientific age. The traditional dietary laws about kosher food, the exclusive use of Hebrew rather than German or English in religious services, and the separation of men and women in synagogues were some of the traditions regarded as outdated and retrograde. German Jews wanted to obliterate the cultural differences between themselves and their non-Jewish neighbors. Only religion should distinguish Jews from non-Jews, but even

on this point, religious differences were reduced since Reform Judaism was purging itself of many ancient and medieval religious practices.

A particularly dramatic declaration of independence from traditional practice occurred in Cincinnati on July 11, 1883. A banquet celebrating the tenth anniversary of the Union of American Hebrew Congregations (a federation of Reform temples) and the first graduates of the Hebrew Union College (a Reform seminary) featured various "abominations of Leviticus," foods prohibited in the Bible to the followers of Moses (Douglas 1966:54–72). The food prohibitions in Leviticus were in part the basis of the ancient kosher laws of Judaism. The banquet menu included clams, crabs, shrimp, and frog legs; additionally nonkosher beef appeared on the table, as well as cheese and ice cream, which, as dairy products, should never be served with meat. This subversion of Jewish religious symbolism provoked Orthodox guests at the banquet to exit en masse.

Cultural assimilation represented a strong value for Reform Jews. They believed their future lay in social integration in the United States rather than social separation. Because such Orthodox practices as strict dietary laws drew sharp boundaries around the faithful, thereby estranging them from non-Jews, the assimilationist-minded German Jews rejected them as added barriers to association and social exchange with other communities. The dietary laws in particular presented a salient object of Reform redefinitions of Judaism, in both its religious and social dimensions. Dispensing with the kosher laws and conventional meanings surrounding food symbolism not only struck a blow for rationality but also celebrated the erosion of social distinctions that had historically alienated Jews from the Christian world. The banquet of 1883 dramatically illustrates how symbols can convey social messages about community boundaries; the messages may be about closure and exclusion or openness and incorporation (Glazier 1993:18–21). In other words, symbolic representations tell us something about a community's attitude toward acculturation and assimilation.

EASTERN EUROPEAN JEWS

The assassination of Czar Alexander II in 1881 set in motion the largest and most consequential Jewish immigration to the United States. Predicting a peasant revolution to topple the Russian monarchy, the assailants instead incited officially supported peasant violence and retaliation against Russian Jewish communities. Known as *pogroms*, these attacks included murder, rape, and the destruction of Jewish property and institutions. The government also enacted the notorious May Laws of 1882, severely curtailing the rights of Jews to gain an education, to live in particular places, to earn a living, or, in short, to eke out even the most meager existence. The bleakness of the Jewish future in Russia was apparent, as periodic violence and official repression continued into the twentieth century. These events triggered the massive Jewish immigration to the United States that continued for approximately four decades.

After some six hundred years in Eastern Europe, the Ashkenazic Jewish communities of Imperial Russia were in turmoil. For centuries they had withstood periodic violence and other state-sponsored repression before embarking on a great exodus to America. On the eve of this momentous immigration, the American Jewish population numbered approximately 250,000. In 1900, 1 million Jews lived in the United States, and by 1924, the American Jewish population had reached 4 million (Goldscheider and Zuckerman 1984:158). This massive movement of Russian Jews—the largest Jewish migration in modern history—established the United States, along with Eastern Europe, as a center of Jewish life. Relatedly, because Russian Jews differed significantly in terms of culture and religion from the American Jewish population of German background, the mass immigration altered the demographic profile and the cultural content of Jewish communal life. Of the approximately 5.9 million Jews now in the United States, the overwhelming majority are the descendants of the immigrants from Russia and Eastern Europe.

While the popular view of the Eastern European Jewish newcomers emphasizes their religious orthodoxy, this picture is incomplete. Indeed, it has been argued that the most religiously observant Jews remained in Europe because they considered America a godless land where people might well lose their faith. To the extent that some Jewish Americans emphasize the ethnic rather than the religious side of their Jewishness, such fears were prescient. The stereotypic view of the deeply religious Jewish immigrant also resolutely ignores the participation of some Jewish immigrants in organized crime.

The new immigrants shared the Yiddish language and the associated Little Tradition culture known as *yidishkayt*. In Eastern Europe, they had also faced widespread intolerance and violence at the hands of the peasantry. Their precarious social and political status provided no reliable protection for themselves or their property. They differed, however, in their religiosity. Some newcomers were Orthodox adherents to Jewish law and custom, while others were secular critics of tradition and rabbinical authority. The latter were often animated by socialist ideals and a general skepticism about all religion. Many were activists in the labor movement and mobilized against the horrific, exploitative conditions in sweatshops. Once in the United States, all the newcomers sought an end to their historic vulnerabilities in order to live on much the same terms as other American citizens. In religion and culture, the Russian Jews collectively were culturally distinct from the established American Jewish population of German background and were accustomed to living in a world suffused by Jewish tradition. Moreover, the religiously observant could not easily disentangle the cultural and religious strands of their lives.

Because German American Jews emphasized cultural assimilation and wanted to guard their own economic and social success, they were apprehensive about the consequences of a rapidly increasing population of Eastern European Jews. They believed that the new immigrants, so unlike themselves in language, values, class, and culture, might provoke anti-Semitism and thus jeopardize the position and security of the established Jewish population. Accordingly, German American Jews appealed to the newcomers to set aside those behaviors marking their peculiar immigrant status—whether it was radical politics or stubborn adherence to traditional religious practices that did not seem to fit well into the new country. Many immigrants, however, resented efforts to transform them culturally; they considered the German American Jews snobbish and condescending, hardly different from Christians. A recurring theme in twentieth-century American Jewish history is the antagonism between the Eastern European Jews and the German Jews over the question of how to reconcile a religious and/or ethnic Jewish identity to American life and citizenship.

Ironically, the apprehension of German American Jews about the capacity or willingness of the Russian Jewish immigrants to adjust to their new country was misplaced. Many of the newcomers from Eastern Europe were not against accommodation and cultural change but, rather, resented the paternalism of German American Jews in promoting assimilation. The newcomers adapted rapidly to American life, but they also wanted to exercise some control over that accommodation. They did not want the German American Jews to define its terms. Many Russian Jews, like earlier Jewish immigrants, went into business. In addition, the children of the Russian Jews attended college and university in steadily increasing numbers. Consequently, a large proportion of immigrant families achieved a rapid economic and social mobility, with accompanying cultural changes, in a relatively short period of time.

Jewish immigrants, often before they left their European homes, knew that they would face great pressures to accommodate themselves to an American life based on some approximation of Anglo conformity. They quickly learned the meaning of "greenhorn," a derisive term applied to immigrants who were either fresh off the boat or slow to adopt "superior" American ways.

Mary Antin, born in Plotzk in Russian-controlled Poland, arrived in Boston in 1897 with her mother and three siblings to join her father. An immigrant's celebration of America, her 1912 volume, *The Promised Land*, details her life in Poland, the six-week journey to the New World, and her rebirth, so to speak, in the United States. From her very first day in Boston, she learns the importance of quickly putting the world of Plotzk behind her. On the ride from the pier to the small apartment Mary's father has set up, he instructs the children "not to lean out the windows, not to point and explained the word 'greenhorn.' We did not want to be 'greenhorns' and gave the strictest attention to my father's instructions" (p. 185). Soon after, they were taken to a department store, "where we exchanged our hateful homemade European costumes, which pointed us out as 'greenhorns,' to the children on the street, for real American machine-made garments." The process continued, as the children also shed their "impossible Hebrew names," for American versions (p. 187).

Even if one were less sensitive than Mary Antin's father to the greenhorn characterization, changes in most traditional lives inevitably came about simply because of economic necessity. The rhythm of the American workweek, for example, immediately created a predicament for the most religious of the Jewish immigrants. Saturday, the Jewish Sabbath, was inviolate, a sacred day requiring the observance of ancient strictures. The suspension of work was essential, but the immigrants soon found out that Saturday was a workday in the United States. They faced the wrenching choice of observing the Sabbath or keeping a job that was essential to the survival of their families. Economic necessity usually won out over spiritual fidelity. It was little comfort to the immigrants that their employers were sometimes Eastern European Jewish immigrants or German Jews who had immigrated a generation before.

The following brief account indicates in very human terms the work pressures facing many immigrants. Set in New York City in 1912, the narrative begins with a Jewish immigrant's desperate inquiry about employment.

> "Mister," he whispers insinuatingly, Have you a job?
> "What kind of a job?" we ask him.
> "I don't know," he answers.
> "What is your trade?" we ask.
> "I'm just a common laborer."
> "A laborer?" we ask in distrust, scanning his wispy body. He shoves out a grimy, hairy hand, the hand of a Volga boatman, hard as a nail. "Where did you work?"

The job seeker then describes a harrowing experience in the West, where he was severely exploited on a labor gang,

> "Do you have a job? But I don't work on the Sabbath. I never work on the Sabbath."
> We explained the difficulty of finding him a job under that condition. He remained rooted to the ground, looked wistful, concentrated his face as though studying a riddle and went away. That afternoon he returned. . . . With him he brought his wife, a little woman, plaintive, battered by life, but with pleasant kindly features.
> "Mister," she said, "I will let my husband work on the Sabbath," and then gulping hard, "I will take the sin upon myself." [IRO Publications 1914:5]

This vignette is typical of many such dilemmas faced by Jewish newcomers. The painful decision to accept a job in violation of religious beliefs represented the beginning of a longer term process of economic acculturation and assimilation.

SEPHARDIC JEWS: THE EARLY TWENTIETH-CENTURY IMMIGRATION

Although Sephardic Jews were the largest Jewish group in the early years of the United States, their community was steadily absorbed into the dominant society through intermarriage and conversion to Christianity. A new Sephardic immigration occurred in the early twentieth century when economic disruption, political conflict, and warfare in the Balkans drove 25,000 Sephardim to the United States. However, this number was only a small percentage of the Eastern European Jewish immigration, numbering annually in the tens of thousands. The Jewish immigrants from the Balkans were descendants of those Jews expelled from Spain by order of the Inquisition. As Columbus sailed westward from the port of Cadiz in 1492 with Sephardic Jewish sailors on board, other Sephardic Jews sailed eastward from that port. They were heading to the areas controlled by the sultan of the Ottoman Empire, who had promised them a refuge following the Spanish edict of expulsion. Eager to enlarge commerce and trade throughout his territories, the sultan believed that the refugees from Spain would serve his purpose. For nearly five hundred years, their descendants flourished in the towns and cities of what would become Turkey, Greece, Bulgaria, and Yugoslavia.

Sephardic Jews constituted a Jewish ethnicity quite distinct from that of the Eastern European Jewish immigrants. Sephardic Jews spoke Ladino, or Judeo-Spanish, rather than Yiddish; like Yiddish, it is written in Hebrew script. They also maintained cultural practices and beliefs that clearly separated them from the Yiddish-speakers. Modern American Sephardic communities emerged in New York, Los Angeles, Atlanta, Seattle, Rochester, and Indianapolis. That these communities are so little known tells us something about the character of Jewish American ethnicity. In popular thinking, Jewish life in the United States is defined overwhelmingly in terms of the Yiddish-speaking Eastern European Jews and their descendants. Constituting by far the largest Jewish ethnicity in the United States, this group has, accordingly, attracted the most attention and shapes the popular profile of Jewish American life.

A common, although not monolithic, religious heritage joined Sephardic and Ashkenazic Jews in the Great Tradition; indeed, among the immigrants, Sephardic Jews were often more religiously minded than some of the Eastern European newcomers. But for each group, their ethnic and linguistic characteristics were as salient as religion in their self-definition as well as in the way they regarded each other.

While many of the immigrant generation of Sephardim were multilingual, their first language was Ladino. It is a vernacular built on the fifteenth-century Spanish spoken by Sephardic Jews when they arrived in the eastern Mediterranean. Like culture, language never remains static, and over the centuries the Ladino lexicon absorbed words from other languages, reflecting the experience of its speakers as they came into social and commercial contact with Turks, Serbs, Greeks, and others. Yet once in America, the legitimacy of their Judaism was disputed by the Ashkenazic majority because the Sephardim did not speak Yiddish, or "Jewish" (Glazier 1988:51; Zenner 1990:233–234). A legacy of rancor against those who were skeptical about their Jewishness is still recalled among older Sephardic Jews.

Beyond language differences, other cultural features defined each ethnic group, further distinguishing their respective immigrant generations. For example, Sephardic and Ashkenazic patterns of naming children contrast in important ways. Neither mode of naming is religiously sanctioned; they are simply ethnic variations, and, like the use of Yiddish or Ladino, did not make people more or less Jewish in religious terms. Still, Sephardic ethnic patterns were mistakenly interpreted by the

Yiddish-speaking majority as indicators of inauthentic Judaism.

Among Ashkenazic Jews, parents name their children after the dead, usually kinsmen. Naming a child after a living person is portentous, for it connects the living person to the world of the dead. It may even imply his or her imminent death. Founded in the folk traditions of Eastern European Jews, the naming pattern commemorates and honors the dead but does so without biblical or other sacred textual authority. If that authority existed, Sephardic Jews would also honor the same religious tradition. Sephardic Jews, by contrast, pay tribute to the living by naming children after them. Derived from two distinct Little Traditions, naming patterns among Sephardic and Askenazic Jews nonetheless resulted in cultural misunderstandings between the immigrant generations.

Cuisine likewise separated Ashkenazic and Sephardic Jews. Food, along with other shared tastes, beliefs, and behaviors represents an important symbol of the ethnic community. Like linguistic and naming distinctions, dissimilar cuisines are an index of social distance and contrast. What are now taken to be conventional Jewish foods—bagels, blintzes, knishes, pickled herring, and so forth—were the particular foods of the Eastern European Jewish majority. They were quite foreign to the tastes of Sephardic Jews, whose cuisine closely resembled that of their Turkish and Balkan neighbors and included *borekas, boyos,* and *bulemas* (three varieties of pastries cooked with meat, vegetable, or cheese fillings), *quajados* (fritadas or soufflés), *yaprak* (stuffed grape leaves), and so on.

While these characteristic cuisines still grace the tables of Ashkenazic and Sephardic Jews, they do so now in a non-exclusive way and are not the singular preserve of either group. Ethnic cuisines continue to be durable cultural symbols, but they have diffused outward from their ethnic origins to the rest of contemporary America (Gans 1979). Bagels, for example, are so widely available in grocery stores that most people are probably unaware of their origin among Eastern European Jews. They are now simply one more item in the American pantry.

ETHNIC CONTINUITY AND DISCONTINUITY AMONG ASHKENAZIC AND SEPHARDIC JEWS

Immigration to America profoundly affected various European ethnicities, for it ruptured continuity with the old country in a mere two generations. The United States certainly offered great economic opportunity and personal security to people whose lives had undergone severe dislocation as a result of the political and economic turmoil in their homelands. But each group incurred major cultural costs in exchange for the benefits of living in America. The Jewish immigrant experience should thus be seen as part of a much larger process of acculturation and assimilation, including the movements promoting a revival of ethnic consciousness in the late 1960s and early 1970s (Glazer and Moynihan 1970; Novak 1971).

Sephardic and Ashkenazic Jews alike have prospered, and certainly Jewish Americans collectively rank among the most upwardly mobile and successful ethnic groups in the United States. No longer self-governing as they were under the Ottomans, the Sephardic Jews in their new American communities found themselves in a novel sociopolitical circumstance. Formal self-governance of ethnic communities was alien to the American political scene. The absence of a political boundary between their ethnic community and others was symptomatic of the weakening of other barriers—social and economic—that had once clearly defined and helped to perpetuate Sephardic communities in Europe. Cultural distinctiveness diminished as well. Likewise, the cultural distance between Ashkenazic Jews and their various neighbors shrank as they came to realize altogether new economic possibilities in the United States. The immigrants no longer

faced the kind of legal restrictions that for centuries had narrowly specified Jewish vocations or places of residence.

At the same time, precipitous linguistic shifts in the course of a generation substituted English for Yiddish and Ladino among the second generation. The fate of these two languages in the United States is a telling barometer of acculturative change since the early 1900s. In other words, Jewish American life has undergone a major transformation in conjunction with the decline in the number of speakers of the ethnic vernaculars. Language codifies a culture and embodies its fundamental systems of classification and nuances of meaning. Linguistic shifts, then, are interconnected to cultural changes. Most of the children of the Jewish immigrants, and especially their grandchildren, do not speak Yiddish or Ladino (Fishman 1966, 1985; Malinowski 1983). Indeed, a sharp decline in native language fluency in a single generation was the norm among European-derived ethnic groups.

The social and cultural divisions that at one time clearly circumscribed Ashkenazic and Sephardic ethnicities are now much diminished. Likewise, the porous borders of each community admit many mainstream cultural currents. American social life has ensured that the ethnic community, unless it made concerted efforts to keep the outside world at bay, could not successfully reproduce itself in ways characteristic of the European experience. European Jewish communities, Ashkenazic and Sephardic, of course, were not static. They had steadily evolved and absorbed various cultural influences from their neighbors. But the changes they underwent were contained by the political and social restrictions imposed upon them. These restrictions effectively negated the possibilities of their cultural absorption into the host society.

In the United States, assimilative changes coursing through the Sephardic Jewish community—numerically small to begin with—have prompted predictions of the imminent disappearance of that community (Angel 1974:136).

Preservation efforts are thus underway and include academic and public programs, college courses, and museum exhibits that aim to revitalize Sephardic Jewish culture. Like other third- and fourth-generation Americans, some Sephardic Jews are actively researching their ethnic history. While such efforts are hopeful, they are simultaneously the worrisome symptom of the rapid cultural changes that sparked the revival in the first place. One must then ask if a culture, preserved primarily through formal institutions, holds the same significance it once did for the immigrants. For them, it was distinctly unself-conscious and an organic part of community living that pervaded every aspect of their experience. For the fourth generation, whose decisions about everything from marriage partners to career choices to place of residence are not dictated by ethnic considerations, it is very doubtful that ethnicity will regain the same influence it once exercised.

The case of the third and fourth generations of Ashkenazic Jews closely parallels that of their Sephardic counterparts. Although much larger, the Ashkenazic generations also are little constrained by ethnic bonds and allegiances. High rates of intermarriage diminish the concentration of speakers of Yiddish that might occasion systematic use of the language and provide the setting in which children could learn it (Alba 1990:100). Likewise, continuity in ethnic culture is ruptured in the same way. Above all, the American embrace of personal freedom and choice works against a sense of social obligation and the authority of an ethnic or religious tradition. Individualism as a fundamental American value is played out in the wide range of options a person can choose from, but it can quite easily act at cross-purposes with the sense of common aims and shared goals that help to perpetuate an ethnic or religious community (Itoh and Plotnicov 1999).

Nevertheless, a minority of Ashkenazic Jews is also attempting to reclaim their ethnic and religious heritage. Part of the revival focuses on the Yiddish language; indeed, many Jewish community centers and other institutions sponsor adult classes in Yiddish. The preservation of books written in Yiddish is also occurring. Interest in Yiddish folklore and culture, including particularly the distinctive music of Eastern Europe's Jews, known as *klezmer*, is widespread. The development of Jewish studies programs offering courses on Eastern European Jewry in many colleges and universities is yet another indicator of cultural concern. But, as in the Sephardic case, these are not spontaneous community developments but, rather, self-conscious attempts by a relatively small number of people to revive and to nurture traditions that once pervaded Jewish communal life.

In the religious sphere, a return to orthodoxy represents a sincere attempt to renew faith and belief while establishing a connection to past generations, but this religious revitalization engages the interest of only a fraction of Jewish Americans. Moreover, Judaism in the United States is very fractious, reflecting a high level of internal diversity ranging from strict religious observance to liberal, modernist practices. Various contentious issues such as conversion, ritual innovation, feminism, homosexuality, intermarriage, and even the adoption of Buddhist or New Age beliefs also divide Jewish Americans.

HASIDIC JEWS

Hasidic Jews are an ultraorthodox segment of the American Jewish population. They number more than 200,000 people, the majority of whom live in New York State. Their communities derive from the settlement of Holocaust survivors from Eastern Europe in the years immediately after World War II. They are easily identifiable by their characteristic dress and appearance. The men are bearded and have earlocks. Their clothing includes black suits and hats. The women must always appear in modest attire, including head coverings and long dresses with sleeves over the entire arm. Hasidic Jews represent a particularly notable exception to the pattern of cultural and linguistic assimilation that has dominated the Jewish American experience. Thus, among this Ashkenazic group, marriages are endogamous and often arranged, gender role separation and hierarchy are normative, and mystical religious beliefs and practices that arose in eighteenth-century Poland flourish. The Yiddish language is thriving, if not the many associated secular features of Yiddish culture such as literature. Hasidic communities are led by charismatic rabbis believed capable of performing miracles.

The Hasidic Jews manage to be "in the world but not of the world." That is, they are not sealed off from their surroundings, and indeed must deal with the realities of living in densely populated urban environments, such as Brooklyn, which has brought about some political involvement. However, Hasidic communities very closely control the kinds of cultural influences that reach them, maintaining formidable social and cultural boundaries around their communities. Consequently, the rigorous culturally self-protective strategies of the Hasidic Jews have ensured a remarkable degree of religious and ethnic continuity compared to that of other segments of the Jewish American population.

RUSSIAN JEWS IN AMERICA SINCE 1975

Unlike the large-scale immigration of Eastern European Jews a century ago, the Russian Jewish immigration over the last quarter century has been linked to American foreign policy concerns. The cold war and the plight of minorities under Communist regimes created sympathetic American immigration and refugee policies—policies much less attentive to ethnic minorities suppressed by governments friendly to the United States. With the end of the cold war, Russian Jewish immigration to the United States

has continued. Numbering some 350,000, the Russian Jewish community now represents the single largest refugee group in the United States. Russian Jews have established themselves in several large metropolitan areas including New York, Los Angeles, San Francisco, Boston, and Chicago, as well as in smaller cities.

The experience of Jews in Russia was conditioned by the Soviet goals of collective absorption into Russian national culture. Relentlessly assimilationist, state policy actively discouraged or punished ethnic and religious activity. Consequently, many Russian Jewish newcomers to the United States have little knowledge of Yiddish or of Jewish cultural or religious traditions. They often lack any prior experience in observing Jewish holidays or rituals.

There is, however, some variation among Russian Jewish immigrants depending on age. The oldest immigrants recall the early years of the Soviet Union, prior to the Stalinist repression of religious and cultural groups. They were socialized by parents into the culture, religion, and Yiddish language of Eastern European Jewry. The next generation came of age when Stalinism was fully entrenched, and they learned little of their ethnic or religious heritage. In accordance with state policy, they aimed to assimilate into Russian society; whatever success they gained in the Soviet Union depended on their ability to distance themselves as completely as possible from their ethnic background and to immerse themselves in Russian national culture. Even if they were inclined, they could not with impunity openly affirm or practice Judaism. The liberalization of Russian society in the late 1980s and the eventual collapse of Communism, however, enabled young people to study Judaism openly in Russia, although anti-Semitism did not suddenly dissipate. Many continued their involvement in Jewish education after immigration to the United States (Gold 1995:7–9).

Russian Jews have encountered many of the same problems that earlier Jewish immigrants confronted in trying to find a place for themselves in a new society and in redefining their identity. Language problems remain formidable, and current immigrant frustrations may be greater than a century ago when very few newcomers were from the professional ranks. Many Russian Jewish physicians, engineers, chemists, and so on work in modest, low-wage jobs because they lack adequate English-language skills to practice their professions. Although some immigrants thus become downwardly mobile, others manage to get good jobs or to start their own businesses.

The adaptation of the new immigrants, like that of their predecessors, also depends on attitudes of the host society as well as their established co-ethnics and coreligionists. In some respects, Jewish American organizations of assistance and support for the Russian Jews reproduce the patron-client relationship between German American Jews and the Russian Jewish immigrants of a century ago. Current Russian Jewish immigrants thus find some of the same condescending attitudes directed toward them. But, unlike the earlier immigrants for whom the national cultures of Eastern Europe held no value, today's Russian Jewish newcomers often have positive feelings toward many aspects of Russian national culture, including its social intensity and the richness of intellectual life among many ordinary people.

Jewish Americans often have difficulty understanding why the newcomers do not want to jettison cultural values and attitudes rooted in Russia. Still, American society as a whole is now more sympathetic than ever before to ethnic groups joining the mainstream while preserving their cultural heritage. Indeed, many Russian Jewish immigrants are attempting to steer this middle course (Gold 1995:120). They hope to shape the terms of their accommodation to the new country. Still, the experience of Jewish immigrants of a century ago may model the future. If that is the case, then the blandishments of American society will further loosen the hold of the ethnic community, thus promoting a cul-tural convergence between the children of the latest Jewish newcomers and the descendants of other immigrants.

REFERENCES CITED

ALBA, RICHARD. 1990. *Ethnic Identity: The Transformation of White America.* New Haven, CT: Yale University Press.

ANGEL, MARC. 1974. *The Sephardim of the United States: An Exploratory Study.* New York: Union of Sephardic Congregations.

ANTIN, MARY. 1912. *The Promised Land.* Boston: Houghton Mifflin.

BOAS, FRANZ. 1938. *The Mind of Primitive Man.* New York: Macmillan.

BRODKIN, KAREN. 1998. *How Jews Became White Folks and What That Says about Race in America.* New Brunswick, NJ: Rutgers University Press.

Cleveland Plain Dealer. 2000. Jewish refugees in NYC put new face on poverty, July 16.

DOUGLAS, MARY. 1966. *Purity and Danger: An Analysis of Concepts of Pollution and Taboo.* London: Routledge & Kegan Paul.

FISHMAN, JOSHUA. 1966. *Language Loyalty in the United States.* The Hague: Mouton.

——. 1985. Mother-tongue claiming since 1960: Trends and correlates. In *The Rise and Fall of the Ethnic Revival: Perspectives on Language and Ethnicity.* Joshua Fishman et al., eds. Amsterdam: Mouton.

GANS, HERBERT. 1979. Symbolic ethnicity: The future of ethnic groups and cultures in America. *Ethnic and Racial Studies* 2(1):1–19.

GLAZER, NATHAN, and DANIEL PATRICK MOYNIHAN. 1970. *Beyond the Melting Pot.* Cambridge, MA: MIT Press.

GLAZIER, JACK. 1988. Stigma, identity, and Sephardic-Ashkenazic relations in Indianapolis. In *Persistence and Flexibility: Anthropological Perspectives on the American Jewish Experience.* Walter P. Zenner, ed. Albany: State University of New York Press.

——. 1993. Subversive Food. Paper presented before Central States Anthropological Society, Beloit, WI.

——. 1998. *Dispersing the Ghetto: The Relocation of Jewish Immigrants across America.* Ithaca, NY: Cornell University Press.

GOLD, STEVEN J. 1995. *From the Workers' State to the Golden State: Jews from the Former Soviet Union in California.* Boston: Allyn & Bacon.

GOLDSCHEIDER, CALVIN, and ALAN S. ZUCKERMAN. 1984. *The Transformation of the Jews.* Chicago: University of Chicago Press.

IRO Publications. 1914. In our application rooms. Distribution. *Monthly Bulletin of the Industrial Removal Office* 1(6):5.

ITOH, REIKO, and LEONARD PLOTNICOV. 1999. The Saturday morning informal service: Community and identity in a Reform congregation. *Ethnology* 38(1):1–19.

KOSMIN, BARRY A., SIDNEY GOLDSTEIN, JOSEPH WAKSBERG, NAVA LERER, ARIELLA KEYSAR, and JEFFREY SCHECKNER. 1991. *Highlights of the CFC 1990 National Jewish Population Survey*. New York: Council of Jewish Federations.

KOSMIN, BARRY A., and JEFFREY SCHECKNER. 1995. Jewish population in the United States. In *American Jewish Yearbook*, vol. 96.

LEVINE, LAWRENCE W. 1996. *The Opening of the American Mind: Canons, Culture and History*. Boston: Beacon Press.

LIPSET, SEYMOUR MARTIN, and EARL RABB. 1995. *Jews and the New American Scene*. Cambridge, MA: Harvard University Press.

MALINOWSKI, ARLENE. 1983. Judeo-Spanish language-maintenance efforts in the United States. *International Journal of the Sociology of Language* 44:137–151.

MYERHOFF, BARBARA. 1979. *Number Our Days*. New York: Dutton.

NOVAK, MICHAEL. 1971. *The Rise of the Unmeltable Ethnics*. New York: Macmillan.

REDFIELD, ROBERT. 1956. *Peasant Society and Culture*. Chicago: University of Chicago Press.

ZENNER, WALTER P. 1990. Chicago's Sephardim. *American Jewish History* 79(2):221–241.

10

HISPANIC AMERICANS/ LATINOS

Ellen Bigler

Rhode Island College

What's in a name anyway? Terms of identity can reflect a people's self-perception and their power to name themselves. Terms of identity can be imposed from outside. They can mask internal differences, and construct new categories that may or may not be accepted by those they seek to label. Terms of identity can change meaning from one generation to another. For Americans who originate from Spanish-speaking cultures, terms of identity—both imposed and chosen—can provide clues to their perceived internal differences and commonalities, as they struggle to find their place in the racialized hierarchy of the United States.

The popular term *Hispanic* is actually an umbrella term used first by the U.S. government in the 1970s and then in the 1980 census to identify U.S. residents originating from Spanish-speaking regions of the world. As such, it is a term fraught with difficulties. It embraces Mexican Americans who trace their roots to families living on the land the United States acquired from Mexico in 1848, alongside Salvadorans who entered in the 1980s as political refugees. It includes Afro-Cubans descended from African slaves and "white" Argentinians whose ancestors originated from Italy. It incorporates the rural indigenous Guatemalans speaking only Kanjobal Maya (an Indian language), and bilingual academics from Peru who immigrate for greater professional opportunities. It embraces U.S.-born Chicanos who don't use or perhaps even understand Spanish. It subsumes Puerto Ricans who enter the mainland as citizens, and undocumented Dominicans who reside in the United States in constant fear of deportation. It is, without question, a term that masks important differences among the groups it embraces.

What can such disparate peoples share? How did such a term come to gain entry and legitimacy in the public discourse? Why is it contested by many Hispanics? How useful a label is it for those it encompasses? Are we perhaps witnessing the creation of a new panethnic group akin to the construction of an "African American," "Italian," or "Indian" identity in the United States? What ultimately does it mean to be Hispanic in the United States today, and what forces have helped shape their existence? These are questions this chapter seeks to address.

HISPANIC OR LATINO? RACIAL OR ETHNIC GROUP? OR NEITHER?

Most people the government classifies as Hispanic, if asked their group membership, won't actually define themselves as such. Typically, Hispanics will identify by their place of origin or by terms for ethnic groups that have become popular in U.S. ethnic communities: Mexican American or Chicano, Nuyorican, Puerto Rican, Dominican, Cuban, and so forth. Panethnic terms like *Hispanic* or *Latino* can be useful, of course, and Hispanics have long recognized the political potential of such a label to unite diverse groups and encourage them to recognize similarities they share with others (Flores 2000; Padilla 1985; Sánchez Korrol 1988). Latino academics express concern, though, about the imposition from outside of such an umbrella term, and its potential to foster stereotyped public perceptions of "Hispanics" (e.g., Gimenez 1997; Oboler 1995; Santos 1997).

The use of Hispanic is also criticized for the term's association with Spanish hegemony and for acknowledging only the Spanish heritage of Latin Americans. This concern with the privileging of Spanish culture has long-standing roots in Latin America. The valuing of the Spanish side of Latin Americans' heritage over their hybridized cultures and their indigenous and African roots has been a topic addressed by intellectuals and political leaders throughout much of Latin America's history. Many Latino academics (e.g., Nieto 2000) argue that if an umbrella term is to be used, *Latino*[1]—a sort of shorthand for *latinoamericano*[2]—at least acknowledges their Latin American roots and therefore the presence of their African and indigenous heritage. Latino currently appears to be more widespread among politically active members of the community, and Hispanic has more currency in the East and Latino in the West. In this chapter both terms are used.

As the opening paragraph suggests, Hispanics do not constitute one "racial" group.[3]

Because of more racial intermixing in Latin America than in the United States, the peoples of Latin America have evolved a broad range of physical appearances that blend to varying degrees their Indian, African, and European roots. While Latin American societies did not escape the privileging of light skin that mar U.S. ethnic group relations, racial boundaries in Latin America are more fluid (Rodríguez 2000). There is a range of intermediary terms used to refer to a person's physical appearance, depending on factors such as skin color, hair texture, and facial features. "Race" is not necessarily viewed as a fixed biological inheritance from parents, as in the United States, but rather is dependent in part on appearance or social status. Children of the same family, therefore, may be classified as members of different racial groups based on their physical appearances. An individual's racial designation can change with that person's change in social status.

The racial category a Latino is designated as belonging to in the United States can be different from the categorization in his or her homeland. It can be disconcerting for dark-skinned Puerto Ricans, for instance, to become "black" on the mainland, or for Dominicans considered *blancos* (whites) in the Dominican Republic to be viewed as "nonwhite" in the United States. The Latino presence, though, is shaking up the dichotomous racial categories that have dominated in the United States for so long (see Rodríguez and Cordero-Guzman 1992). In this respect—and, as we shall see, in other respects—they are "Latinizing" aspects of U.S. culture.

THE LATINO PRESENCE IN THE UNITED STATES: A TROUBLED PAST

Settlers of Spanish and Indian descent were present early on in what is now the United States. Mestizo communities in New Mexico predate the first so-called North American settlement of

Jamestown in 1609, and people with Spanish roots were incorporated with the acquisition of Florida. Mexicans were incorporated into the political boundaries of the United States beginning in the mid-1800s, and since then the numbers and diversity of Hispanics have continued to grow. The rate of growth has been greatest in recent decades, with the population more than doubling since the 1980 census, due to their relative youthfulness, high immigration rates, and higher birth rates. Hispanics, according to the 2000 census, now number 35.3 million and make up 12.5 percent of the U.S. population, roughly equal in size to the African American population (Schmitt 2001). There are more Hispanics in the United States today than there are Peruvians, Chileans, or Canadians in their respective countries. Almost 60 percent, 20.6 million, are of Mexican descent. Second largest are the Puerto Ricans, numbering 3.4 million and almost 10 percent of Hispanics. Cuban Americans are third, numbering 1.2 million. Another 10 million Hispanics hail from elsewhere, including Central and South America.

Mexican Americans, to the 1960s

Mexicans did not originally cross the border to enter the United States; rather, the border crossed over them. Mexico in 1848 lost fully half its territory to the far more economically and militarily powerful United States after Texas declared its independence and Mexico lost the Mexican War. What are now the states of California, Colorado, New Mexico, Nevada, Utah, and most of Arizona were, along with Texas, originally Mexican land. Mexicans thus became part of the U.S. population through conquest, and this means of incorporation profoundly affected Anglos' views of them and their relations with Mexican Americans in the ensuing decades.

Mexicans living on the land when the United States acquired it were promised full rights and protections by the federal government if they chose to remain and become American citizens. That promise, however, was quickly broken. Within a year, the discovery of gold in California led to a massive in-migration of Anglos. The 13,000 original Mexicans there were quickly outnumbered, and by 1849 the Anglo population had reached 100,000. Anglos soon dominated in the state legislature, passing discriminatory laws aimed specifically at the Mexican-origin population. These included an antivagrancy "Greaser" act and a foreign miner's tax of $20 monthly, aimed at all who spoke Spanish—including American citizens. Mexican Americans were driven from their mines, and along with Chinese miners, assaulted and lynched on occasion. Ironically, it was the Mexican miners who brought with them knowledge of mining techniques that aided the Anglo miners, and who performed much of the grueling manual labor (Takaki 1990).

The extent of Anglo–Mexican American conflict varied across the Southwest. In courts throughout the region, Mexican Americans were divested of their preexisting claims to land titles guaranteed them through the 1848 Treaty of Guadalupe Hidalgo. While some Mexican American elites initially succeeded in forging alliances with Anglos, wealthy *californios* in northern California began to lose economic clout early on. Conflict and racial violence were commonplace in Texas. The Mexican Americans of New Mexico were somewhat better off, living in relative isolation for several more decades. They succeeded in retaining some numerical plurality and degree of control in political matters, and Spanish along with English became an official state language of New Mexico. There, too, though, the tolerant mood between Anglos and Mexican Americans began to evaporate by the early 1900s, as resident Mexican Americans were forced into the status of a dependent minority.

Mexicans are overwhelmingly mestizos, an outcome of Spanish and Indian intermixture over the previous four centuries. After 1848,

Mexicans now in the United States found themselves surrounded by Anglo-Americans who brought with them attitudes about white superiority forged in earlier contacts and interactions with Africans and Native Americans. In the eyes of many Anglos, Mexican Americans were an inferior, mongrelized people (Takaki 1993). Even their allegedly superior "Spanish blood" had long been viewed by the English as racially impure due to the *mestizaje* (mixing) between Spaniards and Moors in Spain. Cultural traits were linked to "racial" characteristics, so that Mexicans, for instance, were seen as naturally "superstitious, cowardly, treacherous, idle, avaricious, and inveterate gamblers" (De León 1998:163).

To avoid this stigmatization, wealthy Mexican Americans *(los ricos)* struggled to maintain their status of *pureza de sangre* (pure-blooded [Spanish]) and to differentiate themselves from *mexicanos pobres* in the eyes of Anglos. In New Mexico, as the power and wealth of these elites declined, they began to refer to themselves as *hispanos* and to emphasize their "pure" Spanish (read "European") ancestry.[4] It was, of course, a cultural "invention" that ignored the realities of their own indigenous roots,[5] as they struggled to insert themselves into the "imagined (white) American community" (Oboler 1995; Takaki 1993).

The end of slavery in the United States in 1865 represented an aperture, a moment of opportunity, for re-envisioning the "American" community to be a more inclusive one. It was, unfortunately, a missed opportunity. African Americans continued to be denied equality through a variety of legal and extralegal means. Native Americans were rounded up and put on reservations. Immigration of the Chinese, who had contributed so much to the economy of the West and the construction of the transcontinental railroad, ground abruptly to a halt with passage of the Chinese Exclusion Act in 1882. Mexican Americans continued to be oppressed throughout the Southwest.

Virtually reduced to a class of exploited laborers, most Mexican Americans found themselves stigmatized, socially segregated, and politically marginalized through a variety of means. The southwestern territories were given the power to determine citizenship eligibility requirements when applying for statehood, and could elect to bar Native Americans from citizenship.[6] This became a basis in parts of the Southwest for denying Mexican Americans of predominantly Indian heritage their political rights (see Menchaca 1993). Mexican Americans in Texas were denied the vote by the use of white primaries, poll taxes, and intimidation tactics. While courts sometimes ruled that Mexican Americans be considered "white"—and the Treaty of Guadalupe Hidalgo recognized them as having the right to citizenship at a time when only whites could become naturalized citizens—Anglo cultural constructions forged in European contacts with Africans and Indians oftentimes prevailed.

Mexican Americans and Mexican nationals labored in agriculture and ranching, in mines, and on the railroads. Their labor played a significant role in the expansion of American capitalism into the Southwest, and these contributions to the well-being of the nation were clearly not limited to the Southwest. As Carey McWilliams, in his classic historical analysis *North from Mexico: The Spanish-Speaking People of the United States* (1990) emphasized in a masterfully understated fashion, "One might say . . . that Mexican miners in the copper mines of Arizona, Utah, and Nevada, have played an important role in making possible the illumination of (all) America by electricity" (p. 144).

Mining companies in search of cheap labor in the Southwest developed a caste labor system that exploited these workers. As miners, they were paid an average of 37¢ per day in 1860, compared to $1.25 for Anglos; in 1880, Mexican Americans earned $1.50 and Anglos $2.75. Anglos also usually received board while Mexican Americans were given only a ration of flour.

"Mexicans," one mine owner pointed out in rationalizing such practices, "have been 'peons' for generations. They will always remain so, as it is their natural condition" (Takaki 1990:163).

Both push and pull factors contributed to the growth of the Mexican American population in the early twentieth century. The Mexican Revolution in the 1910s and its aftermath dramatically increased the numbers of Mexicans entering the United States. Agriculturalists and the burgeoning industries came to depend heavily on Mexican Americans as a cheap source of labor, particularly after Southern and Eastern European immigration was severely curtailed in the 1920s. Until the early 1920s there was little policing of the U.S.–Mexican border, and Mexicans generally moved freely back and forth as economic conditions demanded.

Mexican Americans did not passively accept their poor treatment, stereotypes of docility and submissiveness aside. Workers on numerous occasion went out on strike. In one such strike Mexican American farm workers joined forces with fellow Japanese American laborers and formed a successful union. Their bid for affiliation and support from national labor leaders, however, was rebuffed. When they approached Samuel Gompers of the American Federation of Labor to charter their organization, they were told that a charter would be issued under only one condition: that Chinese and Japanese workers not be accepted as members. Mexican American union leaders refused the conditions, and the union, without the support of organized labor, soon passed out of existence (Takaki 1993).

Where Mexican American labor leaders could count on support was from within their own communities. These early labor strikes drew on the ethnic solidarity of Mexican American communities. The merchants provided support, and musicians provided entertainment. Mexican American *mutualistas* (benevolent associations), common throughout the Southwest, were formed to help individual members cope with life on the margins (Acuña 1988). They made loans, raised money for emergencies, and helped cover funeral expenses. Through such organizations Mexican Americans sought to resist labor exploitation and racism when assistance from government or national labor organizations was not forthcoming.

In segregated Mexican American communities their language and cultural traditions, abetted by the continued influx of newcomers and frequent movement across the border, flourished and provided some measure of comfort. Extended families were their primary social networks and their safety nets in times of crisis. Opportunities for their children, meanwhile, were essentially nonexistent; if they had schooling at all, it was typically in segregated schools where they were given inferior educations and discouraged from going on in school (Carter and Segura 1979; Takaki 1993).

The Great Depression dramatically worsened the situation for Mexican Americans. They lost their jobs to Euro-Americans, and were routinely denied welfare benefits. Many were rounded up and deported, others driven "voluntarily" out of the country. In all, over 400,000 Mexicans and Mexican Americans—including legal residents and citizens among them—were repatriated to Mexico, without benefit of formal deportation proceedings (Carrasco 1998).

With the onset of World War II, however, Mexican labor was again in demand. Mexican and U.S. government officials negotiated the Bracero Program to help meet the increased demands for laborers. While the program provided protections for temporary Mexican workers, these stipulations were largely ignored. With no bargaining rights, they lived and worked in deplorable conditions for substandard wages. The Bracero Program also freed Mexican American men to serve as soldiers. Despite the racism they faced at home, they distinguished themselves in the war effort and won more Medals of Honor than any other identifiable ethnic or racial group. They also died in disproportionate numbers; Mexican Americans, for instance, represented one-tenth of the Los Angelinos but comprised one-fifth of the city's casualties (Acuña 1988:253).

What these Mexican American soldiers discovered upon returning home was that their sacrifices for the nation did not end their poor treatment. Sergeant Macario Garcia, recipient of the Congressional Medal of Honor, found, for instance, that he could not purchase a cup of coffee in a Richmond, California, restaurant. Incidents such as the "Sleepy Lagoon" case (1942) and the Zoot-Suit Riots (1943) in Los Angeles dramatized the continuing racism toward Mexican Americans.

The Sleepy Lagoon case began when a group of Mexican American youth, who called themselves members of a *barrio* club, crashed a party at a ranch. A fight soon ensued. When an invited guest was found dead in the road the following morning–without any wounds and a likely victim of a hit-and-run–authorities jailed the entire gang of Mexican American youth, alleging that they had beaten the dead youth. The response of societal institutions was appalling. The press depicted the *barrio* club members as hoodlums. A report by the Sheriff's Department of Los Angeles concluded that Mexican Americans were inherently criminal and violent: they were Indians, Indians are Orientals, and Orientals have no regard for life. In addition, the report went on, Mexican Americans were descendants of the Aztecs who allegedly sacrificed 30,000 victims a day and had an innate desire to wield a knife and spill blood. The report further urged that all club members be jailed. Sleepy Lagoon Defense Committee members, including noted journalist and lawyer Carey McWilliams, were harassed and red-baited by both the press and government agencies. Only in a court of appeals were the verdicts, ranging from assault to first-degree murder despite the lack of evidence, overturned (Acuña 1988).

The Zoot-Suit Riots occurred shortly thereafter. Sailors went on a rampage in Mexican American communities in Los Angeles, and Mexican American "zoot-suited" youth were attacked while police did little to quell the unrest. Sensationalist headlines fanned the flames. In all, over 600 Mexican American youth were arrested without cause. Military shore patrols finally intervened to put down the riot (Acuña 1988). These two incidents came to symbolize the gross injustices that Mexican Americans confronted as they went to war for what was being denied them at home, democracy and equality.

World War II profoundly affected Mexican Americans, as it did African Americans. The soldiers for the first time experienced social climates where they were not treated in a discriminatory manner. The expanding war economy meanwhile drew more Mexican Americans to urban centers and industrial employment, and the rhetoric designed to win support for the war positively depicted Latin Americans in the media. Mexican Americans were proud of their sacrifices and contributions, further increasing their sense of entitlement to equality as Americans (Moore and Pachon 1985). Political activism in turn increased. The American G.I. Forum, for instance, was formed by Mexican American veterans in 1948, when private cemeteries and mortuaries in Texas refused to handle the body of a Mexican American soldier.

Progress in the postwar years, however, was distressingly slow. Like African Americans, Mexican Americans contended with segregated public facilities and schools and discriminatory jury selection procedures. "Operation Wetback," organized by the federal government in 1954 to address the issue of illegal immigration, only worsened Anglo–Mexican American relations. Looking "Mexican" was enough to get someone stopped and told to prove his citizenship. Almost 3.8 million persons were rounded up and sent back to Mexico, most without formal proceedings (Moore and Pachon 1985). Given these sorts of conditions, Chicano historian Rudolfo Acuña and others asserted that Mexican Americans represented an "internal colony" in the United States: they were a colonized people in their own home, with little or no control over their political, economic, and educational destinies (Acuña 1988).

At the same time that Mexican Americans were an oppressed population, a small middle class had established itself. Mexican Americans were also becoming an urban population, and these developments favored greater political activism in the 1950s. The lower profile this activism assumed at the time was likely a response to the McCarthyism of the era and the backlash against Mexican Americans during Operation Wetback (Moore and Pachon 1985). Oppression was challenged through labor strikes, use of the courts when feasible, and political organizations such as the assimilation-oriented LULAC (League of United Latin American Citizens). The continuing racism and marginalization they encountered in turn set the stage for the particular form of political mobilization many Mexican Americans came to adopt in the 1960s and 1970s.

Puerto Ricans, to the 1960s

While the Mexican American presence was initially established in the Southwest and increasingly in midwestern industrial cities like Chicago, the Puerto Rican presence was concentrated in the Northeast, overwhelmingly the New York City area. The Caribbean migration that Puerto Ricans are part of is driven in large measure by the area's proximity and relationship to its powerful northern neighbor.

By the early 1900s, the Caribbean had become effectively a North American lake. Hegemony was mostly exercised through economic power but, when necessary, it took political and military form. . . . The effect of overwhelming external hegemony was the creation of insular economies molded entirely by North American interests and

the emergence of local societies profoundly dependent in their political and cultural outlook. This orientation established the broad framework for subsequent U.S.-bound migration, although the actualization of each individual outflow responded to specific circumstances. [Portes and Grosfoguel 1994:52]

Small communities of Puerto Ricans and Cubans were in place on the U.S. mainland by the late 1800s in Tampa, Key West, New Orleans, and New York City. Many of the men were *tabaqueros*, skilled cigar rollers who were politically active and ardent supporters of the struggle for Cuban and Puerto Rican independence from Spain. Caribbean political activists like José Martí frequented such communities, seeking support for the independence movement.

The status of Puerto Ricans journeying to the mainland changed dramatically in 1898. Spain, in its waning days as a colonial power, had awarded Puerto Rico greater autonomy in 1897. Eight days after the first meeting of the newly elected Puerto Rican legislature, U.S. troops at war with Spain invaded the island. The United States defeated Spain and elected to maintain control of Puerto Rico, an island that represented a desirable possession given its strategic location, potential markets, and agricultural possibilities. Puerto Rican *independentistas* now sought their freedom not from Spain, but from the United States. Puerto Ricans migrating to the mainland after 1898 now entered the United States not as immigrants from another country but, like Mexicans in the Southwest after 1848, as a colonized people. Some 100,000 Caribbean migrants arrived between 1901 and 1910, and the mainland population climbed to 135,000 in the following decade (Portes and Grosfoguel 1994).

Cultural and artistic activities flourished in these mainland Spanish-speaking communities in the Northeast. Spanish newspapers, like other immigrant presses, kept the new arrivals informed. Social organizations formed around shared interests. The Liga Antillana, for instance, was formed in New York City by working-class Cuban and Puerto Rican women related to *tabaqueros*. East Coast attitudes about "racial" mixing, however, conflicted with the interracial complexion of Caribbean communities. While racial intermixing may have been commonplace among island Puerto Ricans and Cubans, on the mainland newcomers entered into another world where "race" separated people and profoundly shaped people's life experiences. Because the Liga Antillana was an interracial group, most meeting halls closed their doors to them (Vega 1984).

When the U.S. government granted them citizenship in 1917, Puerto Ricans became eligible to migrate to the mainland without restriction. As citizens, they constituted a readily available labor pool in the Northeast, and some 12,000 migrated to fill jobs created by the war effort. Another 18,000 were inducted into the military, where they served in segregated units (DeFreitas 1999).

The racialized social order that existed in the United States shaped Americans' relations not only with Puerto Ricans on the mainland but also with Puerto Ricans on the island. In Puerto Rico, American government officials' and businessmen's assumptions of the "racial" inferiority of the Puerto Ricans—they were a mixture of Spanish, African, and Indian—went hand-in-hand with assumptions of Anglo-American cultural superiority. Puerto Ricans were deemed not ready for self-government.

The policy that government officials adopted in relation to the island was to deliberately "Americanize" Puerto Ricans. The island's name was Anglicized to "Porto Rico." A secular public school system was established, with English-only the dominant policy until 1948. Victor Clark, architect of the new educational system, expressed the prevailing sentiments of the time.

> The great mass of Puerto Ricans are as yet passive and plastic. . . . Their ideals are in our hands to create and mold. If the schools are made American

and the teachers and pupils are inspired with the American (spirit) . . . the island will become in its sympathies, views, and attitude . . . essentially American. [cited in Negrón de Montilla 1975:13]

To assist in the process, U.S. heroes, holidays, symbols, and textbooks and curricula were imported. Americans were recruited as teachers, and teacher certification required fluency in English (Negrón de Montilla 1975). Even Puerto Ricans' own Spanish dialect, forged over centuries of separation from Spain, was labeled inferior.

The degree and persistence of U.S. cultural and linguistic imperialism on the island have contributed to a legacy of resistance to Anglo-American dominance that is felt today (Zentella 1981). As sociologist Clara Rodríguez notes, this existence of an "articulation of resistance, defiance, and struggle against oppression" (1989:14) provides a different context from which Puerto Ricans may interpret their relationship to the dominant society on the mainland.

Under U.S. occupation, growing numbers of Puerto Ricans were also displaced from the land to work on plantations established by American entrepreneurs. By 1930, four U.S. corporations controlled a quarter of all the land in Puerto Rico devoted to sugarcane. Puerto Rico had become economically dependent on the United States, which now accounted for 96 percent of its exports and 87 percent of its imports (Centro de Estudios Puertorriqueños 1979).

The consequences of this dependent relationship were devastating. In the early years of the Great Depression, the per capita income in Puerto Rico fell 30 percent. The growth of absentee-owned sugar corporations that displaced small independent growers reduced Puerto Ricans to "virtual economic serfdom," U.S. Secretary of the Interior Harold Ickes noted in 1935. "There is today more widespread misery and destitution and far more unemployment in Puerto Rico than at any previous time in its history" (Dietz 1986:132). The despair of Puerto Ricans fanned the flames of the independence struggle on the island, and contributed to a small but steady growth in migration to the mainland. By 1940, the mainland Puerto Rican population stood at 70,000. Puerto Rican communities were also appearing in cities outside the New York City area that provided job prospects, including Chicago, Illinois (Padilla 1985), and Hartford, Connecticut (Glasser 1997).

What was to become known as the Puerto Rican "diaspora" in the post–World War II period was the product of several interrelated events. Operation Bootstrap, designed to transform Puerto Rico's plantation economy into an industrial one, was set in motion by the U.S. government beginning in 1947. The economic displacement it stimulated occurred at a time when the population was expanding rapidly. With U.S. employers eager to recruit from this ready pool of surplus labor, agreements between the Truman administration and the colonial government were concluded leading to lower airfare from the island to New York City (Grosfoguel and Georas 1996). Puerto Ricans, as citizens, were assured entry. The mainland population between 1940 and 1960 grew over twelvefold, jumping from 70,000 to nearly 900,000. Most of these economic migrants settled in the New York metropolitan area, filling lower-level jobs vacated as Euro-Americans migrated to the suburbs.

To the great misfortune of this growing mainland Puerto Rican community, however, economic changes were simultaneously underway that undermined their opportunities for wide-scale upward mobility (Torres 1995). The U.S. economy, despite the postwar economic boom, was undergoing a massive shift from manufacturing to a service-based economy. Sixty percent of Puerto Ricans were employed in manufacturing in 1960, and New York City lost almost 450,000 manufacturing jobs in the subsequent two decades. The better-paying unionized manufacturing jobs that had allowed earlier generations of European immigrants to establish a solid economic foothold were rapidly disappearing, as manufacturers in search of greater profits sought cheaper labor in the South and then overseas. The growing numbers of informal-sector manufacturing jobs paid substandard wages and relied on new Latino immigrants (Grosfoguel and Georas 1996). Discriminatory policies further reduced opportunities for stable employment. In turn, "white flight" to the suburbs contributed to the erosion of the city's tax base.

The outcome of this was Puerto Ricans' heavy concentration in the secondary labor market and declining urban areas. Yet Puerto Ricans themselves were oftentimes scapegoated for the changing urban environment and blamed for their own poverty. The New York *World Telegram* informed its readers as early as 1947 that "Puerto Ricans are destroying the economy and suffocating the culture of their adopted community. . . . (They) are the cause of the incredibly bad housing situation . . . (and upon arrival head) straight for the welfare offices in East Harlem" (cited in Vega 1984:230).

Puerto Ricans moving to the mainland also confronted a black-white racial binary. In Puerto Rico racial membership is based primarily on physical appearance rather than biological descent, and socioeconomic variables such as education or occupation can affect racial categorization. Membership is more fluid, with more intermediary categories. Intermarriage across "racial" lines is fairly frequent, and members of the same family can be classified as belonging to different racial categories. (There is racial prejudice in Puerto Rico, though generally regarded as not as virulent as that in the United States [see Duany 1998].) Ironically, as sociologist Clara Rodríguez noted,

Puerto Ricans entered a heterogeneous society that articulated an assimilationist, melting-pot ideology, but that, in fact, had evolved a racial order of dual ethnic queues, one White and one not-White. . . . (Yet) Puerto Ricans represented the ideal of the melting-pot ideology–a culturally unified, racially integrated people. [1989:49]

In this situation of extreme residential and occupational segregation and oppression on the mainland, not surprisingly, "the elaboration of ethnic ties provides a ready system of support for groups distinguishable by race, national origin or language" (Nelson and Tienda 1988:51). In addition, the ongoing *va y ven* (back and forth) movement between the island and mainland, propelled by economics, ensured a constant infusion of Puerto Rican culture and the Spanish language. "Ethnicity theory," which assumes that all ethnic groups are in line to assimilate as they move up the social class ladder (see Omi and Winant 1994), failed to recognize how racial formations, the colonial status of Puerto Rico, and the changing economy would play out for many Puerto Ricans. Like Mexicans, they were racialized and excluded from the imagined U.S. community. They became Americans through conquest, and experienced U.S. economic and cultural imperialism on the island; they remain concentrated on the lowest economic rungs on the mainland; and they experience ongoing ethnic revitalization from their home communities. These factors positioned them quite differently from the descendants of Euro-American immigrants in the United States by the 1960s and 1970s.

Cubans, to the 1960s

The United States acquired not only Puerto Rico but also Cuba after the Spanish-American War. By 1902, though, the United States had helped set up an independent, albeit U.S.–dominated, Cuban nation. The numbers of Cubans in the United States grew slowly up through the 1950s; by 1930, an estimated 18,000 to 19,000 Cubans were residents; by 1960, that number climbed to approximately 79,000. But when Fidel Castro overthrew the Cuban dictator Fulgencio Batista in 1959, the numbers of migrants from this island, only ninety miles off the tip of Florida, jumped dramatically. By 1965, 210,000

Cubans had entered the United States, most of them settling in Miami. Between 1965 and 1973, their numbers increased by another 345,000 (Portes and Bach 1985).

Demographic data on these refugees point to significant differences between this early Cuban wave and other Hispanic populations. These differences also help explain their rapid economic ascendancy in the United States. The first wave of post-1959 Cubans to arrive comprised overwhelmingly professionals, government officials, and businesspeople. Under the socialist system that Castro put into place, this group's social and economic positions in Cuba were threatened. Florida was the logical place to "wait out" the Castro years. Before Castro, many of the upper class had traveled regularly for play and work between the island and southern Florida, and for many middle-class Cubans a sojourn to the United States was an annual ritual. Miami, therefore, did not produce "culture shock," nor were the arriving Cubans viewed by established residents as the quintessential "tired and poor" immigrants. Most of these Cubans came to Miami intending to re-establish themselves only temporarily while they waited for Castro to be deposed.

This first wave was also 94 percent white, and averaged 34 years of age and 14 years of schooling (Moore and Pachon 1985). Thus they brought considerable cultural and social capital with them as a result of their professional status and educational backgrounds. At the school level this translated into the establishment in the Dade County public schools of the first bilingual program in the United States since World War I, when German Americans facing anti-German sentiments had abandoned their successful programs (Rodríguez-Morazzani 1997). And because they were deemed political refugees fleeing a Latin American leader the United States wanted overthrown, Cubans were welcomed and given financial assistance from the government to facilitate their resettlement. "Rapid entrepreneurial advance of the Cubans," as Alejandro Portes and Alex Stepick point out, "was not due entirely to their business acumen or community solidarity. U.S. government agencies . . . favored them disproportionately" (1993:46). The Small Business Administration, for instance, granted over $47 million in loans to Cuban-owned small businesses between 1968 and 1980 and only $6.5 million to black businesses, further contributing to ethnic group tensions in the area (Portes and Stepick 1993:46)

Despite a significant federal effort to disperse Cubans across the United States, the overwhelming majority chose to settle in the Miami area. Many who agreed to be relocated in exchange for federal assistance returned to Miami after establishing themselves elsewhere; by 1978, the *Miami Herald* estimated that about 40 percent of Cuban Americans in the Miami area were returnees (Portes and Stepick 1993:104). The ethnic enclaves they established in Miami also provided jobs and assistance for later immigrating waves of Cubans. Although the 1965–73 refugees were less well educated, they benefited from the presence of the 1959–65 refugees and U.S. government support.

TURNING POINTS: THE CIVIL RIGHTS MOVEMENT AND LATINOS

The 1960s marked an important turning point for the nation. People of color and other Americans disturbed by the continued existence of racism gained space on the national stage to confront the nation with the continuing persistence of racism in U.S. society. Government actions in response to community activism helped move their agenda forward. The *Brown v. Board of Education* decision in 1954, the 1964 Civil Rights Act, the Voting Rights Act of 1965, and presidential responses among other initiatives affirmed the greater willingness on the part of the federal government to address racial oppression in the United States.

The black civil rights movement and black power movement of the 1950s and 1960s provided inspiration to many in Latino communities, who saw parallels between the conditions that African Americans struggled against and their own situations. These were also years in which struggles against European colonialism were articulated on the international scene. Views of Chicano and Puerto Rican communities as exploited "internal colonies" gained credence. Challenges to ethnicity theory that assumed the comparability of all groups and their eventual assimilation into the American melting pot were mounted. Community leaders pointed to their long history of "unassimilability" as evidence of the failure of the American "melting pot." Claims of universal accessibility to the American dream, so long given lip service in the United States, were resoundingly challenged in the public sphere. Puerto Rican and Chicano activists and artists challenged the need to abandon their language and cultures, articulating a new vision of the United States as culturally pluralistic, a "salad" or a "tapestry" rather than a "blended soup."

Mexican Americans

Political and social action in Mexican American communities coalesced into *el movimiento*, the Chicano movement, by the later 1960s. César Chávez, whose charisma and political brilliance ultimately led to the creation of the United Farm Workers (UFW), remains perhaps the most well-known Mexican American leader. With Delores Huerta, he sought to address the pervasive poverty and the castelike status of rural Mexican Americans and Mexican immigrant labor by organizing farm workers.[7] Chávez, himself a former migrant worker, drew on their ethnic pride, religious beliefs, and sense of community and history to organize farm workers. He adapted the Mexican eagle, a key symbol in Mexico, for use on the UFW flag and borrowed tactics of nonviolence and the effective use of boycotts from Mahatma Gandhi. Chávez and his followers organized massive consumer boycotts of nonunionized grapes and lettuce to force the agricultural corporations to allow workers to unionize. Their aims were further aided by two other factors: the end of the *bracero* program, thereby reducing growers' access to easily exploitable labor, and the growing urbanization and stabilization of the Mexican American community (Acuña 1988).

Other Mexican American leaders also emerged on the regional scene. Reies López Tijerina formed the Alianza de las Mercedes, a movement that sought to reappropriate lands taken improperly from Mexicans and Mexican communities. Rodolfo Corkey Gonzáles organized the Chicano power youth movement. José Angel Gutiérrez formed a third political party, La Raza Unida, which achieved some political successes in Texas. Mexican Americans were becoming a force to be reckoned with, and the major political parties began to court their vote.

Challenging assimilation. Given the negative stereotypes and anti-Mexican American sentiments that Mexican Americans routinely encountered, many downplayed their Mexican roots ("I'm Spanish") and sought to "pass" where feasible (e.g., Johnson 1999). The use of "Mexican-American," signaling as it did that they were one among many other "hyphenated" immigrant groups, was popular. This more assimilationist orientation, however, was profoundly challenged by the new postwar generation, who were no longer willing to wait for acceptance and equality.

Cultural nationalism challenged the acceptance of assimilation as a goal. It also provided the theme that succeeded in mobilizing and unifying individuals of Mexican descent, strengthening and reinforcing ethnic identity. "Two crucial decisions were made during this period by these guardians of the culture. . . . 'Somos Chicanos.' . . . By using this term the Chicano community consciously and publicly acknowledged

its Native American heritage. . . . 'Aztlán is our homeland' was the second," Chicano writer and activist Rudolfo Anaya asserted a generation later (1989:232). Young and politically active Mexican Americans renamed themselves "Chicanos," a term used earlier to refer to lower-class Mexican Americans. *La Raza*, a term that Latin Americans used to signify their identity as a new hybrid people, also gained popularity. *Spanish*, a euphemism for the more derogatory *Mexican*, meanwhile was challenged for its implicit rejection of Chicanos' Indian heritage.

The Aztec heritage of the Mexican people became a source of pride for Mexican Americans and its emphasis an affirmation of their hybrid roots. Chicano writers, artists, and activists popularized an image of the Southwest as the land of Aztlán,[8] which, according to Aztec myth, was the original homeland of the Aztec people of central Mexico. The idea of the Southwest as Aztlán was a powerful one, as it situated Chicanos not as unwelcome outsiders but as the original inhabitants fully entitled to be there; it asserted ethnic pride in their connections to the civilizations of ancient Mexico; it affirmed their separate identity, in contrast to their Mexican heritage and Anglo environment; and it effectively unified the heterogeneous Mexican American communities in the United States (Klor de Alva 1989). This new terminology, like the evolution in the African American community of "colored" to "Negro" and then to "black" or "African American," affirmed an emerging and positive vision of themselves.

The arts also flourished, used as a vehicle to reinforce a sense of community, to build Mexicans' pride in themselves and their heritage, and to inspire community action. Playwright and film and stage director Luis Valdez organized Teatro Campesino to take these works to the people. Chicano artists took inspiration from Mexican muralists and organized to paint their interpretations of the Chicano experience on walls across the Southwest. Here representations of Donald Duck shared space with traditional

Mexican heros. Singers taught a new generation the traditional Mexican *corridos* (ballads) that told their folk history. At community centers across the Southwest, Chicanos learned the steps of the various Indian and Mexican *ballet folklorico* dances. Chicanos, like African Americans and other politically active minority groups, also challenged their representation in the media (e.g., Cortés 1983) and in school curricula and textbooks (e.g., Martínez 1989; New York State Education Department 1987), a process that continues today.

Puerto Ricans

Puerto Ricans, like Chicanos, African Americans, and Native Americans, also challenged the validity of the melting pot and asserted their entitlement to a distinctive cultural identity beginning in the 1960s. The children of the massive postwar diaspora came of age during the explosive years of the anticolonial and civil rights movements of the 1960s. Puerto Ricans organized around a variety of issues relevant to their communities: decent housing, health care and community services, the elimination of racial discrimination and police brutality, drug abuse programs, and better educational services for their children. One important component of their struggle for better educational services included support for bilingual education (Del Valle 1997). This objective was furthered by the 1973 U.S. Supreme Court case *Lau v. Nichols*, in which the court ruled that non-English-dominant children were entitled to assistance in learning English.

Political activists in the mainland Puerto Rican communities of the 1960s and 1970s recognized the shared concerns of Puerto Ricans and African Americans. Puerto Ricans in New York City live in close proximity to African Americans. As a racialized group in the United States, Puerto Ricans too have experienced prejudice and discrimination. Furthermore, different shades of color within the community translate

into different experiences for darker-skinned Puerto Ricans (Klor de Alva 1989; Rodríguez 1989). Piri Thomas's autobiography, *Down These Mean Streets* (1967), early on traced the significance of skin color in shaping Puerto Ricans' experiences and life opportunities on the mainland. Piri recounts his painful discovery of what it means to be a dark-skinned Puerto Rican when he applied for a sales job. He is told that he will be contacted when something opens up, but his light-skinned Puerto Rican friend who goes in after him is hired on the spot. "I didn't feel so much angry as I did sick, like throwing-up sick. Later, when I told this story to my buddy, a colored cat, he said, 'Hell, Piri, Ah know stuff like that can sure burn a cat up, but a Negro faces that all the time.' 'I know that,' I said, 'but I wasn't a Negro then. I was still only a Puerto Rican'" (p. 104).

The political activists who organized the Puerto Rican Young Lords Party in New York City sought to build connections with the African American community, and to address the racism embedded in the Puerto Rican community itself (Laó 1995). Many of the programs and calls to action by the Young Lords (e.g., their breakfast program, the garbage protest to bring attention to the city's neglect of their neighborhoods) served both Puerto Rican and African American community members. Pablo Guzmán, a leader of the group, spoke for many when he wrote that for "Puerto Ricans like myself, who are darker-skinned, who look like Afro-Americans, (we) couldn't avoid do(ing) that (seeing connections between the Black and Puerto Rican experiences), 'cause to do that would be to escape into a kind of fantasy. Because before people called me a spic, they called me a nigger" (Young Lords Party 1971:74).

Another important rallying point for the mainland community was Puerto Rico's ambiguous status as neither a state nor an independent nation. On the island, the movement for independence waxed and waned over the course of the twentieth century. The granting of commonwealth status in 1952 did little to alleviate the perception that the island still retains its colonial relationship to the United States; Puerto Ricans on the island cannot vote for president, nor do they have voting representatives in Congress. While both islanders and mainlanders remain divided on what Puerto Rico's status should be—independent, continuing as is, or statehood—the struggle for independence provides a forum for asserting the cultural nationalism of Puerto Ricans (Rodríguez 1989). Puerto Ricans today continue to maintain a distinct sense of "peoplehood," both on and off the island (Morris 1995).

Over time, however, Puerto Ricans on the mainland become culturally differentiated from island Puerto Ricans. They may lose their mastery of Spanish, and acquire different cultural preferences and views than their island counterparts. The women's movement on the mainland, for instance, contributed to politically active Puerto Rican women challenging men's domination of their organizations (Laó 1995). As in the Mexican American community, women demanded that they move from being subordinated to men to being treated as equals.

So, too, the differing experiences of mainland Puerto Ricans with "race" and their own racialization on the mainland affected their understanding of such matters. These different sensibilities were apparent in mainland Puerto Rican responses to Mattel's release of "Puerto Rican Barbie" in 1997. The doll was well received in Puerto Rico as a welcome acknowledgment of their presence in American society. On the mainland, however, many were offended by her depiction as light-skinned with Anglicized features, and her colonial-tiered dress. The failure of the accompanying literature to acknowledge the Tainos, the original inhabitants of the island, was also criticized (Navarro 1997).

The cultural and linguistic fusion that grows out of shared spaces and lives is readily visible in literary and artistic productions of New York Puerto Ricans,[9] oftentimes called "Nuyoricans."[10] The poetry of Nuyorican Tato Laviera evokes these interconnections, seen here in his poem "melao"[11] (Laviera 1988:27):

melao was nineteen years old
when he arrived from santurce   (city in Puerto
                        Rico)
spanish speaking streets. . . .
melaíto his son now answered
in black american soul english talk
with native plena sounds   (African-based
                    Puerto Rican
                    music)
and primitive urban salsa beats.

Latino rap also creatively comments on these lived realities when it intermingles Spanish and Black English and addresses shared interests, as the lyrics of KT's "We're Puerto Rican and Proud!" illustrate (Flores 2000):

I rarely talk Spanish and a little
   trigueño   (Spanglish)
People be swearin' I'm a *moreno*   (black)
Pero (but) guess what? I'm *Puertorriqueño*.
Word 'em up.
All jokes aside, I ain't tryin' to dis any race.

When Puerto Ricans do return to the island, the cultural differentiation that arises between these two communities can be brought home all too painfully. Children raised on the mainland may be rejected by their island peers for not being "real" Puerto Ricans. "If I am an American, a gringo, a Yankee down here, and up north I am a Puerto Rican, a spik; what in hell am I really? Who am I? Where do I belong?" asks the main character in Pedro Juan Soto's "Hot Land, Cold Season" (in Seda-Bonilla 1977:115). At the same time that cultural differentiation is taking place, the ongoing movement back and forth across the "air bridge" that links island and mainland also contributes to the movement of elements of culture in both directions, producing heated debates on the island about American cultural influence.

Tato Laviera acknowledges both the cultural

hybridization taking place and the psychic costs that this rejection engenders in his poem "nuyorican" (Laviera 1985, translated from Spanish in Flores 2000:54):

> I fight for you puerto rico, you know?
> I defend myself for your name, you know?
> I enter your island, i feel foreign, you know?
> I enter searching for more and more, you know?
> But you, with your insults,
> you deny me your smile,
> i feel bad, indignant.
> I am your son, of a migration,
> a sin forced on me,
> . . . .
> Now i return with a *boricua*[12] heart, and you,
> you scorn me, you look askance, you attack the
>   way i speak,
> while you're out there eating mcdonalds in
>   american discotheques.

This circular migration from island to mainland that became so pronounced by the 1960s, and that many Puerto Ricans continue to participate in, seems at first glance to be an outcome of individual decisions. When conditions improve on the mainland, migration increases; when conditions decline, migration decreases and more people return (Maldonado 1976). What often goes unnoticed, though, are the macrostructural factors contributing to this movement (Bonilla and Campos 1981; Morales 1986). Puerto Rican analysts point to the economic and political dependence of Puerto Rico and its position in the global economy, and the grave consequences for Puerto Rican migrants. "Direct colonial relations," underlines ethnographer Juan Flores, "as an uninterrupted legacy and ever-present reality, govern the motives and outcomes of the whole migratory and settlement process, and fix a consistently low ceiling on the group's expectations and opportunities" (1996:67). Puerto Rican migrants, Flores points out, might be better categorized as "colonial emigrants," like the Jamaicans in England or Martinicans in Paris, because of this larger context and the consequences of discrimination and economic marginalization in the United States.

Mainland Puerto Ricans have challenged the binary system operating on the mainland that provides no middle ground: a person should speak either Spanish or English, identify as either white or black, be either Puerto Rican or American (Bruce-Noboa 1987; Flores 1985; Flores et al. 1981; Klor de Alva 1988). The rejection of such binary assumptions in Puerto Rican communities, and their renaming of themselves "Nuyoricans," attest to similar processes occurring in both Puerto Rican and Chicano communities. While they remain the poorest ethnic group, they have been the "front line that opened doors for every Latino that came after them" in New York City, points out Susana Torruella Leval, director of El Museo del Barrio:

> After a half century, Puerto Ricans in New York have succeeded in carving out electoral districts and Latino studies programs in universities. They have won bilingual education and civil rights battles and congressional, state and municipal posts. They have created a wide array of organizations, from cultural institutions to nonprofit agencies that now increasingly serve other Latinos. [Navarro 2000]

Puerto Ricans have collectively altered the face of New York. Today almost half of all Puerto Ricans live on the mainland, up from 2.7 million in 1990 to 3.4 million in 2000 (Schmitt 2001).

THE CHANGING U.S. LATINO COMMUNITY: THE 1970s AND BEYOND

The diversity of Latinos in the United States shifted with changes in U.S. immigration law in 1965. The national origins quota system that favored Northern and Western Europeans since its inception in the 1920s was abolished in an effort to address the racism embedded in earlier laws. This effectively opened the door to massive immigration from parts of Asia and the Latin American and Caribbean countries, with undocumented immigrants representing an additional unknown number of newcomers. The Latino population has more than doubled since 1980 (Delgado and Stefancic 1998). Hispanics today number 35.3 million and are 12.5 percent of the U.S. population.

The cultural revitalization and access to the home communities that characterized Puerto Ricans' and Mexican Americans' experiences is ongoing for virtually all newcomers to the United States today. Analysts of immigrant communities in the United States (e.g., Basch et al. 1994) speak of the emergence of transnational communities, "characterized by a constant flow of people in both directions, a dual sense of identity, ambivalent attachments to two nations, and a far-flung network of kinship and friendship ties across state frontiers" (Duany 1994:2). The process of conceptualizing migrants as part of transnational sociocultural systems provides a new model for understanding the immigrant experience:

> Transnational identities cross over territorial boundaries and national cultures in ways that are difficult to grasp from a traditional ethnographic perspective [Appadurai 1991, 1990]. Recent approaches to transnational communities have begun by discarding the conventional image of immigration as a form of cultural stripping away and complete absorption into the host society [Rosaldo 1989]. Rather, immigrants belong to multiple communities with fluid and hybrid identities that are not necessarily grounded in geopolitical frontiers but perhaps in subjective affiliations. Border crossing becomes an apt image for not just the physical act of moving to another country but also the crossover between cultures, languages, and nation-states in which transnational migrants participate. [Duany 1994:2]

Puerto Ricans and, to some extent, Mexicans were in many respects the earliest such communities.

While the Latino population has become more dispersed in recent decades, each of the three largest populations remains geographically concentrated in a particular region of the United States. The majority of Mexican Americans live in the Southwest, with four out of every five residing in California or Texas. One-third of Puerto Ricans are in New York City (Glasser 1997), and two-thirds of Cubans reside in the Miami area. Today's Hispanics are overwhelmingly urbanites and are a significant presence in many cities. Almost 6 million live in Los Angeles, where they will soon become the majority population (Sterngold 2000). Almost 3.5 million Latinos can be found in the New York–northern New Jersey metropolitan area. Over 1 million each reside in the Chicago, Houston, and San Francisco metropolitan areas. Longtime sites are becoming more ethnically diverse as Latino newcomers join established Latino populations. In New York City, for instance, the numbers of Dominicans and Mexican Americans rose dramatically, while Puerto Ricans declined to only 36 percent of the city's Latinos by 2000 (Sachs 2001).

At the same time that Latinos remain concentrated regionally, both the old and the newcomers are spreading out to other nontraditional areas of the country, including Wisconsin, parts of the Midwest, and several southern states. (Cuban Americans remain the exception to this trend; their concentration in Florida has actually increased in recent years [Portes and Grosfoguel 1994].) Over 1 million Hispanics live in Illinois today (National Council of La Raza 2001). The Latino population in Massachusetts grew 104 percent in the 1980s (Frau-Ramos and Nieto 1993), and New Jersey's Latino population increased 35 percent in the 1990s, to over 1 million (Brand 2000). Puerto Rican migration from New York City to elsewhere on the mainland accelerated beginning in the 1980s, as Puerto Ricans left in search of better quality lives for their children and enhanced job opportunities. Puerto Ricans spreading out on the mainland have oftentimes found themselves struggling again over many of the very issues they confronted early on in New York City (e.g., Bigler 1999; Glasser 1997; Soto 1997; Stains 1994).

Many Latino newcomers are also part of the

"brain drain" from less developed nations to the developed nations, as the economic disparities between the "have" and the "have-not" nations continue unchecked. Professionals, including engineers, academics, and entrepreneurs, from Latin American countries are also immigrating and joining established later-generation Latinos further up on the social class ladder. The New Jersey Department of Labor, for instance, reported in 1993 that 30 percent of the state's Hispanics earned from $25,000 to $50,000 per year, and almost 15 percent earned more than $50,000 (Brand 2000).

The Mariel Exodus: Expansion of the Cuban Community

Most Cuban Americans did not participate in the ethnic movements of the 1960s and 1970s. They had little identification with other oppressed groups in the United States,[13] and many viewed themselves as political exiles rather than a racial/ethnic minority. That changed, however, after 1980, with the arrival of 125,000 *marielitos* from Cuba. Cuban president Fidel Castro, embarrassed by a sudden surge of refugees seeking to leave the island through the Peruvian embassy, opened the port of Mariel and declared that anyone wanting to leave could do so. Cuban Americans were invited to pick up their relatives. Castro, deliberately seeking to discredit the refugees, also sent ex-convicts and mental patients among them. While they represented perhaps only 10 percent of the *marielitos*, their presence tarnished the entire group of newcomers, many of whom also wrestled with the difficulties of being poorer and darker-skinned than the initial refugee waves. The *Miami Herald*, controlled at the time by the Anglo population, sensationalized the story. A negative stereotype of *marielitos* quickly crystallized within the established Cuban American community and the larger society. Anglos organized an "antibilingual" referendum that passed overwhelmingly. Earlier Cuban exiles, long considered "model minorities," now found themselves tarnished by negative stereotypes.

This turn of events prompted the transformation of Miami Cuban Americans "from a political exile group into a self-conscious ethnic minority" (Portes and Stepick 1993:105), producing what Portes and Stepick characterize as a process of "reactive formation." Cuban Americans came together to work to redefine the situation positively and to depict themselves as the impetus for Miami's economic transformation. Ethnic organizations formed, and the Cuban American community in Miami became more politically active. A great advantage they enjoyed over other Latino groups seeking similar goals was the economic resources they controlled.

Growing Diversification of the Latino Population

Immigration from other areas of Latin America also increased from the 1980s on, with the largest growth occurring among Dominicans, Guatemalans, Salvadorans, Nicaraguans, and Colombians.

Nicaraguans. Cubans in Miami have been joined by other immigrant groups from Central and South America. Most numerous are the Nicaraguans who, like the Cubans before them, fled a leftist government. Like the Cubans, the earliest were the wealthy, who often had already established roots in the United States; many had also transferred their assets to U.S. banks in the late 1970s. They were soon followed by the middle class, and then the working class in the mid-1980s.

The reception of Nicaraguans in the United States, however, has been quite different from that of the Cubans. While virtually all Cubans up until 1980 had their passages paid for and were automatically granted permanent residence, most Nicaraguans found themselves classified as unwanted illegal aliens. By 1985, only around 10 percent of Nicaraguan applicants had been granted political asylum. The rest remained ineligible for refugee assistance, resettlement aid, welfare, or government loans. This changed briefly as Nicaraguan elites cemented their ties with the Cuban exile community and the Reagan White House courted potential Republican votes. By 1988, however, the policy reverted to its earlier phase, and Nicaraguans were again deported and actively discouraged from migrating (Portes and Stepick 1993:159). In 1997, the U.S. government finally made application for legal residency easier (Brinkley 1999).

Dominicans. Large-scale migration from the Dominican Republic is a more recent phenomenon, beginning in the 1960s when emigration restrictions loosened after the dictator Rafael Trujillo was killed. Since then, emigration has been largely economically driven, responding to rising expectations and economic downturns. Over three-quarters of a million Dominicans live in the United States according to the 2000 census, with New York the major haven for the new arrivals. Dominicans have christened Washington Heights, where so many settled, "Quisqueya," the indigenous term for their island. Dominicans now represent the second largest Latino group, behind Puerto Ricans, and the single largest immigrant group in New York City (Pessar 1995). These newcomers are primarily urban middle class or working class, and, like other immigrants, typically come as part of a preexisting *cadena* (chain) that links immigrants through kinship networks. They are concentrated in manufacturing and wholesale/retail trades, areas where massive job loss has occurred and where desperately poor Mexicans and Central Americans are said to be accepting even lower wages and displacing them (Pessar 1995:40). Dominican unemployment is almost double that of the overall New York City population, and over one-third live below the poverty rate (Hernández et al. 1995:28). Low rates of high school completion—60 percent over age 25 have not completed their secondary educations—further limit job opportunities.

Not surprisingly, Grasmuck and Pessar (1991) found skin color among Dominican Americans to be a very significant predictor of poverty. Fifty percent of Dominicans in the 1990 census identified as "other" and 25 percent as "black." Dominicans, like Puerto Ricans, oftentimes find themselves taken for African Americans, whereas on the island anyone partly "white" is considered nonblack. While it is difficult to document the extent of discrimination, findings from a 1990 Urban Institute report are instructive. When young Anglo men and young Latino men were paired and given identical résumés to apply for the same jobs, their success rates differed by race. Sixty-four percent of Anglos were invited for an interview, compared to 48 percent of Latinos; 43 percent of the Anglo job applicants received job offers, and only 28 percent of the Latinos (Cross et al. 1990, cited in Cordero Guzmán 1993).

Dominicans' placement in a different racial hierarchy in the United States is a challenging one to negotiate. Jorge Duany's 1998 ethnographic study highlights some of the ways in which Dominicans seek to negotiate their identities in the racially divided United States:

> Racial prejudice and discrimination have forced many Dominicans in New York to settle in areas adjacent to African American concentrations. . . . Despite physical proximity, most Dominicans strive to distance themselves culturally from African Americans by speaking Spanish, dancing the merengue, rejecting black hairstyles and speech patterns, and associating primarily with other Latinos. . . . Dominican immigrants strongly resist assimilation into the dominant culture. This tendency is partly a response to racial and ethnic exclusion. [p. 11]

Second-generation Dominican Americans, however, may be more likely to acknowledge the links and experiences they share with African Americans and identify as "Afro-Caribbean" (Pessar 1995). Duany concurs:

(Y)ounger members of the second generation often adopt the black dialect, hip-hop fashion, and rap music popular among African American teenagers. Some dark-skinned Dominicans are following the path of a segmented assimilation in which the main frame of reference is an adversarial African American culture rather than a mainstream white identity (see Portes, 1994). Slowly but surely, Dominican immigrants are developing an awareness of their black roots and reaching out to other Caribbean and Latino peoples. [p. 11]

Many Dominicans, like other immigrants and Puerto Ricans, are choosing, for a variety of reasons, to forge lives both *aqui* ("here") and *allá* ("there") (Pessar 1995). Transportation, communication, and technology enhance access to the homeland. A greater tolerance for ethnic pluralism exists than for earlier immigrants. Economic uncertainties both at home and in the United States make it wise to keep options open. Emigrants are increasingly viewed by the home communities as important resources to be courted. Finally, as people of color, they may feel more valued in their homeland than in the United States. However when they do return, like Puerto Ricans they may find themselves ostracized for being "Americanized." At the same time, "Dominican Yorks" are emerging as a distinctive ethnic group in New York. More politically involved, they are demanding recognition and respect and seeking alliances with other ethnics. If projections hold, Dominicans will become the largest Hispanic group in New York City in the next 10 years (Navarro 2000).

Salvadorans and Guatemalans. Among the estimated 2 million refugees fleeing the conflicts in Central America by the late 1980s were the Salvadorans and Guatemalans. Large-scale immigration from El Salvador north followed the outbreak of civil war in 1979. Salvadorans number about 0.5 million according to the U.S. census, though scholars put the numbers at more like 1 million (Mahler 1995). Perhaps one-quarter million Guatemalans of Mayan descent also fled for their lives from government troops.

(Then-President Bill Clinton recognized the U.S. role in this civil war when he apologized in 1999 to Guatemalans for the U.S. support of right-wing Guatemalan governments that killed tens of thousands of Mayan Indians and rebels in recent decades [Broder 1999].)

Like the Nicaraguans, many of these refugees entered the United States as undocumented immigrants. Unlike the Nicaraguans, the Salvadorans and Guatemalans fled from conflicts where the U.S. government supported their military rulers, and Americans were generally uninformed about the conflicts in their home countries. They thus had no allies like the vocal anti-Communist Cuban American community to advocate on their behalf. Recently, however, the U.S. government reversed long-standing policy and agreed that refugees from right-wing governments will be accorded the same treatment as the Nicaraguans fleeing a left-wing government. They can now apply for legal residency and are spared the earlier difficulties of having to appear before a judge, prove they have been in the United States for seven years, and show that their lives are in danger if they return (Brinkley 1999).

The Maya of Guatemala are the indigenous people of the region, descendants of the ancient Maya that once dominated Central America. They are cultural refugees who came in large family and community groups to the United States (Burns 1993), fleeing the destruction of their communities and widespread murders. Southern Florida, in particular, Indiantown, became a popular destination in the early 1980s, providing work and a safe environment for the refugees.

It was, however, an environment very different from what they had previously known. In the United States the Maya face prejudice and discrimination not only from Anglos but also from other Latinos. Mexican immigrants, for instance, echoing prejudices in Mexico, may disparage them as *indios*. In the United States the Maya also became one among many diverse groups. No longer identifying and identified as indigenous Maya, they have become "migrant workers" or "illegals." After several years in the United States they also become culturally differentiated from the Maya that remained behind (Burns 1993).

The Salvadorans entering the United States, primarily peasants and urban workers, were also uprooted by a civil war. By 1990, they had made their way north, almost half of them to Los Angeles, with significant populations in greater New York, Washington, DC, San Francisco, and Houston. As a whole they are poorer, younger, and less educated than the average American (Mahler 1995). Their status, lack of education, and lack of English limit their employment opportunities primarily to the poorly paid informal and service sectors, and they settle where they find niches for their labor. Large cities are not the only destinations for new immigrants; Sarah Mahler (1995), for instance, found an estimated 60,000 to 100,000 Salvadorans living on Long Island, filling spaces in the labor force created by a growing demand for service jobs and an aging and shrinking native-born population. The limited skills and oftentimes undocumented status of these newcomers, unfortunately, leave them vulnerable to mistreatment from their employers.

CHALLENGES AND OPPORTUNITIES

Latinos are now a numerical force in the United States, yet their troubled past and current social and economic situations combine to limit their access to equal participation in the American mainstream. Particularly problematic are the stubborn disparities in educational attainment, given the changing economy.

Economic and Educational Challenges

A growing number of Latinos have gained access to the middle class, in part due to their mobilization in the 1960s. Most Latinos, how-

ever, continue to confront significant structural barriers to upward mobility that negatively affect the quality of their life experiences and their life chances (e.g., Moore and Pinderhughes 1993; Portes and Grosfoguel 1994; Torres 1995). They suffer the consequences of racial and ethnic discrimination, and of the decline of the central cities. Economic restructuring, with jobs moving overseas and a shift from a manufacturing to a service economy, has meant the elimination of the unionized better-paying blue-collar jobs that provided white ethnics opportunities to establish economic stability and ultimately enter the middle class. Despite the thriving economy of the 1990s, Latinos remained concentrated in the secondary labor market, with its low-wage jobs vulnerable to market swings and with virtually nonexistent benefits (Fletcher 2000). Meanwhile educational requirements for economically viable jobs are increasing, and the economy has experienced a marked downturn.

U.S. News & World Report in May 1997 featured a superhero flying through the air with the caption "The Amazing American Economy." What may be more amazing is how economic trends have led to greater, rather than lesser, income inequality across the U.S. population. Since the 1960s the gap between the rich and the poor has increased, and real wages for those on the lower rungs of the economic ladder have actually declined (Collins and Yeskel 2000). While child poverty rates fell significantly with the 1990s economic boom, nationwide child poverty remains higher than it was 20 years ago, up by some 3 million (Terry 2000). The real value of the minimum wage may have climbed in the 1990s, but it remains down 27 percent since 1968 (Davis 2000).

This situation of stubbornly entrenched income inequality is ominous for all Americans, and groups like Latinos who are disproportionately worse off will feel the impact most. A brief overview of unemployment, income, and education statistics from the 1997 census

Table 10-1   Social and Economic Characteristics of Major Hispanic Groups and Euro-Americans

	Total White[b]	Total Hispanic	Mexican American	Puerto Rican	Cuban
Below poverty level[a]	7.8%	26.4%	27.9%	34.2%	19.6%
And under age 18[a]			36.0%	49.5%	20.7%
Unemployed	2.8%	7.7%	7.7%	9.8%	6.6%
High school graduate (age 25+)	83.1%	54.7%	48.6%	61.1%	65.2%
Completion of college (25+)	24.6%	10.3%	7.4%	10.8%	19.7%
Median family income	$49,636	$26,179	$25,347	$23,646	$35,616

[a]March 1997 Current Population Survey, Table 12.2, U.S. Bureau of the Census.
[b]Non-Hispanic white.

data (Table 10-1) suggests the extent of these different locations in the socioeconomic structure and the challenges confronting us. Taken collectively, over one-quarter of all Hispanics live below the poverty level, including over one-third of Puerto Ricans. The median family income of Hispanics is roughly half that of Euro-Americans. (Cubans, for reasons discussed earlier, fare best.) Differences in education, so critical in today's new economy, translate into differences in access to better-paying employment opportunities.

Recent statistics underline the costs of less education for younger generations. In 1995, male college graduates earned an average of $61,717 and female graduates $37,924. High school graduates earned barely more than half that: $32,708 for males and $21,961 for females. High school dropouts fared even worse: males earned $23,338 and females $16,319. Worse yet, average earnings in 1995 dollars for male high school graduates dropped almost $5,000 and earnings of male dropouts over $6,000 since 1979 (McCormick and Press 1997).

Beyond the immigrant analogy. In many respects, Latinos as a whole are better understood as "racial" rather than "ethnic" minorities. Their limited opportunities as racial minorities in turn differentiate them from their Euro-American counterparts.

(Racial minorities) are less assimilated than their white "ethnic" counterparts. Therefore, these racial groups possess extensive non-Anglo American cultural traits, frequently feel alienated from the political institutions of the U.S., participate disproportionately in working-class cultural activities, and have been kept at a substantial social distance from the white majority. This segregation under conditions of super-exploitation, coupled among some racial groups such as Latinos with the cultural reinforcement provided by continuous immigration from the homeland, have made racial minorities politically and socioeconomically different from ethnic groups like the Irish, Polish, or Italian-Americans. [Klor de Alva 1989:143]

Why Latinos were not culturally and structurally assimilating into the dominant population and ascending the social class ladder like their Euro-American counterparts became a contentious subject of debate by the 1960s. "Cultural deficit" explanations that attributed their low socioeconomic status to "culturally determined" behaviors were prevalent.[14] Hispanic culture (with most early studies based on Mexican Americans) was alleged to be deficient because of its supposed anti-intellectualism, parental indifference, doting child-rearing style, and absence of future orientation, as well as a lack of commitment to the English language.[15] A "noncompetitive, nonprogressive, easily satisfied psychological makeup that caters to a family-oriented fatalistic world view" was defined as the barrier to rapidly ascending the social class ladder (Klor de Alva 1988:116). Fatalism and familism (family needs taking priority over emphasis on the individual's fulfillment) were widely accepted as explanations for Mexican Americans' poverty, without investigating whether these traits existed in urban barrios or, for that matter, led to poverty (Moore and Pinderhughes 1993). These images of Latinos and explanations for their economic situations arose from a variety of sources: popular culture, ethnocentric scholarly analyses (e.g., Heller 1966), and overgeneralization of findings from anthropological studies of isolated rural Mexican American communities (e.g., Madsen 1964; Rubel 1966) to urban settings.

While the idea that cultural and linguistic "deficits" held back Latinos may have been a popular assumption among many educators, social service providers, and policymakers in the 1960s, a growing number of anthropologists and other qualitative researchers—including among them a new generation of Chicano and Puerto Rican academics—took issue with then-popular social science assumptions. Chicano academics attacked depictions of Mexican American culture that portrayed it as static, oppressive, and backwards[16] (Griswold del Castillo 1984). Mexican American anthropologist Octavio Romano's work, published in the Chicano journal *El Grito* from 1967 to 1970, was central:

> In using such words as these (fatalistic, resigned, apathetic, tradition oriented, tradition bound, emotional, impetuous . . .) to describe other people they thereby place the reasons or causes of "inferior" status *somewhere within the minds, within the personalities, or within the culture* [sic] of those who are economically, politically, or educationally out of power. [1967:7]

Romano, noted one Chicano anthropologist, "taught his many readers to argue against cultural determinism, the idea that Chicanos (or any other group) are victims of their own values, such as passivity, fatalism and envy. . . . (These are) new ways to blame the victim" (Rosaldo 1986:8). Chicano folklorist Américo Paredes, in his critiques of portrayals of Mexican Americans (1978), aptly demonstrated how Euro-American anthropologists, as cultural outsiders, easily missed the subtle double meanings in many Mexican oral traditions when arriving at their conclusions.

Puerto Ricans' continuing poverty was also a focus in the social science literature. Anthropologist Oscar Lewis popularized the notion of a "culture of poverty" that reproduced itself in his ethnography *La Vida, A Puerto Rican Family in the Culture of Poverty* (1966). Though Lewis did not intend to equate a culture of poverty with race or ethnicity, many felt that it read as characteristic of Puerto Ricans rather than as an outcome of dislocation in a capitalist economy. Critics attacked it as a "blame the victim" approach to understanding the root causes of poverty, and instead argued for attention to the system that produces such profound poverty. Cultural practices, they argued, needed to be understood as adaptive responses to life difficulties rather than causes of poverty. This sort of understanding would, for instance, see familism as a "smart" choice when resources and opportunities are limited, rather than a barrier to upward mobility. Anthropologists' own tendencies to depict culture as bounded, unchanging, and homogeneous, and to ignore oppression and inequality (Rosaldo 1989), came under attack within anthropology at home as a new generation of scholars, many of them "natives" themselves, came of age and entered the discipline.

Culture, Language, Identity . . . and Education

If greater educational success is increasingly a prerequisite for achieving economic stability in the United States, it is instructive to examine what educational anthropologists have found in exploring disparities in educational performance across groups. The criticism in the 1960s and 1970s of mainstream social science explanations for minority groups' lack of achievement had its counterpart in new theorizing on education and minority student performance coming out of educational anthropology, a field then in its infancy.

Anthropologists working in schools brought a number of strengths to their study of educational institutions. For one, schools and students are contextualized as existing within a larger framework, both historically and societally. For another, anthropologists are interested in how various groups experience and view their worlds, ensuring a broader range of perspectives and understandings. They also seek to distance themselves from their own cultural biases and assumptions and frequently challenge common, taken-for-granted understandings. Both the macro perspective, looking at things from outside the schools, and the micro perspective, close-up ethnographic projects within schools themselves that examine the complex ways in which culture and language differences can enter into educational performance, were utilized. These orientations provided new understandings of how culturally and linguistically diverse students and their communities participate in the school experience.

Refuting cultural deficit notions. Early analyses of Latinos' school performance often took for granted that the practices of the schools themselves were neutral, and that the "problems" lie in the cultural and linguistic practices of nonmainstream families. It was taken as a given that all students had equal educational opportunities. Yet we know that was not (e.g., Carter and Segura 1979; Pedraza 1997), and still is not, the case, when de facto segregation and gross economic disparities across suburban and urban schools make quality education far less likely for Latinos and other urban minorities (Kozol 1991).

The early explanations (e.g., Bereiter and Engelmann 1966; Hess and Shipman 1965) alleged that cultural and linguistic deficits in lower-class homes were the causes of their lower educational performance.[17] This "culture of poverty" explanation, as critics termed it (e.g., Leacock 1971), was flawed for its assessment of these groups from an ethnocentric, middle-class point of view rather than a culturally relativistic point of view that seeks to understand people's behavior from their own perspectives and experiences. Working and living in minority communities, they documented the strengths of culturally different students' home environments (e.g., Au 1980; Labov 1972; Philips 1972) and argued that the issue was not one of cultural deficiencies in their homes, but rather cultural mismatches in interaction and learning styles within the schools. Cultural differences in school settings when teachers are unaware of them can lead to systematic miscommunication and contribute to academic difficulties.

Beyond "cultural difference." But cultural difference alone doesn't always lead to problems, and John Ogbu (1978) took the lead in theorizing the significance of factors beyond the school doors. Put briefly, Ogbu argues that the way that racialized groups have been treated in the United States affects their attitudes toward mainstream institutions. "Involuntary" minorities such as African Americans, Chicanos, or Native Americans, all longtime U.S. citizens, have suffered the consequences of an enduring, ongoing history of discrimination that affects their sense of whether education can improve their lives. They may manifest oppositional behavior in schools. Secondary cultural practices forged in segregated social environments (e.g., dress, ways of speaking) for instance become important markers of identity, and conformity to school rules may be read as "acting white" (Fordham and Ogbu 1986).[18]

"Voluntary" minorities, on the other hand, new immigrants, have a different history and thus a different perspective. They look back to their homelands as the basis of comparison; they see opportunities denied to them there; but if all else fails, they can return. Therefore they are more willing to comply with school expectations, firm in the belief (for the first generation, anyway) that they have opportunities to succeed.

Ethnographic research has found support for Ogbu's theory. Maria Matute-Bianchi, for instance, found an oppositional identity among second- and third-generation Chicano students (1986). Marcelo Suarez-Orozco (1987) found that Central American newcomers–immigrant minorities–had a better track record in schools than their Chicano and Puerto Rican peers. While these students faced significant institutional barriers–a drug-infested environment, low expectations, and placement into non-academic tracks, among them–they saw schooling as their window of opportunity and felt duty-bound to succeed for their suffering parents.

John Ogbu's work is valuable for fostering awareness of how the larger sociohistoric context can affect people's relations to educational institutions, but a number of anthropologists have also pointed out some of the limitations of his theory (e.g., Davidson 1996; Erickson 1987; Foley 1991; Gibson 1997; MacLeod 1995; Tapia 1998).[19] Among them: it assumes the neutrality of schools and can easily be read as deterministic, with nothing to be done about it; it doesn't explain why *some* involuntary minorities succeed, and why *some* immigrant minority youth come to display oppositional identities; it doesn't consider class differences adequately; it doesn't allow for the possibility that students may manifest an oppositional identity and still succeed academically.

The ethnographic findings these anthropologists draw on have a great deal to tell us about Latinos: the variability within any given ethnic group in the United States; the difficulties with assuming a linear progression from "immigrant" to "ethnic" to "assimilated"; and the significance of the ways in which individual actors negotiate and construct new, and oftentimes multiple, identities. Douglas Foley (1990), studying working-

class and middle-class Mexicanos (the regional term for Mexican Americans) in a south Texas town, found significant intragroup differences among the Mexicanos. Both groups expressed "chicanismos," or "pochismos," expressive cultural practices (dress, greetings, etc.) associated with Mexican Americans. Middle-class youth, though, when the situation demanded, put into action mainstream communicative competencies in impression management such as feigning interest in teacher talk or asking questions designed to get teachers "going" on a topic. These practices fostered positive relations with Anglos and authority figures, unlike those of their working-class peers.

Maria Matute-Bianchi (1991) and Katherine Hayes (1992) found immigrant minority youth who acted like involuntary minority youth. Matute-Bianchi documented immigrant Mexican students seeking acceptance by their Chicano peers through adoption of a *cholo* identity (including expressive aspects such as their dress, walk, and speech) and the antischool attitudes that are common among many *cholo* youth. Similarly, Hayes found that the children of Mexican immigrants felt that school offered nothing to them; their classroom behaviors echoed those of involuntary minority students who rejected the symbols, behaviors, and ideals of Anglo-American society. The time of arrival of immigrant youth may be significant, she suggests. Those who come later in elementary school may have positive identities already in place, whereas those who have all their schooling in the United States may have experiences that lead them to see the world in ways more similar to those of involuntary minorities.

Javier Tapia (1998) found considerable variability in academic performance among the children of poor Puerto Rican families in Philadelphia. His ethnographic study documents the critical nature of family stability, in turn influenced by economic stability, for stronger academic performance. This family stability appeared to matter more than the language of instruction and method of teaching. Nilda Flores-González (1999) found Puerto Rican students in an urban Chicago school who displayed an ethnic identity and were also high achievers, without being accused of "acting white" by their lower-achieving peers.

If raising students' academic success rates is an educational goal there is also much that educational anthropologists can tell us about what sorts of conditions affect culturally diverse students' educational engagement. School practices, as we now know from ethnographic research, can negatively affect culturally diverse students' orientations to schooling. Marginalization and alienation can be the unanticipated outcomes of unquestioned school practices, including the choice of instructional language, tracking, differential treatment, speech acts that stigmatize cultural expressive practices, and writing off parents who fail to conform to middle-class ways of showing interest in their children's education (Davidson 1996).

On the other hand, certain conditions appear to foster the educational engagement of minority youth. One major finding, drawing on both international and U.S. cases, is that "minority students do better in school when they feel strongly anchored in the identities of their families, communities, and peers and when they feel supported in pursuing a strategy of selective or additive acculturation" (Gibson 1997:445–446). Students can be academically successful without losing their ethnic identity if the schools are structured in ways that affirm students' identities and sense of empowerment (Mehan et al. 1994). A culturally sensitive pedagogy, a multicultural curriculum, and recognition and utilization of the "funds of knowledge" that all students bring to school can create a more inclusive and empowering environment while educating all students to the diversity of the world around them (e.g., Bigler 1999; Mercado and Moll 1997; Osborne 1996). Schools can adopt multiculturalism as a *process*, whereby all school practices and outcomes are constantly re-

quired to foster more equitable outcomes (Nieto 2000).

Language and identity. Sociolinguists—anthropologists who study language in its social context—also have a great deal to say about the relationships among culture, identity, language, historical processes, and educational well-being.

We take our cues for language usage from those around us, so that our class locations and ethnic roots, particularly in a society like our own that remains very segregated, provide us with diverse understandings of appropriate "ways of speaking." Latinos are linguistically diverse. Some speak only English, some only Spanish, some are bilinguals; various dialects of English and Spanish coexist, and many Latinos use "Spanglish." Code-switching, or moving back and forth between languages or styles of speaking, is common in regions of the world where different speech communities live in close contact. Linguistic borrowing from one language to another is also common, so that Spanish-speaking Puerto Ricans in New York speak of *el bloque* ("the block") and *lonchar* ("to lunch"). English, in fact, is peppered with words that were originally Spanish: *adobe, bronco, canyon, corral, lasso, lariat, mosquito.* Mexican Spanish contains words from Nahuatl, the language of the Aztecs. Some of these "nahuatlismos," in turn, entered English through the Spanish: *cocoa, tomato, coyote, chocolate, chile.* In Puerto Rico, remnants of the Arawak language, spoken by the original inhabitants, are woven into their Spanish and made their way into English: *papaya, yuca, maíz, iguana, barbacoa (barbecue), huracán.* Today English Internet terms make headway in Spanish-speaking countries, as speakers adapt them to their own linguistic rules: *el backup, fordwardear, chatear, la windo* (Dillon 2000). These sorts of processes of linguistic change are normal anticipated responses to contacts with other speakers, not signs of linguistic "deficiencies."

Yet Puerto Ricans and Spanish-speaking Mexican Americans have a long history of being stigmatized for their speech patterns, as well as being pressured to abandon Spanish. There is a hierarchy of Spanish dialects among Latinos, and Puerto Ricans may be told by other Spanish speakers—or even Spanish-language teachers— that their Spanish is ungrammatical. Mexican American children in the Southwest up to the 1960s were required to use only English in school, even when playing with their classmates on the playground. Stories abound among Chicanos of physical punishment or loss of privileges like recess for using Spanish on school grounds (Montoya 1998).

Thus, many Latinos come to believe their own language patterns are inferior (e.g., Urciuoli 1996; Zentella 1997). To be pressured to reject the language of the home and community, with all that implies, is a traumatic experience (Rodríguez 1982), and such acts also have unanticipated consequences. They increase the possible alienation of children from school, particularly when accompanied by other practices such as cultural exclusion, inappropriate evaluation of cultural differences, and the like, so that they come to view school as a "white" institution. If these practices result in language loss, children may be denied important links to their families and communities. And for those caught up in the migrant stream and transnational communities, language loss complicates their return.

Some Latinos are refusing to surrender to this hegemonic evaluation of their languages and dialects, and now proclaim their use of Spanish and Spanglish as positive and as an affirmation of ethnic pride (Anzaldua 1987; Zentella 1997). Bilingualism could be reconfigured not as a deficiency but as a precious national resource given our role in the "global village" and the need for bilinguals to work in linguistically diverse communities. Rather than to assume that there is room for only one language, a common American assumption, linguistically diverse children can be more productively taught to value both

languages and to code-switch when their community dialect differs from the standard.

The negative evaluation of Spanish in public places has grown as anti-immigrant, antibilingual education, and English-only movements have flourished in the 1980s and 1990s. Speaking Spanish in public is viewed by segments of the Euro-American population as "unAmerican" and evidence of speakers' laziness and unwillingness to assimilate (e.g., Bigler 1997; Woolard 1989; Zentella 1988). Bilingual education has increasingly come under attack, despite significant evidence of its benefits when done well.[20] Ironically, arguments that Spanish maintenance threatens the status of English and leads to ethnic fragmentation ignore the linguistic research that indicates that second- and third-generation Americans are losing their native languages at rates comparable to those of earlier immigrants (Crawford 1992). In the 1990 census, the 91.5 percent of the Hispanics who reported that they spoke Spanish also said that they spoke English—three-quarters of them reporting that they spoke it "well" or "very well" (National Council of La Raza 2001). As Ana Zentella notes,

> Blaming linguistic and cultural diversity (for the political, social and economic problems facing the US today) is a smokescreen for the fact that the US has not resolved fundamental inequalities. The root of the problem lies in an inability to accept an expanded definition of what it is to be a US American today. . . . The nation's problems would not disappear if we all spoke the same language, unless by speaking the same language we mean that we have the same rights and obligations toward each other. [1997:286–87]

Past Imperfect, Present Tense, Future Conditional?[21]

As Latinos are changed by their experiences in the United States, so too is the United States changed by the growing presence of Latinos and their increased access to mainstream institutions. Latinos have historically gone unrecognized for their contributions to the national economic well-being, and today's situation remains little changed. The continued economic strength of the United States is in part made possible by the labor and tax revenue contributions that Latinos and the newest immigrants, both documented and undocumented, contribute. Popular impressions notwithstanding, Latinos' contributions exceed their costs to the government. A 1994 report from the Urban Institute, a research organization in Washington, DC, affirmed that for every dollar a recent immigrant pays in taxes, that immigrant receives 37 cents in government benefits (Brand 2000).

Latino immigrants have helped revitalize declining cities and suburbs where they have settled. Many cities, including Boston, Dallas, and Los Angeles, would have declined in population over the 1990s were it not for Hispanics (Schmitt 2001). Many Hispanics, like earlier generations of Americans, also see owning their own businesses as a stepping-stone on the way to the American dream (Fletcher 2000; Kotkin 2000). The number of Hispanic businesses grew from 422,000 to 720,000 between 1988 and 1994 (Chartrand 1996). " 'Without the Latino entrepreneur, New Jersey's cities would be falling into urban decay,' says Guillermo Beytagh-Maldonado, executive director of New Brunswick's Puerto Rican Action Board. . . . 'Latino entrepreneurs are the (New Brunswick) owners of the mom-and-pop shops' " (Brand 2000). Meanwhile, Latinos are rapidly emerging as a significant market, with an estimated $440 billion in annual buying power (Blair 2000), and marketers are quick to seize the opportunity to win their allegiance. To reach this market, they have begun to attend to Hispanic cultural tastes, the images they project in their ads, and even the models they select to sell their products.

The growing Latino population is now more actively courted by political candidates, as recent *New York Times* articles on the 2000 presidential election made clear: "Candidates Courting Hispanic Vote" (6/25/00), "Republicans Open a Big Drive to Appeal to Hispanic Voters" (1/15/00),

"GOP Courting Hispanics with New Spanish Ad" (4/5/00). *"Yo quiero mucho"* (I love you), Vice President Al Gore roared to the National Association of Latino Elected and Appointed Officials during one of his campaign speeches. If the major political parties are going to successfully court Latino voters, they will want to address not only the concerns they share with many other Americans but also their specific interests, including government policies toward Latin American nations and immigration and language policies.[22] Latinos holding public office are also on the increase. Over the 1990s their numbers in Congress grew from 11 to 19, and the 135 Latino state lawmakers grew to 189. Seven Hispanics now hold statewide offices. Over five thousand hold elected office (approximately half of them on school boards) (Janofsky 2000).

The cultural influence of Latinos is, meanwhile, undeniable. By 1988 *Time* magazine was calling attention to the presence of Latinos on the cultural scene. "A Surging New Spirit: In film, music, theater, art, design—the Hispanic influence is exploding into the American cultural mainstream," the feature article proclaimed:

> (Hispanic culture) is diverse and complex, embedded with traditions inherited from baroque Spain, from the Aztecs and Mayans, from the descendants of black slaves who peopled the Antilles, from the mountainous country of Central America. Each winds its way differently into the American imagination, where it gets put to new uses. There are the things that come from tropical sea-bordered places like Puerto Rico, Cuba, the Dominican Republic. African influences are the legacy of the region's old status as a center of the slave trade. They can be heard in the Afro-Caribbean rhythm that the Talking Heads deploy. . . . (A powerful Indian legacy) can be felt in the somber and ceremonial notes of Mexican Catholicism. . . . Hispanic culture offers a counterweight (to American individualism) in the claims of community and the shared impulse . . . (seen) asserting themselves in mainstream life through such means as the outdoor murals . . . that are an essential part of the Los Angeles cityscape. Add to that senti-

ment the claims of family, the primal unit of Hispanic life. [Lacayo 1988:46]

True, these influences are not felt uniformly around the nation, but they are there nonetheless. New crossover artists join other Latinos with national name recognition: Gloria Estafan, Jennifer Lopez, Ricky Martin, and Andy García; Edward James Olmos, Jimmy Smits, Linda Ronstadt, and Rosie Perez. Americans of all backgrounds dance increasingly to a Latin beat. Meanwhile Latin American musicians filter American rock through their own sensibilities, producing the new phenomenon "rock *en español*" that is now winding its way back into the U.S. music scene (Rohter 2000).

A new generation of Latinos, like earlier generations of ethnic writers, pen bittersweet memoirs about their coming of age in the United States: *How the Garcia Girls Lost Their Accents*, by Julia Alvarez (1992); *When I Was Puerto Rican*, by Esmeralda Santiago (1993); *The House on Mango Street*, by Sandra Cisneros (1989); *Always Running: La Vida Loca*, by Luis Rodríguez (1993). Quality movies with Latinos as stars are hailed as box-office successes: *Mi Familia, Stand and Deliver, American Me, The Mambo Kings Play Songs of Love*. Salsa and flour tortillas are ubiquitous, having even gone trendy for "roll-ups" in chic eateries; design and architecture magazines borrow heavily from Hispanic decorating styles in the South and West; Spanish has become the preferred second language in schools across the nation.

A sense of affinity is palpable at times among Latinos when they come together to share their common concerns.[23] But there is no one "Latino" experience, any more than there is one "Chicano" or one "Puerto Rican" experience—or for that matter, one "American" experience. Latinos are taking a variety of paths in the United States. Many, particularly the lighter-skinned, may assimilate into the Euro-American mainstream, as intermarriage across Latino-Anglo lines increases (an estimated one-third of all Latinos intermarry). Not that they will necessarily be absorbed into the dominant society; the assimilation may also be in the opposite direction (Rosaldo 1985). Others may assimilate into the African American urban culture, or children of mixed Latino–African American marriages may choose to identify as Latino. Undoubtedly, the homelands will continue to be not only spiritual but also material realities for many Latinos. And many Latinos, if current trends hold, may be "not neither," as Sandra Maria Esteves (1984:26) puts it, continuing to maintain their claims to the right to distinctive identities, to exist in the "borderlands" (e.g., Anzaldua 1987) and carve out new ways of being "American." Some will have more choice than others.

The very nature of Latinos' experiences has required them to be adept "border crossers," crossing racial borders, ethnic borders, national borders, language borders. But there is one border that will remain particularly problematic: Without the public will to address the continuing and growing inequalities among us that rob so many of a decent quality of life, many will remain on the wrong side of an economic divide that continues to threaten American society into the twenty-first century.

NOTES

1. In Spanish, the ending -*o* is used for the masculine form of a word, and -*a* for the feminine. Much like in the arguments for replacing "mankind" with "humankind," the term *Latino* is also sometimes written as *Latino/a*, or *Latinos/Latinas* to signal more inclusiveness.
2. The word "Latin" would technically incorporate speakers of other Latin-derived languages. Indeed, Portuguese-speaking Brazilians in the U.S. in many respects could be logically grouped with other Hispanic groups but instead fall between the cracks of U.S. racial/ethnic categories.
3. By "racial" group, here I mean it in the sense of those who see distinctive biological races existing. Latinos to varying degrees have white, Indian (Asian), and black ancestry when seen from this perspective.
4. While this reflects to some extent the valuing of "European" ancestry in Latin American countries, it can also be understood in part as a politically expedient choice given the racism toward American Indians in the United States (see Menchaca 1993).

5. Even the federal government could not agree on how to classify Mexicans. When the 1930 census sought for the first time to capture the number of Hispanics in the United States, "Mexican" (meant as a label for Mexican Americans) was placed under the rubric of "other races"; in the 1950 census, Mexican Americans were considered to be whites.

6. Ironically, Indians in Mexico had been eligible for citizenship since 1812 under Mexican law (see Menchaca 1993).

7. The National Labor Relations Act, passed during the Great Depression, had given American workers the right to join labor unions but excluded farm workers.

8. The term is found throughout the political and artistic productions of the day: in the name of a scholarly Chicano journal, in political tracts like the *Plan Espiritual de Aztlán*, and in titles of literary works and organizations.

9. There are many excellent anthologies; for an overview, the reader may want to begin with *Hispanic-American Literature: A Brief Introduction and Anthology*, edited by Nicolás Kanellos (1995).

10. "Nuyorican" refers to Puerto Ricans who grew up in New York City. Alternatively, they sometimes label themselves "neoricans." The term is not universally accepted.

11. The many nuances of this poem are developed in depth in Juan Flores' essay "Broken English Memories" (2000).

12. *Boriquen* was the name the indigenous people called Puerto Rico, and Puerto Ricans oftentimes refer to themselves as *boricuas*.

13. Some Afro-Cubans did see themselves as a racial minority, however.

14. As late as the 1950s, and even into the 1960s, social science researchers were asking similar questions about why Italian Americans were not climbing the social class ladder at the rates of other "model minorities," like the Jews (di Leonardo 1992).

15. A small number of early studies (e.g., McWilliams 1990) did argue that poverty was the result of structural factors rather than the product of "deficient" cultural behaviors, anticipating current understandings.

16. Several people attacked by Romano and other Chicanos subsequently left the field of Chicano studies.

17. See Jacob and Jordan (1993) for a summary of these works and anthropologists' refutations.

18. This sort of oppositional identity is not inherently linked with racial minorities. Paul Willis (1977), for instance, found a similar oppositional identity among disaffected white working-class males in Britain, who believed they had little chance to succeed.

19. Ogbu has begun to address some of these concerns in recent work; see, for instance, Ogbu and Simmons (1998).

20. The merits of bilingual education are well documented in a number of works. See Nieto (2000) for a rationale and an excellent summary of findings on the merits on strong late-exit bilingual programs for students' academic development.

21. This, of course, is a play on words, using real and "imagined" verb conjugations.

22. While Latinos have lower voting rates than other groups, they are also a younger population (median age 26, compared with 36 years for non-Hispanics). In addition, the 25 percent who are not citizens are ineligible to vote (Brand 2000).

23. Numerous academic works address these commonalities, including Bonilla et al. (1998), Flores and Benmayor (1997), and Flores (2000).

REFERENCES CITED

ACUÑA, RUDOLFO. 1988. *Occupied America: A History of Chicanos*. 3rd edition. New York: Harper & Row.

ALVAREZ, JULIA. 1992. *How the García Girls Lost Their Accents*. New York: Penguin.

ANAYA, RUDOLFO. 1989. Aztlán: A homeland without boundaries. In *Aztlán: Essays on the Chicano Homeland*. R. Anaya and F. Lomelí, eds. Pp. 230–241. Albuquerque, NM: Academia/El Norte.

ANZALDUA, GLORIA. 1987. *Borderlands/La Frontera: The New Mestiza*. San Francisco: Spinsters/Aunt Lute.

APPADURAI, ARJUN. 1990. Disjuncture and difference in the global cultural economy. *Public Culture* 2(2):1–24.

——. 1991. Global ethnoscapes: Notes and queries for a transnational anthropology. In *Recapturing Anthropology: Working in the Present*. R. Fox, ed. Pp. 191–210. Santa Fe, NM: School of American Research Press.

AU, KATHRYN. 1980. Participant structure in a reading lesson with Hawaiian children: Analysis of a culturally appropriate instructional event. *Anthropology & Education Quarterly* 11(2):91–115.

BASCH, LINDA, NINA GLICK SCHILLER, and CRISTINA SZANTON BLANC. 1994. *Nations Unbound: Transnational Projects, Postcolonial Predicaments, and Deterritorialized States*. Basel: Gordon & Breach.

BEREITER, CARL, and SIEGFRIED ENGELMANN. 1966. *Teaching Disadvantaged Children in the Preschool*. Englewood Cliffs, NJ: Prentice Hall.

BIGLER, ELLEN. 1997. Dangerous Discourses: Language Politics and Classroom Practices in Upstate New York. *Centro* 9(1):8–25. New York: Centro de Estudios Puertorriqueños, Hunter College, CUNY.

——. 1999. *American Conversations: Puerto Ricans, White Ethnics, and Multicultural Education*. Philadelphia: Temple University Press.

BLAIR, JAYSON. 2000. TV advertising drives fight over size of Spanish audience. *New York Times*, July 17.

BONILLA, FRANK, and RICARDO CAMPOS. 1981. A wealth of poor: Puerto Ricans in the new economic order. *Daedalus* 110 (Spring):133–176.

BONILLA, FRANK, EDWIN MELÉNDEZ, REBECCA MORALES, and MARÍA DE LOS ANGELES TORRES, eds. 1998. *Borderless Borders: U.S. Latinos, Latin Americans, and the Paradox of Interdependence*. Philadelphia: Temple University Press.

BRAND, RICHARD. 2000. The second great wave; Hispanic immigrants are changing the face of central Jersey. *New York Times*, May 28.

BRINKLEY, JOEL. 1999. U.S. acts in behalf of immigrants

who fled right-wing governments. *New York Times*, May 21.

BRODER, JOHN. 1999. Clinton offers his apologies to Guatemalans. *New York Times*, March 11.

BRUCE-NOBOA, JAMES. 1987. A question of identity: What's in a name? Chicanos and Riqueños. In *Images and Identities: The Puerto Rican in Two World Contexts*. Asela Rodrígues, ed. Pp. 229–235. New Brunswick, NJ: Transaction.

BURNS, ALLAN. 1993. *Maya in Exile: Guatemalans in Florida*. Philadelphia: Temple University Press.

CARRASCO, GILBERT PAUL. 1998. Latinos in the United States: Invitation and exile. In *The Latino/a Condition: A Critical Reader*. R. Delgado and J. Stefancic, eds. Pp. 77–85. New York: New York University Press.

CARTER, THOMAS, and ROBERT SEGURA. 1979. *Mexican-Americans in School: A Decade of Change*. New York: CEEB.

Centro de Estudios Puertorriqueños (CENEP), City University of New York. 1979. *Labor Migration under Capitalism: The Puerto Rican Experience*. New York: Monthly Review Press.

CHARTRAND, SABRA. 1996. Women and minorities now account for biggest jump in startup companies. *New York Times*, October 6.

CISNEROS, SANDRA. 1989. *The House on Mango Street*. New York: Vintage.

COLLINS, CHUCK, and FELICE YESKEL (with United for a Fair Economy). 2000. *Economic Apartheid in America: A Primer on Economic Inequality and Insecurity*. New York: New Press. [excerpted in journal on-line]; http://www.tompaine.com/print.php3?id+1245, Internet. Accessed August 8, 2000.

CORDERO GUZMÁN, HECTOR. 1993. The structure of inequality and the status of Puerto Rican youth in the U.S. *Centro* 5(1):100–115. New York: Centro de Estudios Puertorriqueños, Hunter College, CUNY.

CORTÉS, CARLOS. 1983. The greaser's revenge to boulevard nights: The mass media curriculum on Chicanos. In *History, Culture, and Society: Chicano Studies in the 1980s*. National Association for Chicano Studies. Pp. 128–131. Ypsilanti, MI: Bilingual Press.

CRAWFORD, JAMES. 1992. *Hold Your Tongue: Bilingualism and the Politics of "English Only."* Reading, MA: Addison-Wesley.

CROSS, HARRY, et al. 1990. *Employer Hiring Policies: Differential Treatment of Hispanic and Anglo Job Seekers*. Washington, DC: The Urban Institute.

DAVIDSON, ANNE LOCKE. 1996. *Making and Molding Identity in Schools: Student Narratives on Race, Gender, and Academic Engagement*. Albany: State University of New York Press.

DAVIS, ALICE. 2000. What we face: America the divided: Religious leaders find moral imperative to overcome poverty. http://tompaine.com/features/2000/08/01/index.html; Internet. Accessed August 3, 2000.

DE LEÓN, ARNOLDO. 1998. Initial contacts: Niggers, red-skins and greasers. In *The Latino(a) Condition: A Critical Reader*. Richard Delgado and Jean Stefancic, eds. Pp. 158–164. New York: New York University Press.

DEFREITAS, GREGORY. 1999. The emergence of the Hispanic American labor force. In *Rethinking the Color Line: Readings in Race and Ethnicity*. Charles Gallagher, ed. Pp. 237–275. Mountain View, CA: Mayfield.

DEL VALLE, SANDRA. 1997. BPO v. Mills and the struggle for bilingual education. *Centro* 9(9):74–85. New York: Centro de Estudios Puertorriqueños, Hunter College, CUNY.

DELGADO, RICHARD, and JEAN STEFANCIC, eds. 1998. Introduction. In *The Latino(a) Condition: A Critical Reader*. New York: New York University Press.

DI LEONARDO, MICAELA. 1992. White lies, black myths. *Village Voice*, September 22:29–36.

DIETZ, JAMES. 1986. *Economic History of Puerto Rico*. Princeton, NJ: Princeton University Press.

DILLON, SAM. 2000. Click to be subsumed: On the language of Cervantes, the imprint of the Internet. *New York Times*, August 6.

DUANY, JORGE. 1994. *Quisqueya on the Hudson: The Transnational Identity of Dominicans in Washington Heights*. New York: Dominican Studies Institute, City University of New York.

____. 1996. Imagining the Puerto Rican nation: Recent works on cultural identity. *Latin American Research Review*, 31(3):248–267.

____. 1998. Reconstructing racial identity: Ethnicity, color, and class among Dominicans in the United States and Puerto Rico. *Latin American Perspectives* 25(May): 147(26). http://web7.searchbank.com/infotrac/sessions/577/201/6076836w5/7!xm_4; Internet. Accessed February 15, 1999.

ERICKSON, FREDERICK. 1987. Transformation and school success: The politics and culture of educational achievement. *Anthropology & Education Quarterly* 18(4):335–356.

ESTEVES, SANDRA MARÍA. 1984. *Tropical Rains: A Bilingual Downpour*. New York: African Caribbean Poetry Theater.

FLETCHER, MICHAEL. 2000. Latinos missing American dream: Report finds many stuck in low-wage jobs. *San Jose Mercury News*, July 5.

FLORES, JUAN. 1985. "Que assimilated, brother, yo soy asimilao": The structuring of Puerto Rican identity in the U.S. *Journal of Ethnic Studies* 13 (Fall):1–16.

____. 1996. Pan-Latino/trans-Latino: Puerto Ricans in the "New Nueva York." *Centro* 8(1–2):170–186. New York: Centro de Estudios Puertorriqueños, Hunter College, CUNY.

____. 2000. *From Bomba to Hip-Hop: Puerto Rican Culture and Latino Identity*. New York: Columbia University Press.

FLORES, JUAN, JOHN ATTINASI, and PEDRO PEDRAZA. 1981. La carreta made a U-turn: Puerto Rican language and culture in the United States. *Daedalus* 110 (Spring):193–217.

FLORES, WILLIAM, and RINA BENMAYOR, eds. 1997. *Latino Cultural Citizenship: Claiming Identity, Space, and Rights.* Boston: Beacon Press.

FLORES-GONZÁLEZ, NILDA. 1999. Puerto Rican high achievers: An example of ethnic and academic identity compatibility. *Anthropology & Education Quarterly* 30(3):343–362.

FOLEY, DOUGLAS. 1990. *Learning Capitalist Culture: Deep in the Heart of Tejas.* Philadelphia: University of Pennsylvania Press.

___. 1991. Reconsidering anthropological explanations of ethnic school failure. *Anthropology & Education Quarterly* 22(1):60–86.

FORDHAM, SIGNITHIA, and JOHN OGBU. 1986. Coping with the burden of "acting white." *Urban Review* 18(3):176–206.

FRAU-RAMOS, MANUEL, and SONIA NIETO. 1993. I was an outsider: An exploratory study of dropping out among Puerto Rican youths in Holyoke, Massachusetts. In *The Education of Latino Students in Massachusetts: Issues, Research, and Policy Implications.* Ralph Rivera and Sonia Nieto, eds. Pp. 147–169. Amherst: University of Massachusetts Press.

GIBSON, MARGARET. 1997. Complicating the immigrant/involuntary minority typology. *Anthropology & Education Quarterly* 28(3):431–454.

GIMENEZ, MARTHA. 1997. Latino/"Hispanic"—who needs a name? The case against a standardized terminology. In *Latinos and Education.* Antonia Darder, Rodolfo Torres, and Henry Gutíerrez, eds. Pp. 225–238. New York: Routledge.

GLASSER, RUTH. 1997. *Aquí Me Quedo: Puerto Ricans in Connecticut.* Middletown: Connecticut Humanities Council.

GRASMUCK, SHERRI, and PATRICIA PESSAR. 1991. *Between Two Islands: Dominican International Migration.* Berkeley: University of California Press.

GRISWOLD DEL CASTILLO, RICHARD. 1984. *La Familia: Chicano Families in the Urban Southwest, 1848 to the Present.* Notre Dame, IN: University of Notre Dame Press.

GROSFOGUEL, RAMÓN, and CHLOÉ GEORAS. 1996. The racialization of Latino Caribbean migrants in the New York metropolitan area. *Centro* 8(1–2):190–201. New York: Centro de Estudios Puertorriqueños, Hunter College, CUNY.

HAYES, KATHERINE. 1992. Attitudes toward education: Voluntary and involuntary immigrants from the same families. *Anthropology & Education Quarterly* 23(3):250–267.

HELLER, CELIA. 1966. *Mexican-American Youth: Forgotten Youth at the Crossroads.* New York: Random House.

HERNÁNDEZ, RAMONA, FRANCISCO RIVERA-BATIZ, and ROBERTO AGODINI. 1995. *Dominican New Yorkers: A Socioeconomic Profile.* New York: Dominican Studies Institute, City of New York.

HESS, ROBERT, and VIRGINIA SHIPMAN. 1965. Early experience and the socialization of cognitive modes in children. *Child Development* 36:869–886.

JACOB, EVELYN, and CATHIE JORDAN, eds. 1993. Introduction. In *Minority Education: Anthropological Perspectives.* Norwood, NJ: Ablex.

JANOFSKY, MICHAEL. 2000. Candidates courting Hispanic vote. *New York Times,* June 25.

JOHNSON, KEVIN. 1999. *How Did You Get to Be Mexican? A White/Brown Man's Search for Identity.* Philadelphia: Temple University Press.

KANELLOS, NICOLÁS, ed. 1995. *Hispanic-American Literature: A Brief Introduction and Anthology.* New York: Addison-Wesley.

KLOR DE ALVA, JORGE. 1988. Telling Hispanics apart: Latino sociocultural diversity. In *The Hispanic Experience in the United States: Contemporary Issues and Perspectives.* Edna Acosta-Bélen and Barbara Sjostrom, eds. Pp. 107–136. New York: Praeger.

___. 1989. Aztlán, Borinquen and Hispanic nationalism in the United States. In *Aztlán: Essays on the Chicano Homeland.* Rudolfo Anaya and Francisco Lomelí, eds. Pp. 135–171. Albuquerque: El Norte Publications/Academia.

KOTKIN, JOEL. 2000. A revival of older suburbs as ethnic businesses take hold. *New York Times,* February 27.

KOZOL, JONATHAN. 1991. *Savage Inequalities: Children in America's Schools.* New York: Crown.

LABOV, WILLIAM. 1972. The logic of Nonstandard English. In *Language and Social Context.* ed. Pier Paolo Giglioli, ed. Pp. 179–215. London: Penguin.

LACAYO, RICHARD. 1988. A surging new spirit. *Time,* July 11: 46–49.

LAMBERT, BRUCE. 2000. 40 percent in New York City are foreign born, study finds. *New York Times,* July 24.

LAÓ, AUGUSTÍN. 1995. Resources of Hope: Imagining the Young Lords and the Politics of Memory. *Centro* 7(1):34–49. New York: Centro de Estudios Puertorriqueños, Hunter College, CUNY.

LAVIERA, TATO. 1985. *AmeRícan.* Houston: Arte Publico.

___. 1988. *Mainstream Ethics (Ética Corriente).* Houston: Arte Publico.

LEACOCK, ELEANOR, ed. 1971. *The Culture of Poverty: A Critique.* New York: Simon & Schuster.

LEWIS, OSCAR. 1966. *La Vida: A Puerto Rican Family in the Culture of Poverty.* New York: Random House.

MACLEOD, JAY. 1995. *Ain't No Makin' It: Aspirations and Attainment in a Low-Income Neighborhood.* 2nd edition. Boulder, CO: Westview Press.

MADSEN, WILLIAM. 1964. *Mexican-Americans of South Texas.* San Francisco: Holt, Rinehart and Winston.

MAHLER, SARAH. 1995. *Salvadorans in Suburbia: Symbiosis and Conflict.* Boston: Allyn & Bacon.

MALDONADO, RITA. 1976. Why Puerto Ricans migrated to the United States in 1947–73. *Monthly Labor Review* 99 (Summer): 7–18.

MARTÍNEZ, ELIZABETH. 1989. A certain absence of color. *Social Justice* 16(4).

MATUTE-BIANCHI, MARIA. 1986. Ethnic identities and patterns of school success and failure among Mexican-descent and Japanese-American students in a California high school: An ethnographic analysis. *American Journal of Education* 95(1):233–255.

___. 1991. Situational ethnicity and patterns of school performance among immigrant and nonimmigrant Mexican-descent students. In *Minority Status and Schooling: A Comparative Study of Immigrant and Involuntary Minorities.* Margaret Gibson and John Ogbu, eds. Pp. 205–247. New York: Garland.

McCORMICK, JOHN, and ARIC PRESS. 1997. Pomp and promises. *Newsweek*, June 16: 44–46.

McWILLIAMS, CAREY. 1990 [1948]. *North from Mexico: The Spanish-Speaking People of the United States.* New edition updated by Matt Meier. New York: Greenwood Press.

MEHAN, HUGH, LEA HUBBARD, and IRENE VILLANUEVA. 1994. Forming academic identities: Accommodation without assimilation among involuntary minorities. *Anthropology & Education Quarterly* 25(2):91–117.

MENCHACA, MARTHA. 1993. Chicano Indianism: A historical account of racial repression in the United States. *American Ethnologist* 20 (August):3.

MERCADO, CARMEN, and LUIS MOLL. 1997. The study of funds of knowledge: Collaborative research in Latino homes. *Centro* 9(9):27–42. New York: Centro de Estudios Puertorriqueños, Hunter College, CUNY.

MONTOYA, MARGARET. 1998. Law and language(s). In *The Latino(a) Condition: A Critical Reader.* Richard Delgado and Jean Stefancic, eds. Pp. 574–578. New York: New York University Press.

MOORE, JOAN, and HARRY PACHON. 1985. *Hispanics in the United States.* Englewood Cliffs, NJ: Prentice Hall.

MOORE, JOAN, and RAQUEL PINDERHUGHES. 1993. Introduction. In *In the Barrios: Latinos and the Underclass Debate.* Joan Moore and Raquel Pinderhughes, eds. Pp. xi–xxxix. New York: Russell Sage.

MORALES, JULIO. 1986. *Puerto Rican Poverty and Migration: We Just Had to Try Elsewhere.* New York: Praeger.

MORRIS, NANCY. 1995. *Puerto Rico: Culture, Politics, and Identity.* Westport, CT: Praeger.

NATIONAL COUNCIL OF LA RAZA. 2001. Twenty most frequently asked questions about the Latino community, Updated March 2001. http://www.nclr.org/about/nclrfaq.html; Internet. Accessed October 19, 2001.

NAVARRO, MIREYA. 1997. A new Barbie in Puerto Rico divides island and mainland. *New York Times*, December 27.

___. 2000. Falling back: A special report. Puerto Rican presence wanes in New York. *New York Times*, February 28.

NEGRÓN DE MONTILLA, AIDA. 1975. *Americanization in Puerto Rico and the Public School System, 1900–1930.* 2nd edition. Rio Piedras, PR: Editorial Edil.

NELSON, CANDACE, and MARTA TIENDA. 1988. The structuring of Hispanic ethnicity: Historical and contemporary perspectives. In *Ethnicity and Race in the U.S.A.* Richard Alba, ed. Pp. 49–74. London: Routledge.

New York State Education Department. 1987. *The Ibero-American Heritage Curriculum Project: Latinos in the Making of the United States of America: Yesterday, Today, and Tomorrow.* First Annual Meeting Conference Proceedings, Albany.

NIETO, SONIA. 2000. *Affirming Diversity: The Sociopolitical Context of Multicultural Education.* 3rd edition. New York: Addison Wesley Longman.

OBOLER, SUZANNE. 1995. *Ethnic Labels, Latino Lives: Identity and Politics of (Re)presentation in the United States.* Minneapolis: University of Minnesota Press.

OGBU, JOHN. 1978. *Minority Education and Caste: The American System in Cross-Cultural Perspective.* New York: Academic Press.

OGBU, JOHN, and HERBERT SIMONS. 1998. Voluntary and involuntary minorities: A cultural-ecological theory of school performance with some implications for education. *Anthropology & Education Quarterly* 29(2): 155–188.

OMI, MICHAEL, and HOWARD WINANT. 1994. *Racial Formation in the United States from the Late 1960s to the 1990s.* 2nd edition. New York: Routledge.

OSBORNE, A. BARRY. 1996. Practice into theory into practice: Culturally relevant pedagogy for students we have marginalized and normalized. *Anthropology & Education Quarterly* 27(3):285–314.

PADILLA, FELIX. 1985. *Latino Ethnic Consciousness: The Case of Mexican Americans and Puerto Ricans in Chicago.* Notre Dame, IN: University of Notre Dame Press.

PAREDES, AMÉRICO. 1978. On ethnographic work among minority groups: A folklorist's perspective. In *New Directions in Chicano Scholarship.* R. Romo and R. Paredes, eds. Pp. 1–32. Chicano Studies Monograph Series. La Jolla: Chicano Studies Program, University of California at San Diego.

PEDRAZA, PEDRO. 1997. Puerto Ricans and the politics of school reform. *Centro* 9(9):74–85. New York: Centro de Estudios Puertorriqueños, Hunter College, CUNY.

PESSAR, PATRICIA. 1995. *A Visa for a Dream.* Needham Heights, MA: Allyn & Bacon.

PHILIPS, SUSAN. 1972. Participant structure and communicative competence: Warm Springs children in community and classroom. In *Functions of Language in the Classroom.* Courtney Cazden, Dell Hymes, and Vera John, eds. Pp. 370–394. New York: Teachers College Press.

PORTES, ALEJANDRO, ed. 1994. The new second generation. *International Migration Review* 28(4).

PORTES, ALEJANDRO, and ROBERT BACH. 1985. *Latin*

Journey: Cuban and Mexican Immigrants in the United States. Berkeley: University of California Press.

PORTES, ALEJANDRO, and RAMÓN GROSFOGUEL. 1994. Caribbean diasporas: Migration and ethnic communities. *Annals of the American Academy of Political and Social Science* 533 (May):48–69.

PORTES, ALEJANDRO, and ALEX STEPICK. 1993. *City on the Edge: The Transformation of Miami*. Berkeley: University of California Press.

RODRÍGUEZ, CLARA. 1989. *Puerto Ricans: Born in the USA*. Boston: Unwin Hyman.

___. 2000. *Changing Race: Latinos, the Census, and the History of Ethnicity in the United States*. New York: New York University Press.

RODRÍGUEZ, CLARA, and HECTOR CORDERO-GUZMAN. 1992. Placing race in context. *Ethnic and Racial Studies* 15(4):523–529.

RODRÍGUEZ, LUIS. 1993. *Always Running: La Vida Loca: Gang Days in L.A.* Willimantic, CT: Curbstone Press.

RODRÍGUEZ, RICHARD. 1982. *Hunger of Memory: The Education of Richard Rodríguez*. Boston: Godine.

RODRÍGUEZ-MORAZZANI, ROBERTO. 1997. Puerto Ricans and educational reform in the U.S.: A preliminary exploration. *Centro* 9(9):59–73. New York: Centro de Estudios Puertorriqueños, Hunter College, CUNY.

ROHTER, LARRY. 2000. Rock en español approaching its final border. *New York Times*, August 6.

ROMANO, OCTAVIO. 1967. Minorities, history and the cultural mystique. *El Grito* 1(1):5–11.

ROSALDO, RENATO. 1985. *Assimilation Revisited*. Stanford Center for Chicano Research. Working Paper Series No. 9 (July). Stanford, CA.

___. 1986. *When Natives Talk Back: Chicano Anthropology since the Late Sixties*. Renato Rosaldo Lecture Series Monograph. Vol. 2, pp. 3–21. University of Arizona, Tucson.

___. 1989. *Culture and Truth: The Remaking of Social Analysis*. Boston: Beacon Press.

RUBEL, ARTHUR. 1966. *Across the Tracks*. Austin: University of Texas Press.

SACHS, SUSAN. 2001. Hispanic New York shifted in 90's, data shows. *New York Times*, May 22.

SÁNCHEZ KORROL, VIRGINIA. 1988. Latinismo among early Puerto Rican migrants in New York City: A sociohistoric interpretation. In *The Hispanic Experience in the United States: Contemporary Issues and Perspectives*. Edna Acosta-Bélen and Barbara Sjostrom, eds. Pp. 151–162. New York: Praeger.

SANTIAGO, ESMERALDA. 1993. *When I Was Puerto Rican*. New York: Addison-Wesley.

SANTOS, GONZALO. 1997. Somos RUNAFRIBES? The future of Latino ethnicity in the Americas. In *Latinos and Education*. Antonia Darder, Rodolfo Torres, and Henry Gutíerrez, eds. Pp. 201–224. New York: Routledge.

SCHMITT, ERIC. 2001. Census shows big gain for Mexican-Americans. *New York Times*, May 10.

SEDA-BONILLA, EDUARDO. 1977. Who is a Puerto Rican? Problems of sociocultural identity in Puerto Rico. *Caribbean Studies* 17 (April–July):105–121.

SOTO, LOURDES DIAZ. 1997. *Language, Culture, and Power: Bilingual Families and the Struggle for Quality Education*. Albany: State University of New York Press.

STAINS, LAURENCE. 1994. The Latinization of Allentown, Pa. *New York Times Magazine*, May 15.

STERNGOLD, JAMES. 2000. Los Angeles power brokers play catch-up to the city's rapid changes. *New York Times*, August 13.

SUAREZ-OROZCO, MARCELO. 1987. Becoming somebody: Central American immigrants in U.S. inner-city schools. *Anthropology & Education Quarterly* 18(4): 287–299.

TAKAKI, RONALD. 1990. *Iron Cages: Race and Culture in 19th-Century America*. New York: Oxford University Press.

___. 1993. *A Different Mirror: A History of Multicultural America*. Boston: Little, Brown.

TAPIA, JAVIER. 1998. The schooling of Puerto Ricans: Philadelphia's most impoverished community. *Anthropology & Education Quarterly* 29(3):297–323.

TERRY, DON. 2000. U.S. child poverty rate fell as economy grew, but is above 1979 level. *New York Times*, August 11.

THOMAS, PIRI. 1967. *Down These Mean Streets*. New York: Knopf.

TORRES, ANDRES. 1995. *Between Melting Pot and Mosaic: African Americans and Puerto Ricans in the New York Political Economy*. Philadelphia: Temple University Press.

U.S. Bureau of the Census. 1997. Selected characteristics of the population by Hispanic origin: March 1997. http://www.bls.census.gov/cps/pub/1997/int_hisp. htm; Accessed July 31, 2000.

___. 1998. *Statistical Abstract of the United States 1998*. Washington, DC: U.S. Government Printing Office.

___. 2000. http://www.census.gov/press-release/www/2001/ cb01-81.html. Accessed May 23, 2001.

URCIUOLI, BONNIE. 1996. *Exposing Prejudice: Puerto Rican Experiences of Language, Race, and Class*. Boulder, CO: Westview Press.

VEGA, BERNARDO. 1984. *Memoirs of Bernardo Vega*, César Andreu Iglesias, ed. New York: Monthly Review Press.

WILLIS, PAUL. 1977. *Learning to Labor*. Westmead, England: Saxon House.

WOOLARD, KATHRYN. 1989. Sentences in the language prison: The rhetorical structuring of an American language policy debate. *American Ethnologist* May (16):268–278.

YOUNG LORDS PARTY. 1971. *Palante: Young Lords Party*. New York: McGraw-Hill.

ZENTELLA, ANA CELIA. 1981. Language variety among Puerto Ricans. In *Language in the USA*. Charles Ferguson and Shirley Brice Heath, eds. Pp. 218–238. Cambridge: Cambridge University Press.

___. 1988. Language politics in the U.S.A.: The English-only movement. In *Literature, Language and Politics*. B. J. Craige, ed. Pp. 39–51. Athens: University of Georgia Press.

___. 1997. *Growing Up Bilingual: Puerto Rican Children in New York*. Malden, MA: Blackwell.

11 ASIAN AMERICANS

Janet E. Benson

Kansas State University

While significant numbers of Asians have migrated to the United States since the nineteenth century, by far the most dramatic population growth has taken place since the passing of the 1965 Immigration Act. Chinese and Japanese came first during the nineteenth century, followed by Filipinos and Koreans; since the 1960s, however, the numbers of Asian Indians, Vietnamese, and other Southeast Asians have rapidly grown, as well as those of Chinese newcomers from the mainland and Taiwan. The term *Asian American*, created during the 1960s for political purposes by second- and third-generation Americans of Asian descent, implies a homogeneity of culture that does not exist (Cheng and Yang 1996:341). Not only does Asia include more than half the world's population, but people of Asian descent live in the Western Hemisphere (in Latin America or the West Indies, for example) and have emigrated from these regions to the United States. They differ culturally from ancestral groups in the country of origin. An "East Indian" (Asian Indian) person from Trinidad, for example, comes from a very different cultural background than that of his or her contemporaries in India.

Many recent immigrants identify themselves first by nationality of birth or ethnic group and only second, if at all, as "American" (often used as a synonym for "white" in everyday language). However, native-born Americans frequently cannot distinguish among different Asian groups, or even between Asians and Latinos, and hostility toward one ethnic group is often mistakenly directed at another. Generation is another complicating factor. While the Asian groups are predominantly foreign-born, even the post-1965 newcomers have produced a second generation whose members are, to a large degree, culturally American. Other Americans should not assume that a person with an "Asian" appearance is foreign or non-English-speaking. The individual may very well have been born and raised in the United States with little knowledge of any language except English.

The first part of this chapter will focus on Asian immigration from the nineteenth century to 1965; the remainder will emphasize post-1965 immigration. Only the largest groups can be covered here. For our purposes these will include the Chinese, Japanese, Korean, Filipino, South Asian (particularly Asian Indian), and main Southeast Asian groups (particularly Vietnamese). Rates of citizenship vary among the groups, depending on recency of arrival and other factors, but the majority are American citizens today.

EARLY ASIAN IMMIGRATION

The Chinese, who were the first Asian immigrants to enter the United States in significant numbers, arrived in Hawaii in the 1830s to cultivate sugarcane, and in California during the 1840s to work as miners following the discovery of gold. Chinese laborers built the Central Pacific Railroad (1865–69) (Takaki 1990:21, 84–86). Japanese immigrants followed in the 1880s, and other Asians arrived after the turn of the century. The Japanese found employment as agricultural laborers, first in Hawaii and then California (Takaki 1990:42–45). Between 1820 and 1930, newcomers from China numbered 377,245, and from Japan, 275,643; not all of these remained in the United States, however. Other Asian groups were much smaller in total numbers due to racist opposition following the Chinese arrival. Before World War II, the total immigrant flow from Korea, India, and the Philippines numbered less than 150,000 (Reimers 1992:3).

Chinese Americans

Old-stock Americans were historically ambivalent about immigration. They supported the ideology of religious and political freedom and wanted cheap labor, but they also wanted to avoid social contact with newcomers. Immigration peaked during the period 1890–1920, with opposition to Southern European immigrants as well as Asians resulting in restrictions being implemented at the end of that period. As the first Asians to arrive, the Chinese were the first to encounter severe discrimination. The Foreign Miners' Tax (originally created to discourage Mexican and Latin American miners) was imposed on the Chinese in the 1850s; by the 1880s, nativist feelings on the West Coast led to mob violence against them (Reimers 1992:1–2). In 1882, Congress passed the Chinese Exclusion Act, "the first federal law ever passed banning a group of immigrants solely on the basis of race or nationality" (Gyory 1998:1). The act suspended immigration for ten years and was later renewed, with devastating social consequences for Chinese people in the United States. After the Scott Act of 1888, which imposed further restrictions, even the reentry of Chinese with return certificates was prohibited. Men other than merchants were not allowed to bring their wives from China, nor were Chinese allowed to marry "white" women in California until 1948 (Ling 1998:2; Nee and Nee 1972:18–19). As a result, communities of permanent bachelors developed in the western United States. The situation was somewhat different in Hawaii, where planters encouraged families to settle, and intermarriage between Chinese and Hawaiians took place (Takaki 1990:159, 169). After 1943, when Congress repealed the Chinese Exclusion Act and granted the right of naturalization, Chinese men were allowed to bring their wives to the mainland again. Ninety percent of Chinese immigrants between 1948 and 1952 were women (Reimers 1992:27).

Among the causes suggested for discrimination against the Chinese, and Asian Americans in general, are economics and racism. The Chinese worked for lower wages than white miners and laborers, who saw them as competing unfairly. Nativists also accused them of having lower moral standards and being unassimilable due to their race (Reimers 1992:4). Andrew Gyory argues, however, that "the motive force behind the Chinese Exclusion Act was national politicians who seized and manipulated the issue in an effort to gain votes" (1998:1). On the West Coast, the Chinese were systematically excluded from economic sectors where they competed with native-born Americans, such as gold mining, but they were allowed to fill niches such as the laundry business where their services were needed and they did not compete with established Americans. "Chinatowns," today a magnet for tourists in American cities from San Francisco to New York, are relics of nineteenth-century segregation (see Nee and Nee 1972).

During and after World War II, public attitudes toward Chinese Americans improved somewhat. The United States was an ally of China against Japan, which led to the repeal of the Chinese Exclusion Act. Labor shortages during the war created opportunities for Chinese Americans in defense industries; and ethnic and religious groups and voluntary organizations involved in refugee resettlement lobbied against laws restricting Chinese immigration and naturalization. The United States also experienced relative prosperity after the 1940s, which eased racial tensions (Ling 1998:2; Nee and Nee 1972:154; Reimers 1992:11–12).

Japanese Americans

The Japanese initially worked on Hawaii's sugar plantations but migrated to California by the 1880s, where anti-Japanese feelings quickly developed. The San Francisco school board nearly created an international incident by segregating Japanese students in 1905; it rescinded the order in return for the Gentlemen's Agreement of 1908, which was an understanding between the United States and the Japanese government that the latter would withhold visas from laborers headed to the United States (Reimers 1992:5).

Japanese newcomers wanted to move from being agricultural laborers to farmers, but were resisted by white Californians, who passed restrictive land laws. The Alien Land Law of 1913 (amended in 1920–21) barred aliens ineligible for citizenship from owning or leasing agricultural land. In practice, this meant "Orientals," all those not classified as "white" or African American. The laws affected Chinese, Koreans, and Asian Indians, as well (Leonard 1997:41). The Japanese were declared ineligible for citizenship by the U.S. Supreme Court in 1922, which cited naturalization statutes dating back to 1790. Congress then banned virtually all immigration from Asia in 1924 when it passed the Oriental Exclusion Act, declaring all Asians "ineligible for citizenship" (Reimers 1992:5–6).

The worst case of civil rights violation during World War II took place shortly after Pearl Harbor when President Roosevelt interned 110,000 Japanese Americans, many of whom were American-born citizens, in internment camps far from their homes. The action placated racist fears, despite the fact that no sabotage had been committed by this population. The Japanese Americans were not only deeply shamed and disillusioned but also lost most of their property, for which they were never adequately compensated (Reimers 1992:9). After World War II, intermarriage between American soldiers and Japanese women became the main reason for immigration from Japan. Between 1947 and 1975, 66,681 women from Japan joined their husbands in the United States (Reimers 1992:23, 26). In recent years Japanese Americans have been characterized by a high rate of intermarriage with established Americans; they are the only Asian American group in which a minority are foreign-born (Okamura 1998:22).

Korean Americans

The earliest-arriving Koreans were a much smaller group than the Chinese or Japanese. A few students came around the turn of the century, but the main flow began when several thousand laborers were recruited to work on plantations in Hawaii. Some former plantation workers later traveled from Hawaii to the West Coast. Nativists complained to the U.S. government, and Japan, in control of Korea at the time, halted emigration (Reimers 1992:5). After World War II, the American military presence in Asia led to marriages between Korean women and American servicemen: 28,205 Korean women emigrated to join their husbands between 1950 and 1975 (Reimers 1992:23).

Filipino Americans

Filipino Americans share a common historical background with Chinese, Japanese, and Korean Americans as labor migrants, particularly in Hawaii, and as groups experiencing exclusion and discrimination before World War II. Some authors feel that of all the Asian American groups, Filipinos occupy the most marginalized and subordinate status (Okamura 1998:3).

Yen Le Espiritu argues persuasively that Filipino American history must be understood in the context of the colonial and postcolonial relationship between the Philippines and the United States. Following the Spanish-American War in 1898, the United States assumed colonial rule. The U.S. annexation affected all aspects of Philippine life, from the economy to the educational and political systems, and encouraged emigration (Espiritu 1995:2–3, 1996:30). Filipinos were exempted from the Oriental Exclusion Act of 1924 and allowed to immigrate as American nationals, though they lacked full citizenship. The first Filipino newcomers were college students arriving between 1903 and 1910; however, most Filipinos came to Hawaii as plantation workers. The Hawaiian Sugar Planters' Association recruited heavily in the Philippines, bringing 126,000 Filipinos between 1909 (when Japanese workers organized a major strike) and 1946. Although almost half of them eventually returned home, Filipinos numbered 70 percent of plantation workers by the 1930s. They were hit hard by the depression, particularly because,

as a recent immigrant group with little education, they had no means of employment other than agricultural or service work. Chinese and Japanese American residents of Hawaii were already employed in the business and skilled or semiskilled sectors by this time. Since most of the Filipino workers recruited were young single men from rural areas, an imbalanced sex ratio existed (5 men to 1 woman in 1930); this in turn contributed to racial stereotyping of Filipinos as violent and immoral (Okamura 1998:37–39).

Most Filipino immigrants who reached the U.S. mainland were former plantation employees who continued to work in agriculture, following crops up and down the West Coast. There were only 6,000 on the mainland in 1924, but they grew to 30,000 by 1930. Discrimination was much worse than in Hawaii. During 1928–30, race riots directed at Filipinos broke out in farming towns in Washington, California, and Oregon. In 1930, in Watsonville, California, a mob of whites attacked agricultural workers and killed one person (Okamura 1998:39–40). Whites viewed Filipinos as "unfair competition" because they worked for lower wages and courted white women.[1] Organized labor and other conservative groups lobbied for laws (declared unconstitutional in 1948), which were passed in several states in the 1930s, to keep Filipinos from marrying whites (Okamura 1998:40). Although the War Department and Hawaiian sugar planters wanted Filipino labor, opposition grew during the 1920s and 1930s from nativist groups and trade unions. As part of the Philippine independence bill, the country was given an annual quota of only 50 (Reimers 1992:6–7). Between 1946 and 1965, only 34,000 Filipinos came to the United States, 16,000 of them wives of American servicemen.

Asian Indians

Early South Asian, or Asian Indian, immigrants consisted mainly of a few thousand Sikhs (a minority religious group) from the Punjab in north India, farmers who came to California to work as agricultural laborers around 1900. Capital-intensive agriculture and large-scale irrigation led to strong labor demands by the 1870s, with Asian immigrant groups contributing in different ways to agricultural development. The Japanese, for example, came as contract laborers, but many became tenants and specialized in labor-intensive crops like strawberries (Leonard 1997:40–41). The Punjabis cultivated rice in northern California and grapes in central California, and established cotton growing in the southern Imperial Valley. Although they initially worked as laborers, many were soon farming in their own right until the U.S. Supreme Court's Thind decision of 1923. In this ruling, people from India were considered Caucasian but not "white persons" as popularly defined. This made Asian Indians "aliens ineligible to citizenship" (like other Asian groups) and subject to California's Alien Land Laws, discussed earlier. Citizenship was not granted until 1946.

By 1917, Congress had created the Asiatic Barred Zone, an area including India, from which immigration was banned (Reimers 1992:5–6). The farm workers from India were placed in the same situation that the Chinese had faced earlier: they were not allowed to bring wives from India (since immigration was banned and Asians in any case were "aliens ineligible for naturalization"), nor were they allowed to marry "white" women due to miscegenation laws.

Karen Leonard has written a fascinating account of how a new ethnic group, the so-called "Mexican Hindus" (the misnamed "Hindus" were actually Sikhs), developed due to discriminatory laws and practices. Many Punjabi Sikhs already had wives and families in India but were not allowed to bring them to the United States. Because most of the immigrants were male, those who wanted a stable family life had to marry women of an ethnic group other than their own. White justices of the peace would not conduct marriages between Sikh men and white women but would for Sikhs and the darker-skinned Mexican women, with whom Sikhs often worked. Husband and wife could communicate verbally but only in limited ways, neither fully mastering the other's language. Children generally learned Spanish, and grew up culturally more similar to mothers than fathers. The current generation tends to identify more with their Indian ("Hindu") heritage, but has minimal knowledge of it and little in common with recent immigrants from South Asia (Leonard 1997: 47–57).

Almost all of the present Asian Indian population arrived after 1965.

The War Brides Act and Asian Immigration

The passage of the War Brides Act in December 1945 allowed spouses and minor children of American servicemen to join the men and become citizens more easily. In spite of this, Korean and Japanese wives were barred from entering the United States prior to 1952 because they were members of races "ineligible for immigration or naturalization." After Congress changed the law, several thousand Asians (from a total of 117,000 women) entered under the act. The end of racial barriers to immigration and naturalization allowed other wives to join husbands after the end of the War Brides Act in 1952. A total of 165,839 wives came between 1947 and 1975, with by far the largest numbers from Japan, the Philippines, and Korea (Reimers 1992:21–23).

Discrimination and Prejudice

As seen in this account, the early Asian immigrants encountered nativist reactions ranging from negative newspaper editorials to mob violence, restrictive land laws, confinement to internment camps, and denial of citizenship rights. Like other minority groups, Asian Americans experienced segregation in the wider society well into the 1940s and 1950s with regard to public facilities like schools, restaurants, and swimming pools (see, for example, Leonard 1997:61). Because of their small numbers and vulnerable position, individual groups (the Japanese internees, for example) were seldom willing or able to protest effectively against discrimination. This situation changed after World War II, when veterans returned no longer willing to accept second-class citizenship, and especially after the civil rights movement of the 1960s.

POST-1965 IMMIGRATION

The New Asian Americans

By the 1950s, Asian immigration to the United States had slowed to a trickle (about 15,000 per year) due to restrictive immigration laws. However, it dramatically increased after 1965 because of two factors, the Immigration and Nationality Act Amendments of 1965 and the end of the war in Vietnam (Lee 1998:10). The 1965 act reflected new relationships between the United States and Asian countries, less discriminatory attitudes in general, and the effects of the Civil Rights movement. It abolished the old national origins quota system, which privileged Northern European immigrants and severely restricted flows from other countries, and it emphasized family reunification (Takaki 1990:419).

Because Asian Americans were a small minority in 1965, few supporters of the act expected the dramatic increase in Asian immigration that took place. However, Asians tend to have larger families than the American norm, and once established, newcomers often sponsor relatives. As a result, although their numbers are small (an estimated 10.2 million in 2000) (U.S. Bureau of the Census 2000), Asian Americans are increasing rapidly–at a much faster rate than Latinos or African Americans. Although they formed only 3.6 percent of the U.S. population in 1997, they are estimated to grow to 8 percent (32 million people) by 2050 (Lee 1998:15–16).

Some older, established Asian American groups, such as Chinese, Korean, and Filipino, have received an influx of recent immigrants. Chinese from the mainland, Taiwan, and Hong Kong have arrived in the United States, particularly on the East and West coasts, and Korean and Filipino populations have mushroomed. One group, the Japanese Americans, has declined due to current low immigration. Asian American diversity has also increased, as more groups are named in every census. The South Asian immigrant population, for example (which consists largely of Asian Indians but also includes newcomers from Pakistan, Bangladesh, Sri Lanka, Nepal, and Bhutan), is almost entirely a product of the post-1965 period. The ability to sponsor family members has made a dramatic difference to Asian American populations in the United States. With some exceptions, recent immigration involves more families and more women in relation to men than in earlier periods (Chen 1992: 6; Lee 1998:1; Ling 1998:2, 113).

The 1990 Immigration Act increased the numbers of legal immigrants[2] but also created an annual quota for family members brought in by sponsoring relatives. The preference quotas have also been changed to reflect the old national origins quota system of 1925, so that the pool of legal entrants is now dominated by Latin Americans and Asians from only a few countries, particularly China, Korea, the Philippines, and India (see Salins, as cited in Williams 1996:24).

According to the 2000 census, the Chinese (2.4 million) and Filipinos (1.8 million) are the two largest Asian American groups, followed by Asian Indians (1.7 million), Vietnamese (1.1 million), and Koreans (1.0 million). Nearly 1.3 million residents are classified as "other Asian," meaning other Asian groups or those combining two or more Asian categories (U.S. Bureau of the Census 2000). Asian Indians, Koreans, and Vietnamese have outnumbered Japanese Americans (797,000 in 2000) since 1990 (Lee 1998:15–16). Civil war in Vietnam and the neighboring countries of Laos and Cambodia began a massive refugee flow in 1975, which continued into the 1990s and fundamentally altered American demographics. There were only about 20,000 Southeast Asians in the United States in 1975, but by September 1987, they totaled well over 1 million people (Haines 1989:2).

The Vietnam War and the Southeast Asian Refugees

To understand the how and why of the sudden increase of Southeast Asians in the United States, as well as American reactions to the refugees, some knowledge of the Vietnam War is essential. Most of these events seem remote and irrelevant to young people today. However, 15 years of military involvement in Vietnam, Laos, and Cambodia had a profound and lasting effect on both America and the war-torn Southeast Asian countries. By 1975, 60,000 Americans were dead and 300,000 wounded, and the country was deeply divided over the war's morality (Robinson 1998:7). American political involvement in Southeast Asia created military, economic, and personal ties as well as (in the minds of at least some Americans) moral responsibility for the fate of those who had worked for or had been associated with Americans.

Following the withdrawal of the French colonialists in 1954, the partition of Vietnam into North and South, and the creation of Cambodia, Laos, and Vietnam as independent states, the United States became increasingly embroiled in the wars and internal conflicts of these countries (Robinson 1998:12). It was the Cold War era, and American foreign policy emphasized opposition to communist influence. In Vietnam's case, this meant supporting the South Vietnamese government against the North Vietnamese communists led by Ho Chi Minh.

Meanwhile, in neighboring Laos, leftist fighters known as the Pathet Lao opposed the government of Prince Souvanna Phouma, and

North Vietnamese troops moved soldiers and supplies down the Ho Chi Minh Trail into South Vietnam. To interfere with this supply line, in 1961 the American CIA began to train a highland ethnic minority, the Hmong, as guerrilla fighters. By 1967, when the Americans had turned to conventional warfare and guerrilla tactics were becoming increasingly irrelevant, the Hmong guerrillas numbered nearly 40,000. They suffered terrible losses, with 18,000 to 20,000 killed in combat and 120,000, nearly half the population, becoming internal refugees by 1973. Following a cease-fire agreement that year, U.S. forces withdrew and the situation became increasingly desperate for the Hmong. In the spring of 1975, as a communist victory was about to take place in Laos, the Americans finally agreed to rescue Hmong leader Vang Pao, his most important officers, and their families. About 2,500 Hmong were airlifted into Thailand. Abandoned by their former American allies and fearful of retribution, thousands of other Hmong, as well as lowland Lao who were associated with the previous government, sought refuge in Thailand (Robinson 1998:12–14). Attacked by the Pathet Lao and Vietnamese troops in 1977 and 1978, 100,000 Hmong and other highland groups had fled to Thailand by 1980 (Robinson 1998:107).

When Saigon fell to the Vietnamese communists on April 30, 1975, an unprecedented refugee flight out of Southeast Asia began. The U.S. State Department was unprepared for the rapidity of South Vietnam's collapse, and departure conditions were chaotic. Approximately 130,000 Vietnamese refugees managed to escape within the first few weeks of Saigon's fall, including a segment of elite with close ties to the U.S. government. They were quickly settled in America with the help of voluntary organizations, particularly the Catholic church. A second wave peaked in 1980–81 when the new Vietnamese government expelled Chinese from Vietnam; large numbers of Vietnamese fled by sea in small, crowded boats; and lowland Lao and

Hmong escaped from Laos (Haines 1989:2; Rutledge 1992:5–6). Accounts of the "boat people" being repeatedly attacked by Thai pirates, or being pushed back into the ocean by hostile residents of neighboring countries, alarmed the international community and led to increased humanitarian efforts.

Cambodia's government also experienced rapid collapse in April 1975. The Communist Party of Kampuchea (the Khmer Rouge, or "Red" Khmer, supported by the North Vietnamese) took Phnom Penh, the country's capital, on April 17 and immediately began a campaign to empty the cities and move all the people to the countryside. Markets and currency were to be abolished and cooperatives established with communal eating arrangements. Buddhist monks were set to work in the fields, and leaders of the U.S.-backed Lon Nol regime were targeted for execution. The entire Vietnamese minority population (between 170,000 and 270,000 people) was expelled in 1975, many Cambodians and Chinese fleeing with them into Vietnam. Up to 2 million people died in this brutally enforced social revolution (death was the punishment for any fault); many Cambodians witnessed the murder of close relatives (Robinson 1998:10–12).

The U.S. government did not initially plan to admit large numbers of refugees. High-ranking Vietnamese officials and military personnel and their families were to be evacuated, as well as a token number of Cambodians and Laotians. However, conflict in all three states created so many refugees that "first asylum" countries (neighboring states like Thailand, Malaysia, and Indonesia) and the then-British colony of Hong Kong were soon overwhelmed. Because of U.S. involvement in Vietnam, the refugees were seen as an American responsibility. While "first asylum" countries felt that the "displaced persons" should be sent home, the countries of origin did not want them. The use of the term *refugee* for this population allowed the United States to blame communism for the exodus and to draw on international aid (Robinson 1998:7–8). Refugee camps were created and funded, processing centers were set up in the Philippines and Indonesia to resettle refugees more rapidly, and a number of countries, including the United States, agreed to admit more refugees.

The presence of Vietnamese, Lao, Cambodians, Hmong, and other Southeast Asians in the United States cannot be understood without reference to this brief history. At least in the case of the early arrivals, most refugees did not want to leave their homes and relatives, but were forced out by political circumstances. Faced with reprisals in their own countries, or living in spartan refugee camps with no chance of returning home, they chose to start over in a new and unfamiliar third country. For most, this meant separation from family for years if not forever.

In addition to these Southeast Asian ethnic groups, another subset of the refugee population are the *Amerasians*—children of American servicemen and Vietnamese women. As children of the enemy, they were denied education and economic opportunities in Vietnam and relegated to the lowest social status. Special efforts have been made to bring them to the United States. By the 1990s, the last Southeast Asians to enter as refugees (rather than as immigrants sponsored by families) included Amerasians and people who had been confined to Vietnamese communist "reeducation camps" because of their close contact with Americans. The Amerasians and other groups from Southeast Asia have greatly increased the diversity of America's Asian heritage population.

The 1980 Refugee Act

After 1980, a major shift in American policy permitted large numbers of refugees, including Vietnamese and other Asians, to enter the United States for the first time. Prior to 1980, refugee acts or the use of presidential "parole power"[3]—an executive decision made by the president through his attorney general to admit whole groups of people—mainly focused on European refugees fleeing communist countries. (Hong Kong Chinese were, however, admitted in 1962.) Large numbers of Vietnamese were initially paroled, as well as Cubans who fled after Castro came to power in 1959 (Reimers 1992:157–159). Problems with the ad hoc, inconsistent nature of refugee policy and the basically anticommunist definition of "refugee" led to major reforms of the 1980 Refugee Act. The United States formally accepted the United Nations definition of "refugee," namely, any person outside his or her country who is unable or unwilling to return "because of persecution, or a well-founded fear of persecution, on account of race, religion, nationality, membership of a particular social group, or political opinion" (Reimers 1992:194).[4] The act also created refugee programs in the U.S. Department of Health, Education, and Welfare, and allocated funding for refugees (Reimers 1992:195–197). Since then, the Office of Refugee Resettlement has been responsible for allocating federal money to state-level agencies to pay for resettlement costs.

The Significance of Refugee Status

In discussing displaced populations, a distinction is generally made between refugees and immigrants. The United Nations definition applies to individuals unable to return home because of the possibility of persecution or death; they are exempt from immigrant quotas (Rutledge 1992:10). Unlike immigrants, who may have years to plan a move from one country to another, refugees are often forced to risk their lives in a hasty departure. In actuality, it is not always easy to distinguish between political and economic motives for flight. "Refugee" is a temporary legal status that entitles people to enter the United States and to receive medical aid, cash assistance, and other benefits for a limited period of time. From the beginning, the refugee resettlement program has emphasized

self-sufficiency, due to taxpayer concerns about costs. The government also expects that refugees will soon become U.S. citizens. In fact many of the escapees from Vietnam, Laos, and Cambodia are now naturalized Americans, while their children have been born or largely raised in the United States.

The fact that refugees receive government assistance has been misunderstood and often resented by established Americans. It is important to understand that once awarded refugee status by the government, an individual has the legal right to be in the United States and to receive certain types of aid. The government's assumption is that people who have recently fled for their lives will need medical and mental health services, initial financial support, and perhaps language instruction in order to adapt and become self-supporting.

Most recent arrivals from Southeast Asia today are not refugees, but legal immigrants sponsored by relatives. The relatives undertake full legal responsibility for their support, as individuals with immigrant status receive no government assistance. With this background, we turn to a more detailed discussion of contemporary Asian American groups.

ASIAN AMERICANS TODAY

Chinese Americans

Nineteenth-century Chinese immigrants were relatively homogenous culturally, since most came from Kwangtung Province in southeast China, and they lived in Hawaii or the West Coast. As anti-Chinese sentiment peaked, many returned to China. Others moved to the central and eastern United States, which were relatively safer regions and offered more job opportunities. Until the 1960s, highly educated Chinese immigrants were often barred from professional occupations and restricted to menial work (Chen 1992:5).

In his book *Chinatown No More* (1992), the anthropologist Hsing-shui Chen describes a considerably more diverse post-1965 flow of newcomers from China, and argues that contrary to popular stereotypes, most Chinese immigrants do not live in isolated Chinese communities ("Chinatowns"). Some of the first post-1965 immigrants were college students from Hong Kong and Taiwan who were studying in the United States when immigration laws changed and who decided to stay on[5] (p. 6). Many others came through family sponsorship. By the early 1980s, Chinese from Taiwan, Hong Kong, mainland China, Southeast Asia, the Caribbean, and South America were present in New York City, where Mandarin, Taiwanese, and other languages besides Cantonese could be heard (pp. vii–ix). As early as the late 1960s, however, the Chinese American population was divided into "Chinatown Chinese," older immigrants involved in the ethnic economy, and "non-Chinatown Chinese," professionals and university faculty living in white neighborhoods. Examples of outer-city or suburban settlements of Chinese Americans include Flushing and Elmhurst in New York City (the site of Chen's study) and Monterey Park in California (Chen 1992:6–7; Fong 1994).

While the pre-1965 Chinese immigrants had been manual workers, professional and technical workers form the largest group of Chinese immigrants today. In addition, many are entrepreneurs or factory workers. Decreased job discrimination has also meant more opportunities for the second generation of Chinese Americans, born and raised in the United States. Favored locations for new immigrants, because of expanding job markets and good public transportation, have been San Francisco, New York City, and Los Angeles (Chen 1992:8–9). While the Los Angeles region exceeds all other centers in terms of total Asian population[6] (Cheng and Yang 1996:308), by some estimates as many as one-fourth of all new Chinese immigrants are now in the New York City metropolitan area.

Immigrants provide a cheap labor force that has helped revive declining industries like garment manufacturing.[7] Immigrants also invest capital in stores and small retail shops, which produce taxes for the city and provide jobs for native-born Americans as well as other immigrants (Chen 1992:28–32). Though commonly scapegoated as "taking jobs away from Americans," the reverse–job creation–is more likely to be true.

Chen argues that Chinatowns have changed since the 1940s. The repeal of the Chinese Exclusion Act, access to citizenship, voting rights laws, war bride legislation, and the family-reunification policy have all weakened the traditional bachelor organizations of urban Chinatowns. Second-generation Chinese are more assimilated into the majority population and not reliant on ethnic businesses (p. 11). Although New York City's Chinatown has mushroomed in recent years, many new immigrant Chinese live elsewhere.

Chen emphasizes the fact that Chinese Americans are not homogenous. Those born and raised in the United States since the 1950s tend to be highly educated and middle class. They are unlikely to know any language other than English well, and may feel they have little in common with new arrivals. Post-1965 immigrants are very diverse in terms of education attained, level of English spoken, and other characteristics. Chen observes that Chinese of different classes do not interact with each other. Although a "Chinese" ethnic consciousness does emerge in some situations, such as political campaigns, Chen found that the ethnic group concept was not suitable for his purposes. He focused instead on differences within the Queens (Taiwanese) Chinese, who, occupationally speaking, fall into four classes: working class (workers in factories, restaurants, and stores); small business owners; the new middle class (professionals, medical doctors, civil servants, university faculty); and capitalists (owners of businesses with more than 30 employees). Considerable mobility takes place among these classes, with the middle class moving in and out of small business, for example, and workers becoming capitalists (pp. 42–44).

Like many other researchers, Chen found that the revolution in international communications has removed barriers between countries. What is true for Taiwan is no less true for most of the other Asian countries discussed in this chapter: jet travel, the telephone, television, video recorders, and above all the Internet make possible the rapid exchange of information and the maintenance of family relationships across continents (see Cheng and Yang 1996). Travel to the United States is seen as desirable, and friends and relatives who have made the journey can easily give up-to-date information and advice. Modern communications also influence ethnic identity, since people who can travel frequently from one continent to another may be less willing to settle permanently in, and identify with, a new homeland. Especially when first trying to establish themselves, immigrants may maintain family units spread between continents. Among his sample of 100 households, Chen found 19 cases of what he calls "divided family ties" (all among working-class or business-class people)—cases in which a husband or wife cared for children alone while the spouse was back in Taiwan. Taiwan residents refer to these absent spouses as "wife in America" or "astronaut" (in the case of a husband who has to fly frequently back and forth). Some couples come as tourists, leaving children temporarily in Taiwan with grandparents. Child care is extremely expensive in New York City, and both parents must work to support themselves; also, boys older than 16 are of military-service age and are not permitted to travel until the service has been completed (Chen 1992:54–56).

Not only do patterns of migration differ today from those of the early Chinese, with families arriving rather than single males, but motives also differ. Economic gain is not the only consideration. Parents value education highly, want their children to learn English, and some wish to remove their children from Taiwan's high-pressure educational system. Sponsorship is another important factor; 80 percent of immigrant Chinese are said to have come to the United States through kin sponsorship (Chen 1992:59, 65–66). Once in the United States, both men and women work (in 68 of 100 households in Chen's sample), resulting in a median family income that is higher than the national average (p. 76).

Chen found that working-class immigrants, who do not know English, find language so great a barrier that they prefer to work in businesses run by other Chinese: garment and knitting factories, for example, and Chinese restaurants. Immigrants often suffer downward social mobility; women teachers from Taiwan, for example, find it difficult or impossible to work as teachers in the United States. Their children have adjustment problems because parents do not know enough English, or have enough time, to adequately supervise them. For small business owners, earning money is the most important value; they often bring capital from Taiwan, though owners may also start out as workers, accumulate capital, and borrow from banks. Not all of these businesses are successful, and busy entrepreneurs often have problems with their children as well. Professionals, in contrast, have more stable family lives, encounter fewer language problems, usually own their own homes, and frequently start businesses. Female community leaders come from this class (Chen 1992:248–254).

Japanese Americans

Japanese Americans are the only Asian American group that has not had rapid growth during the post-1965 era. They are distinguished by relatively high levels of income and education and high levels of intermarriage with white Americans among the third generation. The degree of intermarriage is especially remarkable given the rampant discrimination they faced before and during World War II. Less than forty years after internment, half of all new Japanese American marriages took place with whites. David O'Brien and Stephen Fugita attribute this assimilation to a number of factors: the postwar economic boom, various government actions, and such cultural factors as high education levels, a strong work ethic, and emphasis on group survival (1991:84–85).

As with other Asian Americans, important generational differences exist. Most Japanese Americans distinguish among three generations: *Issei*, the first generation, born in Japan; *Nisei*, the second generation, born in the United States to Issei parents between 1910 and 1940; and *Sansei*, or the third generation, born in the United States to Nisei parents since World War II (Kitano 1976:5–9). Antimiscegenation laws in California between 1905 and 1948 made legal marriage with whites impossible, so there are very low rates of intermarriage with whites among members of the first two generations. However, such marriages were very common among Sansei (O'Brien and Fugita 1991:98).

Japanese Americans had different postwar experiences in Hawaii and on the mainland. Hawaii, with its tourist industry, military bases, and plantations, offered more limited economic opportunities than the West Coast. On the other hand, Japanese Americans there had not suffered the massive property losses that those on the mainland had, because of their internment. The return of the famous 442nd soldiers, an all-Japanese American combat unit that distinguished itself during the war, also resulted in political changes. The veterans were now unwilling to be treated as second-class citizens, and a number of them went to law school on the GI Bill and became active in politics. By 1950, 40 percent of Hawaii's voters were of Japanese ancestry. The Nisei veterans used the Democratic Party as a vehicle for change (Republicans had been dominated by the sugar plantations), campaigning for Hawaii's statehood[8] and entering the state house and senate. Half of the legislators were Nisei, mostly war veterans and law school graduates (O'Brien and Fugita 1991:87–88).

On the mainland, discrimination had been more severe, culminating in internment and massive loss of property. However, Japanese Americans were able to make a remarkable comeback after 1945. First, American attitudes toward Japan changed. Once defeated, it was no longer a threat but remained strategically important to the United States as an outpost in the Far East during the cold war. The War Relocation Authority, which had been responsible for interning Japanese Americans, encouraged them to disperse upon their release. Many moved to the Midwest or East, where discrimination was less and smaller numbers encouraged greater acculturation. Japanese Americans also had more resources than many other ethnic groups, particularly a high level of education which exceeded that of whites from 1940 on (O'Brien and Fugita 1991:90–94).

After release from the internment camps, mainland Japanese Americans experienced dramatic changes in employment opportunities. Formerly they had been excluded from professional services and public administration, but new openings were available to them in a booming postwar economy. By 1980, 21.8 percent were in professional services (although 35.9 percent were in trade, a common prewar occupation given other constraints on employment), and 4.8 percent were still employed in agriculture versus 3 percent for the general population (O'Brien and Fugita 1991:95).

One issue that eventually united Japanese Americans of different generations and social classes was the redress movement (at first, called the reparations movement), which called for an apology from the U.S. government and financial restitution for the internment of Japanese Americans during the war. It began in the late 1960s on the West Coast, and had become a priority issue by 1974. The Japanese American community was not always united in support of it; some feared a backlash by white Americans or felt that payment would trivialize their experiences. After concerted efforts by Japanese Americans, with help from the Jewish lobby, the Civil Liberties Act of 1988 was finally signed into law by President Reagan. It mandates a payment of $20,000 to all living internees and a formal apology by the government. O'Brien and Fugita note that "only in the 1980s with the discussion and soul searching associated with the successful redress movement has the community as a whole cleansed itself of many of the repressed and unresolved feelings toward the incarceration" (p. 81). Before this, many Japanese Americans were afraid to show reactions that might lead to reprisals from white Americans. Third- and fourth-generation Japanese Americans are not likely to feel this hesitancy in America's more open social climate today.

A current controversy regarding Japanese Americans has to do with the National Japanese American Monument to Patriotism, installed on the south side of the Capitol grounds during the fall of 2000. The memorial is dedicated to Japanese Americans, both those who fought for the United States and those who were interned during World War II. A national committee of Japanese American activists objected to the use of words by Mike Masaoka, who is accused of collaborating with the government during the internment of Japanese Americans. Masaoka was field secretary for the Japanese American Citizens League (JACL) during wartime years.[9] Members of the memorial foundation's board argued that Masaoka had little choice but to cooperate at the time, and felt that it was too late to change the monument. Control of the JACL is passing from second-generation Nisei, who were directly involved in the war as veterans,

resisters, or internees, to third-generation Sansei, who were not (DeMillo 2000).

Filipino Americans

Like the nineteenth-century Chinese immigrants, early Filipino migrants came to Hawaii and California to work primarily as manual laborers. Also, as in the case of Chinese Americans, ongoing immigration since 1965 has resulted in a much more diverse Filipino American population today (Espiritu 1996). Third- and fourth-generation Filipino Americans do not speak any of the Philippine languages, and they tend to have a higher socioeconomic status than the first generation. Like the children of the post-1965 immigrants, they are more integrated into U.S. society than newcomers. On the other hand, almost two-thirds of Filipino Americans are foreign-born and speak a Philippine language at home. The majority (71 percent) live in the western United States, particularly California and Hawaii (Okamura 1998:34–35).

Because of *chain migration*, in which earlier immigrants sponsor other family members, Filipino American numbers have doubled with every census. Since 90 percent prefer to live near relatives, the number of Filipino Americans in specific states and cities increased over time (Okamura 1998:42–43).

Agriculture employed most Filipino Americans until recently; even as late as the 1960s, they made up 47 percent of plantation employees in Hawaii and 31 percent of agricultural laborers in California. Many are also service workers in factories and restaurants. Shortly after the 1965 act was passed, several thousand Filipino doctors, engineers, and scientists arrived to work in the United States, and during the 1980s thousands of Filipino nurses obtained H1-B visas[10] during a nursing shortage in the United States (Okamura 1998:45; Williams 1996:16).

The anthropologist Jonathan Okamura argues that Filipinos have experienced little occupational mobility since 1980, in spite of a relatively high educational status among post-1965 immigrants. In California, Filipinos have the highest high school dropout rate and, in the case of the third and fourth generations are underrepresented in higher education. Service work is still the most important occupational category for men and the second largest for women, especially in Hawaii, where the tourist industry is a big employer. Filipino Americans have very high work force participation rates (75 percent among persons age 16 or older). Median household incomes ($42,600 in 1989) were higher than those of both Asian Americans and whites in the late 1980s, simply because the average Filipino American household had more working adults (Okamura 1998:44–47).

Okamura argues that Filipino Americans have been particularly disadvantaged by the "model minority" stereotype of Asian Americans, the popular assumption that all are highly educated and well-to-do. Beginning in 1986, Filipino Americans were no longer considered a special target group for recruitment and admission in the University of California's affirmative action program. According to Okamura, not only did their acceptance rate decline at UCLA in the 1990s, but Filipino American enrollment at UCLA and Berkeley also decreased. In July 1995, the University of California Board of Regents voted to eliminate affirmative action programs based on racial and other preferences starting in the fall of 1997. Okamura argues that Filipino Americans also face employment discrimination due to their accented English and stereotyping, perpetuated by ethnic jokes in the mass media (Okamura 1998:51–52).

South Asians

South Asia includes India, Pakistan, Bangladesh, Sri Lanka, Nepal, and Bhutan. Asian Indians are by far the largest South Asian group represented in the United States today and will receive most discussion here. Culturally and linguistically, South Asia is one of the world's most complex regions. Although its roots extend back more than 5,000 years to the Indus Valley civilization, it has been periodically invaded by newcomers entering through the northwest passes or by sea; Greeks, Mughals, Pathans, Portuguese, Dutch, French, English—all have left their mark. Within India, there are two major language families, Indo-Aryan (a branch of Indo-European) in the north and Dravidian (consisting of indigenous languages) in the south. Modern states in India and Pakistan have been formed along linguistic lines (for example, Andhra Pradesh in the south is dominated by speakers of Telugu, a Dravidian language), although many people speak more than one language, including English. At least within India and Pakistan, individuals tend to identify strongly with regional cultures of the different states.

Modern South Asia is very much a product of British colonial history. The British came first as traders during the period of Mughal rule and stayed to gradually take control of the Indian subcontinent. By the time India gained independence in 1947, the British had created a system of government and law and a modern infrastructure in the region. It also created a mostly Hindu, English-speaking elite oriented toward the West. At Independence, India was divided; Partition led to the creation of Pakistan with its two wings, East and West, separated by 1,500 miles of territory. Millions of people became internal refugees, and the older generation has never forgotten the violence of that period. Following civil war in 1971, West Pakistan became simply Pakistan and East Pakistan, Bangladesh.

By the time of Sri Lanka's independence in 1948, a Western-educated Tamil elite coexisted uneasily with a Buddhist majority largely educated in the indigenous Sinhalese language. Colonialism created conditions favorable to emigration, including political and economic ties between India and the West and a highly educated, English-speaking professional elite who could adapt quickly to U.S. culture and society. Almost all of the early post-1965 immigrants studied in English-language schools in India (Williams 1996:12). Conflict in the region over the past two decades (civil war in Sri Lanka between Buddhists and Tamils, Sikh separatism in the Punjab) has also spurred minorities to leave South Asia. One important feature of the South Asian diaspora has been the establishment of Hindu temples, Muslim mosques, and Sikh gurudwaras in many American cities, sometimes against the opposition of local established Americans. Indian Christians, some recent converts and others with a two-thousand-year-old religious tradition, have also added new elements to Christianity in the United States (Williams 1996:5).

Some of the Asian Indian Christians were among the first of the "pioneers" to enter the United States after 1965. Numerous Indians were students in American universities at the time and decided to stay on to work in the United States. They were engineers and physicians, scientists and university faculty; many hold prominent positions in their fields today. This pattern continues as every fall, bright young graduate students arrive from India to be welcomed by their American university's India Student Association. Many of them will later work for an American employer and obtain H1-B status. This "brain drain" is the result of India's Western-oriented educational system and stagnant economy. Indians and other South Asians seek better employment, the opportunity to conduct cutting-edge research, and the best education for their children (Williams 1996:12–13).

In the 1960s and 1970s, and again in the 1990s, a growing American economy led to employer demands for certain specialists from foreign countries. Earlier in this period, the beginning of Medicare and Medicaid, coupled with the drafting of physicians and nurses for the Vietnam War, resulted in a shortage of health personnel. Because of India's colonial background, Indians were able to establish professional credentials in the United States and adapt quickly (Williams 1996:13). Today, Indian physicians and nurses can be found working in isolated rural settings and big-city hospitals where most established American physicians prefer not to practice. They provide services to populations who would otherwise go without care.

Indian Christian nurses had a particularly interesting role to play in immigration. A nursing shortage in the 1970s led to the recruitment of nurses in India by agents of American hospitals. Almost all of these nurses were Christian because, until recently, nursing occupied a very low social status in India due to its polluting aspects. The nurses in turn brought their husbands and other family members. In the case of other Asian Indian groups, a man with high professional qualifications usually was offered a job or a position and then returned home to India to marry, or brought his wife and children to join him (Williams 1996:16–18). The sponsorship of relatives in recent decades has brought less highly educated and less English-proficient Indians to the United States, creating a more socioeconomically diverse population, as in the cases of other Asian American immigrant groups. It is more difficult for elderly relatives and non-English-speaking spouses to adjust (although highly educated men often have highly educated wives who are also technicians, teachers, or professionals). In the 1990s, with the growth of the computer industry and a shortage of technically trained American personnel, computer companies have demanded an increase in H1-B visas in order to bring more computer specialists from India to the United States.

Korean Americans

Pre-1965 Korean immigrants shared a number of characteristics with Chinese, Japanese, and Filipino immigrants and endured similar experiences of racial exclusion. Because of U.S.

military involvement in Asia, Korean women married to American servicemen have been one subgroup in the immigration flow since World War II to the present. However, as did other Asian Americans, many came to join close relatives through the family reunification provisions of the 1965 Immigration Act. There are also reports of middle-class people being recruited by Korean brokers to work in low-level occupations like poultry processing. The immigrants pay high fees to the brokers, who require that they stay in the job for a certain period of time.[11] One of the major motivations for emigration is a better future for their children.

Korean Americans are probably best known for running small businesses, such as greengrocer shops and liquor stores, in large urban centers like New York City and Los Angeles. However, they also operate restaurants and stores in many small towns throughout the United States, especially near army bases. The entrepreneurs are often relatively well-educated, middle-class people who lack the English-language skills and credentials to move into professional occupations (though their children may do so); self-employment, which represents downward social mobility for many, is the best option given their constraints. Other Korean Americans, particularly those who came originally as graduate students, do have the English proficiency and skills to enter mainstream occupations.

A great deal has been written about one current issue related to Korean Americans, namely, conflict between Korean shopkeepers and African Americans in urban settings (Abelmann and Lie 1995; Kim 1999; Lie and Abelman 1999; Min 1996; K. Park 1999). On April 29, 1992, South Central Los Angeles flared into flames and violence that continued for three days and attracted a national attention. Sparked by the Rodney King verdict, in which white police officers were acquitted in the beating of an African American suspect, the riots destroyed many businesses in South Central Los Angeles and Koreatown. While the violence began as a protest against white society, the media recast it as group conflict between two minorities; in fact, all ethnic groups were involved, both as victims and looters. Pictures of armed Korean store owners reproduced a negative stereotype of Korean businesspeople as ruthless exploiters and vigilantes (Kim 1999:1). Korean merchants suffered catastrophic economic losses, $350 million to $400 million and approximately 2,300 Korean American businesses out of a total of 4,500 damaged or destroyed. Half could not rebuild at all, and many lost their homes (Kim and Kim 1999:26).

Kwang Chung Kim and others have argued that Korean merchants in Los Angeles were victimized twice, first by economic loss and psychological trauma and again when they were blamed for the destruction of their own property: "Thus, along with African Americans' racism, jealousy, and scapegoating, Korean merchants' rude treatment of customers, prejudice, economic exploitation, cultural misunderstandings, limited assimilation, and foreignness were all identified as sources of the conflict" (Kim 1999:2).

Kim points out that the Los Angeles racial disturbance does not represent the whole Korean American experience; racial relations in other cities, like Chicago and New York, are similar in some ways to those in Los Angeles and different in others (p. 2). One constant is the structural position of Korean merchants, literally "caught in the middle" (Min 1996) between poor urban minorities and dominant white society. White-owned corporations—industries providing "good" jobs as well as large retail stores—had abandoned poor minority urban neighborhoods by the 1970s, just as Korean immigrants were beginning to arrive in the United States. Unable to compete with white-owned chains in middle-class locales, Korean entrepreneurs purchased inexpensive property in inner-city neighborhoods and started small stores. Some African Americans see this situation as exploitative, and feel that banks or the government discriminate against African Americans in favor of Korean Americans. In fact, Korean American researchers argue that merchants compete fiercely with other Korean American entrepreneurs, keeping overall prices down. They find no evidence of bank or government help (Kim and Kim 1999:30; Lee 1999b:123). They argue that native-born residents are often too poor to start their own businesses, or lack the necessary skills.

Given their different experiences in U.S. society, African Americans and Korean Americans take opposing perspectives on the presence of Korean merchants in poor urban neighborhoods and negative responses by African American residents (Kim 1999:4). Both African Americans and Korean Americans explain intergroup conflict in terms of culture, while the media focuses on race and ignores the role of whites in creating the situation (K. Park 1999). Because of their own desperate circumstances, any outside businesses are viewed with suspicion by African Americans living in poverty. Korean American merchants are culturally and racially distinctive, easily labeled as "foreigners."

Intergroup conflict includes interpersonal disputes, boycotts, and (rarely) mass violence. Studies of boycotts of Korean American businesses in New York City (Lee 1999a) and Chicago (Choi 1999) indicate that such boycotts are organized by African American leaders involved in intense political competition. Actual relations between Korean merchants and African American customers are not as bad as suggested by the media and popular stereotypes, although communication difficulties do exist. For example, shopkeepers have been accused of rudeness for not smiling at customers, not looking them in the eyes, and following them around the store. These behaviors are related not only to cultural differences (looking someone in the eyes is regarded as rude behavior in a number of Asian societies) but also to merchants' negative experiences (shoplifting, armed robberies) with customers in high-crime locations.

In Chicago, there have been outbreaks of rioting, endangering store owners of all ethnic groups, whenever the Chicago Bulls basketball team has won NBA championships. Mediation efforts on the part of Korean American and African American representatives, coupled with prompt police action, have helped forestall violence (Choi 1999). The anthropologist Jung Sun Park (1999:216–222) points out that Korean Americans in Chicago were shocked by media coverage of the Los Angeles riots that portrayed Korean Americans as powerless and marginalized "foreigners" (although two-thirds in fact are American citizens). First-generation immigrants in Chicago turned to the second generation for leadership; as a result, the Chicago ethnic community began to identify with the term "Korean American" in order to claim full membership in American society.

Korean immigration has been declining since the early 1990s, and recent immigrants are not entering business. As the present Korean merchants age, many are selling out; their children, often highly educated professionals, are not interested in maintaining retail businesses in high-risk urban areas. Less antagonism will probably be directed against Korean Americans in the future, though it may well affect the Arab and Pakistani American merchants now moving into inner-city locations (Choi 1999:175; Kim 1999:240–241).

Vietnamese and Other Southeast Asians

Southeast Asians are unique among post-1965 Asian groups due to their origin as refugees, the recentness of their arrival, and the problematic fact of their association with the war in Vietnam.

The main ethnic groups from Southeast Asia in the United States today come from Vietnam, Cambodia, and Laos. The largest groups resettling in America are the Vietnamese, Sino-Vietnamese (Vietnamese of Chinese descent, including merchants from Vietnam), Lao and

Hmong from Laos, and Khmer (Cambodian). The Vietnamese are by far the largest group. (The many smaller ethnic groups will not be discussed here.) "Southeast Asian," a broad category used by the government and recent scholars, is not a term applied by most former refugees to themselves. As the anthropologist David Haines points out (1989:8), each of these has its distinct culture, language, and prearrival history; each has also had different experiences resettling in the United States.

Of all the Southeast Asian groups, the Vietnamese were the best educated, the most familiar with English, and the most apt to have technical or professional backgrounds before leaving Vietnam. The Sino-Vietnamese are similar in characteristics but were even more urban as a group. Together with the Vietnamese, with whom they sometimes intermarried, they had relatively small households and fewer children. The Hmong, a hill people who were enlisted by the U.S. military to fight against communist forces in Laos, are just the opposite; the most rural and least educated and with the largest families, they have had the most difficult adjustment problems in the United States. The Lao and Khmer are in between, both having urban and rural people, a moderate education level, and a wide range of occupations. The Khmer, however, suffered the genocidal activities of the Pol Pot regime (1975–78) and have endured the most psychological trauma of all the Southeast Asian refugees (Haines 1989:8).

Considerable diversity exists within, as well as between, the different ethnic groups. The Vietnamese, for example, include Catholics, Buddhists, and members of other religions. Some were white-collar workers in Saigon, and others were farmers or fishermen. Some came from highly educated, well-to-do families; others had an impoverished background. Lao include former military officials and educated professionals, as well as older people, men and especially women, who may be completely illiterate. Education and previous occupation in turn affect individual adjustment in the United States.

The pattern of settlement of the Southeast Asian refugee population in the United States is both similar to and different from that of other Asian groups. At the time of the 1980 census, there were relatively few Southeast Asians in New England, for example, and more on the west coast, as is the case with other Asian Americans. However, a large proportion were living in the west central states, such as Texas, Louisiana, Minnesota, and Iowa (Haines 1989:5–6). This is partly due to the refugee resettlement process, which emphasized dispersal of the refugee population in order to avoid overburdening communities with large numbers of newcomers.

At first, the Southeast Asians had no choice about where to move; they were placed where sponsors and services were available. However, the refugees quickly relocated, often several times, to reunite with kin, seek better employment, and find more congenial locales. While refugees commonly refer to the climate as a reason for moving (not surprisingly, people from tropical countries prefer warmer climates), the presence of relatives and/or a sizable ethnic community is probably a more important concern. The concentration of Southeast Asians, for example, has steadily increased in California (over 40 percent of the refugee population had settled there by 1984), a state with a long history of Asian immigration. Texas has consistently been the second most populous state for 1975 arrivals (Haines 1989:3–5). Former refugees from fishing communities in Vietnam prefer to live on the Gulf Coast, in Texas or Louisiana, where they can be near the water, enjoy a seafood diet as they did in Vietnam, and work in shrimping or seafood processing (Durrenberger 1996).

The Context of Reception

Because the war in Vietnam was such a divisive experience for Americans, and because this refugee flow has been unusually large and long-term, the reception of Southeast Asians by established Americans has not been uniform. Some refugees arrived as late as the 1990s when many earlier refugees were well-established citizens of American communities. A whole generation of Vietnamese American children has grown up in the United States. Though native-born citizens and often more American than Vietnamese in culture, they are likely to be categorized as "foreign" by established Americans of other ethnic groups. "First-wave" arrivals, those who came in 1975, were generally warmly received. Catholic church congregations often sponsored fellow Catholics and developed enduring relationships with refugee families. However, cross-cultural misunderstandings occurred as well. The refugee flow began so suddenly that there was no time to properly train or orient either the refugees or their sponsors, who might be individual families, churches, voluntary organizations, or even companies. Eventually "donor fatigue" set in as numbers increased in the late 1970s and 1980s (Rutledge 1992:41–42).

Other misunderstandings occurred with regard to church attendance. For many established Americans, being Christian is synonymous with being American; but the majority of Vietnamese, as well as Lao and Khmer, are Buddhist. While they might feel obligated to attend a sponsor's church at first out of politeness, in most cases they had no desire to change religion. This was sometimes a source of disillusionment for sponsors. Some ministers and church groups focused on the attempted conversion of Vietnamese and Lao refugees as a mission, even to the extent of learning the language and preaching in it. Because they did not see Buddhists attending temples regularly (often none were available, especially in small towns), Christians tended to assume that the newcomers "had no religion." In fact, just the opposite was true; religion was a great source of comfort and identity as people struggled to re-create their lives in a

new land. A small shelf in the living room often served as an altar on which photographs of deceased relatives were displayed, and offerings of food and drink were made weekly and annually to commemorate deceased individuals (called ancestor worship in the literature, this custom is similar to Memorial Day observations in America). Southeast Asians did travel to temples in other communities on special occasions. But, as one Vietnamese refugee told the author, "I don't need to go to a temple; the Buddha is in my heart."

A persistent response of some established Americans—particularly some Vietnam veterans, though not confined to them and certainly not true of all—is a negative reaction to the Vietnamese (or even Asian Americans in general) because of an association with bad memories of the war in Vietnam. Some veterans suffer from posttraumatic stress syndrome—nightmares, depression, anxiety, and other symptoms resulting from wartime experiences—which can be triggered by seeing an Asian face. Others felt they had been rejected by fellow Americans after their return home because of the war's unpopularity, and they resented the "special treatment" supposedly given to refugees.

The effects of these feelings can range from discrimination in hiring practices to casual insults and harassment in daily life. For example, young Lao men in southwest Kansas in the late 1980s told the author that they were sometimes targets for hostility when driving to work; cars would cut them off and the occupants would spit at them. When asked why this happened, they said: "They think we're Vietnamese and they don't like the Vietnam War." Former South Vietnamese army officers were confused by the behavior of some individuals who apparently thought that they were communists. The established Americans did not distinguish between North and South Vietnamese (enemies during the conflict): "Don't they know we fought on the American side?" asked the Vietnamese newcomers.

However, some white American veterans have formed close relationships with Vietnamese Americans and have reconciled feelings of hostility or guilt over Vietnam by making return visits with them in recent years as the country has opened up to the outside world. Over time, particularly in smaller communities, the Vietnamese and other former refugees have gradually been accepted.

Economic conditions also greatly influenced the reception of Southeast Asians, both generally and in the specific communities where they resettled. Increasing numbers of refugees in the early 1980s coincided with an economic recession in the United States (Haines 1989:11). By 1981, more than 500,000 Southeast Asians had been resettled in hundreds of American communities, and domestic pressure to scale back the U.S. refugee program was growing. Local governments and service providers felt overwhelmed and underfunded (Robinson 1998: 113). Competition grew between refugee groups, and between newcomers and established American minorities, for scarce resources in poor local employment markets. For example, anthropologists Paul Durrenberger (1996) and Paul Starr (1981) have discussed competition and conflict between Vietnamese fisherfolk and established white Americans on the Gulf Coast. Refugees from Vietnam were placed with seafood company sponsors in Florida, Louisiana, and Texas who needed workers for fishing and packing. The Vietnamese soon bought boats, however, and went into business for themselves. The Vietnamese initially broke many boating and fishing regulations, angering local fishermen. Starr suggests that some of the complaints, however, can be understood as jealousy expressed "toward those who work harder, longer, and more efficiently than is regarded as 'normal'" (Starr 1981:233). The Vietnamese came at a time when shrimp supplies were declining and government regulations made it increasingly hard for fishermen to survive.

Racial violence broke out along the Gulf Coast in the early 1980s—boat burnings in Seadrift, Texas; a Ku Klux Klan rally in Galveston, Texas; and a brawl among shrimpers in Gulfport, Louisiana (Durrenberger 1996:37–39). Durrenberger points out that Vietnamese shrimpers were deliberately recruited by Mississippi processors who wanted workers and a reliable shrimp supply (p. 68). By the late 1980s, although competition still persisted, the violence had lessened. Local and immigrant shrimpers adjusted to each other, even uniting in a spontaneous Gulf port blockade in 1989 to protest government regulations (pp. 69–70).

Where jobs were readily available and newcomers were not seen as competing with the established population for employment or resources, as in the meatpacking town of Garden City, Kansas, during the 1980s and 1990s, minimal conflict took place. The newspaper and the local ministerial alliance played a vital role informing the public about reasons for the presence of Southeast Asians, almost all of whom had come to work in local meatpacking plants. Most employers came to appreciate the strong work ethic of the Vietnamese and Lao newcomers. Although discrimination and stereotypes persist, mutual adjustment and accommodation between Vietnamese and other, established groups has been the norm (see Benson 1990, 2001; Stull et al. 1990).

The previous discussion leads us to larger questions about perceptions of Asian Americans—and nonwhite groups in general—by native-born Americans.

PREJUDICE AND ASIAN AMERICAN IDENTITY

In general, American attitudes toward Asian groups mirror America's relationship to the countries of origin at any given time. World War II led to marked antagonism toward Japanese

Americans; the Vietnam War created considerable hostility toward Vietnamese refugees. Most established Americans know little about the post-1965 immigrants, and misinformation and rumors easily spread.

A persistent problem for Asian Americans, and for nonwhite individuals in general, is that regardless of their own perceptions of ethnic identity, they are often inappropriately categorized by established Americans. Prejudices directed against a particular population or ethnic group are generalized and applied to others. Native-born Asian Americans, for example, are confused with recent immigrants from China, India, or other countries. As we have seen, media treatment of Korean American merchants in Los Angeles as "foreigners" led to greater self-consciousness among Chicago's Korean Americans. The September 11, 2001 terrorist attack on the World Trade Center led to hundreds of cases of persecution of Muslims and Asian Americans, particularly South Asians. A Sikh gas station owner was murdered, possibly because he wore a turban vaguely similar to that of the Saudi Arabian terrorist Osama bin Laden, as pictured on television. As long as Asian Americans are considered "others," they are likely to face a certain amount of prejudice and discrimination from established residents. At the same time, it must be recognized that first-generation Asian Americans, many of whom have already absorbed American racial stereotypes from the mass media before emigrating, are also capable of prejudice against outsiders and those they perceive to be of low status in U.S. society.

The longer a group has been in the country, the more politicized it is apt to become in its awareness of the need to protect civil rights. At the same time, the more established the group, the more likely that it has become incorporated into U.S. society, at least economically if not culturally. Here we turn to the issue of achievement among Asian Americans and whether they should be considered a "model minority."

ACHIEVEMENT AND DIVERSITY AMONG ASIAN AMERICANS

As we have discussed, great diversity—economic, cultural, linguistic, generational—exists within the population referred to here as "Asian American." Some are fourth-generation Americans, and others are recent immigrants or refugees not yet eligible for citizenship. Some can speak, read, and write one or more Asian languages, and others are fluent only in English. Some are well-to-do, successful entrepreneurs or professionals; others have difficulty finding employment. Given this diversity, we would expect considerable variation in the degree to which Asian American individuals and groups have been integrated into U.S. society, economically and otherwise.

Income and Occupation

Newcomers enter U.S. society in several ways, most commonly as labor migrants, professionals, entrepreneurs, refugees, or capitalists (Cheng and Yang 1996:325; Portes and Rumbaut 1996). As we have seen, the first Asian immigrants were primarily labor migrants, while post-1965 newcomers came initially as professionals (particularly the South Asians) or refugees (Vietnamese and other Southeast Asian groups). Many others, sponsored by family members, have turned to self-employment in the form of entrepreneurship. For refugees, especially minority groups from rural areas of Southeast Asia, employment has been far more challenging. The Immigration Act of 1990 also granted permanent residence to wealthy investors, a number of whom have settled in the Los Angeles and San Francisco areas (Cheng and Yang 1996:331; Wong 1998:35).

Although the influx of refugees has resulted in more varied public reactions, to a large extent Asian Americans still retain a "model minority" image in the wider society. This term was first used by the press in the mid-1960s to praise

Japanese and Chinese Americans for their achievements (Cheng and Yang 1996:312), and has been a source of controversy ever since. It has been criticized as a racial stereotype which implies that there is no problem with racism in U.S. society because Asian Americans have "made it," creating a standard of behavior that is difficult for other, more stigmatized minorities to match. It also conceals great differences in economic outcomes. Many Asian Americans resent the common assumption that all those of Asian heritage are privileged or not "real" minorities in the same sense as African Americans, Latinos, and Native Americans. Asian Americans are quick to point out that whatever success they have achieved has been the result of extremely hard work and sacrifice, often in the face of discrimination. This is a particularly sensitive point for professionals who compete with other minorities under affirmative action guidelines.

In spite of these criticisms, there is some truth in the stereotype. Compared to other minorities such as African Americans and Latinos, Asian Americans are, in fact, doing relatively well. According to the U.S. Census Bureau (1998), in 1995 the median income ($46,360) of Asian and Pacific Islander families was close to that ($45,020) of non-Hispanic white families.[12] This is partly explained, however, by the fact that Asian American families tend to have more wage earners than do white families. Wives make a major economic contribution in almost all of the Asian groups, while other adults may be present in the household as well (Benson 1994; Ling 1998:168). However, median earnings of adults 25 years old or older with a high school education were less than those of whites, and earnings of Asian and Pacific Islander men with a bachelor's degree or more averaged less than those of their non-Hispanic white male counterparts: $41,370 to $50,240 (U.S. Census Bureau 1998). Asian American professionals feel that they are underrepresented in managerial jobs—that a "glass ceiling" exists—and that this limits their earnings potential (Cheng and Yang 1996).

The overall statistics conceal great variation, with groups who have been in the United States longest generally faring best and the Southeast Asian refugees, who are relatively recent arrivals, having the most difficulty. The general Asian American population is split between those at the top of the socioeconomic ladder (professionals and capitalists) and those at the bottom (service workers). The poverty rate for Asian and Pacific Islander families is double that for non-Hispanic white families: 14.6 percent versus 8.5 percent for non-Hispanic whites (U.S. Census Bureau 1998).

Education

Education is another area in which many Asian Americans excel, although the model minority image is problematic here as well. Although educational levels are high, school completion rates vary greatly among Asian American groups, from 31 percent for Hmong to 88 percent for Japanese (U.S. Census Bureau 1998).

A number of studies have attempted to explain Asian American academic achievement (e.g., Caplan et al. 1991; Gibson 1988; Zhou and Bankston 1998). One study, by Nathan Caplan, Marcella Choy, and John Whitmore, in the early 1980s was a national survey of educational outcomes among Vietnamese, Lao, and Sino-Vietnamese refugee children. These were children of farmers and fishermen, not highly educated people. Most lost between one and three years of formal schooling in the resettlement process, and they lacked English skills and a basic knowledge of American culture. However, at the time of the study, eight out of ten students had a B average or better in terms of GPA, with almost half receiving A's in mathematics. They did not do as well in writing and English, since they had had only about three and a half years of experience with the new language.

Families with four or more children did just as well or better than smaller families, and girls did just as well as boys. The authors attribute this success to cultural values (particularly a high value placed on education), family lifestyle (a low divorce rate, parental involvement, and cooperative learning), and a willingness to seize opportunities. Min Zhou and Carl Bankston (1998) also studied the adaptation of Vietnamese American children and found that the ethnic group is an important source of identity and support. Those children who do best academically are least acculturated and have the strongest ties to their ethnic community (p. 235).

The Future of Asian American Ethnicity

Asian American authors are somewhat ambivalent about the future of their ethnicity. On the one hand, they recognize the need for political unity with regard to civil rights issues; on the other, they recognize that the phrase "Asian American" embodies hope rather than reality. Members of different Asian groups do not necessarily live in the same neighborhoods, interact with each other more than other Americans, or see themselves as having interests in common. They may or may not identify strongly with an ethnic group from a particular country of origin. Class and generation also divide co-ethnics: on certain issues, university professors will have different concerns from those of shopkeepers, recent arrivals from third- or fourth-generation Asian Americans (see Espiritu 1996). This is not to say that national origin groups cannot become politicized and recognize a common identity in certain situations, such as Japanese Americans with reference to the redress movement or Korean Americans in reaction to negative media portrayals. However, a Pan-Asian identity is still in its beginning stages. As long as immigration continues at high levels, and easy travel and communication continue, broad solidarity among Asian-origin groups will not come easily (Cheng and Yang 1996:342–343; see also Espiritu 1992). Intermarriage is a related issue. Rare among first-generation immigrants, it becomes more common over time. It may be that while ethnicity does not disappear, it will become increasingly symbolic as kinship integrates Asian groups into U.S. society (Zhou and Bankston 1998:240).

NOTES

1. California suffered a very unbalanced sex ratio in the 1930s, with 14 men to every woman (Okamura 1998:40).
2. The country quota does not include close relatives, refugees, and special immigrants, so actual numbers coming from a particular country per year may greatly exceed the total.
3. Through the attorney general, the president could grant admission to whole groups of people.
4. In actual practice, previous policies continued; most refugee admissions after 1980 were of persons supposedly fleeing communism, including those from Vietnam, Laos, and Cambodia.
5. The People's Republic of China did not permit emigration until recently (Chen 1992:ix).
6. In 1990, it had more than 1.3 million Asians, or 9 percent of the total population.
7. Many American companies moved their factories to other countries or Sunbelt states in the 1970s to take advantage of cheaper labor and overhead (Chen 1992:31).
8. Hawaii became the fiftieth state on March 12, 1959.
9. Founded in 1929, JACL is the oldest and largest civil rights organization representing Asian Americans (Japanese American Citizens League 2001).
10. H1-B visas allow foreigners temporary residence for employment purposes, and can be converted into the coveted "green card" (no longer actually green) of permanent residence.
11. These newcomers enter with H1-B status as workers fulfilling employer needs.
12. "Asian and Pacific Islander" is the government category used in the 1990 census, with Pacific Islanders representing only a small portion of the total.

REFERENCES CITED

ABELMANN, NANCY, and JOHN LIE. 1995. *Blue Dreams: Korean Americans and the Los Angeles Riots.* Cambridge, MA: Harvard University Press.

BENSON, JANET E. 1990. Good neighbors: Ethnic relations in Garden City trailer courts. *Urban Anthropology* 19:361–386.

___. 1994. The effects of packinghouse work on Southeast Asian refugee families. In *Newcomers in the Workplace.*

Louise Lamphere, Alex Stepick, and Guillermo Grenier, eds. Pp. 99–126. Philadelphia: Temple University Press.

___. 2001. Vietnamese refugees, Mexican immigrants, and the changing character of a community. In *Manifest Destinies: Americanizing Immigrants and Internationalizing Americans*. David W. Haines and Carol A. Mortland, eds. Westport, CT: Praeger.

CAPLAN, NATHAN, MARCELLA H. CHOY, and JOHN K. WHITMORE. 1991. *Children of the Boat People: A Study of Educational Success*. Ann Arbor: University of Michigan Press.

CHEN, HSIANG-SHUI. 1992. *Chinatown No More*. Ithaca, NY: Cornell University Press.

CHENG, LUCIE, and PHILIP Q. YANG. 1996. Asians: The "model minority" deconstructed. In *Ethnic Los Angeles*. Roger Waldinger and Mehdi Bozorgmehr, eds. Pp. 305–344. New York: Russell Sage Foundation.

CHOI, INCHUL. 1999. Contemplating Black-Korean conflict in Chicago. In *Koreans in the Hood: Conflict with African Americans*. Kwang Chung Kim, ed. Baltimore: Johns Hopkins University Press.

DEMILLO, ANDREW. 2000. Japanese Americans spar over message on memorial. *Seattle Times*, June 15.

DURRENBERGER, PAUL E. 1996. *Gulf Coast Soundings: People and Policy in the Mississippi Shrimp Industry*. Lawrence, KS: University Press of Kansas.

ESPIRITU, YEN LE. 1992. *Asian American Panethnicity*. Philadelphia: Temple University Press.

___. 1995. *Filipino American Lives*. Philadelphia: Temple University Press.

___. 1996. Colonial oppression, labor importation and group formation: Filipinos in the United States. *Ethnic and Racial Studies* 19:29–48.

FONG, TIMOTHY P. 1994. *The First Suburban Chinatown: The Remaking of Monterey Park, California*. Philadelphia: Temple University Press.

GIBSON, MARGARET A. 1988. *Accommodation without Assimilation: Sikh Immigrants in an American High School*. Ithaca, NY: Cornell University Press.

GYORY, ANDREW. 1998. *Closing the Gate: Race, Politics, and the Chinese Exclusion Act*. Chapel Hill: University of North Carolina Press.

HAINES, DAVID W., ed. 1989. Introduction. In *Refugees as Immigrants*. Pp. 1–23. Totowa, NJ: Rowman and Littlefield.

Japanese American Citizens League. 2001. About JACL. Retrieved May 23, 2001. http://www.jacl.org/about.html.

KIM, KWANG CHUNG. 1999. Introduction. In *Koreans in the Hood: Conflict with African Americans*. Kwang Chung Kim, ed. Pp. 1–13. Baltimore: Johns Hopkins University Press.

KIM, KWANG CHUNG, and SHIN KIM. 1999. The multiracial nature of Los Angeles unrest in 1992. In *Koreans in the Hood: Conflict with African Americans*. Kwang Chung Kim, ed. Pp. 17–38. Baltimore: Johns Hopkins University Press.

KITANO, HARRY L. 1976. *Japanese Americans: The Evolution of a Subculture*. Englewood Cliffs, NJ: Prentice Hall.

LEE, HEON CHEOL. 1999a. The dynamics of Black-Korean conflict: A Korean American perspective. In *Koreans in the Hood: Conflict with African Americans*. Kwang Chung Kim, ed. Pp. 91–112. Baltimore: Johns Hopkins University Press.

___. 1999b. Conflict between Korean merchants and black customers: A structural analysis.In *Koreans in the Hood: Conflict with African Americans*. Kwang Chung Kim, ed. Pp. 113–130. Baltimore: Johns Hopkins University Press.

LEE, SHARON M. 1998. Asian Americans: Diverse and growing. *Population Bulletin* 53(2). Washington, DC: Population Reference Bureau.

LEONARD, KAREN ISAKSEN. 1997. *The South Asian Americans*. Westport, CT: Greenwood Press.

LIE, JOHN, and NANCY ABELMAN. 1999. The 1992 Los Angeles riots and the "Black-Korean conflict." In *Koreans in the Hood: Conflict with African Americans*. Kwang Chung Kim, ed. Pp. 75–87. Baltimore: Johns Hopkins University Press.

LING, HUPING. 1998. *Surviving on the Gold Mountain: A History of Chinese American Women and Their Lives*. Albany: State University of New York Press.

MIN, PYONG GAP. 1996. *Caught in the Middle: Korean Communities in New York and Los Angeles*. Berkeley: University of California Press.

NEE, VICTOR G., and BRETT DE BARY Nee. 1972. *Longtime Californ': A Documentary Study of an American Chinatown*. New York: Pantheon.

O'BRIEN, DAVID J., and STEPHEN S. FUGITA. 1991. *The Japanese American Experience*. Bloomington: Indiana University Press.

OKAMURA, JONATHAN. 1998. *Imagining the Filipino American Diaspora*. New York: Garland.

PARK, JUNG SUN. 1999. Identity politics: Chicago Korean-Americans and the Los Angeles "riots." In *Koreans in the Hood: Conflict with African Americans*. Kwang Chung Kim, ed. Pp. 202–231. Baltimore: Johns Hopkins University Press.

PARK, KYEYOUNG. 1999. Use and abuse of race and culture: Black-Korean tension in America. In *Koreans in the Hood: Conflict with African Americans*. Kwang Chung Kim, ed. Pp. 60–74. Baltimore: Johns Hopkins University Press.

PORTES, ALEJANDRO, and RUBEN G. RUMBAUT. 1996. *Immigrant America: A Portrait*. 2nd edition. Berkeley: University of California Press.

REIMERS, DAVID M. 1992. *Still the Golden Door*. 2nd edition. New York: Columbia University Press.

ROBINSON, W. COURTLAND. 1998. *Terms of Refuge: The Indochinese Exodus and the International Response*. London: Zed Books.

RUTLEDGE, PAUL JAMES. 1992. *The Vietnamese Experience in America.* Bloomington: Indiana University Press.

STARR, PAUL D. 1981. Troubled waters: Vietnamese fisherfolk on America's Gulf Coast. *International Migration Review* 15:226–238.

STULL, DONALD D., JANET E. BENSON, MICHAEL J. BROADWAY, ARTHUR L. CAMPA, KEN C. ERICKSON, and MARK A. GREY. 1990. *Changing Relations: Newcomers and Established Residents in Garden City, Kansas.* Institute for Public Policy and Business Research. Report No. 172. Lawrence: University of Kansas.

TAKAKI, RONALD. 1990. *Strangers from a Different Shore: A History of Asian Americans.* New York: Penguin.

U.S. Bureau of the Census. 1998. *Population Profile of the United States, 1997.* Current Population Reports P-23 Special Studies No. 194. Washington, DC: U.S. Government Printing Office.

___. 2000. Profile of general demographic characteristics for the United States, 2000. Table DP-1. Retrieved May 23, 2001. http://www.census.gov/prod/cen2000/index.html.

WILLIAMS, RAYMOND BRADY. 1996. *Christian Pluralism in the United States.* Cambridge: Cambridge University Press.

WONG, BERNARD. 1998. *Ethnicity and Entrepreneurship: The New Chinese Immigrants in the San Francisco Bay Area.* Needham Heights, MA: Allyn and Bacon.

ZHOU, MIN, and CARL L. BANKSTON III. 1998. *Growing Up American: How Vietnamese Children Adapt to Life in the United States.* New York: Russell Sage Foundation.

12 ARAB AMERICANS

Barbara C. Aswad

Wayne State University

The Arab world is a large area composed of 21 states, extending from Morocco on the Atlantic Ocean to Iraq and the Persian Gulf. It includes over 200 million persons and exhibits great diversity, which is also reflected in Arab Americans. In reference to Americans of Arab background, the term *Arab* connotes a linguistic, cultural, and sometimes political term used to identify those who have migrated primarily from Lebanon, Syria, Palestine, Iraq, Egypt, Yemen, and Jordan. For historical and cultural reasons, some persons from these areas may not identify with the designation. Also, Americans often confuse "Arab" with "Middle Eastern," a term that refers to an area that includes not only the Arab countries but also Turkey, Iran, and Israel, where languages other than Arabic are spoken by the majority and are official languages. Arabic is a Semitic language, related historically to Hebrew, Aramaic, and Chaldean.

WHERE AND HOW DO ARAB AMERICANS FIT IN?

Areas of settlement from Arabic-speaking countries include major concentrations in the Detroit-Dearborn, New York, Cleveland, Chicago, and Los Angeles metropolitan areas. Ninety-one percent of all Arab Americans are urbanites, and 97 percent of Arab immigrants live in urban areas. Almost 40 percent live in the northeastern United States, 28 percent in the Midwest, 20 percent in the South, and 12 percent in the West (Zogby 1990).

Compared with other ethnic communities, Arab Americans constitute a small group often marginalized in discussions of ethnicity and racism. The 1990 U.S. census documented 870,000, yet scholars maintain numbers of 2 million to 4 million, depending upon whether Chaldean-speakers and speakers of other minority languages from Arab countries are included.[1] The Detroit area, where the Arab American population is among the highest in the United States, at approximately 250,000, people from the Arab countries were the largest group of immigrants in 2000 (*Detroit Free Press*, July 4, 2000).

Nadine Naber insightfully describes four paradoxes of "Arab American invisibility" as an ethnic group: (1) Arab diversity while represented as a monolith, (2) simultaneously racialized as whites and nonwhites, (3) racialized by religion (Islam), and (4) the intersection between the religious forms of identity that Arab immigrants bring to the United States and the racial forms that characterize U.S. society (2000: 37–81). I would add to these a misunderstanding of Middle East history and a misunderstanding of Arab kinship, gender, and family roles in society.

Much of the identification "Arab" has been created within the United States in the last fifty years. During this period, the words *Arab* and *Islam* received numerous negative stereotypes that affect the Arab American communities. As do other minority groups, members of the Arab community know the sting of prejudice and fears of harassment as in reports of international Arab terrorism, or their religion misrepresented as primarily violent, or their women seen as powerless. These attitudes were true before the violent terrorist attacks on the World Trade Center in New York City and the Pentagon in Washington, D.C. on September 11, 2001 attributed to Saudi militant Osama bin Laden, head of the Al Qaeda movement, to the Islamic Jihad in Egypt, and to the Taliban in Afghanistan. The attacks increased some of the fervor of negativism and raised questions about the origins of such an attack and its relation to religious and cultural customs. The American government tried vigorously, and with some success, to separate this horrific deed from the beliefs of most Muslims. President Bush and others spoke against attacking people because they looked Arab, Muslim, or Eastern. Shortly after the attack, a Detroit newspaper headline from a survey of 306 persons stated, "Few blame local Arab Americans for attacks: More than 63 percent say they don't feel hostile; 59 percent support profiling"; 14.7 percent reported feeling "somewhat hostile"; and 4.6 percent "very hostile" (*Detroit News*, September 16, 2001).

Ethnic profiling has become a major problem for Arab Americans. A local poll of 527 Detroit area Arab Americans, half of whom were Chris-

tians, half Muslims, stated, "Arab Americans expect scrutiny, feel sting of bias: 61 percent in poll say profiling is justified." (*Detroit Free Press*, October 1, 2001). This reaction appears to reflect fear in the communities. The poll reported only 22 percent of the Arab Americans said they had felt acts of bias. Of this figure, 22 percent had experienced strange looks, 19 percent nasty comments, 15 percent racial slurs, and 10 percent threats. Few had met with physical assault (2 percent) or objects thrown (2 percent). Imad Hamad, Regional Midwest director of the American-Arab Anti-Discrimination Committee reported that there were 500 incidents nationally, including 5 deaths (personal communication, November 6, 2001). Windows had been broken and threats made in local community centers and mosques, but there were also many messages of support. In Chicago an angry crowd marching on a mosque was stopped by police. A mosque was fire bombed in Texas. The incidents initially, however, seemed somewhat less violent than during the Gulf War. Locally Arab Americans felt the need to proclaim their loyalty and love of the United States (*Detroit Free Press*, October 2001). Imams spoke out explaining their faith and disassociating themselves from the attack and from the El Qaeda organization (*Detroit Free Press*, October 27, 2001).

Initially many Arabs in the Detroit area stayed inside their homes and community and reported that they felt extremely nervous and scared. Many women did not shop; several had their Islamic head scarves *(hijab)* pulled off. A suburban Arab commented that he now knew how African Americans felt walking in a primarily white community. Some Christian Arabs distanced themselves from Muslim Arabs, and some wore large crosses. To strengthen diversity and unity, thirty religious and community groups accepted the local mosque's invitation to enter and learn about Islam in the Claremont and Pomona areas of California. The groups offered support for the Muslims in their community (*Claremont Courier*, September 9, October 22, 2001).

Because of the attack, many thoughtful Americans acquainted themselves with the history, religion, literature, and politics of the Middle East, Afghanistan, Pakistan, and Central Asia. As in the Vietnam War, they also examined America's role in global affairs.

Stereotypes and feelings have been created not only because of the attack. In the last fifty years the dominant industrialized United States has been engaged in a political-economic struggle because of its dependence on Arab oil. The United States inflicted wars and destruction in the Middle East and aided authoritarian governments to control oil. Government officials know that increased stereotypes of Islam could injure relations with highly religious Saudi Arabia and other countries where U.S. military bases exist. Attitudes are also influenced by the Palestinian-Israeli conflict in which the United States allied itself with Israel in its occupation of Palestinian, Lebanese, and Syrian lands, along with the resultant harsh treatment of the peoples of those lands. The hundreds of thousands of casualties suffered by the Iraqi peoples in the Gulf War and the following ten years of economic sanctions are also in the minds of Arab Americans. Many have experienced violence themselves or have relatives who have experienced it. Their worldview includes information from media in the Arab world that the majority of Americans do not receive. There has been a general lack of knowledge in the United States about the history of the Arab world and a selectivity regarding the tenets of Islam, the Arab family, and foreign conflicts.

Arab Americans are well aware of the many contributions in science, mathematics, medicine, literature, and architecture made by Arab and Islamic Empires from the eighth through the twelfth centuries A.D. when Europe was in the Dark Ages. They share a common history of 400 years of Ottoman Turkish control and, more important, two centuries of European colonial control, influence, and suppression, against which they fought wars of liberation in the twentieth century. Thus Arab Americans, proud to be citizens of the United States and having made many contributions in their new country, find themselves with an uncomfortable struggle as they try to explain themselves, exhibit their patriotism, yet show ethnic pride and examine their identity.

In the United States, diverse cultural groups are often lumped together by language. Thus Spanish-speakers include such diverse groups as Cubans, Puerto Ricans, and Mexicans. Similar differences occur with communities from Arabic-speaking areas. The U.S. census categorizes immigrants by language, skin color, and country of origin, which often confounds the process of identification for Arabic-speakers. In the census, they are considered "Caucasian," and with other Middle Eastern groups, are the only Third World peoples not afforded "minority" status. Many could be considered Asian or African since they were born in those geographic areas, but they are not for the purposes of the census or policies of affirmative action.

The privilege of whiteness in the social stratification of the United States and the discrimination against those of darker pigmentation affect members of the Arab communities. Although legally classified as Caucasian, a dark-skinned person from Yemen or Lower Egypt is not granted that privilege by white Americans, who are also ambivalent toward other olive-skinned Arabs. African Americans, on the other hand, generally view Arab Americans as white. Because skin color is not a major social category in the Middle East, being part of the U.S. system of racial stratification has raised debates within the communities as to how they should be classified. Official minority status obviously brings some benefits, especially for those of low income.[2] Still, other members wanting to assimilate speedily, and fearful of many of the negative terms often associated with "Arab," would disassociate themselves and be glad to be considered members of the dominant society. Others decline to identify themselves, fearful of documentation or discrimination.

Naber points out that "Arab-Americans do not always possess the power to choose 'to pass' or 'not to pass' as white" (2000:49). This is especially true during a political crisis. She cites documentation by the Arab American Anti-Discrimination Committee (ADC) of harassment that began in the Nixon era by the FBI, such as visiting homes and making phone calls to individuals as well as to relatives, neighbors, friends, and employers (ADC 1986:2). According to the ADC, "Invariably, no criminal charge is involved and the individuals are being investigated because of their origin and/or political beliefs" (p. 2). Detention camps for Arab Americans were planned by the FBI and the Immigration and Naturalization Service in 1987 in Oakdale, Louisiana (Naber 2000:49). These pressures intensified after the 1991 Gulf War, and most recently there have been trials and deportations based on secret evidence in which the attorney for the accused does not have access to evidence brought against the client. (This will be discussed in more detail later.) The violent response by some members of the Islamic world to U.S. dominance has created much tension for U.S. citizens from Arab countries.

In the introductory essay to their book, *Arab Detroit: From Margin to Mainstream*, Andrew Skryock and Nabeel Abraham discuss Arab American identity.

> They enter the American margins whenever they represent or think of themselves in relation to Arab worlds, private or public, that are not generally accessible (or even intelligible) to a larger, non-Arab society. For some Arab Detroiters, life is mostly a mainstream affair. For others, it is a prolonged study in marginality. For those in between, the leap from margin to mainstreams (and back again) occurs constantly, as though in the twinkling of an eye. [2000:16]

Labels found within the community, such as "old world" and "boaters" (those just off the boat) versus "American born" or "integrationist" or "isolationist," or those used by academics (Abraham 1989), show these processes and a certain consciousness. Outsiders use such derogatory terms as "camel jockey" and "sand nigger" (Charara 2000:405). "Rag head" is often directed at Muslim girls in Dearborn high schools.

As with other immigrants, working out their positions in the U.S. system of stratification includes both acceptance and resistance to Americanization. Sensitive life stories illustrate the variety of identifications and swings back and forth, helping Arab Americans to get around labels of "us," "them," and "others." For example, Nabeel Abraham (2000) recounts the upheavals in his family and homeland from which his parents had to flee after the creation of the Israeli state in 1948. He discusses his initial marginality with his schoolmates, then acceptance, then increased identification with Arabs and Palestine, which he later visits, and his final career choice of studying Arab culture as an anthropologist.

Linda Walbridge and T. M. Aziz (2000), writing about the recently arrived south Iraqi Muslim population, articulate well that building a community is a strategy of survival for these poor refugees who were victims of the Gulf War in 1991. They contrast these immigrants with the well-established Lebanese community in the same area, who distance themselves from these 'boaters' from another region of the Middle East.

Thus identity is found to be a mixture of the changing identities found in the Middle East, the existing and changing perceptions, stereotypes, and stratification in the United States, and the variables found among the different communities and individuals, such as generation, region of origin, religion, urban or rural background, education level, occupation, and economic status.

Now we will examine historical and cultural background factors to identity and community organization, in two sections: first the major immigration periods, and second, specific social factors, such as religion, family, and political organization.

THE IMMIGRATION EXPERIENCES

The Early Settlers

Many empires affected the roots and identities of today's Arab peoples. Arabs lived in the Arabian Peninsula for many years before the rise of the Islamic state in the seventh century under the Prophet Muhammad. At that time, religion, politics, and society were strongly linked, and the Islamic empire spread the Arabic language and Islam religion across North Africa into Europe and into other areas of Asia, where they were incorporated to different degrees into the local customs of many diverse groups.

Formation of subcommunities and identities. It is important to realize, as they do, that Arab Americans form many distinct subcommunities, both abroad and in the United States. The relationships among the groups depend on their historical, social, and geographic relationships and on current events in the Middle East. The usual basis for group identity is, first, the family, then religion, region, economic class, and generation. The importance of religion is seen in that immigrants from the same village in Lebanon nonetheless live in separate areas of Detroit, divided by their religious identities (Aswad 1974). Other examples are seen in the situation in Dearborn between the established Muslim Shiite Lebanese community and the recently arrived Iraqi Muslim Shiite community. The Iraqis settled in Dearborn because the Lebanese Muslim Shiite community was there; however, social, educational, and generational differences between the two communities produced tensions. Most Iraqis reported more affinity with

the Yemeni, who also came from rural, quasi-tribal backgrounds (Walbridge and Aziz 2000).

Despite their differences, immigrants from the Arab world share many characteristics: the Arabic language, art and music, food, myths, and social customs such as patrilineal descent, extensive and intensive kinship obligations, and values of hospitality. They also share a long history.

When and why did they come? According to some authors, among the belongings of Columbus was a book by the Arab geographer al-Idrisi, which mentions that eight Arabs sailed from Lisbon and landed in South America, long before 1492. We are also told that Istephan, a Moroccan Arab, served as a guide to the Spanish explorers and conquerors in what is now Arizona and New Mexico in the 1500s (Mehdi 1978). Arabs had been the major navigators and geographers for centuries before Portuguese and Spanish explorers. Andalusia, in southern Spain, was part of the Arab and Islamic empires for 800 years until the Inquisition in 1492, in which Spain expelled the majority Muslim and minority Jewish populations. The exchange of knowledge, technical and navigational skills, and personnel among these Mediterranean cultures, which settled the Americas, is well documented.

Although a few Arabs settled in the United States during the nineteenth century, the first sizable wave arrived between 1900 and 1914. The overwhelming majority were Lebanese Christian from the Syrian-Lebanese region, and until the mid-1950s identified themselves as Syrians. Although some were urbanites, the vast majority were middle peasants from rural villages or towns. A "middle peasant" is one who is neither a large landlord nor a sharecropper but who owns a medium amount of land and works it with his family. This emphasis on family work assisted them in opening up family-run businesses in the United States.

Because Lebanon was the home of the early group, as well as providing a continuous stream of immigrants, we will discuss it in some detail. Lebanon is a mountainous region, with villages and regions that have a high degree of autonomy and well-developed networks of rural markets. The entrepreneurial skills of the Lebanese, both in the mountains and especially in the coastal communities, are well known. There are 17 religious communities, primarily Christian and Muslim, which are like ethnic groups due to their high degree of endogamy, or marriage within the group, as well as social and economic networking within these communities (see Chapter 15). Quotas in the Lebanese parliament represent these religioethnic communities. They are not as economically stratified as the ethnic or racial groups in the United States; however, in the nineteenth century, when Lebanon was part of Syria, the French colonists, who ruled Syria-Lebanon for a century, used a divide and rule strategy by patronizing a minority, the Maronite Roman Catholics, to control a majority of Muslims. France gave the Catholics privileges, introduced the cash crop and silk into their regions, placed them in government positions, and greatly influenced their culture to a higher extent than that of other Lebanese. The politicization and racialization of religious and ethnic groups in the Middle East by Europeans still affect members of the Arab American communities. These same complicated rules of divide and rule were part of the ruling strategy used by the British and later the Americans in Palestine and Israel.

The mainly Christian immigrants left Lebanon for several reasons. The cash crop gave them the financial means to emigrate (Owen 1992). On the other hand, competition from the Japanese and Chinese silk trade, which had increased after the opening of the Suez Canal in 1856, and a deadly mulberry tree disease, forced many who had specialized in silk which decreased subsistence products, to find other sources of income and migrate. In addition, the population had increased due to cash cropping, where young hands formed a cheap labor pool.

These processes occurred throughout the world with other crops such as cotton in Egypt, rubber in Java, and many crops in Africa. Thus, the result is a larger population, fewer subsistence crops, and less trade. Some populations reacting to these stresses, such as those in Egypt, just became poorer; some, such as the Lebanese, were able to migrate.

Increased military conscription and taxation by the deteriorating Ottoman Turkish administration added to the economic pressure to leave (Khalif 1987). Some Christians reported that the violence of the earlier Christian-Muslim conflicts of the mid-nineteenth century also affected their decisions (Suleiman 1999). The stories of wealth in America, and in many cases the enticements of steamboat agents and the influence of Western missionary educators, were part of the many push-pull factors of early migration (Naff 1985).

Many members of the early communities were single men who wanted to earn money and return to Lebanon; others feared persecution if they returned. They often disagreed regarding the situation back home, but usually kept their politics to themselves (Suleiman 1999). Eventually, they brought their wives, and started families. Rouf Halaby (1985) reports that by 1919, 70,000 immigrants supported nine Arabic-language newspapers. Journals such as *The Syrian World*, published in English in the late 1920s, featured poetry, fiction, essays, and prose. In 1923, the well-known Lebanese immigrant Khalil Gibran published *The Prophet*, which became one of the all-time best-selling books in the United States.

What were their occupations? Many started as peddlers and became small shop owners, industrial workers, and farmers.[3] Later, some enterprises grew into large businesses such as the Haggar and Farah companies. In the early days women worked in the family stores and in factories and textile mills.

American nationalism during and after World War I emphasized assimilation. Restrictive immigration quota laws such as that of 1924 favored European migration and curtailed immigration from Third World countries. Those who spoke a different language were made to feel ashamed, and the melting pot ethos affected the second generation. Consequently, much of the native literature and history was systematically ignored.

Communities adapted differently according to the character of the region in which they settled. The Lebanese Catholics who settled in the southern United States, where Baptists were dominant and plantations and lumber provided the economic base, entered the small-shop niche, a niche not available to poor blacks and stigmatized by upper-class whites. This niche was also entered by Italians, Chinese, and European Jews. All were marginalized from the major economic and political arena. However, in southern Texas, the Catholic Lebanese who had arrived by way of Mexico, spoke Spanish and became a more accepted integrating link between upper-class Anglos and lower-class Mexican Catholics (John 1987). In the northeastern United States bordering Canada, where their French might have been useful, they worked as unskilled laborers in textile mills, because the Quebecois scorned the Lebanese usage of French (Hoogland 1987). Thus, each area affected adjustment differently.

The immigrants and their descendants describe these early migrants as hardworking, and they certainly were. However, it is important to be aware that Europeans and other non-black immigrants were able to "make it" to the middle class, but American blacks did not because of the politics of racial inequality in the United States. In this period, the "not quite white" Lebanese Christians identified with the dominant European Christians if possible. Muslims identified as being Lebanese or Syrians, or Muslims, but had the disadvantage of there being few Muslims in America, a reason many give for the limited numbers of Muslims in the early immigrant groups. They feared a loss of religious faith among their children. Catholic

Christians, meanwhile, often sent their children to Catholic schools, another institution of assimilation. Muslims usually sent their children to the public schools. Names were often anglicized by both Christian and Muslim immigrant groups. Muhammad became Mike, Adnan became Ed, and Salwa became Sally. During the depression years, there was little immigration, and often the Lebanese returned to Lebanon because of unemployment.

Changes in Immigration after World War II

Following World War II, the demographics of Arab immigration changed. Although the Lebanese continued to come, other Arab countries were represented, and there were other reasons for coming. The new geographic areas for Arab emigrants included Palestine, Yemen, Egypt, Iraq, Syria, and Jordan.

A new and influential group of professional members began to arrive in the 1960s. They were part of the "brain drain," a term referring to the expertise lost to the country that provided the professionals' initial education. Changes in the United States immigration laws in the 1960s allowed increased immigration from Third World countries, favoring professionals and family members. Many professionals married Americans and became more secular; their children usually had dual cultures. Yvonne Haddad and Adair Lummis (1987) mention that many of the professionals were influenced by Western ideas before they came. Since the 1980s members of the professional cadre married primarily from their home countries.

During the post–World War II period, there was an increase in the number who were pushed or fled political unrest, oppression, and wars. Palestinians began their diaspora, due to the occupation of their lands by Israel in the wars of 1948, 1957, and 1967, and emigration continues today. The 1980s witnessed major immigration because of warfare in Lebanon and Iraq. A civil war in Lebanon occurred in the 1970s and 1980s. In particular, the Israeli invasion of Lebanon in 1982, which included the bombing of Beirut and occupation of south Lebanon, resulted in massive immigration to the United States. Many came to the Detroit area and other regions where they had relatives. Iraqis fled the Iraq/Iran War in the 1980s and the Gulf War in the 1990s. A sizable number continues to wait in Jordan hoping to immigrate. Struggles between South and North Yemen increased their numbers in the United States. The often-violent treatment of Christian Copts in Egypt in the last twenty years has forced many, primarily of the professional class, to immigrate to the United States. The availability of professionals is useful to social service organizations such as ACCESS in Dearborn, which has numerous doctors, psychiatrists, psychologists, and social workers from the Middle East who are bilingual. This was not the case even twenty years ago.

We mentioned earlier that Arab Americans have experienced a sense of hostility in the United States during the last forty to fifty years— primarily because of the struggle over oil and the political power of Israel and its supporters in the U.S. Congress. Movies and TV in particular portrayed Arabs as villains and terrorists. One could not find an Arab "good guy" in the movies (Shaheen 1984; Stockton 1994). As negative stereotypes of Arabs, Islam, and Arab culture increased, Arab Americans were forced to reconsider their identity, to defend it and reconnect with it, or shun it. New organizations were created to help Arab Americans cope.

In the 1960s, America was also changing. The Civil Rights Movement and cultural protests of the African American communities increased ethnic revival among other communities. In the Arab American community, one could hear, "We want to be called Muhammad instead of Mike in public." It had always been Muhammad in the home.

The social upheavals have also brought a rigor and revivalism of Islam found in the movements of the Middle East. The recent influx of educated Arabs into the United States has increased the literary and artistic character of those local communities that have large populations. Definitions of ethnicity often use art, dance, literature, poetry as well as food in their celebrations and ethnic fairs.

Ethnic identity may change in relation to a number of factors: foreign relations between the communities abroad, the size of the local community here, relations with other American ethnic groups, and how other Americans identify them. For example, if there are few in an area, they may seek out others from their general area or state of origin such as Lebanon. If they are a large community, they may separate on their own, and have their own newspapers, clubs, or organizations. Thus, ethnicity is a fluid variable and, of course, we need to remember that persons have multiple identities, changing them according to the circumstances. Christian Arabs may emphasize their religion, light-skinned Arabs may stress phenotypic characteristics, and those who know English or are educated may identify with other Americans in their economic class.

Factors of religion, such as Islam, or phenotypic characteristics, such as dark skin, rank some Arabs low in the American stratification scheme. Thus, a dark-skinned Muslim from a village who has low educational or occupational skills may experience more discrimination than, for example, an educated light-skinned Christian doctor. However, if the former remains in his community or with other minorities, which share class or education similarities, and does not interact with the dominant Anglo-Americans, he may feel everyday discrimination less than someone in a more affluent predominantly Anglo suburb who is separated from others like him. A person living in a "Little Arabia" also has the psychological satisfaction of speaking his own language and living with those who share his values.

Going to school and college often presents

major challenges to a person's identity. Nabeel Abraham discusses his paths of identity as a youth when his family moved to Detroit.

> My formerly placid world erupted into four confusing and contradictory worlds of home, school, neighborhood and the Arab Community of Dix. Reflecting on this period, I now realize that Mother attempted to preserve a Palestinian Arab Muslim identity at home, while my brothers and I found ourselves increasingly pulled into other worlds, each demanding unconditional conformity. I subconsciously spent the better part of the next three decades trying to keep a strict separation between my home and these worlds. To my chagrin and embarrassment, one world would inevitably collide with another, home with school, neighborhood with home. [2000:430]

Abraham also writes about his increasing intellectual and political interest and identity with the Arab world during his college years and further identity challenges as he studies the Arab world and becomes interested in working there.

SOCIAL DIMENSIONS OF ORGANIZATION AND IDENTITY

Religion

Religion is a major social and cultural boundary among Arabic-speakers in the Middle East, and it has been important in the location of today's Arab American communities. It is the most difficult boundary to marry across, unlike skin color or language or geographic area. Thus, even though there is a considerable amount of identification, organization, and marriage within state, city, and village communities, there is little marriage between Muslims and Christians from the same region. For example, there are fewer stigmas for a Lebanese Muslim to marry a Pakistani or Yemeni Muslim than to marry a Lebanese Christian from his or her village, and vice versa. A Christian Arab could marry an Italian Christian with less negative social pressure from his or her family than a Muslim Arab

from his or her village. Due to the rules of patrilineality, in which the children assume their father's lineage, there are more restrictions on Arab women's marriages than those of Arab males. It is assumed that children will take the father's religion and identity. Consequently, if a Muslim Arab woman wishes to marry "out," strong pressure is placed on the future husband by her family to convert to Islam. It is also easier for a Muslim male to marry a non-Arab Christian than an Arab Christian. In the same fashion, many more Arab Catholics marry Catholics than Protestants, and again it is easier for males to cross these lines than for females.

Many religious groups are represented among American Arabs. Lebanon itself has 17 religious groups, which are all represented. The major Christian Catholic groups include the Maronite (Lebanese), Chaldean (Iraqi), Assyrian (Syrian), Melkite (Lebanese), and Coptic Catholics (Egyptian). Christian Orthodox sects include Byzantine, Antiochian and Syrian Orthodox (from Lebanon, Syria, and Palestine), and Coptic Orthodox (Egyptian). Since the Europeans drew the boundaries of current states in 1922, religious communities and country boundaries do not coincide.

Among the Muslim sects, the largest are the Shi'a from Lebanon and, most recently, southern Iraq, as well as Yemen. It should be noted that the Shi'a are a numerical minority in the Middle East but are a numerical majority, for example, in Detroit, where there are five or six Shi'a mosques. Linda Walbridge (1996), in a sensitive study of the differences among these mosques, comments that at times it is a "battle of the headscarves," referring to how much hair should be covered by women's apparel. The Sunni, the vast majority of Muslims in the Arab world, are also building mosques in the United States, and it should be noted that their number rose after the 1960s, when many professionals and upperclass Muslims came to the United States. Some of this group were secular and often married Americans, and thus their children are often not associated with the mosque as much as the earlier or later arrivals. The Druze, an offshoot of Shi'a Islam, also have active societies in the United States.

Recent and historical conflicts in the Middle East may cause some Arab Americans to minimize socialization with members of another religion. The civil war in Lebanon during the 1970s and 1980s had many dimensions, especially economic, but it also involved military conflicts between religious communities in the Middle East. This caused tensions among Arab communities in the United States. However, because these religious communities usually settle in different areas, the opportunity for interaction was minimized. Although separateness has existed between the Muslims of the African American and Arab American communities, relationships between some groups, both nationally and within communities, has been increasing. Islam is the fasting-growing religion in America.[4]

The church and mosque are major institutions for socialization of young people, and a place to select marriage partners, as well as for religious education. In addition, Christian Arabs, especially Catholics, often attend religious schools. Recently, there has been a major push by Muslims across the United States to open Islamic schools. With the rise of Islamic movements in the Middle East, many Muslim communities in the United States have been faced with stricter adherence to Islamic customs and laws. Yvonne Haddad and John Esposito state that a primary question facing Muslims in America is whether or not to live Muslim lives in a non-Muslim territory. "Islamic law provides the ideal blueprint for society delineating what can and cannot be done" (1998:5). Islamic law was formed in the early centuries of Islamic history and was affected by nineteenth-century reformers who called for reinterpretations. Much of this law pertains to family law, and thus informs everyday decisions.

Mohammed Khan (1998) found that immigrants may adhere more strictly, while those born and raised in the United States are more open, inclusive, and less sectarian. A Lebanese recounts to Sally Howell his dramatic rebirth to Islam while attending a revivalist meeting in which the major Lebanese religious leader, Shaykh Fadlalla, spoke. It was in part a reaction to the political events in Lebanon and Iran.

> I went there and I saw six hundred people, seven hundred people. Everyone I knew was there. And I saw . . . Fadlallah. I knew him since I was a little boy cause he used to be a sheikh right in my neighborhood. For me, that was like I was sleeping and somebody woke me up from a dream. I came back home. I put the Quran in front of me and I started crying. . . . I had forgotten how to pray. I forgot everything. [2000b:251]

Those who came before 1950, during the period of strong assimilationist pressures in the United States, had outwardly accepted many American customs, including Anglo names, marriages to non-Muslims, and often the loss of Arabic. When communities were influenced by immigrants from countries experiencing a reemergence of Islamic laws and Islamic dress codes during the past 30 years, and when the communities experienced growth so that there were many mates to choose from, the push toward assimilation was weakened. The emergence of African American ethnicity since the 1960s raised ethnic pride among other groups as well, Arabs and Muslims among them (Aswad and Bilge 1996:1–14). In fact, the two tendencies of assimilation and revitalization produce conflicts in some areas, especially over female behavior. Still, one sees family and friendship groups where women wear a variety of dress, from Islamic scarves and dresses to typical American, and no one seems to notice.

The role of the clergy is important, due to the significance of religion as an ethnic boundary. They assist members in adjusting to the United States and its laws. They become enforcers of Islamic laws at times, and can be crucial in cases of, for example, domestic violence. The author has heard women complain that some imams side with men. Men have been heard to explain that America is a country that favors women: "they get the custody and welfare." As we discuss the family and women's roles, we will find that members of the family may often be a woman's best protector, and thus complicated dramas between the clergy and the family may be played out.

Early Christian groups sponsored newspapers, some of which continue today, and an increasing number of Islamic newspapers in both Arabic and English are currently published. More recently, there are cable TV and video programs in Arabic, as well as Internet Web pages, which access religious and other programs in the United States and in the Middle East.

In sum, religion is one of the most important organizing factors of identity among Arabs in America; the other is kinship and the family. Sometimes the two are blurred. Of course, Islam was founded in an area of the world where patrilineal rules were customary and it reinforced them. However, among the Arab Christians, family organization is also patrilineal and in most customs parallels that of Muslims. Let us now discover how patrilineality and extended connectivity characterize the Arab family, resembling more the structure of families of Indians and other Asians than that of Euro-Americans.

Family and Kinship

The family is the major social institution in the Middle East, as well as among Arab Americans. Arab families are very gregarious, and visiting among members is expected and frequent (Aswad 1974). In all societies, there are many family types, which may vary among lines of socioeconomic background and individual histories and experiences. However, the ideology and practice of family rules, in Arab culture, include being large and extended, based on intimate social reciprocal relations, and patrilineally organized.

Arabs share with other cultures, such as Indian, Chinese, and Mediterranean, the institution of large families. Socialized as a member of a group rather than in a nuclear family is a basic difference from many American families. The importance of the honor of the family and the rules and obligations of etiquette are opposed to the bilateral, nucleated form of traditional American families, and even more so from the increasingly one-parent households in the United States. An emphasis on individualism and individual space in many American families is also at variance with the idea of shared obligations, hierarchies of power, and living styles of Arab Americans. Andrew Shryock describes the interdependence and cohesiveness:

> The cohesiveness of Arab immigrant families derives, instead, from a worldview in which human society beyond the realm of kinship, filled as it is with nonrelatives, strangers, and unreliable institutions is construed as amoral and fundamentally dangerous, as a domain in which one's resources and affections are drained away from the "loved ones, in-laws, and kin" . . . who truly deserve them. [2000:588]

He adds that this solidarity comes at a price, by discouraging individual pursuits. While "amoral" may be too strong a word, pressures are put on young people to socialize with their relatives, not to live alone, and not to travel far away to college. A youth may ask, "You went to the movies or shopping with your cousins, not your friends?" The Arab youth will respond, "They are my friends." Arab youth may criticize the restrictions but usually come to terms and carry on the teachings of their parents. Life stories bring out the importance of these connections. Lara Hamza writes, "My emerging divided identity troubled and confused me. My family life increasingly appeared 'foreign' to me, and I longed to fit in with the majority, to fully assimilate into the American lifestyle. This displaced loyalty made me resent not only my Arab heritage but, much to my later misfortune, my family life as well" (2000:392). In her essay, she also discusses confusing perceptions of gender roles and arranged marriages in a culture of individual choice. Only later did she come to appreciate some of the values of a philosophy that emphasized the unit rather than strictly individual choices.

In cases of mixed marriages, however, this struggle of dependence and connectivity versus independence and space often presents a problem for the parents and mixed messages for the children. The degree of patriarchy, discussed below, also presents problems.

For most immigrants, the family has been influential in migration. Kinship and marriage are of primary importance in the system of chain migration, whereby one member in a family immigrates to the United States and establishes himself, then brings other members of the family, and so on, until many relatives have settled together. Mohsen Amen says with pride that he has brought 36 families here since he migrated in the 1970s (Howell 2000a:243). Relatives often provide the economic basis for an enterprise such as operating or owning a store. In ethnic villages, members can name 200 or more relatives who live around them. These family networks often span many continents, providing links to Africa, Latin America, the Caribbean, and the United States (Aswad 1974). Members of the professional or upper classes who may not have these large kin groups establish for themselves a circle of friends who operate in a similar fashion regarding visiting and hospitality.

What are patrilineality and patriarchy? *Patrilineality* is being a member of one's father's descent group at birth, sharing many special rights and obligations with this group. This is true for daughters as well as sons. It is not to say that one's mother's descent group is not important; in fact, migration may increase dependence on the mother's kin. However, one traces his or her descent through the father and is known to the community as a member of that line of descent; one's behavior reflects favorably or unfavorably on that name and group, not just

upon oneself or merely on one's parents. In tribal cultures of the Middle East, this group will defend one's life. The honor or reputation of the family acts very much as a mechanism of social control.

In the United States, where the dominant pattern of descent brought from Europe is bilateral descent, kinship is constructed through both mother's and father's lines, is more flexible, and identity is often characterized by whom you live close to, whom you see, or other circumstantial variables. Under situations of industrial capitalism, individual achievement is stressed more than family or group achievement. In meeting someone in the United States, people often ask, "What do you do (referring to an occupation)?" Arabs usually want to know what family and region you are from.

Males have more privileges in patrilineal systems—plural wives, more inheritance, fewer restrictions on sexuality, and the like—and more power is given to males, especially elders, in the patriline. This is called *patriarchy*. Regarding male privilege, Shryock comments, "Most Arab immigrants accept as a fact of life that a man should be head of the house, even if 'the mother is the neck that moves the head'" (2000:586). Fathers are treated with respect in public and often get preferential treatment at home. What is often seen by the outsider is the modesty or public restriction placed on some females. The patriline also pressures the behavior of men, often influencing their occupations and marriages.

Patrilocality, in which men live near their fathers and brothers after marriage, reinforces male power, since women then are separated from their own patriline. Cousin marriage within the patriline, a tradition in the Middle East, mitigates against this separation. It is important to distinguish patrilineality (male descent) from patriarchy (male power). Most Americans see only the latter. In the United States there is also patriarchy despite the ideology of equal partnership and it certainly exists in the corporate and governmental structures. Arab women in the Middle East and in the United States are challenging many of these rules, forming groups to seek protection from abuse and entering public roles more often.

Patrilineality explains restrictions placed on female sexuality, in order to preserve the legitimacy of the male line. This is especially true where lineages are a major form of organization, such as India and the Middle East. One does not find such restrictions on females in matrilineal systems, where the identity of the child is obvious. It is also less in countries where other institutions such as age grade or associations offer alternative forms of organization, such as in sub-Saharan Africa. The emphasis on female virginity before marriage helps to explain the double standard where dating is tolerated for males but not for females. When placed in the American situation where dating is common for mate selection, this area of inequality between brother and sister becomes obvious. Immigrant parents, fearful of American styles of behavior, especially dating, alcohol, and drugs, usually feel the need to protect their daughters even more than in their countries of origin. Several interesting books and studies have been written on Arab American women caught in the tug of war between American "freedoms" for women and the restrictive nature of their homes.[5]

Shryock (2000:583–584) notes that in the Arab world gender segregation in public is the norm and breaks down in the privacy of the home or with close friends. In America, however, things change, but he says: "Still, among all recently arrived immigrants groups, cross-sex socializing is encouraged only among close kin" (2000:584). In U.S. suburbs there are often fewer relatives or neighbors to depend upon to enforce cultural norms. Instead, cultural groups are formed around religious institutions or regional or friendship groups that help to reinforce these customs. It is also within these groups that socializing and marriages are encouraged.

In Western societies, there is a stereotype that women in the Arab family have very little power. However, women get their status and reputation in the same way as men, through their patriline. For example, Pakistan's prime minister, Benazhir Butto, followed her father to power, as did Indira Gandhi, both from patrilineal systems. (So far there has been no woman president of the United States.) In Arab society, women continue to belong to their patriline after they marry, thus preserving protection from their brothers and fathers. It is important to distinguish patrilineality (male descent) from patriarchy (male power).

In her discussion of negative stereotypes of Arab women in the Western media, Suad Joseph (1999:165) comments.

> In particular, the veil, polygyny, clitoridectomy and honor crimes are all represented as evidence of backwardness of Arab society. We know that polygyny is pre-Islamic and widespread through the world and practiced by a very small percentage of Arab males, clitoridectory is not Islamic, rather is primarily an African sub-Saharan ritual, practiced in few Arab countries. Honor crimes also are not uniquely Islamic or Arab, they are features of Mediterranean culture, found in Spain, Italy and Greece.

Fadwa el-Guindi (2000), in an engrossing and comprehensive analysis of the head scarf (*hijab*) and veil, challenges Western and feminist ideas, and indicates how dress serves to establish a woman's identity and status, as well as its use in the contemporary political context.

Due to the extended nature of family relations, women are a major part of social configurations and have most of the power in running the household and raising children. They negotiate their positions through sons, brothers, fathers, education, alliances with other women, gossip, and other mechanisms of power. Families influence marriages to a great extent, especially in the case of girls. In extreme cases, where it is felt that a youth is violating family rules, he or she may be sent "back home" for a mate (Aswad

1991). The differences between Christian and Muslim rules is notable in the lack of polygyny among Christians, but most rules are the same. Divorce is viewed as unfavorable among all Arabs and the rate found by John Zogby (1990) was 4.5 percent in the 1980 census, although recently it is said to be rising. Due to the importance of the family, children, and patrilineality, homosexuality is viewed with extreme disfavor, stigmatized, and usually not discussed.

Caring for the elderly is a requirement in the ideology of the extended family. When the author inquired regarding a retirement home, Arab Americans in Dearborn reacted with negative surprise, saying it brought "shame." Later, some added, "Well, if it was right in the middle of the community, maybe." It is the exceptional family that does not care for their elderly in the home. In describing the needs of elderly Muslims, Mary Sengstock (1996) found a discrepancy between the subjects' perceptions of their own needs and the perceptions of the (generally non-Arab) interviewers. The interviewers' vision of the elderly was that of being surrounded by family members and community, yet the elderly reported being "lonely." They missed the members of the extended family who were abroad.

Mental illness is stigmatized in many cultures, and it is in Arab culture. Organizations like ACCESS provide assistance to families and consumers, and communities are slowly beginning to discuss it publicly. As with other family-oriented cultures, mental illness is often accommodated or hidden but not discussed in public.

There are some problems when Arab family customs meet with the American legal system. They will be discussed later.

Language

Language, folktales, literature, and expressions are primary ethnic identifiers. There are numerous dialects in the Arab world, and likewise among the immigrants. There is also a standard Arabic used in the media, so people from different parts of the vast region can understand each other, except for certain vocabulary. In the Detroit area, language distinguishes the Arab communities from the Chaldean community. Chaldean is a dialect of Aramaic, which, like Arabic, is a Semitic language. Many Chaldeans also know Arabic because they grew up in Iraq, but the language, as well as the origin of their homeland in northern Iraq, creates a major social boundary for the community. Many non-Arab or non-Chaldeans confuse the two communities, usually calling them both Arab. And, indeed, some bilingual Chaldeans regard themselves as Arabs, which definitely confuses those outside the communities.

There are also certain languages that are liturgical languages, spoken by priests in churches but not by the communities outside the church. These include the Coptic language in the Egyptian Coptic church and Assyrian in the Lebanese Maronite Roman Catholic church. In places such as Michigan, which has a large Arab community, Arabic had a first-language status early on and changed to become an ethnic language, understandable primarily to that community (Rouchdy et al. 1992). With recent increases in immigration, the first-language status has returned for many, and many are learning standard Arabic in school.

Arabic is not a language easily learned by Americans, and although it has become a major language in the international realm, few Americans know it compared for example with Spanish or French. Preserving the language is seen as important to most immigrants, since many members see its loss as a major loss of the culture. Aleya Rouchdy (forthcoming) reports that as many of the young study classical (or standard) Arabic in schools, it revives their sense of pride in the language and increases their desire to learn the colloquial. But they also know the importance for their future of learning the dominant language of the host country. For students who immigrate not knowing English, it can be very problematic and bilingual programs in areas of Arabic speakers have had some successes. The negative perceptions and racism of non-Arabs in the local communities have often made it difficult to fund such programs.

Literature has been an equally vital part of the Arab communities. The immigrants brought books and stories from the Arab world, but until recently, there has been little translation into English. Newspapers, magazines, and books are now being translated. American Arab writers in the diaspora such as Naomi Shihab Nye, Larry Joseph, Antoun Shammas, Gregory Orfalea, and others have become popular. The worldwide proliferation of cable TV has infused local communities with new and old movies, cultural events, and news analysis from the Arab world. New immigrants and increased technology have revived an interest in Arabic so that the older generations are pushing the younger to learn Arabic. Mosques have been active in offering Arabic courses and Koranic studies. At the university level, classes at Wayne State University, for example, have risen from 20 students in the 1980s to 200 today (Rouchdy, personal communication).

Overall, the challenge of maintaining the Arabic language increases as generations pass. Generational problems, caused by lack of knowledge of the parental language, are well known in all immigrant cultures. Parents and children alike often feel the culture is diminished if the language is not known. Young people have been heard to comment, "My parents say I am not an Arab because I don't know the language well." Children may understand but not speak or read. Parents may be disappointed and children may feel inadequate in meeting their parents' expectations, or embarrassed in front of their friends. Feelings of alienation can arise on many levels. This is especially true in mixed marriages, where children often don't know the language. On the other hand, if parents don't know English well, and children do, there can be cases of "role reversal," where children gain power over

parents in some situations, or are called on to translate.

The predominance of Arabic as a language in a working-class community where Arabic is a primary language may present a problem in school success for some children. Some of their parents may not have had much schooling in Arabic as well. Organizations such as ACCESS have instituted tutorial programs to assist the children and offer classes for adults (Aswad and Gray 1996). Rouchdy (forthcoming) comments that because of classical (or standard) Arabic, Arabs have a great respect for the language and they do not feel it is subordinate, fundamental to its revival and maintenance in the community. The increased importance of Islam and the Qu'ran would assist this in Muslim communities.

Economic Class and Occupations

We mentioned earlier that many Arabs began by peddling and running grocery stores and dry goods stores, and then changed to other occupations (Sengstock 1974, 1996). The entrepreneurial spirit is still strong. Zogby indicates that 25 percent are involved in retail trade, substantially higher than the 16 percent of the U.S. population (1990:15). In small shops, one doesn't need much English to get by, and, more importantly, family networks, family labor, and community networks make it possible to start a business with few financial resources. The patrilineal and extended nature of the family, plus long hours of work, have assisted many in becoming successful. Those without the networks might suffer a handicap unless they have professional training. Gary David (2000) notes that the Chaldeans in Detroit trace their history of small store ownership back to Iraq, where Muslims couldn't have liquor licenses and Christians could and did. In Toledo and Detroit, however, Muslims do own liquor shops. The nature of kin corporations is seldom understood by other ethnic groups, such as those in whose neighborhoods they operate. Stores become an area of interracial and cross-cultural interaction, and there may be conflicts, some of them violent. The community becomes suspicious and resentful as the foreign culture profits from the community, then leaves without doing anything to economically help the neighborhood residents (Shadroui and Bahhur 1995).

In the upheavals in Detroit in 1967 and in Los Angeles in 1988, stores were burned. In Detroit, Chaldean merchants work behind bulletproof glass cages and often complain of the feeling of separation from their customers (David 2000). While teaching in Detroit, the author has heard complaints by local non–Middle Eastern people of feeling exploited by Arab American merchants, their lack of cleanliness, food that wasn't fresh, rude behavior by clerks, talking in Arabic or Chaldean, and their encouraging liquor consumption. Also, they feel that the merchants should hire them. Of course hiring local persons undermines the cheap labor of family members. Merchants who have stayed in areas without hostile feelings do, in fact, find ways of serving their communities by having clean stores, extending credit, having good merchandise, offering food to the poor, hiring local people, and contributing to scholarship funds. Comments by the local community are very positive for these merchants.

When large sums of money are necessary for start-ups, trust and reciprocity are primary, and those are found in the family and community, seldom outside it. Store owners working in another culture work many hours, only trust each other for sums of money to start up businesses, and owe each other. They also run the risk of murder. More than 80 shopkeepers have been shot over the years in Detroit. Store owners prefer to operate within their cultural enclaves, such as Atlantic Avenue in Brooklyn or Warren Avenue in Dearborn, where there are 125 shops of every nature (Abraham 2000). Sometimes saturation occurs, and stores and restaurants go out of business. Even within a large city such as Detroit, a saturation point emerges, and store owners encourage their children to go into other professions (David 2000; Sengstock 1999). Gas stations are another niche for Lebanese and Yemeni. Factory work was a major tradition in Detroit. With mechanization, such work has become less available; however, the high wages still attract immigrant workers if they are able to find networks offering them jobs.

There are also an increasing number of large and wealthy Arab American entrepreneurs who trade with the Middle East. This class lives in spacious homes in the suburbs, and in most cases supports Republican politics in their communities. As a group, they have not been studied as much as smaller entrepreneurs have. Likewise, the richer members of the kin corporations, who have gone into wholesale and ownership of large food businesses, and have benefited from the small shopkeepers, have received less attention. The brain drain, begun in the 1960s, still continues, along with the increased education of generations raised in the United States, so that today many Arab Americans are in the professional class. Significant groups include doctors, lawyers, engineers, and professors. Among women in the Detroit area, a major profession of choice is pharmacy. Zogby (1990:18) found that Arab Americans are twice as likely as the national population to be health professionals and more likely than most other ethnic groups. They are less likely to be in agriculture, forestry and fishing, construction, and manufacturing

Thus there is an increasing wealth differential within the Arab American communities, with a growing class of wealthy professionals and large entrepreneurs, a growing middle class, and a growing poorer, less skilled class of rural immigrants. These last may, in fact, be quite poor. Zogby's (1990) study found a higher disparity among household and economic status for Arabs than for other ethnic groups. For example, they have a high mean income, yet have a larger percentage below the poverty level than the U.S. population as a whole and than those of European background. On the other hand, he found that Arab Americans as a whole, both native-born and immigrant, had a higher educational achievement level than the U.S. population as a whole and many European groups. His figures represent populations before immigrants reacting to the recent Iraqi war migrated to the United States. This corresponds to a greater poverty level among those most recently arrived and those who are American-born (p. 10).

Arabs and the American Legal System

Fatima al-Hayani found that many Arabs and lawyers feel the law can be and is sometimes negatively biased against Arab Americans, and she reports that many lawyers avoid jury trials because they feel "juries are affected by the negative depiction of Arabs" (1999:80). Particular areas that present a lack of understanding of social customs involve custody cases and Arab parenting practices and domestic violence. Racial profiling and targeting by police are also felt by the community and lawyers. Cases of child abuse obviously do occur in the community; however, sometimes misunderstandings of language and custom have resulted in children being taken from their homes, so that people fear involvement with the law. Adoption is not a policy of patrilineal families because it is the close patrilineal relatives who care for children in cases of abuse or death of parents, with the result that few Arabs become foster parents. Some Muslim children were put in Christian foster homes where Muslim dietary laws and religious beliefs were not observed.

In the area of domestic violence cases, al-Hayani (1999) found that cultural problems result in the police either ignoring the wife's complaints or overreacting. Al-Hayani contends that this is due to the erroneous view that wife-beating is acceptable Arab behavior and custom, a reason found in police statements for non-

involvement (p. 74). In some cases women are afraid that their husbands will be deported and thus do not report mistreatment. The author is often asked about how domestic violence in the Arab community is compared to that in other groups in the United States. Without comparable statistics, I would venture that the stress of adaptation to another culture will certainly present increased chances for violence among immigrant families. On the other hand, it seems through observations that the nature of the extended family attempts to limit the degrees of violence. There are usually relatives or others who will try to intervene in cases of violence. They feel this is their obligation. This intervention scheme is not part of many American two-parent families or neighbors, who feel they "should mind their own business." Community organizations such as ACCESS and ACCSSA in the Detroit area have been extremely important as culture brokers and in assisting members of the Arab community with these kinds of problems (Aswad and Gray 1996).

Welfare is another area in which American laws may affect family relations. The author found that it provides an alternative means of support for some women who are mistreated. However, the majority use it to improve their power in the home by gaining access to revenue. The additional money is useful to men also and although it may give women more decision-making power, it does not always cause conflicts. Changes in the laws, which require recipients to find jobs or take classes after two years, will probably affect those families in which husbands do not want their wives to work outside the home. In some poor communities, women also do not have the educational level or linguistic ability to hold jobs or even to apply for job training (Aswad 1999).

Several recent pieces of legislation have particularly affected Arab immigrants. The Anti-Terrorism and Effective Death Penalty Act was signed into law in 1996. Under the terms of this law, "the government may deport an immigrant even if she or he has not committed any crime" (Moore 1995). A new court, called the removal court, hears the government's deportation cases behind a cloak of secrecy. Kathleen Moore, a legal scholar, states that "while the court accepts the government's case against a suspected alien terrorist, the defendant receives an unclassified summary of the evidence against her or him, without showing the identity of informants, which could be used in preparing a defense" (p. 85). This ruling affects other immigrants as well, but targets Arabs in particular (Hajjar 2001:8). Moore contends:

> The members of Congress constructed this law and the legal classification of "alien terrorist" on which it turns, for apparently irreconcilable ends: first to combat terrorism by removing so-called aliens, and finding permanent residents and citizens who support or are affiliated with a "terrorist" organization, and second, to preserve a modicum of due process guarantees, including very limited summary disclosure of classified information, for "alien" targets of deportation proceedings. Congress effectively has formed a new class of persons who are defined as deportable merely because of their association with a disfavored group, not because they personally committed a terrorist act. [p. 84].

After the World Trade Center and Pentagon attacks, the USA Patriot Act of 2001 [H.R. 3162] was passed by Congress and signed by President Bush with limited opportunity for debate or committee hearings. Many civil rights groups are concerned that civil rights could be compromised in the rush to put in place new laws to fight terrorism. The issues regard longer detention, increased use of secret evidence, expanded federal electronic surveillance authority, and deportation for acts vaguely defined as "terrorist." In a summary of issues affecting Arab Americans, Anton Hajjar (2001:10) quotes U.S. Senator Russ Feingold (D-WI) on October 25, 2001:

> Although the Administration requested the power "to detain immigrants indefinitely," including legal permanent residents, "the Senate bill required the detainee to be charged with a criminal or immigration violation within seven days or release the detainee." Under the Act, however, "immigrants who win their deportation cases could continue to be held if the Attorney General continues to have suspicions." . . . The bill also continues to deny detained persons a trial or hearing where the government would be required to prove that the person is, in fact, engaged in terrorist activity." [H.R. 3162, Sec. 411–412]. "To avoid deportation, the immigrant is required to prove a negative; that he or she did not know, or should not have known, that the assistance would further terrorist activity . . . Groups that might fit this definition could include Operation Rescue, Greenpeace and even the (Afghan) Northern Alliance . . ." [H.R. 3162, Sec. 411–412]. Feingold concludes "In the wake of these terrible events, our government has been given vast new powers and they may fall most heavily on a minority of our population who already feel particularly acutely the pain of this disaster" (p. 11).

There has also been extensive discussion on political processes in the Arab world. In a 1999 article examining inaccuracies and myths in the media and in some academic circles, Joseph finds that political processes in the Arab world are described as undemocratic, and as part of Islam. They are frequently represented as resistant to modernity, blindly traditional, hierarchical, and opppressive to women. Little is shown of the relationships that occur, especially kinship and family systems, even under conditions of authoritarian regimes. Arabs and Arab Americans are becoming more critical of these regimes.

Ethnic and Political Organizations

Arab identity was revitalized in the United States after the 1967 Arab-Israeli War, in which Israel occupied the territories of Lebanon, Syria, Egypt, Jordan, and Palestine. These events motivated the establishment of organizations that cut across religious and regional groups, such as the Association of Arab-American University Graduates (AAUG) in 1967. The National Association of Arab Americans (NAAA) was founded in

1972, and the Arab-American Anti-Discrimination Association (ADC) was formed in 1980 to combat discrimination. Later, the Arab American Institute (AAI) was founded in 1985 to increase Arab American participation in the U.S. political system. At a national level these organizations have attracted notable speakers at their conferences. These organizations were very active after the September 11 attacks.

On the local level in concentrated communities, before the September attacks, there had been increased protests and celebrations of political events. For example, thousands of Lebanese (most from south Lebanon) held a two-week celebration in the streets after Israel quit its occupation of south Lebanon in June 2000. One of the largest villages in occupied territory, Bint Jbail, has perhaps 3,000 members living near Dearborn, Michigan. Visits to Lebanon were planned immediately. During the same month, 200,000 persons attended an annual Arab street festival. Sally Howell (2000a) documents how traditional art, dancing, and food are revitalizing the communities. She also notes that the vast number of artists using Middle East themes are recent immigrants from the Arab world.

Music is another venue that has energized and expanded in the Arab American community, and Anne Rasmussen discusses how "memory and imagination are fueled by musical style, textual references, and regional repertoires" (2000:568). And it has become an ethnic occupation. In an attempt to be more inclusive and less insular, some organizers are including performances of other ethnic groups, such as Hispanic and African American.

In sum, there are strengths and challenges for Arab Americans, in their varieties of adaptations and identities. Their identity has been acutely challenged, especially Muslim Arab Americans, since the terrorist attack on September 11, 2001. The event has also caused Christian communities to further distance themselves from Muslim communities. One particuliar strength that Arab Americans have is the sense of family and kinship with reciprocal relationships, connectivity, and generosity. Those visiting the communities feel a vibrancy and enthusiasm. However, strains are also apparent because of its misfit with much in the United States, especially the legal and religious systems, where Arabs feel discrimination and misunderstanding. Yet kin relations form their own adaptations, thereby contributing to American values, as do other minority ethnic groups. Kin corporations have been beneficial in some economic niches, yet may be restraining in other areas since time and finances must be shared. Arab Americans are considered both white and non-white by U.S. culture and are thus often marginalized. They feel they are a Third World minority, yet do not receive the benefits of special programs. This is especially true for the poor. Muslims feel that their religion is attacked in the United States.

A special area of discomfort for Arab Americans has been the political realm due to tensions between the United States and the Middle East, the U.S. support of Israel, the Gulf War, and tensions between groups within the Middle East. They feel their history has not been given exposure in textbooks. But as they increase in numbers, Arab Americans and Muslims will undoubtedly become more evident in the U.S. ethnic, social, and political arenas. Their culture, religion, and literature will continue to add to the culture as much as their food has.

NOTES

1. For studies in this area, see John Zogby (1990) and Michael Suleiman (1999).
2. Some social service organizations for Arabs, such as ACCESS in Dearborn, Michigan, receive funds under the title of "special populations."
3. Read the stories by Alixa Naff (1985) and Nabeel Abraham (2000) to see how they went back and forth between peddling and shopkeeping.
4. See Yvonne Haddad (1991) and Yvonne Haddad and John Esposito (1998).
5. See examples of these life stories in Barbara Aswad and Barbara Bilge (1996), Evelyn Shakir (1997), Joanna

Kadi (1994), and Nabeel Abraham and Sameer Shryock (2000).

REFERENCES CITED

ABRAHAM, NABEEL. 1989. Arab-American marginality: Mythos and praxis. In *Arab Americans: Continuity and Change*. Baha Abu-Luban and Michael Suleiman, eds. Pp. 17–43. Belmont, MA: Association of Arab-American University Graduates.

———. 2000. To Palestine and back. In *Arab Detroit*. Nabeel Abraham and Andrew Shryock, eds. Pp. 425–462. Detroit: Wayne State University Press.

ABRAHAM, SAMEER, and NABEEL ABRAHAM, eds. 1983. *Arabs in the New World*. Detroit: Center for Urban Studies, Wayne State University.

AJROUCH, KRISTINE. 1999. Family and ethnic identity in an Arab-American community. In *Arabs in America*. Michael W. Suleiman, ed. Pp. 129–139. Philadelphia: Temple University Press.

AL-HAYANI, FATIMA AGHA. 1999. Arabs and the American legal system: Cultural and political ramifications. In *Arabs in America*. Michael Suleiman, ed. Pp. 69–73. Philadelphia: Temple University Press.

American Anti-Discrimination Committee (ADC). 1986. *Report on the FBI and Civil Rights of Arab Americans*. Washington, DC.

ASWAD, BARBARA C., ed. 1974. *Arabic-Speaking Communities in American Cities*. Staten Island, NY: Center for Migration Studies Press.

———. 1992.The Lebanese Muslim community in Dearborn, Michigan. In *The Lebanese in the World*. Albert Hourani and Nadim Shehadi, eds. Pp. 167–188. London: I. B. Tauris.

———. 1998. Arab American families. In *Families in Cultural Context*. Mary Kay DeGenova, ed. Pp. 213–238. Mountain View, CA: Mayfield.

———. 1999. Attitudes of Arab immigrants toward welfare. In *Arabs in America*. Michael W. Suleiman, ed. Pp. 177–191. Philadelphia: Temple University Press.

ASWAD, BARBARA C. 1991. Yemeni and Lebanese Muslim immigrant women in southeast Dearborn, Michigan. In *Muslim Families in North America*. Earle Waugh, Sharon McIrvin Abu-Laban, and Regula Burchkardt Quershi, eds. Pp. 256–281. Edmonton: University of Alberta.

ASWAD, BARBARA C., and BARBARA BILGE, eds. 1996. *Family and Gender among American Muslims*. Philadelphia: Temple University Press.

ASWAD, BARBARA, and NANCY GRAY. 1996. Challenges to the Arab-American Family and ACCESS (Arab Community Center for Economic and Social Services). In *Family and Gender among American Muslims*. Barbara C. Aswad and Barbara Bilge, eds. Pp. 223–241. Philadelphia: Temple University Press.

CAINKAR, LOUISE. 1991. Immigrant Palestinian women evaluate their lives. In *Family and Gender among American Muslims*. Barbara Aswad and Barbara Bilge, eds. Pp. 41–58. Philadelphia: Temple University Press.

CHARARA, HAYAN. 2000. Becoming the center of mystery. In *Arab Detroit*. Nabeel Abraham and Andrew Shryock, eds. Pp. 401–424. Detroit: Wayne State University Press.

DAVID, GARY. 1999. *The Mosaic of Middle Eastern Communities in Metropolitan Detroit*. Detroit: United Way Community Services.

———. 2000. Behind the bulletproof glass: Iraqi Chaldean store ownership in Metropolitan Detroit. In *Arab Detroit*. Nabeel Abraham and Andrew Shryock, eds. Pp. 151–178. Detroit: Wayne State University Press.

EISENSENLOHR, CHARLENE. 1996. Adolescent Arab girls in an American high school. In *Family and Gender among American Muslims*. Barbara C. Aswad and Barbara Bilge, eds. Pp. 250–270. Philadelphia: Temple University Press.

EL-GUINDI, FADWA. 2000. *Veil: Modesty, Privacy and Resistance*. New York: Berg Press.

ELKHOLY, ABDO. 1966. *The Arab Moslems in the United States: Religion and Assimilation*. New Haven, CT: College and University Press.

HADDAD, YVONNE Y., ed. 1991. *The Muslims of America*. New York: Oxford University Press.

HADDAD, YVONNE Y., and JOHN L. ESPOSITO, eds. 1998. *Muslims on the Americanization Path?* New York: Oxford University Press.

HADDAD, YVONNE, and ADAIR LUMMIS. 1987. *Islamic Values in the United States*. New York: Oxford University Press.

HAJJAR, ANTON GEORGE. 2001. *Selected Legal Issues Affecting Arab Americans*. Washington, DC. The Division of United States Studies of the Woodrow Wilson Center. (Manuscript).

HALABY, ROUF. 1985. Introduction. In *Arabic Speaking Immigrants in the United States and Canada*. Muhammed Sawaie, ed. Lexington, NY: Mazda.

HAMZA, LARA. 2000. Coming home. In *Arab Detroit*. Nabeel Abraham and Andrew Shryock, eds. Pp. 391–400. Detroit: Wayne State University Press.

HOOGLUND, ERIC, ed. 1987. *Crossing the Waters*. Washington, DC: Smithsonian Institute Press.

HOWELL, SALLY. 2000a. The art and artistry of Arab Detroit. In *Arab Detroit: Detroit*. Nabeel Abraham and Andrew Shryock, eds. Pp. 487–514. Detroit: Wayne State University Press.

———. 2000b. Finding the strait path. In *Arab Detroit*. Nabeel Abraham and Andrew Shryock, eds. Pp. 241–278, Detroit: Wayne State University Press.

JOHN, SARA E. 1987. Arabic speaking immigration to the El Paso area, 1900–1935. In *Crossing the Waters*. Eric Hooglund, ed. Washington, DC: Smithsonian Institution.

JOSEPH, SUAD. 1999. Against the grain of the nation–the Arab. In *Arabs in America*. Michael Suleiman, ed. Pp. 256–271. Philadelphia: Temple University Press.

KADI, JOANNA, ed. 1994. *Food for Our Grandmothers. Writings by Arab-American and Arab Canadian Feminists*. Boston: South End Press.

KHALIF, SAMIR. 1987. The background and causes of Lebanese/Syrian immigration to the United States before World War I. In *Crossing the Waters*. Eric Hooglund, ed. Pp. 17–36. Washington, DC: Smithsonian Institute Press.

KHAN, MOHAMMED A. MUQTEDAR. 1998. Muslims and identity politics in America. In *Muslims on the Modernization Path?* Yvonne Y. Haddad and John L. Esposito, eds. Pp. 87–104. New York: Oxford University Press.

MEHDI, BEVERLEE TURNER. 1978. *The Arabs in America, 1942–1991*. Dobbs Ferry, NY: Oceana.

MOORE, KATHLEEN M. 1999. A closer look at anti-terrorism law: *American-Arab Anti-Discrimination Committee* vs. *Reno and the Construction of Aliens' Rights*. In *Arabs in America*. Michael Suleiman, ed. Pp. 84–99. Philadelphia: Temple University Press.

NABER, NADINE. 2000. Ambiguous insiders: An investigation of Arab American invisibility. *Ethnic and Racial Studies* 23(1):37–61.

NAFF, ALIXA. 1985. *Becoming American: The Early Arab Immigrants' Experience*. Carbondale: Southern Illinois University Press.

OWEN, ROGER. 1992. Lebanese migration in the context of world population movements. In *The Lebanese in the World*. Albert Hourani and Nadim Shehadi, eds. Pp. 32–40. London: I. B. Tauris.

RASMUSSEN, ANNE. 2000. The sound of culture, the structure of tradition. In *Arab Detroit*. Nabeel Abraham and Andrew Shryock, eds. Detroit: Wayne State University Press.

ROUCHDY, ALEYA, ed. 1992. *The Arabic Language in America*. Detroit: Wayne State University Press.

___. forthcoming. *Language Contact Phenomena in Arabic: Variations on a Sociolinguistic Theme*. Richmond, UK: Cuzon.

SAMHAM, HELEN. 1999. Not quite white: Race classification and the Arab American experience. In *Arabs in America*. Michael W. Suleiman, ed. Pp. 207–226. Philadelphia: Temple University Press.

SEIKALY, MAY. 1999. Attachment and identity: The Palestinian community of Detroit. In *Arabs in America*. Michael W. Suleiman, ed. Pp. 25–38. Philadelphia: Temple University Press.

SENGSTOCK, MARY. 1974. Iraqi Christians in Detroit: An analysis of an ethnic occupation. In *Arabic Speaking Communities in American Cities*. Barbara C. Aswad, ed. Pp. 21–38. New York: Center for Migration Studies.

___. 1996. Care of the elderly within Muslim families. In *Family and Gender among American Muslims*. Barbara C. Aswad and Barbara Bilge, eds. Pp. 271–297. Philadelphia: Temple University Press.

SHAHEEN, JACK. 1984. *The TV Arab*. Bowling Green, OH: Bowling Green State University Popular Press.

___. 1999. *Chaldean Americans*. New York: Center for Migration Studies.

SHADROUI, GEORGE, and RIAD BAHHUR. 1995. *Arab American Merchants and the Crisis of the Inner City: Cleveland—a Case Study*. Washington, DC.: Arab American Institute.

SHAKIR, EVELYN. 1997. *Bint Arab: Arab and Arab American Women in the United States*. Westport, CT: Praeger.

SHRYOCK, ANDREW. 2000. Family resemblances. In *Arab Detroit*. Nabeel Abraham and Andrew Shryock, eds. Pp. 573–610. Detroit: Wayne State University Press.

SHRYOCK, ANDREW, and NABEEL ABRAHAM. 2000. On margins and mainstreams. In *Arab Detroit*. Nabeel Abraham and Andrew Shryock, eds. Pp. 15–38. Detroit: Wayne State University Press.

STOCKTON, RONALD. 1994. Ethnic archetypes and the Arab image. In *The Development of Arab-American Identity*. Ernest McCarus, ed. Pp. 119–154. Ann Arbor: University of Michigan Press.

SULEIMAN, MICHAEL W. 1988. *The Arabs in the Mind of America*. Brattleboro, MA: Amana.

———. 1999. Introduction. In *Arabs in America*. Michael W. Suleiman, ed. Pp. 1–24. Philadelphia: Temple University Press.

WALBRIDGE, LINDA. 1996. Sex and the single Shi'ite: Mut'a marriage in an American Lebanese Shi'ite community. In *Family and Gender among American Muslims*. Barbara C. Aswad and Barbara Bilge, eds. Pp. 143–154. Philadelphia: Temple University Press.

WALBRIDGE, LINDA, and T. M. AZIZ. 2000. After Karbala. In *Arab Detroit*. Nabeel Abraham and Andrew Shryock, eds. Pp. 321–342. Detroit: Wayne State University Press.

ZOGBY, JOHN A. 1990. *Arab America Today: A Demographic Profile of Arab Americans*. Washington, DC: Arab American Institute.

13

LATIN AMERICA AND THE CARIBBEAN

Ronald Kephart

University of North Florida

Latin America and the Caribbean provide one of the richest tapestries of human biological, linguistic, and cultural diversity on earth. Anyone who travels to any part of this vast region witnesses an astonishing variety of skin colors, hair forms, facial features, and overall body types. They see dark-skinned, very curly-haired "African"-looking people in Port-au-Prince and Bridgetown; brown-skinned East Indians with straight black hair in Port-of-Spain and Georgetown; Europeans with light skin and thin straight or wavy hair in Buenos Aires and Bogotá; and Native American peoples with eyes and hair similar to those of many Chinese in La Paz and Cuzco.

At the same time, travelers may suspect that many of the people they encounter appear to be a "mixture" of some or all of these groups, and they are correct. In Latin America and the Caribbean, people from all major parts of the world—the only exception being indigenous Australians—came together and mixed to form what is essentially a new, modern human gene pool. Those who pay close attention in their journey are also impressed by the variety of languages and cultural practices they encounter. Of course, they may hear any number of standard European languages, such as Spanish, English, Portuguese, French, and Dutch. But they may also hear languages as diverse as Jamaican Creole English, which has been spread worldwide by Bob Marley and other performers of reggae music; Garifuna, spoken in Central America by descendants of "black Caribs"; and Quechua, the imperial language of the Incas at the time of the Spanish Conquest. And this is only the tip of the iceberg, because hundreds of languages are spoken all over Mexico and Central and South America. People are often surprised to learn that only about one-third of the population of Bolivia speak Spanish as their first language: the other two-thirds are native speakers of Aymara, Quechua, or other Native American languages, as well as Japanese, German, and the like.

Similarly, observers may see diverse cultural practices, such as Mayans blessing the corn seed; or Carriacouans honoring their African ancestors by setting out a special table of food called the *saraka*; or perhaps a group of Aymara offering a llama fetus to the *awki* spirits. And, if the travelers are North Americans, they may be puzzled by the fact that people who they would call "black" in the United States are not always called "black" in the Caribbean and in Latin America. We shall return to this important observation later.

Obviously, this is a vast topic, and organizing it into a coherent and meaningful presentation is not easy. I have chosen to follow anthropologist Charles Wagley, who, for broad purposes of discussion, suggested that we think of the New World in terms of three basic "culture spheres": Euro-America, Indo-America, and Plantation America (Wagley 1957). Euro-America consists of those regions whose present-day populations consist primarily of people of European descent: Argentina and Uruguay, for example. The population of Indo-America is primarily of Amerindian or mixed Amerindian-European origin. Plantation America consists of the regions to which the majority of African slaves was imported, and is distinguished by populations that are largely of African and African European descent. It is important to note that the borders between these "culture spheres" do not always correspond to national borders. For example, southern Brazil, like neighboring Argentina and Uruguay, is essentially Euro-America, whereas northern Brazil with its strong African presence is clearly part of Plantation America.

In this chapter I shall be concerned primarily with Plantation America and Indo-America, which I prefer to call Amerindian America. After making a few comments about the Amerindian background and Native American notions of ethnicity, I shall move on to survey Latin America and the Caribbean. Here and there, I will focus more sharply on particular problems in ethnicity or "race," as illustrations of the broader generalizations.

Before going on, I want to make explicit a couple of crucial assumptions underlying my presentation. As indicated within this textbook, it has been convincingly demonstrated that "race," as it is popularly constructed, is a part of the *folk model* of Western culture, and that an *analytic model* of human biological variation does not support this folk model (see Chapters 1, 2, and 4). Folk models are culturally constructed descriptions and explanations of the natural and social worlds that do not depend for their validity on the scientific method. Folk models typically take their validity from an authority, often a religious authority of some sort. In contrast, analytic models are products of scientific investigation, which is grounded in empirical evidence, hypothesis formation and testing, replicability, and so on. As we shall see, the folk models of "race" we find in Latin America and the Caribbean are sometimes quite different from that of the United States. We shall also see that the differences between the U.S. folk model and the Caribbean and Latin American folk models sometimes cause conflicts, especially in the areas of culture contact.

As indicated in this textbook (see Chapter 4), the standard anthropological notion of *ethnicity* is self-identification centered on belonging to a group whose members believe that they share a history, culture, and language. People who differ biologically may belong to the same ethnic group, and people who are biologically very similar may belong to different ethnic groups. In other words, within their analytic models, anthropologists recognize ethnicity and biology as independent variables, which may or may not correlate. We shall see examples of both these situations in Latin America and the Caribbean.

People, however, in constructing their folk models, frequently confuse or conflate notions of "race" and ethnicity, resulting in the *essentializing* of ethnicity. Ethnicity is then viewed as resulting from *descent*, rather than from *enculturation* (Gil-White 2001). For example, in the United States *Hispanic* is sometimes referred to as a "race" rather than an ethnic group. And then, when *Hispanic* is taken to be an ethnic group, there is the question of whether it represents a single ethnic group or many: Are Cubans the same, ethnically, as Argentines, just because both speak Spanish? From our perspective, of course, the answer must be "no."

When it seems appropriate, I offer some statistical data on various ethnic groups of Latin America and the Caribbean, taken from the *Encyclopaedia Britannica* online (www.britannica.com).

THE COLUMBIAN EXCHANGE

The biological, linguistic, and cultural diversity found throughout Latin America and the Caribbean is, ultimately, the result of one fateful event in the history of humankind. On October 12, 1492, Christopher Columbus and his followers, in their three tiny sailing ships, arrived at an island in the region that is now called the Bahamas. Columbus's arrival set in motion a process that is sometimes referred to as the "Columbian exchange," the transfer of peoples, languages, and cultures (both ideal and material) between the Old World and the New (Crosby 1972).

Most evidence suggests that the New World was peopled initially by migrants from northeastern Asia who traveled across the Bering Strait during periods of intense glaciation, between about 20,000 and 10,000 years ago. The date for the earliest of these migrations is in dispute, but about 10,000 years ago the melting Ice Age glaciers ended the possibility of walking from Asia to North America. And, by around 8,000 years ago, and probably earlier, the descendants of these early migrants had reached the far corners of the vast territory at their disposal. Physically, the indigenous peoples of the Americas were relatively homogeneous, suggesting that the number of original migrants was small. Similar outward physical appearance, and the very high frequency (100 percent in many populations) of type O blood throughout the Americas, attest to the probability of a genetic "founder's effect" at some point in the past.

The relative lack of physical differences among Native American peoples is dramatically counterbalanced by the cultural and linguistic differences we find among them. In Latin America and the Caribbean, people are organized into bands subsisting on foraging like the Ciboney, Siriono, and Ache. We also find societies subsisting on a mix of foraging and horticulture, such as the Yanomama of Venezuela and Brazil and the Shuar (Jívaro) of Ecuador. Historically, there were chiefdoms based on more intensive horticulture, such as the Taíno of the Greater Antilles. And finally, before and at the outset of the Columbian exchange, complex, stratified, state societies based on intensive agriculture had developed, the most well known of which are the Maya of Central America, the Inca of the central Andes, and the Aztec of Mexico.

Presently, there are no Native American states; most indigenous peoples now find themselves, for better or worse, integrated into European-dominated state societies as peasant farmers, like the Maya or the Aymara of Perú and Bolivia. Many have also come to be part of an ever-growing rural and urban proletariat. Relatively few have managed, like some Yanomama communities, to maintain their traditional lifeways.

Linguistically, we find literally hundreds of indigenous languages across the Caribbean and Central and South America. The relationships between and among these languages are often difficult to determine, but linguists generally agree that most belong to one of the following groups (O'Grady et al. 2001):

- *Uto-Aztecan* (Mexico, northern Central America, southwestern United States). Many speakers of these languages, especially Nahuatl and related languages, are descendants of peoples who were organized into states at the time of the arrival of Europeans. Other related languages include Hopi and Papago (Tohono O'odham) of the southwestern United States.
- *Mayan* (southern Mexico, Guatemala, Belize). Varieties of Mayan include Yucatec, Kekchi, Tzeltal, and Tojolabal. Most present-day Maya are peasant farmers.
- *Andean-Equatorial* (the Andes, other parts of South America). Many scholars place Aymara and Quechua into this group; however, the two languages are not historically related, and their exact relationship is contested. The Inca used both as imperial languages: languages related to Aymara had been replaced by Quechua just before the Spanish arrived. Arawak is still spoken in northern South America; and Guaraní, along with Spanish, is an official language of Paraguay.
- *Ge-Pano-Carib* (South America). Languages in this group include Carib (Guyana, Surinam, French Guiana, and also formerly the Lesser Antilles) and several minority languages of Perú, Brazil, and Argentina.
- *Macro-Chibchan* (northwestern South America, southern Central America). Languages include Cuna (Panama and Colombia), Warao (Venezuela), and some others.

It seems that among most of these Native American groups, classification of people is based on linguistic and cultural factors rather than on any visible biological traits that might qualify as "racial." For example, the Yanomama, who are forager-horticulturalists of the upper Orinoco (northwestern Brazil and southern Venezuela), classify people into *Yanomama*, those who speak the Yanomama language and who also know how to operate within Yanomama culture; and *nabuh*, those who don't. Kenneth Good (1991), who studied the Yanomama for 15 years, reports that at first his hosts called him "Ghost Tongue," meaning that he was like a child who had not yet learned to talk, until he was able to speak Yanomama fluently. In the Andes, similar concepts exist. For example, the native people living around Tupi, Perú, speak a language they call *Jaqaru*, from the words *jaqi* "human being" and *aru* "speech"; they also refer to themselves as *Jaqaru* people. Thus, their concept of self-identity is tightly bound up with their language and culture (more about this later). Similarly, Ecuadoran Quechua speakers call their language *runa shimi*, "human language" (Carpenter 1983).

In the Columbian exchange, the Old World received from the New World many new foods, including corn, potatoes, tomatoes, peanuts, squash, beans, chili peppers, manioc (yuca, or casava), and turkeys. Some of these have become supremely important in the Old World. (Who can imagine Italian cooking without tomatoes, the Swiss without chocolate, or the Irish without potatoes?) Indeed, there are now parts of the Old World, especially in Africa, that could not feed their people without the New World crops they gained from the Columbian exchange. And finally, we might mention the millions of people around the world addicted to the nicotine in tobacco, a New World product.

In the reverse direction, the Old World contributed important food and work animals (cattle, horses, pigs, sheep, goats, donkeys), although these were frequently more destructive than beneficial. But perhaps the most consequential Old World product introduced to the New World was sugarcane. Its arrival and subsequent development into one of the New World's most important tropical exports had enormous consequences for the human component of the Columbian exchange and for European constructions of "race."

The consequences of the Columbian exchange included the decimation and outright disappearance of many Native American groups, the oppression and exploitation of others, and their reduction to marginalized existences within newly formed state societies dominated by Europeans. In addition, over 10 million Africans were enslaved and transported to the New World to provide labor for the growth and expansion of European capitalism. Later, when these African slaves were freed, people of other diverse origins—India, Indonesia, the Middle East, and even Africa—were brought, sometimes by enticement, sometimes by trick-

ery, sometimes by force, to take their place. All the while, Europeans themselves came to labor, not always willingly and not always as members of an elite ruling class. The Caribbean, along with some parts of the South American mainland (especially northeastern Brazil and the Guianas), provided the settings for the first large-scale experiments in tropical plantation agriculture. These in turn provided the model, and also much of the investment capital, for the development of the Industrial Revolution in Europe and the United States (Williams 1994).

Meanwhile, the Columbian exchange also gave the peoples of the New World something they had never had before: an all-inclusive name for themselves. Columbus, mistakenly thinking that he had sailed all the way to the Indies, called the people he encountered *indios*, or "Indians." Before this, they had defined themselves according to their languages and cultures; after Columbus, they were defined by the Europeans as people from a place they had never heard of, much less visited. Over time the word became, like *nigger* in the United States, a term of deprecation, and most Native American peoples today prefer to be called by their ethnolinguistic name (Aymara, Maya, etc.), or even *indígena*, meaning "indigenous." Further confusion arises when we realize that in a number of places, such as Guyana and Trinidad, there are people who really qualify as "Indians," that is, people from India. They are often referred to as "East Indians" to distinguish them from Native Americans.

As we continue our survey, we shall see that the fates of Native American peoples were different in different areas of Latin America and the Caribbean. They all but disappeared from the Caribbean islands, but in other areas, such as Mexico, Guatemala, Paraguay, and the Andean countries, they remain significant, although often abused and exploited, segments of society. And in some regions, notably the drainage basins of the Amazon and Orinoco Rivers, small populations attempt to hang on to their traditional ways of life in the face of the ever-increasing challenges of "development" and their ever-intensifying integration, willing or not, into the economies of state societies.

AMERINDIAN AMERICA

Amerindian America consists primarily of those regions that had relatively large and dense populations of indigenous peoples at the time of Columbus's arrival. These regions include Mexico, the interior of Central America, and the cordillera of the Andes. Indigenous peoples in these regions had created complex societies with all the characteristics of states: a ruling elite; a full-time priesthood that managed the state religion; a bureaucracy; a middle class of tradespeople and artisans; and an army to defend and, if possible, extend the dominion of the state. At the time of the Spanish Conquest, the Aztecs of Mexico and the Inca of the central Andes had created empires, in the latter case an empire of greater extent than the Roman Empire. A smaller but equally complex state society, that of the Maya, had existed previously in Central America and Mexico, but this society had collapsed and the Mayans whom the Spanish encountered were living in essentially village-scale communities.

The dense populations of these Amerindian states ensured that relatively high indigenous populations would survive to be incorporated into the new Spanish domains, and it is indeed in these areas that we find the highest percentages of people claiming Amerindian status, as shown in Table 13-1. In contrast, we will see later that the percentages of Amerindians in the

Table 13-1. Amerindian populations, as percentage of total population, for selected countries of Amerindian America

Country	Bolivia	Perú	Guatemala	Ecuador	Mexico
Percent	55	54	43	40	30

countries making up Plantation America approach or equal zero.

The incorporation of Amerindians into the newly created Spanish domains typically entailed becoming a *peón*, or serf, on a plot of land granted to the conquerors and their allies by the Spanish rulers as part of the *encomienda* system. Under this system, the Spanish *encomenderos* had rights to the land and its produce, as well as to the labor of the Amerindians, who came attached to the land as a result of their *reducción* (reduction) to territories determined by the colonizers. The labor extracted was typically in the form of mining, as well as public works such as road building and the like, in addition to their obligation to grow crops portions of which were owed to the landowners. Hence, in many places the system closely resembled the feudalism that was disappearing in other parts of Europe at the time but that was still a vital part of the Spaniards' worldview.

As we have seen, Columbus called the people he encountered *indios* (Indians) because he thought that he had reached the Indies. From the beginning, most of the Spanish who came to the New World were males, looking for adventure and wealth; they were not averse to finding mates also. The term *blanco* refers to people of European descent, who are generally rare in the highlands, except in the larger towns and cities, where they are concentrated. In Spanish, the word *mestizo* was applied to the offspring of matings, and it is still used to refer to someone who is a mixture of European and Amerindian descent. *Mestizaje*, the mixing of Amerindians and Europeans, has been the subject of differing ideologies over the centuries. As Martínez-Echazabal (1998) reports, the Amerindians were at first viewed as even more savage and less human than Africans, and it was thought by some that mestizaje would result in the disappearance of "civilized" European society in the Americas. As time went on, however, mestizaje became part of an ideology centered on creating new societies distinct from the European

Table 13-2.   Mestizos as percentage of total population, for selected countries of Amerindian America

Country	Honduras/ El Salvador	Nicaragua	Venezuela	Mexico
Percent	90	69	67	60

colonizers, as in the ideology of *la raza* (the race) in Mexico.

The result of mestizaje is that in those areas that had the largest indigenous populations, populations that were not obliterated early on, mestizos form a very significant portion of the population, as illustrated in Table 13-2.

The Andes

In the Andes, the distinct, yet interdependent, nature of these three groups is especially well illustrated by the relationships among the indigenous Aymara and their mestizo and blanco neighbors. The Aymara were, before the Spanish arrived, one of the principal groups in the Inca Empire. There is evidence that a language related to Aymara was used by the Incas in their first territorial expansion along the Andean chain; just prior to the conquest, however, Quechua had replaced Aymara as the imperial language.

Today, the Aymara live in scattered communities throughout a large region surrounding Lake Titicaca, where Perú, Bolivia, and Chile come together, a region known as the *Altiplano* ("high plain"). They occupy an ecological niche similar to that of the Sherpas of Tibet, with crops and animals adapted to high altitudes and extreme daily fluctuations in temperature. Frequently, in the preconquest Andes, indigenous peoples used an "archipelago" system of farming, under which each family had plots at different altitudes from near sea level to around 12,000 feet. This allowed families access to foods and products from tropical, temperate, and alpine environmental niches. After the Spanish imposed their limited European view of land-

holding, sometimes in rather arbitrary and capricious ways, this spectrum of resources was closed off to most native groups, with far-reaching consequences for their subsistence strategies.

Before the Bolivian revolution of the 1950s, many Aymara were essentially serfs in a feudal system that tied them economically as well as physically to large haciendas owned by the Spanish-speaking elite. Presently, they typically work their own small plots, planting especially potatoes (some 2,000 varieties) and quinoa using traditional technology such as the foot plow. They also herd sheep and camelids, and they keep guinea pigs for food as well. Many Aymara have gone beyond this, however, by integrating themselves into the national marketing system connecting rural producing areas to consumers in the cities.

To supplement their income, they may also hire themselves out to work on the mestizos' land, which is usually better than their own, more marginal land. The *misti*, as the Aymara call them, need the Aymara's labor; the Aymara need the misti's cash. There is a certain element of mutual distrust and deprecation: the Aymara may feel that the misti are too lazy to work their own land; the misti complain about the Aymara's addiction to cycles of fiestas. For the Aymara, the sponsorship of a fiesta, which impoverishes the sponsors but at the same time binds them to their community, is an essential part of adult life; for the misti and the blancos, the fiestas are distractions from work.

The Aymara have maintained many elements of their traditional religion, and these are practiced alongside Roman Catholic rites and ceremonies: the Catholic god and saints must be invoked, as well as the *awki*, the spirits of high places, and also the ancestors. Crucially, both the Aymara and the misti need the "white" priest for the blessing of the Virgin. The Aymara sometimes use the term *viracocha* to refer to the white elites, a reference to the light-skinned, bearded god who in Andean myth was supposed to have gone away and then returned in the form of the Spaniards.

Because many people in the highlands are mestizos who may be physically indistinguishable from the indios, the principal markers of "Indian-ness" are language and clothing. The colorful and "exotic" clothing worn by "traditional" Native Americans in the Andes frequently represents costumes originating in medieval Spain that were imposed by the Spanish in the years of the conquest. In any case, to "pass" into mestizo society Native Americans may need only to put on European-style clothes and speak Spanish instead of Quechua or Aymara (Buechler and Buechler 1971; Hardman 1981).

The Aymara language is co-official with Quechua and Spanish in Bolivia; Quechua is co-official with Spanish in Perú. These languages, plus Guaraní, which is co-official with Spanish in Paraguay, are the only Amerindian languages that enjoy official status in Latin America and the Caribbean.

PLANTATION AMERICA

Plantation America encompasses primarily the tropical and subtropical lowland areas that were best suited for the development of export agriculture based on tropical cultigens. This includes most of the Caribbean islands, as well as the low-lying Caribbean coastal regions of Central and South America: the Guianas (Guyana, French Guiana, and Surinam) and northern Brazil. The distinguishing demographic feature of these areas is the large presence of the descendants of African slaves, people who in censuses are referred to as "black" or "African." Figures for some selected countries of Plantation America are given in Table 13-3.

These regions, especially the French and British territories in the Caribbean, are special in any discussion of "race" and ethnicity. It was here that Europeans put into place the system of

Table 13-3. People reported as "black," as percentage of total population, for selected countries of Plantation America

Country	Haiti	Barbados	Antigua	Grenada
Percent	95	93	91	85

using enslaved West Africans as labor for the production of sugar and other tropical staples. However, this in itself might not have produced the virulent racist ideology that developed, had not the particular social, political, and economic context for this contact been as it was. Within this context, a tiny European "white" elite dominated a much larger African "black" population that was enslaved and that existed as chattel property of the white elite. The labor of this enslaved work force was directed toward the planting, cultivation, and processing for export of tropical staples, with sugarcane being especially important.

The virtual elimination of native peoples in these areas, itself a principal reason for the importation of African slaves, had another consequence: the early and continued reproductive mixing of Europeans and Africans, usually the outcome of mating between African females and European males. The result was an ever-growing population of people of mixed descent, whose status was, historically, often ambiguous. At first, it was thought that the offspring of such matings would be infertile, like mules, the product of mating between horses and donkeys. Hence, they acquired the labels *mulato* (Spanish and Portuguese) and *mulatre* (French), words that found their way into English as *mulatto*; the corresponding process is sometimes referred to as *mulataje*, on a parallel with *mestizaje*. Of course, any photograph of a crowd of people in Cuba or Brazil refutes the notion of their infertility! Table 13-4 lists the percentages of people classed as mulatto or "mixed" for selected countries of Plantation America.

An additional aspect in this context was the rise of empiricist science in the West, and with it

Table 13-4.   Percentages of mulatto or "mixed" for selected countries of Plantation America.

Country	Martinique	Dominican Republic	Cuba	Brazil
Percent	94	73	51	40

Table 13-5.   The sentence "I am eating" as translated into three creole languages of Plantation America

Language	Subject I	Progressive (am)... -ing	Verb eat
Jamaican Creole	Mi	a	nyam
Haitian Creole	M	ap	manje
Papiamentu	Mi	ta	kome

the quest to classify things, living and nonliving, into orderly categories. In the eighteenth century, Linnaeus' classification of humans into four types (white, black, red, and yellow) was soon followed by Blumenbach's revision, which included a fifth category (Ethiopian, Caucasian, Mongoloid, American, and Malay; see Chapter 3). Soon, schemes with many more categories were proposed. But, most importantly for our topic, in addition to the supposed physical traits that separated these alleged "races," mental and behavioral traits were also concocted, mostly out of the clouded pseudo-scientific world of European ethnocentrism. In this way, an ideology of racial inferiority, inferiority represented not just in physical features but also in linguistic and cultural forms, developed as a means of justifying slavery, or at least making it easier for the slave owners and traders to live with the system they had created. As the historian and former prime minister of Trinidad and Tobago Eric Williams (1994), argued, in this view African slavery was the cause of the racist ideology that developed in its support, not the other way around.

One outstanding feature of Plantation America is the predominance in nearly every country of a *creole* language. Creole languages take the majority of their vocabularies from one of the European languages (Spanish, Portuguese, French, English); they take their syntax, to at least some degree, from the West African languages spoken by the slaves who were brought to the New World. Linguists disagree about the details of their genesis, but it is clear that they are the product of the linguistic creativity of West Africans. Table 13-5 provides a sample sentence in the Jamaican (English) Creole, Haitian

(French) Creole, and Papiamentu, a Spanish/Portuguese Creole spoken in parts of the Netherland Antilles. All the words are from European languages except the Jamaican *nyam*, which is from a West African language. The structure, which in all cases places the progressive marker corresponding to the English *-ing* suffix before the verb, is typical of a number of West African languages spoken by the slaves.

Creole languages are the majority languages throughout Plantation America, with the exception of the Spanish countries and Brazil (although some linguists claim semicreole status for Brazilian Portuguese). The lack of creole languages in Cuba, the Dominican Republic, and other Spanish-speaking areas is generally thought to be due to the fact that in the early years of settlement only small numbers of African slaves were brought to these places. Furthermore, these slaves mostly worked on small farms alongside their Spanish-speaking owners, and thus had access to more or less normal acquisition of Spanish as a second language. Their descendants were able to pass on Spanish to the slaves who arrived later and in larger numbers. In contrast, in the French- and English-speaking territories, the European population was typically very small and the slaves interacted mostly with each other, rather than directly with Europeans, reinforcing the separateness of the creole languages from the European ones.

Despite their ubiquity, creole languages enjoy official recognition only in Haiti, where Haitian *Kreyòl* is co-official with French. A standardized writing system and materials for literacy education have been developed for Kreyòl, and books, both fiction and nonfiction, have been written in Kreyòl. In other areas, and, for that matter, even in Haiti among some elite circles, the debate about the appropriate use of creole languages continues, and children are expected to deal with the official European language from the time they enter school, often in a sort of sink-or-swim way (Holm 1989).

Brazil

It was in northeastern Brazil that the Portuguese, in the sixteenth century, established the first sugar plantations in the New World. These plantations were modeled on those they had already been operating, with African slaves, on the Azores and other islands near the coast of Africa. The Native Americans who inhabited Brazil, especially the part of Brazil that forms the Amazon drainage basin, were (and are) generally foragers and small-scale slash-and-burn farmers living in villages scattered through the rain forest. Hence, they were not available for plantation labor. To provide labor for the plantations, then, more than 3.6 million African slaves were taken to Brazil between the sixteenth and nineteenth centuries (Richardson 1992). Hence, the area making up primarily the state of Bahia is the region of Brazil with the strongest African presence. Population figures for Brazil are given in Table 13-6.

Afro-Brazilians, like people of African descent in Haiti, Cuba, and elsewhere, have conserved and also embellished important aspects of their African culture. This is especially true in the domain of religion. Many Brazilians participate in religious activities and rituals associated with *Candomblé*, a syncretism of West African and European Catholic religions similar to the Haitian *Vodoun* and the Cuban *Santería*. In these religions West African spirits are identified with Catholic saints; important components include the veneration of ancestors and possession by spirits during intense ceremonies.

As slaves, of course, Afro-Brazilians were subject to the same aspects of "race" ideology as were Africans in other parts of Latin America and the Caribbean. This ideology includes the devaluing of Africans' physical features and also their mental abilities, and these attitudes are present today. Nevertheless, Brazil promotes itself as a sort of racial democracy, a "mixed-race nation," an idea that was expressed widely in 1988, the centennial of the abolition of slavery in Brazil. But the popular saying, "Every Brazilian male needs three women in his life: a white woman to bear his heirs, a black woman to cook for him, and a *mulata* to make love to" suggests that Brazilians are not as color-blind as they might like to think (Winn 1999). It may be true that Brazilian culture is different in terms of the way it models and interprets "racial" differences, but these differences still play an important role in Brazilian culture.

While doing research in Brazil in the 1950s, the anthropologist Marvin Harris (1964) noticed that Brazilians used a much greater variety of terms to refer to people of different physical types. To explore this phenomenon, Harris showed Brazilians photographs of people and asked them to tell what "race" the person in the photo belonged to. Surprisingly, he found that the same person could be categorized differently depending on the context in which they were observed. For example, a person called *preto* (black) when wearing old clothes and standing in front of a poor-looking house might be called *moreno* (brown) or even *branco* (white) when seen dressed up in front of a wealthy-looking house.

In an attempt to attack this problem systematically, Harris designed a set of cards, each of which contained a simple drawing of a person. There were 36 male and 36 female portraits.

Table 13-6. Brazilian ethnic groups as percentages of total population

Category	White	Mulatto	Black	Other
Percent	54	40	5	1

The portraits differed by three skin tones (light, medium, dark), three hair types (straight, wavy, curly), two nose widths (narrow, wide), and two lip types (thin, full). All 36 combinations were represented for each sex. Harris showed people the cards and asked them to characterize each drawing, with the hope of uncovering the rules Brazilians use to place people into "racial" categories. Harris found a wide variety of terms available to Brazilians which allows them to call attention to different combinations of physical traits (skin color, hair form, etc.). In addition, as shown by the earlier experiments with photographs, Brazilians can also take into account social and economic circumstances in calculating their "race." The result is that the Brazilian system is a continuum, from preto at one end to branco at the other and a number of categories in between.

In contrast, North Americans, at least as far as "black" and "white" are concerned, produce a simple dichotomy. The North American rule is called a *hypodescent* rule because it places people into the category that has the *lower* prestige in the society. Under the hypodescent rule, people with *any* known African ancestry can be considered "black."

Harris's explanation for the difference between U.S. and Brazilian folk models involves taking into account the different socioeconomic conditions that prevailed in these places during colonial times. In the United States, during the period of slavery, the ratio of slaves to Europeans was relatively small; only in places like coastal South Carolina, where rice (to help feed Caribbean slaves) was grown on large plantations, were the ratios anything like those of Brazil or the Caribbean. There were plenty of European immigrants available to fill the middle-level jobs, such as blacksmith, carpenter, and wheelwright, as well as to work on small farms providing food for the plantations, and even to serve as militia. The strict categorization of both slaves and former slaves, as well as people of "mixed" descent, into a "black" (Negro, Col-ored) category, helped keep them from competing for these jobs. At the same time it helped keep the power of the planter class secure, by ensuring that poor whites saw themselves as belonging to a category distinct and separate from both slaves and ex-slaves, and thus preventing the two groups of exploited people from joining together against the planters.

In Brazil, in contrast, there were relatively fewer Europeans available to do these sorts of jobs, which still needed to be done. Harris concluded that this led to a more open system that allowed people to move around and occupy a greater variety of roles in the society. In Brazil, and in other parts of Plantation America, there was less need to maintain a strictly defined boundary between the Europeans and everyone else.

This is not to suggest that Brazilians are "color-blind" or that skin color and other physical features do not make any difference to Brazilians. In Brazil, light skin and European features are valued over darker skin and non-European features. In fact, Brazilians are probably more consciously aware of these differences than North Americans typically are. The saying quoted earlier, about men needing white women to give them heirs (i.e., as legal wives) and black and brown women to cook for them and to give them (extramarital) sex, has no analog in U.S. culture. What it does suggest is that in Brazil people are spread out along a continuum with many more points on it, rather than being squeezed into two mutually exclusive categories.

More recently, Francisco Gil-White (2001) has called Harris's conclusions into question by pointing out that Harris did not follow up to discover whether the terms he elicited actually represented "racial" or ethnic groups, that is, groupings based on descent or enculturation. Instead, they may have simply represented sorting by physical features. This is an important criticism, and more work needs to be done in this area. We will revisit this issue when we discuss concepts of "race" in the Caribbean.

The Caribbean

The Amerindians. When Columbus arrived in the Caribbean in 1492, several ethnolinguistic groups inhabited the region. Small numbers of a foraging people known as the Ciboney could be found on Cuba. However, by about 700 A.D. most of the Greater Antilles and the Bahamas were occupied by Arawakan-speaking peoples who had migrated northward from South America along the chain of islands. They called themselves by various names such as *Taíno* (Hispaniola), *Lucaya* (Bahamas), and *Iñeri* in the Lesser Antilles. These Arawakan-speaking groups were organized into villages that subsisted on fairly intensive horticulture supplemented by fishing and hunting. They had a ranked system of social hierarchy, and their word for their leaders gave us the Spanish word *cacique*. Some other words that entered European languages from Arawak are *hammock* and *hurricane*. The Dominican Spanish word *bohío*, meaning a rural shack, was the Arawaks' name for the island that the Spanish called *Hispaniola*.

The Arawaks essentially disappeared from the Greater Antilles within half a century or so of Columbus's first visit. Their disappearance was due in part to their lack of immunity to certain diseases, especially smallpox and influenza, to which both Europeans and Africans carried some immunity. Their immunity was a result of their long association with domesticated animals, like cattle, sheep, poultry, and so on, from which these diseases migrated to humans in the Old World (Diamond 1998). However, abusive and even genocidal behavior on the part of the colonists also factored in their disappearance, as it did in parts of North America.

In the Dominican Republic, the Taíno are gone but by no means forgotten. In Santo Domingo, the capital, there is a statue of a woman named Anacaona, who is revered as a symbol of the Arawak people. She was hanged in 1503, after participating in an unsuccessful uprising against the Spanish. The Arawaks on Puerto Rico called their island *Borikén*, and this is the name used by the Puerto Rican independence movement as a symbol of their desire to break from past colonial relationships. The group works to preserve and increase awareness of Taíno language and culture (Rouse 1992). Arawak-speaking people today live along the northern fringe of South America. They include the Guajiros of the Guajira Peninsula between Colombia and Venezuela and the Locono of Venezuela.

Just prior to the European encounter, another group, the Caribs, had invaded the Windward and Leeward Islands from the region of South America near the mouth of the Orinoco River. In the Lesser Antilles, the indigenous peoples survived, marginally, on some of the Leeward and Windward Islands. These small islands, while claimed initially by Spain, did not offer the gold and other riches that the Spanish adventurers sought and thus were mostly ignored by the Spanish. After 1600, the French and English began to settle them and set up sugar and other plantations. By this time a culture had developed that consisted of a mixture of the Arawaks, who had arrived earlier, and the more recent Caribs; this culture came to be known as Island Carib and extended from Grenada in the south to Dominica in the north.

At first, the Island Carib society was probably bilingual, with both women and men speaking Arawak while Carib was maintained as a men's prestige language. Eventually, though, a "new" language developed that was essentially Arawakan in structure but that contained some dual vocabulary: Arawakan for women, Carib for men. For example, to this day women and men use different pronouns meaning "I": *nuguya* for women and *aw* for men. Historically, there were other differences. The new language came to be known as *Garifuna*.

On Grenada, French forces eventually drove the Island Caribs to the very northern tip of the island, where they jumped off a cliff into the sea rather than face defeat. The place where this happened is called Morne des Sauteurs, "hill of the jumpers"; the nearby town is called Sauteurs. In contrast, on Dominica, which is a larger and more rugged island, a community of Island Caribs has survived on the windward (east) coast. These are "true" Caribs, and their reserve was set aside for them by the government of Dominica in 1903. The reserve serves as the focal point for their ethnic revitalization (Hulme and Whitehead 1992).

As a further complication, the Island Caribs on St. Vincent were joined at some point by African slaves who had escaped from a shipwreck and managed to reach shore. The resulting group came to be known as the Black Caribs. As on Grenada, there was a years-long conflict between these people and the British, who wanted to make the island safe for settlement. In 1797, in one of the more bizarre stories from the Caribbean past, most of the remaining Black Caribs were rounded up and put on vessels that carried them to the Bay Islands lying between Belize and Honduras. The British left them there, charitably, with some supplies.

These forced migrants and their descendants prospered, spreading to the neighboring mainland territories of Belize, Guatemala, Honduras, and Nicaragua. They have maintained the Garifuna language and many elements of their culture, and see themselves as distinct from the "Creole" population, which consists of Anglophone West Indians. In Nicaragua, they mixed to some extent with the Miskitu, who occupy the region known as the Mosquito Coast (Gonzalez 1988). The Garifuna are renowned as "linguists," that is, people who have a facility for languages; they are prominent in the teaching profession in Belize. They maintain important aspects of their culture, which include the *punta* drumming and singing in honor of their ancestors. They also retain in their ethnohistory knowledge of their homeland, St. Vincent.

Although it is sometimes claimed that there are no longer any Caribbean Amerindian people, on Puerto Rico there exists a group who call themselves the *Jatibonicu Taíno*. Furthermore, the Caribbean Amerindian Centrelink is an Internet site maintained to "focus upon or shed light upon the Native peoples of the Caribbean and circum-Caribbean."[1]

"Whites," "blacks," and others in the Caribbean. As a result of the African slave trade, and the subsequent mating of Europeans and others with Africans, approximately two-thirds of the people of the Caribbean can claim at least some African ancestry, making them, for census purposes, either black or mulatto. Because the Spanish territories didn't import large numbers of African slaves until the second half of the nineteenth century, the numbers there are fairly low, but note the high percentage of the populations that is mixed, as shown in Table 13-7.

In contrast, on Haiti the black population is about 95 percent, with whites and mulattos making up the other 5 percent. This is a direct result of the fact that Haiti was a French sugar colony almost from the start. Then, during the Haitian revolution (1790–1894), most of the already small white elite were either killed or forced to flee the country.

Other Caribbean countries fall somewhere in between the extremes of Haiti, on the one hand, and Cuba and the Dominican Republic on the other. For example, Table 13-8 provides figures for blacks, whites, and mulattos for a selected sample of Lesser Antillean states.

When I was doing my ethnographic and linguistic research I thought it would be interesting to use Harris's method to investigate Caribbean racial categories. I supposed that most places in

Table 13-7. Ethnic groups as percentage of population for two countries of the Hispanic Caribbean

	White	Black	Mulatto	Other
Cuba	37	11	51	1
Dominican Republic	16	11	73	–

Table 13-8. Ethnic groups as percentage of population in selected countries of the Lesser Antilles

	Barbados	Grenada	St. Lucia	Trinidad
Black	92	85	90	40
White	3	1	1	1
Mulatto/mixed	3	11	6	18
Other	2	3	3	41

the Caribbean ought to follow a pattern more like the Brazilian one than the North American pattern, since the Caribbean belongs mostly to Plantation America. Nevertheless, the Caribbean subsumes a number of differently structured societies. As pointed out by David Lowenthal (1972), social stratification in Caribbean societies may take place along lines of "color" (i.e., "race") or "class" (social and/or economic position). Some societies are stratified along one or the other dimension; some are stratified along both; a few are relatively unstratified, or homogeneous.

Following Lowenthal, then, I formulated the following hypotheses regarding the way in which people from the Caribbean would deal with Harris's drawings:

- Societies that are stratified both by color and social class, like Trinidad and Barbados, should show the most "racial" terms. In these societies, people in the upper classes tend to be "white" or light-skinned, while people in the working classes tend to be "black" or dark-skinned. However, there are wealthy upper-class "blacks" as well as poor lower-class "whites."
- Homogeneous societies, like Carriacou, should show the fewest "racial" terms. In these societies there is little or no stratification along lines of color or class.
- Societies stratified by class or color but not both should fall somewhere between the two extremes. Examples of these societies are Grenada and Dominica, which have no "white" elite and in which there is little or no correlation between skin color and social class.

I borrowed a set of Harris's cards and made photos of them. I began by trying the portraits out on both "black" and "white" North Americans. Without exception, they placed most of the portraits into discrete categories labeled white, black, and Indian or Asian. What happened after that varied; usually there were one or two extra categories like Hispanic, American Indian, or Australian Aborigine, into which they put the portraits that didn't seem to fit the three basic categories.

I then used the portraits on informants from Barbados, Trinidad, Jamaica, Bahamas, Dominica, and Grenada; I also tried them out on people in Carriacou. In general, I found an overall pattern that more closely resembled Harris's Brazilian pattern than the North American pattern. I also found that the hypothesis about the correlation between social stratification and complexity of categorization was confirmed: Trinidad and Barbados had the most categories, Grenada and Dominica had fewer; Carriacou had the fewest of all.

Trinidad. Trinidad (the larger part of the state of Trinidad and Tobago) is a complex society stratified along the lines of both class and color. It was Spanish for a while, then French, and then British. It became an independent state in 1962. Because of its historical background, the ethnic makeup of Trinidad is especially complex. The Spanish, French, and British all brought African slaves to work in the sugarcane fields. After emancipation (1835), when many ex-slaves preferred working their own small farms rather than continuing to work on the sugar plantations, tens of thousands of East Indians, as well as a number of Chinese, were brought in as indentured laborers. Consultants from Trinidad offered the following seven basic terms in response to the portraits: *negro, indian, dogla* (a mixture of East Indian and African), *mestizo, panyol* (i.e., Venezuelan), *Spanish* (i.e., European), and *white*. In addition, nine compound terms occurred: *madrasi-Indian, kuli-indian, Tobago-negro, chinee-negro, French-creole* (= local-white), *clearskin-dogla, koko-panyol, half-white* (= mulatto), and *local-white*.

Dominica. Dominica, in the Windward Islands, is a society stratified by economic class rather than by color. This means that there are social classes, but the classes are based on wealth rather than "racial" affinity, and there is no substantial "white" elite as there is in places like Jamaica, Barbados, and Trinidad. The Dominican consultant offered the following five terms in response to the portraits: *nèg* (= black), *blan* or *beke* (= white), *kuli* (= East Indian), *black-and-kuli*, and *chaben*. Besides these four terms, the consultant offered the descriptive modifier *fairskin-*, which can be used to modify the first three terms. None of Harris's faces elicited the term *Carib*, which is an important ethnic group within Dominica.

Carriacou. Carriacou is a relatively homogeneous society with a strong cultural ideal of egalitarianism that is reinforced in a number of ways, including informal food sharing and more formal redistributive feasts at special occasions such as boat launchings, weddings, and the like. Harris's faces elicited no single-word terms such as "white" or "black" to identify the portraits. Instead, the Carriacouans used color terms as descriptive adjectives: they were always accompanied by a noun such as *people, woman, man, girl,* or *boy.* The terms included *dark-/black-, brown-/brown-skin-, red-/redskin-, pink-* (i.e., albino), and *white-.*

On Carriacou, the term *white people* is sometimes used to describe the people of Windward, a village that was traditionally inhabited by descendants of British and French indentured workers. Until well into the twentieth century this group was a "closed community"; however, for some time now there has been intermarriage between the "white people" and the much more numerous people of African descent. Still, for most Carriacouans, "white" implies someone not born on Carriacou; no one born and raised in Carriacou is normally thought of as "white."

My research reported here, which used Harris's drawings of faces, is equally open to Gil-White's (2001) criticism of Harris: Were my informants simply sorting by physical features visible on the cards, but not really telling me anything about any "racial" or ethnic categories they might have had? This is really a question for further research. However, it seems clear that the way in which the faces are approached varies significantly, both between the United States and the Caribbean and also within the Caribbean itself. In the United States and Trinidad, people used terms that could be plugged into a sentence, like "The *x* live on that side of town," where *x* might be *whites* or *blacks*, and so on. The principal difference between the United States and Trinidad (and other societies stratified by both class and "race") seems to be the number of terms given. In the United States, the faces can be fitted pretty easily into four or five categories; in Trinidad, more categories are available.

On the other hand, I do think that my Carriacouan informants were simply sorting or, rather, describing in the way that they might use to call attention to someone. They provided not terms, but adjectives: "You know Mary; she is the *brown-skin* one." This was their response to the physical features presented in the faces. And yet, they clearly also have ways of constructing for themselves identities that set them apart from other people in the world, and that also divide them into groups internal to Carriacou.

First, Carriacou people see themselves as distinctive, by virtue of having been born and raised on Carriacou of parents who were also born and raised on Carriacou, and so on. This sets them apart from everyone else in the world, even nearby Grenadians. They are *Carriacou people*: more honest, thrifty, and hardworking than people from other places.

Carriacou people are also very aware of their African ancestry. They conceptualize at least some of their behaviors and beliefs as "African," and they contrast these with "white" behaviors and beliefs. One such behavior is the food sharing mentioned earlier. One evening when I had prepared a little fish broth, an elderly friend dropped by just as I was about to eat. So I shared out all the broth between the two of us. As we were about to eat, a young man happened by; I asked if he had eaten, and he said no. So, after asking permission, I took enough broth from each of us to make a plate for him. The elderly Carriacouan commented that I was behaving "like *negro people*," since everyone knew that *white people* would not share their food in this way.

Finally, Carriacou people traditionally categorized themselves as belonging to different African *nations* or *bloods*. This is described in the next section.

Whatever is going on, sorting or categorization, the situation is not significantly different for the Hispanic and Francophone Caribbean. For example, in Spanish America, the term *negro* tends to be reserved for people with very dark skin; it is not a hypodescent term. The classificatory term *mulato*, which was formerly used as a term for someone of mixed African and European descent, has been mostly replaced by descriptive terms such as *trigueño* (wheat-colored), *acanelado* (cinnamon colored), and *cobrizo* (copper-colored). In addition, the term *moreno* can be used for anyone, from European brunettes to people with dark skin. All these terms can be modified in various ways. For example, a person might be *moreno claro* (light brown), or *blanco quemado* (sunburned white), or *negro fileno* (dark-skinned with a straight nose) (Solaún et al. 1987).

It is worth mentioning that in some Hispanic areas, *negrito* and *negrita* (literally "little black") are used as terms of affection. Similarly, on Haiti the Creole term *nèg* (from French *negre*) means something like "guy" or "buddy" and can be used with people of any skin color.

African Ethnicities: Carriacouan "Nations"

One frequently ignored aspect of Caribbean ethnic identity is that different African ethnolinguistic groups were represented among the early

slave populations. In early censuses, slaves born in Africa were designated by a given name (George, Mary), as well as by the name of the ethnic group they belonged to (e.g., "Georges Bambara"). Slaves born in the New World were designated as "creole." The 1750 census of Carriacou easily identified several African ethnolinguistic groups (Brinkley 1978): Bambara, Congo, Ibo, Arada, Anan. A number of others were added to the culture later.

On Carriacou, people were classified traditionally by the African "nation" (ethnic group) into which they were born, as determined by the nation of their mother (a matrilineal descent rule). There was a hierarchy of nations, with the *Kromanti* and *Mandingo* at the top. The term *Kromanti*, sometimes spelled *Cromanti*, refers to the port city of Cormantyn, in what is now Ghana, which served as a holding area for many Africans on their way to enslavement in the New World. At a *Big Drum* ceremony, which is performed on special occasions and involves summoning the ancestors back from Africa, the *Mandingo* and *Kromanti* songs are the first of the actual nation songs to be played. Each nation has its own drumming pattern and associated songs. There were also stereotypical beliefs about physical and mental attributes of particular nations, for example: *Kongo* people are very dark; *Kromanti* women are independent and prefer to remain single (Hill 1977). This knowledge of one's African ethnic roots is less important today than it was in the traditional society; traditionally, it set limits on possible marriage partners, because a person was not supposed to marry someone from the same nation (Hill 1977; Kephart 2000; McDaniel 1998; Smith 1962).

The "Redlegs" of Barbados

In the earliest years of the developing Barbadian sugar industry, planters tried to satisfy their need for labor by recruiting workers from the British Isles. Sometimes, workers were enticed by promises of a plot of land after serving their period of contract; sometimes, they were shipped out involuntarily for a variety of reasons. On Barbados, once their contract was completed, they found that virtually all the decent land was already in sugar production; they were thus forced to accept marginal lands on the windward side of the island. Those who did developed a closed community of small farmers similar to, but if anything more closed than, the one at Windward, Carriacou.

For many years, these "redlegs," as they came to be called, were the poorest group on Barbados; they nevertheless took pride in the fact that they were "white," and therefore united by color, if not by class, with the planters. By the middle of the twentieth century, some of them had begun to mix with the "African" population; and some became successful as merchants. Still, some redlegs retained their prejudicial attitudes toward the African population (for an in-depth history of the redlegs see Sheppard 1977).

Some European indentured laborers who were unable to obtain land on Barbados migrated westward to the Windward and Leeward Islands, where they founded communities similar to that on Barbados. Two such communities are the one at Windward, Carriacou, and another at Mount Moritz, Grenada. These white nonelites are known as *mongmong* (from Creole French *moun-mòn*, "mountain people") on Grenada. As on Barbados, historically, they have been looked down upon by other segments of the population. Interestingly, on Carriacou, until they began intermarrying with the "African" population, they belonged to no nation; this limited the extent of the social networks available to them. (See Howard Johnson and Karl Watson [1998] for essays on these and other white minorities in the Caribbean.)

The East Indians

After emancipation, many ex-slaves refused to work for their former masters on the sugar plantations. To supply the need for labor, the industry turned again to indentured laborers, imported this time from India and other parts of Asia. The majority went to Trinidad and the Guianas. In Trinidad they are about 40 percent of the population; in Guyana, 50 percent; in Suriname, they are about 33 percent, but the number rises to 49 percent if the Javanese, also East Asians, are included. The anthropologist Morton Klass (1988) has written about the East Indians of Trinidad.

The indentured laborers were frequently able to complete their period of indenture and acquire a farm or shop or, eventually, a business. Their descendants have been relatively successful in the societies in which they are a substantial part of the population and have integrated themselves into the social, political, and economic spheres of the countries where they live. In the process, they have maintained much of their culture. This success has come at a price, however. The price is a long-standing, and sometimes violent, relationship with the descendants of African slaves. Afro-West Indians at times felt that the East Indians had kept them from making a living by selling their own labor at a price lower than the former slaves were willing to do. In turn, East Indians have often seen Africans as lazy, unwilling to work hard in order to get ahead. In both Guyana and Trinidad, especially, East Indians and Africans have vied with each other for political power (Eriksen 1992).

The Maroons

Whenever and wherever possible, the African slaves ran away from their plantations and founded *maroon* communities (from Spanish *cimarrón* "wild"), documented extensively by anthropologist Richard Price (1979). This *maroonage* was feasible on the larger islands, like Jamaica, and the South American mainland, where ample unsettled land was available outside the reach of the authorities. One area where this occurred, and where the descendants of the original maroons continue to maintain an existence separate from the larger society, is the so-called "Cockpit Country" of Jamaica, settled in the eighteenth century and described by anthropologist Zora Neal Hurston (1990). Another is San Basilio de Palenque, near Cartagena, Colombia. A third, and perhaps the most famous, consists of various groups, including the Saramaka, Ndjuka, and others, inhabiting the interior of Suriname (see also Herskovits 1966).

Perhaps more than any other Africans in the New World, these maroon groups, by separating themselves early on from the plantation culture, were able to maintain aspects of the African cultures from which they had come. These include religious practices, various arts and crafts, verbal performance, horticultural methods, and so on. In all cases, they speak creole languages, languages that contain European vocabulary grafted onto West African sentence structures.

ETHNIC REVITALIZATION

As is evident throughout much of the world, in the Caribbean and Latin America contemporary humans have adjusted to living in large-scale societies influenced by globalization and nationalization trends. Within these once traditional societies, many of the human interactions that occur are anonymous. There is, too, often a culturally homogenizing trend reinforced by the declaration of particular languages (usually the languages of the former European colonists) as "official." National systems of education attempt to reinforce this by teaching in the "national" language and emphasizing a "national" ideology. People are encouraged through a long process of enculturation to speak Spanish, English, or whatever the national language happens to be; to identify with the flag; and to behave in ways that are indicative of nationhood, be it Cuban, Jamaican, or Haitian.

At the same time, from the perspective of anthropology, nation-states like these are relatively new in the history of humankind. Before this, people had lived for tens, perhaps hundreds, of thousands of years in small-scale societies in which nearly all interactions were face-to-face and usually with someone known or even related. Given these facts of history, and especially given the relatively short time (about 5,000 years) that humans have lived in large-scale societies, it seems reasonable to assume that we have not had time to adjust biologically to our new living arrangements. In particular, we almost certainly retain from our not that distant past a proclivity for life in small, face-to-face societies. Within such societies, it is easy to construct ethnic markers that help let us create an identity for ourselves as a group, in contrast to others who don't share those ethnic markers and therefore are outside the group. The ethnic markers may be linguistic (as in some of the cases we noted earlier among Native Americans); they may be cultural (beliefs, behaviors, dress, tattooing, or other body decorations); they may include aspects of physical appearance, such as skin color or hair form. One anthropologist has referred to this predisposition among humans toward the formation of relatively small in-groups as the *social imperative* (Cring 1992).

The social imperative provides us with an explanation for why, all across Latin America and the Caribbean, people have sought, and continue to seek, ways of forming themselves into more manageable groups than the large-scale states they find themselves in tend to provide. When we couple this with the fact that most Caribbean and Latin American societies contain within themselves minority groups that are in structurally subordinate positions (economically, socially, politically), we have a situation ripe for the development of *ethnic revitalization movements* or *ethnonationalist movements*.

Often, ethnic revitalization movements are centered on religion, and while this is true for the Caribbean and Latin America, it is also possible to identify a component of ethnicity in some cases. Let us look briefly at a case that illustrates these ethnic (rather than strictly religious) revitalizations.

The Rastafarians

As we have seen, Africans in Jamaica are descended from slaves who were brought there by the Spanish and then the English to work on plantations. After emancipation, the ideology of African as inferior, European as superior, was maintained, and, as often happens, found its way into the worldview of even the slaves' descendants. All things European were prized: hair, dress, language, religion. All things African were devalued.

In the 1930s, a movement to revalue all things African began, largely under the impetus of Marcus Garvey. Garvey found passages in the Christian Bible that allowed him to declare that Haile Selassie, the newly crowned emperor of Ethiopia, was a living god. Black people should worship him and turn away from the Christian god. Haile Selassie's title was *Ras* ("king") *Tafari*, so the movement's followers came to be known as *Rastafarians*.

One of the ethnic markers Rastafarians (or Rastas, for short) used to set themselves apart not only from the European elite but also the masses of African descent was by their hairstyle. Rastafarians refused to cut their hair, allowing it to grow into long "dreadlocks." They also refused to comb their hair in the conventional European way. It must be understood that this was not the copying of an African custom; no Africans wore their hair this way traditionally (those that wear "dreads" now are copying the Rastafarians!). The growing of dreadlocks, then, began as an explicit rejection of European cultural norms–a defiant symbol of resistance to the cultural values and norms imposed by the white Europeans (Barrett 1977).

Another ethnic marker setting Rastas apart is language. Although Rastas essentially speak Jamaican Creole English, locally called *Patwa*, they consciously made some changes to it, especially in vocabulary. One noticeable shift is the Rastas' use of the first person pronoun *I*, pronounced [ay], for all functions of the pronouns (Patwa speakers use *mi* for all functions). So, a Rasta might say, "Give I a book," where speakers of both English and Patwa would say, "Give me a book." Rastafarians also creatively alter the forms of words to make a political point, such as using *overstand* for *understand* and *downpress* for *oppress*. The use of *I* also makes a point, since it is homophonous with *eye*, the organ of sight.[2]

A third ethnic marker is *reggae* music, which developed from urban *ska*, played in the poor sections of Kingston, the Jamaican capital. The music was first carried out of Jamaica by artists like Jimmy Cliff, Peter Tosh, and especially Bob Marley. It is heard and copied all over the world.

The Illogic of "Black Power"

The Rastafarians were successful in rekindling a consciousness of Africa and Africa-ness among many Caribbean people. However, the *black power movement*, which attempted to do the same thing in the United States beginning in the 1960s, found little sympathy in the Caribbean. Our earlier discussion of the meanings and use of "black" and "white" among West Indians should make the answer obvious. For Caribbean people, "black" is a descriptive term used for people with very dark skin color, not a term for a descent group, as it is in the United States.

SUMMARY

In this chapter, we have provided an overview of the physical, cultural, and linguistic diversity displayed by the peoples of Latin America and the Caribbean. We have noted that in some areas (the Caribbean, for example) the Native American populations were almost totally obliterated. In others (Perú, Bolivia) they remain an important, even dominant, segment of the population, although they are integrated, principally as peasant farmers and urban and rural proletariat, into national (and even global) economies. In some scattered regions, especially the Amazon and Orinoco river basins of Brazil and Venezuela, indigenous groups like the Yanomama attempt to carry on their traditional life ways largely separated from their respective national cultures. And yet, even these groups have become integrated, if only at arm's length, into larger economies by their acceptance of and increased dependence on products of Western technology, such as machetes and firearms.

The descendants of people who came from Europe, Africa, and Asia as part of the Columbian exchange dominate large portions of Latin America and the Caribbean. Some regions display their history of plantation slavery in the large numbers of people who claim African descent. As with the majority of surviving Amerindians, these peoples have mostly been integrated into national cultures, but some groups of descendants of African slaves, like the Saramaka of Suriname, have managed to carry on cultural and linguistic traditions that tie them directly to Africa. People of European descent are the majority in some regions, such as southern Brazil, Argentina, Uruguay, and Chile. In other places, like Barbados, Europeans form minorities that, perhaps paradoxically, are divided into elite and nonelite classes.

However, the overall theme uniting the peoples and cultures of Latin America and the Caribbean is *mestizaje*, or "mixture." First, there is mixture of gene pools: Amerindian, European, African, and Asian. Secondly, the languages and cultures found throughout the region reflect the creation of new from old, so that "Cuban," "Barbadian," and "Haitian," to mention three examples, are all distinct, in their own ways, from the

cultures of their founding populations (see Yelvington 2001).

NOTES

1. The Web address for the Jatibonicu Taino is http://members.dandy.net/~orocobix/index.html. The Web address for the Caribbean Amerindian Centrelink is http://www.centrelink.org.
2. The observations on Rastafarian language are from a presentation by Mervyn Alleyne during a conference on San Andrés, Colombia, in May 1999.

REFERENCES CITED

BARRETT, LEONARD E. 1977. *Rastafarians: Sounds of Cultural Dissonance*. Boston: Beacon Press.

BRINKLEY, FRANCES. 1978. An analysis of the 1750 Carriacou census. *Caribbean Quarterly* 24(1–2):44–60.

BUECHLER, HANS, and JUDITH-MARIA BUECHLER. 1971. *The Bolivian Aymara*. New York: Holt, Rinehart & Winston.

CARPENTER, LAWRENCE. 1983. Social stratification and implications for bilingual education: An Ecuadorian example. In *Bilingualism: Social Issues and Policy Implications*. Andrew W. Miracle, ed. Pp. 96–106. Athens: University of Georgia Press.

CRING, DAN. 1992. The ontogeny and phylogeny of discrimination. Paper presented at the Annual Meeting of the Louisiana Academy of Science.

CROSBY, ALFRED. 1972. *The Columbian Exchange: Biological and Cultural Consequences of 1492*. Westport, CT: Greenwood Press.

DIAMOND, JARED. 1998. *Guns, Germs, and Steel: The Fates of Human Societies*. New York: Norton.

Encyclopaedia Britannica. Electronic document, http://www.britannica.com.

ERIKSEN, THOMAS H. 1992. *Us and Them in Modern Societies: Ethnicity and Nationalism in Trinidad, Mauritius and Beyond*. Oslo: Scandinavian University Press.

GIL-WHITE, FRANCISCO. 2001. Sorting is not categorization: A critique of the claim that Brazilians have fuzzy racial categories. Unpublished manuscript.

GONZALEZ, NANCY. 1988. *Sojourners of the Caribbean: Ethnogenesis and Ethnohistory of the Garifuna*. Urbana: University of Illinois Press.

GOOD, KENNETH. 1991. *Into the Heart: One Man's Pursuit of Love and Knowledge among the Yanomama*. New York: Simon & Schuster.

HARDMAN, M. J., ed. 1981. *The Aymara Language in Its Social and Cultural Context*. Gainesville: University Press of Florida.

HARRIS, MARVIN. 1964. *Patterns of Race in the Americas*. New York: Norton Library.

HERSKOVITS, MELVILLE. 1966. *The New World Negro: Selected Papers in Afroamerican Studies*. Frances S. Herskovits, ed. Bloomington: Indiana University Press.

HILL, DONALD. 1977. *The Impact of Migration on the Folk and Metropolitan Society of Carriacou, Grenada*. New York: American Museum of Natural History.

HOLM, JOHN. 1989. *Pidgins and Creoles*, vol. II. *Reference Survey*. Cambridge: Cambridge University Press.

HULME, PETER, and NEIL WHITEHEAD, eds. 1992. *Wild Majesty: Encounters with Caribs from Columbus to the Present Day*. Oxford: Clarendon Press.

HURSTON, ZORA. 1990. *Tell My Horse: Voodoo and Life in Haiti and Jamaica*. New York: Perennial Library.

JOHNSON, HOWARD, and KARL WATSON, eds. 1998. *The White Minority in the Caribbean*. Kingston: Ian Randle.

KEPHART, RONALD. 2000. *"Broken English": The Creole Language of Carriacou*. New York: Peter Lang.

KLASS, MORTON. 1988 [1961]. *East Indians in Trinidad: A Study in Cultural Persistence*. Prospect Heights, IL: Waveland Press.

LOWENTHAL, DAVID. 1972. *West Indian Societies*. London: Oxford University Press.

MCDANIEL, LORNA. 1998. *The Big Drum Ritual of Carriacou: Praisesongs in Rememory of Flight*. Gainesville: University Press of Florida.

MARTÍNEZ-ECHAZABAL, LOURDES. 1998. Mestizaje and the discourse of national/cultural identity in Latin America, 1845–1959. *Latin American Perspectives* 25(3)21–43.

O'GRADY, WILLIAM, J. ARCHIBALD, M. ARONOFF, and J. REES-MILLER. 2001. *Contemporary Linguistics: An Introduction*. 4th edition. Boston: Bedford/St. Martin's Press.

PRICE, RICHARD, ed. 1979. *Maroon Societies: Rebel Slave Communities in the Americas*. Baltimore: Johns Hopkins University Press.

RICHARDSON, BONHAM. 1992. *The Caribbean in the Wider World: A Regional Geography*. Cambridge: Cambridge University Press.

ROUSE, IRVING. 1992. *The Tainos: Rise & Decline of the People Who Greeted Columbus*. New Haven, CT: Yale University Press.

SHEPPARD, JILL. 1977. *The "Redlegs" of Barbados*. Millwood, NY: KTO Press.

SMITH, M. G. 1962. *Kinship and Community in Carriacou*. New Haven, CT: Yale University Press.

SOLAÚN, M, E. VÉLEZ, and C. SMITH. 1987. Claro, Trigueño, Moreno: Testing for race in Cartagena. *Caribbean Review* 15(3):18–19.

WAGLEY, CHARLES. 1957. Plantation-America: A culture sphere. In *Caribbean Studies: A Symposium*. Vera Rubin, ed. Pp. 3–13. Seattle: University of Washington Press.

WILLIAMS, ERIC. 1994. *Capitalism and Slavery*. Chapel Hill: University of North Carolina Press.

WINN, PETER. 1999. *Americas: The Changing Face of Latin America and the Caribbean*. Berkeley: University of California Press.

YELVINGTON, KEVIN. 2001. The anthropology of Afro-Latin America: Diasporic dimensions. *Annual Review of Anthropology* 30:227–260.

14

AFRICA

Sheilah Clark-Ekong

University of Missouri, St. Louis

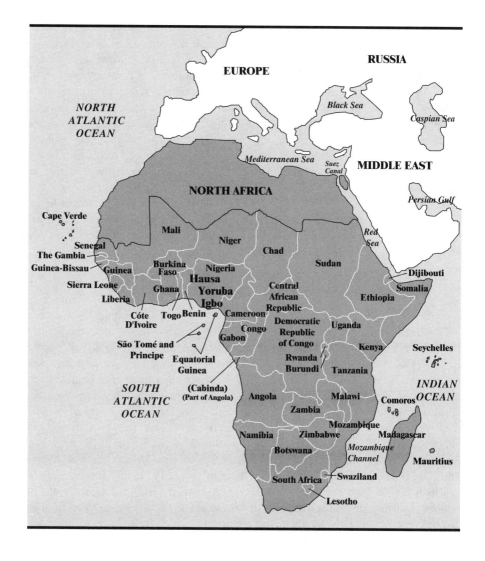

Many North American students and their teachers have only a limited interest or understanding of Africa. Thus, there is a good amount of misinformation about the continent and its inhabitants. For starters, there is no distinguishable African race, no mono-African language (written or spoken), and the African continent comprises 56 sovereign countries. Fifty-two of these nation-states make up sub-Saharan Africa, the most likely area of focus when the topic of Africa comes up for discussion. Within these independent countries are approximately 650 million people. Sub-Saharan Africa is home to the largest populated country, Nigeria, with an estimated population of 120 million, and Seychelles, the smallest country, with only 75,000 people, as well as Zambia, with an urban population of nearly 50 percent, and Burundi, with only 6 percent city dwellers (Middleton 2000). Africa gave us the world's earliest civilizations, and hominid fossils found in Africa date the origins of humankind. This is a continent that still houses some of the few remaining hunting and gathering societies, the longest sustaining subsistence pattern of human record. We also know now that these societies might well have been referred to as "gathering and hunting" societies, as the women's gathering activity supplied at least 80 percent of the caloric intake. Making generalized statements about Africa is a risky business, but anthropologists take the challenge with their focus on comparative cross-cultural analysis.

Our interest in the developing world is often driven by our own local ethnocentric agenda of the processes of globalization as it impacts Western economic and political well-being. When thinking of Africa, we may likely have images of famine, poverty, and violence, these reinforced by portrayals of starving women and children and "tribal-ethnic" violence that come across the airwaves of Western media. Although there are a number of hot spots in Africa, neither African civil strife nor civil wars can or should be totally reduced to tribal or ethnic conflicts. It would also be incorrect, though, to suggest that ethnic

hostilities are not a serious problem in parts of the continent.

Some current conflicts are struggles for power among rival factions. In several African countries (Liberia, Sierra Leone, Somalia, Angola), rival forces often recruit heavily from one region or clan (giving rise to the notion that these are ethnic conflicts) in order to make use of local leaders and loyalties to control their followers. Many sources of conflict may have cultural components, but these are often manifested through political and economic arenas. Villages, regions, ethnic groups, nationalities, religious groups—all have distinct cultures at different levels of cultural and social heterogeneity. It is the number of ethnic groups and their relationships to power, not diversity, per se, that strongly affect political stability. Interactions among peoples of different societies and backgrounds may very well enhance their "ethnic" consciousness and restimulate differences and animosities stretching back deep into their history. Another way of thinking about the dynamic nature of ethnicity, according to anthropologist Jack David Eller, "is that ethnic groups do not fight about culture but with culture—with culture as a weapon in a struggle of a different kind, whether it is political, economic, religious, or irredentism" (1999:3).

As indicated throughout this textbook, the idea that the world's current conflicts are fueled by age-old ethnic loyalties and cultural differences without due consideration for other social, economic, and political dynamics is an oversimplification. If ethnicity does not necessarily mean conflict, neither is conflict everywhere traceable to politicized ethnicity. Somalia, one of the most conflict-ridden states anywhere in the continent, is a case in point. Ethnically and culturally, Somalia is one of the most homogeneous countries in Africa. The real diversity for Somalia, a country slightly smaller than Texas, might have been during the colonial period when the French, the Ethiopians, the British, and the Italians all took a part for themselves.

In Somalia, family loyalty is the premier value. Clans, a systematic genealogical structure, with numerous branches called lineages, constitute the heart of Somali society. By the twelfth century, the ancestors of some clan families were already established in their present locations. The major challenge facing modern Somalia is how to unify a country whose people often give greater allegiance to their lineage and clan than to the nation-state. The contemporary situation continues to show the importance of clans in that by the mid-1980s, government and opposition movements were still clan-based, as they were prior to colonization in the nineteenth century. The primary divisions in the Somali nation are based on kinship, culture, economy (occupation), history, and geographic location. The northern Somali are those clans and lineages primarily engaged in nomadic subsistence strategies. The southern Somali are settled in the arable regions and practice either agriculture or agro-pastoralism (Putman and Noor 1993).

Conflict, like any other social dynamic, must be looked at holistically. Unfortunately, the phrase *ethnic conflict* has become a shorthand way to speak about any and all violent confrontations between groups of people living in the same country. Indeed, some of these conflicts may involve ethnic and cultural identity, but many are about equitable resource distribution and allocation (Bowen 2001:356).

Africa, the second largest continent of the world's seven, presents both similarities and certain uniqueness when one examines topics of identity. Colonialism, military coup d'état, the HIV/AIDS epidemic, mineral reserves, ethnic strife, tribalism, genocide, and apartheid and postapartheid are just some of the issues shaping both the insider's and outsider's perceptions of Africa. In reality, Africa's history, as well as its contemporary evolution, reflects the complexity of the entire world, from the most technologically advanced to the most marginal.

In this chapter we will examine some of the more significant expressions of ethnicity in

Africa, as a social construction of identity that serves many people around the world. We will also give consideration to some of the historical legacies that help sustain this form of identity in contemporary Africa. Africans, like all people, have multiple levels of identity and symbols of representation. Examples that readily express this "situational selectivity" are many. An Ibibio may be a mainland Ibibio or an Ibibio from Ibesikpo clan, when the reference point is the southeastern region of Nigeria. In Lagos, the commercial capital, he is simply an Easterner. In London, he is a Nigerian. In Missouri, he is an African. Having several "ethnic" identities also holds true for some Tanzanians within their own country. Postcolonial policy encouraged the use of KiSwahili as the national lingua franca and socialism (*ujaamaa*) as a means of uniting the citizens. "Thus, a man in Tabora, a center of the nineteenth century Arab slave trade, may point to distant Arab origins of his father and Sukuma or other Bantu origins of his mother, and may speak both Swahili and the Sujuma language, according to the situation" (Middleton 2000:90).

In anthropological terms, the use of the comparative method makes multiethnicity and statehood part of the same process. Multiethnicity becomes a way of adding power through numbers of supporters, which overrides chance demographic factors. In such instances claims of common ethnicity can be used to mobilize previously autonomous groups under a unified leadership. According to Paul Bohannan, "When states developed to become nation-states, a new dimension of difficulty was added: the idea that the state should be associated with both a specific ethnic group and with a specific territory" (1995:180). The fact that almost no states were actually of this sort made no difference to creating this imaginary model and policy implementation (Lemarchand 1999). The idea appeared early among the Portuguese in the fourteenth century. It logically led to the proposition that the state should be the representative of what we today would call a dominant ethnic group, which should occupy and control its own property. Its members become the only people with full rights within the territory (Cohen 1993).

Ethnicity is just one way of categorizing a group of people. It is not an immutable phenomenon but a changing feature of society. Just as people are able to self-define, they are able to redefine themselves, and as a result ethnic compositions and boundaries do change. Knowing that culture is primarily adaptive, it is reasonable to conclude that identity can be and is often situational, and may change in response to any number of extenuating historical, territorial, economic, or political factors. An individual or group attachment to shared ethnicity can also set moral boundaries and values determined by rules of tradition (Maybury-Lewis 1997).

ETHNICITY OR TRIBALISM?

The conventional use of the word *tribe* stems in part from a view that African cultures have remained largely static and fixed at some pre-twentieth-century stage of development. "Tribe" comes from the Latin *tribus*. Throughout time, this term has been tied to classical Judeo-Christian biblical images. Many nineteenth- and early twentieth-century Europeans and Americans who used Latin and English Bibles adopted the term for the 12 lineages of Hebrews who settled the Promised Land. This link of tribes to the glorified periods of early Western culture supported the notion that "the tribe" had some universal validity in social evolution. According to David Wiley, "It is no accident that the contemporary uses of the term 'tribe' were developed during the nineteenth century rise of linear evolutionary and racist theories to designate alien non-white peoples as inferior or less civilized" (1999:56). From 1885 on, the colonial partition and conquest of Africa divided communities, created new ones, and fostered new identities.[1]

There is sufficient evidence that in the pre-colonial era, Africans thought of themselves primarily as members of descent-based lineage groups. Personal identification arose first out of familial sentiment and socialization, reinforced by community membership and respect for recognized authority figures (Falola 2000; Williams 2001). The renowned Igbo novelist and social critic Chinua Achebe says that the proverb, "*Nku di na mba na-eghelu mba nni*,"—Every community has enough firewood in its own forests for all the cooking it needs to do—underscores the importance of community (2000:7). At yet another level, the occupational or subsistence niche associated with many groups is basic to distinguishing them from neighboring groups. Ethnic groups occupying the Horn of Africa are classically distinguished by their subsistence patterns. Among peoples with established chieftaincy institutions, such as the Yoruba of Nigeria, loyalty to the chiefdom provides an active identity marker. While modernity tends to play down the influence of customary law, chieftancy is an identity above and beyond any secular constitutional arrangements and/or mandates. The chieftancy institution as a repository of tradition and customary law was incorporated into the colonial administration, making traditional rulers the middlemen. Colonial rule very often subordinated indigenous African authority.

Among the Asante of Ghana, distance to or from the royal lineage sustains group identification. The coastal Fante are very keen to impress other Ghanaian groups with their level of Western education and long-term European exposure. We might also see groups sharing so much in common, like the Lele and Bushong of the former Belgian Congo, that outsiders would hardly notice any difference. Both peoples recognize a common ancestry, share similar customs, live in the same geographic zone, and speak languages very closely related. The major distinguishing feature, the Kasai River, provides for rich and poor soils. The Lele are poor subsistence farmers; their soils support only steppe-like vegetation. The Bushong, even before colonialism, produced for exchange, and their native economy was noted for its use of money and its specialized traders and markets (Douglas 1997:101–102).

In the mergers of colonial and indigenous political systems, we begin to see the linkage between politics and kinship. The Nuer of southern Sudan were scattered over an immense area of land and seemed to have no discernible system of relationships linking them together. With more than 200,000 persons over an area of more than 30,000 miles there were fewer than seven people per square mile. E. E. Evans-Pritchard (1940) concluded that one could make sense of the Nuer world—that they had a well-organized political system uniquely suited to their ecological and social needs and one that operated according to genealogy and kinship relations (Grinker and Steiner 1997:5).

The examples cited here show that in all the different articulations and manifestations of group identity and affiliation relationships are sustained and/or diminished and subsequently reinforced and understood in relation to other similar and dissimilar groups, situations, and events.

For Africa, where much of the early history was passed down orally, there is still considerable uncertainty about the nature and forms of social interaction before the colonial era. The areas most discussed are what these native peoples called themselves and the relationship between different groups. Social anthropologist S. Nadel (1942) presents evidence that affirms the existence of specific forms of self-group identification in the precolonial era. "The Nupe ethnic group was not different from the Nupe State. A Nupe was anyone—whether warrior, peasant, pastoralist, or craftsman—who was defined as a subject of the Nupe sovereign" (Middleton 2000:84).

From a different point of view, and drawing insight from official colonial documents and missionary records from the early 1900s, David Simmons (2000) asserts that there was a colonialist need to ascribe identities to native peoples as a means of reordering the native perception of reality. This also provided a justification for allocating resources to some and excluding others. An example includes the following account of a British War Office official in 1917 who reportedly assessed the situation as such:

> [The] spirit of nationality, or perhaps it would be more correct to say, of tribe, should be cultivated and nowhere can this be done with better chance of success than in British East Africa and Uganda, where there are numerous tribes ethnographically quite distinct from one another. It is suggested that in each ethnographically distinct district the schools should, as far as possible, form integral parts of the tribe and centers of folklore and tradition. . . .
>
> A method may also be found whereby the efforts of missionaries may also assist in the cultivation of national spirit. This it seems might be done by allowing only one denomination to work in each demographic area and by not allowing the same denomination to work in two adjacent areas. [Malawi National Archives, GOA 2/4/12, "Mohammadanism and Ethiopianism" (circular letter, Lt. Col. French to Governor Smith, 7 Aug. 1917)]

The colonial powers—Belgians, Spanish, Germans, French, British, and Dutch—also realized that, given their small numbers in their colonies, they could only effectively govern and exploit by making "partners" from among local people, sometimes from minority or Christianized groups. After affirming this relationship, the state then had to separate its partners from all others, thereby creating firmly bounded "ethnic groups" (Bowen 2000:358; Middleton 2000).

When introduced by European missionaries and anthropologists, and used strategically by colonial officials, the concept of "tribe" in Africa became an effective mechanism for implementing colonial policies. These policies determined the relationship between ruler and subject, exploiter and exploited. Commonly referred to as "indirect rule or divide and rule," the British policy was designed to leave traditional leaders and local institutional structures essentially intact. Indirect rule in northern Nigeria aimed to maintain British economic interests in a castelike structure in which the Fulani were to serve as allies. The British official Frederick Lugard endeavored to enlist the conquered Fulani as captains, ensure their loyalty through the establishment of a taxation system that would give them appropriate compensation, control the collection of taxes through partnership, and guide the people on the road to "civilization." Inherent in the process was the need for centralization, all sources of separate identity being either destroyed or subdued. It was then directed that European officers or their Fulani delegates would work within this framework to extract resources for the British Empire. There was little interest on the side of the British to have Africans take on their masters' cultural attributes or values.[2] However, with the change in institutional structures and the imposition of new authority figures, new cultural values did come into existence.

The French had a different approach for administering their African colonies. Their policy of assimilation was much more obtrusive to local leadership and critical of local institutional structures. Africans under French colonial rule were encouraged to "become French" by relinquishing indigenous cultural beliefs and values. Taking on French cultural attributes and achieving competency in spoken French became the markers of "civilization" and elite status (Grinker and Steiner 1997; Simmons 2000; Southall 1997:41–43). The Portuguese and Belgians were notably the most authoritarian and rigid in their native-rule policies (Scupin 2000). Whether for administrative convenience or as part of the civilizing mission, colonialism had a systemic and fundamental impact on Africa's indigenous social order. Over time, and often unwittingly, Africans also began to think of themselves in terms designated by their colonial masters.

Compounding our lack of understanding is confusion about the term *tribalism*, often used, even by academics, interchangeably with ethnicity, as if they were one and the same. Try to imagine, if you will, a news release announcing tribal violence breakouts between the Israelis and the Palestinians, or ethnic clashes between the Irish Catholics and Protestants. This with a full description of white-on-white violence!

Although ethnic violence is commonplace in many parts of the world today, ethnicity in Africa is often treated differently and frequently dismissed as tribalism among native peoples. Increasingly, scholars of African area studies are promoting the view that the conflicts commonly attributed to tribalism are as much an outgrowth of such modern phenomena as political instability, urbanization, and economic hardship as they are a continuation of age-old traditional alliances (Bowen 2001).

So the question remains: Are there tribes in Africa, and if so, what function do they fulfill? Yes, there are tribes in Africa. Many terms change meaning over time in social science discourse, and anthropologists are particularly sensitive to this phenomenon as we attempt to explain the reality of our informants. Tribe can refer to groups with a range of social realities such as a common language, a common culture, common ancestral lineages, or recognition of the same authority figure. Tribe may also appropriately refer to types of subsistence, such as horticulture and pastoralism (Scupin 2000).

It was only in the 1960s that the concept of tribe came under criticism from the academic community as part of a critique of Eurocentric perspectives and analyses. Because the word was also normally used in conjunction with describing rural peoples, there was the unfortunate implication that it explained some largely unchanged and or stagnant stage of development. Many scholars now agree that the word *tribe*, in sociological and anthropological literature, as well as in the popular press, is essentially derogatory, ambiguous, and imprecise.

ETHNICITY: THE AFRICAN PARTICULAR

In Africa, one finds, in addition to cultural pluralism, *syncretism*, that is, the co-existence of different beliefs and practices without necessarily being merged into new entities. Among Africans, an ethnic group is defined both by common objective elements, such as ancestry, kinship and descent, language, history, religion, customs (i.e., even food and initiation rights), institutions, and physical type, and by subjective self-identification. Increasingly, the inherent struggle for political power as it revolves around the state allocation of resources is also equally important in modern times. According to Rene Lemarchard, in an article titled, "Ethnicity as Myth: The View from the Central Africa," "Ethnicity is never what it seems. What looks to the profane like ancestral atavism others identify as a typically modern phenomenon, anchored in the impact of colonial rule. Where neo-Marxists detect class interests parading in traditional garb, mainstream scholars unveil imagined communities. And what many see as the bane of the continent others view as the basis of a moral social contract that carries the seeds of accountability and transparency" (1999:1). Myth or not, "Ethnicities arose from the people's varied experience of migration and urbanization, subordination and competition, religious belief and conversion. These brought people into new relations and differentiated them in new ways. What multiple forms have in common is access to public resources" (Williams 2000:3).

Ethnic groups are meaningful entities, and while the lines between them are seldom sharp, they are, nonetheless, real (Harf and Lombardi 2001:341). According to Susan Greenbaum, ethnicity is a process rather than a finite set of categories. "What endures, however, is kinship. Ethnic groups are basically ancestral groups, in which shared origins provide the basis of a common identity. Ethnicity is both voluntary and imposed. Both elements reflect a continuum,

and divided ancestry represents choice as well as ambiguity" (1992:8). The Yoruba of southwestern Nigeria say, "*Ajobi a gbe wa o*"—May the bond of our common ancestry bless, protect, and nurture us all!

Most Africans identify themselves in terms of their local societies, not as members of any monolithic ethnic groups. Within Africa and among its many diverse communities, a critical part of the contemporary articulation of ethnicity includes a "we-group feeling," sustained by land tenure/ownership, subsistence patterns, language proficiency, and chieftaincy. Whether self-defined, attributed by others, or both, these usually descent-based associations constitute a process of ethnic identification dependent upon real-world causes. The most widespread and apparent expression of this "we/them" worldview comes into play and is defined by the presence of an outsider, "the other(s)." Other indicators of group affiliation include a real or putative common historical experience (i.e., colonialism, migration, etc.) that provides a sense of shared fate. African leaders may also facilitate notions of group membership in an effort to build constituencies by using ethnic loyalties and fears to mobilize supporters. And as Ronald Cohen emphasizes, "The competition for scarce resources intensifies allegiance to racial or ethnic groups" (1978:402).

Anthropologists, responsible for many of the early African ethnographies, have been key participants in the effort to understand the concept of ethnicity in Africa. The focus on ethnicity took hold with the study of rapidly changing communities, many of them African cities. Urban anthropologists, such as Clyde Mitchell, Max Gluckman, A. L. Epstein, and Abner Cohen, set the stage and made some of the most important strides in the transition from tribal to ethnic studies (Grinker and Steiner 1997:6; Toland 1993:233). Additionally, a number of different explanations were given for the sustainability of ethnic groups, such as socially constructed groups' efforts at boundary maintenance

(Barth 1969), primordial ties of language and culture (Geertz 1973), and a group's instrumental strategies (Cohen 1969).

Frederik Barth (1969) wrote a treatise entitled *Ethnic Groups and Boundaries*, in which he challenged prevailing views of how ethnicity operates in the modern world. Barth argued that ethnic identification reflects neither cultural inertia, nor the incomplete process of integration in modern nation-states but, rather, that those persistent ethnic distinctions are an essential feature of such political systems. He observed that boundaries remain between groups in spite of groups' frequent interactions, including intermarriage. In his terms, ethnicity serves as a "vessel" for the mobilization of group interests. The articulation of such interests is a dynamic, ongoing process, not a historical artifact. Barth's ideas strongly influenced a generation of anthropologists and other social scientists interested in the subject of ethnicity (Greenbaum 1992; see also Chapter 4).

Two distinct strands of thought on the nature of ethnicity have emerged. On the one hand, ethnicity is presented as a "primordial" sentiment embedded in human nature (Stack 1974; see also Chapter 4). And that given this inherent nature of ethnicity it actually thrives in societies that extol group values over individual rights. Here we consider ethnicity as to how it relates mainly to the abstract symbol system of a group, functioning largely as a repository of social categories that play an important role in group boundary maintenance and identification. On the other hand, ethnic identification represents a strategic axis around which groups and individuals organize to compete for resources and power. Here we acknowledge that ethnicity is about group consciousness and exclusivity and manifests itself in interethnic discrimination. But ethnic identification and solidarity need to be activated before they can assume relevance as a vehicle for social action. Ethnic diversity need not mean ethnic conflict, but in the modern African state, ethnicity has been commonly

mobilized and exploited by elite groups to advance or defend their positions within the political economy. Although somewhat contradictory in their implications, both perspectives emphasize the fact that ethnic divisions are permanent forces in modern society. These newer conceptions also make it more difficult to define exactly what is an ethnic group.

In the African context this meant that the national integration thesis that became so prominent was hinged on the wrong assumption that ethnic loyalties are temporal survivals from the past that will wither away in the course of urban and industrial development and modernization. With this development, attention shifted from the "detribalization" thesis, which assumes that ethnic ties would be eliminated by modernization, to the "retribalization" or "supertribalization" thesis, in which ethnicity is seen as a consequence of modernization and is heightened by it. According to John Middleton, "Ethnicity is rarely a mere classification system of parallel groups operating at the same level of power, esteem, and privilege. It usually implies an element of vertical subordination: ethnic group membership is a status position in a hierarchy of political-economic power and prestige, and ethnicization aims at improving the position of the entire ethnic group" (2000:93).

We anthropologists were much more comfortable with issues of ethnicity that stressed group solidarity and explaining cultural phenomena in terms of the "ethnographic presence," even if perpetuating, at times, ahistorical perceptions. We now know that ethnicity is realistically a process, both voluntary and imposed. Elements reflecting a continuum and divided ancestry represent choice as well as ambiguity. Fragmentation and intensification can, in fact, be part of the same process.

The fluid nature of ethnicity in Africa is particularly interesting from an anthropological perspective. Changes in political, economic, and occupational positions have led to changes in identities leading to stability in interethnic relationships. From ancient times trade encouraged a symbolic interethnicity among people who regularly came into contact with one another (Falola 2000). African ethnicity is syncretic, multilayered, and transitional. It may be the most adaptable component of anything close to a pan-African phenomenon.

In Africa, indigenous group identities are, more often than not, negotiable. Interesting examples of the fluidity and the negotiable nature of ethnicity include the Diakhanke, inhabitants of the Senegambia hinterland, who specialized in trade, carrying goods from the Upper Niger to the Senegal and Gambia Rivers and establishing trading colonies throughout West Africa (Falola 2000:29–30). And a more systematic ethnic manipulation was evident in apartheid South Africa, where eugenicists, with the assistance of the academic community, codified ethnic boundaries for political and economic advantage (Gates 2000).

Ethnicity and Ritual

Reinvention, resynthesis, and appropriation of cultural forms all influence the expression of ethnicity. Culture helps us organize a worldview. Many of the customs and associated rituals in Africa reinforce a sense of belonging to communal living and the importance of group membership. There are many examples throughout Africa. We now find "ethnic" associations that enable urban dwellers to organize themselves for mutual aid and benefit. These associations are an important source of security for those finding themselves away from the comforts of lineage and community. In Migwani, in central Kenya, local identity is expressed outwardly in distinctive traits such as styles of dress and body decorations, hairstyles, popular songs and dances, and nuances of language. For the Kaguru of Tanzania, East Africa, the initiation of adolescent boys and girls defines them as a culturally unique people. The rituals and symbolism associated with this transformation of children into

adult members of society mark them as a distinct ethnic group (Beidelman 1997).

The ritually important festival in contemporary Ghana is a funnel to history that keeps alive much that people have lost; it supplies what modernization and Westernization have eroded and allows participants to look into their past with joy and pride. In addition, there exists a link to tradition where the rites somehow embody what only a few select individuals are privileged to know, thus marking it with prestige. Being scarce, this selective knowledge is cherished. The tenacity of age-old tradition has preserved some archaic language forms, used by select individuals, that few others are able to understand or appreciate. This has effectively become a ritual and performance language that provides an added sense of authenticity to cultural events and displays. Among African governments that now encourage the revitalization and reinvention of tradition, those proficient in select areas gain renewed status. The ability to improvise becomes key to the continuity and genius of it all. Interesting are the analogies that are made to Christendom, as Ghanaians convert to this tradition, to ensure that the net of inclusive grows larger as times goes on. The main concern is to attract the largest possible following and support by winning over the community.

In contemporary Ghanaian society, some festivals take the place of traditional rites of passage, dictating rights and obligations of a new generation to the past and as enforcers of values for the future. Many of the more extensive traditional ceremonies that once marked major transitions in the lives of young men and women have, for the most part, been replaced by Western schooling and other local institutional arrangements for passing on knowledge.

Historical events also represent oneness of society, ethnic unity and togetherness. For example, the Hogbetsotso festival is a celebration to commemorate the migration of the Ewes from Notsie and to rekindle a keener appreciation of the cultural heritage and traditional values of Anlo. It is also meant to foster a sense of belonging and ethnic unity (Kodzo-Vordoagu 1994). From traditional times, Anlo, like other Ewe states, has been a monarchy, the chief being the constitutional head (that is, he reigns rather than rules). In traditional times, a hierarchy of officials ranging from the lineage–head through the ward chiefs, sub-chiefs, chiefs (*dufia*) to the paramount chief–conducted the administration of the state.

IMPORTANCE OF POLITICAL CHOICES

Clifford Geertz, best known for *The Interpretation of Cultures* (1973), wrote in an essay:

> At the political center of any complexly organized society (to narrow our focus now to that) there is both a governing elite and a set of symbolic forms expressing the fact that it is governing. No matter how democratically the members of the elite are chosen (usually not very) or how deeply divided among themselves they may be (usually more than outsiders imagine), they justify their existence and order their actions in terms of a collection of stories, ceremonies, insignia, formalities, which they have inherited or, in more revolutionary situations, invented. [1985:15]

The state, through its nature of incorporation of the many into a united one, articulated with an official origin myth, charter, and dominant system of values and beliefs, has always constituted a more or less believable, stable-unstable entity at the ethnic level. Precolonial Africans may have formed something analogous to ethnic units within a compact territory but not as a political unit. Leadership and political authority in African societies within state development, at least comparable to Europe, was never defined exclusively by ethnic terms. It has been argued that colonialism-interrupted political autonomy left the continent with bitter ethnic, class, and intercountry hostilities, which have been at the root of many contemporary problems (Evans-Pritchard 1951).

Other forms of changing inter-ethnic contact, especially in the context of the social-political changes associated with colonial rule include: (1). Peripheral Contact, people exchanging goods without much interaction, (2). Institutional Contact, a mostly peripheral contact based upon some institutionalized meeting point such as trade or conflict; (3). Acculturation, a partial merging, where the weaker society makes more adjustments than the stronger and accepts some of the outward manifestations of identity of the dominant group; (4). Dominance, a single society with two categories distinguished primarily by non-ethnic characteristics such as income, education and religion; (5). Paternalism, a specialized form of institutional contact which, unlike domination, involves the retention of distinctiveness among the interactive societies; (6). Integration, a reduction of identifying with ethnic group and instead the establishment of a larger unity based upon association ties; and (7). Pluralism, similar to an integrated situation, but the distinction being the existence of a larger order without the clear dominant-subordinate relation. [Paden and Soja 1970:26]

Contemporary sub-Saharan Africa presents some interesting case studies. Nigeria is a good example of the inherent intricacies of ethnicity in public and private life. In early contact with the British, an ideology developed in which the Hamitic Hausa-Fulani became models for "civilization" and partners in its spread. An example is the Yauri emirate, located in the northwest part of Sokoto State, Nigeria. By the time of the British conquest, it was the smallest of the Hausa emirates, and the westernmost station along the Niger River. Yauri never was a Fulani state, although it had paid tribute to the Fulani sultan Sokoto. Its rulers have generally been careful to stress their separate Hausa identity and, therefore, their distinction from the Fulani. Yauri's rulers form a Hausaized minority among an ethnically heterogeneous population. Changes in political, economic, and occupational position have led to changes in such identities. The stability resulting from the imposition of British rule frustrated resistance to the emir's power. The traditional patterns of migration into Yauri were changed and the Hausa population grew significantly. In addition, there was an increase in the number of people changing ethnic identities from Reshe to Yaurawa and then to Hausa (Salamone 1974, 1985).

People are strength. Ethnic group enclaves reproduce their heritable cultures (and traditions) with the polity while assembling more slowly alliances. In comparative and historical perspective, uni-ethnic states are the exception, not the rule. It was the colonial powers, and the independent states succeeding them, that reinforced the concept that each and every person had an "ethnic identity" that determined his or her place within the colony or the postcolonial system. Even such seemingly innocent events as the taking of a census created the idea of a colony-wide ethnic category to which one belonged and had loyalties.

In the postcolonial period, most African countries have, like other world areas, tried to integrate their diverse peoples. It is a policy that has risks and sometimes runs into difficulties. At the beginning of the colonial period, Frederick Lugard, a British military-trained administrator, realized the value of governing this protectorate through local rulers, if possible. Nigeria was initially divided into north and south, for administrative purposes. In the north, the emirs, who held religious and political influence, were recruited, especially those who had been defeated, to cooperate with and work for the British government. In return, the British government would confirm them in office. In the southwestern region, largely occupied by another major ethnic group, the Yoruba, officeholders were identified among traditional kingdoms and chieftancies. The problem came when assessing centralized leadership and/or authority holders in the eastern region. Many of the groups in the southeastern part of the country had decentralized authority frameworks. Important leadership positions were held at very local

levels, such as clan and village heads. A new and foreign officeholder, the district officer, was created by the British to administer colonial rule in these areas.

At the dawn of independence Nigeria was divided into three regions: north, south, and east—each with its own party supported by ethnic allegiances. In 1963, the midwestern region was created in response to minority interests within the former western region. The intensity and discord of this three-way division, a pogrom against the Igbo in the north, and a feeling of disenfranchisement drove the Igbo in the southeast region of Biafra to attempt to break away from Nigeria in 1967. The traumas of the civil war and those that followed led politicians to try a new system in the politically and ethnically divided country. They carved the country into 12 states, the boundaries of which cut through the territories of the three largest ethnic groups (Hausa, Yoruba, and Igbo), encouraging a new federalist politics based on multiethnic coalitions.

Nigeria's 1979 government put in place *the Federal Character Principle*. The principle was grounded in sensitivity to ethnoregional representation in the federal government and its agencies.[3] The policy of federal character representation was nurtured by the Mohammed/Obasanjo regime, which introduced the concept as a panacea to the problem of ethnic balancing in federal government appointments. The basis of representation now, however, was states rather than geographic regions, which nevertheless continued to be important. In 1976, the Nigerian government, under military rule, further divided the country by creating seven more states. By creating 19 states, it was hoped that ethnic coalitions would be weakened, and even disappear. Once again, the ruling government decided to renegotiate the sharing of national resources (Diamond 1988; Joseph 1987). In 1991, 11 more states were created, and in 1996 the number rose to, and is currently holding at, 36. The Federal Territory was situated strategically to avoid ethnic domination by any one group and is located centrally within the country's middle belt.

The facts of ethnic differentiation in terms of language, culture, territory, and even loyalty as an "objective" reality remain problematic from the point of view of governance. The problem is only made worse by the competition for scarce resources between the groups. Increasing the number of states was a direct response to the demands and agitation of groups that were not satisfied with their positions in the federation. Initially, it was the minorities who agitated for more states, but in 1990 the need for states had changed. They were no longer needed to protect group identity and autonomy. Any group that sought a share of the "national cake" or that wanted to maximize its share of the cake demanded more states, although states were not designed to have an ethnic basis. An example of the latter was the Igbo, who constituted the majority in only two states, Anambra and Imo; the other major groups, the Hausa/Fulani and the Yoruba, represented majorities in about five states each. The Igbo had persistently pressed for equality with other major groups by demanding new states. Realizing that the creation of states could go on endlessly, the federal government tried to bolster local governments as another way of meeting the demands. The subordinate status of local governments, however, coupled with the continued use of the states as units for distributing national resources, made demands for more states a recurrent theme in Nigerian federalism (Udogu 1999).

Elections can and will stir up intergroup tensions. African governments have taken different approaches to the problem. In the 2000 presidential election in Ghana each candidate had to secure a percentage of votes from each of the country's 11 regions. At the other extreme, Kenya's Daniel Moi has created an ethnic electoral base that excludes most Kikuyus, thus increasing the relevance of ethnicity in politics and therefore the level of intergroup tensions.

RELIGION

A person can be half-African and half-Arab and simultaneously a citizen of two countries, but it is more difficult to be half-Catholic and half-Muslim. As people define their identity in ethnic and religious terms, they are likely to view their world in an "us versus them" basis (Huntington 2001). Mobilizing support and forming coalitions on the basis of ethnic and religious ideology has become a powerful tool among some African governments.

Islam was introduced into West Africa during the fifteenth century. The people in northern Nigeria who accepted Islam took on the name "Hausa," and those who did not remained "Maguzawa." This process of fission essentially divided the community into two distinct ethnic societies. On the other hand, in the nineteenth century, after the Fulani conquered the area, there was a merger of the urban Hausa and Fulani into a new group called "Hausa-Fulani." All these people are now referred to as Hausa by people in the south.

In contemporary times, the link between religion and politics has become very complex. Muslims in Nigeria are about 47 percent and Christians make up 35 percent of the population. Nigeria now has 11 states with Shari'ah law in place. Muslims are also members of the dominant political and ethnic group in the country. Islam is generally associated with the Hausa-Fulani segment of the population, though an increasing number of Yoruba are now practicing Muslims. With the political amalgamation of the various ethnic groups in Nigeria into one political entity, and since Hausa-Fulani ethnicity and the Islamic religion pioneered a political party for central political power, no major decisions are ever taken without prior consultations and approbation of certain powerful emirs. No Christian equivalent exists within the political arena (Assimeng 1989:245–246).

People who "became" Hausa in order to reap the benefits of affiliating with that religion: political centralization, administrative organization, trade, connections with a far-reaching network of states sharing a common civilization and religion. In attempting to overcome the various hazards of trade, traders had to build relations of trust and confidence with those whom they encountered during their journeys. Learning languages was common. Next, intermarriage was a social bond and alliance-building mechanism for promoting shared interests (Falola 2000:29; Salamone 1974). Bonds were also created through "blood brotherhoods." In northwestern Uganda during the nineteenth century, the salt trade became a very contentious one, with struggle over control of the trade. Religion was used to facilitate trade. The Hausa, also long-distance traders, used Islam to create an effective bond of unity among themselves in order to control trade (Cohen 1969).

RELIGION AND ETHNICITY IN SUDAN

Sudan is the largest nation in Africa, covering nearly a million square miles. The population is estimated at 34 million, and 70 percent are Muslim, 5 percent Christian, and 25 percent animist. Many different ethnic groups occupy the country, and over 400 languages are spoken. Northern Sudan represents Arabic Islamic culture, with both pastoralists and agriculturists. Southern Sudan is composed primarily of more "African" people who follow indigenous animist beliefs and/or Christianity. The country is effectively divided between the north and the south, with all real power, both economic and political, residing in the north. Sudanese have engaged in destructive civil wars for years (Middleton 2000).

The British colonized the Sudan in 1896–98. They allowed for Anglo-Egyptian administration until 1924, when they introduced "indirect rule" through local chiefs. The tensions and disparities between the north and south in large part emerged as a result of British colonial policy, which sought favor with the northerners, bringing Western education and infrastructure developments, with benign neglect and control as the overall approach toward southerners. The British southern policy led to a depopulated no-man's land between the two regions, which kept peace during the colonial era. When Sudan gained independence in 1956, the better educated and Western-trained northerners were the beneficiaries of almost all of the government and administrative positions; only 4 such positions out of 800 went to southerners (O'Ballance 1977:70). The frustrations and insults felt among southerners led to the first Sudanese separatist movement. A 16-year civil war ensued, ending with autonomy for the south, which devolved into chaos.

Military and civil governments seized power alternately, until in 1969 a coup d'état brought in a military government headed by Colonel Jaafar Nimeiri. In 1972, his government sanctioned a constitution that mandated a single political party, the Sudan Socialist Union. A second southern revolution broke out in 1983, when the military government introduced Shari'ah law for the entire country, which is still in progress, the impasse halted only by an uneasy cease-fire. As a result, the Sudan People's Liberation Army (SPLA) was formed in the south, with its goal of a "unified, secular, democratic Sudan." Martial law was enacted in 1984 as southern Sudan sank into full-scale famine, partially caused by drought but primarily by political troubles. The religious-based ethnic struggle between the north and south continues today.

GENOCIDE IN RWANDA

Rwanda has experienced Africa's worst attempted genocide in modern times and is still recovering from the shock. Even where mass murder appears aimed at a specific ethnic community, questions still arise as to the meaning of ethnicity where the groups in conflict share the same language, the same national territory, the same customs, and for centuries have lived more or less peacefully side by side. The country has been beset by ethnic tension associated with the traditionally unequal relationship between the dominant Tutsi minority and the majority Hutus. Mass conflict began when Belgian colonial rulers gave the Tutsi a monopoly of state power. (Middleton 2000). Using "ethnicity" as a political weapon is a product of modern politics that often reflects a real or imagined inequity of resource distribution and allocation (Bowen 2001; Falola 2000; Middleton 2000).

Before the modern era some Africans did consider themselves Hutu or Tutsi, Nuer or Zande, but these labels were not the characteristic of everyday identity. A woman living in Central Africa drew her identity from where she was born, from her lineage and in-laws, and from her wealth. Tribal or ethnic identity was rarely important in everyday life and could change as people moved over vast areas in pursuit of trade or new lands. Conflicts were more often within tribal categories than between them, as people fought over sources of water, farmland, or grazing rights.

In Rwanda and Burundi, German and Belgian colonizers admired the taller people called Tutsis, who formed a small minority in both colonies. The Belgians gave the Tutsis, the minority group, privileged access to education and jobs, and even instituted a minimum height requirement for entrance to college. To enable colonial officials to distinguish Tutsi from non-Tutsi, everyone was required to carry identity cards with tribal labels. Fortunately, people cannot be forced into the neat compartments that this requirement suggests. Many Hutus are tall and many Tutsis short; furthermore, many Hutus and Tutsis had intermarried to such an extent that they were not easily distinguished physically (nor are they today). They spoke the same language and carried out the same religious practices. In most regions of the colonies

the categories became economic labels: poor Tutsis became Hutus, and economically successful Hutus became Tutsis. Where the labels Hutu and Tutsi had not been much used, lineages with lots of cattle were simply labeled Tutsi; poorer lineages, Hutu. Colonial discrimination against Hutus created what had never existed before: a sense of collective Hutu identity, a Hutu cause. In the late 1950s Hutus began to rebel against Tutsi rule (encouraged by Europeans on their way out) and then created an independent, Hutu-dominated state in Rwanda; this state then gave rise to Tutsi resentments and to the creation of a Tutsi rebel army, the Rwandan Patriotic Front.

In Rwanda, the continuing slaughter of the past few years stemmed from efforts by the dictator-president Juvenal Habyarimana to wipe out his political opposition, Hutu as well as Tutsi. In 1990–91 Habyarimana began to assemble armed gangs into a militia called Interahamwe. The militia carried out its first massacre of a village in March 1992, and in 1993 began systematically to kill Hutu moderates and Tutsis (Bowen 2000:356–366; Lemarchand 1999).

Paul Kagame, the current president of Rwanda, grew up in Uganda where his parents fled to escape Hutu violence. He has attempted to play down any ethnic agenda in Rwanda, presenting himself as a Rwandan and not a Tutsi. Like other African countries, Rwanda is attempting to forge a national identity that will supersede any ethnic identity (Scupin 2000).

SOUTH AFRICA IN TRANSITION

In some ways South Africa is a mirror reflection of all other countries in the sub-Saharan region, and at the same time, it is very different. In many countries, colonial authorities exploited and exacerbated ethnic differences for their own ends, and the white regimes of southern Africa pursued an aggressive policy of retribalization (Bowen 2001; Wiley 1999).

The Republic of South Africa, also referred to simply as South Africa, came into being in 1961. It is the most populous country in southern Africa. It is also the most industrialized and has the largest white population in sub-Saharan Africa. Population estimates show that South Africa has 34.5 million blacks, 5 million whites, 3.5 million coloreds, and 1 million Asians. Eight million people, mostly blacks, live in the squalor of squatter settlements. Many blacks were resettled into reservation areas called "homelands." About 18 million black families earn less than $220 a month. Half the black population is illiterate and half of its work force is unemployed. The urban population continues to grow, while the infrastructure of social services and amenities fails to meet urgent needs. Currently, only 15 percent of the urban population have access to potable water; about 8 million have access to only minimal sanitation; about 17 million do not have electricity and about 8 million do not have formal road access to their homes. Of the white population, 60 percent are Afrikaans-speaking. These are descendants of Dutch, Huguenot, and German ancestry. Forty percent are English-speakers, descendants of British rule in the Cape Province (Middleton 2000).

For most of South Africa's contemporary history, social identity has been tied to a political agenda of legitimized racial separation and discrimination. In apartheid South Africa, race or skin color was enclosed within the net of ethnicity, thus clouding the issues particular to each.[4] This is even more problematic because the social categories of apartheid were defined by crude racial measures (see Chapter 4). Phenotype, as perceived by those in power, was the most salient component of apartheid social categories.

The white minority population was privileged by the state. Blacks, members of the native populations of South Africa, were largely disenfranchised, while those designated as colored fell somewhere in between. Some coloreds were able to pass for white; some were accused of being black.[5] Whites took all that was good; blacks were denied all that was good. The colored population was systematically relocated over a period of 40 years, at the whim of how much privilege they were deemed deserving of to serve the needs of the apartheid system. Residential patterns, school attendance, job niches, and entertainment venues still, for the most part, represent the social structure of apartheid, lagging behind the rapid ideological changes mandated by the "postapartheid era." Those designated as "colored" are, perhaps, the most interesting of apartheid's creations: white is privilege, black is disenfranchised, colored is neither.

According to Jamie Gates (2000:58), Birgit Pickel (1997) argues from the literature that the colored category was constructed as a buffer between privileged white and subjugated black South Africans. The colored category, as with the white, black, and Indian categories, was reified and given the meaning most conducive to the goals of apartheid. A colored identity remains, in some ways, a disclaimer. It is the perception that one is not black, white, Indian, Chinese, or a member of any other socially meaningful category—in other words, it is more a perception of what coloreds are not than what they are.

About 1995, nine new provincial capitals, the dissolution of the ten black homelands, successful national/local government elections, the inauguration of the human rights commission, and other transformations of the social order set the stage for new dispensations. The new flag of six colors symbolizes the people, their blood, their land, the gold under the ground, the sky, and peace. The importance of language is expressed in the interim constitution, which accords official status to 9 of South Africa's 11 indigenous languages (isiZulu, Setswana, North Sotho, South Sotho, Xhosa, Swazi, Ndebele, Venda, Shangan), putting them on a par with English and Afrikaans in all spheres of life. This document, referred to as a "model" by many a news correspondent, has left out in the cold the "language of apartheid,"–the words, phrases, and idiomatic expressions that continue to color daily interactions among South Africans.

The language of the "new" South Africa stresses the need for a nonracial, nonsexist society and provides hope for a positive transformation. The African National Congress's Reconstruction and Development Program (RDP) promises transparency, socioeconomic restructuring, growth, and equity. The National Government of Unity has put in place the Truth and Reconciliation Commission, the Human Rights Commission, and the Anti-Corruption Commission. National and local decisions are being taken on affirmative action, gender equity, house subsidy grants, industrial development, and the integration of universal primary education. Workers now have the Labor Relations Act and a Commission of Conciliation, Mediation and Arbitration (CCMA), which is independent of the state, trade unions, and employers, to resolve disputes through conciliation.

Crossroads, the built-up shanties of the blacks that have been marginalized by the system of institutionalized racism of apartheid, are appalling. In these slum conditions there is no plumbing, no electricity, and no waste collection. Homes are made of battered aluminum, cardboard, and wood strips salvaged from demolished construction sites. In contrast, the designated areas for resident Indians are crowded with some massively impressive building, showing the entrepreneurial successes of the owners. Locked into small plots with nowhere else to go, they overbuilt. Mitchell Plain is one model community for Indians. Bishops Court, the exclusive reserve for whites, is all that wealth can afford. High walls shield occupants from the eyes of those who pass on the surrounding roadways, as each house is self-contained with a state-of-the-art security system.

The real problem for contemporary South Africa is the urgency to meet the needs of its many ethnic and communal groups, especially those facing dramatic social, political, and economic changes for which their history has not prepared them. People will be drawn into groups with which they feel an affinity, for mutual assistance and in reaction toward hostility against them. South Africans who are making a public claim for a nonracial, nonsexist society that forbids discrimination will have to find a way to bargain for an equitable division of the state's resources if they hope to avoid the ethnic clashes being played out in many other parts of the African continent.

CONCLUSION

All cultural concepts are inherently interconnected in complex and often complicated ways. Ethnicity is just one cultural construct for self- and group identity with both historical and contemporary references. In Africa, traditional ethnic categories were influenced by changes in the social-economic structure attendant to the colonial and postcolonial eras, leading to a complex identity paradigm. Communal self-perception and identification by others are equally powerful issues to contend with in Africa. An assessment of "ethnicity" in the present day requires an evaluation of (1) ethnic minorities who are nationals, (2) ethnic minorities who are migrants and/or refugees, (3) ethnic majority populations who are politically dominant, (4) ethnic majority populations who are politically subordinate, and (5) ethnic minority populations who are politically dominant.

Most African instrumental and symbolic features sustain the continuing value for ethnic association and affiliation. Ethnicity in Africa is now being used to integrate the trajectories of political power, prestige, and privilege through access to economic resources. Attendant issues include spatial integration and social boundaries, physical expressions, and symbolic representations.

Group and individual identity that is now based along ethnic lines serves to secure a community's place in the nation-state, as well as the nation-state's preeminence in the lives of communities. Among Africa's multiethnic societies this means bargaining for the group's share of the resources available in the state against other groups, defending the group against discrimination, and, in general, maximizing its members' chances and minimizing their disadvantages (Hobsbawn 1991).

NOTES

1. At the Berlin Conference of 1884–85, European countries with interests in expanding into the African continent met to determine the rules that would guide them. This is sometimes referred to as "the scramble for Africa."

2. Flora Shaw (Lady Lugard) (1964) developed an elaborate scheme for racial ranking.

3. Chronology of major events in Nigeria's 40 years of nationhood:

October 1960	Nigeria gains independence from Britain
October 1963	Nigeria becomes a republic
January 1966	First military coup led by Major Chukwuma Kaduna Nzeogu
July 1966	Counter coup by Lieutenant Colonel Yakubu Gowon
May 1967	Nigerian civil war starts
1967	Gowon divides four regions into 12 states
January 1970	Nigerian civil war ends
July 1975	Brigadier Murtala Mohammed topples Gowon in military coup
1976	Murtala increases states to 19
October 1979	Obasanjo hands power to Shehu Shagari, second republic begins
December 1983	General Muhammadu Buhari topples Shagari in military coup
August 1985	General Ibrahim Babangida ousts Buhari in military putsch
1987	Babangida increased states to 21
1991	Babangida creates nine more states, bringing total to 30
June 1993	Babangida reneges on handover plan, annuls presidential poll
1993	Ernest Shonekan assumes office as head of interim government
November 1993	General Sani Abacha seizes power from Shonekan
1996	Abacha increases states to 36

Source: From "Landmarks in Nigerian History." Copyright © 2001. Reprinted by permission of Panapress.

4. Apartheid, "apartness," was maintained by a massive legal and institutional structure to ensure the perpetuation of white rule. Some of the laws:

1893	Indians disenfranchised
1902–1909	Location laws (Jim Crow in the United States)
1905	Schools Board Act in the Cape
1902	Native Reserve Location Act
1904	Locations Act
1909	South Africa Act, basis for Constitution Act of

1961; established places for prime minister and parliament government; coloreds and blacks could elect whites to represent them in parliament until this "privilege" was abolished for Africans in 1959 and for coloreds in 1968.

1913	Native Land Act (scheduled areas)
1923	Natives (urban areas) act
1910–24	Definitive legislative acts to institutionalize segregation, politically, territorially, and residentially. First restriction of black and colored voters to the Cape alone, and the exclusion of blacks everywhere from parliament.
1949	South African Citizen Bill
1949	Prohibition of Mixed Marriages Act; repealed in 1985
1946	Asiatic Land Tenure Act
1950	Immorality Act
1950	Population Registration Act
1950	Group Area Act; Urban Areas Act and Bantu Homelands Citizenship Act (migrant workers)
1951	Prevention of Illegal Squatters Act
1951	Separate Representation Voters Act; only certain South Africans can now vote
1952	Natives Services Levy Act
1953	Natives Abolition of Passes and Coordination of Documents Act
1953	Bantu Education Act and the University Education Act
1954	Natives Resettlement Act
1959	Bantu Self-Government Act
1960	ANC officially banned
1969	Terrorism Act; backdated to 1962. Terrorism now receives death penalty; no appeal.
1984	New Constitution Act, creating a three-chamber parliament dominated by the white chamber with subordinate chambers for coloreds and Asians. Africans, making up 73 percent of the population, were still excluded. Prime minister position abolished and a "president" position, which is now head of state and head of government, is new government profile.

5. Racial Classification Act, Population Registration Act, Colored Labor Preferential Act. South Africa Apartheid Racial Classification and Reclassifications: In South Africa, the state chooses to classify people according to race rather than shoe size, class, or educational attainment. The Population Registration Act requires that all South Africans be classified according to race at birth. It is possible to apply for reclassification. The Minister of Home Affairs, Stoffel Botha, disclosed in 1985:

702 coloured people turned white
19 whites became coloured
One Indian became white
Three Chinese became white
50 Indians became coloured
21 Indians became Malay
30 Malays went Indian
249 blacks became coloured
20 coloureds became black
Two blacks became "other Asians"
One black was classified Griqua
11 coloureds became Chinese
Three coloureds went Malay

One Chinese became coloured
Eight Malays became coloured
Three blacks were classed as Malay
No blacks became white and no whites became black

Source: Reprinted by permission of *The Johannesburg Star*, part of Independent Newspapers Network.

If you read the progressive press you will find Indians and coloureds referred to as blacks, or quotation marks are used (as in "coloured" schools), or else a qualifier is introduced: "so-called coloured areas."

REFERENCES

ACHEBE, CHINUA. 2000. *Home and Exile.* Oxford: University Press.

ADEJUMOBI, SAHEED A. 2000. Politics and government. In *Africa*, vol. 2. *African Cultures and Societies before 1885.* Toyin Falola, ed. Pp. 149–161. Durham, NC: Carolina Academic Press.

Africa South of the Sahara. 2001. 30th edition. London: Europa.

ASSIMENG, MAX. 1989. *Religion and Social Change in West Africa: An Introduction to the Sociology of Religion.* Accra: Ghana Universities Press.

BARTH, F., ed. 1969. *Ethnic Groups and Boundaries: The Social Organization of Cultural Differences.* Boston: Little, Brown.

BEIDELMAN, T. O. 1997. *The Cool Knife: Imagery of Gender, Sexuality, and Moral Education in Kaguru Initiation Ritual.* Washington, DC: Smithsonian Institution Press.

BOHANNAN, PAUL. 1995. *How Culture Works.* New York: Free Press.

BOWEN, JOHN R. 2001. The myth of global ethnic conflict. *Journal of Democracy* (October 1996). *Taking Sides: Clashing Views on Controversial Global Issues.* James E. Harf and Mark Owen Lombardi, eds. Guilford, CT: McGraw-Hill/Dushkin.

CASTELLS, MANUEL. 1998. *End of Millennium: The Information Age.* Oxford: Blackwell.

COHEN, ABNER. 1969. *Custom and Politics in Urban Africa: A Study of Hausa Migrants in Yoruba Towns.* Berkeley: University of California Press.

COHEN, RONALD. 1978. Ethnicity: Problem and Focus. *Annual Review of Anthropology* 7:379–403.

___. 1993. Ethnicity, the state, and moral order. In *Ethnicity and the State. Political and Legal Anthropology Series*, vol. 9. Judith D. Toland, ed. New Brunswick, NJ: Transaction.

DIAMOND, LARRY. 1988. "Nigeria: Pluralism, statism, and the struggle for democracy." In *Democracy in Developing Countries: Africa.* Larry Diamond, Juan J. Linz, and Seymour Martin Lipset, eds. Boulder, CO: Lynne Rienner.

DOUGLAS, MARY. 1997. Lele economy compared with the Bushong. In *Perspectives on Africa: A Reader in Culture, History, and Representation.* Roy R. Grinker and Christopher B. Steiner, eds. Cambridge, MA: Blackwell.

ELLER, JACK D. 1999. *From Culture to Ethnicity to Conflict: An Anthropological Perspective on International Ethnic Conflict.* Ann Arbor: University of Michigan Press.

EVANS-PRITCHARD, E. E. 1940. Time and space. In *The Nuer.* Oxford: Clarendon Press.

___. 1951. *Kinship and Marriage among the Nuer.* Oxford: Clarendon Press.

FALOLA, TOYIN, ed. 2000. *Africa: African Cultures and Societies before 1885*, vol. 2. Durham, NC: Carolina Academic Press.

GATES, JAMIE. 2000. Review of coloured ethnicity and identity: A Case study in the former coloured areas in the Western Cape, South Africa. *Transforming Anthropology* 9(1):58–60.

GEERTZ, CLIFFORD. 1973. *The Interpretation of Cultures.* New York: Basic Books.

___. 1985. "Centers, kings, and charisma: Reflections on the symbolics of power." In *Rites of Power, Symbolism, Ritual and Politics since the Middle Ages*, Sean Wilentz, ed. Philadelphia: University of Pennsylvania Press.

GREENBAUM, SUSAN. 1992. *Race/Ethnicity/Culture.* Essay produced under sponsorship for USF Center for Teaching Enhancement, Resource Guide for the General Education Curriculum, Department of Anthropology, University of South Florida.

GRINKER, ROY RICHARD, and CHRISTOPHER B. STEINER, eds. 1997. Introduction: Africa in perspective. In *Perspectives on Africa: A Reader in Culture, History, and Representation.* Cambridge, MA: Blackwell.

HARF, JAMES E., and MARK OWEN LOMBARDI, eds. 2001. *Taking Sides: Clashing Views on Controversial Global Issues.* Guilford, CT: McGraw-Hill/Dushkin.

HOBSBAWN, E. J. 1991. *Nations and Nationalism since 1780: Program, Myth, Reality.* Cambridge: University of Cambridge Press.

HUNTINGTON, SAMUEL P. 2001. The clash of civilizations? In *Taking Sides: Clashing Views on Controversial Global Issues.* James E. Harf and Mark Owen Lombardi, eds. Guilford, CT: McGraw-Hill/Dushkin.

JOSEPH, RICHARD A. 1987. *Democracy and Prebendal Politics in Nigeria: The Rise and Fall of the Second Republic.* New York: Cambridge University Press.

KODZO-VORDOAGU, J. G. 1994. *Anlo Hogbetsotso Festival.* Accra, Ghana: Domak Press.

LEMARCHAND, RENE. 1999. Ethnicity as myth: The view from the Central Africa. Occasional paper. Centre of African Studies, University of Copenhagen.

MAYBURY-LEWIS, DAVID. 1997. *Indigenous Peoples, Ethnic Groups, and the State.* Boston: Allyn & Bacon.

MIDDLETON, JOHN, ed. 2000. *Encyclopedia of Africa: South of the Sahara*, vol. 2. New York: Simon & Schuster/Macmillan.

NADEL, S. F. 1942. *A Black Byzantium: The Kingdom of Nupe in Nigeria.* Cambridge, MA: Blackwell.

O'BALLANCE, E. 1977. *The Secret War in the Sudan, 1955–1972.* London: Faber & Faber.

PADEN, JOHN, and EDWARD SOJA, eds. 1970. *The African Experience,* vol. 2. Evanston, IL: Northwestern University Press.

PICKEL, BIRGIT. 1997. *Coloured Ethnicity and Identity: A Case Study in the Former Coloured Areas in the Western Cape/South Africa.* Hamburg, Germany: Lit Verlag.

PUTMAN, DIANA, and MOHAMOOD C. NOOR. 1993. *The Somalis: Their History and Culture. CAL Refugee Fact Sheet No. 9.* Washington, DC: Refugee Service Center.

SALAMONE, FRANK A. 1974. *Gods and Goods in Africa. Persistence and Change in Ethnic and Religious Identity in Yauri Emirate, Northwestern State, Nigeria.* HRA Flex Books, Ethnography Series FF 36-001. New Haven, CT: Human Relations Area Files.

___. 1985. The social construction of colonial reality: Yauri emirate. *Cahiers d'Etudes Africaines* 98, XXV-2:139–159.

SCUPIN, RAYMOND. 2000. *Cultural Anthropology: A Global Perspective.* 4th edition. Upper Saddle River, NJ: Prentice Hall.

SHAW, FLORA L. (Lady Lugard). 1905. *A Tropical Dependency: An Outline of the Ancient History of the Western Soudan with an Account of the Modern Settlement of Northern Nigeria.* London: J. Nisbet.

SIMMONS, DAVID. 2000. Signs of the times: Missionaries and tribal genesis in southern Rhodesia. *Transforming Anthropology* 9(2):3–18.

SOUTHALL, AIDAN W. 1997. The illusion of tribe. In *Perspectives on Africa: A Reader in Culture, History, and Representation.* Roy R. Grinker and Christopher B. Steiner, eds. Cambridge, MA: Blackwell.

STACK, CAROL B. 1974. *All Our Kin: Strategies for Survival in a Black Community.* New York: Harper & Row.

Teaching Tolerance magazine. 2001. No. 19, Spring. Southern Poverty Law Center.

TOLAND, JUDITH D. 1993. *Ethnicity and the State: Political and Legal Anthropology Series,* vol. 9. New Brunswick, NJ: Transaction.

TWUM-BARIMA, K. 1982. *The Cultural Basis of Our National Development.* J. B. Danquah Lectures, fifteenth series. February 1982. Accra, Ghana: Academy of Arts and Sciences.

UDOGU, IKE E. 1999. Ethnicity, the state and the issue of nation-building in Nigeria's fourth republic. *Scandinavian Journal of Development Alternatives and Area Studies* 18(4):5–22.

WILEY, DAVID. 1999. If it's Africa, this must be a tribe. In *Capturing the Continent: U.S. Media Coverage of Africa.* Special 1990 edition of *Africa News.*

WILLIAMS, GAVIN. 2001. Reforming Africa: Continuities and change. In *Africa South of the Sahara.* 30th edition. John Middleton, ed. London: Europa.

15

THE MIDDLE EAST

Laurie King-Irani

Indiana University, Bloomington

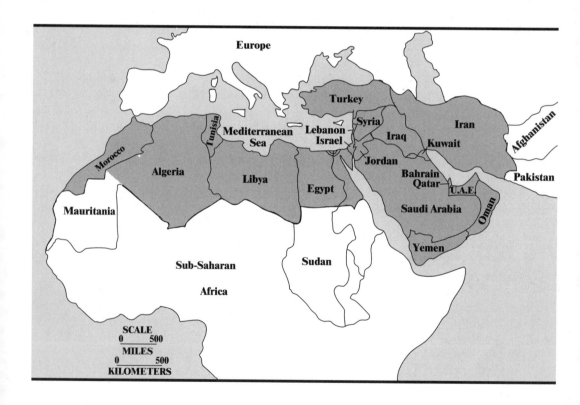

Scarcely a day passes without a dramatic news report about violence in the Middle East. Whether an Islamic group massacring villagers in Algeria; clashes between Israeli soldiers and Palestinian youths; civil war, famine, and population displacements in the Sudan; or the Iraqi government attacking its own Kurdish citizens, the region seems to endure more than its fair share of political strife and ethnic conflict. And perhaps it does. The unique historical, strategic, and geographic aspects of this region, as well as the interplay of these aspects with a multiplicity of local political interests and goals, may well predispose the societies and states of the Middle East to a greater degree and variety of political conflicts than many other regions of the contemporary world.

Along with Central Africa and the Balkans, the Middle East registers in the consciousness of most Westerners as an area of chronic conflict, political volatility, and dangerous divisiveness, all of which, it is assumed, arises from age-old ethnic disagreements or religious antagonisms between the human components of the supposedly static and eternal Middle Eastern mosaic of communities (Coon 1961). The mainstream media's depictions of such conflicts as being rooted in ancient tribal animosities might lead casual observers to conclude that ethnic tensions in this large and diverse region are simply inevitable—encoded in the very genetic makeup or cultural "programming" of Middle Eastern populations. It is easy to assume that the sharp edges of the individual pieces of the Middle East mosaic are immutable, inherently antagonistic, and fated to "rub each other the wrong way" forever. Yet nothing could be farther from the truth.

In contrast to these popular—and mistaken—notions about ethnicity and ethnic conflict in the contemporary Middle East, this chapter will examine the emergence, mobilization, consolidation, and institutionalization of the region's ethnic identities not as examples of unchanging biological predispositions or cultural "essences" but, rather, as humanly shaped and strategic responses to specific environmental, geographic, historical, political, and economic realities. Changing configurations of ethnic identity and the dynamics of majority-minority relations in the various states in this region offer valuable lessons in the contingent and political—and therefore constructed and strategic—nature of ethnicity in the Middle East.

To understand the genesis, nature, and trajectory of Middle Eastern ethnic phenomena, we must first survey the region's ecological, historical, geographic, and administrative contexts. In other words, we must investigate the politics of identity. The formation of ethnic groups in the Middle East, as well as the dynamics of collaboration and competition among and between such groups and the states in which they are located, arise from ever-changing balances of power and shifting frameworks of decision making and resource distribution at the local, national, regional, and international levels. Such political processes are present in every region of the world, but in the Middle East, long a "crossroads" of diverse cultures, languages, economies, and environments, political phenomena arising from the cross-fertilization of diverse peoples have taken distinct forms. Since ancient times, and indeed, up until the present, the region has been a key prize for various world powers, from the ancient Roman and Persian empires, to the European colonial powers of the nineteenth and early twentieth centuries, and ultimately to the multinational corporations and high-tech Western armies of the present era.

Thanks to its marked strategic importance, the Middle East and its peoples are no strangers to the intrigues and interventions of local, regional, and global politics. As we shall see in some of the case studies presented here, the most harrowing episodes of interethnic conflict in the Middle East have occurred when all three dimensions of competition for political power and economic resources—global, regional, and local—have coincided, as they did in Lebanon during its long and bloody civil war, which was also a regional war fought out on Lebanese soil (Hanf 1992; Harf 1993; al-Khazen 2000; King-Irani 2000b), or more recently in Iraq, where the nation's marginalized Shi'i and Kurdish communities rose up in a bloody, but ultimately futile, challenge to the ruling Sunni Ba'athist regime of Saddam Hussein in 1991 (Abd al-Jabber 1992; Graham-Brown 1999; Hiltermann 1999).

DEFINING THE TERMS

Before embarking on a journey through the ethnopolitical map of the Middle East, we shall first clarify what is meant by such easily taken-for-granted terms as the "Middle East" and "ethnicity."

The *Middle East* or *Near East* has been characterized as such in relation to the "Far East" (China, Southeast Asia, and Japan), indicating that the vantage point for determining these locations was not indigenous but Eurocentric. The perspective from which this label was coined was that of Britain and France, former colonial powers. Here, we find an initial, and telling, indication of the historical tensions and conflicts surrounding issues of identity and power in the Middle East: the region has been defined and represented from the outside, not from within (Said 1978). This discomfiting reality has sparked various nationalist and religious movements over the years to assert regional or national autonomy from Western political and cultural domination.

Even many decades after the end of colonial rule, Western interests and interventions can still evoke deep emotions and great controversies. The West's direct or implicit role in some of the continuing tensions and injustices in the region, particularly those associated with Israel's occupation of Palestinian territory and Israeli military attacks on Lebanon, or the U.S. role in the current militarization of the Arab Gulf region, are interpreted through a lens of suspicion, out-

rage, and anger. Ironically, although direct colonial rule has long since ended, the dynamics of the current global capitalist economy and the Middle East's weak role therein replicate relationships of dependency between the region and the leading industrialized nations of the West (Barakat 1993; Halliday 1999; S. Makdisi 1990; Pfeifer 1998).

The imperialist roots of the region's geographic labeling notwithstanding, the Middle East is conventionally described as stretching from Morocco and Mauritania in the west to Iran in the east, and from Turkey in the north to Sudan in the south. The area of this large and culturally diverse region, which is double the size of the continental United States, encompasses territory on three continents (Africa, Europe, and Asia) and is home to over 370 million people, among whom Muslims constitute 82 percent of the population, Christians 9 percent, and Jews 7 percent[1] (Eickelman 1999). The region also includes other religious groups that do not fit neatly into the categories of the three monotheistic faiths, such as followers of the Druze faith,[2] adepts of the ancient Zoroastrian faith (found in Iran and India), and followers of the relatively new Baha'i faith that originated in Iran, where it is now subject to repression (Sanasarian 2000).

Despite Islam's crucial historical and cultural roles in unifying most of the region between the seventh and the ninth centuries (Esposito 1991), no less than its contemporary galvanizing role as a basis of political mobilization and ideological guidance in a rapidly changing world, the Islamic world is far from unified and harmonious: Sunni and Shi'i Muslims have been known to fight each other more ferociously than either has fought against Christians and Jews.[3] Furthermore, with the rise of politicized Islam throughout the region during the last quarter of the twentieth century, there have been ideological divisions and disagreements between members of the same Islamic sects over the proper role of religion and religious organizations in contemporary Arab society (Silverstein 1996) as well as within the Iranian government.

In addition to the region's multiplicity of religions, the diversity of languages is also pronounced and frequently corresponds to religious distinctions: Arabic, Persian, Turkish, Hebrew, Kurdish, Berber, and Armenian are spoken in the region, in addition to lingering colonial languages: French in North Africa, Syria, and Lebanon; English in Egypt, Jordan, Palestine, and Iraq; and Italian in Libya. Some languages, such as Berber (Tamazight) and Kurdish, are subdivided into a variety of dialects, some of which have yet to be standardized.

Because the newly formed states of the region did not emerge as a result of long-term, organic economic and political processes but from the quick sketching of colonial powers' pens (Fromkin 1988; Manners and Parmenter 2000; Tibi 1989), few Middle Eastern states' boundaries coincide with preexisting geographic, linguistic, or cultural borders. (Egypt is the only exception.) Consequently, a variety of identity crises and ethnic conflicts were built into the new states—and thus into the new regional state system—of the postcolonial Middle East from the outset.

The crisis of national integration has been a continuing theme (Drysdale and Blake 1985), expressed through a variety of permutations: military coups, politicized religious movements, strict language policies, and the sedentarization or transfer of population groups that posed direct or indirect challenges to the legitimacy of state borders or the control of state resources. Although few states in the Middle East can boast ethnic, linguistic, or cultural homogeneity, nearly all have tried to achieve it (Bengio and Ben-Dor 1999; Drysdale and Blake 1985; Eickelman 1999; Tétreault 2001), some by force, particularly in the Sudan (Lesch 1997; Ronen 1999), and usually at the expense of weaker ethnic groups.

Although fabulous oil wealth can easily be found in the Middle East, particularly in the countries of the Arab Gulf (Saudi Arabia, Kuwait, Qatar, Bahrain, the United Arab Emirates, and Oman), the vast majority of Middle Eastern peoples are more familiar with poverty or the fear of its imminent arrival (World Bank 1996). The gap between the region's haves and have-nots is profound, dramatic, and deepening. Perceived and actual economic inequalities influence the formation and mobilization of ethnic groupings, particularly in those countries in which the rich and poor live in close proximity, such as Lebanon, Egypt, and Turkey.

In assessing *ethnicity* in any region, including the Middle East, we must avoid the easy assumption that ethnic differences are essentially physiological differences. The conclusion that ensues from this view—that is, that ethnic groups are determined primarily by objective biological criteria such as hair, skin, and eye color, or height and physique, and only further distinguished by such characteristics as language, cultural patterns, and religious faith—has facilitated racial stereotyping and racism in many societies. Social scientists examining the phenomenon of ethnicity stress that it is a strategic more than a genetic phenomenon (Anderson 1983; Cohen 1978; Eller 1999; Royce 1982).

Identity is neither programmed nor preexisting; it is constantly being shaped by the interplay of contexts and the dynamics of power inherent in such contexts. If identities were determined by virtually immutable genetic realities alone, then we would expect to see the same categorizations, symbols, and expressions of identity enduring over time in the same place, regardless of economic, cultural, or political developments. This is clearly not the case in the Middle East, a region that has experienced rapid metamorphoses from empire to colonial regimes to modern nation-states in less than a century, and in which organized ethnic and religious groupings have emerged in different periods to compete for power, resources, and privileges, thus highlighting the contingency and relativity of identity.

Under conditions of empire, familial and religious (sectarian) identities were most significant in the region. Under conditions of centralized state administrations, new regional, class, cultural, and ethnic identities—and, consequently, new conflicts—have come to the fore as laws and policies imposed identities on people that were new, uncomfortable, and even, in some cases, objectionable.

A dual dynamic of identity is evident in the context of the modern nation-state in the region. One aspect of this dynamic is that identities can be claimed actively by people affiliating as members of a particular group in order to secure access to scarce resources or threatened rights, or in competition with other groups for control of the state's resource-distribution mechanisms. The opposite aspect of this dynamic is identification as an involuntary process, as in those situations in which the state, desiring to safeguard or project a vision of its own ethnic purity or religious unity, imposes limited and limiting identities from above while forbidding the expression of contradictory identities from below.

The phenomenon of Middle Eastern ethnicity presents a number of definitional and methodological challenges for researchers because ethnic groups often behave like kin-based groupings, such as lineages and tribes, especially in the way they mobilize their members by invoking a common historical identity and ties of mutual obligation (Tibi 1989). At the same time, ethnic differences frequently correspond closely to socioeconomic distinctions. For example, in Israeli society, Western-oriented Ashkenazi Jews (who emigrated from Central and Eastern Europe), though numerically the minority community, are the dominant group with respect to wealth and control of the state's decision-making bodies. This in comparison with the more numerous Sephardic Jews (Arab, Iranian, and Turkish), whose cultural attitudes and practices have long been denigrated as "backwards" by Ashkenazi Jews (Avruch 1987).

Prior to the convulsions of the Lebanese civil war (1975–90), wealthy power brokers and owners of factories, banks, and businesses in Lebanon tended to be Maronite Christians, while the poorer, less powerful agricultural communities in Lebanon were invariably populated by Shi'i Muslims in the south and Sunni Muslims in the north (Salibi 1988). In Iraq, a country cobbled together from three distinct ethnoreligious groups—Sunni Kurds, Shi'i Arabs, and Sunni Arabs—divisions of wealth and poverty have historically mirrored the divisions between Sunni and Shi'i communities, with Sunni Arabs enjoying a far greater share of power and wealth than either the Sunni Kurds or the more numerous Shi'i community. This political and economic configuration predates the Iraqi nation-state, as Sunnis have enjoyed a greater scope of economic and political power than Shi'i Muslims since Ottoman times and were the "favored community" during the period of British colonization.

To understand how ethnic groupings became key players in the contemporary Middle Eastern political scene, we now turn to an examination of the ecological, historical, and political processes that have shaped individual and collective political perceptions, organizations, and actions in the region. Important factors have been the dismantling of the Ottoman Empire (1359–1918), European colonization and its repercussions, the regional economy's incorporation into a world capitalist system, and last but not least, the formation of nation-states. All of these developments have exacerbated inequalities, mobilized groups, catalyzed competition, and thus occasionally engendered conflicts in the region.

CONTEXTS AND CATALYSTS OF ETHNICITY IN THE MIDDLE EAST

The peoples of the Middle East are no strangers to harsh and uncertain environments, whether natural, economic, or political. Inhabiting an ecological zone characterized by aridity, steep valleys, rugged mountains, few rivers, scant rainfall, and poor soils, Middle Eastern communities were traditionally compelled to combine a variety of modes of subsistence, such as pastoral nomadism, small-scale agriculture, commerce, and fishing, in order to make a living. Groups dwelling in this arid and semiarid region also developed distinctive cultural patterns and sociopolitical institutions that served to minimize the hardships and uncertainties of their natural environment. Up until the present era, the peoples of the Middle East have remained justly famous for loyal attachment to their families and religious communities, and distinctive rituals of hospitality and conflict mediation. They have a preference for shifting and fluid coalitions rather than enduring, corporate sociopolitical organizations and for flexible kin-based collectivities, such as the lineage and the tribe, which until quite recently performed most of the social, economic, and political functions of communities in the absence of centralized state governments (Khoury and Kostiner 1989; King-Irani 2000a).

Before the nation-state system, and even before the colonial era, most of the peoples of the region (with the exception of those living in Morocco, Mauritania, and Iran) lived under Ottoman rule in the sociopolitical framework of a vast and multiethnic Islamic empire. Day-to-day matters of administration and basic governance were overseen and discharged by local political elites chosen by the Ottoman rulers, as well as the local clergy.

The Ottoman Empire was organized not according to ethnic or national principles and categories but according to religious distinctions (Bosworth 1982). Subjects of the Ottoman sultan did not identify themselves as Ottomans, Turks, Arabs, Azeris, Berbers, or Kurds but as Muslims, Christians, Jews, or Druze. The crucially distinguishing social categories were religion, class, and gender. Accordingly, Muslims, men, and the well-to-do enjoyed power and privileges that women, the poor, and non-Muslim communities could never hope to attain.

Within this sociopolitical setting, Muslims constituted the majority, both in terms of absolute numbers and in terms of power, rank, status, and opportunities. Christians and Jews were formally recognized as respected religious minorities—"Peoples of the Book"—and categorized as *dhimmi* communities (literally, "on the conscience" of the larger and more powerful Muslim community). Christians and Jews were to be protected from harm or persecution by the majority Muslim community in return for their acceptance of a subordinate social and political status, payment of a special head tax (*jizya*) in exchange for their exemption from military service, and refraining from any public display of their religions, such as processions and liturgical ceremonies.

Dhimmi communities were under the jurisdiction of Islamic courts in the event of criminal cases and some property disputes, but otherwise obeyed the jurisdiction of their own communities' religious laws and precepts concerning any issues touching upon religious and family matters. As non-Muslims, Christians, Druze, and Jews were not subject to the rulings of *Shari'ah* (Islamic law) in matters of personal status, such as marriage, divorce, inheritance, adoption, and other family issues. Instead, Christian sects and Druze and Jewish communities sought guidance, mediation, and rulings from their own religious leaders, who had the power to make binding judicial decisions in the domain of family law and to represent their religious communities in official dealings with the Ottoman authorities. This system of legally recognized, non-Muslim communal autonomy was known as the *millet* system (meaning "people" or "community" in Turkish).

The Middle East's cultural heterogeneity stemmed from geography as much as from Ottoman social categorizations, however. The ecological characteristics of the region, combined with the prevalence of rugged mountains, deep valleys, and virtually impassable desert expanses, compelled different communities to live in small, close-knit family groupings widely separated from each other with no overarching political or economic organization (Meeker 1979). This facilitated pronounced diversity in the region. For example, the three key cities of present-day Iraq, all of which are linked by rivers (Mosul, Baghdad, and Basra), had completely different systems of weights and measures and currencies until the late nineteenth century (Batatu 1978). Until the advent of advanced communications technology and the construction of paved roads and railways in the late nineteenth and early twentieth centuries, some areas of the Middle East were virtually inaccessible. Existing independently of each other for so many centuries, it was only natural that marked linguistic, cultural, and religious differences would develop among the dispersed populations of the Middle East.

During the Ottoman era, the rugged mountainous areas of the eastern Mediterranean became a refuge for various Christian sects and Islamic splinter groups seeking to escape persecution by orthodox religious authorities. Dwelling high atop these mountains, minority groups such as the Maronites, Druze, Shi'a, and Alawites could pursue their religious traditions free of interference from either Christian or Muslim authorities. Religious refugees thus rendered the mountainous zones of the region culturally and religiously diverse: not only the mountains of Lebanon and Syria but also the mountainous regions of northern Iraq and eastern Turkey, as well as those of North Africa, have traditionally been home to minority groups such as the Kurds, Assyrians, and Berber tribes.

Middle Eastern cities have always evidenced cultural and religious heterogeneity. The plural nature of Middle Eastern urban space is inscribed in the very towers, walls, and gates that marked off the various named sections of traditional urban settlements (the "Muslim Quarter," the "Armenian Quarter," the "Jewish Quarter," the "Orthodox Quarter"), as we find in such ancient cities as Jerusalem, Cairo, Damascus, and Baghdad. The spatial separation of different religious and ethnic groups in the traditional Middle Eastern city was paralleled by a division of labor among these distinct communities. Muslims, Christians, and Jews occupied different professional categories in the Ottoman social and economic structure.

The city's traditional division of labor was usually characterized by accommodation, complementarity, and integration rather than by competition and conflict. Muslims held influential positions in religious courts and schools as well as in the military and in local government administration. Non-Muslims were primarily doctors, merchants, advisers, artisans, and religious and legal specialists for their own sectarian communities. The Ottoman era division of labor is recorded to this day in the names of many Christian families from Lebanon, Palestine, and Syria designating the professional and artisan roles that their ancestors played in Ottoman society: *sabbagh* (dyer), *hakim* (doctor), *khabbaz* (baker), *sayigh* (goldsmith), *hayek* (weaver), *najjar* (carpenter), *khoury* (priest), and *shammas* (sexton).

Thus, the cultural and religious heterogeneity of the Middle East is neither a new phenomenon associated with rapid urbanization nor a function of the creation of modern nation-states. Nor is cultural diversity a by-product of colonialism (although colonial powers certainly employed "divide and rule" tactics to consolidate their control of local societies and political systems under their rule). Different ethnic and religious groups have been living side by side in the Middle East for centuries, occasionally in conflict, but more often than not in harmony.

What *is* new is a transformed structure of relationships among the different ethnic and religious groups within the contemporary Middle Eastern nation-state. Here we see the aforementioned interplay of context and ethnic identity: in the administrative context of the nation-state, the social, political, and economic frameworks in which different groups interact, work, and struggle are no longer characterized by traditional guidelines of complementarity but by the uncertainties of competition. Although the Ottoman Empire was hardly a model of economic efficiency or social justice, it nevertheless encouraged intercommunal accommodation and cooperation to a greater degree than did subsequent colonial regimes or the imposed nation-state.

The relative balance and insularity of the Ottoman social universe was increasingly disturbed in the eighteenth and nineteenth centuries by European peoples, processes, and events. By the late eighteenth century, Ottoman authorities had grown alarmed by Europe's increasing military prowess and administrative efficacy, and accordingly attempted to copy European developments and practices so as to enhance their own control over the empire's far-flung territory and resources (Drysdale and Blake 1985; Goldschmidt 2000).

By the middle of the nineteenth century, European powers were lobbying the Ottoman sultan for better treatment and even protection of particular *dhimmi* communities, as well as special protections for European commercial agents and representatives in the region and for their local employees and contacts among the Ottoman Christian and Jewish population. Under European pressure, the Ottoman sultan issued a decree giving Christians and Jews legal equality with Muslims in the empire (Goldschmidt 2000), just at a time when the region's incorporation into a European-dominated market economy and the resulting transformation of the local economic system (particularly the shift from subsistence to cash crops) were having a noticeable impact on social and economic relations in the Ottoman world.

European powers' concerns about the local non-Muslim population stemmed not from charitable impulses alone. Aiding and allying with local Christian and Jewish interests enabled European states to get their "foot into the door" of the declining Ottoman Empire. European actions in the empire were part and parcel of the "Great Game"—the race among various European powers to control the routes to and the extraction of resources from the East, particularly India, where the British enjoyed—and naturally endeavored to maintain—a decided strategic advantage (Fromkin 1988).

In their pursuit of the "Great Game," the European powers backed different communities' interests, thereby establishing, whether by design or happenstance, the groundwork for the "divide and rule" policies so effectively implemented during the colonial period following the Ottoman Empire's collapse at the end of World War I. The British supported the Druze and the desert tribes of the Hejaz region of what is now Saudi Arabia (dramatized in David Lean's epic film, *Lawrence of Arabia*), the French backed the Maronites in the Levant and the Berbers in North Africa, and the Russians backed the Greek Orthodox in what are now Lebanon, Palestine, and Syria. During the colonial era, different groups received differential treatment from the British and French authorities. The colonial policy of playing various groups off against one another was later echoed in the practices and policies of the new nation-states that the colonial powers carved out of the region—heedless of any coincidence of ethnic, natural, or linguistic borders. Those who had been favorites during the colonial era frequently became scapegoats after independence.

CRUCIBLE OF COMMUNITY OR CAULDRON OF CONFLICT? THE NATION-STATE IN THE MIDDLE EAST

Although the bureaucracies of most Middle Eastern states are well entrenched and heavily subsidized, few have succeeded in distributing resources equitably, administering justice fairly, protecting and advancing the interests of the majority of their people, establishing a strong sense of common identity and mission, and thereby winning public support and popular participation through legitimate means (Ayoubi 1995; al-Khafaji 1995). Most states in the Middle East serve narrow elite interests rather than the broad common good (Barakat 1993; Tibi 1989). The overwhelming majority of the region's population does not participate in the economic and political decision-making processes that greatly influence their and their children's lives. Middle Eastern states usually rule rather than govern their populaces, employing coercion, manipulation, and co-optation of various ethnic groups to achieve control and compliance (Bengio and Ben-Dor 1999).

As an externally imposed, internally weak, and relatively new form of sociopolitical organization lacking roots, precedents, and traditions, the Middle Eastern nation-state still cannot claim the same kind or degree of support, loyalty, and legitimacy that Middle Eastern kin, ethnoreligious, and patron-client networks have always claimed. Even half a century after the nation-state's appearance in the region, kinship relations (including ethnic relations modeled on a kinship pattern) mediate individuals' personal, economic, and political lives to an extent almost unimaginable to anyone who has grown up in Western Europe or North America.

For example, individuals' interactions with state bodies and government bureaucracies take place primarily through patron-client relationships mediated by ties of kinship (actual or fictive lineages, or, as in Palestine, the *hamoula*, a patronymic association; see Eickelman 1999) or ethnic and sectarian affiliation (Cunningham and Sarayrah 1993). In most Middle Eastern societies, full government services are available only to those who have connections (*wasta* in Arabic, *protektzia* in Hebrew), and such links are usually contingent on one's family or ethnic networks. Citizenship, an identity category deriving its significance from the jural relationship of each individual to the nation-state, carries much less emotional, moral, legal, and political weight

in the Middle East than do the identity categories of kinship, ethnicity, and religion.

Understanding the reasons why peoples throughout the Middle East preserve and value pre-state social and political institutions based on primordial affiliations such as kinship, ethnicity, and religion can help us appreciate the genesis of intrastate turmoil and interstate hostilities. Discovering how Middle Eastern peoples strategically invoke and manipulate ethnic affiliations will give us a new awareness of the creative and effective means individuals and groups have developed in order to survive and thrive in a challenging socioeconomic environment while preparing for future contingencies.

PUTTING IT ALL TOGETHER: SOME CONTEMPORARY CASE STUDIES

We will now examine the emergence, mobilization, and institutionalization of ethnic identity in relation to the historical, geographic, economic, and political contexts described above by examining the following case studies: Copts in Egypt, Berbers in Algeria, the multiconfessional Republic of Lebanon, and the Kurdish tragedy in Iraq. These examples are presented in order of increasing complexity as well as according to the degree of conflict and violence associated with each, from least to most conflictual given present realities.

Copts: Original Egyptians and Non-Muslim Minority

The Copts (whose name is etymologically related to the ancient name "Egypt") are indisputably Egyptians and Arabs; indeed, they are the original Egyptians. Yet their non-Muslim status is a sensitive issue that is seldom discussed openly and frankly in Egyptian society. Egypt experienced less virulent ethnic and religious unrest than virtually any other Arab state in the immediate postindependence period. Indeed, Copts, 5 percent of the country's population, played an important role in the Egyptian struggle for independence from British colonial rule, achieved in 1922. For the next thirty years, Coptic-Muslim relations in Egypt were fairly unproblematic, but the nationalization of Egypt's private industries and businesses after the 1952 revolution affected Coptic interests disproportionately. Many wealthy Coptic families left the country during this period.

A key complaint of Egypt's Coptic community over the last several decades has been the difficulty—in some cases, the impossibility—of obtaining the requisite official permits to undertake the construction of new churches or the repair of old ones. In 1972, a Coptic church that had been built without government authorization was mysteriously burned to the ground, sparking violent riots.

The government's policy was to move carefully, quietly, and judiciously in protecting the rights and answering the demands of the Copts. To focus too much attention on the nature of the Copts' minority status would have the effect of activating Islamists' concerns and emotions. In other words, defining and treating the Copts publicly as a religious minority would implicitly define Egypt as a religiously based—that is, an Islamic—state, and the government did not wish to give this impression, internally or externally. Coptic expatriate communities in Europe and North America did not take so circumspect an approach to the debate, however, and many pressured their adopted Western governments to look into the issue of Coptic rights in Egypt. In 1997, when radical Islamist groups massacred several Copts in villages in Upper Egypt, some felt that the heightened attention to the Copts, although intended as a positive measure, had in fact led to a very negative conclusion.

The situation of Egypt's Copts says as much about regional and international politics and ideological developments as it does about internal Egyptian issues and problems. Strong anti-Western sentiments and associated tensions throughout the region as a whole, largely in response to U.S. policies universally perceived as unfair in the Islamic world (notably U.S. support for Israel and the United States' leading role in applying harsh sanctions on Iraq that have had no impact on Saddam Hussein but have caused suffering to the most vulnerable of Iraq's people), can and have had tragic repercussions for Coptic Christians in remote Egyptian villages (Graham-Brown 1999).

Here we have an illustration of the *transnational* character of ethnic sentiments and political movements in the region. Islamist movements are not geographically constricted or delimited. Events in one country can and frequently do have immediate and unpredictable echoes in other countries, despite national borders that have been in existence for over half a century. The dilemmas of the Egyptian Copts are but one example of the challenges of national integration and the crisis of citizenship in the states of the region. This case study also shows that many states in the region are fearful of actual or potential Islamist mobilization within or outside their borders.

Berbers in Algeria: Creatively Reclaiming Colonial Stereotypes

The shocking episodes of violence in Algeria over the last decade, most notably a series of heinous massacres in several cities and remote villages, is only tangentially related to Algeria's mixed ethnic composition, in which Arabs are 75 percent of the population and Berbers[4] (representing four different tribal groups, the largest and most influential of which are the tribal groups from the mountainous region of Kabylia) constitute 25 percent.

Algeria's ten years of torment stem from sharp ideological and political differences over the benefits and drawbacks of an Islamic form of government. In 1991, Algerians went to the polls to elect a new government. It soon became clear that Islamist parties were poised to win the elections in a landslide. Fearing their ascension to power, the incumbent Algerian government and its military apparatus cancelled the election results and ultimately seized control of the country, ironically in the name of protecting democracy. Thus was set in motion a vicious cycle of attacks and counterattacks whose protagonists are often ambiguous. Rumors abound that some Islamist-orchestrated massacres may in fact have been carried out by army units disguised as Muslim radicals. In the current atmosphere of violence, fear, and chaos, public trust and common points of reference have been badly eroded (Silverstein 1997).

In this troubled setting, the country's Berber minority has creatively reworked an identification imposed upon it by the French colonial authorities in the nineteenth century. In an effort to divide and rule the Algerian population, France, like all colonial powers everywhere, had selected some groups for favored treatment, particularly in the areas of legal rights, educational opportunities, and employment in the colonial administration. In Algeria, Berbers and Jews represented the chosen, colonial favorites (Maddy-Weitzman 1998). French officials considered Berbers to be more refined, educable, and civilized than their Arab counterparts, and therefore more promising candidates for France's "civilizing mission." As such, Berbers were afforded special educational opportunities, were not supposed to learn Arabic, and in 1874 were exempted from the rulings of Islamic law and encouraged to use customary law instead. All of these moves were meant to wean Berbers away from "primitive" cultural, social, and political behaviors in preparation for being "civilized" according to French tastes and specifications.[5] Berbers ultimately became overrepresented in the ranks of the colonial era elite—bureaucrats, teachers, lawyers, and so on.

Because France treated Algeria differently than its other colonies—considering it an integral part of France and turning over most of the country's cultivable land to French settlers—human traffic between France and Algeria was constant and significant in both directions. Berbers and Jews, more than their fellow Arab Muslim Algerians, went to study, work, and live in France, many of them remaining for their entire lives. To this day, Algerian political movements, organizations, and events frequently originate from—and impact upon—Algerian communities in France as much as the Algerian homeland.

Upon independence, the Algerian government wanted to stress the country's Arab and Muslim heritage first and foremost. This desire was a natural psychological reaction to France's inherently racist "civilizing mission," which had denigrated, marginalized, and denied Arab culture, language, and history. Yet this emphasis also sidelined and marginalized the Berbers, who began organizing, first among their expatriate community in France, to protect and advance their own cultural interests and the teaching of their language, Tamazight (Goodman 1996; Maddy-Weitzman 1998; Silverstein 1996, 1997). The initial crux of Algeria's Berber issue was the language issue. The Berbers were fighting to preserve a respected place in the new Algerian nation-state for their own unique cultural heritage. In the 1960s, this was particularly urgent, as the state forbade parents to give their children Berber names and repressed the public use of Berber dialects.

The Berbers have never demanded political autonomy, secession, or self-rule, only the right to be considered a legitimate and integral component of the Algerian nation-state. In advancing this goal, Berber activists and cultural groups promoted a view of Algeria as Arabic *and* Berber. The key vehicles for communicating this vision in the 1970s were the new Kabylian Berber popular songs (Goodman 1996; Silverstein 1996) and the Berber cultural movement, composed primarily of Kabylian students and expatriate Berber intellectuals in France (Maddy-Weitzman 1998). In addition to advancing Berber linguistic and cultural expressiveness and heritage, this movement also called for Western-style political liberalization and democratization because, "at bottom, the Berberists saw democratization as the only way to guarantee their cultural and ethnic rights within the Algerian state" (p. 39).

With the rise of the Islamist movement, the Berbers' identity in the Algerian context took on new dimensions, as some Berber groups and spokesmen invoked their unique cultural and historical role as a countervailing force to the drive for Islamization. Artists and singers were particularly prominent in this effort, particularly members of the Rassemblement de la Culture et la Démocratie (RCD), a movement that espoused an explicitly modernist/secularist Berber stand in the face of the violence tearing the country apart.

The RCD's guiding agenda was a new vision of modern Algerian culture that would include "the Kabylian synthesis of village customs and rituals, many undoubtedly pre-Islamic in origin, an attenuated Islam, Tamazight, and French-centered modernity, epitomized by the French language spoken by much of the intelligentsia and the middle and upper classes" (Maddy-Weitzman 1998:43). This agenda represented an intriguing reworking of the French colonial image of the wise and noble Berbers in comparison to the less cultured Arab Muslims of Algeria. Paul Silverstein (1996) argues that the Berber movement "consciously selected and reworked elements of this colonial era myth, or stereotype, of the essential Berber character to stake out a position between the Algerian military regime and the Islamists" (p. 11).

This strategic choice of identification seems to have been fruitful initially. In 1994, a well-organized, extended school strike on behalf of the Tamazight language as a vehicle of educational instruction took place throughout

Kabylia. By the spring of 1995, Tamazight's role and legitimacy in the Algerian social, cultural, and political contexts received official recognition after a series of negotiations to end the strike. The Algerian government announced that it would create a "body with executive powers, attached to the presidency, [and] charged with the rehabilitation of Tamazight culture, one of the foundations of Algerian culture" (Embassy of Algeria 1995).

Perhaps the Algerian government perceived a strategic value in aligning with Berber demands for inclusiveness and cultural plurality at a time when militant Islamic factions were attempting to impose a strict form of religious and cultural homogeneity and purity on the Algerian populace by force of arms. Nonetheless, as dramatic as these developments were in the history of Berber struggles in Algeria, the regime's new open-mindedness regarding Berber demands did not endure: "Although the new draft constitution [of 1995] recognized that Amazighité (Berber identity) was part of Algeria's common heritage, along with Islam and Arabism, it failed to recognize Tamazight as Algeria's official second language" (Embassy of Algeria 1995:47). As long as significant segments of Algerian society remain committed to emphasizing a strictly Muslim or Arab identity, Berber cultural aspirations are not likely to be fully realized.

Lebanon: A Living Remnant of the Ottoman *Millet* System

Moving east to the Levant, we find another nation-state in which French colonial policies of preferential treatment influenced interethnic relations in the postcolonial period. Lebanon, a country marked by profound ethnic diversity, first, because its mountainous terrain was historically so attractive to religious and ethnic minorities fleeing persecution, and second, because of the manner in which it was patched together as an administrative territory following the collapse of the Ottoman Empire, represents a living remnant of the Ottoman *millet* system disguised as a centralized nation state. Lebanon began as the autonomous region of Mount Lebanon that the French exacted from the Ottoman authorities in the 1860s to protect the Christian *dhimmis* (primarily the Maronites, an Eastern Rite church that was always in communion with Rome and thus had more of a Western orientation than the other Christian sects).

Before Lebanon's independence in 1943, the French colonial powers had attached to Mount Lebanon the northern regions of Akkar Province, the city of Tripoli and its surroundings, the capital city of Beirut, and the southern cities of Sidon and Tyre. This deft carving of territories added Sunni, Greek Orthodox, Armenian Orthodox, Jacobite, Assyrian, and Shi'a communities to the largely Maronite and Druze communities of Mount Lebanon. France's creation of the Republic of Lebanon did not sit well with Syrian leaders or the Syrian populace, who had always considered some of the new territories of Lebanon, particularly the northern provinces and the Beqa'a Valley, its territory. To this day, Syria, which plays an active role in Lebanese affairs behind the scenes, does not have an embassy in Beirut.

Adding to the inherently unstable mix of religious groups in the newly forged Lebanese Republic (which, at independence, was said to be 51 percent Christian and 49 percent Muslim by some manipulations of statistical data) was the arrival in 1948 of tens of thousands of Palestinian refugees fleeing war and violence between Palestinian Arabs and European Jews who had been living and settling in Palestine since the last decades of the nineteenth century. The Jews obviously won that battle, founding the State of Israel in 1948 and forbidding the return of the majority of the refugees who had fled or who had been driven out.

The presence of the Palestinian refugees in Beirut presented not only a logistical and economic problem of immense proportions for a new state lacking in resources. The biggest threat posed by the refugees' presence was the potential demographic and political significance of a large Sunni Muslim group in a state dominated by Christians. Many Christian—and even a few Muslim—leaders of the new republic feared that the refugees might one day tip the delicate religious balance and the verbal national pact that enabled Western-oriented Christians to coexist and collaborate with Muslims who looked to the Arab and Islamic world for their identity and ideological influences.

The Lebanese political system is based on religious (sectarian) power-sharing (called *taa'ifiyya* in Arabic, from the word *ta'ifa*, meaning "sect"). As Barbara Harf (1993) has noted, no single Lebanese group constitutes a majority; Lebanon is unique in being a country composed solely of minorities—18 officially recognized ethnoreligious groups, to be precise. Each group has its guaranteed number of seats in the parliament, and each expects to receive its fair share of ministerial posts. The three largest groups— the Maronites, the Sunnis, and the Shi'a—get the presidency, the prime ministerial, and the speaker of the parliament positions, respectively.[6] Theory and practice rarely coincide in politics, however, and the Christian Maronite community's historic domination of Lebanon's political and economic power structures since before the state's establishment, no less than the context of relative and absolute deprivation and economic inequalities, rising regional Arab nationalist sentiments (particularly pro-Palestinian feelings), and the polarizing influences of the cold war between the United States and the USSR in the region—all led to the eventual conflagration of the war.

In Lebanon, the entire population, being a mosaic of contending minorities, was thinking and feeling like potential victims even before war broke out on April 13, 1975. It is no wonder, then, that the war was so violent, so bitter, and so protracted. As Theodore Hanf describes the nature of the conflict in his Lebanon, "It was a macabre game of musical chairs in which no one wanted to be the only one left standing. . . . The fear of being the ultimate loser is the motivating force in [Lebanese] politics" (1992:1–2). Long before the war began, the Lebanese were enmeshed in a political and psychological "economy of scarcity" that left everyone feeling both vulnerable and opportunistic, and thus prone to aggressiveness.[7]

Clearly, many of Lebanon's 18 sects had valid reasons to worry about scarcities of power, security, and resources. *Taa'ifiyya*, however, actually obstructs power-sharing at the grass-roots level and gives rise not to a nation of fellow citizens but to an arena of pronounced conflict and competition among many anxious and agonistic minority groups. Because of Lebanon's religiously based system, every individual is encouraged to think of himself or herself as a Maronite, a Shi'i or a Sunni first, and only secondarily as a Lebanese citizen. By emphasizing the group over the individual (and thereby minimizing the individual's choice, power, and sense of responsibility), and by privileging the sect over the state (thus contributing to the fragmentation of the polity), *taa'ifiyya* cannot but set the stage for future violent conflicts.[8]

In the Middle Eastern context, Lebanon represents an extreme example of the triumph of the ethnic group over both the individual citizen and the overarching state. Lebanese sociologist Samir Khalaf notes that the tragedy of Lebanon lies in the fact that "the very factors that account for much of the viability, resourcefulness, and integration of the Lebanese are also the factors that are responsible for the erosion of civic ties and national loyalties. . . . In short, the factors that enable at the micro and communal level, disable at the macro and national level. This is, indeed, Lebanon's predicament" (1985:14).

Not only has Lebanon's system of religious power-sharing had detrimental effects on national identity and the consolidation of the institution of citizenship, it also has complicated Lebanese conceptions, attitudes, and behaviors associated with power. In Lebanon, power is not vested in the individual; rather, individuals can only attain power through their community, or, more specifically, through the leader (*za'eem*) of their community. The *za'eem* usually wields absolute power (backed up by credible threats of force) in the context of his ethnoreligious group, which is also a kinship group, so family obligations and duties also influence individual and communal political behavior and choices.

It is often observed that "absolute power corrupts absolutely," and in most cases in Lebanese history this has, unfortunately, been true. The concentration of power in the hands of a few individuals (and families) in Lebanon's political system has increased the sense of powerlessness and dependency that is already so prevalent among the members of the contending minority communities. If two communal leaders become embroiled in a personal conflict, the strife can quickly spread to their supporters in each respective community. The good of the community is thus sacrificed for the political or economic interests of corrupt and grasping leaders, who often have more in common with each other than they do with the wider communities they supposedly represent.

The complexities and tragedies of the long and destructive Lebanese civil war, which took 150,000 lives, were profound and mind-boggling and seemed to necessitate a complex, elaborate, and carefully calibrated solution to effectively end the fighting. This was a mistaken notion. What finally ended the war was a blunt, unambiguous, and decisive show of force by the Syrian military in 1990. In a land beset by a plethora of armed bullies (a wide variety of warlords representing different confessional communities), the Syrians stopped the war in its tracks simply by acting as the biggest bully of all.

Although hostilities seem to have come to a decisive end, the underlying sociopolitical reasons and dynamics of the war have yet to be addressed in a comprehensive and constructive manner. Given the existence of multiple regional tensions that could destabilize Lebanon once again, particularly the growing gap between rich and poor and the unresolved problem of the 350,000 Palestinian refugees in Lebanon, more violence is not only possible but probable in the land of the cedars.

Iraq's Ethnic Trio: Kurd, Sunni, and Shi'a in a Weak State System

At the end of the United States–led Gulf War against Iraq to free Kuwait from Iraqi occupation, few could have predicted that the Ba'thist regime of Saddam Hussein, a Sunni who seized power in 1978, would still be firmly ensconced in Baghdad a decade later. Although Saddam and his regime and inner circle have survived— and according to some, have even thrived—since the Gulf War (Graham-Brown 1999), the Iraqi people, be they Kurds in the north, Shi'a in the south, or Sunnis and Christians in the central area, have suffered from both externally imposed sanctions and internally imposed oppression.

Iraq under Saddam Hussein constitutes the extreme example of the crises of national integration and representative governments in the Middle Eastern context. Today, Iraq remains an integrated nation-state only by the narrowest of definitions: both the Kurdish-dominated north and the Shi'i-dominated south are under constant Western (United States and British) aerial surveillance and have been transformed into "no-fly" zones in which Iraqi air force planes and helicopters can venture only at their own risk. The Kurds, who are part of a larger, stateless ethnicity spread out over five nation-states (Iraq, Iran, Turkey, Russia, and Syria), now look to foreign assistance programs, primarily that of the United Nations, rather than to the central Iraqi bureaucracy in Baghdad for their basic social needs. The Shi'a suffer from the imposed sanctions as well as from the regime's brutal repression and their historically marginal status in Iraq.

The British cobbled Iraq together as a nation-state following World War I by joining the provinces of three distinct cities into one territorial unit: Mosul in the north, Baghdad in the center, and Basra in the south. In patching together this new state, the British colonial powers were far more interested in their own needs and aims than those of the Arab and Kurdish, Shi'i and Sunni, peoples of the new, hybrid nation-state. The Kurds had wanted to have their own state, one that would have joined various, dispersed Kurdish tribal groups, speakers of various languages and subdialects, and communicants of several different religions,[9] into one territorially delimited state (Eller 1999). Britain's strategic interest in oil, which is particularly prevalent in the region around Mosul, meant that this Kurdish-dominated region, which had been linked with Turkey through trade, language, culture, and administrative structures and networks during the Ottoman era, would be given to the new state of Iraq, against the wishes of the Kurdish population (Batatu 1978).

The British placed a compliant ruler (King Faisal, a Sunni who was not even an Iraqi but a member of the Jordanian Hashemite family) on a newly created Iraqi throne in 1921. Nine years later, the nation-state of Iraq—a newly minted monarchy—gained its independence from the British. For the next 20 years, Iraq was run by a British-backed monarchy and an elite class of tribal landlords. This system, in which the gap between rich and poor grew ever more pronounced, did not encourage national integration.

King Faisal's solution to this problem, for which he received help from the British, was to build up a strong army capable of maintaining internal order, representative of all Iraqi ethnic and regional groups but commanded by Sunnis. The strength and consolidation of the Iraqi armed forces were to prove decisive to state unity in the coming years. Indeed, by the time Saddam Hussein came to power, the army, particularly key units known as the special protection forces, already had a well-entrenched role as the keystone of Ba'thist state power.

The Ba'thist regime that took power in 1968, the forerunner of the current regime, survived longer not because it had achieved national integration but because it relied upon tribal and ethnic integration to consolidate the ruling inner circle of the regime in a matrix of overlapping, mutually supportive ties at the expense of the nation as a whole. Kurds and Shi'a were largely excluded from these networks, which meant that they had little power, little say over resource allocation, and little control over the coercive mechanisms of state power and surveillance, all of which remained in the hands of the Sunnis.

The leaders and the rank and file of the post-1968 regime were composed of interlocking networks of tribal members from a limited number of Sunni towns and villages in the central part of the country (Abd al-Jabbar 2000; Bengio 1999; Graham-Brown 1999). Relying on and invoking their own tribal and family ties, they shored up the regime while playing different tribal and ethnic factions off against one another to the regime's advantage, particularly in the very fragmented social milieu of Kurdistan, where tribal, linguistic, regional, and political divisions fragmented Kurdish political demands and rendered coordinated action impossible.

While manipulating tribal and ethnic ties to consolidate power, Saddam Hussein also attempted to manipulate regional politics to his regime's advantage by using warfare to build up the state and focus national attention on expansionary and adventurist projects, such as Iraq's war with Iran (1980–88) and the ill-fated Iraqi invasion of Kuwait in 1990. In addition to squandering Iraq's considerable oil wealth and political capital on such disastrous campaigns, Hussein also used the army against recalcitrant or unruly ethnic groups in Iraq, most notoriously during the Iraqi government's *anfal* campaign in the late 1980s, the goal of which was to control Kurdish elements through ethnic cleans-

ing, population transfers, village demolitions, mass murder, and torture in the Kurdish north.

Similarly, following the failed uprisings against the regime after Iraq's rout from Kuwait in the spring of 1991, Saddam Hussein used the army to drain the swamps of southern Iraq (causing dramatic ecological damage) in order to flush Shi'i rebels out of hiding. Many participants in the Iraqi *intifada* ("uprising") of 1991 were summarily executed. Although Western powers and neighboring Arab states were well aware of the Iraqi regime's massive human rights abuses against its own people, they never interfered, despite the fact that the United States had urged Kurds and Shi'is to rise up against the Iraqi regime in early 1991.

The failure of the Kurdish and Shi'i uprisings attests to the deeply fragmented nature of Iraqi society and the relative advantage this fragmentation gives to a highly centralized, powerful army composed mostly of Sunnis. Since 1991, the fragmentation of the Iraqi population along ethnic, and even subethnic, tribal lines has rendered all potential and actual opposition to the regime unlikely. The army, though feared and hated, is still well entrenched enough to crush future uprisings. Furthermore, the impact of the United States–led economic sanctions against Iraq has served to enrich the regime (through black market economies dominated by Hussein's family) while weakening the Iraqi population physically, economically, psychologically, and politically (Graham-Brown 1999).

MIDDLE EASTERN ETHNICITY ASSESSED: STRATEGY OR STRAITJACKET?

Perhaps it is not too farfetched to argue that extensive, overlapping kin and ethnic-based networks and patron-client relationships constitute the actual "glue" that holds the Middle Eastern nation-state together. Rather than being sustained by a sense of shared identity, the formal institution of citizenship, and broadly shared interests and goals, the nation-state in the Middle East survives because of the public's considerable investments of time, energy, resources, and money in the cultivation and maintenance of innumerable dyadic relationships (often utilizing the idiom of ethnicity or kinship) with influential incumbents of the government bureaucracy.

Although resorting to primary identities and traditional relationships in order to survive in a challenging world is instrumental, logical, and strategic, it also entails costs and consequences that can have negative repercussions on individuals and collectivities in the region. Relying on kin, rather than the state; affiliating with narrowly defined ethnoreligious groups, rather than forming broad-based coalitions and solidarities; and participating in patron-client exchanges of goods and services that perpetuate socioeconomic inequalities while consolidating age-old forms of political domination—all serve to impede economic, cultural, and political integration on the regional and national levels while also discouraging processes of empowerment, the attainment of social justice, and the implementation of democratic reforms on the local level. Also, a public that has fragmented into separate, competing blocs of kin ethnoreligious communities is facilitating its own control, exploitation, co-optation, and manipulation by repressive state governments. A divided population is much easier to rule, as the colonial powers so deftly proved.

The institutionalization of ethnic and religious identities for legal and administrative purposes, seen most clearly in states such as Lebanon and Israel, can be a double-edged sword. Official recognition of cultural heritage and religious laws may provide answers to individuals' psychological needs and communal organizational problems. However, it can also trap individuals (particularly women[10]) in the vise of inflexible identity categories not of their own choice or making, thus limiting their personal options and opportunities while preventing the development of a more inclusive sense of overarching national loyalty and identity.

CONCLUSION

This chapter has analyzed and interpreted ethnicity as a dynamic process in the contemporary Middle East by showing how identities and the political agenda associated with them are influenced by ecological, economic, historical, administrative, and political realities. We have learned that sociopolitical categorizations and behaviors in the Middle East have historically been affected by the limitations of a harsh natural environment in which economic scarcity and pronounced political competition were constants, and sustained and enduring relationships of mutual trust and permanent, broad-based, sociopolitical formations were rare. Furthermore, we noted that the region underwent rapid economic and political changes in the nineteenth century, which permanently altered the traditional class structure and gave rise to sharp socioeconomic inequalities that were exacerbated by colonialism and the incorporation of the region into a competitive world capitalist economy. These inequalities and sociopolitical disparities remain unresolved to this day.

Lacking satisfying representation or assistance from the nation-states of the region, Middle Eastern peoples have resorted to primary identity categories and traditional organizational structures in an effort to make a living—and to discern meaning—in the challenging world that confronts them. Although they have succeeded in this effort, it has not been without costs and consequences. In the long run, resorting to kinship, ethnicity, and ties of patronage based on subnational identifications may have a negative effect on societies that are increasingly pressured to reconcile their segmented and fragmentary nature with increasing demands for political and economic integration, coordination, and cooperation in the global economy. In the current era of dramatic cultural and technical innovations and global economic fluctuations, we should not be surprised to see new political configurations and identities emerging in the Middle East.

NOTES

1. Although most Jews in the region now live in Israel, it is an oft-neglected fact that small but vibrant Jewish communities continue to live in Morocco, Tunisia, Lebanon, Iran, Syria, and Yemen.

2. The Druze faith is sometimes categorized as an Islamic sect, but Sunni Muslims do not consider it as such. It is an offshoot of Ismaili Shi'a Islam that incorporates Neoplatonic doctrines as well as a belief in reincarnation. Druze communities are found in mountainous regions of Syria, Lebanon, and northern Israel. Although all Druze are ethnically and linguistically Arabs, in Israel they are categorized as a separate ethnic group from Muslim and Christian Arab citizens of the state and are required to serve in the Israeli defense forces. Just 80 miles north, in the Shouf region of Lebanon, the Lebanese Druze community was aligned with Arab nationalist, socialist, and pro-Palestinian factions during the Lebanese civil war, thus illustrating the flexibility and fluidity of ethnic politics in this region (Firro 1999; Hajjar 2000).

3. The Shi'i branch of Islam traces its leadership to the cousin of the Prophet Muhammad, 'Ali ibn Abi Talib. Shi'ites are the largest Islamic community after that of Sunni Muslims. Shi'ism originated from a split in the early Muslim community over the issue of succession in the leadership of the Islamic community (the *ummah*). After the assassination of the Caliph Uthman, 'Ali, a blood relative of the Prophet, who was married to the Prophet's daughter Fatima, acceded to the caliphate. 'Ali was opposed by some of the surviving companions of the Prophet, and this disagreement began a conflict between those who opposed his role as leader of the faithful and those who supported him, known as the partisans of 'Ali (*shi'at 'Ali*, in Arabic). Since many tribal groups in Syria and Mesopotamia opposed 'Ali, he moved the caliphate from Damascus to Kufa, a city in what is now southern Iraq. Ali was assassinated in 661, and his martyrdom continues to be a powerful organizing theme in Shi'i faith and tradition. Shi'i communities are found today in Lebanon, where they are numerically the largest of all of Lebanon's confessional sects, as well as in Iraq, where they are a majority of the population, concentrated in southern Iraq, though they are marginalized from centers of political power; and last but not least in Iran, where virtually the entire Muslim population is Shi'i.

4. The name "Berber" is not used by this community. "Berber" derives from the Greek word for "barbarian," or perhaps from a colloquial Arabic expression, "*ber-ber*," which indicates that a person does not speak properly (i.e., does not speak Arabic correctly). The name used by Berbers among themselves is *Amazigh* (plural, *Imazighen*), meaning "free man"

in the Tamazight language. Before the advent of Islam in North Africa, the entire population was Imazighen, speaking several different dialects of Tamazigh. Today the largest and most influential Amazigh tribal group is that of the Kabylian Berber community. All Amazigh are Sunni Muslims, with few exceptions, and are distinguished from non-Amazigh primarily by their spoken language, which was standardized only in the twentieth century.

5. Although Berbers played a key role in Algeria's independence struggle, many Arab nationalists and Islamists cited the Berbers' special treatment under the French, particularly their exemption from Islamic law, as marks against this community's loyalty, patriotism, and steadfastness. Despite the special treatment accorded them by the French colonial regime, the Berbers did not profit economically or politically in the long run. As revealed in a series of 11 essays by Albert Camus that appeared in the *Alger-Republicain* newspaper in 1939 under the title "Poverty in Kabylia," the Berbers were as impoverished as ever in the years leading up to World War II (Maddy-Weitzman 1998:50).

6. Religious affiliation in Lebanon is not a matter of individual choice but something one is born into. In Lebanon, individuals are considered to belong to the religious sect of their father. This conflates a patrilineal (and patriarchal) kinship system with the state's confessional system of government and resource allocation. In Lebanon, religion determines one's relationship to the state, and since religious affiliation determines how one will be married, buried, divorced, and inherited, family membership is intimately tied to political membership. At the national level, this is evident in the "dynasties" of various sectarian leaders and their sons, who have assumed the mantle of power for their respective religious communities generation after generation—for example, the Cham'oun and Frangieh families among the Maronites, the Jumblatt and Arslan families among the Druzes, the Husseinis and Asads among the Shi'ites. Conflicts frequently erupt *within* religious communities when members of these families compete for the role of the lead family within their respective sects. During the civil war, the rise of militias and the breakdown of the state's role as guardian of civil order exacerbated these interfamily, intrasectarian conflicts, particularly among the Maronites.

7. The author, who lived and worked in Lebanon for five years in the postwar period, often heard colleagues and friends refer to Lebanon's tragedy as being analogous to "one hundred dogs trying to chew on the same bone," the bone here being the state and its various material and nonmaterial resources.

8. The Ta'ef Accord, an agreement that set the terms for the end of the Lebanese conflict in 1989 (and which takes its name from the Saudi Arabian city where the negotiations were held), clearly stipulated that the Lebanese system would be deconfessionalized in an orderly progression of steps, culminating in complete deconfessionalization by the mid-1990s. To date, this process has scarcely been initiated or attempted (U. Makdisi 1997).

9. Kurds in Iraq are primarily Sunni Muslims, but there are also Shi'i, Christian, and Jewish Kurdish tribes in neighboring countries.

10. Because both Israel and Lebanon have retained elements

of the *millet* system and Ottoman legal specifications concerning ethnoreligious groups, most notably the retention of "personal status laws," which give different religious communities' leadership effective legal and moral control over issues such as marriage, divorce, inheritance, and adoption, women are particularly disadvantaged by the lack of modern, liberal laws concerning alimony, child-support payments, and fair inheritance practices. Neither Israel nor Lebanon recognizes civil marriage. All couples must marry in a religious ceremony, and if they are from different religious backgrounds, this implies that one must convert to the faith of the other. Usually, it is the woman who converts. In such cases, however, it is far more common that the couple will go to Cyprus, marry there in a legally binding civil ceremony, and return to either Lebanon or Israel, where the state does recognize civil marriage certificates originating in other states.

REFERENCES CITED

ABD AL-JABBAR, FALAH. 1992. Why the uprisings failed. *Middle East Report* 176:2–14.

___. 2000. Shaykhs and ideologues: Detribalization and retribalization in Iraq, 1968–1998. *Middle East Report* 215:28–31.

ABRAMSON, DAVID. 2000. Muslim selves and Uzbek citizens. Paper presented at the 99th Annual Meeting of the American Anthropological Association, San Francisco, November 16.

ANDERSON, BENEDICT. 1983. *Imagined Communities: Reflections on the Origins and Spread of Nationalism.* London: Verso.

AVRUCH, KEVIN. 1987. The emergence of ethnicity in Israel. *American Ethnologist* 14(2):327–339.

AYALON, AMI. 1999. Egypt's Coptic Pandora's box. In *Minorities and the State in the Arab World,* Ofra Bengio and Gabriel Ben-Dor, eds. Pp. 53–72. Boulder, CO: Lynne Rienner.

AYOUBI, NAZIH. 1995. *Overstating the Arab State.* London: I. B. Tauris.

BARAKAT, HALIM. 1993. *The Arab World: Society, Culture, and State.* Berkeley: University of California Press.

BATATU, HANNA. 1978. *The Old Social Classes and the Revolutionary Movements of Iraq.* Princeton, NJ: Princeton University Press.

BENGIO, OFRA. 1999. Nation building in multi-ethnic societies: The case of Iraq. In *Minorities and the State in the Arab World.* Ofra Bengio and Gabriel Ben-Dor, eds. Pp. 149–170. Boulder, CO: Lynne Rienner.

BENGIO, OFRA, and GABRIEL BEN-DOR, eds. 1999. *Minorities and the State in the Arab World.* Boulder, CO: Lynne Rienner.

BOSWORTH, C. E. 1982. The concept of dhimma in early Islam. In *Christians and Jews in the Ottoman Empire,* vol. 2. Benjamin Braude and Bernard Lewis, eds. Pp.

37–54. *The Arabic Speaking Lands.* New York: Holmes & Meier.

CINAR, ALEV. 1999. Cartel: The travels of a German-Turkish rap band. *Middle East Report* 211:43–45.

COHEN, RONALD. 1978. Ethnicity: Problem and focus in anthropology. *Annual Review of Anthropology* 7:379–403.

CONNELL, DAN. 1999. What's new in the new Sudan? *Middle East Report* 212:2–3.

COON, CARLETON. 1961. *Caravan: The Story of the Middle East.* New York: Holt, Rinehart & Winston.

CUNNINGHAM, ROBERT, and YASIN K. SARAYRAH. 1993. *Wasta: The Hidden Force in Middle Eastern Culture.* Westport, CT: Praeger.

DRYSDALE, ALASDAIR, and GERALD H. BLAKE. 1985. *The Middle East and North Africa: A Political Geography.* Oxford: Oxford University Press.

EHSANI, KAVEH. 1999. Municipal matters: The urbanization of consciousness and political change in Tehran. *Middle East Report* 212:22–27.

EICKELMAN, DALE. 1999. *The Middle East and Central Asia: An Anthropological Approach.* 3rd edition. Upper Saddle River, NJ: Prentice Hall.

EL-GAWHARY, KARIM. 1994. Copts in the Egyptian "Fabric." *Middle East Report* 200:21–22.

ELLER, JACK DAVID. 1999. *From Culture to Ethnicity to Conflict: An Anthropological Perspective on International Ethnic Conflict.* Ann Arbor: University of Michigan Press.

Embassy of Algeria. 1995. Amazighté–communiqué de la présidence. Washington, DC, April 3, 1995.

ESPOSITO, JOHN. 1991. *Islam: The Straight Path.* 2nd edition. New York: Oxford University Press.

ETHELSTON, SALLY. 1999. Water and women: The Middle East in demographic transition. *Middle East Report* 213:4–8.

FIRRO, KAIS M. 1999. *The Druzes in the Jewish State: A Brief History.* Leiden: Brill.

FROMKIN, DAVID. 1988. *A Peace to End All Peace: The Fall of the Ottoman Empire and the Creation of the Modern Middle East.* New York: Avon.

GOLDSCHMIDT, ARTHUR JR. 2000. The historical context. In *Understanding the Contemporary Middle East.* Deborah J. Gerner, ed. Pp. 33–80. Boulder, CO: Lynne Rienner.

GOODMAN, JANE. 1996. Berber associations and cultural change in Algeria. *Middle East Report* 200:16–20.

GRAHAM-BROWN, SARAH. 1999. *Sanctioning Saddam: The Politics of Intervention in Iraq.* London and New York: I. B. Tauris, in association with MERIP.

HAJJAR, LISA. 2000. Speaking the conflict, or how the Druze became bilingual: A study of Druze translators in the Israeli military courts in the West Bank and Gaza. *Ethnic and Racial Studies* 23(2):299–328.

HALLIDAY, FRED. 1999. The Middle East at the millennial turn. *Middle East Report* 213:4–7.

HANF, THEODORE. 1992. *Coexistence in Wartime Lebanon: The Decline of a State and the Rise of a Nation*. London: Center for Lebanese Studies, in association with I. B. Tauris.

HARDIN, RUSSELL. 1995. *One for All: The Logic of Group Conflict*. Princeton, NJ: Princeton University Press.

HARF, BARBARA. 1993. Minorities, rebellion, and repression in North Africa and the Middle East. In *Minorities at Risk: A Global View of Ethnopolitical Conflicts*. Ted Gurr, ed. Washington, DC: United States Institute of Peace.

HILTERMANN, JOOST. 1999. Clipped wings and sharp claws: Iraq in the 1990s. *Middle East Report* 212:58–60.

AL-KHAFAJI, ISAM. 1992. State terror and the degradation of politics in Iraq. *Middle East Report* 176:15–21.

___. 1996. The destruction of Iraqi Kurdistan. *Middle East Report* 201:35–38.

KHALAF, SAMIR. 1985. *Lebanon's Predicament*. New York: Columbia University Press.

AL-KHAZEN, FARID. 2000. *The Breakdown of the State in Lebanon: 1967–1976*. Cambridge, MA: Harvard University Press.

KHOURY, PHILIP, and JOSEPH KOSTINER, eds. 1989. *Tribes and State Formation in the Middle East*. Berkeley: University of California Press.

KING-IRANI, LAURIE. 2000a. Kinship, ethnicity and social class: Strategies of diversity in the Middle East. In *Understanding the Contemporary Middle East*. Deborah J. Gerner, ed. Pp. 263–292. Boulder, CO: Lynne Rienner.

___. 2000b. Rituals of forgiveness and processes of empowerment in Lebanon. In *Traditional Cures for Modern Conflicts: African Conflict "Medicine."* I. William Zartman, ed. Pp. 129–140. Boulder, CO: Lynne Rienner.

___. 2001. Maneuvering in narrow spaces: The political construction and existential constriction of Palestinian citizens of Israel. Ph.D. thesis, Department of Anthropology, Indiana University, Bloomington.

LESCH, ANN. 1997. *The Sudan: Contested National Identities*. Bloomington: Indiana University Press.

MADDY-WEITZMAN, BRUCE. 1998. The Berber question in Algeria: Nationalism in the making?" In *Minorities and the State in the Arab World*. Ofra Bengio and Gabriel Ben-Dor, eds. Pp. 31–52. Boulder, CO: Lynne Rienner.

MAKDISI, SAMIR. 1990. The Arab world and the world economy: An overview. In *The Economic Dimensions of Middle East History: Essays in Honor of Charles Issawi*. Hala Esfandiari and A. L. Udovich eds. Pp. 123–146. Princeton, NJ: Darwin Press.

MAKDISI, USAMA. 1997. The modernity of sectarianism in Lebanon. *Middle East Report* 200:23–26.

MANNERS, IAN, and BARBARA McKEAN PARMENTER. 2000. The Middle East: A geographic preface. In *Understanding the Contemporary Middle East*. Deborah G. Gerner, ed. Pp. 5–32. Boulder, CO: Lynne Rienner.

McMURRAY, DAVID, and TED SWEDENBURG. 1991. Rai tide rising. *Middle East Report* 169:39–42.

MEEKER, MICHAEL. 1979. *Literature and Violence in Early Arabia*. London: Cambridge University Press.

PFEIFER, KAREN. 1998. How Tunisia, Morocco, Jordan, and even Egypt became IMF "success stories" in the 1990s. *Middle East Report* 210:23–27.

RONEN, YEHUDIT. 1999. Religion and conflict in the Sudan: A non-Muslim minority in a Muslim state. In *Minorities and the State in the Arab World*, Ofra Bengio and Gabriel Ben-Dor, eds. Pp. 73–90. Boulder, CO: Lynne Rienner.

ROYCE, ANYA PETERSON. 1982. *Ethnicity: Strategies of Diversity*. Bloomington: Indiana University Press.

SAID, EDWARD. 1978. *Orientalism*. Harmondsworth, UK: Penguin.

SALIBI, KAMAL. 1988. *A House of Many Mansions: The History of Lebanon Reconsidered*. London: I. B. Tauris.

SANASARIAN, ELISE. 2000. *Religious Minorities in Iran*. Cambridge: Cambridge University Press.

SILVERSTEIN, PAUL. 1996. Realizing myths: Berbers in France and Algeria. *Middle East Report* 200:16–20.

___. 1997. "The rebel is dead! Long live the martyr!" Kabyle mobilization and the assassination of Lounes Matoub. *Middle East Report* 208:3–4.

TÉTREAULT, MARY ANN. 2001. International relations. In *Understanding the Contemporary Middle East*. Deborah J. Gerner, ed. Pp. 129–160. Boulder, CO: Lynne Rienner.

TIBI, BASSAM. 1989. The simultaneity of the unsimultaneous: Old tribes and imposed nation states in the modern Middle East. In *Tribes and State Formation in the Middle East*. Philip S. Khoury and Joseph Kostiner, eds. Pp. 127–152. Berkeley: University of California Press.

USHER, GRAHAM. 1998. The fate of small nations: The Karabagh conflict ten years later. *Middle East Report* 213:19–22.

World Bank. 1996. *The Middle East and North Africa*. Washington, DC.

16

ASIA

Raymond Scupin

Lindenwood University

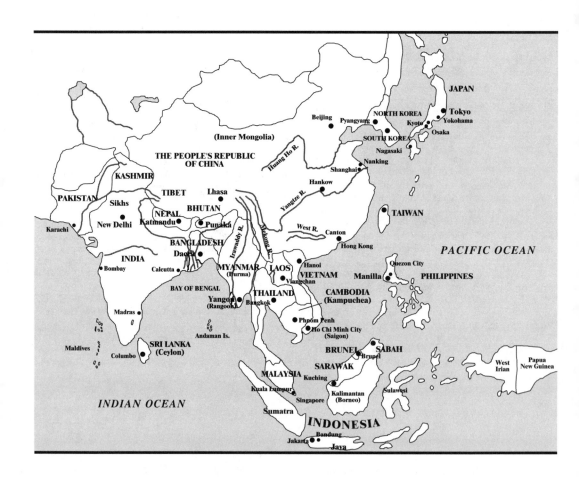

Asia is a culturally diverse region with a wide variety of languages, ethnic groups, and religions. This chapter focuses on race and ethnic relations in three general regions: South Asia, East Asia (China and Japan), and Southeast Asia. These regions contain most of the world's population—over 3 billion people. Different forms of societies have developed in these regions, ranging from hunter-gatherer and horticultural societies of the tropical rain forests, to the pastoral nomads of northern China, to vast, complex, intensive agricultural societies, to the advanced industrial societies such as those in Japan. As we will see, race and ethnic relations have been shaped by the traditional cultural beliefs, worldviews, and ideologies, as well as Western concepts and the rapid globalization processes affecting these different regions.

SOUTH ASIA

South Asia is a distinct geographic region extending from the Himalaya Mountains in the north, through the tropical forests and vast agricultural plains of India, and south to the island-nation of Sri Lanka. The major countries of South Asia include Pakistan, India, Bangladesh, Nepal, and Sri Lanka. To some extent, the geographic locations of the populations of South Asia have influenced the development of diverse ethnic identities. Historically, as various groups were separated by mountains, tropical forests, and other geographic barriers, regional ethnic and linguistic differences emerged within these countries. Additionally, these peoples began to classify and distinguish their own local identities from one another. Therefore, each of these countries has distinctive ethnic groups that differ in their linguistic, historical, and cultural experience. And, for the most part, the ethnic identities of the peoples of South Asia do not correspond to the nation-states or countries. For example, within the country of Pakistan the major ethnic groups are the Punjabi, Sindhi, Pathan, Baluch,

and others who maintain distinct languages and cultural traditions.

India, a country that contains over a billion people, has tremendous ethnic, linguistic, and cultural diversity. A recent ethnographic survey of India has identified over 324 distinct languages (Norton 1999). The major languages of northern India include Hindi, Bengali, Punjabi, Gujarati, and Bihari, all part of the Indo-European language family. Southern India has languages such as Tamil, Telugu, and Malayalam that belong to a completely different language family, the Dravidian. Officially, the government of India recognizes 18 different languages; however, no single language is spoken by more than 40 percent of the population. Thus, India does not have a uniform language that serves to unite all of its various ethnic groups.

South Asia also includes various religious traditions that result in ethnic complexity. For example, although Hinduism is the religion of 80 percent of the population in India, over 100 million Muslims reside in the country. In addition, religious minorities include Sikhs, Jains, Christians, and a wide variety of Buddhist traditions. Pakistan and Bangladesh are Islamic countries, whereas Nepal and Sri Lanka have both Hindu and Buddhist traditions that are widely divergent. All of these religious faiths have been a source of boundary markers of ethnic identity in different regions of South Asia. Combined with linguistic differences, this religious diversity has produced an immense variety of cultural traditions and ethnic complexities throughout South Asia.

THE CONCEPT OF RACE IN SOUTH ASIA

As has been emphasized in earlier chapters, the scientific concept of "race" is problematic within anthropological research. Anthropologists find that there is much too much physical and genetic complexity to identify clearly bounded, easily separated "races" throughout the world. However, as we have seen (Chapter 3), as the concept of "race" began to be formulated by scientists in European society in the eighteenth and nineteenth centuries, it held many misconceptions about the relationship between biology and culture. It led to stereotypes and essentialist constructions of "racial identities" based on blood or inheritance combined with cultural or ethnic traits. These early European scientists, including anthropologists, were conflating physical characteristics with cultural attributes. Today, we would consider these notions as "folk" or "pseudo-scientific" constructions of race.

As we have seen, many people throughout the world have maintained nonscientific folk concepts of race and ethnicity within their cultural traditions (Chapter 4). Thus, some people classify groups into separate categories based on skin color or other traits, including cultural attributes. These folk concepts of race have been identified within the various cultures of South Asia. Though the English term *race* or the German word *Rasse* does not appear in South Asia until after European colonialism, there are close equivalents of this notion of race found in earlier popular or indigenous traditions in the area. These folk categories of race were not based purely on biological characteristics but also indigenous notions of cultural "essences" as well. Subsequently, in many cases, following European colonialism and the introduction of Western concepts of "race," indigenous folk categories were often combined and synthesized into new forms of "race" categories in South Asia.

Some of the indigenous concepts that are close equivalents to the concept of race are intimately connected with the caste system of India. Most scholars associate the origins of the caste system with the Indo-Aryan peoples who settled in northern India after about 2000 B.C.E. The Indo-Aryan peoples were a pastoralist society that gradually gained control of the Punjab region and most of northern India by 600

B.C.E. Prior to the settlement of the Indo-Aryans, agricultural civilizations developed by peoples speaking Dravidian languages existed throughout northern India. Gradually, these peoples were absorbed into the political and cultural system of the Indo-Aryans.

Between 1800 and 600 B.C.E, the Indo-Aryans had produced a massive collection of sacred texts known as the Vedas, the earliest texts of the Hindu religious tradition. In the oldest text of the Vedas, the *Rig Veda*, the term *varna* is introduced to distinguish the Indo-Aryan people from others who were designated as slaves. *Varna* is translated as "color" or "complexion," but it refers primarily to linguistic and cultural differences between the populations (Klass 1997; Trautmann 1997).[1] Within a sacred hymn, the *Purusha-Skuta* ("Hymn of Man") in the *Rig Veda*, the creation of the universe and of humans is described. According to the myth, four social orders, or *varnas*, are associated with different types of humans who are born from the cosmic giant *Purusha*, the primeval man. The *Brahman*, priests or ritual specialists, emerge from the head or mouth of *Purusha*; the *Kshatriya*, warrior princes and chieftains, from the arms; the *Vaisya*, a group of agriculturalists, merchants, and traders, from his thighs; and the *Sudras*, laborers and servants, come from his feet. The levels of origins implied that these various groups had different natures, temperaments, behaviors, and personalities.

This fourfold *varna* scheme provided the ideological framework for organizing thousands of diverse groups within Indian society. Eventually, the functional groupings in the *varna* ideological scheme imposed categories that became the castes and subcastes, or, more precisely, what Indians refer in Hindi as *jatis*, of which there are several thousand. The *jatis* are hierarchically ranked in accordance with descent, occupational, marital, and ritual-religious factors. One is born within a specific family determining one's caste. Ideally, one is supposed to practice the same occupation associated with one's caste, marry within one's caste, and practice Hinduism as a member of a particular caste. As the religious tradition of Hinduism evolved in India, *varnas* were associated with the doctrinal concepts of reincarnation and *karma*. The doctrine of reincarnation refers to how after death one's soul transmigrates to another being to be reborn. Popularly, the doctrine of *karma* suggests that one inherits a particular type of soul that will influence one's temperament and lifelong destiny (Daniel 1983). In other words, an individual will be born within a high-ranking or low-ranking *varna* based on one's *karma*; and, one will inherit a particular "essence" that will shape one's personality and behavior. To some extent, the term *jati* is equivalent to "species," which would imply a concept of a "race" (Dumont 1970).

As is obvious, this indigenous concept of inherited temperament and behavior associated with a particular rank based on one's family and birth is somewhat equivalent to a folk concept of race. In this folk concept, an individual inherits a particular status and "essence" that are connected with specific behaviors and culture. Although the caste system is extremely varied, differing from one region to another and from one village to another, and is constantly being transformed, the basic ideals tend to associate biological inheritance and the determination of one's status, temperament, and behavior.[2]

With Western colonialism, the early European concepts of race were imported into South Asia. During the eighteenth and nineteenth centuries, as the British were colonizing India, colonial officials along with ethnographers and scholars were ordering, counting, and classifying various populations according to "racial," tribal, and caste identities (Bayly 1995; Trautmann 1997). These processes were part and parcel of the colonial project in order to exert political and economic control of the different regions of India. This colonial project also led to the circulation of ideas of "race" that became the predominant myths of European society. For example, the British linguistic scholar William Jones discovered that the Indo-Aryan language of Sanskrit was historically related to other European languages such as Greek and Latin. Jones deduced from this that the "Aryan" peoples represented a conquering "race" that built the civilizations of Greece, Rome, and later European countries (Bayly 1995; Trautmann 1997). This Aryan conquest myth provided the fodder for the theories of the scientific racists such as the French thinker Joseph Gobineau, whose thesis later influenced the Nazi beliefs about the superiority of the so-called Aryan race (see Chapter 3). Other early British scholars, relying on the Hindu texts, distinguished the Aryans from other peoples in India by skin color. In addition, the upper castes were distinguished from the lower castes based on skin color. Thus, the Brahmans, the upper caste associated with the Aryans, were lighter in skin color than the lower castes. The British colonial project resulted in essentialist stereotypes about the hierarchy of various "racial" and caste groups in India, which influenced European conceptions of India for generations (Bayly 1995; Inden 1990).

The European concepts of race were imported by a number of Indian thinkers and were synthesized with indigenous conceptions of "race" and "caste." As more native people became literate in English, and Indian nationalism developed in the nineteenth and twentieth centuries, various essentialist ideas of race and caste began to percolate into Indian thought. Racist beliefs about the superiority of the Aryan race were incorporated into a Hindu revivalist and nationalist movement known as *Hindutva*. One of the important leaders of the Hindutva revivalist movement, V. D. Savarkar, wrote about how Hindus "share a common blood of the mighty race of Aryans," and that this "blood" should be the basis of a nationalist consciousness (Jaffrelot 1995). Later Hindu nationalist ideologues adopted modified myths of Aryan racial superiority to help provide the foundation of a postcolonial independent nation in India. Though, eventually, the Hindutva nationalist ideologies minimized the "racial" aspects of Hinduism and emphasized the cultural and religious traditions, they promoted the dominance of the Hindu majority over other ethnic groups in the building of the Indian nation.

Recently, in the 1980s and 1990s, the Hindutva movement resurfaced as an integral aspect of contemporary Indian politics. A political party, the Bharatiya Janata Party (BJP), which is linked with the Hindutva movement, managed to gain control of the political system. The Hindutva movement emphasizes a resurgence of Hindu religiosity and ethnic purity against other ethnic and religious groups in India. Hinduism is interpreted as a unified ethnic and religious tradition as distinct from other minority religions such as Islam. The BJP and the Hindutva movement were associated with the destruction of a Muslim mosque in Ayodhaya, India, in 1992. Hindus claim that the mosque was actually the temple and birthplace of the Hindu god Rama, prior to the settlement of the Muslims in India. Hindu mobs violently attacked and burned the mosque. The Muslim minority community in India, consisting of over 100 million people, are fearful of the status of their mosques and their ethnic and religious identity in India.

The Hindu ethnic and religious resurgence is partly a response to the globalization process that has fragmented and divided the traditional regional, village, religious, and ethnic communities in India. The basic aim of the Hindutva religious and ethnic resurgence is to restore an "original" ethnic and organic community that represents a harmonious India. This ethnic and religious Hindu movement has created conflict among different ethnic communities in India. The BJP took pride in the explosion of a nuclear device in 1998, which they perceived as a symbol of the political power of the Hindutva agenda. This has exacerbated geo-political relationships with India's Islamic neighbor Pakistan,

which then detonated its own nuclear devices. Ethnic and religious resurgence within this South Asian region may have consequences for the entire global community.

The Sikhs

Another ethnic problem that has confronted India involves the Sikh community. The Sikhs are a population of about 18 million who live in the Punjab region bordering India and Pakistan. The Sikh religion developed in the fifteenth century as a blend of Hindu and Islamic beliefs. Sikhism is a mystical religious tradition centered on venerated leaders who founded a military fraternity that offered protection from both Muslims and Hindus. The Sikhs pride themselves on their warrior spirit. Every male carries the name Singh, which translates as "lion." The Sikhs have built a major house of worship—the golden temple of Amritsar—in the Punjab.

Anthropologist Richard Fox (1985) conducted ethnographic research among the Sikhs in 1980–81. Using historical material and ethnographic data, he focused on the development of Sikh ethnic and religious identity as a response to external pressures. The Sikhs, who had freed themselves from Muslim and Hindu domination, were confronted with colonialism and the capitalist world system that penetrated the Punjab. The British viewed the Sikhs as an important military shield that could be used for extending their control over India. Colonial and military officials, therefore, treated and classified the Sikhs as a separate "race" of warriors.[3] These British conceptions tended to reinforce Sikh ethnic separateness from Muslims, Hindus, and other groups.

Eventually the Sikhs recognized that the incorporation of their territory into the British empire would reduce their political and economic autonomy. Therefore, they initiated reform movements that sought to unify urban workers and rural peasants. These movements led to violent resistance against the British and, following national independence in 1947, to secessionist movements against the Indian government. The Sikhs wanted their own nation-state called Kalistan based on their ethnicity in the Punjab region. This ethnonationalist movement accelerated during the 1970s and 1980s, and was met with increased police and military repression by the Indian government.

In 1984, a group of militant, armed Sikhs took refuge in the golden temple of Amritsar, demanding political autonomy from India. The Indian government responded by sending military troops into the Punjab, some of whom entered the temple. The temple complex was destroyed and hundreds of Sikhs were killed. This violation of their sacred temple outraged many Sikhs, many of whom were not militant. Later in 1984, as resistance to Hindu domination grew, a Sikh militant assassinated Prime Minister Indira Gandhi. This event was marked by wide-scale violence, and Hindus killed over 3,000 Sikhs in the capital city of Delhi. Conflict between Sikhs and Hindus will undoubtedly remain a problem in the twenty-first century.

Ethnic Problems in Sri Lanka

Another South Asian country facing severe and troubling ethnic problems is Sri Lanka. For many years, this island country south of India was called Ceylon. It became known as Sri Lanka in 1972. The indigenous majority population of Sri Lanka is the 12 million or so Sinhalese-speaking Buddhists. Sinhalese is a Sanskrit-derived Aryan language. The Sinhalese Buddhists are concentrated in the central, southern, and western portions of the island. Under British colonialism, Tamil-speaking Hindus were imported from southern India to work on rubber plantations. Tamil is one of the languages of the Dravidian family in India. Although the majority of Tamil-speaking Hindus were already in residence in Sri Lanka, British policies increased their population. There are some internal ethnic divisions between the original Tamil

settlers and the later immigrants (Daniel 1997). By 1995, the Tamil Hindus made up 18 percent of the population, about 3 million people, and constituted a majority in northern Sri Lanka. Both the Tamil Hindus and Sinhalese Buddhists are internally differentiated by caste differences that have played a role in the development of their ethnic identities.

The history of the ethnic conflict between the Tamil Hindus and the Sinhalese Buddhists is extremely complex.[4] Anthropologists have been studying how the myths of nationalism and religion have been used to accentuate ethnic differences in Sri Lanka (Kapferer 1988; Spencer 1990; Tambiah 1992). They indicate how the Sinhalese have employed an ancient Buddhist cosmological tradition known as the *Mahavamsa*, which is interpreted to demonstrate that they are clearly the dominant group. This Buddhist tradition suggests that the original inhabitants of the island were demons ruled by the demon-king Ravana. According to this tradition, the first human settlers were the Sinhala (Sinhalese), "people of the lion." Thus, this cosmological tradition is used as a charter myth to justify claims of ownership of the entire island by the Sinhalese. The myth also emphasizes how after Buddhism was established in Sri Lanka, under a Sinhalese Buddhist king, a Dravidian-speaking Tamil Hindu usurped the throne. Therefore, the Tamils are introduced in the chronicle as an enemy of the Sinhalese people. The Tamils are also associated with the decline of the original Sri Lankan Buddhist civilization. This sets up a cosmic struggle between the Tamil Hindus and Sinhalese Buddhists within the myth.

During the period of British colonialism in Sri Lanka (Ceylon), a number of factors developed that resulted in intense ethnic tensions between the Sinhalese and Tamils. As part of the resistance to British colonial domination, both the Sinhalese and Tamils began to publish newspapers, books, and pamphlets in their respective languages to reform and revitalize their own ethnic and religious traditions. As we have seen elsewhere (Chapter 4), print media is an important stimulant to the development of ethnonationalism. The Sinhalese emphasized the Buddhist traditions such as the *Mahavamsa* to claim their ethnic domination and rights over the entire island. In addition, they also drew on the British colonial scholarship and notions of the "Aryan race superiority" that were circulating among Europeans, suggesting that the Sinhala were the superior race of Sri Lanka. The Tamil ethnonationalism movement produced its own interpretations of the Hindu chronicles to suggest that the Sinhalese identity is not really "Aryan" but rather a mixture of various cultures, and that their own Tamil language and religion are superior to those of the Sinhalese. In addition, an economic factor influenced the ethnic relationship between the Tamils and Sinhalese. Generally, the Tamil adopted the English language rapidly and tended to be favored by the British for high-status positions within the colonial regime. The Sinhalese perceived this tendency, and were fearful of losing their majority control of the island following independence. All these factors crystallized the ethnic division between the majority "Sinhala/Buddhist/Aryan" and minority "Tamil/Hindu/Dravidian" populations.

In 1948, after independence from the British, the Sinhalese were able to dominate politically and elect people to office from their own community. During the 1950s, to extend their ethnic hegemony they began to promote a Sinhalese-only language policy. In addition they emphasized that Buddhism was the official religion of the country. Tamils demonstrated against these policies, and interethnic violence erupted. Eventually, in the 1970s Tamil militants formed an organized paramilitary group, the Tamil Tigers, who called for the liberation of northern Sri Lanka as an independent Tamil nation-state. Extensive violence broke out between Tamils and Sinhalese in the north. The Sinhalese army responded with an invasion and indiscriminate killings in the Tamil communities. The Tamils

responded in kind. In 1987, India sent soldiers to quell the violence. Pressured by the Sri Lankan government, India withdrew in 1989. Today the violence continues, and over 30,000 people have been killed as a result of this interethnic warfare. As anthropologist Stanley Tambiah notes (1986), the ethnic fratricide that is ongoing in Sri Lanka is exacerbated by the continuing delivery of strategic arms from the industrialized world into the hands of these ethnic groups.

RACE AND ETHNICITY IN EAST ASIA: CHINA AND JAPAN

At first sight, unlike South Asia, the East Asian countries of China and Japan appear not to have great ethnic diversity. Many people assume that these countries have been dominated by one ethnic group for centuries, and the percentage of people who are not part of the dominant ethnic group is fairly small. For example, China (mainland China, not including the island of Taiwan), with over a billion people, includes 104 million people (9.1 percent of the population) who are referred to as "national minorities." These minorities are ethnically distinct from the Han majority population, which make up 92 percent of the population. These official national minorities consist of 55 groups, 18 of which have more than 1 million members. Japan appears to have even more ethnic homogeneity. The Japanese make up 99.4 percent of the population of 126 million people, with only 0.6 percent of the population being ethnic minorities (mostly Korean).

Thus, both of these countries appear to have more cultural and ethnic homogeneity than many other areas within Asia. Nevertheless, as we will see, they do have interethnic tensions, and the appearance of cultural homogeneity is rather superficial. And, most recently, global factors have begun to stimulate more ethnic diversity in these areas. Anthropologists have been doing research on the ethnic relations in China and Japan to investigate how these countries deal with their interethnic tensions, and how the dominant majority has to maintain its ethnic and cultural dominance.

The Concept of Race in China and Japan

As in South Asia and many other areas of the non-Western world, within China and Japan "folk" concepts of group membership were equivalent to the pseudo-scientific concept of "race" that was developed in European society in the eighteenth and nineteenth centuries. In both China and Japan these folk notions of race were related to family, blood relationships, and descent. From the earliest centuries of Chinese civilization one's social identity revolved around membership within a particular family, a family that had deep historical roots. In traditional China a family was part of a patrilineage, or *zu*, a group of people who could demonstrate through written records or oral history that they were descended from particular ancestors. A group of patrilineages was referred to as a *clan*. Clans shared the same surname, such as Li, Mao, or Chang, and often shared property, such as an ancestral temple, cemetery, or common land. In some regions of China this emphasis on patrilineal clans led to villages where almost all the inhabitants shared the same surname.

Throughout much of traditional Chinese history these patrilineal clans were involved in competition and conflict over land, power, and status. They became militarized, and struggled with each other for leadership. Those patrilineal clans that attained leadership success and were able to rule over various regions gained higher status. To justify their claims to high status, various concepts of descent, blood ties, and kinship solidarity were developed. Cults and folk notions of patrilineal descent emphasizing specific families as superior "peoples" and "culture" were acknowledged. As expected, the Chinese emperor's patrilineal clan was superior to all.

Various people outside the confines of traditional Chinese civilization were classified as "barbarians," *yongxiabianyi*, and the physical characteristics of these people were conflated with cultural attributes (Dikötter 1992). The barbarians living beyond the realm of Chinese civilization were classified as nonhuman animals. The only people who were *ren*, "human beings," were the Chinese. Skin color was often used as a marker of animality and bestiality for the barbarians. In both the mythological and elite literate traditions of China, color consciousness was used to classify different peoples outside the empire. When trading activities took the Chinese to areas such as Southeast Asia, Africa, and Central Asia, they encountered people of different skin colorations. This resulted in linking skin coloration with cultural characteristics, and defining these peoples as nonhuman and uncivilized. Thus ideologies that emphasized the "purity" of the Chinese versus the "impurity" of barbarians based on natural "essences" emerged. One of the principal duties of the Chinese emperor was to keep the boundaries between these groups distinct. Thus, folk-based ideologies of "racial" taxonomies were being formed well before European intrusions into China (Dikötter 1992).

Likewise, the Japanese had similar folk and ideological notions that were parallel to the early European pseudo-scientific concepts of race. Purported links between blood, descent, and status were inextricably tied together in Japanese myth and cultural traditions. During the Classical period in Japanese history (400–1200 C.E.) cultural traditions, including writing, literature, religion, and political forms, were borrowed from China and grafted onto the indigenous traditions within Japan. Political institutions, including the institution of the emperor, were adopted from China into Japan. The notion that the bloodline of the imperial family was superior became even more important in Japan than in China. The Japanese emperor and his family were associated with cosmological traditions that designated them as divine beings. The emperor's family and clan were at the top of a traditional hierarchy of families, resembling the caste system of India, that distinguished between pure and impure individuals. Therefore, rank, status, and hierarchy were believed to be determined by birth, blood, kinship, and descent in traditional Japanese society. This was similar to the folk concepts of race found in other areas of the world.

Western Influence and Race

With the exception of the colonization of Hong Kong and nearby regions by the British, neither China or Japan were taken over as colonies by European powers. However, with Western penetration into Asia, European pseudo-scientific beliefs about race were diffused and integrated with indigenous concepts into China and Japan. In China, the Western pseudo-scientific category of "race" and the purported evolutionary superiority of specific "races" were fused with folk models of patrilineal descent and the pure origins of the emperor (Dikötter 1992, 1997). The term *zu* for patrilineage was eventually redefined as *minzu*, which integrated people (*min*) and descent (*zu*) to refer to the people, "race," or nation of China.

The term *minzu* was introduced into China from Japan in the late nineteenth century when other Western concepts were translated into Japanese and transmitted to China. In particular, the "Han race" was identified with the most pure "race" descended from the emperor. The leader and first president of the Republic in China, Sun Yat-sen, promoted a racial nationalism as a basis for the nation-state in the early twentieth century. He wrote about how the Han had common blood, common language, common religion, and common customs, and was a single, pure race. Sun believed that groups such as the Mongols, Manchus, Tibetans, and Mohammedan Turks were different *minzu*, or peoples or nationalities. Textbooks were used to educate the children of China about these "races." For example, one elementary textbook

of 1921 asserts: "Mankind is divided into five races. The yellow and white races are relatively strong and intelligent. Because the other races are feeble and stupid, they are being exterminated by the white race. Only the yellow race competes with the white race" (cited in Dikötter 1992:163). Following the Communist revolution in China led by Mao Zedong in the 1950s, racialized notions were still perpetuated. Mao perceived the Chinese nation (*minzu*) as a biologically distinct group, a matter of "culture" as well as "race."

Japanese nationalists also adopted the European pseudo-scientific concepts of race to reinforce indigenous concepts of blood and descent. A conjunction of blood, culture, history, and political form became the dominant discourse of Japanese intellectuals during the Meiji period (1868–1912). During the Meiji period many Japanese studied Western traditions as a means of inducing rapid modernization. As the Japanese investigated Western writings on "race," these ideas were incorporated and synthesized with indigenous conceptions. "Japaneseness" became associated with a particular "race" of people who were part of one family nation (*kazoku kokka*), with the emperor as a semidivine father. Various Japanese intellectuals identified the nation, or *minzoku*, as a manifestation of common blood and ancestry as well as culture (Weiner 1997; Yoshino 1998). Ultimately, this racialistic thinking was extended in the Japanese notion that they were the superior "race" of Asia, and this became the basis for an ethnonationalistic movement and imperialistic expansion in the twentieth century resulting in World War II. Many Japanese began to believe that they were a superior "race" compared to the inferior races of China, Korea, or their own indigenous native population of Ainu in northern Japan (Ohnuki-Tierney 1998; Weiner 1997). Family, kinship, blood, and culture became inextricably bound to produce a sense of superior Japaneseness. Following World War II, with the U.S. occupation and the ideological attack on these notions of the superior Japanese race and blood, these beliefs became muted. Yet, as sociologist Kosaku Yoshino says, in the Japanese subconsciousness the nation as "imagined kinship" and metaphors of blood remain alive and well (1997:201).

The Muslim Minority in China

Anthropologist Dru Gladney has been conducting ethnographic research on the Muslim minority in China illustrating how ethnic relations between the national minorities and Han majority have evolved and persist (1991, 1998). Sun Yat-sen, the nationalist leader, had divided China into five different peoples: the Han, Man (Manchu), Meng (Mongolian), Zang (Tibetan), and Hui (all Muslims in China). He used the term *Han minzu* to refer to the majority group, in contrast and opposition to these other "internal foreigners." After the Communist revolution in China, the 56 different nationalities, including the Han majority, were recognized by government authorities in order to control and consolidate the nation-state. Included within these 56 nationalities are 10 Muslim nationalities: Hui, Uygur, Kazak, Dongxiang, Kirghiz, Salar, Tadjik, Uzbek, Baonan, and Tatar—consisting of over 17 million people.

The earliest Muslim groups in China were descended from Arab, Persian, Central Asian, and Turkish peoples who migrated into China and settled in the northwest and southeast coastal regions. As noted, prior to 1949 the term *Hui* was a general term for "Muslims." However, following the Communist revolution, the Muslims were separated into the 10 separate groups, based on language. The Hui, who are the largest Muslim group, have a population of over 8 million people and are widely distributed throughout China. They did not have a separate language of their own, and spoke the language (mostly Chinese Mandarin) where they lived. The Hui reside in most of the counties and cities throughout China, including the large cities of

Beijing and Shanghai. Unlike the other Muslim nationalities in China, the Hui speak the dialects of the other ethnic groups among whom they live, primarily the Han. Some of the Hui, however, reside in areas such as Tibet or Mongolia, where they speak the Tibetan or Mongolian language. Since the Hui did not reside in one locale in China, Gladney had to do multisited ethnographic work. This enabled him to investigate how the Hui have managed to maintain and emphasize their ethnic identity in different cultural contexts throughout China.

The focus of Gladney's research was on the ethnogenesis of the Hui. How have these widely dispersed people been able to develop and sustain an ethnic identity that differentiates them from other people in China? Before the 1950s, the Hui were not recognized by the state as a distinctive nationality. Instead, they were referred to in general terms as "Muslims," along with other groups of Muslims. In order to examine the question of how they became "Hui," Gladney concentrated his ethnographic research on several different regional locations where the Hui resided. He studied the Hui in the city of Beijing, in Ningxia, a rural area in the northwest, in a rural community on the outskirts of Beijing, and in the southern city of Chendai in Fujian Province. Gladney discovered that it was only after the Chinese state began to categorize and designate these people as "Hui" for political purposes that these people began to objectify their own ethnicity. Though they previously related to one another on a local level as fellow Muslims, after government classification and designation, the Hui began to think of themselves as "*Hui minzu.*" However, as Gladney discovered from his research in these four areas, the expression of ethnicity was dramatically different in these various locales.

One important expression of ethnic and religious identity does appear to cut across the dispersed Muslim population in China. The notion of belonging to the Islamic faith, which is the "pure and true" (*qing zhen*) religion, is emphasized by all Hui Muslims. This phrase *qing zhen* is found wherever Hui Muslims reside, and it refers to such Islamic dietary rules as the avoidance of pork consumption. To some extent, it is similar to Jewish notions of "kosher" and approximates the Arabic concept of "halal." Among the approximately 200,000 Hui Muslims in the capital city of Beijing, the most important expression of ethnic identity is based on their dietary restrictions, especially the absence of pork, which is maintained through their own ethnic restaurants. Pork is the staple meat of the Han majority in Beijing and throughout China, and many of the Han cannot fathom why the Hui do not eat pork. Thus, the pork taboo has become the most significant aspect of Hui identity within Beijing. Muslim restaurants where the phrase *qing zhen* is displayed openly are the foremost centers of cultural and religious identity for the Beijing Hui. The Hui meet in the restaurants to discuss religious and other community issues while maintaining their *qing zhen* lifestyle. Young Hui go to restaurants to socialize and meet prospective spouses. Though the Hui of Beijing do not wear traditional Muslim clothing, and are more secular than Muslims in rural areas, Gladney found vibrant signs of ethnic identity within this community.

Gladney resided in the Hui rural community in Ningxia, which is representative of many of the Muslim communities of northwest China. Ningxia is the Ningxia Hui Autonomous Region, one of the five minority autonomous regions in China (including Tibet, Uygur, Inner Mongolia, and Zhuang in Guangxi). The Ningxia Hui community has a completely different form of ethnic expression than that of the Beijing Hui. Within this community, the emphasis on *qing zhen* is sought through a close identity with the Islamic religious tradition. They maintain a rigid notion of *qing zhen*, which results in strict rules of pure and impure behaviors. These pure and impure regulations divide the Hui from the Han in the northwest area. For example, Hui Muslims cannot accept food from their Han neighbors because of pure/impure cultural

norms. In addition, an Islamic resurgence movement has developed among these Hui Muslims. Increases in religious education, mosque attendance, traditional restrictions on male-female interaction, decreases in Hui-Han intermarriages, and extensive contact with other areas of the Islamic world are recognizable signs of an enhanced ethnic and religious identity among these Hui Muslims in Nangxia.

In the two other Hui communities Gladney discovered other indications of ethnic identity. In Chang Ying village, on the outskirts of Beijing, Hui Muslims maintain their identity primarily through marriage arrangements. They practice a strict form of ethnic endogamy (marriage within their own ethnic group) as a means of preserving their identity. To live the *qing zhen* "pure and true" Islamic life among the Hui in Chang Ying is to marry only within one's own ethnic group. In order to maintain this ethnic endogamy, the Chang Ying Hui have had to develop extensive marriage networks throughout China. Though this ethnic endogamy has sometimes resulted in birth defects, it reinforces their identity with their original purported Muslim ancestors.

In contrast to this mode of ethnic expression, Hui Muslims of the town of Chendai, in southern Fujian Province, have another understanding of *qing zhen*. The Chendai Hui consist of one patrilineal group with the surname Ding. The Ding do not practice Islam, they consume pork, and they are the most highly assimilated Hui within China. However, the Chendai Hui do assert their ethnic affiliation with Arab and Persian ancestors through various tombs of Muslim saints in their city, and ancient texts that refer to their Ding patrilineal group. Various rituals surrounding the use of these texts and graves are maintained to reinforce their own unique interpretation of *qing zhen*, an identification with their ancient Arab and Persian ancestry.

Through his ethnographic research Gladney demonstrates how ethnic expression varies within the group classified as "*Hui minzui*" in China. However, he also illustrates how Chinese nationality, and Han nationality, are "imagined" by both the Chinese state and scholars of China. He shows how the assumptions of cultural and ethnic homogeneity regarding China are misconceived, in that they underestimate the degree of ethnic and cultural diversity within China. Aside from his own case studies of the Hui, Gladney notes that with the new forms of globalism and economic expansion in southern China, different groups from within the Han majority have begun to reassert, reinvent, and rediscover their own ethnic and cultural differences. The Cantonese (in southern China and Hong Kong), the Hakka (*Kejia*), and the Hokkien-speaking people are beginning to distinguish themselves from other Han. As these groups benefit from the opening of China to the global economy, and freedom from the severe political restraints of Maoism, they are beginning to emphasize their own local histories, genealogies, and cultural traditions. These new ethnic movements belie the traditional assumptions about China being a monocultural and culturally homogeneous society.

Japan as a Multiethnic Society

The perception of Japan as one of the most ethnically homogeneous societies in the world is not just an outsider's stereotypical understanding of Japan but is also the dominant Japanese perception of their own society. The Japanese tend to believe that they are a distinctive "race" and that they differ from the other "races" of Asia. They imagine themselves as all related with one another "by blood," and this metaphor of "Japanese blood" (*Nihonjin no chi*) is used to strengthen their ethnic identity. Although the Japanese, like all other peoples, are the result of a long evolutionary history of mixture of different groups, this racialized notion of ethnic identity remains a myth of cultural identity for the Japanese (Diamond 1998; Yoshino 1992, 1998). These social constructions of "race" are similar to other peoples' "folk" notions of "race" that we

have encountered (see Chapter 4). This social construction of "race" is also the basis of the *Nihonjinron* (works on Japanese distinctiveness) that have been promoted within the media and intellectual circles in Japanese society. In the media and in the *Nihonjinron* literature, the Japanese economic miracle and absence of social problems were attributed to this "racial" and ethnic uniqueness. These folk notions of "race" maintained within Japanese society also resulted in various ethnic problems.

In a provocative essay, anthropologist Emiko Ohnuki-Tierney (1998) suggests that the construction of Japaneseness is related to the dominant symbols and metaphors of nature, which include rice and animals. She argues that Japanese ethnic identity is tied to the traditions of agrarian Japan, where peasants produced rice on the land. This form of agricultural production lasted for some two thousand years and provided the foundations for the nation-state in Japan. Additionally, the Buddhist tradition, with its strong prohibition on the killing of animals, became integral to Japanese culture. In fact, until after World War II, most Japanese did not consume meat. As Ohnuki-Tierney emphasizes, the Japanese vision of nature does not have much room for "wild nature," in contrast to European cultures in which hunting and pastoralism have been important (1998:35). These two traditions of agricultural rice production and taboos against the killing of animals have had negative consequences for two different ethnic minorities in Japan: the people known as the *hisabetsu burakumin* and the indigenous Ainu.

Ohnuki-Tierney underscores the fact that during the medieval period in agrarian Japan there were categories of people associated with different occupations, ranks, and statuses that were classified as "pure" or "impure." This stratified society was composed of low-status peoples: cleaners of temples, entertainers, prostitutes, undertakers, plasterers, carpenters, arms manufacturers, butchers, tanners, and leather workers. All of these low-status occupations and peoples were considered impure, and all were nonagrarian (Ohnuki-Tierney 1987, 1998). Later, during the Tokugawa period (1603–1868), this stratification system evolved into a rigid caste system of warriors, farmers, manufacturers, and merchants, with an "outcaste" group at the bottom. This lowest outcaste group has become known as the "*etta*," or *hisabetsu burakumin*, who were employed as leather workers, fur processors, or butchers. This nonagricultural occupation was associated with "death and violence" against animals, and the people were considered as the most "defiled" and "impure" group in Japan.

Presently, the *burakumin* consist of about 3 million people, and remain a discriminated ethnic minority in Japanese society. They are sometimes referred to as "Japan's invisible race," because no physical characteristics distinguish this population from other Japanese. Nonetheless, they reside in separate ghetto areas in Japan, and most still work primarily in shoe shops and other leather-related industries. Marriage between *burakumin* and other Japanese is still restricted, and other patterns of ethnic discrimination against this group continue (DeVos and Wetherhall 1974). This ethnic discrimination has resulted in poverty, lower education attainment, delinquency, and other social problems for the *burakumin*, just as it has for some ethnic minorities within the United States. The *burakumin* also score lower on IQ tests. Since these people are not biologically or racially different from other Japanese people, this finding indicates, as was emphasized in the discussion in Chapter 3, that ethnic discrimination, poverty, and related environmental conditions are more responsible for differences in intelligence than any purported biological differences.

The indigenous Ainu people of the northern island of Hokkaido in Japan are also considered another "race" distinctive from the Japanese. They are referred to as *Kyuudojin* ("aborigines") or *Dojin* ("natives") in colloquial Japanese. The Ainu have some physical traits that distinguish them from the Japanese population, but there has been extensive intermarriage between these people and other Japanese. Because of the intermarriage, it is difficult to estimate the population of the Ainu, which ranges from 20,000 to 300,000 (Sjoberg 1993). However, the offspring of marriages between other Japanese and Ainu are classified as "Ainu" by the majority population. The fraction of "foreign" blood in a child's veins is sufficient to deny it "pure" Japaneseness (DeVos and Wetherhall 1972). Traditionally these people were hunters and gatherers, and, like many indigenous peoples elsewhere in the world, were conquered and eventually incorporated into the expanding imperial agrarian state of Japan. According to Ohnuki-Tierney (1998), the fact that these people were engaged in hunting animals and were nonagriculturalists reinforced their low status and resulted in negative stereotypes against them. The Ainu are sometimes referred to as *gaijin* ("outside person," "non-Japanese," "foreigner") by other Japanese. Until the 1930s the Japanese government maintained separate schools for the Ainu, which reinforced their minority status. Presently, they remain in the lowest income bracket in Japan, and only 8.1 percent graduate from high school (Sjoberg 1993). Although the Japanese government has been reluctant to recognize the social and cultural problems that have faced the Ainu, the local government in Hokkaido has opened an Ainu research center in 1994 to gain an understanding of these people.

Other ethnic minorities, such as the Koreans, Chinese, and Okinawans, have had their share of difficulties in Japanese society. These groups have experienced widespread discrimination, even though they have adopted the Japanese language, norms, and values. A common attitude found in Japan is that because these people do not share "Japanese blood" they do not think like "us" (Yoshino 1992, 1998). The fact that some Korean well-known entertainers and sports figures are accepted as "ethnically Japanese" has not dislodged this racialistic thinking.

The metaphor of "Japanese blood" is embedded strongly within Japanese culture. The blurring of race and culture, and the beliefs regarding the genetic transmission of Japanese uniqueness, have been perpetuated for centuries. These folk beliefs have a tenacious hold on the minds of both Japanese lay people and intellectuals (Yoshino 1992, 1998).

Globalization trends, however, are beginning to have an effect on the indigenous folk notions of Japanese blood, descent, and race. Despite official policies that restrict immigration of foreigners into Japan, the country has witnessed a growing number of immigrants in recent years. Since the mid-1980s Japan has faced a labor shortage, and many immigrants are coming to seek work. Many of these jobs are unskilled or low-skilled, and the Japanese government is willing to open its doors to immigrants to work in jobs that most Japanese will not accept. These newcomers work in so-called 3-K jobs: work that is *kitsui* ("hard"), *kitanai* ("dirty"), or *kiken* ("dangerous") (Wehrfritz and Takayama 2000). Koreans, Chinese, Indians, and smaller numbers of people from Africa and the Middle East are now immigrating to Japan for these jobs, as well as many illegal and undocumented immigrants.

Faced with new ethnic minority problems, in 1989 the Japanese government gave special residency status to *Nikkeijin*, descendants of Japanese emigrants, mostly from Brazil and Peru. By the end of 1998, some 222,000 Brazilians and 41,000 Peruvians of Japanese ancestry had established residency in Japan. The assumption of the government is that these people will be able to assimilate into Japanese society more easily than other foreigners (Potter and Knepper 1998). However, the folk notion that Japanese culture is the exclusive property of the Japanese race is being challenged by new immigrants, who, though different in physical appearance, can speak Japanese as well as native Japanese. The concept of Japan as a culturally and ethnically homogeneous society is less likely to be maintained in the face of these new globalization tendencies.

ETHNICITY AND RACE IN SOUTHEAST ASIA

Southeast Asia is divided into two geographic zones: mainland and island Southeast Asia, which include countries with different environments and histories that have contributed to cultural and ethnic complexity. The countries of mainland Southeast Asia include Myanmar (Burma), Thailand, Kampuchea (Cambodia), Laos, and Vietnam. The countries of island Southeast Asia are Malaysia, Singapore, Brunei, Indonesia, and the Philippines. All of the mainland Southeast Asian countries have a dominant ethnic majority with various ethnic minorities. For example, Myanmar consists of ethnic Burmese, who make up 65 percent of the population of 47 million, and a variety of other ethnic groups, including Shans, Karens, Mons, Indians, and Chinese. Ethnic Thais make up 75 percent of the population of Thailand of 62 million, with a number of other ethnic minorities such as Chinese, Malay, Indian, and smaller numbers of "Hill tribes" residing in the mountain areas bordering southern China. The countries of Vietnam, Kampuchea, and Laos have ethnic majorities with smaller populations of ethnic minorities residing in different regions.

Island Southeast Asia has countries that range from extreme ethnic diversity to those that have ethnically homogeneous populations. The most ethnically diverse country is Indonesia, which encompasses over 13,000 islands extending over three thousand miles from west to east. Indonesia has a total population of about 210 million people. The largest ethnic group, the Javanese, on the major island of Java, makes up 45 percent of the population. Other ethnic minorities on different islands of Indonesia include the Sundanese, Achenese, Madurese, Alorese, Timorese, Sumatrans, Balinese, Moluccans,

Iban, Dani, and many others. Altogether there are over 100 different ethnic groups speaking some 300 different languages extending throughout the Indonesian archipelago. The country of Malaysia consists of the ethnically Malay population, 58 percent of the population of 21 million people, and other ethnic minorities, such as the Chinese, Indian, and other smaller groups. In contrast, the country of Singapore has a Chinese majority of 77 percent of its 3 million plus population, along with Malay and Indian minorities. The small country of Brunei, with approximately 300,000 people, also has an ethnic Malay majority, a Chinese minority, and smaller numbers of other ethnic groups. The ethnic majority, the lowland Filipinos, are 90 percent of the 77 million people in the Philippines, where nine different languages are spoken, including Tagalog, Cebuana, and Ilocano. Minorities such as the Chinese and Muslims and smaller upland ethnic groups also reside in the Philippines.

Other factors that have complicated ethnic relations throughout most of Southeast Asia are the historical experience of European colonialism and the Japanese occupation during World War II. During the nineteenth century, to extend its Asian empire from India the British colonized the countries of Burma and Malaysia. At about the same time, to compete with the British the French colonized Indo-China (Cambodia, Laos, and Vietnam). Earlier, the Dutch colonized the various islands of Indonesia. Spaniards were the colonizers of the Philippines in the 1500s, but following the Spanish-American war in 1898, the United States took control over the Philippines. In World War II Japan controlled most of the countries of Southeast Asia. Following World War II most of these countries developed independence and nationalist movements, gradually resulting in their liberation from their colonial masters. However, colonialism in Southeast Asia had major consequences for the content and form of ethnic relations in these societies. For examples of the dynamics of ethnic relations in

Southeast Asia, we will concentrate on the countries of Thailand and Malaysia.

Thailand

Thailand is an atypical country in Southeast Asia because it was not directly colonized by European powers. The Thai monarchy, which had some experience with Western interests, developed economic and political strategies to play European rivals against one another while adopting Western innovations. European business interests were allowed to aid in the development of some goods, but not to exercise direct political control. To some extent, this suited the geopolitical strategies of both the British and the French, who preferred Thailand as a buffer state between their colonial domains of Burma and Indo-China.

To some degree, Thailand, like China and Japan, is perceived as an ethnically and culturally homogeneous society (Winichakul 1994). Siam, Thailand's original name, was established through the expansion of monarchical rule beginning in the sixteenth century. Gradually, as the Siamese state developed from its centers in Sukothai, Ayudhaya, and finally Bangkok, it incorporated bordering regions in the north, northeast, and south. Within these geographic regions were people who were different ethnically, linguistically, and culturally from the ethnic Tai. For example, in the north were many tribal minorities speaking different languages, in the central region there were Mon- and Khmer-speakers, and in the south was a large number of Malay-speaking people. Even within the capital city of Bangkok ethnic minorities resided among the majority Tai.

Despite the ethnic diversity within the country Siamese nationalist leaders and state officials promoted a uniform ethnic collective identity based on notions of race, culture, and what has been referred to as the "Three Pillars." Various Siamese monarchs promoted the Three Pillars of national and ethnic identity for the country. The

Three Pillars of this Thai collective identity were the "Nation" (*chat*), "Religion" (*sasana*), and "Monarchy" (*phramahaksat*). This Siamese political and cultural code represented a symbol of a unified ethnic identity that was formulated to mediate the actual ethnic ambiguities and contradictions within the country.

The first pillar, *chat* (derived from the Sanskrit-Hindi *jati*, which translates roughly as "caste"), is used by the Siamese majority to refer to birth, race, lineage, and origin. Historically, the second pillar, *sasana*, religion, was synonymous with Theravada Buddhism, which is practiced by the majority of people in Thailand. The third pillar, *phramahakasat*, is an honorific term for "king" or "monarch" and embodies the vertical or hierarchical symbolic relationship between the ruler and the people in Siamese society.

These Three Pillars were cultivated as the basis of ethnic and national identity within Siamese society. In particular, *chat* (nation) also has the connotations of biology, birth, lineage, and descent, which makes it somewhat equivalent to the European concept of race. In linguistic usage *Chon Chat Thai* was used to refer to the Thai race/nation/culture. This racialistic term of identity became the basis of ethnonationalism in Thailand (Barmé 1993; Vella 1978). It was also used to promote government policies that affected ethnic relations. For example, by the twentieth century, approximately 10 percent of the population in Thailand was Chinese who had immigrated for economic and political purposes. Many of the Chinese had become successful in the Siamese economy. For many years, unlike other citizens, the Chinese were not subject to head taxes because the Siamese economy was dependent on their labor. When, in 1910, the Chinese were required to pay the head tax, they organized a general strike and closed all their businesses and shops. Also, some of the Chinese community had been involved in a political plot against the royalty.

In response to these perceived economic and political threats, the king, Rama IV, wrote two

books outlining his fears of the Chinese: *The Jews of the Orient* and *Wake Up Siam: A Reminder to the Thais*. Obviously, his perceptions were based on Western racial stereotypes perpetuated in the early twentieth century. However, understanding the important role that the Chinese had played in developing the Siamese economy, the king did not implement restrictive immigration policies. Additionally, he initiated a Thai nationality law in 1913 which stated that everyone born in Siam, regardless of parentage, was Thai. This official policy tended to encourage the assimilation of the Chinese and other ethnic minorities.

Later developments in Thai history provoked extreme nationalistic policies that were based on notions of "race" drawn from European and Japanese sources. In particular, Luang Wichit Wathakan, who was director general of the department of fine arts during the years 1932–41, drew on racist and fascist ideas from Europe and Japan to promote nationalism in Thailand. During World War II he became minister of foreign affairs. Wichit, like Hermann Goebbels of Germany, with whom he was compared, became the major propaganda minister in Thailand. He provided a conceptual framework that was sanctioned by the state to create a racial and nationalistic identity for the Thai people (Barmé 1993). Wichit propagated the idea that the Thai were a heroic and martial "race." The Thai "race" was conceptualized to be different from that of the Chinese, Indian, European, or American. There were specific behaviors and cultural conventions that were assumed to be associated with the Thai "race." Thai culture and race (*Thai Rathaniyom*) and a cultural policy based on "Cultural Rules" (*Kot Wattanatham*) were publicized and propagated through the educational system and media.

At this same time, the name of the country was changed from Siam to Thailand. Part of the reason for this name change was to distinguish the Thai "race" from the Chinese and other ethnic minorities and to encourage a more unified basis for this ethnonationalist movement. The promotion of "Thainess," emphasizing various behaviors and etiquette, was used along with other national symbols such as the Three Pillars to emphasize an ethnically homogeneous society. Official legislation was passed to expand the use of the Thai language and reduce the use of other languages such as Chinese, Lao, Shan, and Malay within Thailand. All of these policies have had consequences for ethnic minorities in Thailand up to the present.

The Muslim Minority in Thailand

In Thailand, one of the largest ethnic minorities is the Muslim population. Muslims are approximately 4 percent of the population. About 4 million Thai citizens profess the Islamic faith and maintain over 2,700 mosques. Muslims in Thailand include the Malay Muslims, who speak the Malay language and reside primarily in south Thailand in a number of provinces bordering on Malaysia. The Malay Muslims of south Thailand make up over 70 percent of the population in that region. A second category of Muslims sometimes refer to themselves as Thai Muslims, or, *Thai Isalam*, and reside in central and north Thailand. The Thai Muslims are smaller heterogeneous ethnic and religious minorities in these regions and speak Thai. Historically, the Muslims of south Thailand lived in a region imbued with a Malay-Indonesian Islamic political and religious cultural ethos, whereas the Muslims of central and north Thailand have been influenced by the political-religious culture of the Theravada Buddhist traditions. However, because of the administrative practices and policies of the Thai state during the course of the twentieth century, all Muslims in Thailand have been largely affected by the dominant Buddhist political and religious culture.

The Malay-speaking Muslims are in south Thailand as a result of the expansion of the Thai state into that region. The four southern provinces of Patani, Narathiwat, Satul, and Yala bordering on Malaysia have been gradually integrated into Thailand since at least the sixteenth century. These Malay Muslims identify themselves as *ore nayu* (the Malay people), and they refer to the Thai Buddhists as *ore siye* (the Siamese people). The Thai Buddhists, or *chat Thai*, use the ethnic category *khaek Musalayam* to refer to the Malay Muslims, which was perceived as a pejorative term by the native Muslims in the south. In the early twentieth century, the Thai government aggressively began to incorporate this Malay Muslim population through the appointment of Thai Buddhist bureaucrats throughout southern Malay regions (Pitsuwan 1985; Thomas 1975). In addition, Thai authorities began to interfere directly with the religious practices of the Muslims in the South. Bangkok authorities attempted to assume all legal matters under Thai law. In effect, this meant that the Muslim legal code, structured by the *Shari'ah* and *adat* (Malay custom) and administered by the local *qadi* (Muslim judge), was to be controlled by Thai Buddhist officials.

During the 1930s, the Thai government promoted education as the means of integrating this region into the Thai nation. This created a dilemma for the Malay Muslims in the south, because the Thai educational system was based on Buddhist values, and the language of education was Thai. Therefore, to become involved in the Thai educational process necessitated a rejection of one's language and religion, the primordial basis of ethnic identity for these Malay Muslims. To resolve this dilemma, the *ulama*, the local Muslim religious leaders and the source of political legitimacy, played a prominent role in mobilizing political support around Islamic religious and cultural symbols. However, the Thai government, based on the racist notion of *chon chat Thai*, attempted to enforce central Thai "race" and culture at the expense of other minority groups in Thailand. As part of these policies, the Malay Muslims were not allowed to wear their traditional clothing, elements of Islamic religion that applied to marriage and inheritance were banned, non-Buddhists were deliberately discriminated against in government, and conscious attempts at proselytization of the Buddhist faith in the south were to be carried out within the government-sponsored educational system. All in all, an aggressive attempt at forced assimilation.

Eventually, in the 1950s and 1960s the Thai government began to develop socioeconomic programs as an instrument of assimilation. Nonetheless, these national integrationist policies continued to include the imposition of Thai Buddhist cultural ideals in the southern Malay areas. The result was resentment among the Malay Muslim minority.

A number of Islamic-based factions emerged during the 1960s and 1970s in south Thailand, reflecting a diversity of political views and engaging in secessionist activities. One of the most influential secessionist groups, PULO, the Patani United Liberation Organization, emerged in the late 1960s and became the most well known and most effective guerrilla and separatist movement in the region. PULO was devoted to preserving "Malayness" and the Islamic way of life in south Thailand. Their militant activities created deeper divisions between the Malay Muslims and the Thai Buddhists associated with central Thai authorities. The overall goal of PULO was to create an autonomous Islamic state. Although there have been sporadic skirmishes in the recent past, since the 1990s the Malay Muslim communities of Patani have largely turned away from extremist separatist movements. Increasingly, they have changed their political strategies by actively mobilizing their communities and seeking a voice in the Thai political system. Malay Muslim leaders continue to promote their ethnic and religious identity while pressing for more pluralism and fair treatment from Thai authorities.

The Muslim Minority in Central and Northern Thailand

Because of historical and cultural conditions the experience of Muslims in central and northern Thailand has been much different than that of their Islamic affiliates to the south. Historically, these Muslims of the central and northern corridors of Thailand migrated, either voluntarily or by force, into these regions bringing distinctive ethnic, social, and religious conventions. Thus, these Muslim communities are much more heterogeneous than the Muslims of the south. And, unlike their Islamic brethren to the south, these Muslims are ethnic minorities residing in the centers of a predominantly Thai Buddhist cultural environment.

The largest group of Muslims in central Thailand, especially in the capital city of Bangkok, is the descendants of peoples from the southern provinces of Thailand and parts of Malaysia. Their presence in Bangkok and surrounding areas resulted from the forced relocation policies of the Thai state in the nineteenth century in its attempt to integrate the southern Malay Muslim provinces. Part of the state integrationist policies was to weaken the antagonistic southern Malay areas by transferring hostage populations from the Malay areas to central Thailand. The majority of these Muslims were resettled in Bangkok. These Muslim war captives were organized to provide labor on major projects for the Thai state. Of the more than 150 mosques in Bangkok, over 70 percent were built by Malay Muslims and their descendants. Although precise statistics are not available to calculate the exact number of these descendants, considering demographic factors such as fertility, mortality, migration, and intermarriage, this population is about 250,000 (Scupin 1998).

Several communities of Muslims in central Thailand, including Chams, Indonesians, and Iranians, have a long history that extends back to the Ayudhyan period (1351–1767 C.E.). The

Cham settled in Ayudhya, in central Thailand, the Thai capital at that time. As a result of their loyalty in serving in the Thai military, the royal family gave the Cham a tract of land in Bangkok. Some Indonesian Muslims migrated to Ayudhya as traders. Later, a small percentage of Indonesian Muslims migrated to Bangkok during the nineteenth century. There was no mass migration of Indonesians to Thailand in any particular era; they tended to come as individual traders and established small businesses related to the Thai-Indonesian trade. Gradually, a settlement of Indonesians, most of them Javanese, clustered in an inner-city area of Bangkok. One of the most influential trading communities in seventeenth-century Ayudhya was composed of Iranian Shi'a Muslims or Persian Muslims. Eventually, a number of the families related to the Iranian Muslims from Ayudhya settled near Bangkok. The Iranian Muslims played an important role in early Thai politics and intermarried among the royal and noble families. Some of the leading aristocratic families of Bangkok are descendants of these Iranian Muslims.

Muslims from South Asia and the Middle East have also migrated to central Thailand. South Asian Muslim migrants came from various linguistic and geographic areas of the subcontinent. Punjabi-, Sindhi-, Gujerati-, and Bengali-speakers came from north India, as well as Pathans- or Pushto-speakers from Peshawar. From south India came Tamils, Madrasis, and others from the Malabar coast. In addition, since the late 1970s and 1980s, many Muslims have migrated to Bangkok from the Middle East. Initially, some came as tourists and remained for business, trade, or religious purposes. As bilateral trade between Thailand and the Middle East increased, especially during the 1980s, a number of Muslims from Lebanon, Yemen, Egypt, and other Arab areas arrived in Bangkok. Middle Eastern restaurants and hotels developed to provide for Muslim Arab visitors and residents. One area of Bangkok has become known as the Arab Quarter and is sometimes referred to as mini-Beirut of the East. Arabic calligraphy, Arabian music, coffeehouses, belly dancing, and other signs of Arabic culture became recognizable in the evolving cosmopolitan city of Bangkok.

Muslim communities were also established in north Thailand. Many of the Muslims in north Thailand came from the Islamicized portion of China. Most of the Chinese Muslims in Thailand came from the southwestern part of Yunnan and are part of the Hui community studied by Dru Gladney. Historically this ethnic group operated an expansive trading network between the Shan states, China, and North Thailand. Later, in the 1950s, as a consequence of the Chinese revolution another wave of Yunnanese refugees fled into northern Thailand, many settling in Chiangmai Province. These recent migrants have their own Sunni mosque and a modern religious school, both built in the early 1970s. Other migrant groups from South Asia also settled in north Thailand. The majority of the South Asians in north Thailand are third- and fourth-generation descendants of the settlers of the nineteenth century. In addition to the Chinese and South Asian Muslims and their descendants, a small community of Malay Muslims from south Thailand was relocated by the Thai government into north Thailand during the nineteenth century.

Though the degree of assimilation of the Muslims in central and north Thailand varies among the different ethnic groups, and even within families within the ethnic groups, many refer to themselves as Thai Muslims. Most of these Muslims have not taught their native languages to their children, and thai has become their first language. Although some of the descendants of the Malays, South Asian, or Chinese Muslims can speak their native language, it is not used in everyday affairs in central and north Thailand. Through the educational system and intermarriage between these Muslims and other Thais, traditional ethnic differences among these early Muslim settlers were, to some extent, partially erased. A number of the Muslim migrants married Thai women, who then converted to Islam. An aphorism often heard in these Muslim communities is that "the children of these mixed marriages would adhere to the dress, manners, and language of their Thai mothers, but to the religion of their Muslim fathers."

One colloquial Thai term of reference for the Muslims in central and north Thailand is *khaek*, which was used liberally to refer to South and Southwest Asians, Arabs, Malays, Indonesians, and Persians. Thus, instead of *chat Thai*, Muslims in Bangkok are sometimes referred to as *khaek Isalam* or *khaek Musalam;* Hindus and Tibetans are also included within the *khaek* category. Until recently, *khaek* in central and north Thailand did not have a pejorative connotation. However, this ethnic designation, *khaek*, was not used to categorize the children of Muslims in a rigid manner. And, historically, despite mutual misunderstandings between Buddhists and Muslims, there appears to be no aggressive anti-Muslim hostility in central or north Thailand. Consequently, a good deal of structural assimilation has occurred among these Muslims in their accommodation to residing in a Thai Buddhist environment. Although the Muslim communities in these Buddhist regions are identifiable by their needs for an Islamic-based diet and mosques, they tend to participate in the same institutions as their Thai Buddhist neighbors.

Despite the great degree of structural and cultural assimilation, recently there have been some tendencies toward traditional ethnic expression and assertiveness among Muslims in central and north Thailand. For example, ethnic expression is seen within the context of Islamic activities during the celebration of holidays. During these events various ethnic groups such as the Pathans or Indonesians will set up booths to serve their own foods and participate in a combination of ethnic and religious celebrations. In recent times,

Cham Muslim ethnicity and religious identity were mobilized in a form of political ethnic protest against the Thai government. The Bangkok authorities wanted to develop a highway system that would destroy the traditional Cham neighborhood. Demonstrations mobilized many Muslims, and the Cham began to assert their ethnic ties. In some senses, the Cham Muslim community represented a model of a moral community standing together against the forces of globalization, corporate capitalism, vested interests, and corrupt government-inspired development.

Additionally, in both central and north Thailand, Muslims from different ethnic backgrounds have begun to assert their ethnic and religious identities in certain contexts when dealing with their Buddhist neighbors. The Islamic resurgence in the Middle East and elsewhere has resulted in an enhanced awareness and reawakening of ethnic and religious identity among these Muslims. However, in general, this new assertiveness and the cultural expressions of one's religious or ethnic identity have usually not been mobilized toward political ends.

Malaysia

Malaysia is an ethnically plural society. Before the fourteenth century the Malay archipelago consisted of a number of small states each of which had its own ruling monarch. These states were influenced strongly by the religious traditions of Hinduism and Buddhism, which, since the first century C.E., had diffused to this region through trading and political contacts with India. The rulers of these small kingdoms were believed to be semi-divine. The peoples residing in the interior regions of what was then known as Malaya were mostly peasants who cultivated rice; most of the coastal peoples were involved in fishing, trading, and piracy. During this period, there were active trading contacts among different Asian countries and the Malaya region. Following the fourteenth century, Islamic traders from the Middle East and South Asia entered the region of Malaya. Gradually, some of the rulers of Malaya began to convert to the Islamic tradition, and in most cases the people converted to the religion of their rulers. Though Islam coexisted with the traditions of Hinduism and Buddhism for many years in Malaya, eventually the Islamic religion began to predominate. During the sixteenth century Western expansion into Malaya began with the Portuguese. The religious tradition of Islam became a means of mobilizing and unifying different Malay principalities as the Western colonial powers arrived on the scene. Eventually, during the nineteenth century, the British took control of the region of Malaya as one of its primary colonies in Southeast Asia, and British colonialism persisted there until the 1950s.

Under the British, new patterns of ethnic relations in Malaya developed. As a means of developing the colonial economy in Malaya, the British actively recruited and imported cheap labor from China and India. The native population of Malaya was reluctant to work in the tin mines and on the rubber plantations developed by the British. Thus, thousands of Chinese, mainly from the southeast area of China, came to work in mines, commercial businesses, and other occupations. Indians were imported from colonized India to work on the rubber plantations. These groups from China and India were themselves linguistically and ethnically diverse. The Chinese included Cantonese, Hakka, Hainanese, Kwongsai, Hokkien, and other different linguistic groups. The Indians comprised Tamil, Telegu, Punjabi, Bengalis, Sikhs, and others. There were also migrant workers from many different ethnic backgrounds in Indonesia. The effects of these developments in British Malaya were to create a plural society that would result in ethnic divisions and tensions in postcolonial Malaysia.

Prior to Western colonialism in Malaya, as in the other areas of Asia we have examined, an indigenous concept was used to categorize people that closely resembled a notion of "race." The Malay term *bangsa* was used to refer to the common culture, descent, and origin of a particular group of people. *Bangsa* is derived from the Sanskrit word *vamsa*, which is translated as "line of descent" or "blood" (Hirschman 1987; Nagata 1981). Originally, the term *bangsa* was used to differentiate different families, and in particular to distinguish the royal family from other patrilineages. Thus, the term had similar connotations of a folk concept of "race," referring to blood, birth, biological inheritance, and origins. When the British colonized the region of Malaya, colonial officials, census takers, and scholars imposed their nineteenth-century pseudo-scientific conception of race onto the various populations. Thus, the racially conscious British divided the major populations into the Malay, Chinese, and Indian races, with other subdivisions based on language, religion, and culture. These racial categories hopelessly confused "race" with "culture." Eventually, these British notions were combined with indigenous beliefs of *bangsa* to crystallize into racial ideologies that were to become the foundation of the nationalist and independence movements in Malaysia (Hirschman 1987; Milner 1998). They continue to influence ethnic relations today.

The Ethnic Struggle in Malaysia

Following independence and the withdrawal of the British in 1957, a major challenge confronted the Malay majority. Despite the fact of the Malay's slight majority in population, the Chinese had become the dominant ethnic group in the private sector of the economy. Thus, as in most of the other areas of Southeast Asia, the Chinese population became extremely successful in businesses and entrepreneurial activities. Though the Malay majority gained control of the political institutions, the Chinese tended to control the economy. The various reasons for the economic success of the Chinese in Southeast Asia have been studied by many scholars over the years. In Malaysia during the colonial period various stereotypes were perpetuated by the British regarding the Malay and Chinese "races." The Malay were considered "lazy and indolent," whereas the Chinese were assumed to be "industrious and hardworking."

Modern researchers have examined the various factors that resulted in Chinese economic success in Southeast Asia and have debunked these racist stereotypes. Historians emphasize the business experience that the Chinese had at home, which preadapted them for success in Southeast Asia. The fact that the Chinese had some prior experience in small and medium-scale businesses and in handling money and loans gave them advantages in comparison with native populations in Southeast Asia (Mackie 1998). However, this explanation tends to underestimate the traditional economic activities that native populations of Southeast Asia had been engaged in prior to the arrival of the Chinese (Hefner 1998; Mackie 1998). Later research compared the "overseas Chinese" in Southeast Asia to other ethnic groups such as the Jews of Europe as "middleman minorities." Because of their business skills, the various governments drew on these "middleman minorities" to act as intermediaries between them and the native peoples. For example, the Chinese were recruited to collect taxes and work in a variety of state-owned businesses. Other scholars note how the patrilineal kinship system of the Chinese, which involves the commitment of all members of the family in family businesses, was significant in stimulating economic development. In addition, traditional practices of personal patron-client networks, or *guanxi* relationships, for building trust and community ties within the Chinese business community played a significant role in success in Southeast Asia (Hefner 1998; Mackie 1998).

After independence, the economic success of the Chinese (and, to some extent, the Indian population) compared with that of the Malaysian majority resulted in ethnic tensions.

As the majority of the Malays were rural farmers and were not benefiting from the modern industrializing economy, they felt deprived compared to the Chinese and Indian segments of the country. During the late 1960s, riots ensued directed against the perceived ethnic inequalities and lack of opportunities within the newly developing economy. Two thousand lives were lost, mostly Chinese. As a result of these demonstrations, in the 1970s the Malaysian government designed an affirmative action plan that gave preference to ethnic Malays in education and employment in the private sector of the economy. The aim of the government was to reduce the "structural barriers" that prevented the Malays from enjoying the benefits of the economic boom taking place in Malaysia. The government set a target of Malay participation in 30 percent of Malaysian businesses. In addition, to reinforce these ethnically based policies the government introduced a new Malay term, *Bumiputras* ("sons of the soil"), to distinguish the Malay from the immigrant communities of Chinese and Indians. Although this system of preferential treatment has resulted in some success for Malay involvement in the economy, the Chinese and Indian communities are concerned that the privileges given to the *Bumiputras* are being abused by the government to discriminate against them. These ethnic tensions are reflected within the political party system in Malaysia presently. Each of the major ethnic groups has its own political party that competes with the others in elections.

Ethnicity and Religion in Malaysia

Anthropologist Judith Nagata has been engaged in a long research project on ethnicity and religion in Malaysia. In one of her ethnographic studies in the 1970s she observed ethnic interaction in the Malaysian city of George Town, Penang (1974, 1981). George Town, a port city, is ethnically diverse, with the Chinese population making up 71 percent and smaller communities of Indians, Malays, Indonesians, Arabs, and Europeans. The Chinese population was mostly Buddhist, the Indians mostly Hindu, and Malays, Indonesians, and Arabs were Muslims. Traditionally, in rural areas to become "Malay" meant converting to Islam and becoming a practicing Muslim and speaking Malay. In fact, the constitution of Malaysia is based on a salient definition of "Malay": it is a person who is a Muslim and speaks the Malay language and follows the traditional customs *adat* of Malay culture (Nagata 1974:335). Nagata, however, found that the ethnic interaction among these different communities was marked by tremendous fluidity and modifiability in various social contexts. In some situations, people descended from the Arab or Indian Muslims considered themselves Malay and at other times classified themselves as Arabs or Indians. Thus, the Islamic religious tradition was used to unify their ethnic identity in some circumstances, while other traits were utilized to distinguish themselves from others. Nagata found that the variances in self-categorization were dependent on whether individuals wanted to express social solidarity or distance from one another, or to expedite social or political benefits, or a consideration of social status. For example, in some contexts, Arabs would claim higher ritual purity by referring to their ancestors associated with the "Holy Land" versus the lower impure status of "Malays."

At the same time, some "primordial" features of ethnicity were used to demarcate boundaries among various groups. Nagata found that people distinguish between different types of Muslims: Arabs, Indian, and a variety of groups from Indonesia. In addition, some Chinese Muslims who lived in George Town had intermarried with Malay and had adopted Malay culture, including dress, diet, and other norms. These Chinese Muslims were not considered Malay. Usually Malays revert to the racialistic term *bangsa*, to refer to these Chinese Muslims. In this case a commonality of religion and culture does not become a primordial charter for ethnicity.

Thus, Nagata found that some ethnic traits have become primordialized for identity purposes, but others do not. Regardless of religious and cultural practices, the notions of race (*bangsa*) would enter into Malay discourse when discussing Chinese Muslims. Thus, in some contexts, the building blocks of ethnicity appear to be based on irreducible givens, whereas in other situations group economic, social, and political interests result in permutations of ethnic identity.

Another dimension of ethnicity and religion that Nagata (1984) emphasizes has to do with the emergence of Islamic revitalization in Malaysia. During the 1970s, an Islamic movement known as *dakwah* (Islamic revival) developed in Malaysia, primarily among young Malays who had moved from rural areas into the cities and were adapting to the new demands of education and modernist developments. The *dakwah* movement led to an increasing emphasis on religious ritual, mosque and religious school attendance, the introduction of Arabic dress and language, and political Islamic themes. Despite the fact that Islam is perceived as a universal religion that is antithetical to racism, nationalism, and parochial identities, the *dakwah* movement has tended to be bound with the ethnic identity of "Malayness." Though the religious leaders espouse the universality of Islam in their discourse, the reality of ethnic politics and ethnic categorization constrains this universalism in Malaysia.

The *dakwah* movement tends to concentrate on the Malay community, and tends to be associated with the politics of that ethnic bloc. Even though some Chinese convert to Islam, as a means of assimilating to Malay culture, they are not integrated within the Malay ethnic community. Islamic religious revitalization has exacerbated the ethnic divisions among the Malay, Indian, and Chinese populations in Malaysia. Additionally, religious revitalization has been developing among the Chinese (Buddhist and Christian) and Indian (Hindu), which tends to reinforce ethnic segmentation and polarization. The overtly pro-Malay and pro-Islamic programs of the Malaysian government have revived apprehensions among the non-Malay communities. Whether Malaysia can adopt a more tolerant civic form of nationhood that will provide the basis for a multiethnic society is a challenge for the future.

CONCLUSION

Throughout the region of South, East, and Southeast Asia are found indigenous concepts similar to notions of race emphasizing the intimate connections between biology and culture. Following contact with Western countries, the pseudo-scientific concept of race was incorporated and synthesized with earlier native conceptions. These concepts of race were promoted by the different governments, both colonial and postcolonial, to distinguish among various ethnic majorities and minorities. These concepts of race persist, perpetuating specific patterns of ethnic interaction and dynamics throughout Asia. Presently in Asia many different ethnic and cultural traditions are colliding with the rapid process of globalization. Globalization is disrupting the traditional values and practices within the region. In some cases, the overall reaction is to revert to a nostalgic past in which the traditional ethnic or "racial" community, the extended family, and other communal practices provide sustenance. This reaction has at times led to tensions among ethnic groups. Continuing ethnographic research is needed to help people understand each other's traditions as one major step in helping to reduce these tensions.

NOTES

1. The indigenous Indian tradition was not immune to considerations of skin color and the classification of different peoples. In one classic work, the *Mahabhasya*, the people of northern India are "fair," those of eastern India are "dusky," those of the south are "dark," and those of the west are "pale, yellowish-white." The people of the central areas are mixed. But these "folk" constructions of peoples by skin color were not the basis of any type of scientific objective notion of race (Trautmann 1997).

2. The Indian caste system is not the only social structure that connects birth with status and rank. As we saw in Chapter 3, the Greek philosophers maintained similar ideas regarding the relationship between inheritance of different types of souls and "essences." This type of classification, based on the idea of inherited blood, essences, and humors, continued to influence many people during the medieval period in Western society, and resulted in simplified stereotypes of behavior and temperaments of people around the world. In the medieval period it was accepted that there was a "Great Chain of Being," which posited natural essential categories based on a hierarchy established by God and nature. Thus, the social differences among aristocrats and serfs were purportedly based on innate biological characteristics and birth.

3. The Sikhs were not the only people used for military and strategic purposes by the British. Lionel Caplan (1995) discusses how the British classified the Gurkhas of Nepal as a "martial," "warlike," "masculine" "race," and recruited them into the Indian army. This nineteenth-century racial essentialistic discourse about the Gurkhas has had very real economic and political effects for these people.

4. For a thorough summary of the literature and history of the Sri Lankan ethnic conflicts, see chapter 3 in Jack Eller's *From Culture to Ethnicity to Conflict: An Anthropological Perspective on International Ethnic Conflict* (Ann Arbor: University of Michigan Press, 1999).

REFERENCES CITED

BARMÈ, SCOTT. 1993. *Luang Wichit Wathakan and the Creation of a Thai Identity*. Singapore: Institute of Southeast Asian Studies.

BAYLY, SUSAN. 1995. Caste and "race" in the colonial ethnography of India. In *The Concept of Race in South Asia*. Peter Robb, ed. Pp. 165–218. Delhi: Oxford University Press.

CAPLAN, LIONEL. 1995. Martial Gurkhas: The persistence of a British military discourse on "race." In *The Concept of Race in South Asia*. Peter Robb, ed. Delhi, Oxford University Press.

DANIEL, VALENTINE E. 1983. Conclusion: Karma, the uses of an idea. In *Karma: An Anthropological Inquiry*. Charles F. Keyes and Valentine Daniel, eds. Pp. 287–300. Berkeley: University of California Press.

_____. 1997. *Charred Lullabies: Chapters in an Anthropography of Violence*. Princeton, NJ: Princeton University Press.

DEVOS, GEORGE, and WILLIAM WETHERHALL. 1972. *Japan's Minorities: Burakumin, Koreans, and Ainu*. New York: Minority Rights Group.

DEVOS, GEORGE, and HIROSHI WAGATSUMA. 1972. *Japan's Invisible Race*. Berkeley: University of California Press.

DIAMOND, JARED. 1998. Japanese roots. *Discover* (June): 86–94.

DIKÖTTER, FRANK. 1992. *The Discourse of Race in Modern China*. Stanford: Stanford University Press.

___, ed. 1997. *The Construction of Racial Identities in China and Japan: Historical and Contemporary Perspectives*. Honolulu: University of Hawaii Press.

DUMONT, LOUIS. 1970. *Homo Hierarchicus: An Essay on the Caste System*. Mark Sainsburg, trans. Chicago: University of Chicago Press.

FOX, RICHARD G. 1985. *Lions of the Punjab: Culture in the Making*. Berkeley: University of California Press.

GLADNEY, DRU C. 1991. *Muslim Chinese: Ethnic Nationalism in the People's Republic*. Cambridge, MA: Harvard University Press.

___. 1998. *Ethnic Identity in China: The Making of a Muslim Minority Nationality*. Orlando, FL: Harcourt Brace.

HEFNER, ROBERT W., ed. 1998. *Market Cultures: Society and Morality in the New Asian Capitalisms*. Boulder, CO: Westview Press.

HIRSCHMAN, CHARLES. 1987. The meaning and measurement of ethnicity in Malaysia: An analysis of census classifications. *Journal of Asian Studies* 46(3):555–582.

INDEN, RONALD. 1990. *Imagining India*. Oxford: Oxford University Press.

JAFFRELOT, CHRISTOPHE. 1995. The ideas of the Hindu race in the writings of Hindu nationalist ideologues in the 1920s and 1930s: A concept between two cultures. In *The Concept of Race in South Asia*. Peter Robb, ed. Pp. 327–352. Delhi: Oxford University Press.

KAPFERER, BRUCE. 1988. *Legends of People, Myths of State: Violence, Intolerance, and Political Culture in Sri Lanka and Australia*. Washington, DC: Smithsonian Institution Press.

KLASS, MORTON. 1997. *Caste: The Emergence of the South Asian Social System*. Prospect Heights, IL: Waveland Press.

MACKIE, JAMIE. 1998. Business success among Southeast Asian Chinese: The role of culture, values, and social structures. In *Market Cultures: Society and Morality in the New Asian Capitalisms*. Robert Hefner, ed. Pp. 129–146. Boulder, CO: Westview Press.

MILNER, ANTHONY. 1998. Ideological work in constructing the Malay majority. In *Making Majorities: Constituting the Nation in Japan, Korea, China, Malaysia, Fiji, Turkey, and the United States*. Dru C. Gladney, ed. Pp. 151–172. Stanford: Stanford University Press.

NAGATA, JUDITH A. 1974. What is a Malay? Situational selections of ethnic identity in a plural society. *American Ethnologist* 1(2):331–350.

___. 1981. In defense of ethnic boundaries: The changing myths and charters of Malay identity. In *Ethnic Change*. Charles F. Keyes, ed. Pp. 88–116. Seattle: University of Washington Press.

___. 1984. *The Reflowering of Malaysian Islam: Modern Religious Radicals and Their Roots*. Vancouver: University of British Columbia Press.

NORTON, JAMES H. K. 1999. *India and South Asia*. 4th edition. Guilford, CT: Dushkin/McGraw Hill.

OHNUKI-TIERNEY, EMIKO. 1987. *The Monkey as Mirror: Symbolic Transformations in Japanese History and Ritual*. Princeton, NJ: Princeton University Press.

___. 1998. A conceptual model for the historical relationship between the self and the internal and external others: The agrarian Japanese, the Ainu, and the special-status people. In *Making Majorities: Constituting the Nation in Japan, Korea, China, Malaysia, Fiji, Turkey, and the United States*. Dru C. Gladney, ed. Pp. 31–54. Stanford: Stanford University Press.

PITSUWAN, SURIN. 1985. *Islam and Malay Nationalism: A Case Study of the Malay-Muslims of Southern Thailand*. Bangkok: Thai Kadai Research Institute.

POTTER, DAVID, and PAUL KNEPPER. 1998. Comparing official definitions of race in Japan and the United States. In *The Social Construction of Race and Ethnicity in the United States*. Joan Ferrante and Prince Brown, Jr., eds. Pp. 139–156. New York: Longman Press.

SCUPIN, RAYMOND. 1998. Muslim accommodation in Thailand. *Journal of Islamic Studies* 9(2):229–258.

SJOBERG, KATARINA. 1993. *The Return of the Ainu*. Switzerland: Harwood Academic Publishing.

SPENCER, JONATHAN, ed. 1990. *Sri Lanka: History and Roots of Conflict*. London: Routledge.

TAMBIAH, STANLEY. 1986. *Sri Lanka: Ethnic Fratricide and the Dismantling of Democracy*. Chicago: University of Chicago Press.

___. 1992. *Buddhism Betrayed: Religion, Politics, and Violence in Sri Lanka*. Chicago: University of Chicago Press.

THOMAS, LADD. 1975. *Political Violence in the Muslim Provinces of Southern Thailand*. Singapore: Institute of Southeast Asian Studies.

TRAUTMANN, THOMAS R. 1997. *Aryans and British India*. Berkeley: University of California Press.

VELLA, WALTER F. 1978. *Chaiyo! King Vajiravudh and the Development of Thai Nationalism*. Honolulu: University Press of Hawaii.

WEHRFRITZ, GEORGE, and HIDEKO TAKAYAMA. 2000. The Japan that can say yes. *Newsweek*, June 5:34–35.

WEINER, MICHAEL. 1997. The invention of identity: Race and nation in pre-war Japan. In *The Construction of Racial Identities in China and Japan: Historical and Contemporary Perspectives*. Frank Dikötter, ed. Pp. 96–117. Honolulu: University of Hawaii Press.

WINICHAKUL, THONGCHAI. 1994. *Siam Mapped: A History of the Geo-Body of a Nation*. Honolulu: University of Hawaii Press.

YOSHINO, KOSAKU. 1992. *Cultural Nationalism in Contemporary Japan: A Sociological Inquiry*. London: Routledge.

___. 1998. Culturalism, racialism, and internationalism in the discourse on Japanese identity. In *Making Majorities: Constituting the Nation in Japan, Korea, China, Malaysia, Fiji, Turkey, and the United States*. Dru C. Gladney, ed. Pp. 13–30. Stanford: Stanford University Press.

17

THE PACIFIC ISLANDS

Karen Brison

Union College

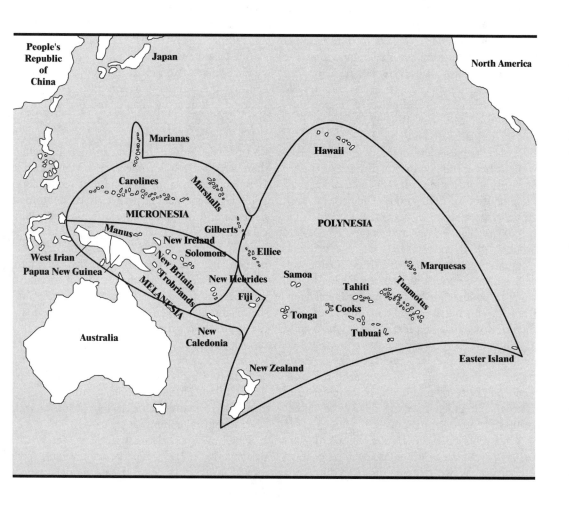

On May 19, 2000, as my husband, son, and I were getting ready to wrap up ten months of anthropological research in the Pacific island-nation of Fiji, George Speight, a disgruntled businessman from the indigenous Fijian ethnic group which makes up just over half of Fiji's population, stormed parliament with a small group of armed supporters. Speight and his supporters took hostage the entire parliament, including Mahendra Chaudhry, the first Fijian prime minister to come from the Indo-Fijian ethnic group, which constitutes about 44 percent of Fiji's population. Many of the members of parliament, including Chaudhry, were to remain hostage for almost two months as Speight negotiated with various groups about the proper relations between ethnic groups within the nation of Fiji.

Many Indo-Fijians, backed by international opinion, had for decades maintained that the only proper form of government in a modern nation was democracy based on "common roll" elections where each individual cast one vote, regardless of his or her ethnicity. People are people, so they argued, and should be free to consider their interests and opinions as individuals, without being trapped by the dictates of culture or of traditional authorities. Speight, along with the majority of indigenous Fijians, however, argued that such a system was unsuited to the culture of Fiji where indigenous Fijians are brought up to respect hereditary chiefs and where their status as the host, or original, group of the nation entitles indigenous Fijians to primacy in politics. In the indigenous Fijian view, ethnic groups must forever remain separate and should elect ethnic representatives who would develop policies for the common good. Furthermore, indigenous Fijians could only be properly governed by a system that recognized the God-given authority of traditional Fijian chiefs and the right of indigenous Fijians as the "host" group to control the nation.[1]

The events in the tiny Pacific nation of Fiji are at best peripheral to the consciousness of most Americans, as we quickly discovered on our return home one week after Speight's takeover. Yet the struggles of the Fijians and the peoples of other small South Pacific nations like Samoa, Tonga, Papua New Guinea, and the Federated States of Micronesia to decide the proper relationship between ethnic groups can provide Americans with valuable insights into the factors that shape ethnic identity worldwide. Likewise, the struggles of native Hawaiians and New Zealand Maori to define their place in the larger societies that encompass them are not at the forefront of American popular consciousness but can help us understand ethnicity in our own society and elsewhere. Specifically, ethnicity in Pacific Island societies provides an instructive contrast for Americans because so many of our taken-for-granted assumptions about ethnicity and ethnic relations are not shared by many Pacific Islanders.

First, most Americans assume that at least some degree of assimilation into a common national culture is inevitable, and perhaps desirable. For many Pacific Islanders, on the other hand, experience has shown that greater interaction between ethnic groups can increase rather than decrease ethnic differences. Many Pacific Islanders also assume that cultural assimilation will relegate indigenous peoples to the bottom of national and international economic and political systems. Second, while the majority of Americans are committed to the idea of universal human rights regardless of ethnicity, for many Pacific Islanders people are, first and foremost, members of particular cultural communities and their rights can never be divorced from their status as an ethnic group member. A nation, in this model, comprises a collection of ethnic groups whose leaders negotiate a common good, not a collection of individuals with inalienable rights. This kind of "pluralist" model of ethnic relations is typical of many Pacific Island countries with several cultural communities.

Finally, and closely related, many Americans, particularly in the scholarly community, have moved away from "essentialist" models, which see ethnic differences as immutable, rooted in the very nature of ethnic populations. Many Pacific Islanders, in contrast, embrace such "essentialist" views, arguing, for instance, that Western democratic institutions are unsuited to the nature of Pacific Islanders, who have lived since time immemorial according to a very different "Pacific way" handed down through the generations (Lawson 1996). What is suitable in the West, many argue, is contrary to the essential principles governing Pacific life. Taken as a whole, then, the ideas about race and ethnicity popular in many Pacific Island societies treat cultural differences as vitally important and immutable facts. People are, first and foremost, members of cultural groups.

Through exploring ethnicity in the Pacific, this chapter will investigate the causes and consequences of Pacific notions of ethnicity. It is tempting to conclude that Pacific Islanders have strong "primordial" loyalties to their ethnic cultures because so many of them grow up in small rural villages where kin ties and commitment to a common cultural tradition are emphasized. Such deeply rooted local cultures could easily lead to clashes with other groups with different values. Furthermore, the overarching pan-ethnic institutions of a nation are often remote in daily life, so do not establish a common, extralocal, identity and value system. One can also trace ideologies that root individuals in cultural groups to Pacific beliefs and values that prompt individuals to think of themselves always as part of a community and to work for the good of that community (Becker 1995; Kirkpatrick and White 1985; Lutz 1988). It is not surprising that people who have been brought up to think of themselves as playing their proper role in preserving a harmonious community would be inclined to see these communities as essential building blocks to a nation. The idea that a nation is made up of individuals each pursuing his or her own interests is much more alien to local views of the relationship between individual and society.

But looking closely at Pacific histories shows that the primacy of ethnic identity does not just stem from isolation in rural villages or from deeply rooted cultural values that are incompatible with those of the West or with those of competing ethnic groups. Instead, loyalty to ethnic cultures, as well as the values thought of as central to these ethnic cultures, has been forged (as circumstantialists like Fredrik Barth would argue) in the process of struggles for political and economic power with colonizing European powers and with other ethnic groups within the same nation. In cases like Fiji, colonizers directly contributed to defining traditional ethnic culture and convincing people that preserving both this culture and traditional authority structures was vital to their survival in the contemporary world. The colonizers also put into place a political and economic system that made ethnic solidarity key to political and economic survival. In the contemporary Pacific, tourism has had a similar impact on ideas about ethnicity. Tourists flock to small Pacific Islands looking for idyllic societies, free of the tensions of modern life, where people live simple, happy lives, content with few material possessions and revering nature through exotic rituals. Pacific Islanders have latched onto such images, restaging ceremonies that have not been practiced for generations and even inventing a few in order to attract tourists (Buck 1993; Keesing 1989; Sissons 1997). In some cases, national governments even have exhorted islanders to preserve their traditional cultural practices, particularly when these involve things like "friendly smiling faces," which are attractive to tourists. Once tourism prompts a renewed interest in traditional culture and identity, however, Pacific Islanders have then taken up these ideas about deeply rooted and distinctive ethnic cultures for other purposes. As we shall see, for instance, some Pacific Island nations have argued that only their own political tradition is suited to the essential nature of their citizens in order to fend off attempts by outside groups to take power or to assert themselves against more powerful groups within the same country.

Looking at Pacific models of ethnic relations can alert us to both the strengths and to the pitfalls of stressing immutable cultural differences. Seeing the world in terms of essential differences between cultural and racial groups can protect the rights of minority groups and foster group pride. But it can also lead to the suppression of differences within each ethnic group and can lead to intolerance and even violence between groups (Keesing 1989; Lawson 1996; Said 1993). Indeed, as I write, not only is Fiji politically and economically paralyzed in the aftermath of the coup, but another Pacific Island country, the Solomon Islands, has also been crippled by a recent coup stemming from ethnic tensions.

PACIFIC CULTURES

The South Pacific is conventionally, though somewhat arbitrarily, divided into four main areas. First, the Melanesian islands of the southwestern Pacific include (among others) Papua New Guinea, the Solomon Islands, Vanuatu, and New Caledonia. Melanesian nations are characterized by extreme linguistic and cultural diversity and by small-scale, relatively egalitarian political structures. Second, Polynesian cultures of the eastern and central South Pacific include (among others) the Maori of New Zealand and the indigenous peoples of Hawaii, Tahiti, Tonga, Samoa, the Marquesan Islands, and the Cook Islands. Fiji is technically considered to be part of Melanesia but has a culture and a colonial history that in many ways are closer to those of Polynesian nations. Polynesian cultures were characterized by more hierarchical political systems with powerful chiefs who, in some cases, united large areas under their power. The more centralized political systems of Polynesia resulted in larger groups of people who were united by a sense of sharing a common cul-

ture and belonging to the same group. Third, the islands of Micronesia lie scattered across the western Pacific, north of Melanesia. As in Polynesia, many Micronesian cultures had hierarchical political systems in which the population was divided into chiefs and commoners. However, perhaps due to the fact that the islands of Micronesia are geographically scattered, Micronesian cultures generally did not have high chiefs who ruled over as large areas as did their Polynesian counterparts. Finally, the Aboriginal peoples of Australia are generally also included in surveys of the indigenous cultures of the Pacific but do not fit into any of the three larger groups.

Because the cultures and historical experiences of these many Pacific cultures are diverse, I will not attempt a comprehensive survey here but, instead, will trace general patterns in each of the four areas and focus on a few specific cases. I will deal primarily with the indigenous peoples of the Pacific, although, of course, there are numerous groups of Asian and European ancestry in the Pacific who have also struggled to define a positive sense of ethnic identity.

CELEBRATING ETHNIC DISTINCTIONS IN MELANESIA

The nations of Melanesia draw together many small linguistic and cultural groups. Papua New Guinea, for instance, is renowned for having 760 different linguistic groups with a population of 3 million and an area about the size of California. Thirty-five percent of these linguistic groups contain fewer than 500 people (Kulick 1992:1). This extreme linguistic diversity goes along with egalitarian and small-scale political structures. Most Papua New Guineans, for instance, live in small rural villages where there was, traditionally, little in the way of regional political structures beyond the village level. In 1984–86, when my husband, Stephen Leavitt, and I did our doctoral research in the northeastern part of Papua

New Guinea, we lived in villages about five miles apart. The residents of these two villages, however, spoke languages from different linguistic families, and most people knew only a smattering of words from the language of their neighbors. My neighbors and friends, of the Kwanga language group, commented admiringly on Steve's mastery of the neighboring Bumbita Arapesh language, saying that this language was much too difficult for any Kwanga-speaker to be able to learn more than a few words. While the two groups had traditionally intermarried and had participated occasionally in each other's rituals, they had no sense of belonging to the same community. Nor did residents of the village where I lived, Inakor, feel that they belonged to the same group as residents of the next village of the same language group, Asanakor, a mere quarter-mile away.

It was striking to us that people took great pleasure in pointing out and exaggerating what sometimes seemed to us to be minor differences between groups. Papua New Guinea illustrates *par excellence* anthropologist Fredrik Barth's (1969) famous statement that people's consciousness of ethnic difference is not necessarily determined by the objective differences in their cultures (cited in Poyer 1990). People, in other words, may feel themselves to be part of very different ethnic communities even when, to the outsider, the cultures appear very similar. In Papua New Guinea, we were impressed by the fact that people who thought of themselves as coming from different cultural groups had a great deal in common. They all were subsistence gardeners who grew the same array of crops using the same techniques. They all had very similar beliefs about sorcery and magic and, in fact, traded supernatural paraphernalia and knowledge with each other. They all also shared a cult where males were initiated, as they matured, into a series of five cult grades where they accumulated ritual power and secret knowledge.

While we were impressed by the regional similarities, however, the local people would fix on small differences between groups as emblems of ethnic dissimilarity. Despite the fact that the people of Inakor, for instance, were in daily contact with people from the next village, Asanakor, I soon learned that there were minor (but in local eyes significant) differences in the languages of the two groups. Both spoke the Kwanga language, but the people of Asanakor used the consonant *v* when they spoke, and this sound was not used in the Inakor version of Kwanga. This meant that some of the most commonly used words, such as the word for coconuts, were pronounced differently in the two groups. In Inakor, a coconut was a *tuwa*, in Asanakor it was *tiva*. It was hard to avoid concluding that the residents of the two villages had purposely devised different ways of pronouncing common words to assert their distinctiveness. After all, virtually everyone had close family members in both villages and, indeed, the two villages had originally been one village that had separated just fifty years before I arrived. One unfortunate result of this celebration of cultural difference was the local reaction to "*Kwanga Godri Mwanchi*"—a portion of the New Testament painstakingly translated into Kwanga by missionary linguist Takashi Manabe, who lived in the Kwanga-speaking village of Yubanakor, about four miles away from Inakor. Inakor and Asanakor residents claimed not to be able to read this translation at all, saying that the Yubanakor dialect was just "wrong" and unintelligible to them. The possessive marker *ri* (as in GodRI Mwanchi—"the talk of God") in Yubanakor, people said, was different, for instance, from the possessive *hi* (GodHI mwanchi) used in Inakor and Asanakor. In reality, the differences between Yubanakor and Inakor Kwanga were slight.

Theodore Schwartz (1975), who worked in Manus Province of Papua New Guinea, has labeled this process of purposefully focusing on, and accentuating, minor cultural differences as emblems of identity as "cultural totemism." Schwartz argues that increased contact between neighboring cultural groups in Melanesia magnifies and reinforces cultural differences instead of diminishing them. Groups ignore the many similarities between them and celebrate the minor differences. Don Kulick, a linguistic anthropologist, suggests that this process contributes to maintaining Papua New Guinea's extreme linguistic diversity: when groups come into contact, they embrace symbols of difference and magnify these differences instead of forming a common culture and assimilating into a single group (1992). What creates these patterns?.

It is tempting to conclude that Papua New Guineans' primordial attachment to their local group is bound to be overwhelmingly strong since their daily experience impresses upon them the importance of kin ties and ties within their own village. Indeed, it is true that individuals work and live as parts of kin groups through which they all get access to land and to which they look for protection of their rights and interests. However, it is strikingly evident that the celebration of cultural differences is not the product of isolation but the product of interaction between groups. Logically, it is only through interaction that people become aware of difference. Furthermore, people's kin groups span village and linguistic divides and yet these close ties between relatives do little to diminish the strong sense of difference between groups. Rather, it is the political and economic conditions under which groups interact that has produced the celebration of cultural differences in Papua New Guinea.

Economically, most rural Papua New Guineans are horticulturalists who produce most of their own food and other necessities of life. People grow a few cash crops (coffee in the area where I worked) that they sell in order to obtain money to buy clothes, salt, kerosene, and a few other products. But even cash cropping is mostly a family operation in many areas of the country. The upshot is that people are not dependent to any great extent on people from other groups to make a livelihood. Furthermore,

there is a rough equality between neighboring groups in access to resources (though this situation has changed somewhat with the development of new technologies and industries that give some groups access to much more valuable resources than others). In addition, there is a rough political equality between groups in most areas of the country, with few groups having a regional dominance over others.

In this situation, there is no particular incentive to adopt the culture of another group. In some cases, immigrants to the United States willingly left aside distinctive ethnic cultures and encouraged their children to assimilate to mainstream culture. They did this to help their children escape discrimination and to gain access to the economic and political opportunities monopolized by the majority. In Papua New Guinea and other Melanesian nations, however, traditionally there was no dominant culture monopolizing access to wealth and power. The Bumbita Arapesh can offer the Kwanga no resources that the Kwanga don't already have, nor can the Bumbita provide political patronage to subservient Kwanga.

Furthermore, neighboring groups were traditionally enemies in many areas. Inakor villagers gleefully told me, for example, about the time when they had chased away the residents of Asanakor and burnt their village to the ground. In situations where neighbors are enemies and rivals, each group wants to prove that they are at least as good, if not better, than their neighbors. This situation produces a reluctance to adopt the practices of neighboring groups; it would be like admitting the neighbors were better. Rather, people magnify and celebrate the differences to show that they are strong and autonomous (Schwartz 1975). As Barth (1969) suggested, then, it is not the degree of cultural difference that produces ethnic divides; instead, it is the nature of the situations in which different cultural groups interact that causes them either to notice and even magnify cultural differences in some cases or to ignore them in others.

Both colonialism and more recent efforts to forge new independent nations have introduced new problems and complexities to ethnicity in Melanesia. Papua New Guinea, for instance, became independent in 1975 after having been an Australian colony since the early twentieth century. Some parts of the country had been a German colony before that. The Solomon Islands were a British colony until attaining independence in 1978; and Vanuatu (the former colony of the New Hebrides) became an independent nation in 1980, ending a complicated arrangement in which some parts had been administered by the British and others had been under French power. New Caledonia remains a French colony. Colonial administrators did such things as suppress warfare between groups and establish regular (though not frequent) patrols for the purposes of taking census and providing rudimentary medical and law enforcement services.

Colonialism also brought coastal plantations of copra and other crops where villagers from all areas were recruited (sometimes forcibly) to work. These plantations, and, later, the recruitment of islanders to help Allied armies in World War II, led to an unprecedented degree of contact between islanders from distant cultural groups. These early plantation environments also led to the development of *pidgins*, trade languages with simple grammars and vocabularies drawn from English, German, and local languages. The trade languages allowed islanders to communicate both with plantation bosses and with fellow laborers from other linguistic groups. As colonial powers started to move their Melanesian colonies toward independence, they also introduced widespread education, at least in the primary grades, and such institutions as village courts and councils to help increase villagers' sense of participation in their own government.

One obvious effect of colonialism was to introduce a group—the colonizers—with superior access to wealth and power. Potentially, this cre-

ated a situation where villagers would have an incentive to assimilate to the dominant culture instead of celebrating and identifying with their local culture. Indeed, the infamous "cargo cults," which swept through Melanesia in the early and mid-twentieth century, seem to represent an attempt to get rid of local culture and adopt that of powerful colonizers. Cargo cults were religious movements aiming to bring a new world in which Melanesians would have all the wealth and power that were then monopolized by Europeans. Villagers emulated the outward symbols of Western culture, doing things like insisting that everyone build their houses in neat, orderly rows and put tablecloths and flowers on tables. They built airstrips and bamboo airplanes, in the hope that these airplanes would somehow take off and come back with the same "cargo" that European airplanes brought for Europeans. Villagers were also encouraged to throw away traditional magical and ritual items in the belief that this kind of contact with traditional spirits might block the way of a new communication with more powerful ancestral spirits who held the power to deliver Western cargo. Cargo cults, however, had limited potential to transform local cultural and ethnic identity since followers tended to abandon them when the cargo did not arrive. Some cargo cults like the Paliau movement of Manus Province, in northeastern Papua New Guinea, have been long lived but these long-lived movements tend to move away from wholesale emulation of European culture and incorporate elements of celebrating local culture.

The postcolonial era has also brought some signs of emulation of a national elite culture. Linguistic anthropologist Don Kulick (1992), worked in Gapun, in northeastern Papua New Guinea, a village of some two hundred people who are the only speakers of the language Taiap Mer. Gapun parents complained that although they wanted their children to learn Taiap Mer, most children spoke only Tok Pisin, the Papua New Guinea trade language, first developed in the plantations. Kulick's investigation confirmed that Gapun children did not speak Taiap Mer. Why? He found that Gapun villagers associated Tok Pisin with character qualities of wisdom and self-control. These traits had always been valued in Gapun but were now even more highly prized, since, in the Gapun view (shared by many Papua New Guineans), it was these very qualities that had allowed Europeans to prosper to a much greater extent than Papua New Guineans. Europeans were peaceful and cooperative and so could work together to build large-scale businesses. Gapun villagers who wished to win the respect of their children and fellow villagers adopted what they perceived to be the language of Europeans, Tok Pisin, in order to demonstrate these same authoritative personal qualities. The result was that children heard Tok Pisin as much as they heard Taiap Mer, and quickly picked up that Tok Pisin was the language that people respected. And so the children grew up as monolingual Tok Pisin–speakers.

Overall, however, the colonial and postcolonial experiences have had the effect of rigidifying commitment to local identities instead of diminishing these. While rural villagers may sometimes admire and seek to emulate what they perceive to be European ways, this does not in any way alleviate the tensions between ethnic groups or help to form of sense of common identity between ethnic groups within nations. National elites speak of a shared "Melanesian" or "Pacific" way that unites diverse cultural groups and involves sharing with each other, egalitarian political systems, and reverence for the environment (Keesing 1989). But these rhetorics appear not to resonate with rural villagers who still worry about traditional rivals and enemies and fear that more remote groups may try to monopolize state power (Clark 1997). In fact, colonial, and now postcolonial, conditions have introduced new sources of tension between groups as they rival each other for economic and political power. Groups, for instance, that traditionally were relatively equal in terms of access to basic economic resources now find

themselves to be fundamentally unequal as some others have superior access to education, political power, and new resources such as mineral deposits and land suitable for cash cropping. Often the less privileged groups find themselves closed out of access to new opportunities as more powerful groups continue to prefer members of their own cultural group. These inequalities exacerbate tensions between groups.

In some cases, groups that have been marginalized reassert local culture and identity as a means of resisting domination and fostering group pride. Anthropologist Roger Keesing, for instance, studied the Kwaio of the interior of the Solomon Islands over some thirty years. The Kwaio, along with other interior groups in the Solomons, had become increasingly cut off from political power and good jobs because access to education and European services had come much earlier to more accessible coastal people. As a result, the Kwaio were looked down upon by coastal people and were underrepresented in government and civil service jobs. Partly in response, the Kwaio began a movement to revive and preserve traditional culture. They established a Kwaio cultural center and began a long process of trying to write down local laws and traditions. They also tried to regain control of their own lives by insisting that this newly codified *Kastom lo* ("Custom law") should be the one to govern local life. They also began to celebrate the Kwaio tradition of warfare, claiming that the Kwaio, unlike coastal people, were strong and autonomous and, therefore, had resisted European pressures and preserved their traditional way of life.

Actually, this kind of rhetoric is common not only in Melanesia but across the Pacific. For instance, young men often wear T-shirts with pictures of muscular young men carrying spears and wearing warrior attire. In fact, a T-shirt I bought my husband in Fiji in 1999 portraying a muscular young Fijian warrior under the slogan *Kai Viti power* ("Fijian" power) was virtually identical to one I had bought my young nephew over ten years previously in Hawaii except that this T-shirt had celebrated "Hawaiian Warrior Strength." Both shirts would have gone over well with both the Kwaio and young Kwanga men, who used to boast to me about Papua New Guinean "black power." The Kwaio Custom movement, then, like other similar such movements among marginalized groups, attempted to build local pride and autonomy through resurrecting a distinct local tradition and an identity based on autonomy and strength (Keesing 1992).

Clearly, however, ethnic identities are also being transformed at the same time that they are reinforced. This again shows how ethnic divisions are fueled less by value conflicts between cultures than by the nature of the interaction between them. Groups, in fact, redefine their identities and values to make sense of the particular situations in which they find themselves. As many Pacific scholars have pointed out (e.g., Linnekin 1990; Thomas 1992), we tend to think of ethnic traditions as practices and values that are important to people because they have been passed down through the generations. In fact, however, what more often gives certain ethnic values and practices their symbolic salience is the ways in which these beliefs help people to understand their contemporary lives. People everywhere pay more attention to those aspects of their ethnic heritage that help them make sense of the present.

The Kwaio, for instance, may always have contrasted themselves with their neighbors; they surely also always had a warrior tradition. But it is unlikely that they viewed themselves as strong, autonomous iconoclasts who refused to give in to the outside oppressors, for, indeed, no such powerful oppressors existed in the precolonial era. Likewise, the appeal of muscular, warrior icons to young Fijians and Hawaiians surely owes a lot to their current situation where they are often put in the position of having to be polite, subservient underlings to outsiders like wealthy tourists who seem to hold all the cards. The colonial and postcolonial situations intro-

duced not only new sources of tension between ethnic groups but also a whole new field of international relationships (with colonial powers and with international tourists) that cause islanders to re-evaluate their identity.

Furthermore, current senses of ethnic identity are also informed by relatively new ideas. The celebration of warriors was undoubtedly traditional in Melanesia, but warrior images are obviously influenced by colonial rhetoric. Archaeologists, for instance, have long argued that the gourd helmets sported by young Hawaiian warriors on the famous T-shirts were never worn by Hawaiian warriors (what good would a gourd do if someone clubbed you over the head?). These images are based on early explorers' drawings of "savage" priests. Colonial officials and missionaries in Melanesia and elsewhere in the Pacific often viewed islanders as savages whose warfare and black magic made their lives "nasty, brutish, and short" (Brison 1995). Colonial and missionary policies reflected these views: the first act of colonial regimes was generally to suppress warfare; some (though not all) missionary groups encouraged islanders to give up their magical paraphernalia. Islanders have (correctly), however, picked up on the idea that the purported savagery of their ancestors made them fearful and dangerous to Europeans. Docile Christian islanders who follow the rules get some money and power (though nothing near the equivalent of that possessed by Europeans), but they can be nothing more than an inferior version of Europeans.

Savage warrior islanders, however, with "black power" can strike fear in the hearts of the outside world. I frequently heard Kwanga villagers, for instance, comment longingly on precolonial times when they claimed that people were much bigger (the adults today are like the children of the past, they would sigh) and lived to such an old age that mushrooms would grow on their skin as they sat quietly in their houses. It was only when Europeans came and forced New Guineans to give up their magic and fighting, people claimed, that they became small and started to die soon. Europeans, they said, had prospered due to their peaceful ways, but these ways were not, they claimed, suited to New Guineans. New Guineans were naturally aggressive and bold; capitalizing on these qualities would never bring them wealth on the scale enjoyed by Europeans, but at least it would restore New Guineans to their former glory and pride (Brison 1991, 1995). Such views are not just idle talk. Particularly in the highlands of Papua New Guinea there has been a resurgence of tribal warfare over the past 25 years.

Colonial rhetoric has also transformed the identity of relatively privileged groups. Bougainville and Buka islands are geographically part of the Solomon Islands group but became a part of the colony of New Guinea due to a deal forged between the colonial powers of the time, Britain and Germany. Later, Buka and Bougainville became the North Solomons Province in the new nation of Papua New Guinea. Plantations were established on these islands earlier than in many other parts of Papua New Guinea. Buka and Bougainville residents, with a longer history of contact with Europeans, soon became favored by the European owners, who generally hired them as overseers and brought in laborers from other parts of Papua New Guinea. The influx of these people from other areas soon generated tensions with the people of Bougainville and Buka. Undoubtedly influenced by the rhetoric of Europeans, the local people saw outsiders (who had had less contact with Europeans) as backward and savage (Nash and Ogan 1990) and claimed that they themselves were more sophisticated and peaceful. Tensions came to a head after the North Solomons Province was incorporated into Papua New Guinea in 1975. Local people resisted this move, saying they had little in common culturally or geographically with the savage New Guineans.

Tensions again escalated when a big copper deposit was discovered in Bougainville a short time later, and a huge mine was built that threatened the ecology. Large numbers of laborers came from other areas of Papua New Guinea to work there. The Bougainville people were understandably upset and demanded the lion's share of the revenues from the mine since they suffered most of the costs. When negotiations broke down, Bougainville people began to sabotage the mine and, in response, the Papua New Guinea government first sent in troops to pacify the area and then withdrew the troops and imposed a blockade on the islands. Bougainville residents resented these actions as evidence that Papua New Guinea "tribal culture" had been transferred to the government (Havini 1992:164). Some claimed that Papua New Guineans would never have treated members of their own "race" (Nash and Ogan 1990) in such a manner. Here, again, new sources of tension have rigidified ethnic boundaries. And the ethnic identities mobilized are clearly ones that have been defined in the context of colonial and postcolonial struggles.

Ethnic cultures and identities have also been transformed in other ways. Roger Keesing and Robert Tonkinson (1982), for instance, brought together a group of anthropologists, mostly working in the Melanesian nations of Vanuatu and the Solomon Islands, who had observed a range of similar movements to resurrect and preserve local cultures in the era closely following national independence. In some cases villagers would refer back to the work of early anthropologists to try and reconstruct a local culture that was no longer practiced (Larcom 1982). Why were they doing this? Sometimes, as among the Kwaio, marginal groups were attempting to reassert local autonomy. Other groups, though, seemed to think that they were simply following the instructions of the national government. National leaders attempted to promote a sense of national pride and identity by speaking of a unique "Melanesian way" involving many distinct cultures that must be preserved. Local leaders took this to mean that they should resurrect their distinct local ways. In the process of preserving their traditions, villagers subtly transformed them by, for instance, writing down as law principles of dispute settlement that traditionally would have been much more amorphous and flexible.

I observed some of this kind of thinking, for instance, among the Kwanga, who had been exposed to a government rhetoric and policy encouraging them to return to traditional ways of settling local disputes instead of relying on new government institutions. Local leaders (who often felt that local people had traditionally settled disputes through fighting and sorcery attacks!) felt impelled to "discover" some kind of traditional Kwanga way of settling disputes that looked more like the village courts that the government seemed to be encouraging (Brison 1999; Westermark 1986). They understood that the traditional ways of doing things were supposed to be good and that they were supposed to return to these ways, but they did not feel that their local ways had anything to do with the "Melanesian way" of consensus building praised by the national government.

The continued commitment of Melanesians to local identities illustrates both the capacity of these identities, rooted in kin ties and shared culture, to exert a powerful hold on people and the ways that overall political and economic conditions can enhance the salience of these primary identities. In most areas of Melanesia, the local group is an overwhelming presence in people's lives; at best, the nation is a remote and abstract entity. There are few opportunities for long-term wage labor, so most people remain rural subsistence farmers. Those who have become wealthy, for instance, through mining or coffee plantations, have done so primarily by using resources controlled by traditional kinds of groups. So, again, local group identity is reinforced. However, cases such as the Kwaio and the Bougainville peoples also show that a commitment to local identities can be fueled through a process of struggle with other groups. As in precolonial Melanesia, commitment to local differ-

ence does not come about solely through isolation. Nor do ethnic divisions always arise from fundamentally incompatibilities in values. Instead, struggles with other groups for political power and economic resources prompt people to focus on, and even magnify, differences in values and practices between groups.

Furthermore, it is clear that in Melanesia the rigidifying of ethnic boundaries has led to significant political and economic problems. The Papua New Guinea government was crippled by the long Bougainville crisis, which both undermined the legitimacy of the national government and decimated its tax dollars. More recently, ethnic tensions came to a head in June 2000 in the Solomon Islands when the Malaita Eagle Force, an armed group representing people from the island of Malaita, took the Solomon Islands prime minister hostage and took control of the capital city, Honiara. The actions of the Malaita Eagle Force were the culmination of 18 months of ethnic fighting on the Solomon island of Guadalcanal. Guadalcanal natives had organized themselves into an armed group that harassed Solomon Islanders not native to Guadalcanal who had settled there. The Guadalcanal group was particularly hostile to people from Malaita, who dominated business and held many important jobs in Honiara. After many Malaitans were killed and forced to flee Guadalcanal, the Malaitans organized their own protection. The prime minister was released on June 8 (after promising to resign), but a peace agreement was not reached until October 15. The extended period of unrest seriously undermined tourism, the main industry of the Solomon Islands.

FORGING REGIONAL IDENTITIES THROUGH POLITICAL STRUGGLE IN POLYNESIA

In the Polynesian cultures of the southeast Pacific, hierarchical political systems divided the populations into chiefs and commoners. In many cases, high chiefs united large areas under their power. In most cases, Polynesian monarchs only succeeded in uniting large areas under their power in the period following contact with Europeans. Resourceful chiefs were able to manipulate their relationships with Europeans, and to take advantage of European firepower.

Close inspection shows that Polynesian national unity often overlays a complex situation where people have strong local loyalties, similar to those found in Melanesian nations. When my husband and I, for instance, started a new research project in Rakiraki Fiji in 1997, we were struck by some similarities in the behavior of the Fijians and the Papua New Guineans, whom we had studied a decade before. One of the attractions of Fiji for us had been the fact that Fijians all over the country spoke the same language, so we would not have to deal with the logistical difficulties that we had encountered in working in the extreme linguistic diversity of Papua New Guinea. But as we e-mailed around to friends and colleagues to try and pin down potential sites for our study, we quickly became aware that the linguistic situation was more complex than we had initially thought. Colleagues cautioned us that we had better situate ourselves in the Rewa Delta, in the southeast of the country, since this was the only area where the national standard, the Bauan dialect of Fijian, was routinely spoken in day-to-day life. In other areas, people warned us, people learned Bauan in school but spoke local dialects in most contexts.

When we arrived in Fiji and chose Rakiraki (in the northeast of the main island of Viti Levu) as a field site, we were strongly reminded of Papua New Guinea. The Rakiraki people spoke "Ra dialect," which sounded quite different from Bauan. Closer examination, however, showed that the differences, although substantial, were also quite superficial. The grammars of Ra dialect and Bauan dialect were, for example, virtually identical. Many of the words of Ra dialect were also the same as its Bauan counterparts.

What made Ra dialect so hard to understand was a heavy local accent that involved, for instance, dropping all *t*'s and replacing all *k*'s with a throaty, almost Germanic *h*. And, of course, where the vocabulary of Ra dialect did differ from Bauan it was in the common words, most likely to be used in day-to-day life, such as the words for "pig," "chicken," and "no," and common verbs like "to hear" and "to see." Local people were very familiar with the differences between their dialect and Bauan and could easily switch back and forth between their local pronunciation and the Bauan version. The more I studied the differences between Ra and Bauan dialects, the more it seemed that I was dealing with a New Guinea–esque situation in which people were purposely focusing on and magnifying small differences in language in order to assert a distinctive local identity.

And the triviality of some of the distinctions did not make them insignificant. In fact, it was hard for an outsider to understand Ra dialect, and local people would take advantage of this (as I quickly learned) in order to exclude outsiders from discussions of sensitive issues. Ra dialect was also extremely important to local people. Villagers gossiped incessantly about the few local people who refused to speak Ra dialect, saying that these people thought that they were better than everybody else and were trying to act like they were better educated. Villagers also made sure to speak Ra dialect when performing their most important traditional ceremonies, such as presenting kava root (a mild narcotic that is a popular ceremonial drink across the Pacific) to honored guests. One of the most popular and gifted orators from Rakiraki even went so far as to open his speeches in formal occasions involving people from other areas with a preamble asking the guests to forgive him: he would have to speak in Ra dialect because he was not familiar with Bauan. I soon found out that this was untrue; this man could speak Bauan very well and did so when asked to give public prayers (everyone considered Bauan the appropriate dialect for prayer). His public insistence that he couldn't speak Bauan, then, was a polite way of indicating that he was going to show the guests that Ra people were quite as good as everyone else by speaking in Ra dialect.

The persistence of Ra dialect and other regional dialects in Fiji, despite the fact that people have been educated in Bauan and English for over fifty years now, attests to their importance. Unlike Papua New Guinea, Fiji offered enough opportunities for outside wage labor that most adult villagers had lived outside of Ra for extended periods of their lives and everybody had relatives living in other areas of the country. Furthermore, intermarriage with speakers of other dialects was common. Yet despite this mixing of people from different areas of the country, local dialects remain robust and they are celebrated. As in Papua New Guinea, the celebration of emblems of difference between groups in frequent contact is alive and well in Fiji and other areas of Polynesia.

Furthermore, in some contexts regional rivalries among Fijians were very active. Fiji, for example, is divided into three large confederacies, mostly for the purpose of determining representation on the Great Council of Chiefs. The north and west parts of the country (an area that includes Rakiraki) share a common culture and economic base but are split between two different confederacies, both of which are controlled by high chiefs from the southeast. It was evident to us that this symbolic subjugation of the north and west to the southeast rankled with the Rakiraki people. In fact, during our stay in Rakiraki there was a meeting of all the chiefs of the north and west areas to discuss establishing a separate, fourth confederacy. This had in fact been proposed several times before. Ra people thought that this was generally a good idea, but the chiefs eventually decided against it. Why? It turned out that establishing a north-west confederacy would involve having to choose one high chief to represent the area, and regional rivalries were too strong for any group to feel comfortable choosing a neighboring chief as their leader. After we left Fiji, however, the idea of a separate western government once again surfaced. After Speight and his supporters released the hostages in mid-July 2000, negotiations started to appoint a new interim government to keep peace while Fijians reconsidered their constitution to pave the way for new elections in a couple of years. People in the west, however, generally disliked the suggested interim governments (which excluded Indo-Fijians) and threatened several times to form their own government, which would include many members of the deposed Chaudhry government, including Chaudhry himself.

In contrast to Papua New Guinea, however, in Polynesia strong regional identities are generally embedded in a robust sense of cultural identity transcending the local region. Samoans, for instance, speak of *fa'asamoa* ("Samoan way"), and native Hawaiians celebrate the way of life of the "children of the land." In Fiji, similarly, Ra people and people of other regions think of themselves as sharing a common Fijian culture, and many of the central symbols of ethnic identity such as the *sevusevu*, the ceremonial presentation of kava, are shared by Fijians of all regions. They also speak quite comfortably about a way of life shared by all Fijians, which they contrast to the ways of the Europeans and of the Indo-Fijians.

On our second research trip to Rakiraki in 1999–2000, we took along seven undergraduates from our American institution, Union College, on a field term abroad focusing on learning anthropological methods and analyzing Pacific cultures. One of the students, Stephanie Sienkiewicz (2000), studied ethnic identity and relations. Sienkiewicz found that indigenous Fijians generally agreed on the differences between themselves and the Indo-Fijians. In fact, these views were so generally shared (and by Indo-Fijians as well) that Sienkiewicz soon found herself looking for ways to get people to go beyond the same old line about indigenous

Fijian identity. Indigenous Fijians, everyone seemed to agree, were marked by a commitment to community and culture. Indo-Fijians (and Europeans) were always thinking about how to get ahead. But indigenous Fijians had too much respect for each other and for the community as a whole to focus on making money. Indigenous Fijians, everyone said, would spend hours just talking with each other and participating in long ceremonies, even if that meant that they were neglecting their farms or jobs. They just had to do this because of their great respect for other people and for their village. Indigenous Fijians (unlike Europeans and Indo-Fijians) also thought nothing of giving away money and other possessions to help others out. And they expected no return for their generosity. Nicholas Thomas (1992) found similar views in another area of Fiji where people also commented on Fijian generosity as a key trait that made them different from other ethnic groups. It is clear, then, that indigenous Fijians have a clear sense of sharing a common culture and identity across the nation.

And, in fact, the extent of cultural and linguistic diversity is much less in Fiji and other areas of Polynesia than in Papua New Guinea. Fijian dialects, for instant, do not vary as much from each other as do the many languages of Papua New Guinea. And, I suspect, differences between dialects as spoken in day-to-day life have been decreasing over the last century. In listening to Rakiraki people speak, for instance, it was striking that while most people adopted the distinctive Ra accent when talking to fellow villagers, they did not always use special Ra vocabulary. People sometimes used Bauan words and other times Ra words. Regional markers of identity, then, were firmly embedded in a robust sense of culture shared with other indigenous Fijians. Regional identities are, however, alive and well and they emerge as important factors in certain contexts.

It is interesting to consider why pan-local ethnic identities have emerged in Polynesia to a greater extent than in Melanesia. The particular histories of each place show how complex political and economic factors interact to shape ethnic identities. In part, the robust pan-local identities of Polynesia stem from the fact that there were larger political confederacies than in Papua New Guinea. But much of the sense of shared culture in Polynesian nations has arisen since European contact and, in some cases, colonization. The fact that there were more powerful rulers, whose authority extended over larger areas, in Polynesia in many cases caused the colonizing powers to develop different kinds of policies in Polynesia than they had in Melanesia. The British, particularly, worked through existing political figures because it was cheaper and easier to do this than to replace them with entirely new systems. This strategy, practiced by the British in many areas, was known as "indirect rule." The British also relied to a certain extent on indirect rule in the Solomon Islands. But because there were fewer powerful chiefs there to begin with, the strategy had a lesser impact.

In Polynesian nations such as Fiji and Tonga (Tonga was never a British colony but was a British protectorate), indirect rule had the impact of valorizing traditional culture but also homogenizing it over larger areas and establishing it as a national tradition. The role of the British in creating a homogeneous Fijian culture is clear. Fiji became a British colony in 1874 when a group of chiefs who had successfully consolidated much of the south and east of the country signed a deed of cession where they became subjects of Queen Victoria in return for the British agreeing to protect Fijian interests from encroaching Americans. The first British governor of Fiji, Sir Arthur Gordon, was, for his time, an enlightened thinker (and a fan of anthropology). He took seriously his mission to protect Fijian culture, doing such things as halting the sale of Fijian land to European colonists and even requiring some Europeans to return land to Fijians. He then declared some 83 percent of the land of Fiji to be a possession of Fijian descent groups and mandated that, as he thought was traditional, this land could never be alienated from those descent groups; in other words, it could not be sold or given away. Gordon, in consultation with eastern chiefs, argued that Fijians believed that there was an inviolable connection between descent groups and land, with land being passed down from generation to generation and inhabited by the *vu* (ancestral spirits). Fijians, Gordon said, believed that human society could only prosper if people continued to live on their ancestral land and play their proper role in the *vanua*, or community, that inhabited that land. Fijian society, Gordon believed, had been divided into ranked lineages under a chiefly authority, with each lineage playing a necessary role to perpetuate the community: some were fishermen, some were carpenters and boat builders, some were warriors, some were priests or administrators, and so on.

Gordon sought to preserve Fijian society not only by registering the land according to descent group but also by setting up a Fijian administration with laws governing Fijian life. Fijians, for instance, were said to owe a certain amount of labor to their community in accordance with traditional expectations. They could be fined or beaten by local chiefs if they failed to perform this labor. Fijians should be committed to their community and had to apply for special permission to leave the village to farm or take a job. Gordon, and his successors, also set up a native land trust board to preserve the hierarchical structure of Fijian society. Much of the land, which could not be sold, was eventually leased out. A complex system of rent distributions was established whereby various levels of chiefs received 30 percent of the rent monies, 25 percent went to maintain the bureaucracy that settled land issues, and the remaining 50 percent was divided among the ordinary members of the lineages owning the land. A Great Council of Chiefs from all over the country was also set up to advise the colonial government.

Gordon's remarkable system had the effect of homogenizing Fijian culture. The British failed to understand the fact that there were substantial differences in the cultures and social structures of the various Fijian groups. Particularly, groups in the interior and western areas of the main island of Viti Levu had more egalitarian and flexible political systems than those typical of the southeast at the time Fiji became a British colony (Norton 1977). The result was to create a national Fijian culture, codified in law and supported by a Fijian administration that was, at least initially, regarded by people in some areas of the country as a new kind of law brought in by the British! One man, for instance, in Rakiraki, quietly confided in my husband that the Rakiraki people did not traditionally have a particular kind of joking relationship between cousins that is common in other areas of Fiji. Such a relationship requires some cousins to do a kind of bawdy joking (such as coming up and squeezing each other's genitals) when they meet, which runs quite counter to the generally restrained tenor of Fijian relations. Steve was confused, having heard about this kind of joking relationship many times from Ra people. But the man just smiled and said that Ra people were generally embarrassed to admit that they did not have this joking relationship, since they knew that it was supposed to be a Fijian way. Younger generations, he continued, learned about Fijian culture in school, so thought that this joking relationship was traditionally a Ra practice.

The Fijian commitment to a shared national culture was not mandated by the British, however. Instead, Fijians became committed to the idea of a shared Fijian tradition in the context of political struggles for economic and political power over the next century and a quarter. It was clear to us that local identities remained alive and well. Given these strong regional rivalries, then, why are Fijians in so many contexts willing to act as a united group and believe they share a common tradition? The obvious answer is that they came together against the perceived threat of another group.

One key to Gordon's plan to preserve traditional Fijian culture was the importation of indentured servants from India to work on European-owned plantations. Gordon felt that recruiting Fijians for plantation labor would undermine their communal way of life and political system by taking able-bodied men away from the village and would also give them a source of income not controlled by chiefs and other authority figures. Interestingly, however, the British did not extend their respect for traditional cultures to the Indian indentured servants. The Indians came from many castes and religious groups, but they were all expected to live and eat together, and there was little support for their religion. This forced many Indians to (according to their beliefs) pollute themselves by mixing with people of lower castes. For this reason, many decided to remain in Fiji after their contracts were finished because they feared that they would become outcastes if they returned home in their polluted state. Others remained because they did not have the funds to return home or because they had little to return to.

As a result, a large Indo-Fijian population began to grow. Because this population was not subject to the same regulations to preserve their culture as were the indigenous Fijians, they were, through their own hard work and ingenuity, able to prosper economically in a way that the indigenous Fijians were not. Some went into business for themselves, but the majority had been small farmers in India and so continued farming in Fiji. Since they could not buy land in Fiji, however, they rented land from Fijian lineages on long-term leases. These Indo-Fijian farmers thus helped to establish the sugar industry, which is now a mainstay of the Fijian economy. Eventually, through hard work, the Indo-Fijian community prospered: the average educational attainment of the Indo-Fijian is much higher than that of the indigenous Fijians, as is the Indo-Fijian average income level.

British colonial policy not only valorized traditional Fijian culture. Colonial policy also set up a situation where indigenous Fijians felt that they needed to hang on to their culture in order to avoid becoming an oppressed and despised class of laborers in their own land. The sense that indigenous Fijians need their common culture and authority to protect them is prevalent. One of my main informants, for example, was a middle-aged woman who was deeply ambivalent about Fijian culture. She felt that many chiefs siphoned too much of the land rents for themselves and that Fijian communities were oppressive. The natural human way, she argued, was to change all the time. But in Fijian villages everyone gossiped about anyone who strayed in any way from the traditional norm. Furthermore, ceremonial and religious life took so much money and time that no one had the resources to try out any new economic schemes. These kinds of complaints were common among Rakiraki villagers. But despite her ambivalence about Fijian tradition as lived, my informant was adamant that Fijians must retain their culture and their chiefly system. If we lose a sense of a common culture and political system, she argued, then Fijians will not vote as a bloc. If that happens, the Indo-Fijians (who did tend to vote as a bloc) could easily take over the government and change land regulations. If Fijians could sell their land, then soon they would be reduced to a class of landless laborers.

This woman's views were shared by many national politicians, who preached unity through a shared pan-Fijian culture (Lawson 1991; Norton 1977:105). Furthermore, since Fiji became an independent country in 1970, three elections have voted in governments supported by a majority of Indo-Fijian voters and a minority of indigenous Fijian voters. In each of these three elections, Fijians split their vote while Indo-

Fijians voted as a bloc. Although these three governments (each of which was displaced within a few weeks, once by the governor-general and the other two times by coups) probably would not have been able to threaten Fijian ownership of land, they might well have made moves to change such things as preferential hiring of indigenous Fijians in civil service positions and in the military—the main avenues for upward mobility among Fijians over the past several decades.

Our Fijian research also showed how ethnic identities can have a deep psychological salience for people in situations where there is an uneven distribution of wealth and power. Fiji is an interesting case because British policy set up a situation where there were striking inequalities in wealth and power between indigenous Fijians and Indo-Fijians but where neither group clearly had the upper hand. Under British policy, which restricted Fijian economic enterprise and education in the name of preserving traditional culture, Indo-Fijians, who were relatively free of such restrictions, were able to prosper in agriculture and business. On the other hand, indigenous Fijians were clearly privileged by the British in the government and the civil service. The British had separate representatives for each of the major ethnic groups (a tradition that was preserved when Fiji became independent). Indigenous Fijians (and, of course, the British) always had more representatives per capita population than did the Indo-Fijians. These policies set up a situation where each group had sources of discontent (indigenous Fijians do not like being poorer than Indo-Fijians, while Indo-Fijians do not like the discriminatory political system), but each also had something of which it could be proud. Stephanie Sienkiewicz's research showed strongly how each group had internalized ideas about the essential differences between the two cultures to explain and justify its situation. Both indigenous Fijians and Indo-Fijians, for instance, maintained that indigenous Fijians had a lot of "culture" and that they were embedded in strong communities. Both groups also agreed that Indo-Fijians (like Europeans) had no culture; furthermore, they were completely individualistic and had no community.

We were all surprised by the degree to which these ideas were shared by both groups, particularly since they seemed to fly in the face of observable reality. Indo-Fijians, for example, to our minds had a great deal of culture and were quite unlike Europeans. Most of the Indo-Fijian families we knew arranged marriages for their children and held frequent and elaborate festivals connected with weddings and religious events. Indo-Fijians also appeared to have a robust sense of community. Indo-Fijians in Rakiraki and other areas of Fiji, for instance, with little support from the British, established and maintained the best primary and secondary school system in the country. Their schools were so much superior to indigenous Fijians' schools that many indigenous Fijians sent their children to Indo-Fijian schools, despite disliking Indo-Fijians. So why did both sides continue to subscribe to stereotypes that distorted reality? It was evident that both sides used the stereotypes to maintain a sense of worth in face of a larger threat from the outside. For an Indo-Fijian to announce proudly that he or she had no culture was a way of pointing out what advanced people Indo-Fijians were: they were shrewd and smart and had succeeded despite being discriminated against in government policy because they (unlike the indigenous Fijians) had thrown off the shackles of "primitive culture." For an indigenous Fijian, on the other hand, to talk about what "cultural" people Fijians were was to say that Fijians had chosen to remain poor because they valued human ties and community tradition over money. For both sides, then, maintaining a strong sense of cultural identity was a way of building a sense of pride and self-worth.

While the presence of a large minority ethnic community has forged a sense of unity among indigenous Fijians, a similar sense of unity has been forged in the Polynesian nations of Tonga and Samoa by outside threats to their autonomy. Tonga prides itself on being one of very few Pacific nations that was never a European colony (though it was a British protectorate from 1900 to 1970). Tongans also have a deep reverence for their culture, which divides the population into two groups, chiefs and commoners, each with its role to play in the community (Lawson 1996:113–114). Commoners are expected to display obedience, loyalty, love of land, and good behavior, whereas nobles are expected to show bravery, prowess, chiefliness, and dominance. Tongans see this distinct tradition as central to their identity and to their survival as an autonomous people.

Many Tongan leaders have argued, for instance, that democracy is unsuited to the Tongan way, which revolves around respect for the monarchy. Commitment to Tongan tradition was forged in a process of struggle to maintain autonomy. When Tongans saw neighboring countries like Fiji becoming British colonies, they devised a strategy of maintaining their political autonomy by codifying their laws and government system in a way that would satisfy the British. Many Tongans believe, with some justice, that it was their strong monarchy that allowed them to avoid becoming a colony and later to win independence from being a British protectorate. Samoa, similarly, takes pride in the way its strong traditional political system enabled it to argue for independence from its colonizer, New Zealand. In both nations, it is clear that people are proud of having a national culture and identity that differentiates them from Europeans.

International tourism has been another force molding commitment to distinct ethnic cultures in many Polynesian nations. Tourism has had a strong impact on ethnic identity in the small Polynesian nation of the Cook Islands (Sissons 1997). There are distinct cultural differences across regions in the Cook Islands. In fact, when the Cook Islands attained independence in 1965, their first government made no claims that

the islands were united by a common culture, thinking that this would have the potential to aggravate local jealousies. As tourism began to make a significant contribution to the national economy in the 1980s, however, the government began to encourage people to revive traditional ceremonies and handicrafts and to follow the Cook Islands way of presenting "friendly smiling faces," in order to attract tourists. Although the government policies were designed to unite the islands behind a common economic cause, some regions of the country have taken the new celebration of local cultures to heart. Movements have formed in some areas to fight for regional rights on the basis of their distinct regional cultural identities. A similar process also occurred in Tahiti, where traditional festivals were revived in the 1980s, largely to attract tourists. Art historian Karen Stevenson (1990), however, has shown that the large cultural festivals that were originally staged to attract tourists are now primarily aimed at a local audience. Tahitians gain a sense of group pride through festivals that glorify their distinct cultural tradition.

The indigenous Hawaiian sovereignty movement, which has blossomed over the past three decades, also shows the way indigenous peoples can reappropriate commercialized cultural symbols in order to foster group pride and fight for group rights. Key symbols of Hawaiian ethnic identity such as hula chants have been used to cater to the fantasies of international tourists looking for a simpler, less sexually inhibited, "primitive" lifestyle. But this marketing of a distinct Hawaiian culture in part paved the way for activists to try to boost Hawaiian pride and fight for Hawaiian rights through arguing that Hawaiians had a distinctive cultural tradition that should be respected in contemporary life. Prior to European contact, Hawaii had a hierarchical political system similar to those of Tahiti and Tonga in which a few high chiefs united large areas under their rule. There was a clear division between chiefs and commoners, with the commoners owing allegiance and tribute to chiefs. Religious beliefs justified this system by portraying chiefs as the human conduits of *mana* (power). Hula dances and chants were an integral part of this system, containing histories that justified the leadership of powerful chiefs and glorifying the person and deeds of the chiefs (Buck 1993).

European contact had a dramatically different impact on Hawaii than it had on Fiji and Tonga. Captain James Cook was the first European to visit Hawaii in 1778. Less than one hundred years later, the Hawaiian population had decreased to less than half its precontact numbers due to introduced diseases. The Hawaiian political and religious system had also been shaken to the core. The Hawaiian nobility gradually lost their position through dealings with European and American traders. Nobles tried to maintain their local prestige and power by trading with Europeans for firearms and prestigious luxury goods. They soon, however, went deep into debt and had to gouge the commoners in order to amass valued resources like sandalwood to pay the traders. The nobles also eventually sold vast tracts of Hawaiian land to Europeans and Americans in order to pay their debts.

The Hawaiian monarchs led a mass conversion to Christianity in order to escape the oppressive prohibitions associated with traditional religion and to ally themselves with European powers. Christianization led to a mass suppression of traditional Hawaiian culture. Hawaiian children were forbidden to speak their language in schools. The missionaries considered many Hawaiian practices, notably the hula dances and sacred chants through which Hawaiians preserved their histories and celebrated their chiefs, to be lewd and indecent and successfully ended these practices. The last Hawaiian monarch, Queen Lili'uokalani, was overthrown in 1893 by a group of American businessmen and marines who feared that the queen would oppose American plans for political and economic expansion into the Hawaiian Islands. Annexation by the United States followed a few years later, in 1898.

European penetration of the Hawaiian Islands also brought many new immigrant populations as Europeans and Americans established plantations and then imported indentured servants, first from Portugal, then later from China and Japan, to work on the plantations. The descendants of these indentured servants have remained in Hawaii, each establishing their own ethnic niche. The Japanese, for instance, are popularly stereotyped in Hawaii as the political powers; the Chinese Hawaiians, on the other hand, have prospered through small business. The native Hawaiians were relegated to the bottom of this new ethnic hierarchy. Until the early twentieth century, many lived in small rural villages where they practiced communally based subsistence agriculture. However, as large plantations and facilities for tourists took over more and more of the Hawaiian land, many drifted to cities, where they worked predominantly in unskilled, low-wage jobs or were unemployed. Today native Hawaiians have the lowest levels of income and education among the Hawaiian ethnic groups. For years, key aspects of Hawaiian culture such as hula dancing survived only in glitzy, Hollywood-style imitations designed to lure tourists through play into their fantasies about sexy, fun-loving primitives living in a paradise and free of desires for material possessions.

The 1970s, however, brought a resurgence of interest in traditional Hawaiian culture and active movements to fight for native Hawaiian political rights. Interestingly, one major impetus for these movements was the success of some Native American groups in winning large settlements and limited political autonomy. The Navajo, for instance, took the U.S. federal government to court and won not only a huge financial settlement but also the right to form a Navajo Nation with authority to establish and enforce laws within its boundaries. In the 1980s native Hawaiians began to push for similar recognition of their rights as a distinct nation within a nation. Some dream that Hawaii could once again become an independent nation, governed by the descendants of Hawaiian monarchs. Most, however, are pushing for more modest goals, such as the restoration to the Hawaiian people of lands ceded by their monarchs to Americans, and native Hawaiian control over the Hawaiian homelands that have already been awarded to indigenous Hawaiians. For instance, the Ka Lahui (Nation of Hawaii), an organization with over 12,000 members, in 1992 advocated negotiating with the federal government to establish Hawaii's status as a "nation within a nation" (Buck 1993:185–186).

One of the most interesting features of the Hawaiian sovereignty movement has been the way certain key symbols of Hawaiian ethnic identity have been reappropriated in order to build a sense of ethnic pride. The 1970s, for example, brought a renewed interest in hula and ancient chants among the native Hawaiian population. Hula halau (schools) sprang up all over the country, where hula adepts trained young Hawaiians in the ancient styles. These halau carefully distanced themselves from the glitzy, Hollywood-style hula by stressing the deep spiritual and political importance of hula to Hawaiians. While Waikiki hula dancers, catering to tourists, for instance, sport bare midriffs, more traditional halau dancers generally wear loose-fitting, form-concealing, blouses designed to emulate the ancient tapa cloth costumes of the past. Furthermore, while hula performances for tourists generally involve slender young women (who are often part Asian, as is much of the Hawaiian population), more traditional performances often feature women of all ages and body types—in fact, the best dancers are often older women—and muscular young men who reenact war dances. In short, hula performances for tourists portray Hawaiians as young, sexy, and happy; more traditional hulas, in contrast, portray Hawaiians as deeply spiritual people with a distinctive religious and political system.

They also celebrate the power and aggression of male warriors.

The Hawaiian renaissance shows clearly the way people everywhere formulate their ideas about their ethnic identity in an effort to make sense of their current situation. Native Hawaiians, for instance, now speak of the importance of *ohana* (family) and *aloha* (love and generosity) in Hawaiian culture. Hawaiians, they argue, unlike the other ethnic groups of the Hawaiian Islands, treat everyone as part of their family. They respect social ties over economic gain and are always willing to help each other out. Native Hawaiians also point to the egalitarian nature of Hawaiian culture in which decisions are made by consensus, and to the deep reverence of Hawaiians for their land (Linnekin 1990). A recent attempt to tap the geothermal energy of Hawaii's volcanoes, for instance, led to a protest by some native Hawaiian groups which argued that tapping volcanoes violated the native Hawaiian respect for the goddess of the volcanoes, Pele.

The thumbnail sketch of Hawaiian history presented is only a selective portrayal of the historical realities of precontact Hawaiian culture. Certainly, communal work groups were important among commoners and so was *ohana*, the tradition of respect for family. But precontact Hawaiian culture was also very hierarchical. Native Hawaiians, like people everywhere, have latched on to aspects of their cultural tradition that are most salient in helping them understand and adjust to their current circumstances. Like indigenous Fijians, native Hawaiians raise group pride by assuring each other that if Hawaiians are poor it is because they value human relations over money. Furthermore, the Hawaiian rhetoric of respect for land is a viewpoint likely to win support from a wider American population that also values (more often in words than in deeds) environmental conservation. Hawaiian statements about their identity, then, show well the process of selective valuation of aspects of a cultural tradition that help people to understand and adjust to their current situation.

Similar patterns are evident among the Maori, the indigenous people of New Zealand. Maori chiefs ceded New Zealand to Britain in 1840 through signing a treaty that, in their understanding, gave them the rights and privileges of British subjects while protecting their chiefly authority and control of land and fishing rights. Over subsequent decades, however, increasing amounts of Maori land were taken over by British settlers. Eventually, as the economy of New Zealand was transformed in the twentieth century, large numbers of Maori moved into cities, where they were clustered at the bottom of the socioeconomic scale. Like their counterparts in Hawaii, the Maori were inspired by movements among indigenous people in the United States and other parts of the world in the 1970s to assert their rights. They won concessions from the New Zealand government which recognized that British settlers had violated the 1840 treaty on numerous occasions and set up tribunals to hear Maori suits. The New Zealand government also set up targeted programs to help improve the socioeconomic position of the Maori. These programs, however, were cut in a period of economic stagnation in the 1980s, with the result that the contemporary Maori still remain at the bottom of the socioeconomic ladder in New Zealand.

Interestingly, the Maori cultural revival focuses on many of the same cultural values as are celebrated by indigenous Hawaiians. One way for urbanized Maori who do not otherwise participate in a distinctively Maori lifestyle to assert their distinctive culture, for instance, is through funerals (Sinclair 1990). Funerals involve drawing extensive networks of relatives back to tribal *marae* (meeting places), even when the deceased did not live on the tribal lands. During funerals, people celebrate their distinctive Maori identity by reminding themselves and each other that Maori, unlike the *Pakeha* (New Zealanders of European ancestry), are willing to invest a lot of time and energy into maintaining ties with large networks of relatives. Like the

Hawaiians and the Fijians, the Maori comment on the way that they value human ties over material gain. In this instance, it is again clear how people's sense of ethnic identity is formed in the particular circumstances of interaction between groups. The Maori, Hawaiians, and Fijians have all come to view their celebration of social ties as central to their identity because this is a trait that distinguishes them from another, more powerful, group. Furthermore, they focus on this particular cultural trait because it helps them understand and maintain a sense of self-respect in their current situation.

As Pacific peoples have become increasingly conscious of the value of their distinctive cultures in fostering group pride and fighting for national and international recognition of their rights, heated debates have arisen over the right to define those cultures. Interestingly, such debates have often focused among anthropologists. As anthropologist Rob Borofsky puts it, "[The] right of Western anthropologists to translate or speak for others . . . is very much under attack" (1997:263). Anthropologist Roger Keesing was, for example, severely criticized by Hawaiian historian Haunani-Kay Trask (1991), for suggesting that indigenous Hawaiian ideas about cultural tradition borrowed on romantic European fantasies of primitives living in communal harmony. Trask suggested that Keesing and other non-Hawaiian scholars had a strong impact on the fate of indigenous Hawaiians and other peoples because scholars were viewed as experts by the general public. These outside experts, however, often did not take into account oral traditions, genealogies, and other cultural knowledge available to group members. Furthermore, on principle, any group should have the power to define its own identity for the outside world. Too often, Trask and others have argued, members of indigenous minorities are reduced to informants who must rely on powerful outside experts to give them voice. The general public, steeped in a tradition requiring academic credentials to convey authority, accords little legitimacy to the lived knowledge of insiders to a culture.

While Trask and others make valid points about the ways international and national inequalities have privileged the voices of some people over those of others, reserving the right to comment on a culture for members of that culture is problematic in several ways. As Borofsky points out, erecting

> such barriers means that little sharing, little conversation, takes place across the borderlands of difference. This is a shame because there are serious issues to be addressed here. There is the question of to what degree being born and raised in a locale leads to effective knowledge of that locale's history. . . . Just as critical, the loss of conversation means that we rarely learn from our differences. We become frozen into positions and less able to move beyond the complacency of our own constructions toward increased knowledge. [1997: 263–264]

Perhaps the solution, as suggested by Hawaiian activist Herb Kane (1997:267), among others, is not to muffle the voices of outside scholars but instead to empower the voices of indigenous peoples by encouraging the trend for members of indigenous minorities to attain higher education degrees and add their own voices to the academic disciplines that define indigenous cultures for the general public.

THE POLITICS OF IDENTITY IN MICRONESIA

The islands of Micronesia lie to the north of Melanesia and Polynesia in the southwestern and central Pacific. There are four major island groups: the Mariana Islands (which include Guam), the Caroline Islands (including Palau, Yap, Truk, Pohnpei, and Kosrae), the Gilbert Islands, and the Marshall Islands. The cultures of Micronesia were in many ways similar to those of Polynesia. Societies were ranked, and there was continual competition for rank

through hosting feasts and through warfare. Micronesian societies, unlike those in Polynesia, however, were generally matrilineal. Large areas of Micronesia were under the influence of the Spanish in the eighteenth and nineteenth centuries, but the Spanish gave way to the Germans in the late nineteenth century. German colonizers were, in turn, displaced by the Japanese in 1914. The Japanese administered the region until 1945, when, in the negotiations following World War II, the Micronesian islands were designated a U.S. trust territory. In 1986, Yap, Truk, Pohnpei, and Kosrae and the smaller islands that were part of their administrative districts negotiated a compact of free association with the United States and became the Federated States of Micronesia. At the same time, Palau, the remaining group of Caroline Islands, became the Republic of Palau. The Northern Mariana Islands also signed a compact of union with the United States in 1975 and became the Commonwealth of the Northern Marianas. The Marshall Islands now constitute the Republic of the Marshall Islands, and the Gilbert Islands, once a British colony, are now the independent country of Kiribati.

Since the 1960s, the U.S. territories have also seen an influx of American funds, though often these funds are used to support building facilities rather than promoting economic development. United States aid has undoubtedly raised the standard of living of Micronesians, but in many areas it has also left them with a sense of dependency (Marshall 1979). American occupation also brought nuclear testing, particularly in the Marshall Islands. Such testing has resulted in the relocation of many groups and in ecological damage. Since the various republics of Micronesia have attained independence, there have also been large influxes of foreign populations and foreign capital. Palau, for instance, now has a substantial Filipino population and a good number of Bangladeshis. Many Americans are living and working there, as well as Chinese and Japanese (including Okinawans). And Guam and Saipan are even more diverse. Micronesian governments and private individuals have entered into partnerships with foreign capital to build hotels and other businesses. In fact, a large resort is due to open on Guam, built by a partnership of local residents and Chinese businesspeople. The ultimate effect of this relatively recent diversification of the Micronesian population is not yet clear.

Colonialism, and now postcolonialism, have had differing impacts on the various areas of Micronesia. The Mariana Islands, the northernmost island group of Micronesia, experienced the most drastic changes due to colonization. The Spanish established a permanent settlement in the Marianas in 1668 and thus issued in an era of massive change. Introduced diseases, warfare, and massive emigration to escape from Spanish-led Mexican and Filipino troops led to a drastic population reduction, from a high of perhaps 50,000 people prior to Spanish occupation to a low of 1,500 in the early 1700s (McPhetres 1992). The Spanish also forced the indigenous people, the Chamorro, to convert to Catholicism. The Spanish campaigns to conquer and convert the Chamorro led to more male than female deaths (since the men were the warriors). When the Chamorro were finally subdued there were many marriages between Filipino soldiers and Chamorro women, so the present-day Chamorro population of the Marianas is of mixed ancestry. Not surprisingly, traditional Chamorro religious beliefs and social structure were largely lost during the Spanish period. The Chamorro experience under the subsequent German and Japanese administrations were less devastating. The Germans and the Japanese introduced a minimal education system, but were primarily interested in reaping whatever strategic and economic benefits they could realize from the colonies rather than in developing the indigenous peoples through promoting general education and resource development.

Under the U.S. trusteeship and later under the compact of union with the United States, the Marianas have experienced economic development that has raised the local standard of living above that of many areas of the Pacific. Mariana Islanders were also the recipients of a huge financial settlement from the United States to compensate for lives lost and damage suffered during World War II. This prosperity, however, has come at a distinct cost. The Marianas and also Guam (which remained an unincorporated territory of the United States) have been inundated with foreign investment, much of it from Asia, to build hotels and garment factories. Asian investors are attracted to the Marianas and Guam because their association with the United States makes it possible to manufacture in these areas and then export products, duty-free, to the United States mainland. Indigenous landowners have made lucrative deals to lease out their land to foreign investors. However, foreign investors also bring with them a huge foreign labor force. The Chamorro are once again a minority in their own land due to huge influxes of Americans, Filipinos, and laborers from Asia. This has led to tensions between Chamorro and foreign laborers, and there have even been some attacks by Chamorro youth on foreign communities. Reliance on foreign investment has also brought a dependency on foreign economies. Recent downturns in the Asian economies have led to massive layoffs in Guam and the Marianas. Interestingly, these various developments have led to a resurgence of consciousness in Chamorro identity. Despite their mixed heritage, and despite the fact that their culture was virtually wiped out by the Spanish, the Chamorro have retained a strong sense of ethnic pride and identity, perhaps because they have always had to fend off domination from a series of powerful groups within their borders.

Colonization was a more benign experience in the Caroline Islands. Pohnpei, for instance, did not become a colony until the late nineteenth century. Colonial policies were much less severe than in the Marianas and, as a result, much of the ranked social structure of Pohnpei remains intact (Moses and Ashby 1992). The survival of the indigenous system of political authority is clearly a source of pride for the people of Pohnpei, as well as a central part of their identity. While Pohnpei society has sustained many changes (including the privatization of land and the introduction of a system of elected government), Pohnpeians stress that these changes have been peacefully and gracefully incorporated into their society without undermining the basic values stressing respect for traditional hierarchy (Moses and Ashby 1992). This is a good example of the ways that ethnic identities selectively interpret history in order to foster local pride: instead of focusing on the ways they have been influenced by foreign powers, Pohnpeians emphasize the ways that they have taken control and incorporated outside elements into the fabric of their "unique" society (Moses and Ashby 1992).

Many of the processes shaping ethnicity in other areas of the Pacific are also evident in Micronesia. As in Melanesia, colonization had the effect of bringing together under one government groups that did not traditionally feel that they had a common identity. The Japanese and German administrations sometimes even relocated populations from the outer islands to the administrative centers. The various administrations also located key medical, educational, and government facilities in the administrative center, and, in the process, increased interaction between groups. As in Melanesia, however, increased interaction does not necessarily bring with it an increased sense of common identity. Indeed, as in Melanesia, when groups who once jealously guarded their autonomy and may even have been enemies are brought together under a common power, the new situation tends to strengthen regional identities and rivalries, and each group fears the other will take advantage of the new situation to become dominant.

For instance, people from the outer islands such as Pulap, an atoll in the Truk district (Flinn 1990), continue to dwell on the differences between themselves and residents of neighboring atolls. They also contrast themselves to people from the administrative center, Truk, who are criticized for failing to preserve their traditional culture. The Pulap people, in contrast, take their own adherence to traditional ways of dress and subsistence horticulture as a sign of their more independent and strong nature. Lin Poyer (1990) describes a similar relationship between the administrative center Pohnpei and one of the outer islands of this district, Sapwuahfik. As was also evident in Melanesia, ethnic boundaries do not always arise from clashes in key values between cultures. Instead, groups that are quite similar will attach great significance to what appear to the outsider to be minor differences in generally similar cultures. Consciousness of ethnic difference, then, arises from the historical situation that brings groups together rather than from the degree of objective cultural difference.

Like people in other areas of the Pacific, Micronesians form ideas about ethnic identity in a struggle to maintain a sense of pride and autonomy in the face of overwhelming economic and political domination from outside groups. Mac Marshall (1979) found an interesting expression of this in the high rates of alcoholism among Trukese men. Marshall observed that not only were rates of alcoholism among young Trukese men between the ages of 15 and 30 very high, but that Trukese drunks were exceptionally prone to violence and fighting compared to drunks in other cultures. Although people considered alcoholism in young males to be a problem it was also clear that it was considered only natural for young men to drink. In fact, those who did not drink were viewed suspiciously and considered to be somewhat lacking in male potency. After examining the Trukese cultural associations with drunkenness, Marshall realized that, when they were drunk, young men exhibited a characteristic of bravery and ability to flaunt outside authority that was highly prized in Trukese males. Traditionally, young men had been warriors who had proved their virility and the power of their group through fighting. Now that warfare had been banned, however, Trukese males found themselves with few avenues to demonstrate their power and autonomy in a world dominated by white American outsiders. Alcoholism, then, provided one of the few ways that the Trukese could show that they were aggressive, autonomous people who could not be subjected to outside control. Drinking to excess, in short, was for Trukese men a way of expressing their distinctive ethnic identity. High rates of male alcoholism in other areas of Micronesia likely have a similar source.

THE ABORIGINAL PEOPLES OF AUSTRALIA

As in New Zealand and Hawaii, the last three decades have seen an upsurge in ethnic consciousness and pride among the Aboriginal peoples of Australia. The Australian case shows well what has also been apparent in other areas of the Pacific, that ethnic revivals are very much influenced by international ideologies and movements. Like their counterparts in Hawaii and New Zealand, Aboriginal activists in Australia were inspired in their efforts by the successes of minority groups in the United States and in other areas of the world in winning some (limited) recognition of their rights as members of distinctive cultures. The Australian government was also influenced by pressures from the world community to redress past wrongs committed against its Aboriginal peoples. Perhaps the most intriguing aspect of the shift in Australian policy, however, has been the impact of an international ideology celebrating the distinctiveness and wisdom of encapsulated cultures perceived as possessing a superior quality of spirituality and being in harmony with the environment. The "Millennium" series of the early 1990s put together by anthropologist David Mabury-Lewis, for instance, uses the Australian Aborigines as one of several "tribal cultures" who, the show claims, have a superior grasp of the cosmic force informing humans and environment. As shows such as the "Millennium" series celebrate the wisdom of tribal peoples, governments, such as that of Australia, move to preserve this distinct cultural heritage and define it as a central part of the national heritage (Lattas 1991; Merlan 1998). Indigenous peoples like the Aborigines, in turn, can take advantage of the new trendiness of their culture in order to push for greater autonomy.

The Aborigines traditionally lived by foraging for food in the vast deserts of inland Australia. The inhospitable conditions of much of the country required that groups cover vast amounts of territory in order to take advantage of seasonal foods available in different areas (Tonkinson 1991). Supporting this mobile lifestyle was a system of religious beliefs, "the Dreaming," which defined paths traveled by ancestral animals that created key landmarks along these paths. The Dreaming also suggested a close relationship between humans and lands, with the belief that creation involved a woman being fertilized by an ancestral spirit located in the territory where she conceived.

The experience of Aboriginals with the intruding European (largely British) settlers and administrators varied a great deal with the nature of the territory they occupied. Aborigines who occupied tracts of fertile ground found themselves pushed off the land. They suffered greatly from introduced diseases and settler campaigns to subdue them. In contrast, groups who occupied the interior desert of Australia often managed to continue their hunting and gathering way of life well into the twentieth century. Some chose voluntarily to settle in camps where they could work seasonally for European ranchers, since this life was less arduous than the traditional ways of foraging. By the 1970s, most Aboriginal groups had moved to settlements and towns or to camps near these settlements. While many people continue to forage, few rely primarily on such means for survival.

The twentieth century also brought great shifts in attitudes toward Aborigines among white Australians. Up to World War II, Australia was dominated by an infamous "white Australia" policy that promoted the idea of Australia as a British culture, to be protected from incursions of Asian and other "colored" immigrants (Merlan 1998). Clearly, this formulation of Australian identity marginalized Aboriginal peoples, who, in fact, were not even officially recognized as citizens of Australia until after World War II. The Australian national image, however, began to shift after the war, when Australia recognized the importance of its ties with other Pacific nations and opened its doors to Asian immigration. Gradually, these new policies also led to shifts in ideas about Australian national identity. The 1970s brought a new rhetoric portraying Australia as a multicultural society, tolerant of difference.

The 1960s and 1970s also brought new policies recognizing the rights of the Aborigines to determine whether they wanted to remain a distinct culture or to assimilate into the dominant society. These policies show how limited have been the real gains of Aboriginal peoples despite the national appropriation of their culture as a symbol of "Australianness." In part, these policies were inspired by efforts to win the approval of the world community after the General Assembly of the United Nations passed a 1960 resolution proclaiming the rights of all peoples to determine their political status and to pursue their economic, social, and cultural development. The 1970s brought the creation of a Department of Environment, Aborigines, and the Arts, as well as the passage in 1976 of the Aboriginal Land Rights Act, which allowed Aboriginal groups to claim their ancestral lands, provided these were unoccupied lands owned by the Crown. In fact, many Aboriginal groups did make land claims, with varying degrees of success. In the Northern Territory and in Western

Australia there has been a major shift of land into Aboriginal hands. Some groups, however, have had a difficult time proving their claims, since these involve demonstrating that an Aboriginal clan has enjoyed rights of use over a particular stretch of land and has a spiritual association (as demonstrated by Dreaming myths) over that land. Such claims can be difficult to establish, since in many groups, clans have been disrupted by contact with white settlers. The idea that Aborigines had been organized into clans with control over distinct territories was also probably a distortion of the traditional situation where both group membership and territory use were determined in more flexible ways (Merlan 1998). The 1980s also brought government legislation designed to increase Aboriginal autonomy by setting up and providing funds for indigenous groups.

Going along with these changes in policy have been shifts in Australian national identity that define the Aboriginal peoples as more central to the national heritage (Lattas 1991; Merlan 1998). Films such as *Crocodile Dundee* celebrate the independent "outback" spirit of Australia and link this to the Aboriginal traditions of living on the land. These films, of course, involve unrealistic, "Hollywood" visions of Aboriginal life. They do more to perpetuate romantic western fantasies of the primitive than to improve Aboriginal life. National art museums also accord privileged places to collections of Aboriginal art, now seen as central to the unique Australian heritage (Morphy 1991). As the Australian economy declined in the 1980s, however, funding to support programs targeting the Aboriginal peoples was cut (Merlan 1998).

Aboriginal groups, in turn, have taken advantage of the new celebration of Aboriginal culture to push for their rights. But coming up with practical solutions is difficult: some groups have established back-to-the-land movements, but it is hard for people who have been brought up in camps to return to a traditional foraging lifestyle, cut off from things like modern medicine. Furthermore, there are differences of opinion within the Aboriginal community: women, for instance, have made use of government support programs for single mothers to win autonomy from men (Tonkinson 1991) and do not support some moves to resurrect traditional gender roles.

PACIFIC ETHNICITIES

Examining ethnicity across the Pacific shows well how ethnic identity "unlike personal identity, community cultural identity . . . has meaning only in the context of a set of regional identities of which it is a part" (Poyer 1990:127). There are cultural differences between neighboring groups all over the Pacific. But the particular significance that is attached to these cultural differences varies with the relationships between these groups over time. In many cases, people celebrate and magnify fairly trivial differences to separate themselves from their neighbors; in other cases, people are willing to ignore larger differences in order to claim solidarity with their neighbors. Furthermore, the makeup of people's ethnic identities—that is, the beliefs, values, and practices that they take to define their essential selves and make them different from other groups—is transformed over time. People come to view as highly significant aspects of their culture tradition that make them different from other groups and allow them to feel good about their current situation. Other aspects of traditional ways, handed down through the generations, become lost.

I started out this chapter by suggesting some points of difference in the common American view of ethnicity and the common Pacific view. While there are obviously profound differences in ethnicities in the various islands of the Pacific, there are also some common themes. In general, Pacific Islanders view ethnic differences as persistent over time. Many also believe that ethnic differences should be preserved: it is only as

members of cultural communities that individuals can hope to live fulfilling lives and realize their desires. Again, in many areas, this search for autonomy through ethnicity has led to essentializing rhetorics of ethnic differences. People in various areas claim that members of different cultural communities live according to fundamentally different values that are perhaps rooted in their very nature. What suits one cultural community does not suit another.

My examination of the histories of ideas about ethnicity all over the Pacific has suggested that such ideas are generated in the process of struggle. In many areas of the Pacific, cultivating and preserving cultural difference was traditionally part and parcel of a continual struggle to assert autonomy. In the colonial and postcolonial eras, appeals to a distinctive cultural tradition have also been used to unite groups and to fight for autonomy. But these newer rhetorics differ in important ways from the older celebration of cultural differences between neighbors. Scholars have argued persuasively that Pacific Islanders traditionally tended not to trace cultural differences to biology (e.g., Linnekin 1990; Watson 1990). Adoption of refugees and migrants was, for instance, common, and people placed greater importance on behavior reflecting commitment to a group than they did on blood ties. The new Pacific ethnicities, however, tend to have a more essentialist cast, focusing on immutable differences between groups, as when New Guineans argue that they are essentially aggressive people and unsuited to European ways or when Fijians and Tongans assert that they are essentially people who must live according to their traditional hierarchy in order to prosper and be blessed by God.

It is not hard to understand where these ideas come from. Most Pacific Island cultures were dominated for long periods by European colonial regimes that, themselves, were generally racist, insisting on essential biological differences between races. Not surprisingly, when islanders began to fight for their rights, they worked within the same racist ideology. The best argument, after all, is one that adopts the basic premises of the opponent but reaches the opposite conclusion. People like the Maori and the native Hawaiians, for instance, who were for years considered to be biologically inferior to European colonizers, can now use the claim to distinctiveness to fight for their rights. If we are a distinct population, essentially different from other elements of the population, then we should have special provisions to meet our needs. If we are essentially different from Europeans, then we should be able to live in different ways. These claims have also been made by the people of new independent countries.

Appeals to cultural distinctiveness have done much to build pride among Pacific Islanders and to help them fight for their rights. But potential problems with this kind of ethnic rhetoric should not be ignored. Ideologies that stress essential differences between ethnic groups often suppress the expression of differences within each group (Lawson 1996). In Fiji, for instance, when indigenous Fijians band together in face of a perceived threat from Indo-Fijians, this suppresses discussion of differences in values, interests, and opinions within the community of indigenous Fijians. People from the north and west feel that they are unfairly dominated by people from the southeast of Fiji, but often feel that they must suppress these differences in order to unite against the Indo-Fijians.

Furthermore, ideologies that appeal to the essential differences between groups have the potential to foster intolerance of other groups and even violence (Said 1993). The Solomon Islands, for example, have been brought to a standstill several times in recent years by rioting in the capital city by people like the Kwaio who feel that they have been discriminated against by other groups (Akin 1999). Similarly, we were shocked in our last week in Fiji by the lack of human sympathy expressed toward Indo-Fijians, many of whom had grown up as neighbors and

playmates of the indigenous Fijians among whom we lived. On the night that Speight and his men took the Fijian parliament hostage, an Indo-Fijian elementary school on the outside of Rakiraki burned to the ground. When my research assistant came to work the next day she told me that she had been awakened by the fire in the middle of the night and had gone with some villagers to watch the school burn. On the way they passed the house of an Indo-Fijian and some of the villagers jokingly called out that they would burn his house down if he didn't tie up his dog. On the way back, my research assistant continued, they noticed that the dog had been tied. She was amazed that the Indo-Fijian man had taken them seriously. She was also amused but seemed at the same time slightly ashamed. No one, however, expressed any regrets over the school. Some even went so far as to suggest that the Indo-Fijians must have burned the school down themselves in order to make the indigenous Fijians look bad. When we tried this interpretation out on an Indo-Fijian friend who was a member of the committee of the school, he looked disgusted.

After our return to the United States, the situation in Fiji degenerated. Indo-Fijian houses were burned in some parts of the country. In various areas groups of armed men took over police posts, a factory, a power plant, and a resort in efforts to assert that their rights as owners of the land were not being respected. I received a letter from my research assistant written on July 8, a few days before the hostages were finally released. She wrote: "Even for us Fijian or real Fijian we are living with fear nowadays. If we go in town, we are not walking like before, we are walking fast and rushing to which ever place we are going to. Oh Karen and Steve, we miss our beloved Fiji as it is known before, BEAUTIFUL FIJI, no more." While the situation in Fiji is currently worse than in many other Pacific nations, these words eloquently summarize the plight of many islanders who now live in nations comprising many groups whose differences have only been reinforced by colonial and postcolonial experiences.

NOTE

1. In fact, the constitution of Fiji, which had been ratified in 1997, did mandate separate representatives for each "racial" group. Indigenous Fijians were delegated the majority of representatives, a number out of proportion to their percentage in the overall population. The 1997 constitution, however, also provided for a number of open seats where Fijians of all races voted for a common set of representatives. Chaudhry's government had been elected with the backing of a majority of Indo-Fijians and a minority of indigenous Fijians after the indigenous Fijians split their vote between two other parties. Speight and his supporters were pushing for a new constitution which would mandate that the prime minister be an indigenous Fijian. It should also be noted that most of the negotiations following the hostage taking were not between indigenous Fijians and Indo-Fijians but rather among various indigenous Fijian groups (such as the Great Council of Chiefs, the military, the president, and so on) that had different ideas about how the constitution should be amended.

REFERENCES CITED

AKIN, DAVID. 1999. Compensation and the Melanesian state: Why the Kwaio keep claiming. *The Contemporary Pacific* 11:35–68.

BARTH, FREDRIK, ed. 1969. *Ethnic Groups and Boundaries: The Social Organization of Cultural Difference.* Boston: Little, Brown.

BECKER, ANNE E. 1995. *Body, Self, and Society: The View from Fiji.* Philadelphia: University of Pennsylvania Press.

BOROFSKY, ROBERT. 1997. Cook, Lono, Obeyesekere, and Sahlins. *Current Anthropology* 38:255–265.

BRISON, KAREN J. 1991. Community and prosperity: Social movements in a Papua New Guinea village. *The Contemporary Pacific* 3:325–356.

___. 1995. Changing constructions of masculinity in a Sepik society. *Ethnology* 34:155–175.

___. 1999. Imagining a nation in Kwanga village courts, East Sepik Province, Papua New Guinea. *Anthropological Quarterly* 72:74–85.

BUCK, ELIZABETH. 1993. *Paradise Remade: The Politics of Culture and History in Hawaii.* Philadelphia: Temple University Press.

CLARK, JEFFREY. 1997. Imagining the state, or tribalism and the arts of memory in the highlands of Papua New

Guinea. In 65–90 *Narratives of Nation in the South Pacific.* Ton Otto and Nicholas Thomas, eds. Amsterdam: Harwood Academic Publishers.

FLINN, JULIANA. 1990. We still have our customs: Being Pulapese in Truk. In *Cultural Identity and Ethnicity in the Pacific.* Jocelyn Linnekin and Lin Poyer, eds. Pp. 103–126. Honolulu: University of Hawaii Press.

HAVINI, MOSES. 1992. A Bougainvillean perspective on the crisis. In *The Bougainville Crisis: 1991 Update.* Pp. 161–169. Bathurst: Crawford House Press.

KANE, HERB KAWAINUI. 1997. Comment. *Current Anthropology* 38:265–267.

KEESING, ROGER. 1989. Creating the past: Custom and identity in the Pacific. *The Contemporary Pacific* 1:19–42.

___. 1992. *Custom and Confrontation: The Kwaio Struggle for Cultural Autonomy.* Chicago: University of Chicago Press.

KEESING, ROGER, and ROBERT TONKINSON, eds. 1982. Kastom in Melanesia. *Mankind* 13.

KIRKPATRICK, JOHN, and GEOFFREY M. WHITE. 1985. Introduction: Pacific ethnopsychologies. In *Person, Self and Experience: Exploring Pacific Ethnopsychologies.* Geoffrey M. White and John Kirkpatrick, eds. Pp. 1–34. Berkeley: University of California Press.

KULICK, DON. 1992. *Language Shift and Cultural Reproduction.* Cambridge: Cambridge University Press.

LARCOM, JOAN. 1982. The invention of convention. *Mankind* 13:330–337.

LATTAS, ANDREW. 1991. Nationalism, aesthetic redemption and aboriginality. *TAJA* 2:307–324.

LAWSON, STEPHANIE. 1991. *The Failure of Democratic Politics in Fiji.* Oxford: Clarendon Press.

___. 1996. *Tradition versus Democracy in the South Pacific: Fiji, Tonga and Western Samoa.* Cambridge: Cambridge University Press.

LINNEKIN, JOCELYN. 1990. The politics of culture in the Pacific. In *Cultural Identity and Ethnicity in the Pacific.* Jocelyn Linnekin and Lin Poyer, eds. Pp. 149–174. Honolulu: University of Hawaii Press.

LUTZ, CATHERINE. 1988. *Unnatural Emotions: Everyday Sentiments on a Micronesia Atoll and Their Challenge to Western Theories.* Chicago: University of Chicago Press.

MARSHALL, MAC. 1979. *Weekend Warriors: Alcohol in a Micronesian Culture.* Mountain View, CA: Mayfield.

MCPHETRES, SAMUEL F. 1992. Challenges to democracy in the Commonwealth of the Northern Mariana Islands. In *Culture and Democracy in the South Pacific.* Ron Crocombe, Uentabo Neemia, Asesele Ravuvu, and Werner Vom Busch, eds. Pp. 217–238. Suva: Institute for Pacific Studies.

MERLAN, FRANCESCA. 1998. *Crying the Rainbow: Places, Politics and Aborigines in a North Australia Town.* Honolulu: University of Hawaii Press.

MORPHY, HOWARD. 1991. *Ancestral Connections: Art and an Aboriginal System of Knowledge.* Chicago: University of Chicago Press.

MOSES, RESIO S., and GENE ASHBY. 1992. Tradition and Democracy on Pohnpei Island. In *Culture and Democracy in the South Pacific*. Ron Crocombe, Uentabo Neemia, Asesela Ravuvu, and Werner Vom Busch, eds. Pp. 205–216. Suva: University of the South Pacific Press.

NASH, JILL, and EUGENE OGAN. 1990. The red and the black: The Bougainvillean perceptions of other Papua New Guineans. *Pacific Studies* 13:1–17.

NORTON, ROBERT. 1977. *Race and Politics in Fiji*. New York: St. Martin's.

POYER, LIN. 1990. Being Sapwuahfik: Cultural and ethnic identity in a Micronesian society. In *Cultural Identity and Ethnicity in the Pacific*. Jocelyn Linnekin and Lin Poyer, eds. Pp. 127–148. Honolulu: University of Hawaii Press.

SAID, EDWARD. 1993. *Culture and Imperialism*. New York: Vintage.

SCHWARTZ, THEODORE. 1975. Cultural totemism: Ethnic identity, primitive and modern. In *Ethnic Identity: Cultural Continuities and Change*. George DeVos and Lola Romanucci-Ross, eds. Pp. 106–131. Mountain View, CA: Mayfield.

SIENKIEWICZ, STEPHANIE. 2000. To make a balance: Ethnic relations in Fiji. Undergraduate thesis, Department of Anthropology, Union College.

SINCLAIR, KAREN P. 1990. Tangi: Funeral rituals and the construction of Maori identity. In *Cultural Identity and Ethnicity in the Pacific*. Jocelyn Linnekin and Lin Poyer, eds. Pp. 219–236. Honolulu: University of Hawaii Press.

SISSONS, JEFFREY. 1997. Nation or desti-nation? Cook Islands nationalism since 1965. In *Narratives of Nation in the South Pacific*. Ton Otto and Nicholas Thomas, eds. Pp. 163–188. Amsterdam: Harwood Academic Publishers.

STEVENSON, KAREN. 1990. Heiva: Continuity and change of a Tahitian celebration. *The Contemporary Pacific* 2:255–278.

THOMAS, NICHOLAS. 1992. Substantivization and anthropological discourse: The transformation of practices into institutions in neotraditional Pacific societies. In *History and Tradition in Melanesian Anthropology*. James G. Carrier, ed. Pp. 64–85. Berkeley: University of California Press.

TONKINSON, ROBERT. 1991. *The Mardu Aborigines: Living the Dream in Australia's Desert*. 2nd edition. Chicago: Holt, Rinehart & Winston.

TRASK, HAUNANI-KAY. 1991. Natives and anthropologists: The colonial struggle. *The Contemporary Pacific* 3:159–167.

WATSON, JAMES B. 1990. Other people do other things: Lamarckian identities in Kainantu Subdistrict, Papua New Guinea. In *Cultural Identity and Ethnicity in the Pacific*. Jocelyn Linnekin and Lin Poyer, eds. Pp. 17–42. Honolulu: University of Hawaii Press.

WESTERMARK, GEORGE. 1986. Court is an arrow: Legal pluralism in Papua New Guinea. *Ethnology* 25:131–149.

18

EUROPE

Pamela Ballinger
Bowdoin College

This chapter examines race and ethnicity in Europe, situating contemporary understandings in broad historical processes of state building, ethnic and nationalist movements, and colonialism. We first look at the historical diversity of nationalist movements in Europe and their associated ideas of ethnic and racial identity; the types of nationalism explored range from romantic, national liberation movements in the nineteenth century to the Nazi race regime and state socialist experiments in multiethnic federalism in the twentieth century. We then consider two cases that demonstrate the close and sometimes explosive relationship between religious and ethnic identities, those of Northern Ireland and the former Yugoslavia (with a focus on Bosnia-Herzegovina). In both examples, violent conflict reflects the interplay between long-standing tensions and new challenges confronting Europe after the cold war and the integration of the European Union (EU).

Whereas the EU implies a model of inclusion designed to overcome the ethnic and nationalist hatreds that ravaged Europe with two bloody world wars in the last century, a European identity also appears to exclude many "nonwhite" immigrants, as well as those peoples from Eastern Europe whose states remain outside of the EU. How are notions of "European" identity changing, and how can we understand a pan-European identity in terms of ethnicity, and race? What is the relationship among "culture," ethnicity, and race in the "old" and "new" Europes? Answering such questions illuminates the differences, as well as the similarities, between European societies and the United States as they struggle to build multicultural polities in a globalized world.

THE IDEA OF EUROPE AND THE IDEA OF NATION

Notions of race and ethnicity in contemporary Europe cannot be understood without reference to ideologies of nationhood, commonly said to have originated in Europe in the eighteenth and nineteenth centuries (see Chapter 4). The broad historical circumstances in which nationalism came to the fore as a political ideology included the European conquest of much of the world and the Industrial Revolution, both of which reflected and facilitated the creation of centralized states and bureaucracies. As a result, peoples living within what we today call Europe began to view themselves as "Europeans," as well as members of a specific nation or state.

From Christians to Europeans

The very notion of "Europe" was made possible by radical transformations from the fifteenth century onward. Inhabitants of medieval Europe typically identified either at a narrow, local level, on kinship lines (genealogies, dynasties) or as part of a religious community. Prior to the Protestant schism, to be a Christian in Europe generally meant to view oneself as part of a universal, religious kingdom. (This held true despite the split between Catholicism and Orthodox Christianity in 1054, which followed the division between the Western and Eastern halves of the old Roman Empire.) In the Christian mind, the world was made up of Christians and infidels; in theory, then, any pagan could join the Christian community through a process of religious conversion. This understanding built upon an older worldview that distinguished citizens of the Roman Empire (as well as the earlier Greek polities; see Chapter 4) from so-called "barbarians," who nonetheless might potentially become Romans. Such perspectives contrast sharply with modern understandings of ethnicity and, above all, "race," in which one is said to be literally born into a community and where identity does not prove a matter of choice.

The medieval division of the world into Christians/pagans had already begun to change even before "Europeans" ventured out in transoceanic sailing ships to encounter other peoples. The geographic expansion of Christian states followed upon the humanistic rediscovery of the ancient Greek and Roman past, which had been largely forgotten, condemned, or misunderstood during the medieval period. Just as the explorers encountered strange peoples separated from Europeans in space, the humanists discovered exotic peoples (the ancient Greeks and Romans) separated from Europeans in time. Eventually, the Greeks and Romans were embraced as "ancestors" who laid the foundations of Europe. From this dual encounter in time and space, there emerged a notion of being "European" that built upon and yet reconfigured the older Christian-pagan distinction. The label "Europe" stood for a geographic space, as well as a moral entity, distinguished from a host of other peoples and ways of life (Chabod 1991). These other peoples eventually came to be understood as belonging to diverse nations (*nationes*, from the Latin *natio*) and races.

The purity of this emerging European identity had to be policed from within, as well as from without. Internal "others," like the Jews and Moors (Muslims), were increasingly recognized as alien and expelled from various parts of the European continent, most notably from the Iberian Peninsula with the *Reconquista* of 1492. The timing of this violence coincides with Columbus's first voyage to the New World, further underlining the ways in which the consolidation of forms of European and national identity went hand in hand with the identification, labeling, and frequent persecution of "racial" and religious "others." The brutality of the Iberian reconquest prefigured the tragic genocide carried out in the New World, whereby Spanish violence, enslavement, and other harsh labor policies and diseases decimated native populations.

As Spain and other European powers carved out empires in the New World in the sixteenth and seventeenth centuries, fierce debates ensued over the policies to be adopted toward native populations and over how to classify such peoples (and, by extension, oneself). When Europeans first encountered different plants, animals, and peoples, they sought to incorporate them into their traditional classification systems (Todorov 1987). No matter how exotic or odd other peoples appeared to such Europeans, for Christians all men were thought to be descendants of a common ancestor (Adam) and thus fundamentally the same (Hodgen 1963:386–426). Yet not all Europeans were heterodox Christians, or even believers at all; indeed, the secularizing impulse of Renaissance humanism created a space for questioning an older view of the universe centered on the notion of a "Great Chain of Being" linking the divine to the most minute forms of life. Thus, when European conquistadors, missionaries, traders, and scholars encountered other peoples in the New World, Africa, and Asia, their responses were not uniform.

One reaction was to view other peoples in terms of devolution. This understanding followed out of a traditional Christian belief that Man, perfect at his creation, had subsequently been exposed to different environments after his expulsion from the perfect and balanced climate of the Garden of Eden. These different climates not only modified Man's temperament (thereby explaining cultural diversity) but also led to his degeneration or devolution (Hodgen 1963). According to this theory, peoples like the American Indians could be seen as the most degraded and hence in need of European administration. An opposing but related view held that these natives were the least degenerated of peoples and thus in their childlike and pure state required protection from the corrupting influences of the European colonizers. The French philosopher Jean Jacques Rousseau would later reformulate and secularize this idea as that of the "noble savage."

Others, however, began to question that all these peoples had a common ancestor or even their basic humanity. Some thinkers suggested that these populations represented either a transitional form between Man and other animals or a type of human very far removed from modern European Man. This shift was accompanied by a new interest in taxonomy and "scientific" classification, what became known as natural history. Though Carolus Linnaeus, the founder of modern taxonomic systems, continued to believe that species were immutable or fixed (as given by God), contemporaries like Comte de Buffon suggested that change could occur between forms. In the nineteenth century, the seeds of such thought would blossom into a fully developed theory of biological evolution that profoundly challenged traditional religious worldviews.

The traditional Christian perspective viewed not only species but history as fixed, with time unfolding toward a preordained end point (the Last Judgment). From the eighteenth century onward, however, this view of sacred history increasingly gave way to a secular understanding of history and a search for general laws governing the development of society and culture. New forms of classification—given tangible form in encyclopedias and museums—broke with medieval and Renaissance systems of arrangement according to outward resemblance or "similitude" and instead sought to organize things from simple to complex. This entailed a shift from seeing Man's development in terms of devolution to viewing it as a process of (social) evolution.

With the secularization of older, Christian views of sacred history, time now became something standardized, marked out on a clock. This reflected not just Enlightenment philosophizing but the beginnings of industrialization in Europe, which profoundly altered individuals' rhythms and sense of identity and belonging. The peasant-turned-factory-worker now measured time by the clock (punching in and out) rather than by the position of the sun in his field (Thompson 1967). Changing understandings of time, together with what Benedict Anderson (1987) calls "print capitalism"—the development of the printing press and the subsequent spread of the printed word—helped create new senses of community and belonging (see also the discussion in Chapter 4).

Our having just seen how "(white) Europeans" began to identify themselves as such in relation to other populations of the globe, Anderson's discussion helps us to understand how Europeans simultaneously came to differentiate themselves in ethnic and national terms from their more immediate neighbors. The advent of print capitalism made possible the proliferation of books and newspapers in vernacular, or local, languages. Now that writings were widely available in, say, French or Spanish rather than Latin, the reading public greatly increased. This helped create a sense of identification, for example, between French-speakers as a group as opposed to Spanish-speakers and also served as a vehicle for elites interested in welding diverse local dialects into one "national" language, like French.

Anderson cites the newspaper as a primary means by which such "national" identities were created. He suggests that the newspaper also fostered a new sense of time: that of simultaneity. Each reader of the paper knows that many others are reading the same news at the same moment. Even if the reader will never meet most of these fellow newspaper consumers, he or she has a sense of what Anderson deems an "imagined community" of readers. Since the nineteenth century, this community has been imagined primarily in terms of the nation. According to Anderson, the idea of the sovereign nation that embodies the will of the people ultimately supplanted the older understanding of a "universal" kingdom of God. As we shall see in subsequent sections, this did not mean that religious identities lost all salience in Europe. Religion, ethnicity, race, and nationhood continue to intersect in dramatic and sometimes tragic ways. Let us now untangle the complicated intersections in Europe of the ideas of nation, ethnicity, and race.

The Idea of Nation

Although the idea of the nation is thoroughly modern, it drew upon older understandings about people and place (Kedourie 1993; Kohn 1965, 1967). The word *nation* derives from the Latin *natio* ("to be born"), suggesting a sense of naturalness rooted in time immemorial (Verdery 1993). Not surprisingly, the nationalist movements that arose in early modern Europe often drew upon traditional symbols, at times using them to confer authenticity on "invented" national histories, heroes, and rituals. One famous example is that of the coronation ceremonies associated with the British monarchs. Though seemingly age-old, ceremonies like that for the coronation of England's Queen Victoria were newly minted but nonetheless suffused with an antique air (Cannadine 1983).

Other traditions that became part of a "national heritage" included folk poetry and songs. In some instances, these poems were fabricated by scholars and presented as newly discovered ancient traditions, as in the case of the Ossian poems "recovered" by the Scottish scholar James Macpherson. In many cases, traditional folk forms were edited and selected by scholars (most famously, the Grimm brothers) in a creative process of reworking (Cocchiara 1952; Ellis 1963). The intense interest in these popular traditions proved one of the enduring legacies of the Romantic movement in philosophy and art. Broadly speaking, Romanticism proved a response to the Enlightenment faith in reason and progress. Belief in the perfectibility of Man and society had been profoundly shaken by the events of the French Revolution in which the cult of reason and liberty ultimately descended into tyranny. The dehumanization and degradation of Man wrought by the Industrial Revolution further disillusioned a generation of intellectuals. Romanticism exalted emotion, irrationality, and the sublime together with those things rejected by Enlightenment thinkers: the "primitive," the folk, and the past.

For the development of romantic nationalism in Europe, among the most outstanding intellectual figures are Jean Jacques Rousseau (1712–78) and Johann Gottfried Herder (1744–1803). Skeptical of the Enlightenment's universal histories, search for laws, and belief in an ever better society, the French philosopher Rousseau instead valorized the simple and the "primitive" (i.e., the noble savage). He also addressed himself to broad questions of sovereignty (expressed in the "general will" of the people) and the specific issue of the Polish nation. Like those philosophers he criticized, however, Rousseau proved less interested in the way of life of actual "savages" than in the figure or metaphor of the savage. Rousseau used this image of the pure native uncorrupted by the conceits of society in order to critique the contemporary European societies around him.

In contrast to Rousseau, Herder's interest in the primitive extended to studying the actual examples he found at hand in contemporary Europe. Primarily a philologist (scholar of language), in later life Herder stressed the diversity of culture (*kultur*). He argued that each people, or *volk*, had a unique history and cultural development, which resulted from the interaction of the environment and the innate creative spirit or genius of a people. According to Herder, this genius was expressed in folk arts, in particular folk poetry and songs. Herder dedicated himself to collecting such folk traditions, especially among the Slavic peoples of southeastern Europe, and encouraged other scholars to engage in hands-on fieldwork (Barnard 1965, 1969; Herder 1966, 1968).

Herder's insistence that culture could best be understood through ethnological work, rather than from the comfortable armchair of the philosopher in his salon, constitutes an important precedent for later anthropological practice. Herder also contributed to anthropology the idea that cultures were plural and that each culture must be studied with respect and in relation to its own unique development. These ideas come into American cultural anthropology in a fairly direct fashion (though a century after Herder) through the work of German-born Franz Boas, the "father of American anthropology" (Duden 1989).

Scholars like E. B. Tylor incorporated Herder's focus on popular traditions into the British tradition of social anthropology (Cocchiara 1952:392). Tylor not only contributed to the nascent discipline of anthropology an influential definition of culture but also founded the field of folklore studies in Britain. Although the role played by anthropologists in studying colonial populations and creating racial and ethnic hierarchies has received considerable attention in the last twenty years, the similar involvement of anthropologists in nation-building projects within Europe has been underexplored (Herzfeld 1987). Anthropology proved just as significant to the articulation of ethnic and national differences within Europe as to those distinctions between Europeans and other peoples. Though folklore studies only developed in the late nineteenth century in Great Britain, for example, they blossomed in continental Europe in the second half of the eighteenth century as a result of the researches of Herder and his disciples.

Folklore quickly became wedded to nation- and state-building projects, particularly in the multiethnic Hapsburg Empire. This occurred despite Herder's own rejection of the idea that a people (*volk*) proved synonymous with a state (*staat*) or territory. Herder also denounced *ethnocentrism*, the idea that one people proved superior to another. He did, however, believe in the Slavs' particular mission to regenerate Europe, a theme picked up by intellectuals who identified with their respective Slavic ethnic groups.

Slavic-speaking groups (including Czechs, Slovaks, Poles, Slovenes, Serbs, and Croats) constituted the majority of the peoples dominated by the German-speaking Austrian Hapsburgs. Other sizable populations included Hungarian Magyars and Latin-speaking Italians and Romanians. Vienna, the cosmopolitan capital of this multiethnic empire, became the center for both Slavicist and folklore studies under the Czech scholar Abbé Josif Dobrovski and his student, the Slovene Jernej Kopitar. As subject peoples within the empire began to demand autonomy or independence, the revival of folk traditions underwrote emerging senses of belonging to a nation or people. In most Slavic languages, the word *narod* stands for both "nation" and "people," blurring the distinctions between the two that exist in English and Romance languages. The view that the boundaries of a territorial state must coincide with the *narod* or *volk* (the people or ethnic group)—that is, nation = ethnic group—may have as its extreme consequences the removal of those populations who do not belong to the "national"/ethnic group.

The ambiguities created by this understanding of nation as ethnic group are illustrated by the view of Serbian identity put forward by the folklorist and philologist Vuk Karadžić. Encouraged by Kopitar, Karadžić began in 1814 and 1815 to record the epic folk songs of Serbian peasants, such as those of the Kosovo cycle, detailing the Serbs' legendary defeat by the Ottoman Turks in 1389 on the Field of Blackbirds in Kosovo (Wachtel 1998:32). These traditions had been preserved both by the (Serbian) Orthodox church and the folk singers who recounted the ballads to the accompaniment of the one-stringed instrument known as the *gusle*. In collecting these folk traditions, Karadžić helped codify the Serbian language, publishing a Serbian grammar and dictionary in 1814 and 1818, respectively (p. 26). The Serbian tongue, however, proved similar to other Slavic variants, such as Bulgarian and Croatian. Thus, when Karadžić declared that "Serbia is wherever Serbian is spoken," he included as Serbs those individuals whom others might identify as Bulgarians or Croats. Karadžić's work helped foster a sense of Serbian identity, which both reflected and contributed to the struggle for an independent Serbian state. The Serbs attained complete autonomy within the Ottoman Empire by 1830 and formal independence in 1878.

In roughly the same period, there arose in the Hapsburg lands the South Slav, or Yugoslav (Jugo or Yugo means "south"), movement whose intellectual proponents understood Karadžić's researches in a more inclusive manner. The Yugoslav idea had its origins in the 1830s with the cultural movement known as Illyrianism. Although various understandings of Yugoslavism competed, and some peoples (like the Bulgarians) were at times included or excluded as Yugoslavs, its advocates agreed that a South Slav cultural and linguistic unity existed and should be recognized by a corresponding Yugoslav political unit. Scholars worked to codify a standard language of this cultural expression, Serbo-Croatian (which took the Štokavian dialect as its base). For proponents of Yugoslavism, then, those traditions of epic poetry that Karadžić saw as mapping out a distinctly Serbian nation instead characterized a broader South Slav unity (pp. 38–45). Yugoslavists similarly interpreted lyric poetic forms common to Catholic "Slovenes" and "Croats" as South Slav cultural expressions, whereas for anti-Serbian nationalists like Ante Starcevic and Josip Frank all South Slavic culture (and peoples) were instead "really" Croatian. Politically, these various forms of identity (Serbian, Croatian, Yugoslav) have coexisted for more than a century, at times proving compatible and at other times mutually exclusive, depending on the form of statehood envisioned and the imagined relationship between ethnic identity and nationhood. This example reveals how the same ostensible past and folk tradition can be understood in very different ways. In the course of the recent Yugoslav wars, the insistence that territory and ethnic group coincide culminated in the policy known as "ethnic cleansing," whose tragic results we will examine later.

"Old" and "New" Nations: States before Nations, Nations before States

In considering the historical development of nationalism in what we today call "Eastern" and "Western" Europe, scholars often distinguish between the romantic, *Volkish* nationalism common to the area of the Hapsburg and Ottoman empires (as in the Serbian case) and the liberal, civic nationalism of the type associated with the French Revolution or the Italian Risorgimento (Gellner 1987; Hobsbawm 1990). Sometimes this distinction is rephrased as that of nation understood as ethnicity versus nation as citizenship (Verdery 1993); on this, see also Chapter 4. Other scholars map onto these types of nationalism different understandings of citizenship such as *jus sanguinis*, with belonging based on blood and ethnic group (as in Germany), and *jus soli*, based on common political participation (as in France) (Brubaker 1992). However scholars label the distinction, basically they contrast a "bad" nationalism, which confuses nation and ethnic group, to a "good" (or better) nationalism, which envisions the nation as a political community and hence as something more than an ethnic group.

At the most general level, these distinctions help us delineate the different experiences of nation-state building in Europe. These categories highlight, for example, the challenges faced by national independence movements in the nineteenth century where a sense of belonging to an ethnic or national group often underwrote demands for a state. This contrasts with the experience of the so-called old states and nations, like France and England. Here, political dynasties consolidated and centralized power relatively early. Inhabitants of these polities initially identified themselves as subjects of the Crown more than as French or English (Breuilly 1985:44–82). Over several centuries, centralized institutions like the bureaucracy, educational system, and army served to make "peasants into

Frenchmen" (for France, see Weber 1976; on Britain, Corrigan and Sayer 1985).

Certainly, the long-term process of building national identities in centralized states/monarchies like those of Britain and France contrasts with those national liberation movements, often inspired by the French Revolution, which quite literally had to build states (together with educational systems and militaries) overnight. Yet scholars now recognize that the process of state building in supposedly "old" nations took much longer than previously believed, was always incomplete, and was accompanied by considerable violence (much of it now conveniently forgotten). Furthermore, the assumption that in many parts of Eastern Europe "nation" came before "state" needs to be tempered. Certainly, for *volk*-minded intellectuals like Vuk Karadžić, "nation" did exist before state. There usually exists a significant difference, however, between the sentiments of the well educated and the peasants whose culture the intellectuals codified and then exalted.

Recent historical work also reveals that in cases like those of the Serbian and Greek revolutions, where a sense of nationhood inspired intellectuals in their fight against the Ottoman Empire, considerable time and effort were nonetheless required to build a sense of national identity *after* the achievement of independent states (Herzfeld 1982; Kitromilides 1989). "Serbs" or "Greeks" thus had to be made in a similar manner to "French" or "English," although in considerably less time. This suggests that, while useful in some ways, the distinction between states before nations and nations before states should not be exaggerated. To do so takes the rhetoric of romantic nationalists—that the nation has awoken and must find its expression in a political state—at face value.

Overstating such differences may also lead us to neglect the many similarities between processes of identity formation in both "Eastern" and "Western" Europe, wrongly seeing nationalism in the East as something destructive or violent (at least potentially) in contrast to nationalism in the West. The complicated process of Italian unification illustrates some of the dangers in overdrawing these distinctions. Scholars often describe the Risorgimento, the movement that led to the creation of an Italian state in 1861, as an example of a civic or liberal (i.e., Western-style) nationalism. Unification movements such as that in Italy are typically thought to have put a "political roof over a culture (and over an economy)" (Gellner 1987:99) in a benign manner far removed from the messiness of Central and Eastern Europe, where the lack of a crystallized national culture necessitated brutality in the attempt to render state and nation congruent.

Undeniably, a sense of Italianness did exist among intellectuals, despite the Italian peninsula's political division. The metaphor of a resurgence or reawakening implied by the term *Risorgimento* and the battle cry "Italy, awake!" reflected the deeply romantic impulse of much Italian nationalism (particularly in the thoughts of Giuseppe Mazzini and Giuseppe Garibaldi). This contrasted, however, with the reality of widespread linguistic diversity and extremely localized identities. Indeed, after the Italian state's establishment as a constitutional monarchy, its leaders recognized the necessity to "make Italians."

Although Italy has often been deemed an ethnically homogeneous state (at least until recent immigration), in fact there were ethnically different "others" (in addition to the division between northern and southern Italians, which in everyday life is often posited as a racial difference) who posed a problem to the project of "making Italians." The 1866 war between Austria and Italy, which brought the provinces of Veneto and Friuli into the new Italian state, for example, also incorporated a sizable population of Slovenes located in the Valli di Natisone. Many of these Slovenes assumed that the new Italian state would extend to them the same administrative, judicial, and linguistic "autonomy" they had once enjoyed under the Venetian Republic (Clavora and Ruttar 1990:13). This expectation soon proved mistaken, however, as the Italian state undertook a deliberate policy of Italianization.

An 1866 newspaper article outlined this policy: "These Slavs need to be eliminated, by means of benefits, progress and civility. We will adopt the language and culture of a dominant civilization, that of Italian civilization, in order to Italianize the Slavs in Italy" (cf. Clavora 1988:7). In the twentieth century, the Fascist regime continued and intensified such policies, which were bound up with Italian desires for coastal territories inhabited by Slovenes and Croats. In Italian frontier areas, anti-Slav chauvinism proved strong, and still does today, in border cities like Trieste. Such chauvinism speaks a language of both ethnicity and race, as suggested by an 1884 article in a Triestine newspaper. Entitled "A Microbe," the article compared the Slovenes to a "barbaric" African people, the Hottentots.

Such comments, together with the experience of minorities like the Slovenes, points up what might be called the myth of Italy's lack of racism (examined in the next section), as well as the often idealized image of Italy's benign process of state formation. Though we should not go too far in the other direction in viewing Italian unification as particularly brutal, we should be aware that the processes of nation and state building in "Western" and "Eastern" Europe are not as different or unrelated as scholars have sometimes made them out to be. Indeed, contrasting Western nationalisms to Eastern nationalisms represents one means by which negative images of Eastern Europe (and Eastern European ethnic groups) are perpetuated. As we shall see in the final section, currently such images work to exclude some East European peoples from the very definition of "European."

In understanding ethnic and racial identities in Europe, the distinction between old and new nationalisms proves somewhat more helpful than does that between Western and Eastern nationalisms. Not only did states like France and England have more time in which to build national identities out of diverse ethnic and regional identifications than did those like Italy or Serbia, these long-standing states developed a sense of nationhood in tandem with colonial empires. In contrast, newer nation-states like Italy and Serbia were formed *out of* imperial structures. Yet, as nineteenth-century European national-imperial discourses developed in tandem with bourgeois notions of respectability and normality, the imperial experience shaped interrelated identities—those of ethnicity, race, nationality, and gender—within *and between* the European metropole and colony, as well as between the European core and its internal peripheries. Racial classifications based on supposed signs of deviance (such as certain skull shapes or noses) reveal a direct link between how internal European "others"—including Jews, Gypsies, prostitutes, and homosexuals—and colonial subjects were differentiated by means of a shared vocabulary of criminality and medical hygiene (Gilman 1985; Mosse 1985). This racialized language of "otherness," derived in part from the colonial experience, proves central to the discourses and practices of nationalism, even in those European countries like Italy and Germany that achieved statehood late and lacked significant empires. The next section explores the interpenetration of racial, national, and militaristic ideologies for German Nazism and Italian Fascism.

NATIONALISM AND AUTHORITARIAN REGIMES IN TWENTIETH-CENTURY EUROPE: THE CULMINATION OF NATIONALISM AND RACE?

Nazism and Fascism

Scholars continue to debate the origins of National Socialism and Italian Fascism, the differences between the regimes's racial policies, and the degree of consensus obtained by the regimes among "everyday" Germans and Italians, respectively. The "final solution," Hitler's systematic campaign to exterminate the Jews, understandably provokes the most heated discussion. In a recent and controversial book, Daniel Goldhagen has argued that the Germans' deep tradition of anti-Semitism made them "Hitler's willing executioners" (1996). Picking up on Hannah Arendt's well-known thesis regarding the "banality of evil," Christopher Browning has instead suggested that the supposedly deeply anti-Semitic, willing executioners who actually carried out massacres of Jews were merely "ordinary men" (1992). Such a view reminds us that the potential for genocide cannot be neatly circumscribed to a particular time, place, or culture (like Hitler's Germany).

In questioning pervasive claims that Germans were culturally predispositioned (by anti-Semitism, authoritarian cultures/personalities, and so on) toward genocide, other historians have countered that anti-Semitism proved pervasive in much of Europe and perhaps was strongest in France rather than Germany. Certainly, the negative associations of Jews with rootless cosmopolitanism, capitalism, and effete decadence had currency throughout much of Europe. The nineteenth-century Italian criminologist Cesare Lombroso even claimed to see in Jewish physiognomies signs of an innate criminality or illness (Gilman 1985:154–157; Mosse 1985:133–147).

Although we cannot hope to definitively answer here the question of the origins of the "final solution" or the degree of complicity of ordinary Germans in the Holocaust of the Jews, we can pin down the official ideology of Nazism within which this particular genocide unfolded. Hitler conceived of National Socialism as an anti-Bolshevik revolution. He created a ritual state based on spectacles that invoked Teutonic pagan glories, as with the famous rally at Nürnberg, and ceremonies like the German Harvest Festival and German Summer Solstice. Despite the Nazis' hatred of Jews, the regime proved ambivalent (and at times even hostile) to Christian traditions and sought to reinterpret the meanings attached to Christian holidays like Christmas. Regime folklorists argued that, historically, ethnically German festivals had been Christianized; accordingly, "German" folktales and songs were trotted out to replace Christian ones (Gajek 1990). The regime thus represented this pagan past as a thoroughly German one, a German ethnic or national identity here understood in racial terms as synonymous with "Aryan." Other citizens of the German state, like those who self-identified (or were identified by others) in cultural or religious terms as "Jews," were excluded from this ethnic/racial understanding of German.

As part of their program to instill "German pride" after the nation's humiliating defeat in World War I and the economic chaos of the postwar Weimar Republic, Adolf Hitler and other Nazi leaders codified an elaborate racial hierarchy. At its apex were Aryans, at its bottom Jews. Other "deviant" groups included Gypsies (Roma), homosexuals, and Slavic peoples (the so-called "slave races"). The Nazis thus read various ethnic, cultural, religious, and sexual differences as "racial," that is, inherently rooted in biology. The obsessive fear of homosexuality's contamination of the German "race" led to a purge of the SA (storm) troops in 1934 and the murder of its chief, Ernst Röhm; to prevent the military cult of masculinity from degenerating into male-male sex, soldiers were encouraged to seek out female prostitutes (Mosse 1985:157). Aryan women were, in turn, enjoined to produce children and thereby contribute to a healthy (and superior) *volk*, or people, what one scholar has deemed a "racist sexism" (Bock 1984:288).

This racial and sexual hierarchy informed the Nazi policy of negative eugenics, begun as a program of forced sterilization of those individuals with "undesirable" genes: the physically and mentally disabled.[1] Preventing "asocial" and undesirable elements from reproducing constituted the flip side of "racist sexism," that is, "sexist racism" or the prohibition of procreation by racially inferior women (Bock 1984.) The Nazis soon extended their eugenic policies to the Jews. By the time of World War II, Jewish and Gypsy women in Nazi concentration camps were subject to mass sterilizations. The Nazis also forced many women in the conquered eastern territories to submit to sterilization and/or abortions (Bock 1984).

As the preeminent "other," the Jews became subject to discrimination and violence from almost the moment Hitler assumed power as German chancellor in 1933. Pogroms, expropriations, and laws stripped German Jews of their property and rights. The 1935 Nürnberg laws denied German Jews citizenship and forbad intermarriage with "Germans." Any possible contamination by Jews had to be cleansed; the Nazis went so far as to condemn avant-garde art as degenerate due to its association with cosmopolitanism and the "mad" genius of the artist and hence with Jewishness (Gilman 1985: 233–237). The infamous "Night of the Broken Glass," or *Kristallnacht*, in 1938 made clear the Nazis' determination to destroy all remnants of Jewish life in Germany; on this one night, Nazi supporters vandalized or destroyed Jewish synagogues, homes, and shops. In the years following *Kristallnacht*, Jews were forced to wear the Star of David as an identifying mark. Hitler announced as his goal the physical removal of Germany's Jewish population and, through psychological and physical intimidation, "encouraged" Jews to emigrate.

From 1936 on, a four-year-plan detailed a plan of increasing "living space" (*Lebensraum*) through conquest of territories to the east. Initially, the lands targeted were those with a sizable German-speaking population, which provided the pretext for "unification" with the German motherland. After 1939, the German master race (*Herrenvolk*) turned its attention to neighboring Slavic lands. This program of war and territorial expansion facilitated the Nazi plan of ridding Germany and, later, the occupied territories of their Jewish populations. Jews were confined to restricted areas (ghettos) or concentration camps where they often died of exhaustion, hunger, or disease. In the territories conquered by the Nazis, SS death squads massacred entire villages of Jews.

At the Wannsee Conference of 1942, Nazi leaders, including SS (black shirts) head Reinhard Heydrich, drew up plans for the "final solution" of the "Jewish question." Jewish populations from Nazi-occupied areas throughout Europe were transported to concentration camps in the eastern lands of the Reich. In death camps like Auschwitz and Treblinka, specifically designed to exterminate Jews, Nazis carried out their policies with bureaucratic efficiency. Methods of murder included mass shootings and gassings in chambers disguised as showers. Some scholars have seen in the gas chambers the literal culmination of the Nazi obsession with (racial) hygiene. After the Allies liberated survivors of the concentration camps, the horrors of the Holocaust were condemned, and a number of Nazi war criminals put on trial at Nürnberg.

How have German and Jewish identities been understood in the post-Nazi era? The Nazis' crimes largely discredited expressions of nationalism and racism in Germany, although the country's cold war division into two states (West Germany and the socialist German Democratic Republic) prompted different responses to the Nazi past (Herf 1997). After an initial silence and a desire to return to "normality," a younger generation of West Germans began to critically explore the Nazi past. In particular, this examination focused on the genocide of the Jews, German responsibility, and the admonition to "never forget." The dominance of the Holocaust narrative in West Germany to some extent mirrors forms of identity expressed by many Jews of European origin (including those who resettled in Israel or the United States). Increasingly, many Jews understand the Holocaust as the central Jewish experience, sometimes to the neglect of other aspects of Jewish history (Young 1988:187).

In socialist East Germany, by contrast, the historiography of the war interpreted Nazism as a form of monopolistic capitalism (the merging of big business with the military industrial complex) whose victims included working-class organizations, Slavic peoples, and Jews. In this reading, the Holocaust of approximately 6 million Jews represented one piece of the larger picture of Nazi crimes but not necessarily the dominant or defining aspect of Nazism. The issue of the Holocaust's centrality to the German experience and to what degree and in what ways it should define contemporary German identity remains a source of debate among Germans, particularly after West and East Germans were reunited in a single state in 1990. The appearance of neo-Nazi groups and violence against "immigrants," particularly in the eastern parts of Germany, suggest that the process of (re)defining German national identity proves fraught with difficulties. Despite recent changes in laws that permit some nonethnic Germans to acquire citizenship, German identity remains understood primarily in terms of blood and ethnicity.

Whereas the Nazi obsession with race (and the blurring of categories of religious and ethnic identity with those of race) proves well known, the story of the contemporary Italian Fascist regime and its understandings of nation and race has received less attention. All too often, scholars use the label Fascism or totalitarianism but then look only at the experience of German National Socialism. Rightly criticizing this tendency, in the 1970s one of the premier historians of Fascism argued for a sharp differentiation between Italian Fascism and German Nazism (De Felice 1976). According to this influential interpretation, Italian Fascism differed from Nazism in a key way: Italy lacked a racist tradition. Anti-Semitic policies were said to have

come about only as a late result of the unequal partnership between Mussolini and Hitler, with the Germans imposing racial laws on the Italians.

That significant numbers of Italians defied the 1938 racial laws by sheltering and helping Jews is well documented and confirms the thesis of the different receptions in Germany and Italy of anti-Semitic measures. An estimated 85 percent of Italy's Jewish population survived the Holocaust, making Italy one of the occupied countries with the highest survival rates of Jews (Zuccotti 1987:272). Italian efforts to rescue Jews within Italy and beyond have rightly been lauded as "something unique in the annals of the Holocaust" (Shelah 1989:205; see also Steinberg 1990).

The insistence on Italians' lack of anti-Semitism, however, glosses over the Italian interest in race well before alliance with Germany. Not only did some Italians wholeheartedly embrace anti-Semitism (Stille 1991), but other forms of racism existed, as evidenced by pro-natalist (literally, pro-birth) concerns with reproducing the nation and expressions of racial superiority over and violence toward Italy's colonial populations in Africa and the Balkans.

As occurred in Nazi Germany, the Italian Fascist regime took an obsessive interest in the health and reproduction of the Italian people (particularly in light of declining birth rates in northern Italy). Fascist leader Benito Mussolini's 1927 Ascension Day speech launched a series of demographic campaigns to increase the Italian population (what Mussolini phrased in militaristic terms as the "battle for the births"). A language of hygiene linked what Ferdinando Loffredo, a Catholic fundamentalist and prominent proponent of a racist totalitarianism, deemed "a politics of family and a politics of race" (in *Difesa della Razza*, November 20, 1939). Far from merely imitating German ideas and policies, this demographic policy possessed deep roots in Roman Catholicism and the Italian social sciences. These policies also proved part and parcel of the regime's expansionist aims in Africa and the Balkans prior to World War II. The 1935 Italian conquest of Ethiopia (together with the colonization of Somaliland, Libya, and Albania), for example, raised concerns over miscegenation (racial mixing) and prompted laws forbidding intercourse (social and otherwise) between Italians and Africans.

Italian colonialism was also driven by the desire to stem massive Italian emigration to the Americas by providing land to "settler colonists." Unlike Nazism, where negative eugenics culminated in the medical experiments and scientized mass death of the concentration camps, the Italian regime made sheer numbers the measure of demographic strength (sometimes deemed "euthenics"). This reflected the fact that sterilization, birth control, and other techniques for preventing undesirables from reproducing could not be reconciled with Catholic tenets. In keeping with Catholic beliefs, the regime outlawed abortion and birth control while simultaneously increasing social welfare legislation. In contrast to the almost total control enjoyed in Germany by Hitler after 1938, the Italian Fascist regime needed the support of the Church, although the relationship between the two often proved ambivalent. Despite the regime's sometimes conciliatory stance toward the Church, the two came into conflict over specific issues like education (Koon 1981) and more generally over the regime's attempts to collapse the public and private spheres.

Pointing up the understandings of race and nation that came to the fore during the Fascist regime does not imply that we should now view Italian Fascism just like Nazism where it was once seen as relatively benign in comparison to its German counterpart. The differences between German Nazism and Italian Fascism are significant and should not be overlooked, especially since the prevailing understandings of race, ethnicity, and nation did not prove identical in each case. Furthermore, the response by everyday people to the respective regimes' categories of identity and policies proved distinct; Germany lacked the kind of large-scale resistance movement, for example, found in northern Italy from 1943 on. Having said this, however, it proves important to go beyond clichés about the insignificance of race to Italian Fascism and instead to see exactly what types of understandings—of gender, family, race, and national identity—operated during the twenty years (1922–43) in which the Fascists held power.

Doing this proves particularly important for examining identity in contemporary Italy. The pervasive self-image of Italians as "good people" (*brava gente*)—which rests on an interpretation of Fascism as relatively benign—shapes current Italian responses to immigration. In the final section of this chapter, we examine the issue of "new racisms" in a Europe coping with large-scale immigration.

Socialist Multiethnic Experiments

In contrast to German National Socialism and Italian Fascism, where returning the nation or the people to greatness proved an explicit and fundamental goal, communist states in Europe organized themselves according to the principle of international working-class solidarity. Marxist theory predicted that the realization of a socialist state would overcome the pernicious ideologies of race, ethnicity, and nation that had in the past served the bourgeoisie in manipulating the working classes. According to this line of thinking, members of the working class had been duped into identifying on narrow ethnic or national lines (a "false consciousness"); this prevented workers from seeing their "true" solidarity with other members of the proletariat in other countries. Although various Marxist positions on nationalism existed,[2] in the period before World War I many communist intellectuals did not take seriously enough the enduring strength of nationalist feeling.

In laying the groundwork for the first communist state, achieved in Russia in 1917 with the

Bolshevik Revolution, Vladimir Ilich Lenin did address himself to the troubling nationalities question. Lenin's theoretical writings reflected pragmatic concerns: not only had nationalism hampered previous attempts at working-class revolution, but the Bolsheviks had assumed control of a multiethnic Russian Empire. As Lenin put it, "Russia is a state with a single national center—Great Russia. . . . The specific features of this national state are, firstly, that 'alien races' (which, on the whole, comprise the majority of the population—57 per-cent) inhabit the border regions" (1951:29).

Lenin treated the problem of nationalism together with colonialism, discussing both in terms of self-determination. United States President Woodrow Wilson had enshrined the principle of self-determination, the idea that each national group had the right to its own state, in his Fourteen Points at the Versailles Conference at the end of World War I. As a socialist solution to the issue of self-determination, Lenin promised, "Complete equality for all nations; the right of nations to self-determination; the amalgamation of the workers of all nations—this is the national program that Marxism, the experience of the whole world and the experience of Russia, teaches the workers" (p. 110).

At the same time, Lenin laid out a pragmatic three-pronged political strategy. He argued that prior to assuming power in a particular state, communist parties needed to promise all national groups the right to self-determination (i.e., to secede) and guarantee rights of national equality to those who chose to remain within the state. After obtaining power, the communists would then terminate the right to national secession. In its place, the party would either offer territorial autonomy to compact national groups or assimilate other ethnic and national groups. Finally, Lenin sustained that the party itself should be kept above any national interests (Connor 1984:36). Lenin's different statements point to the fact that under state socialism, the relationship between nationalism/national minorities and communism was one thing in theory but another in practice (refer also to Chapter 4).

If anything, the Marxist-Leninist regime in the USSR institutionalized, rather than abolished, the national question. At the official level, for example, Soviet passports listed the holder's ethnic/national identity, and average Soviet citizens were acutely aware of their neighbors' ethnic affiliation. At a more popular level, ethnic jokes were one means by which group distinctions became known. Such cultural markers included way of dress, codes of morality, physical appearance, and language. Initially, the Soviet regime had promoted plurilingualism; the reality of a central "Russian" state, however, facilitated linguistic assimilation by non-Russian-speaking peoples. After 1938, Stalin reversed these more open linguistic policies and required Russian in schools throughout the Soviet Union. Only in 1959 did schooling in native languages again become possible (Connor 1984:256), although Russian remained the lingua franca until the demise of the USSR. As we have seen, a vocabulary of ethnicity and nation also remained a common language, together with that of communism. This helps explain why between 1989 and 1991 nationalist movements emerged so quickly after the fall of state socialism in both the USSR and in the Soviet-dominated states in the East European bloc.

Those European states that adopted socialist governments after World War II under the "tutelage" of the Soviet Union often followed the Soviet model in addressing the national question. As the Yugoslav and Romanian examples demonstrate, national sentiment by no means disappeared under socialism but rather was harnessed to Marxist-Leninist ideology. In both these cases as well, initial support for the Soviet Union gave way to resistance and explicitly national-based forms of socialism.

The Yugoslav state formed after World War II by Marshal Josip Broz ("Tito") was initially modeled on the Soviet federation. By the eve of the 1941 Axis invasion, the first Yugoslav state—

a Serb-dominated monarchy formed in 1918–had virtually collapsed due to Serb-Croat disagreements. When Tito and his communist partisans emerged as the victors from the bloody civil war carried out within occupied Yugoslavia, they built a socialist federation composed of constituent republics with the legal (albeit fictive) right to secede. In reality, the central party exercised tight control. Following the Stalinist model, Tito also sought to collectivize agriculture and institute a five-year economic plan.

Within three years after the war's end, however, Stalin and Tito had fallen out over a number of issues, notably Tito's pursuit of an independent ("nationally" minded) foreign policy. Against Stalin's wishes, Tito pressed Yugoslav territorial claims to Trieste and Istria (formerly Italian), sought a Yugoslav-Albanian federation, and gave support to the communist side in the Greek civil war. When in 1948 Stalin expelled Tito and the Yugoslav communist party from the international association of socialist states (the cominform), he expected Tito's base of support to collapse immediately. Although the reasons for Tito's political survival are multiple, one primary factor lay in Tito's ability to appeal to a supra-national Yugoslav sentiment in opposition to the Soviet Union. With the help of party leaders like Edvard Kardelj, Tito made a virtue out of necessity and articulated a "Third Way" of socialism, that of the Yugoslavs. The threat (real or imagined) of invasion by the Soviet Union helped foster a sense of defending socialist Yugoslavia, which in contrast to Soviet-imposed regimes had been built with genuine popular support.

As Yugoslavia pursued its own "nonaligned" path independent of both the Soviet Union and the United States, the sense of being a "Yugoslav" with respect to an external threat coexisted with ethnic and national distinctions such as Serb, Croat, Slovene, Macedonian, and (Bosnian) Muslim. Over time, Tito developed an elaborate system, known as the "ethnic key," for apportioning positions to members of various ethnic groups. In doing this, Tito sought to avoid any one ethnic group from dominating the federation, as had occurred in the first Yugoslavia. Identities such as "Macedonian" and "Muslim" were officially recognized as national ones for the first time (in 1945 and 1971, respectively) in order to further balance long-standing Serb-Croat tensions.

This ethnic key in no way abolished ethnic or national sentiments but rather kept them firmly in place. The new constitutions introduced in 1963 and 1974, respectively, moved Yugoslavia toward a decentralized model, giving greater power to the "national" republics (Slovenia, Croatia, Bosnia-Herzegovina, Serbia, Montenegro, and Macedonia). As we shall see in the section devoted to Bosnia, when political and economic conditions changed in the 1980s, nationalist leaders would skillfully manipulate these preexisting forms of identity. In doing so, they helped to destroy Tito's multiethnic, socialist state.

The Romanian mix of socialist and nationalist ideologies shares certain parallels with the Yugoslav case, even though the map of ethnic relations in Romania differed dramatically. In contrast to Yugoslavia, where no one ethnic group made up an absolute majority, Latin-speaking Romanians constituted the ethnic majority in Romania. (Romanian scholars have long argued, however, as to whether contemporary Romanians descend from the original inhabitants, known as Dacians, the subsequent Roman conquerors, or some combination of the two groups.) In the border region of Transylvania, there also exists a sizable population identifying as ethnically Hungarian (and, until the end of World War II, many ethnic Germans). In the postsocialist era, tensions have periodically flared between Romania and Hungary over Transylvania.

Though Romania lacks the extreme ethnic complexity that characterized socialist Yugoslavia, in both places a language of nation informed that of socialism. Anthropologist

Katherine Verdery (1991) has illuminated the important role played by "national ideology under socialism" in Romania. Romania's strongman communist leader, Nikolae Ceaucescu, embraced this national vocabulary in the 1960s and 1970s in the process of distancing Romania from its Soviet master.

At the end of World War II, Romania possessed only a small communist party organization; the eventual triumph of communism in Romania depended directly on Soviet support. As a consequence, Soviet leaders expected Romanians to specialize in those items (agricultural and consumer goods) that suited Soviet needs. In 1964, General Secretary Ceaucescu made what amounted to a "declaration of independence," demanding that the Soviet Union respect the state sovereignty of the bloc members. Ceaucescu thus took up a language of nation that appeared to resonate with average Romanians more than the "foreign" Marxist-Leninism imported from the Soviet Union (Verdery 1991:103–105).

Intellectuals and artists elaborated this "national" language. Although competing schools and interpretations arose in fields like history, they all shared a common conceptual vocabulary centered around nationhood. This vocabulary focused on traditions and ancestors, thereby emphasizing relations of kinship into which the socialist state increasingly intervened. Verdery has called the quasi-familial forms of dependency created between the socialist state and its subjects *socialist paternalism* (1993:39; 1996:61–82). Unlike with other forms of nationalism where a sense of kinship and community generates solidarity, socialist paternalism explicitly operated to create dependency and hierarchy.

Key to this relationship, which made citizens like needy children, were gendered images that represented the state and party like patriarchal family heads (i.e., as fathers). In a manner similar to that of Nazi Germany and Fascist Italy, the Romanian state glorified the role of women as "mothers of the nation," outlawing abortion as an attack on the nation itself (Kligman 1998; Verdery 1996:61–82). The nation's heroes consisted of those virile workers and soldiers ready to sacrifice themselves for the (female) nation. This rhetoric became widespread, despite the increased presence of women in the workplace and the feminization of certain fields, like agriculture. The prominent role of women in "traditional" ways of life like peasant agriculture only furthered the image of women as the bearers (literal and figurative) of national tradition, that is, that of the folk (Kligman 1988).

The work of Verdery and other anthropologists helps us make sense of the ongoing transformations of ethnic and national identities in European postsocialist societies like Romania and the former Soviet Union. Their research demonstrates that, contrary to one popular belief, communism did not put a lid on ethnic and national sentiments which then "boiled over" or erupted after the fall of socialism. Rather, understandings of ethnicity and nation coexisted with these socialist regimes. Ironically, the socialist regimes that sought to use these languages ultimately failed to control them. Verdery suggests that in Romania, the socialist state's opponents ultimately turned the language of nation against it. In places like Poland, a sense of religion (Catholicism) strongly tied to a sense of national identity fueled opposition to the Soviet-backed regime. With the demise of that Soviet regime and the socialist bloc, we are now witnessing the sometimes violent transformations of such ethnic and national sentiments.

THE RESURGENCE OF ETHNICITY

After the horrors of World War II, both nationalism and "scientific racism" were roundly condemned in Europe. With the cold war division of Europe (and the world) into ideologically opposed capitalist and communist blocs, many scholars predicted the declining importance of ethnic and national sentiment in Europe. The creation of a West European common economic structure or market with the explicit aim of preventing future conflicts among European nation-states buoyed such optimism. In addition to those Marxist thinkers who predicted the triumph of class identifications over ethnonational ones, many other observers thought that only in the developing world did narrow ethnic or "tribal" divisions still hold sway.

In the 1960s, however, it was precisely in those "old" European states with supposedly well-consolidated national identities where regionally and linguistically based ethnic identifications emerged as political movements. In France, a movement of Breton-speakers from the northern region of Brittany put into question the success with which Frenchmen had been "made." Similarly, in the United Kingdom there emerged Scottish and Welsh ethnonational movements that criticized England's "suppression" of minority cultures.

The political language used by these minority or regional movements directly drew upon the independence struggles waged by the peoples in Europe's overseas colonies. The Bretons, for example, contended that they had been underdeveloped and exploited in a manner similar to that of the Algerians, who in 1963 had waged a hard-fought war for independence from the French. In line with this, scholars began to talk about processes of "internal colonialism" and underdevelopment (Hechter 1975; Nairn 1977). Many of these scholars worked from a political economy framework, seeking to address Marxist theory's former blind spot for nationalism.

According to the "internal colonialism" interpretation, European nation-states came into being in part as a result of the periphery's exploitation by the center. This exploitation occurred overseas (the European center extracting resources from the colonies) and at "home" in parallel and interrelated processes with similar results: cultural and economic impoverishment of the periphery. Admittedly, some scholars questioned the appropriateness of this analogy for understanding the regional ethnicities emerging in places like France (McDonald 1986) or the United Kingdom; Scotland, for example, did not represent a classic case of economic underdevelopment but rather a well-developed region within a less developed hinterland (Nairn 1977:203). Nonetheless, the idea of internal colonization proved politically useful in fostering a sense of identity within these "new" ethnic movements.

Breton activists, for instance, identified the educational system as a key means by which linguistic "colonization" and "cultural genocide" had been accomplished at home (McDonald 1989:86, 190). Although language represented the key marker of Breton identity, aspects like kinship and ancestry also lent this form of ethnicity a quasi-biological sense (p. 120; see also McDonald 1986). Bretons defined themselves ethnically as Celts, in contrast to the Latin French, and made common cause with other oppressed Celtic minorities, like the Welsh. Folkloric traditions such as dances and festivals became key to expressions of this pan-Celtic identity, as well as a more specific Breton one.

As the Breton example suggests, the ethnic identifications that (re)emerged in Europe in the 1960s and 1970s often drew upon nineteenth-century understandings of a *volk*, or people, as nation. Although Herder focused on shared culture rather than shared biology when he used the term *volk*, others who took up the idea often blurred the lines between race, ethnicity, and nation. In the 1960s and 1970s, the term *ethnic group* assumed many of the quasi-biological meanings associated with the now unpopular terms *race* and *tribe*. Although scholars recognized that ethnicity followed out of shared culture and a shared sense of descent rather than actual biological continuity, in practice "ethnic group" often came to imply a population linked together in some biological fashion (Just 1989). Increasingly, the concept of culture itself has taken over some of these old associations, at times appearing as inescapable as one's genetic makeup.

RELIGION, ETHNICITY, AND NATIONAL IDENTITY

Just as many social scientists expected ethnic distinctions to weaken or even disappear in Europe, they also predicted the decline of religious identifications. Almost every one of the classical social theorists—from Karl Marx to Max Weber to Emile Durkheim—expected religion to give way to a secular (communist, "disenchanted," scientific) worldview. At the same time when "new ethnicities" emerged in Europe in the 1960s and 1970s, however, there arose what scholars labeled "new religions," reflecting interest in alternative forms of spirituality. These beliefs often intersect with new kinds of identities, such as feminism and environmentalism, that complicate older distinctions based on class, ethnicity, and national identity.

Although individuals attracted to these "new" faiths expressed dissatisfaction with traditional churches, religious identifications with Catholicism, Orthodox Christianity, Judaism, various Protestant sects, and Islam nonetheless continue to have significance for many contemporary Europeans. In some instances, ethnic and national identities largely coincide with religious identities. In places like Yugoslavia and Northern Ireland, long-standing ethnic-religious identities acquired new salience in the 1960s, the same period that political movements centered around the new ethnicities made their presence felt in Europe. In Bosnia, for example, the ethnic and national identifications of Serb and Croat have long been associated with Orthodox and Catholic religious identities, respectively. Beginning in the 1960s, the Yugoslav state also recognized "Muslim" as an official ethnic grouping, regardless of individuals' actual religious observances. In Northern Ireland, the late 1960s and the organization of a Catholic civil rights move-

ment signaled the beginning of the period known as "the Troubles."

The Bosnian and Irish cases reflect the enduring legacies of empire within Europe, as well as the dilemmas inherent in the building of "modern" nation-states. In both instances, religious identities have intersected social, economic, and political ones, in sometimes violent ways. To some degree, these contemporary "religious wars" have roots in the religious conflicts (Christianity versus Islam, Catholic versus Protestant) that divided early modern Europe at the same time that this violence proves thoroughly modern in its form and content.

Northern Ireland

In explaining violent conflict in Northern Ireland, a body of recent scholarship de-emphasizes its religious dimensions in favor of economic and political explanations that stress Ireland's role as Britain's "first" and oldest colony (see the discussions in Feldman 1991:19; Galliher and DeGregory 1985:53; Miller 1998). The popularity of the socioeconomic interpretation may reflect the declining significance accorded to religion in much classic social theory and hence that theory's difficulty in explaining the Northern Irish paradox: the coexistence of industrialization, advanced capitalist development, and high levels of participation in traditional religious practices (Fulton 1991:5). This paradox reflects the peculiarities of Anglo-Protestant colonization of Ireland, which ultimately created a series of nested cores and peripheries.

For much of the modern period, the northern part of the island generally possessed a more industrialized economy than the agrarian south; furthermore, within Northern Ireland, an agrarian area surrounded an industrialized core centered on the city of Belfast. The politically and economically dominant Protestants reinforced their status by restricting access to jobs in industry. Material deprivations, together with political disenfranchisement, facilitated the eventual alignment of Catholicism with Irish nationalism. Conflicts over identity in contemporary Northern Ireland thus reflect the ways in which the politics of religion historically unfolded within the context of industrialization and national "revival." Ireland's uneven economic development, which became mapped onto ethnic and religious distinctions, followed out of the island's colonization. This colonial past, and the settlers it left behind, continue to shape contemporary structures of power and group relations, as well as collective memories and myths.

The colonization of Ireland has its distant roots in the twelfth century, at which time Normans from England and France invaded the island, whose population had been overwhelmingly Gaelic (Celtic). Ireland's formal colonization occurred in the late sixteenth and seventeenth centuries, with the emigration of significant numbers of Scot and English settlers to the six counties of Ulster (in the northern part of Ireland), a policy encouraged by the English monarchs Elizabeth I and James I. These policies failed, however, in their aim of creating "Irish" loyalty to an English Crown, which now differed from its Irish subjects not just in ethnic or national terms but also in religious ones, following Henry VIII's break with the Catholic church and the establishment of the Protestant Anglican church. Abandoning efforts to create loyalty, English monarchs subsequently oversaw a campaign (the "plantation policy") in which Protestant settlers received land confiscated from Catholic landholders. By the second half of the seventeenth century, Catholic-owned lands had declined from three-fifths to one-fifth of all land in Ireland (Fulton 1991:27). The defeat of the Catholic King James II, who sought to reverse these policies, by the Protestant William of Orange (husband of James II's daughter, Mary) further reduced Catholic landownership in Ireland to a mere one-seventh of all landholding by 1707 (p. 33).

During the final decades of the eighteenth century, the battle lines between "Catholic" and "Protestant" identities in Ireland hardened. This followed out of both economic and political developments. In the northern part of the island, there emerged a prosperous commercial class made up of drapers, bleachers, and bankers. This class laid the foundations for industrialization in the nineteenth century, which would widen the economic gap between the more prosperous north and the impoverished agrarian south. Ethnic Scottish and English settlers, many of them subscribing to Calvinism (a Protestant sect), largely composed this commercial elite. The traditional landholding elite instead generally self-identified as English and belonged to the Protestant Church of Ireland.

Political events at the end of the 1700s muted any potential solidarities between the ethnically and religiously diverse components of the lower classes. By the end of the 1770s, a Protestant militia unit known as "the Volunteers" formed to resist the "Catholic threat." The Protestant-controlled parliament (relatively independent from England since 1782) sanctioned these Protestant volunteers, as well as stridently Protestant associations like the "Orange Boys," formed by James Wilson in 1793 (pp. 41–49). In response, some Catholics became militiamen known as "the Defenders." Together with the political movement the United Irishmen, the Defenders led a failed insurrection in 1798. As a result, the 1800 Act of Union restored direct English control over Irish affairs.

The nineteenth century witnessed the growing development of an Irish nationalist movement that variously demanded "home rule," or independence from Britain, and a Protestant religious revival. The growth of Irish nationalism reflected a cultural "renaissance," sometimes referred to as the "Celtic twilight." This entailed the intellectual "discovery" of the folk common to romantic movements, with particular emphasis on the linguistic revival of Gaelic and the search for cultural expressions (old and new) such as Gaelic songs and poetry. The Protestant revival embraced diverse Protestant sects and stressed enthusiastic practices such as "spirit possession" (p. 60); these understandings reflected Protestant beliefs in a direct, unmediated relationship with God and thus highlighted fundamental doctrinal differences between Catholics and Protestants. Some Irish Protestants not only saw Catholics as belonging to a different religious or cultural tradition, however, but even a different race. As Charles Darwin's ideas about biological evolution gained popularity, images of the "wild" or savage Irish often depicted them as apelike; as members of a supposedly lesser breed, the Irish were associated with criminality, sloth, and drunkenness (Curtis 1971). These racist views of the Irish were not restricted to Northern Ireland or Great Britain but also circulated widely in North America, where many Protestant-Anglos looked with disdain upon Irish Catholic immigrants (see Chapter 6).

Racialized depictions of the Irish "Paddy" became prominent in newspaper cartoons as debates over home rule unfolded in the last two decades of the nineteenth century. As pressure for some form of home rule grew, particularly under the Liberal English Prime Minister W. E. Gladstone (who in 1886 introduced the first home rule bill in Parliament), Irish Protestants prepared to resist any change that would make them a minority in an Irish Catholic state. Orangeism, dedicated to preserving Protestant ascendancy and the Irish-British Union, became a mass movement. In 1914, the home rule bill finally passed. Although a special act excepted the six counties of Ulster from home rule for a period of six years, Ireland appeared to be on the brink of a civil war.

Only the beginning of the Great War and the postponement of home rule delayed the civil conflict for which Protestant paramilitary groups—many of whose members had sworn the Solemn League and Covenant to defend the Union—had been preparing. In 1913, a group of Catholics formed the Irish Volunteers in order to forcibly prevent a possible secession by Ulster unionists. During the World War, Protestants and Catholics alike loyally defended Britain. A faction of the Irish Volunteers, however, refused to serve what they saw as the interests of an oppressive empire. Led by the poet Padraic Pearse and Tom Clarke, a small group of the Volunteers (forming the Irish Republican Brotherhood) participated in the Easter Rebellion of 1916.

Pearse and his nationalist supporters seized the Dublin post office in what was supposed to be the beginning of a country-wide revolt. Many Irish families had a son or loved one serving in the British imperial forces, however, and Pearse's call for revolution against the colonial oppressor found little support. British forces quickly crushed the uprising, court-martialing and executing 14 of its leaders. The brutal British response ultimately galvanized Irish nationalist sentiment, and Pearse and his fellow conspirators became widely recognized as martyrs to the Irish cause. This may have been Pearse's intent; realizing the lack of widespread support for such a rebellion, he might have desired to make a "blood sacrifice" that would ultimately regenerate and liberate the nation. Pearse drew heavily on Catholic imagery, envisioning himself as a crucified Christ whose sacrifice would redeem the Irish nation (Hughes 1994:39–41).

At the conclusion of World War I, the Irish state Pearse had died for came into being by means of the Government of Ireland Act of 1920 and the subsequent Anglo-Irish Treaty of 1921–22. Though Pearse dreamed of a unitary Irish state, the civil war that followed led to the creation of two separate units: the Republic of Ireland in the south and a Protestant-dominated Northern Ireland (made up of six of Ulster's nine counties). These agreements did not entail meaningful guarantees for the protection of the Protestant minority in the south (many of whose members emigrated) or the Catholic minority in the north.

From its creation in 1921, the state of Northern Ireland pursued undeniably discriminatory policies against its Catholic citizens. The institution of a Special Powers Act in 1922–an "emergency" measure that remained in place for almost half a century–facilitated Protestant dominance. The police force, known as the Royal Ulster Constabulary (RUC), together with the Ulster Special Constabulary (the B Specials), operated in paramilitary fashion. They enforced the religious discrimination that existed in the realms of voting, the legal and justice system, public housing allocations, and the private and public sectors of employment (Rowthorn and Wayne 1988:28–37).

In the late 1960s, Catholics (often referred to as "Nationalists") began to challenge this institutionalized discrimination. Inspired by the African American civil rights movement, in 1968 the Northern Ireland Civil Rights Association (NICRA) led a campaign of civil disobedience. By the summer of 1969, tactics of peaceful protest had given way to violent clashes. This led some Catholics to abandon the politics of nonviolence, forming paramilitary groups known as the Provisionals. The Irish Republican Army (IRA), a guerrilla group that had advocated violence in order to attain Irish independence, also re-emerged. Protestant paramilitary groups replied with equal violence. The use of terror by both sides in the conflict prompted intervention by the British army in 1971.

Although initially welcomed by some Catholics as protectors from the Ulster Protestants, the British soldiers soon became the agents of repression and martial law in Northern Ireland (Rowthorn and Wayne 1988:41). The army oversaw the internment without trial of individuals "suspected of terrorism." In what became known as the "Bloody Sunday" massacre (1972), the British army killed 13 protesters marching at Derry. Later that year, Britain suspended Northern Ireland's constitution and parliament and instituted direct rule. Direct rule ended only in 1999, leaving bitter memories among Catholics of human rights abuses like unconstitutional house and strip searches. The fate of Catholics imprisoned by the British provided a powerful focus for Nationalist resistance. As anthropologist Allen Feldman has argued, "The experience of arrest and interrogation is central to the political culture of violence in Northern Ireland" (1991:85).

Initially, the government accorded both imprisoned Nationalists and Unionists a "special category status" as political prisoners. Grouped together in a manner that facilitated organizing, "politicals" were not required to wear prison uniforms. In 1975, the policy of internment came to a halt. In 1976, various privileges and political prisoner status altogether were revoked. This reflected an attempt to criminalize the paramilitaries and to render the national and religious question in Northern Ireland merely one of "law and order" restricted to unruly ghettos (Aretxaga 1997:84). British media often described Catholic paramilitary volunteers as "hardmen," an image invoking fanatical "gunmen" dedicated to radical violence (Feldman 1991:47). Negative media images accompanied ever more intrusive forms of surveillance, including strip searches. Anthropologists like Feldman and Aretxaga have demonstrated how the bodies of individuals (symbolic of the body politic) became the sites of both repression and resistance.

Jailed Nationalists, for example, wielded their bodies as "protest weapons." Together with well-publicized hunger strikes, one of the most powerful uses of the body for resistance consisted in the so-called "blanket protest." When denied their political status and ordered to wear prison uniforms, Catholic political prisoners responded by wearing only blankets in their cells. Forbidden to wear blankets outside of their cells, and with their naked bodies exposed to physical and verbal abuse, the prisoners undertook a new, "dirty protest." This entailed a refusal to wash or leave their cells, even to use the toilets. When authorities prevented prisoners from discarding their bodily waste through the windows, the prisoners took to smearing feces on the cell walls.

Aretxaga has told the parallel but lesser known story of Catholic women's resistance. Although female activism began during the civil rights and march phase of the Nationalist movement, it crystallized in response to the disruption of family and civil life wrought by British army rule. Members of the security forces often targeted women for sexual harassment (1997:131). When house searches became daily occurrences, women organized a system of whistles and banging garbage-can lids to alert other families. In a more dramatic example, female members of the IRA in Armagh jail organized a "protest of dirt" to demonstrate their solidarity with incarcerated male members of the IRA. This women's protest, all too often treated as a mere footnote to that of the men, proved particularly disturbing for Protestant and Catholic men alike.

The sight of women in their own excrement and menstrual waste violated cultural taboos of various sorts. It also challenged the more traditional role set aside for women in Nationalist discourse: that of mothers supporting (or grieving for) their heroic sons. The IRA relied on a conservative ideal of the activist, republican male and the passive, devoted wife and mother (p. 151). The pervasive image of Mother Ireland drew upon not only a common nationalist language but also the prominence accorded to Mother Mary in popular Catholicism (p. 112). The leader of the Easter Rebellion, Padraic Pearse, had powerfully combined these two languages, reconfiguring an older poetic image of Mother Ireland as a worn-out hag into that of a proud mother sacrificing her sons (like Mary) to the national cause. Aretxaga notes that the Armagh women's protest not only questioned the prevailing ethnic and religious hierarchy in Northern Ireland but also the gender regime. She suggests that the fragility of this feminist project parallels that of the prospects for peace in Northern Ireland at the same time that it represents the possibilities for change (p. 175).

The Anglo-Irish Agreement of 1985, which gave the Republic of Ireland a voice in Northern Ireland politics, marked the beginnings of a drawn-out peace process. Despite sporadic violence, the IRA and the Unionist paramilitaries generally agreed to end the use of violent tactics in 1994. Soon after, Sinn Féin, the political branch of the IRA, began to participate directly in the peace process. The Belfast Agreement of 1996 provided for devolution of government responsibilities to an elected assembly of Northern Ireland; devolution became a reality in December 1999. Though definitive peace has not yet been achieved in Northern Ireland, significant change has occurred. This has been facilitated by Ireland and Northern Ireland's incorporation into the European Union, which has created further impetus to end sectarian violence in Northern Ireland (Hume 1993).

Bosnia-Herzegovina

The conflict in Northern Ireland reflects the dilemmas inherent to state building in Europe's supposedly "old" nations, offering an example in which the framework of an integrated Europe may facilitate resolution of (post)colonial conflicts. Yugoslavia's violent dissolution, by contrast, unfolded within the context of an integrating Europe and raises questions about how ethnic and religious conflicts may develop in those states bordering on, but denied the privileges of membership in, the "new" Europe. Furthermore, in many contemporary societies within the European Union, the relatively recent arrival of immigrants who are not just ethnically but also religiously distinct raises new questions about the future of "national" ways of life; often these "others" come from former colonies or the postsocialist European states, sometimes as refugees.

In particular, Muslims appear to put into question the values associated with both the "West" and "Christianity." Regardless of their actual beliefs and practices, many individuals from Muslim societies are assumed to be proponents of "Muslim fundamentalism"; this label implies a whole host of negative images, such as the principle of theocracy (merging of religious and political rule), subordination of women, and rigid religious strictures. Such contemporary stereotypes draw upon long-standing European fears of the Muslim "other," which date back to the medieval confrontation between Christianity and Islam in Europe and the Near East. Like the Jew, the "Moor" or the "Turk" represents the "other" whose specter has haunted Europe.

After the completion in 1492 of the brutal Christian Reconquest of the Iberian Peninsula, which entailed the expulsion of both Moors and Jews, the Balkan Peninsula remained the last frontier within Europe between Christianity and Islam. In the Balkans generally and on the territory of the South, or Yugo, Slavs especially, met competing religions (Islam and Christianity, as well as Catholicism and Orthodoxy) and empires (those of the Austrian Hapsburgs, the Venetians, and the Ottoman Turks). In the European territories controlled by the Ottomans for several centuries there lived not only large populations of Muslims who had emigrated from the imperial center (Constantinople) but also ethnic Slavs who converted to Islam. When the Ottomans withdrew and "European" nation-states came into being in the nineteenth and twentieth centuries, these Muslim populations remained. One of the largest populations of such "Islamicized Slavs" lives in the territory of Bosnia-Herzegovina; non-Slavic Albanians, thought to be descendants of the peninsula's original Illyrian inhabitants, also converted in large numbers to Islam.

Despite the extensive religious and ethnic mixture that characterized the Yugoslav territory, when the multiethnic federation dissolved in 1991 it broke into states defined on narrow ethnonational lines. In the course of the wars of the 1990s by which these new states came into being, many populations (such as Croatia's Serbs, Bosnia's Muslims, and Kosovo's Albanians) have been "ethnically cleansed" through expulsion and/or massacres in an attempt to make the boundaries of ethnic group and territory contiguous.

Perhaps more than any of socialist Yugoslavia's other republics (Slovenia, Croatia, Serbia, Montenegro, and Macedonia), Bosnia-Herzegovina embodied the multiethnic Yugoslav mix. In Bosnia lived ethnic Serbs (generally Orthodox), Croats (mainly Catholic), Jews, Vlachs, Gypsies, and Muslims (sometimes called Bosnians). The fate of Bosnia-Herzegovina illustrates the tragic failure of the Yugoslav experiment, as well as the ways in which religious affiliation may overlap with ethnic and national identity.

Nationally minded historians in the Balkans often claim that during the centuries of Ottoman domination, the Christian churches kept national sentiment and heritage alive. Serbian monasteries, for example, are said to have nurtured the memory of the medieval Serbian state, and in particular its defeat by the Ottomans in the 1389 battle of Kosovo. In reality, the historic relationship between religious and ethnonational affiliation in the former Yugoslavia proves more complex. In overseeing a vast empire of persons belonging to different ethnic and religious groups, the Ottomans did not generally attempt to assimilate or convert whole populations. Rather, they created a system for administering the different religious communities, known as the *millet*. This system gave a degree of autonomy to the various religious faiths, permitting members to practice their own religious laws and follow their own leaders (although the Ottoman sultan had ultimate authority).

As a consequence, individuals within the European territories of the Ottoman Empire defined their identity primarily in religious terms, at least until the eighteenth and nineteenth centuries. At this time, European ideologies of nationalism came into the Balkan Peninsula via Jewish and Greek traders who traveled in the West, intellectuals schooled in Europe, and various contacts with the world of Russian Orthodoxy. The Orthodox *millet*, headed by the patriarchate in Constantinople, looked with disfavor upon nationalism, given its negative associations with Western secularism. Furthermore, the patriarchate feared losing its control over the empire's Orthodox faithful as various "acephalous" churches—such as the Serbian Orthodox church and the Bulgarian Orthodox church—were restored or created.

Contrary to one commonplace assumption, then, the Orthodox church was not the unproblematic "cradle" of Serbian (or Bulgarian or Macedonian, etc.) nationalism. That said, however, these Christian identities undoubtedly informed resistance to the Ottoman Empire, specifically demands to create European nation-states. The Serbs and Greeks carved out the first independent states within Ottoman Europe. Many other peoples in the South Slav area, including some Catholic Slovenes and Croats in the Hapsburg Empire, looked to the Serbs as possible leaders for some kind of pan-Slav or Yugoslav unification (see the section on "old" and "new" nations). What place would "Muslim Slavs" occupy within such a future state? The first Yugoslav state, formed at the end of World War I with the collapse of both the Hapsburg and Ottoman empires, recognized as its three founding "peoples" the Serbs, Croats, and Slovenes. At this time, neither Muslims nor Bosnians were recognized as separate ethnic groups. Serb and Croat nationalists alike claimed the Bosnian Muslims as Islamicized Serbs or Croats, respectively. In practice, however, there existed a defined Muslim political/cultural community in Bosnia, one that resented the new Yugoslav state's centralizing tendencies (Malcolm 1994:163–173).

In the first Yugoslavia, the major source of ethnic tension derived from the differing visions of the Croats and Slovenes, on the one hand, and of the Serbs, on the other. The role of Bosnia's Muslims did not occupy center stage, although Serbian leaders devoted considerable attention to the majority population of Albanian Muslims in Kosovo; a plan for the forced trans-fer of the Kosovars to Turkey was halted only by the outbreak of World War II (Malcolm 1998:283–286). When a coalition of the Axis powers, led by Nazi Germany and Fascist Italy, invaded Yugoslavia in April 1941, the state rapidly collapsed, in part because Serb-Croat quarreling had weakened any sense of solidarity. The Axis powers partitioned Yugoslavia into occupied zones; in addition, Italy and Germany backed an "independent" Croatian state headed by Ante Pavelić. Founder of the extremist movement known as the Ustaśa, Pavelić advocated the national "purification" of Croatia. The Ustaśa carried out a campaign to exterminate Serbs, Jews, and Gypsies so brutal that it shocked even some Nazi observers. In some cases, Bosnian Muslims also participated in the persecution of ethnic Serbs, though many Muslims also fought with the communist partisans (Malcolm 1994: 89–191). During the war, then, Yugoslavia not only suffered from foreign occupation but also civil war and genocide from within.

Building a socialist Yugoslavia at war's end demanded reconciliation of Yugoslavia's diverse peoples. Tito actively suppressed the memory of some of the worst interethnic fighting during the war (as well as the violence committed by the communists in consolidating their power). In the 1980s and 1990s, interethnic conflict would again tear apart Yugoslavia, fueled by nationalist leaders who invoked past ethnic and religious violence, including that of World War II (Denich 1994; Hayden 1994).

Ironically, many observers expected that Yugoslavia—long independent of the Soviet bloc and more open and prosperous than the bloc states—would make the smoothest transition to a market democracy. Instead, the reverse occurred. Why did Yugoslavia's breakup occur with such violence? In particular, why did Bosnia become the site of expulsions and massacres that many persons believed could never happen again in Europe? The reasons for Yugoslavia's destruction lie in the economic and political character of socialist Yugoslavia, as well as changes in the broader political economy.

In the 1960s and 1970s, Tito transformed the centralized Yugoslav state into a much more loosely organized federation. Despite the growing weakness of the federal center vis-à-vis these republics (with considerable economic and political decision making at the republican, rather than federal, level), Tito and the communist party managed to hold the fragile federation together. Tito's death in 1980 not only left a power vacuum but also coincided with an economic crisis, the result of Yugoslavia's reliance on credits and loans from international banking institutions like the International Monetary Fund and the World Bank (Woodward 1995: 47–81). In the 1980s, once prosperous Yugoslavs had to cope with skyrocketing inflation, unemployment, and shortages. In this context, nationalist demands—which in Tito's time had been suppressed, as occurred in 1971 after the "Croatian Spring"—became a common way to express dissatisfaction.

Usually this nationalism was couched in terms of victimization, the specific ethnic-national group claiming that its interests had been sacrificed to those of Yugoslavia and/or some other national group. Whereas Serb-Croat conflict had dominated much of Yugoslavia's history, in the 1980s the competing and intertwined nationalisms of Serbia and Slovenia first came to the fore. In Slovenia, articulations of national identity and demands for independence rooted in a sense of victimization as a small nation coincided with the flourishing of an underground, avant-garde youth scene; to many Western observers, Slovenia appeared to be enjoying an opening up of "civil society."

Many Slovenes and members of Yugoslavia's other ethnic groups complained that Serbs had disproportionate power in the socialist Yugoslavia (just as they had dominated the first Yugoslavia). Serbs, however, countered that Tito's state had victimized the Serbs, denying them rights and privileges in pursuit of an ethnic quota system. In a 1986 memorandum, intellectuals associated with the Serbian Academy of Arts and Sciences gave expression to a pervasive view of Serb "martyrdom," one that drew upon deeply rooted images from Serbian history and also contemporary events in the province of Kosovo. In the 1980s, Albanian Yugoslavs began to protest discriminatory treatment at the hands of the Serbs and demand that Kosovo, an autonomous province under the control of Serbia, become a full-fledged republic within the federation.

Serbian nationalism found its focal point in the question of Kosovo. The poorest region of Yugoslavia and one inhabited primarily by Muslim Albanians, Kosovo held a special place in narratives of Serb identity. The presence of important Serbian Orthodox monasteries in the region and the memory of the Serbs' 1389 defeat to the Ottomans on Kosovo's Field of Blackbirds, popularly viewed as signaling the end of the medieval Serbian kingdom, underwrote the belief that Kosovo represented Serbia's "Jerusalem" and, by extension, that Serbs shared with the Jews the status of a chosen, yet persecuted, people (Živković 2000). In this line of thinking, the Serbian people had been martyred again and again throughout their history. Serbian nationalists like Slobodan Milošević (taking up well-rehearsed arguments) argued that the growth of the Albanian population in Kosovo and the proportionate decline of the Serbian population there represented the latest act of martyrdom. Albanians were said to be engaging in a plan of ethnic or demographic cleansing that would drive out remaining Serbs from Kosovo; nationalists often represented these Muslim Albanians as akin to the Ottoman Turks who had forced Serbs to submit to the "Ottoman yoke" for centuries. Reports and rumors, never substantiated, charged Albanians with undertaking a systematic campaign of "nationalist rape" of Serbs (young and old, male and female). In actuality, it would be Serbs in Bosnia who would actually first use mass rape as a systematic weapon in the Yugoslav wars (Bracewell 2000).

Although Kosovo appeared the likely place in which these wars would begin, violence first occurred when Slovenia and Croatia declared independence from Yugoslavia in 1991. The Yugoslav national army, increasingly identified as the instrument of Serbian rather than Yugoslav interests, moved to prevent secession. After a ten-day war in Slovenia, Serbian leader Milošević agreed to let Slovenia leave the federation. He then turned his full attention to Croatia, home to a sizable minority population of ethnic Serbs; some of these Serbs had already declared an independent republic in the Krajina region (the mountainous zone adjacent to the Dalmatian coast). These Serbs refused to become a minority within the new Croatian state. They feared that Croatian nationalists and their leader, Franjo Tudjman (elected president of Croatia in 1990), would undertake a genocide of Serbs like that which had occurred during World War II. The revival of symbols (such as the flag, the currency) associated with Pavelić's Ustaśa state and the mass firing of Serbs from the civil service and police fed such fears.

Groups of paramilitary volunteers (many of them from Serbia itself) formed in support of these Croatian Serbs. These volunteers often committed the worst violence of the wars. Although they were likely motivated by ethnonational hatred, other factors such as class antagonism and an aggressive masculinity also came into play (Ignatieff 1993; Woodward 1995). Such militias played a major role in the siege and destruction of the city of Vukovar. Here, ethnic Croatians were driven out or killed in the process that became known as "ethnic cleansing." The violence of Vukovar offered a blueprint for the war in Bosnia, which began in 1992 after that state's declaration of independence.

In the period leading up to Bosnia's first free elections, parties formed largely (though not exclusively) on ethnic lines. The major parties represented the Bosnian Serbs (SDS), the Bosnian Croats (HDZ), and the Bosnian Muslims (SDA). Under the leadership of Aliya Izetbegović, the SDA continued to express support for a multiethnic Bosnia. Without a doubt, however, the SDA was associated with the Muslims; not only had Izetbegović been imprisoned under Yugoslavia for writing a pan-Islamic tract but the SDA adopted the Islamic symbol of the crescent moon. This reflected the way in which, under Tito, "Muslim" had become a recognized cultural or ethnic identity. Whereas Bosnian Muslims had previously been counted in censuses as either ethnically Serb or Croat, the 1961 census defined Muslim as an ethnic identity, and the 1971 census recognized Muslim as a national identity on a par with those of the Serbs and Croats (Malcolm 1994:198–199). This change followed out of a desire to balance Serb and Croat rivalry in Bosnia. In addition, it helped divest a Muslim identity of those religious meanings that might make it a counterpoint for opposition to the communist state (p. 200).

In general, Bosnia's Muslims were among the most secularized in the world. Differences in the practice of being Muslim did, however, mark Bosnia's urban and rural areas. The Muslims of Bosnia's capital city, Sarajevo, possessed a reputation for their cosmopolitan ways. Little, if anything, outwardly distinguished these urban Muslims from their Serb or Croat neighbors. In some rural villages, like that studied by anthropologist Tone Bringa (1995), Muslim women wore traditional headscarves and *dimije* (baggy pants). Here Muslims lived alongside their Croat neighbors and shared bonds of friendship (symbolized by the women's coffee-drinking groups). The two groups nonetheless remained distinct, and intermarriage was infrequent. Even in this case, though, Muslim identity had a situational aspect, as village women wore Western-style clothes when going to the nearby market town; in addition, younger women sometimes adhered to Muslim ways less strictly.

In spite of this, some Serbs in Bosnia argued

that the SDA of Izetbegović represented a party of Islamic fundamentalists. Bosnian independence was declared in 1992 after a referendum that the Serbs of Bosnia boycotted on the grounds that it violated the still-valid constitution of the Socialist Republic of Bosnia and Herzegovina (Hayden 2000:92–93). The Bosnian Serbs instead proclaimed their own independent republic, Republika Srpska. Under the political leadership of Radovan Karadžić and the military leadership of General Ratko Mladic, who had made a name for himself (and his ethnic cleansing tactics) in the Serb-Croat war, the Bosnian Serbs began to drive non-Serbs out of those areas they claimed as Serbian. Together with the expulsions, the Serbian military and paramilitary volunteers also massacred Muslims, often burying them in secret grave sites that international observers later discovered; forensic work on such sites continues, providing important evidence for the International War Crimes Tribunal at the Hague.

Many more Muslims were interned in centers where they suffered from torture, malnourishment, and disease. Paramilitary squads targeted Muslim women as the objects of a systematic campaign of mass rape, designed to physically and psychologically degrade the enemy. All these tactics had a common aim: to make it impossible for Serbs, Croats, and Muslims to live together again after the war and hence to render ethnic cleansing a permanent reality.

Initially, the Croats and Muslims of Bosnia formed a military alliance against the Serbs. By 1993, however, the Muslim's former allies had become their enemies. Bosnia's Croats, concentrated in the region of Herzegovina, increasingly sought incorporation into the neighboring state of Croatia. As chronicled in Tone Bringa's moving film, "*We Are All Neighbors*," Croats and Muslims who yesterday had lived together as neighbors now regarded one another suspiciously as Croat and Muslim militaries advanced toward their villages. In the village depicted in the film and in many other parts of

Bosnia-Herzegovina, Croats ethnically cleansed Muslims. Muslims thus found themselves pressed on both sides by the Serbs and Croats.

Media images of Muslim victims created growing outrage in the United States and Europe, prompting demands for both humanitarian and military intervention. Although Serbs and Croats also suffered ethnic cleansing, Bosnian Muslims were perceived by many in the West as Yugoslavia's greatest victims. The persecution of Jews during the Holocaust offered a key analogy for such media coverage and for arguments that this time the West could not stand idly by. The Yugoslav case thus revealed the powerful moral capital attached to the Holocaust narrative—a narrative referenced by various parties (Serbs, Muslims, Albanians, members of the international community and media) during the conflict—but also the danger that use of the Holocaust metaphor might obscure understanding of what actually happened in former Yugoslavia (Hayden 1996:731; Živković 2000:83). Furthermore, the view that events in Yugoslavia were anomalous in "civilized," late twentieth-century Europe also obscured the extensive violence which historically accompanied state and nation building in Europe, as we have seen.

Anthropologist Robert Hayden has argued that "'ethnic cleansing' is a logical corollary of self-determination in situations in which the existence of a minority can be presented as potentially threatening to the national state of the majority" (1996:735–736). If so, an understanding of events in Yugoslavia requires attention not only to nationalist ideologies espousing purity but also an international system that embraces contradictory principles like those of self-determination and inviolability of borders. The insistence on both principles may lead, as it did in the former Yugoslavia, to violent expulsions designed to render territorial and ethnic borders congruent (Woodward 1995). The extensive role played in the Yugoslav conflict by the international community—from the United Nations peacekeepers to the debates over the arms embargo on Bosnia to the series of limited air strikes conducted by the United States on Serb targets to the NATO campaign in Kosovo—proves too complicated to detail here. What should be stressed, however, is that the Dayton Accords, which ended the Bosnian fighting in 1995, largely resulted from outside pressure being brought to bear on the warring sides within Bosnia.

The Dayton Accords created a Bosnian state in name only, made up of a Croat-Muslim federation and the Serbian entity (Republika Srpska). In reality, these units tend to function like autonomous states that often have little interest in fulfilling all the clauses of the treaty such as that providing for the return of refugees to their homes. Although some refugees have returned, the end result of the ethnic cleansing carried out during the war appears to be the permanent "unmixing" of the peoples of Bosnia. Currently, the existence of the fragile Bosnian state that emerged from the conflict depends on the presence of an international peacekeeping force. While what will happen when the peacekeepers leave Bosnia remains to be seen, the fate of a Bosnian identity will have consequences that extend far beyond that state's territorial boundaries. As in Northern Ireland, the Bosnian conflict has left as its legacy bitter memories of ethnic and religious hatred, as well as a culture of specifically *masculine* violence.

CONCLUSION: THE "NEW" EUROPE AND THE "NEW" RACISM

In the early 1990s, the collapse of socialism and the integration of the European Community (today the European Union) held out much promise for a peaceful and prosperous Europe in which the violence associated with nationalism, racism, and ethnicism would be just a distant memory. As we have seen, however, the violent dissolution of the former Yugoslavia has tem-pered optimism about a smooth transition to the "new" Europe. The cases of Bosnia and Northern Ireland explored here point to unresolved difficulties entailed by the projects of state making (past and present) and raise the question of whether the legal, administrative, and diplomatic apparatus of the "new" Europe (i.e., the European Union) can provide effective solutions. These cases also reveal the way in which the very notion of Europe itself may fuel, rather than diminish, ethnic and national divisions. The issue of what defines Europeanness and who belongs in that category has created new differentiations within contemporary Europe.

During the cold war, the internal boundary within Europe was closed from the eastern side: with the exception of Yugoslavia, socialist states sought to prevent their citizens from traveling or emigrating to Western Europe. The economic and political collapse of the socialist bloc has reversed the equation: today West European states seek to control the flows of individuals from generally poorer Eastern European countries. The wars in Yugoslavia and the opening up of impoverished states like Albania have intensified fears of a literal flood of political and economic refugees. In prosperous countries like Italy, Austria, and Germany, which border on former socialist states, coping with these arrivals has become a concrete, political reality. These European emigrants are increasingly joined by individuals from Asia and Africa, often from former European colonial possessions. Some Europeans now talk about how to strictly control these population movements, prompting the image of a "Fortress Europe" with open internal borders and rigid external ones.

At the state level, this has prompted intense competition among the former socialist states to officially enter into "Europe," understood as synonymous with the European Union. In practice, the label "European" has acquired a positive meaning and its opposite (whether "Oriental," "Eastern," or "Balkan") a negative one. On the one hand, "European" has become a value judgment made by those within the EU about how to understand (and whether to admit) those looking in. On the other hand, various groups within the new states of Central and Eastern Europe (for example, in the former Yugoslavia) adopt this same rhetoric in their efforts to position themselves as more or less European; they simultaneously depict their political opponents as non-European, creating prevalent new forms of chauvinism.

Since the 1980s, many Slovenes and Croats have emphasized their Hapsburg past and Catholic identities in depicting themselves as European peoples. They contrast themselves to "Balkanic" Serbs, said to be saddled with a dual Oriental legacy from the Ottoman Empire and from Orthodox Christianity (Bakić-Hayden 1995; Hayden and Bakić-Hayden 1992). European here implies a cultural heritage of democracy and civil society. Similar distinctions came into play in the dispute between Greece and the newly independent Republic of Macedonia over the name Macedonian and the memory of Alexander the Great; Greeks view themselves as heirs of Alexander and the founders of Europe, in contrast to Balkanic Slavs who claim the name Macedonian (Danforth 1995; Herzfeld 1997; Karakasidou 1997).

In the articulation of identity, many Europeans (as well as Americans) increasingly view cultural heritage as exerting a hold akin to that which a previous generation had imagined race playing. Ironically, then, the socially acquired patterns of culture—what anthropologists like Franz Boas and Margaret Mead used to argue against the primacy of "nature" in the historic nature-nurture debate—may now appear as fixed and fatal as our genetic makeup. Scholars like Verena Stolcke (1995) and Paul Gilroy (1987) have demonstrated how, within the new Europe, this blurring of the once distinct boundaries of culture and nature takes place. Stolcke discusses "cultural fundamentalism" and Gilroy the "new racism," but they essentially make the same point: that identity is no longer necessarily

understood or described in primordial terms, such as race, but instead is often seen as culturally constructed. The trick, however, is that culture is increasingly seen as a given and inescapable, almost as if it were a genetically given or racial characteristic.

At the beginning of the new millennium, fears of such "culture wars" largely supplanted the anxieties about racial degeneration that haunted many European intellectuals at the beginning of the twentieth century. In an influential but controversial article, political scientist Samuel Huntington (1993) has predicted the "coming clash of civilizations" in an apocalyptic language reminiscent of degenerationist rhetoric. Such fears suggest not that racism in Europe has disappeared but that it has assumed new forms and a new vocabulary, all the more difficult to combat because it is disguised within the language of culture.

Writing about the politics of blackness in contemporary Great Britain, for example, Gilroy examines the historic development of notions of race in relation to those of class and nation. Respect for the law proves fundamental to images of English nationality. Identified with criminality, blacks in England (particularly young males) thus appear to stand outside of and threaten the boundaries of the nation. In the 1970s, racist leader Enoch Powell went so far as to declare mugging a "racial crime." Increasingly, though, such leaders attribute supposed criminality and anti-authoritarianism to black culture rather than to any innate characteristics (Gilroy 1987:73–110). This permits such leaders to disingenuously declare, "But we're not racist!" while nonetheless putting forward racist ideas in a new form and promoting repressive measures to deal with presumed criminality.

Ironically, the opponents of such new racism often employ the same language of culture and community. This reveals the conceptual and political challenges contemporary Europeans face in articulating alternative forms of multicultural identity. The ethnographic examples in this chapter have highlighted many of the key dynamics involved in refashioning identities in the "new" Europe. Whether confronting the problems of large-scale immigration for the first time, the impact of nonwhite refugees, or the legacies of violent partition and civil war, contemporary Europeans draw upon older understandings of race and ethnicity even as they struggle to create new forms of identity in a world characterized by increased population flows of all sorts. As we have seen, the very issue of what defines Europeanness and who belongs in this category has proven crucial to the historical development of notions of ethnicity, race, and nation in Europe. Today, the notion of Europeanness continues to constitute an ethnic and moral boundary, as well as a geographic one, highlighting both continuities and transformations of identity.

NOTES

1. Those sterilized in order to avoid "lives unworthy of life" included alcoholics and poor Germans. The latter group, including prostitutes, housewives, and female servants, made up the majority of those subjected to forced sterilization (Bock 1984:281–282).
2. Intellectuals of the "Austro-Marxist" school devoted considerable attention to the "nationalities question," which dominated politics in the late Hapsburg Empire. Thinkers like Otto Bauer and Karl Renner argued for a socialist solution of the nationalities question within the bounds of empire, a proposal that differed from the more "orthodox" interpretations of Marx and Engel's writings on nationalism.

REFERENCES CITED

ANDERSON, BENEDICT. 1987. *Imagined Communities*. London: Verso.

ARETXAGA, BEGONA. 1997. *Shattering Silence: Women, Nationalism and Political Subjectivity in Northern Ireland*. Princeton, NJ: Princeton University Press.

BAKIĆ-HAYDEN, MILICA. 1995. Nesting orientalisms: The case of former Yugoslavia. *Slavic Review* 54(4): 917–931.

BARNARD, F. M. 1965. *Herder's Social and Political Thought*. Oxford: Clarendon Press.

——. 1969. Culture and political development: Herder's suggestive insights. *American Political Science Review* 62: 379–397.

BOCK, GISELE. 1984. Racism and sexism in Nazi Germany: Motherhood, compulsory sterilization and the state. In *When Biology Became Destiny*. R. Bridenthal, A. Grossman, and M. Kaplan, eds. Pp. 272–288. New York: Monthly Review Press.

BRACEWELL, WENDY. 2000. Rape in Kosovo: Masculinity and Serbian nationalism. *Nations and Nationalism* 6(4):563–590.

BREUILLY, JOHN. 1985. *Nationalism and the State*. Chicago: University of Chicago Press.

BRINGA, TONE. 1995. *Being Muslim the Bosnian Way*. Princeton, NJ: Princeton University Press.

BROWNING, CHRISTOPHER. 1992. *Ordinary Men: Reserve Police Battalion 101 and the Final Solution*. New York: HarperCollins.

BRUBAKER, ROGERS. 1992. *Citizenship and Nationhood in France and Germany*. Cambridge, MA: Harvard University Press.

CANNADINE, DAVID. 1983. The context, performance and meaning of ritual: The British monarchy and the "invention of tradition," c. 1820–1977. In *The Invention of Tradition*. Eric Hobsbawm and Terence Ranger, eds. Pp. 101–164. Cambridge: University of Cambridge Press.

CHABOD, FEDERICO. 1991. *Storia dell'Idea di Europa*. Bari: Laterza.

CLAVORA, FERRUCCIO. 1988. *L'Unione Emigranti Sloveni al Servizio della Propria Comunità*. Cividale: Unione Emigranti Sloveni del Friuli-Venezia Giulia.

CLAVORA, FERRUCCIO, and RICCARDO RUTTAR. 1990. *La Comunità Senza Nome: La Slavia alle Soglie del 2000*. Udine: Juliagraf di Premariacco.

COCCHIARA, GIUSEPPE. 1952. *The History of Folkore in Europe*. John N. McDaniel, trans. Philadelphia: Institute for the Study of Human Issues.

CONNOR, WALKER. 1984. *The National Question in Marxist-Leninist Theory and Strategy*. Princeton, NJ: Princeton University Press.

CORRIGAN, PHILIP RICHARD D., and DEREK SAYER. 1985. *The Great Arch: English State Formation as Cultural Revolution*. Oxford: Blackwell.

CURTIS, PERRY. 1971. *Apes and Angels: The Irishmen in Victorian Caricatures*. Washington, DC: Smithsonian Institution.

DANFORTH, LORING. 1995. *The Macedonian Conflict: Ethnic Nationalism in a Transnational World*. Princeton, NJ: Princeton University Press.

DE FELICE, RENZO. 1976. *Fascism: An Informal Introduction to Its Theory and Practice*. Michael Ledeen, ed. New Brunswick: Transaction.

DENICH, BETTE. 1994. Dismembering Yugoslavia: Nationalist ideologies and the symbolic revival of genocide. *American Ethnologist* 21(2):367–390.

DUDEN, BARBARA. 1989. Rereading Boas: A woman historian's response to Carl N. Degler. In *Culture versus Biology in the Thought of Franz Boas and Alfred L. Kroeber.* Pp. 24–28. New York: Berg.

ELLIS, JOHN. 1963. *One Fairy Story Too Many: The Brothers Grimm and Their Tales.* Chicago: University of Chicago Press.

FELDMAN, ALLEN. 1991. *Formations of Violence: The Narrative of the Body and Political Terror in Northern Ireland.* Chicago: University of Chicago Press.

FULTON, JOHN. 1991. *The Tragedy of Belief: Division, Politics and Religion in Ireland.* Oxford: Clarendon Press.

GAJEK, ESTHER. 1990. Christmas under the Third Reich. *Anthropology Today* 6(4):3–9.

GALLIHER, JOHN, and JERRY DEGREGORY. 1985. *Violence in Northern Ireland: Understanding Protestant Perspectives.* Dublin: Gill & Macmillan, Holmes & Meier.

GELLNER, ERNEST. 1987. *Nations and Nationalism.* Ithaca, NY: Cornell University Press.

GILMAN, SANDER. 1985. *Difference and Pathology: Stereotypes of Sexuality, Race and Madness.* Ithaca, NY: Cornell University Press.

GILROY, PAUL. 1987. *There Ain't No Black in the Union Jack: The Cultural Politics of Race and Nation.* London: Hutchinson.

GOLDHAGEN, DANIEL. 1996. *Hitler's Willing Executioners: Ordinary Germans and the Holocaust.* New York: Knopf.

HAYDEN, ROBERT. 1994. Recounting the dead: The rediscovery and redefinition of wartime massacres in late- and post-communist Yugoslavia. In *Memory, History and Opposition under State Socialism.* Rubie Watson, ed. Santa Fe, NM: School of American Research Press.

___. 1996. Schindler's fate: Genocide, ethnic cleansing, and population transfers. *Slavic Review* 55(4):727–748.

___. 2000. *Blueprints for a House Divided.* Ann Arbor: University of Michigan Press.

HAYDEN, ROBERT, and MILICA BAKIĆ-HAYDEN. 1992. Orientalist variations on the theme "Balkans": Symbolic geography in recent Yugoslav cultural politics. *Slavic Review* 51(1):1–15.

HECHTER, MICHAEL. 1975. *Internal Colonialism.* Berkeley: University of California Press.

HERDER, JOHANN GOTTFRIED. 1966. *Outlines of a Philosophy of the History of Man.* T. Churchill, trans. New York: Bergman.

___. 1968. *Reflections on the Philosophy of the History of Mankind.* Frank E. Manuel, ed. Chicago: University of Chicago Press.

HERF, JEFFREY. 1997. *Divided Memory.* Cambridge, MA: Harvard University Press.

HERZFELD, MICHAEL. 1982. *Ours Once More: Folklore, Ideology and the Making of Modern Greece.* Austin: University of Texas Press.

___. 1987. *Anthropology through the Looking Glass: Critical Ethnography in the Margins of Europe.* Cambridge: Cambridge University Press.

___. 1997. *Cultural Intimacy: Social Poetics in the Nation-State.* New York: Routledge.

HOBSBAWM, ERIC. 1990. *Nations and Nationalism since 1780: Programme, Myth, Reality.* Cambridge: Cambridge University Press.

HODGEN, MARGARET. 1963. *Early Anthropology in the Sixteenth and Seventeenth Centuries.* Philadelphia: University of Pennsylvania Press.

HUGHES, MICHAEL. 1994. *Ireland Divided: The Roots of the Modern Irish Problem.* New York: St. Martin's.

HUME, JOHN. 1993. A new Ireland in a new Europe. In *Northern Ireland and the Politics of Reconciliation.* Dermot Keogh and Michael Haltzel, eds. Pp. 226–233. Cambridge: Cambridge University Press.

HUNTINGTON, SAMUEL P. 1993. The clash of civilizations? *Foreign Affairs* 72(3):22–49.

IGNATIEFF, MICHAEL. 1993. *Blood and Belonging.* London: BBC Books.

JUST, ROGER. 1989. Triumph of the ethnos. In *History and Ethnicity.* Elizabeth Tonkin, Maryon McDonald, and Malcolm Chapman, eds. Pp. 71–88. London: Routledge.

KARAKASIDOU, ANASTASIA. 1997. *Fields of Wheat, Fields of Blood.* Chicago: University of Chicago Press.

KEDOURIE, ELIE. 1993. *Nationalism.* Oxford: Blackwell.

KITROMILIDES, PASCHALIS. 1989. "Imagined communities" and the origins of the national question in the Balkans. *European History Quarterly* 19:149–194.

KLIGMAN, GAIL. 1988. *The Wedding of the Dead: Ritual, Poetics and Popular Culture in Transylvania.* Berkeley: University of California Press.

___. 1998. *The Politics of Duplicity: Controlling Reproduction in Ceaucescu's Romania.* Berkeley: University of California Press.

KOHN, HANS. 1965. *Nationalism—Its Meaning and History.* New York: Van Kreiger.

___. 1967. *The Idea of Nationalism.* New York: Macmillan.

KOON, TRACY. 1981. *Believe, Obey, Fight.* Chapel Hill: University of North Carolina Press.

LENIN, V. I. 1951. *The Right of Nations to Self-Determination.* New York: International Publishers.

MALCOLM, NOEL. 1994. *Bosnia: A Short History.* London: Papermac (Macmillan).

___. 1998. *Kosovo: A Short History.* New York: New York University Press.

MCDONALD, MARYON. 1986. Celtic ethnic kinship and the problem of being English. *Current Anthropology* 27:333–341.

___. 1989. *We Are Not French! Language, Culture and Identity in Brittany.* London: Routledge.

MILLER, DAVID, ed. 1998. *Rethinking Northern Ireland: Culture, Ideology and Colonialism.* London: Longman.

MOSSE, GEORGE. 1985. *Nationalism and Sexuality.* Madison: University of Wisconsin Press.

NAIRN, TOM. 1977. *The Break-Up of Britain.* London: New Left Books.

ROWTHORN, BOB, and NAOMI WAYNE. 1988. *Northern Ireland: The Political Economy of Conflict.* Boulder, CO: Westview Press.

SHELAH, MENACHEM. 1989. The Italian rescue of Yugoslav Jews, 1941–1943. In *The Italian Refuge: Rescue of Jews during the Holocaust.* Ivo Herzer et al., eds. Pp. 205–217. Washington, DC: Catholic University of America Press.

STEINBERG, JONATHAN. 1990. *All or Nothing: The Axis and the Holocaust, 1941–1943.* London: Routledge.

STILLE, ALEXANDER. 1991. *Benevolence and Betrayal: Five Italian Jewish Families under Fascism.* New York: Summit Books.

STOLCKE, VERENA. 1995. Talking culture: New boundaries, new rhetorics of exclusion in Europe. *Current Anthropology* 36(1):1–13.

THOMPSON, EDWARD P. 1967. Time, work-discipline and industrial capitalism. *Past and Present,* 38:22–60.

TODOROV, TZVETAN. 1987. *The Conquest of America: The Question of the Other.* Richard Howard, trans. New York: Harper & Row.

VERDERY, KATHERINE. 1991. *National Ideology under Socialism.* Berkeley: University of California Press.

___. 1993. Whither "nation" and "nationalism"? *Daedalus* 122(3):37–46.

___. 1996. *What Was Socialism, and What Comes Next?* Princeton, NJ: Princeton University Press.

WACHTEL, ANDREW BARUCH. 1998. *Making a Nation, Breaking a Nation.* Stanford: Stanford University Press.

WEBER, EUGEN. 1976. *Peasants into Frenchmen: The Modernization of Rural France, 1870–1914.* Stanford: Stanford University Press.

WOODWARD, SUSAN. 1995. *Balkan Tragedy: Chaos and Dissolution after the Cold War.* Washington, DC: Brookings Institution.

YOUNG, JAMES. 1988. *Writing and Rewriting the Holocaust: Narrative and the Consequences of Interpretation.* Bloomington: Indiana University Press.

ŽIVKOVIĆ, MARKO. 2000. The wish to be a Jew: The power of the Jewish trope in the Yugoslav conflict. *Cahiers de l'URMIS* 6:69–84.

ZUCCOTTI, SUSAN. 1987. *The Italians and the Holocaust: Persecution, Rescue, and Survival.* New York: Basic Books.

19

CANADA

Norman Buchignani
University of Lethbridge

RUSSIA

NORWAY

North ★ Pole

Arctic Ocean

Greenland
Sea

UK

Ellesmere
Island

Alert

North
Magnitude
Pole

Kalaallit Nunaat
(Gronland)
(Denmark)

ICELAND

Beaufort
Sea

Banks

Resolute

Baffin Bay

Alaska
(USA)

Dawson

Glva
Hoveo

Victoria
Island

Baffin
Island

Yukon Territory

Whitehorse

Great
Bear
Lake

Iqaluit

Pacific
Ocean

Northwest Territories

Nunavut

Baker
Lake

Labrador Sea

Yellowknife

Fort
Nelson

Great Slave
Lake

CANADA

Atlantic
Ocean

British
Columbia

Fort
McMurray

Nain

Newfoundland

Alberta

Saskatchewan

Hudson
Bay

Prince
George

Churchill

St. John's

Edmonton

Manitoba

Victoria

Vancouver

Calgary

Saskatoon

Sandy
Lake

Innos
Bay

Quebec

Sept-Îles

Regina

Ontario

Quebec

P.E.I.

Sydney

New
Brunswick

Winnipeg

UNITED STATES

Thunder
Bay

Fredericton

Halifax

Montreal

Nova Scotia

Lake
Superior

Ottawa ⊛

LEGEND
⊛ National Capital
Calgary • City
—— International Boundary
—— Provincial Boundary
Quebec Province Name

Toronto

Lake
Michigan

Lake
Huron

Lake
Ontario

Lake
Erie

Scale
500 km

0   500 Miles

When they think of them at all, Americans tend to think stereotypically about their northern neighbors. Images of Mounties and hockey aside, Americans typically harbor a sense that Canada is a fairly homogeneous place; one populated with nice, if somewhat unimaginative, folk, pretty much like those next door but with a residue of British "civility." Some may be aware of Québec and of separatist sentiments there. However, few Canadians in this century, and even fewer in this generation, would have such an impression. Each in their own way, they would have sensed and experienced a country whose social diversity is now fully as great as that in the United States. This is markedly so of ethnic and "racial" diversity. Ethnic and race relations have played a central role in shaping Canada since before the arrival of Europeans, and this role has been enduring and increasing. Today, 42 percent of individuals in the country's largest city (Metro Toronto, 1996 population, 4.2 million) are foreign-born, as are 17.5 percent of all Canadians. Current annual immigration rates are proportionally double those in the United States, and over 800,000 Canadians claim First Nations (native) origins.[1] A new northern territory (Nunavut) run by and for Inuit people was created by mutual consent only two years ago.

It is often said that Canada and the United States share the longest militarily undefended border in the world. They share much more than this, and many parallels can be made between the two countries. Some are the result of the border being "undefended" in many other respects: they are mutually dependent societies of unequal power and influence. Huge flows of goods and people move across the border every day, and with them move ideas and values.[2] Similar ecologies and historical forces have led to the evolution of broadly similar regional cultures on each side of the line, from west to east: British Columbia shares much with the Pacific Northwest, Alberta with Montana, and the Maritime provinces with New England.

Other parallels have more general sources. Both have their roots as nation-states in Protestant colonial settler societies. Both are prosperous, highly urban societies based on fairly open capitalistic economies. Both have English as a national language (although Canada has two of them), and what English has brought with it: broadly similar notions of citizenship, the individual and the role of the state in people's affairs. Both have had a long-term dependence on immigration and are home to large native populations. As a consequence, contemporary ethnic and race relations in Canada also share a number of parallels with those in the United States (Reitz and Breton 1994). For example, both societies now positively affirm ethnic and racial equality and diversity, and the pressures of assimilation and acculturation faced by immigrants are broadly similar in each.

Even so, in other important ways ethnic and race relations in Canada have always been very different, and differently framed, than those to the south. Folk and government responses have differed as well. In what follows, I purposely highlight some of these main distinctions, bringing in key similarities with the United States where appropriate.

A STRONG AND ENDURING FIRST NATIONS PRESENCE

What was to become Canada was home to an extremely diverse set of First Nations. Some of these societies were as culturally and linguistically different from each other as Chinese and English. They often *felt* different and acted accordingly. A sense of "us and them" that was often as strong as anything seen today was incorporated into complex relationships between members of one First Nations collectivity and another. In these senses, ethnic relations in Canada predate the arrival of Europeans by thousands of years. When they did appear, Europeans were quickly integrated into ongoing local systems of ethnic and political relationships. Such relations thereafter were critical to the development of fledgling European colonies. Settlers, the military, and colonial administrators in New France (founded in 1608) were highly dependent on the goodwill and support of some First Nations from the onset–particularly in their struggles with the English over who would control the northeastern part of the continent.

French settlers quickly established a form of "Latin" or "Catholic" race relations with the original inhabitants of New France and Acadia. A person's status and authority depended not only on "biology" (conceived of by all Europeans very differently than now) but also on one's class and culture. This logic led to the quick rise of intermarriage and informal liaisons between settlers and natives, to the consequent creation of a large Métis (literally, "mixed") population (now numbering more than 210,000; see Purich 1988) and to a continuum of European and First Nations lifestyles and cultural traditions on the frontier. New France was conquered by the British in 1759 and amalgamated into the nascent British Empire (1763). British entrepreneurs (chiefly Scots) then quickly developed the fur trade (from which comes Canada's animal totem, the beaver). By 1820, the fur trade extended right across what is Canada today and far into the North. The fur trade was a polyethnic enterprise that tied local ethnic relations into a global economic system: "Indians" and Métis were the chief trappers. Métis and "French Canadians" were the *voyageurs* who transported the furs and trade goods back and forth to Montréal. Almost all the owners, factors, and other functionaries were British.

As was intended, the fur trade led to increasing First Nations dependence on Europeans for food, tools, clothing, and weapons. In the nineteenth century this dependence was greatly increased by population losses from imported diseases, by advancing European settlement and political hegemony, and by settler resource extraction activities. The initial subordination of

First Nations people was a relentless, ongoing (if rarely overtly violent) process that extended far more recently into the modern era than similar processes did in the United States. Much of the Canadian prairies (which became Alberta, Saskatchewan, and Manitoba) were only extensively settled by Europeans after 1895, and some Inuit only came under definitive European control in the 1950s.

The sole late nineteenth-century exceptions to the "Canadian way" of colonizing and otherwise repressing First Nations people through nonmilitary means involved Métis settlers and Cree in what were to become Manitoba and Saskatchewan. Fearful of losing their political, cultural, and land rights in the upcoming transfer of the Red River Settlement and the rest of the North-West from the Hudson's Bay Company to the federal government, long-established Métis settlers resisted in 1869. Under the charismatic leadership of highly religious and well-educated Louis Riel, they stopped federal land surveys, seized Fort Garry, and established a provisional government. Unable to mount a swift military response, the federal government was conciliatory, and in 1870 passed legislation (the Manitoba Act) granting Métis rights to 1,400,000 acres of land and providing for a limited range of bilingual rights and services in the new province. Vilified in Ontario but seen as a hero and defender of the faith in Québec, Riel fled to the United States in response to a military force of occupation sent out the same year. Fourteen years later, he returned to Saskatchewan in response to solicitations from local Métis settlers. Within a year, Riel mounted another rebellion centered at the Métis settlement of Batoche. This time, the railway facilitated the quick arrival of Canadian troops, and the rebellion was crushed after a series of fierce engagements. Riel and a number of Métis and Cree leaders were tried for treason. Riel was convicted and hanged, thereby making him an enduring symbol of British Canadian oppression for francophones and Québec separatists.

Both early French and British colonial leaders mapped European international relations practice onto their relations with native people. Some (including Champlain, the founder of New France) treated natives seriously as nations and established political treaties with them. This practice was continued after 1867 by the autonomous Canadian government, which legally recognized extant treaty commitments made by the British. The last comprehensive treaty was signed with a range of peoples in the North in 1921.[3] In the end, few of the provisions of these treaties were consistently honored by the government, save perhaps in regard to the establishment of a system of band lists and reserves (reservations) upon which certain First Nations people were thereafter to live. There are currently about 550 such bands sprinkled across the country, controlling roughly 2,200 reserves.

The period 1870–1960 illustrates many parallels with the United States. "Status" or "registered" Indians (those whose names were entered on a band list, whose descendants numbered 488,000 in 1996) were relegated to reserves and excluded from full participation in Canadian society.[4] There, they functioned as a reserve army of agricultural and resource extraction labor, an economic option that, along with subsistence bush economies, evaporated after World War II. While "nonstatus" Indians and Métis had the same legal rights as other Canadians, status Indians (reflecting a dubious notion that they were still members of autonomous societies) could not vote. Neither could they control their own local affairs, and their cultures and languages were inexorably repressed through such means as forced attendance at residential schools. Most First Nations people in the southern part of the country had to deal primarily with a negative, paternalistic stereotype of themselves as "fallen" Indians—in contrast to a much more positive (but highly romantic) stereotype of what "Indians" were like before contact. Highly individualized notions of citizenship, independence, and responsibility marginal-

ized First Nations people and were used to blame them for their own misfortunes.[5]

Since the 1960s there has been a remarkable increase in the power and influence of First Nations people. In the vanguard were a set of increasingly effective status Indian leaders and organizations (Dyck 1985, 1991). Initially, organizations such as the Assembly of First Nations pressed for and often secured a wider interpretation of government treaty responsibilities more appropriate to modern times. Almost all residential schools were disbanded by the end of the 1960s, and since the mid-1980s band councils have secured increasing control over how reserve-based services are delivered; many are now entirely provided by local native personnel (Driben 1985). These national organizations also helped local band councils to move forward on outstanding land claims—in essence, reopening treaties to reconsider what lands and land-use rights (such as fishing and logging) continue to be the preserve of First Nations. In British Columbia, serious negotiation over land rights began for the first time (Ponting 1997).

During 1975–78, the Inuit and Cree of northern Québec negotiated and signed major agreements with the governments of Québec Province and Canada that exchanged aboriginal title over some lands for confirming those of others, increased local sovereignty, and money (Salisbury 1986). In 1993, the federal government and the Inuit of the eastern Arctic signed an agreement to create Nunavut, a new, Inuit-run northern territory. Nunavut was established in 1999, with all the powers and responsibilities of the Yukon and Northwest Territories. Further south, these processes also led in 1999 to the comprehensive Nisga'a land claims settlement in northern British Columbia. This settlement is now looked to by many as the model for resolving the hundreds of other land claims that are still outstanding. It gives the Nisga'a many autonomous political and economic powers within the land ceded to them, powers that elsewhere would be the sole prerogative of the provincial or federal government. Recent court interpretations of British era treaties have secured important fishing and other resources-collection rights for certain Indian bands in the Maritimes.

By the 1980s, representatives of status Indian and Inuit people were sufficiently influential to demand and secure political representation at key national forums at which important Canadian constitutional issues concerning them were addressed. As a result, significant First Nations *group* rights were affirmed in the Constitution Act of 1982 (Asch 1984). Section 25 of the Canadian Charter of Rights and Freedoms (part of the Constitution) explicitly subordinates all other constitutional provisions to the treaty and other rights of First Nations. First Nations representatives also pressed to have a voice in subsequent efforts to amend the Constitution to address Québec separatism, arguing that First Nations rights would be affected by any such new arrangements. These concerns were paramount when Elija Harper, a Cree representative in the Manitoba provincial legislature, played a significant role in blocking assent to the Meech Lake Accord. Representatives from four First Nations organizations later sat with provincial and federal representatives to hammer out the unsuccessful Charlottetown Constitutional Agreement.

Most other Canadians hold radically more positive notions of natives and native cultures than were prevalent a generation ago. These changes are the result of several factors: a general moderation of prior ethnic and racial sensitivities; ideological connections made between First Nations people, ecological lifestyles, and nature; and a sense that First Nations people are actively and appropriately moving to address historical injustices. Overall, First Nations people today have a public presence and impact across Canada that they do not have in the United States. At the same time, most First Nations people continue to face many significant disabilities and disadvantages in everyday life.

Some of these are ethnic and racial (and are considered later), a distinction that, as with African Americans, is somewhat arbitrary to employ regarding a population whose life chances today are profoundly affected by past inequities.

TWO PERSISTING EUROPEAN CHARTER GROUPS

Every large landmass conquered by Europeans was at some point occupied by more than one colonial power. In the United States, this included the Spanish, Dutch, British, French, and Russians. In every case this has had some impact on subsequent race and ethnic relations. Canada, therefore, is not unique in being occupied and settled by two European powers: the French in New France and Acadia and the British initially in Newfoundland. Neither is it unique that one–the British–eventually prevailed through a combination of military conquest and political negotiation.

What makes Canada atypical of the nations that arose out of European settler societies is that the "losers"–the French, established in what would eventually become part of Canada–were not reduced to an ethnic minority in the general population.[6] Such was the fate of Mexicans in the U.S. Southwest and California after their forcible incorporation into the United States. British, British immigrants, and Canadian-born people who subsequently styled themselves "British Canadians" did come to hold a preponderance of political, economic, and cultural power after the Conquest. Like British-origin Americans after the American Revolution, they became a *charter group*–a population whose interests, culture, and language shaped the core institutions and values of society.

But in a significant, albeit more limited, way, so did the French. The British faced a political dilemma immediately after the Conquest: how to govern and control a large and disaffected French population without an equally large number of British foot soldier–settlers. Very few British had yet immigrated to these northern regions, as compared with those who had sought a new home in the American colonies. The British government, therefore, strategically extended rights and privileges to the residents of former New France that were not even available to Catholics in England. Informally, and through the Québec Act (1775), the British established an early kind of indirect colonial rule in Lower Canada (later, Québec). The French-speaking inhabitants thereby maintained much local autonomy in language, culture, religion, and politics. Extant French institutions were supported and maintained, including the French language, much of the legal system, Catholic schools, and the powerful everyday role of the Catholic church.

The nominally British population of what was to become Upper Canada (Ontario), New Brunswick, and Nova Scotia first swelled with the influx of United Empire Loyalists who fled the American Revolution and its aftermath. It is interesting to note that while the Loyalists were long portrayed as epitomizing the British founders of Canada, a large minority were Germans, free African Americans, and natives. British control ensured that the number of English, Scots, Irish, and "white" Americans in subsequent generations slowly grew through immigration while French immigration was negligible.

Through the decades, tensions between French Canadians and the growing anglophone minority of Lower Canada grew episodically. These came to a head during the economically depressed mid-1830s, when local francophone patriots and politicians first tried, unsuccessfully, to secure control over provincial revenues and increase local representation, and then, in 1837–38, escalated their actions to mount a disastrous insurrection. In 1841, Upper and Lower Canada were merged into a single political entity, with the British in the majority. However, high birth rates (that would be later termed the "revenge of the cradle") helped to ensure French

demographic continuity and selective political power. Control of the growing urban economy was almost exclusively in the hands of British Canadians, whose elite dominated Montréal.

The British North America (BNA) Act (1867), which enabled Canadian Confederation and consequent formal independence from Britain (along with subsequent federal legislation), enshrined certain French-language and (Catholic) education rights. It also gave significant powers to the confederating political entities like Québec that thereafter became provinces. Although a numerical minority, francophones could not be ignored by federal politicians, for no one could form a government majority in Parliament without their significant support. Roughly half of all Canadian Prime Ministers have been Québec francophones, and every Prime Minister since the 1950s has been fluently bilingual.

Then as now, French-speakers in Québec (and secondarily, in New Brunswick, where francophones are roughly one-third of the population) maintained all the necessary elements for their long-term persistence—demographically, culturally, linguistically, and in regard to personal identity (Eller 1998:299–300). Most Québec francophones lived in communities with a high degree of *institutional completeness* (Breton 1964): virtually everything in one's daily orbit of activities could be done using economic, political, religious, educational, and other parallel institutions where French was spoken and that were used by others maintaining broadly the same core ethnocultural identity. While chronically poor economic conditions generated an ongoing exodus from these communities, such losses were more than compensated for by new births. As a consequence, 5.7 million people in Québec still consider French their mother tongue, and use it as a home language. Four million are monolingual French-speakers.

The francophone communities in other provinces and territories were never as institutionally complete, lacking a full range of institutions parallel to those of the anglophones that often surrounded them. Roughly 900,000 francophone individuals live outside Québec, 479,000 of them in Ontario and 239,000 in New Brunswick. However, francophone community institutions outside Québec, New Brunswick, and some parts of Ontario now appear to be rapidly disappearing. This does not bode well for the long-term persistence of local francophone populations outside Québec.

Confederation did little to mitigate a persistent sense of disadvantage among Québec francophones, which in turn helped maintain distinctive local identities. This discontent episodically rose to critical levels in response to British Canadian political insensitivities, as in the conscription crisis of World War I.[7] Since the formation of the first overtly separatist government in 1976, Québec politicians have used their extensive powers to ensure that francophones are the dominant charter group in that province.

NO HISTORY OF EXTENSIVE RACIALLY GROUNDED SLAVERY

Slavery was legal and was practiced in New France, as it was during the early days of British rule. However, it was not economically viable and so was not widespread. Within sixty years of the Conquest (1807), the British home government banned the slave trade in British ships, and slavery was outlawed throughout the empire in 1833. Thereafter, anyone enslaved elsewhere became legally free simply by virtue of setting foot in Canada. This augmented the Underground Railway, through which an estimated 50,000 African American political refugees fled north to freedom during 1830–65 (Dirks 1977:23). Although many returned to the United States after the Civil War, others joined a small Afro-Canadian population that had been previously established through the immigration of Loyalists and free "blacks" from the Caribbean and the United States. Significant

"black" immigration did not again occur until the 1960s, and then came primarily from the Caribbean. Today's Afro-Canadian population is very diverse, including a few individuals who are eighth- and ninth-generation Canadian-born, as well as immigrants from over thirty countries. However, Afro-Canadians today are a far smaller proportion of the population than are African Americans in the United States: 574,000 people, or roughly 2 percent of all Canadians.

Because of this very different history, Canadians have not had to generate or maintain the kind of radical racial notions some Americans historically used to justify the enslavement of other Americans based on the latter's supposed biological inferiority. Neither have Canadians had to deal so directly with slavery's sorry legacy of racial thought and practice. To this day, social race—the erroneous notion that the world's people can be divided into biologically distinct, largely self-reproducing populations—does not have anything like the salience and naturalized, take-it-for-granted status it has in the United States. Instead, since World War II both Canadians and their governments have preferred to frame intergroup relations in terms of ethnicity (that is to say, in terms of perceived cultural differences and attendant identities), even when they *do* have clear racial dimensions. With the priority that Canadians currently place on ethnicity typically comes an assumption of mutability: whether or not the perceived "ethnic" differences of others are thought desirable, they are believed to be cultural things that can be altered by the efforts of those who practice them. Racial ideas of the sort prevalent in the United States do not as extensively incorporate such assumptions.

This is not to suggest that racial perceptions are irrelevant. Canadians have always employed a mix of both perceived cultural and biological criteria to distinguish each other. Perceived biological difference was a significant disability for historical First Nations, Métis, and Afro-Canadian people, even when they were culturally indistinguishable from others. Asians and African Americans were the only populations that faced explicit Canadian immigration bans in the past. Almost all Japanese Canadians were interned during World War II, but few German Canadians were. Canadians have long embraced hierarchically evaluated stereotypes of ethnocultural populations that locate most of those perceived to be "nonwhite" lower than others (see Table 19-3). Such attitudes have moderated greatly over time, and no governmental, institutional, or personal form of discrimination based on race has been legal in Canada for almost two generations. Even so, members of the culturally heterogeneous Afro-Canadian population in particular do often continue to contend specifically with race.

AN ENDURING TIE WITH BRITAIN, REAL AND IMAGINED

Both Canada and the United States arose out of British colonialism and had their core institutions framed by British immigrants and their descendants. In contrast to the United States, Canada had no Revolution that separated it from the mother country. The British government exerted direct control over all the entities that were to become Canada, and the explicit tie with Britain remained powerful long after Confederation. Indeed, although by then formally independent for almost a hundred years, significant British connections persisted into the 1950s. Even now, Queen Elizabeth remains the titular ruler of Canada (although with no significant powers) and her likeness can be found on some Canadian currency, stamps, and government office walls. Until supplanted by the ethnically neutral "O Canada" in 1980, the de facto national anthem was the ethnically exclusive "The Maple Leaf Forever," which explicitly valorizes the British. A national flag modeled on the British one was only replaced in 1965. Just fifty years ago, Canadians were legally British subjects resident in Canada, rather than Canadian citizens.

This enduring tie has had a profound effect on both the makeup of the country and ethnic relations. As in the United States, most immigrants (chiefly excluding those of British or generically "white" American origin) and First Nations people historically faced profound, overt pressure to acculturate and assimilate. In Canada, even French Canadians faced such pressures. What these individuals were supposed to conform to in each country was, however, claimed to be quite different. In the United States they were under pressure to conform to an anglophone, "white" constructed ideal of an "American" that, by the 1890s, had no overt ethnic or national associations. Linked ideologies asserted that those who were not "colored" could consequently achieve full "Americanness" by abandoning their ethnicity, even if this goal was not always achievable in practice. Similar folk in Canada had to contend with an explicitly British image of the ideal Canadian—in both an ethnic and a racial sense. They faced a regime of language and cultural *anglo conformity* without even the supportive ideological fiction that by conforming they could become fully Canadian. One could not, after all, ever become "biologically" British.

This historical conflation of Canadianness with Britishness had many other consequences. Powerful imperial ethnic and racial stereotypes were imported through the British link. For a long time, these helped justify and maintain a "vertical mosaic" of ethnic individuals, groups, and populations (Helmes-Hayes and Curtis 1998; Porter 1965), with those most closely matching the British ideal at the top, and those who were perceived to be culturally and physically the most different at the bottom. As late as the 1950s, British immigrants were numerous and benefited greatly, while other immigrants faced disabilities in rough proportion to how much they were perceived to diverge from the ideal. French Canadians, of course, felt both threatened and marginalized by the ethnic content of this "national" image and by their exclusion from the nation's key symbols. This in turn directly fueled separatist sentiments.

The British tie also shaped the nature of Canadian institutions outside Québec, almost all of which were founded and developed in the image of the British charter group. One result was much *institutional discrimination*; those who differed in language and culture faced public and private institutions that did little to accommodate them. As late as 1970, immigrant children who did not know English were routinely placed into the general school population to sink or swim, without any special language training. Even inside Québec it was then common for urban francophones to have to communicate in English at work or to receive effective service in many retail businesses.

Until the 1960s this long-standing British connection also impeded the development of an all-encompassing Canadian identity. Uncertainties over "what it means to be Canadian" continue to be both a running joke and the subject of serious discussion. Nevertheless, since the 1960s this uncertainty has allowed a large degree of flexibility in reshaping national symbols and ideologies. It would be fair to say that in the intervening generation the explicitly British dimension of anglophone symbols and ideologies of the nation has been largely eliminated.

Finally, the British connection has also profoundly shaped immigration: who was desired, who came, and who stayed. Four hundred thousand Irish rendered destitute by the potato famine of the 1840s followed imperial ties to Canada (Knowles 1997:44), but the Catholics among them found British Canadian prejudices so strong that most subsequently moved on to the United States or merged into the francophone Catholic population. There were, nonetheless, more Irish than English in Canada at the time of the first national census in 1871; yet anglo-conformity pressures were so strong that today one sees few parallels with the strong Irish American presence. When in 1896 the government first began to consistently use immigration as a tool for national development, its British biases were overt. It first solicited the "right class" of British and "white" American agriculturalists to help settle the Prairies. When their numbers proved insufficient, agents focused on what were then perceived as the "Aryan" cousins of the British in Holland, Germany, and Scandinavia. Only after that did they turn reluctantly to Eastern Europe. French farmers were not solicited, and neither southern Europeans, African Americans, nor Asians need apply.

The last British biases and preferences in immigration were eliminated in the 1960s. Nevertheless, the aftermath of this historical connection can still be seen in today's population makeup and immigration patterns. In 1996, 655,540 Canadians were immigrants from the United Kingdom, most of whom arrived before 1970. Immigrants are now extremely diverse and come from virtually every country on earth, and immigration from Britain itself is now low. Even so, most of the countries that consistently send large numbers of immigrants to Canada (see Table 19-1), such as India and Hong Kong, have some kind of historical British imperial connection.

A PROFOUND ROLE FOR IMMIGRATION

Few rich countries today willingly accept large numbers of immigrants and asylum seekers. Among this select company, only in Canada, the United States, and Australia does immigration intentionally play a long-term role in national development. Immigration may have played an even more significant role in Canada than in the United States. Prior to World War II, attracting European settlers to Canada was easy. Push factors motivating many Europeans to emigrate were numerous and powerful. In contrast, ensuring

Table 19-1. Top Ten Source Countries of Immigrants, 1996–98

Country of Last Permanent Residence	Number of Immigrants, 1996–98	Percentage of All Immigrants
Hong Kong	60,292	9.8
India	56,222	9.1
China	55,828	9.1
Taiwan	33,701	5.5
Philippines	32,198	5.2
Pakistan	27,071	4.4
United States	15,676	2.5
Sri Lanka	14,554	2.4
United Kingdom	14,140	2.3
Iran	13,981	2.3

Source: Canada. *Citizenship and Immigration* 1999:7.

that they—and native-born Canadians—stayed in the country was a challenge. Until the 1930s the border between Canada and the United States was essentially open in both directions to "white" migrants. What at least looked like superior U.S. economic opportunities attracted many Canadian residents. A huge flow of immigrants to Canada during 1851–1901 (1,892,000 people) was required simply to partially offset those leaving for the United States (2,190,000). Improved perceived prospects in Canada and more effective U.S. border control subsequently severely reduced the movement of people south. Even so, rates of legal immigration continued to be higher than in the United States, initially (1947–67) in order to develop the urban economy, then (1968–90) to supply specific occupational demands, and, most recently, to compensate for a population that is aging and producing few children. Five million of 30 million Canadians today are immigrants, and about 0.8 percent of the total Canadian population arrives each year, as compared with 0.4 percent in the United States (including undocumented U.S. immigration).

Immigration to Canada over the last century can also be distinguished from that to the United States by its much more coherent and effective use by the state as a tool for national development. In this, it is also marked by an equally

long-term trend with important implications for national diversity: a pattern of decreasing ethnic, national, and racial immigration criteria and increasing economic and other adaptive ones. These two trends are closely linked. When the federal government set out in 1896 to develop the prairie West, it sought farmers—ideally, British and "white" American ones. However, in the end, in order to achieve this economic objective, the government sequentially relaxed its ethnic preferences. This resulted in a doubling in the proportion of Canadians who were neither British, French, nor First Nations between 1900 and 1930, to about 20 percent of the population. These economic objectives also resulted in a different national mix of immigrants than were then arriving in the United States: fewer Italians and Jews but many more British, Germans, and Ukrainians. Immigration criteria based on race were not as flexible, and like their U.S. counterparts, the government of the day actively used a range of means to limit, then virtually stop, "nonwhite" immigration. Chinese, Japanese, and Indian immigration into British Columbia was extremely controversial (as it was along the U.S. Pacific Coast), and was effectively banned during 1921–47. After 1910, African American farmers were informally but routinely denied entry.

Immigration policy and practice became increasingly intertwined with other national concerns after World War II. Canada came out of the war profoundly altered. Temporarily the fourth largest industrial economy in the world, it was dramatically more urban and had a much greater international focus than before. These changes were reflected in immigration patterns, and in ever-increasing ethnic diversity. A mix of economic, human rights, and political criteria soon led the government to establish a large program of refugee settlement. This program became worldwide by the 1970s, and has brought hundreds of thousands of increasingly diverse individuals to Canada. In the 1950s a great demand for urban workers led the government to expand the range of significant source countries to include Italy and Portugal, while international concerns led to a slow elimination of specifically national, ethnic, and racial immigration restrictions. A desire to tailor immigration even more closely to the economy led to the complete elimination of such barriers in 1962, chiefly to emphasize further class criteria of entry. After 1967, immigrants were to be selected individually, primarily on the basis of personal skills, national language proficiency, health, age, employment demand, and whether they had sponsoring relatives already in Canada. In reality, continuing means to sponsor one's overseas relatives have ensured that chain migration has been extensive and, accordingly, that very large numbers of new immigrants have come from certain countries and regions at particular times.

Immigrant source countries have dramatically shifted over time. As recently as the mid-1960s, about three-quarters of immigrants came from Europe or the United States. In contrast, of 616,194 immigrants who arrived during 1996–98, over 48 percent came from Asia and the Pacific, and another 19 percent were from Africa or the Middle East. European countries now contribute only 22 percent to the total flow, and Asian countries strongly predominate among the top ten sources (Table 19-1).[8]

Postwar immigration has significantly increased the ethnic diversity of the Canadian population. Exactly how diverse, and how strongly felt their own ethnicity is to Canadians today, are difficult to assess with any precision. If one takes an anthropological orientation toward ethnicity, one thing that must be kept central are ethnic identities in action: What kind of individual, personally felt attachments to group, culture, population, or nationality does a person have, how central are they to self, and how often are they activated? While many detailed ethnographic studies have demonstrated that such identities are very significant to many individuals in certain ethnic groups and populations, anthropologists in Canada have tended to focus

their attention on groups that have been strongly marked by others *as* different (now, chiefly, First Nations people, members of various Asian groups, and Afro-Canadians; see Buchignani and Letkemann 1993). They have also tended to focus on the immigrant generation, who are often marginalized by immigration itself. The designers of the Canadian census appreciate the need for relevant identity data but consider such information uncollectable under the constraints of doing a mass census. Instead, census takers now ask Canadians a completely open-ended question about what they see as their ethnic *origins*. Respondents can fill in more than one group if they wish. Table 19-2 summarizes this information derived from the last (1996) census; single responses presumably are the best indication of ethnic identity.

Ethnic diversity is highly concentrated in those prosperous urban areas that attract immigrants, particularly in Metro Toronto, Vancouver, and Montréal. In contrast, cities in economically depressed parts of the country such as St. John's, Newfoundland, have almost no ethnic diversity.

Immigration has been more of a positive, ongoing symbol of the nation than it has recently been in the United States. For over a century, immigration and an idealized image of the "good immigrant" have been tightly intertwined in national mythology. The good immigrant has long been deemed worthy of support because he or she has helped develop the country through hard work and law-abiding enterprise. For the last thirty years federal multiculturalism policy has helped broaden and further integrate this ideology into that of the nation.

At the same time, certain types of immigration have episodically been very controversial. There has never been much citizen input into the formation of immigration policy (which contributes to its partial coherence). Neither has the government spent much effort to explain its policies to those affected by it. Practical support for

Table 19-2. Canadian Ethnic Origins, 1996

Ethnic Origin	Total Responses	Single Responses	Multiple Responses
1 Canadian	8,806,275	5,326,995	3,479,285
2 English	6,832,095	2,048,275	4,783,820
3 French	5,597,845	2,665,250	2,932,595
4 Scottish	4,260,840	642,970	3,617,870
5 Irish	3,767,610	504,030	3,263,580
6 German	2,757,140	726,145	2,030,990
7 Italian	1,207,475	729,455	478,025
8 Aboriginal	1,101,955	477,630	624,330
9 Ukrainian	1,026,475	331,680	694,790
10 Chinese	921,585	800,470	121,115
11 Dutch	916,215	313,880	602,335
12 Polish	786,735	265,930	520,805
13 South Asian	723,345	590,145	133,200
14 Jewish	351,705	195,810	155,900
15 Norwegian	346,310	47,805	298,500
16 Welsh	338,905	27,915	310,990
17 Portuguese	335,110	252,640	82,470
18 Swedish	278,975	31,200	247,775
19 Russian	272,335	46,885	225,450
20 Hungarian	250,525	94,185	156,340
21 Filipino	242,880	198,420	44,460
22 American	211,790	22,085	189,705
23 Spanish	204,360	72,470	131,895
24 Greek	203,345	144,940	58,405
25 Jamaican	188,770	128,570	60,200

immigrant integration has increased greatly, but little has been done to help those already in Canada adjust to newcomers or to the greatly changed neighborhoods, cities, and economic structures that result. One consequence has been periods of focused intolerance toward some newly arrived immigrant populations, typically directed toward those seen to be the most culturally and biologically different.

FEW ILLEGAL IMMIGRANTS, MANY REFUGEES AND ASYLUM SEEKERS

One thing that has definitely helped maintain positive support for immigration and immigrants has been the prevalent belief that the government maintains firm control over an orderly process of immigrant selection. Canadians are very intolerant of illegal immigration, but they have not actually had to face the high levels of formally illegal immigration that typify many areas of the United States (Buchignani and Indra 1999). No attractive underground economy supports many undocumented workers; few illegally resident in the United States prefer to cross the border into Canada; and the only way many can otherwise arrive in Canada is by plane, and the government vigorously controls air access through a system of visas.

In 1985, the Supreme Court of Canada (in Re: Singh and the Minister of Employment and Immigration [1985] 1 SCR 177) ruled that illegal immigrants and asylum seekers could not be detained without cause. If they were detained, they had to be promptly given the reason for their arrest and detention, had the right to counsel and habeas corpus, and could appear personally to state their case to remain in the country. It also ruled that any minimally credible in-country claim for political asylum had to be duly considered by the government. In addition, Canada is a signatory to a number of international conventions (including the 1951 UN

Convention Relating to the Status of Refugees and the 1967 Protocol) that acknowledge that asylum seekers have the right of *nonrefoulement*– the right not to be returned against their will to a place in which they may be at risk. Because of these legal and policy constraints, deportation is rarely used to control undocumented immigration.

Since 1981, tens of thousands of individuals have tried to secure residence in Canada by claiming political asylum (Buchignani and Indra 1999; Gilad 1990). Some clearly do not meet the legal definition of a political refugee, but the way that the government deals with them has the effect of ideologically converting these potentially illegal immigrants into a category of person that is much more acceptable to the public: asylum seekers.

Direct challenges to Canada's geographic borders by small numbers of people continue to generate very negative public reactions. Public disapproval of the arrival by chartered ship of a mere 174 Sikhs in 1987 was so strong that the Prime Minister recalled Parliament to deal with the issue (Buchignani 1993). Most recently, despite generally positive Canadian attitudes toward Chinese immigrants, in 1999 there was almost no public support for 500 asylum seekers from China who arrived in British Columbia on leaky freighters. Should large numbers of individuals seek residence in Canada by such means in the future it is likely to dramatically increase hostility to the national populations in question.

Like the ideal of the good immigrant, Canadians have strongly supported an image of the ideal political refugee: a person who, through no fault of his or her own, faces oppression by government agents at home. In actuality, the circumstances of those seeking asylum are rarely so clear. Nevertheless, public support for a large program of refugee settlement has persisted since 186,000 "displaced persons" were accepted in the decade after World War II. This public support has sometimes been concrete, as when groups of Canadians financially carried the full first-year cost of settlement for 50,000 Southeast Asian refugees during 1979–81 (Chan and Indra 1986; Chan et al. 1988; Dorais et al. 1987). In 1986, the people of Canada received the UN's Nansen Medal in recognition of their assistance to refugees, an award previously given only to individuals.

Refugee policy up to the 1970s in both Canada and the United States strongly reflected a persistent anti-communist theme in foreign policy. Since then, this bias has decreased to a far greater extent in Canada than it has in the United States, with the result that the percentage of current world distribution of refugees and asylum seekers is very different than in the United States. During 1996–98, refugees most often came from Bosnia-Herzegovina, Sri Lanka, Afghanistan, Iraq, India, Somalia, and Pakistan.

The impact of refugee arrivals on ethnic diversity has been far greater than that which has arisen simply through their actual numbers. Refugees often form new national and ethnic communities or else dramatically increase the number of individuals in these communities. Group-specific chain migration through normal immigration channels almost always continues to augment these populations for a long time thereafter.

ONGOING QUÉBÉCOIS NATIONALISM

The historical establishment of two unequally powerful charter groups within the Canadian state has had several important consequences for ethnic and race relations. The most noticeable of these has been the rise of a reactive form of nationalism in the 5,800,000-strong francophone population of Québec.[9]

A curious mix of civic and ethnic nationalism prevailed across anglophone Canada from Confederation through the 1960s. This accreting national origin myth increasingly stressed civic, nonethnic nationalism: the creation of a uniquely Canadian nation through the efforts of all its past and present citizens. Even so, neither this national myth nor government policy informed by it were in fact actively inclusive of all Canadians. Almost all the key actors in the national myth were British, and attempts to weaken the everyday power of anglo conformity were few. Federal government accommodation to the specific concerns of francophones was limited, and that of provincial governments other than Québec and New Brunswick was even more so. The Canadian economic elite was monolithically British.

Even in the nineteenth century this state of affairs provided fertile ground for the development of Québec-based ethnic nationalism among clerics and other francophone intellectuals. Separated by language and religion and shut out of many avenues to economic or political success *as French*, they generated an alternative national creation myth. The Conquest was constructed as the decisive event in national history. Either before the "Fall" or in the rural *habitant* way of life thereafter, early nationalists evoked a lost Eden: a stable, homogeneous, pastoral way of life grounded in French and Catholicism—one where "Québécois" individuals fixed to the soil of their ancestors participated in an authentic, unique culture that could be traced back to New France (Eller 1998:313; Handler 1988). By the early twentieth century some of the explicitly Catholic elements of this national myth were being downplayed and its cultural dimensions highlighted—in part by anthropologists like Marius Barbeau using what today would be considered a timeless, overly holistic and anthropomorphic notion of Québec folk culture. These images of a past rural life were highly attractive—and nostalgic—for by the 1920s few francophone residents of Québec actually practiced anything like it. Half its population and the driving forces of its economy were already urban-based, even if some cultural elements derived from rural life such as strong informal kinship relations persisted (Garique 1956).

In what has come to be known as the Quiet Revolution (1955–70), a new set of urban, well-educated francophone leaders, spokespersons, and theoreticians swept away the explicitly Catholic dimensions of this nationalist vision (Gold 1975). The explicitly ethnic and racial dimensions of Québécois nationalism were backstaged, replaced by an awkward kind of civil nationalism based on protecting the rights, language, and culture of those who were French-*speaking*. This move reflected their own experiences and aspirations as cosmopolitan individuals who believed that speaking their native French was a disability, even "in their own land." The federal Bilingualism and Biculturalism Commission (struck in 1963) concluded that these Québec nationalists were correct in their opinion. It found that while anti-French personal prejudices were weak, monolingual francophones across Canada faced massive institutional language discrimination, which had ramifying implications for their life chances.

One consequence of the commission's work was federal legislation creating official bilingualism (1969). This set of programs proposed to make the federal government bureaucracy thoroughly bilingual by the solicitation of more francophones, by providing French-language training for anglophones, and by making more public federal government communications bilingual. Over the next twenty years, an increasing number of programs and powers constitutionally within the preserve of the federal government (such as tax collection, some social programs, and immigration) were partially or wholly transferred to the Québec provincial government. French immersion school programs (and entire schools) sprung up across the anglophone parts of the country.

These responses did little to slow the rise of separatism, and in 1976 the charismatic René Lévesque brought the Parti Québécois to power in Québec. Their parliamentary majority gave the Parti Québécois the power to make fundamental changes in the fabric of Québec society, which they immediately exercised. The new government argued that the province's 6 million francophones were an island in a sea of 300 million anglophones (anglophone Canada and the United States), and that their language would be quickly lost without compensatory state action. This was more than an argument about language. Separatists claimed that language distinctiveness had allowed Québécois to craft their own distinctive culture: lose the language, lose the everyday culture that went with it. The previous provincial government had passed legislation in 1974 making French the sole official language of Québec. The Parti Québécois government followed with a series of bills enforcing the primacy of French—chiefly Bills 101 (1977), 178 (1988), and 86 (1993). All large and medium-sized businesses must now provide a francophone workplace and customer service in French. All outdoor public signs are to highlight French. While anglophones maintain the right to educate their children in English, "allophones"—chiefly immigrants whose first language is neither English nor French—are required to send their children to French schools. The provincial government moved aggressively to solicit francophone immigrants, using its own parallel immigration program.

The first Parti Québécois government also had a referendum on separation. Although what was asked for in 1980 was only a mandate to discuss "sovereignty-association" with the federal government, voters rejected the proposal 60 percent to 40 percent. Virtually all Québec anglophones, allophones, and First Nations people voted against it. This referendum on separation nevertheless served as a wakeup call to the national and other provincial governments, which then made several attempts to increase Québec's powers and highlight its special status. In 1982, the Canadian Constitution was "repatriated" from Britain and rewritten to highlight the charter status of francophones. However, because the Québec government was not part of the repatriation process, in 1987 the federal and

all the provincial governments assembled at Meech Lake in order to further address Québécois nationalist concerns. While all of the Québec government's demands made there were met, two provincial governments subsequently changed, and refused to support the necessary constitutional amendments. Excluded from the Meech Lake process, most First Nations representatives were strongly against its passage. All the provincial governments and four First Nations organizations met in 1992 in Charlottetown, Prince Edward Island, to try yet again. A national referendum defeated the solution they proposed.

Stung by these rebuffs, in 1995 Québec voters barely sent down to defeat a much more directly worded referendum proposal. Increasing economic prosperity, francophone self-confidence, and voter concern over conventional provincial issues like budget overruns, taxes, and the provision of services seem to have put separatism on the back burner for a while. However, it remains the chief distinguishing political characteristic of the current provincial government, and will not disappear.

Québécois nationalism is a political movement that cannot be considered a primarily ethnic phenomenon. It nevertheless has many ethnic (and some racial) dimensions. Up to the 1960s, separatism was clearly based on a highly exclusive sense of the nation: "Québécois" meant almost exclusively those who lived in Québec, who still spoke French, and whose ancestors either founded New France or else had married into that population. The gloss of civic nationalism added in recent times remains problematic for both adherents and detractors. If "Québécois" is now meant to refer only to a movement to guarantee that those who speak French and live in Québec have full civic rights, much of the separatist rationale for national autonomy based on the historical oppression of, and threat of cultural loss to, the descendants of New France evaporates. Moreover, nationalists have not convinced many anglophones or allophones that one can actually do what this ideology suggests: become Québécois by virtue of becoming a francophone (Handler 1988: 175–181). They argue that (like historical anglo conformity elsewhere in the country) the ethnic (and racial) dimensions of nationalism remain sufficiently powerful that even complete franco conformity does not allow full incorporation of an individual into the nation. In this, they point to the claimed difficulties in becoming Québécois faced by fluently French immigrants such as Vietnamese and Haitians. Over the last twenty years, hundreds of thousands of anglophones and allophones have found the potential trade-offs in making the attempt unrewarding and have voted with their feet by leaving the province.

Perhaps the most knotty problem of an ethnic nature currently facing Québecers concerns First Nations people. Like most ethnic nationalist movements elsewhere, that of francophones in Québec is based on a widely prevalent theory of the rights of peoples. So this argument goes, a people that share origins, language, history, culture, and territory ought to have the right of national self-determination. But there is no natural level at which such claims are either authentic or inauthentic. Ironically, First Nations can–and do–make at least as strong claims of this sort contra the Québec government as Québécois do contra the federal government. Several northern First Nations currently are actively preparing their cases for separation from Québec and re-affiliation with Canada, should Québec separate from the rest of the country (Grand Council of the Crees 1998).

MULTICULTURALISM AND MULTIRACIALISM

National ideologies in Canada and the United States have historically characterized cultural diversity quite differently. When Americans were idealizing the United States as a melting pot of cultures, out of which was cast "an Amer-

ican," nationalist ideologues to the North spoke of a Canadian cultural "mosaic" (Foster 1924)–a nation composed of the contributions of a number of persisting, discrete cultures and groups.

This metaphor of a Canadian cultural mosaic had far less salience and impact than its U.S. counterpart until the late 1960s. By that time, those ethnocultural populations that had been founded or greatly expanded by immigrants during 1896–1930 had generated an articulate, educated, well-placed, middle-class elite. These were chiefly the children of immigrants. When the federal government established the Bilingualism and Biculturalism Commission, these spokespersons were able to raise an effective objection: What about the one-third of Canadians who were then neither British nor French? Where did they fit in a regime of bilingualism and biculturalism? In response, the commission hastily cobbled together another volume to its report titled *The Contributions of the Other Ethnic Groups.* Unsatisfied, spokespersons kept up the pressure, which in 1971 resulted in the promulgation of the Trudeau government's initial policy of *Multiculturalism*–coining a word that has since become ubiquitous. Some dimensions of Multiculturalism were incorporated into the (1982) Constitution Act and subsequently into the world's first Multiculturalism Act (1988).

The government initially had a very limited vision of what federal Multiculturalism was going to be. A minor cabinet portfolio was created to oversee programs having two basic goals: facilitating immigrant adaptation and integration, and securing more public and official recognition of the "achievements" of ethnic groups. However, ethnic group spokespersons, academics, and federal bureaucrats almost immediately established a far larger agenda for Multiculturalism. Within three years, those involved with Multiculturalism policy were committed to changing the substance and image of the Canadian nation: to be more reflective of the diversity of groups and populations in Canada, to reflect a kind of civic nationalism that did not privilege certain ethnicities, to provide positive support for the ethnic identities of Canadians, and to make Canada's laws and practices consistent with Canada's international commitments.

This entailed much social reengineering of Canada's key symbols and origin myths. In 1982, the Canadian national holiday (July 1) was converted from Dominion Day to the ethnically neutral Canada Day–a holiday now marked primarily by local and national celebrations of ethnic and regional diversity. The current Governor General of Canada (i.e., the British Crown's symbolic representative) is a woman of Chinese descent who grew up in Burma. Federal government–supported research initiatives radically expanded core knowledge about, and public awareness of, ethnic group history, current situations, and contemporary achievements and difficulties.[10] Federal financial support was also extended to revise provincial school curricula and curricular materials to make them more inclusive of French Canadians, immigrant groups, and First Nations–all of whom had been almost absent from school texts earlier.

A second major objective of federal Multiculturalism programs (and provincially created similar ones) has been the provision of financial and informational support for a range of symbolically significant ethnic group activities. Here, the rationale is threefold: to support prideful, nonexclusionary ethnic identity, to support effective integration, particularly of new immigrants, and to support the positive public acceptance of ethnocultural diversity. Such financial support has facilitated the teaching of "heritage" languages to the children of immigrants and the establishment of heritage schools, in which students receive a bicultural and bilingual experience. Government money has also been forthcoming for a range of ethnic performances and celebrations aimed at the general population.

A third main goal extends far beyond the range of responsibilities of federal Multicultural-

ism, per se. This is to facilitate more effective access to social, health, educational, and other services by Canada's culturally and linguistically diverse citizenry. This goal remains an ongoing challenge.

In the early 1980s the federal government responded to a series of racial incidents directed toward South Asians and Afro-Canadians with an attempt to address social race through its Multiculturalism machinery. This proved difficult, as the government wished to address folk fictions about race without unintentionally adding credibility to the erroneous idea that there actually *are* biological human races. One unique Canadian government semantic strategy was to generate the term "visible minority groups" (VMGs) to refer to those populations that some other Canadians who viewed themselves as "white" or "invisible" might perceive to be biologically distinct from themselves. In this, the government wished to stress that in Canada, as elsewhere, race is a *perceptual*, not a biological, issue. Visible minorities in Canada encompass several broad categories of person, and represent about 11 percent of all Canadians:

1. First Nations people (800,000–1,100,000 individuals, depending on what criterion is used)
2. Visible minority immigrants and their descendants (roughly 3,200,000 people), including:

    Afro-Canadians (574,000 individuals, chiefly immigrants from nations in the Caribbean and their descendants, long-term residents, and some African immigrants)

    Asian Canadians (2,061,000 individuals), including:

    Chinese (860,000 individuals)

    South Asians (30+ groups, and 671,000 individuals)

    Filipinos (224,000 individuals)

    Vietnamese, Khmer, and Lao (173,000 individuals)

    Japanese (68,000 individuals)

    Koreans (65,000 individuals)

    Arabs and West Asians (245,000 individuals)

    Latin Americans (177,000 individuals)

Federal Multiculturalism and similar provincial and municipal efforts have been quite successful, with three important qualifications. Across Canada–including among francophones in Québec–these programs have established a strong consciousness among Canadians that Canada arose out of, and has been built upon, diversity. Most Canadians today also believe that a limited degree of behavioral diversity is not inconsistent with the goal of creating a harmonious, effective society offering equal treatment to all. These have been very positive developments for the 40 to 50 percent of Canadians who may have some kind of ethnic identity. Critically, virtually all Canadians now believe that one can positively feel "Canadian" and "ethnic" at the same time without contradiction (Canada. *Multiculturalism and Citizenship Canada* 1992; Kalin and Berry 1995). Historical anglo conformity did not allow this. Today's Québec regime of franco conformity may not either.

Even so, the qualifications are significant. First of all, the spokespersons and leaders of two key populations have never accepted the premises of Multiculturalism (Bauhn et al. 1995): representatives of Québec francophones (whether separatist or not) and those of First Nations people. In each case, the leadership has accepted and strongly identifies with the rhetoric of their special, national character. Québécois and First Nations spokespersons feel–some theorists (Kymlicka 1998) claim with justification–that they are more than "merely" another ethnic group. They are also adamant that this fact should be reflected in group-specific rights and privileges and in special relations to governments and governance. In this light, some Québécois and First Nations spokespersons have viewed Multiculturalism as a federal plot to negate their national claims and reduce them to the same status as immigrant-origin ethnic groups. While this assertion is largely unfounded insofar as the subsequent policy trajectory of Multiculturalism is concerned, the overall position of Prime Minister Pierre Trudeau was to strongly affirm individual rights while deprecating ethnocultural and subnational group rights; this stance may have played some role in the policy receiving initial governmental support. Moreover, in their affirmation of Multiculturalism, immigrant-origin ethnic group spokespersons often *do* assert an equivalency among their groups, First Nations people, and Québécois (Kymlicka 1998). Surprisingly, public support for Multiculturalism has been higher in Québec than in most other parts of the country (Mata and Hennebry 1997:6).

Second, although many ethnic group spokespersons fault it as a "failing," Multiculturalism was never intended, and could not possibly have had the resources, to support the full-blown behavioral perpetuation of "ethnic" cultures in Canada. With very few exceptions (such as Mexican Mennonites and Russian Old Believers in rural Alberta; see Scheffel 1991), virtually all recently established Canadian ethnic groups and populations are urban-based. Even in rural areas the few groups that have persisted and grown over the generations play a unique card: like communal Hutterites in the west (Bennett 1967; Hostetler and Huntington 1996), they are bound together by both cultural and religious factors. Extremely powerful acculturative pressures and desires operate on urban immigration-based populations. In a behavioral sense, recent immigrants must conform to much "Canadian" everyday practice from the day they arrive in order to achieve their personal goals and to function effectively. Some unwanted elements of their source cultures and social systems were, of course, among the things that motivated them to immigrate in the first place. These forces of acculturation operate particularly strongly on the young. In the absence of profound discrimination or enforced ethnic separation, the second generation in most groups exhibit very selective maintenance of source country cultural practices. This does not mean that they have ceased to identify with their roots. Multiculturalism programs are designed primarily to support positive ethnic identity through *symbolic* cultural maintenance and through language training.

Third, and by extension, Multiculturalism has not been able to profoundly transform the behavioral dimensions of ethnic and race relations through direct programming. Multiculturalism programs are grounded on the thesis that one can significantly change unwanted behaviors (in this case, ethnic and racial discrimination) by changing people's beliefs and values. There is merit in this thesis when it operates slowly on a large stage, as when programming alters the general sense of what it means to be Canadian to make it more inclusive. Even so, ethnic and racial discrimination (that is to say, discriminatory behavior) is often most effectively combated directly, not through attitude change (Buchignani 1983). Multiculturalism's concentration on attitudes rather than behavior exemplifies the indirect way the state generally approaches the promotion of social justice issues pertaining to ethnicity and race.

AN INCREASINGLY STRONG COMMITMENT TO INDIVIDUAL HUMAN RIGHTS

Historical Canadian governments rarely placed legal constraints on ethnic and racial minorities. In the twentieth century, the most glaring exception was the discriminatory legal treatment of those First Nations people who were registered on tribal band lists. Status Indians could neither vote nor leave reserves without permission. Their children were sent to residential schools whether this was the desire of their parents or not. Perhaps the second most significant exception was the treatment of certain minorities in wartime. Germans, Ukrainians, and some other "enemy aliens" faced many constraints during

World War I, and some were arbitrarily jailed. During World War II the Canadian and American governments coordinated efforts to incarcerate virtually every mainland resident of Japanese origin for the duration, including citizens (but ironically excluding those in the armed forces). The government then sold their property. Several thousand residents of other nationalities were also sent to camps. Some national and ethnic immigration restrictions (most notably against Chinese, Japanese, and Indians) remained in place until after World War II. Among provincial governments, only British Columbia's extensively used the law to limit the rights and activities of immigrants once they had arrived in Canada. Most Chinese, Japanese, and people from India in British Columbia could not vote prior to 1947. They were also banned from provincial jobs, crown contracts, and certain professions.

These actions were legal prior to the promulgation of the Canadian Bill of Rights in 1958. So also were informal discrimination and overt expressions of prejudice. Since then, a series of legislative and court actions have rendered illegal virtually all forms of discrimination against individuals on the grounds of nationality, ethnic origin, and race; the right to protection against these forms of discrimination is overtly asserted in the Canadian Constitution and the Charter of Rights and Freedoms. Section 15.(1) of the latter states: "Every individual is equal before and under the law and has the right to the equal protection and equal benefit of the law without discrimination and, in particular, without discrimination based on race, national or ethnic origin, colour, religion, sex, age or mental or physical disability."[11] The federal and provincial governments have also passed human rights legislation empowering commissions to address complaints of discrimination through mediation and civil law. The elimination of discrimination and injustice is now a stated responsibility of Canadian citizenship.

FEW INSTITUTIONALIZED MEANS TO ADDRESS DISCRIMINATION

Racial and ethnic discrimination in Canada have never been anything near as big a public social issue as they have in the United States. One consequence of this has been that Canadian courts have not played the same activist role in addressing or redressing discrimination that courts did in the United States during 1950–80. Strong commitments to individual human rights notwithstanding, the only court-mandated forms of redress of significance have addressed solely the treaty and other aboriginal rights of First Nations people. Even in the case of First Nations, courts have done little to specifically address historical inequities faced by *individuals*; perhaps the sole significant exception has been a series of civil suits and criminal prosecutions relating to the treatment of children in residential schools, orphanages, and other publicly funded institutions.

This has put the issue squarely in the court of government, which has been reluctant to act aggressively, either to punish discriminators or to actively protect its potential victims. The argument that historical injustices have significant, lingering consequences that must be addressed by compensatory programs such as affirmative action has been repeatedly asserted by visible minority spokespersons, but this has had few important consequences in law or government practice (Loney 1998). The provision of extensive (if still profoundly inadequate) services to First Nations people is, for example, rarely justified by such arguments. The federal government initiated a policy of preferentially advancing francophones in the 1970s, and thereafter has instituted a basic form of affirmative hiring and advancement that also covers visible minorities in the federal government workplace (through the Employment Equity Act 1986/1996). Public institutions such as universities that receive federal funds and companies that receive federal contracts are also supposed

to comply but often do not (Henry et al. 1995, chapter 8). Similar provincial and municipal government efforts have been episodic and lackadaisical. Some metropolitan police departments have instituted targeted searches for visible minority recruits, but the proportion of visible minority officers in no urban police force today is even one-quarter that of the population they serve. A few big-city forces have liaison officers who interface with particular urban ethnocultural groups. Some large school districts have put zero tolerance antidiscriminatory policies in place. With the exception of some resource extraction companies that operate in areas primarily populated by First Nations people, few private companies have initiated any kind of affirmative action.

In addition, Canada has no effective legislation in place that criminalizes discrimination. Its federal Hate Crimes legislation is supposed to offer some redress from explicit expressions of race hatred, but few prosecutions have been made under it and almost none have been successful. Human rights legislation based on civil law has proved to be slow, cumbersome, and ineffective in materially addressing the ethnic or racial disabilities of a significant number of Canadians.

Instead of seeking to punish or otherwise directly address the actions of discriminators, the Canadian way has been to put money and effort into programs that better prepare potential victims of discrimination to succeed, to affirm the morality and legality of equality, and to support intergroup tolerance. Here, the focus has clearly been primarily on immigrant-origin visible minority groups.

CONTEMPORARY ETHNIC AND RACE RELATIONS PROBLEMS

Like Americans, Canadians have become increasingly tolerant of immigrant-origin cultural diversity over the last fifty years. One key factor here has been a form of sequential desensitization to cultural difference that has been an unintended result of increasing immigrant diversity. Many less tolerant urban Canadians of the 1950s thought of so-called DPs—displaced persons arriving from Europe—as quite strange. They did not look so strange when many thousands of Italian and Portuguese immigrants arrived a decade later. When South Asians, Jamaicans, Chinese, and other visible minorities began coming in force in the 1970s, reservations against southern Europeans evaporated.

Another factor reducing intolerance toward immigrant-origin populations has been their quick and easily apparent integration into the social and economic mainstream. No modern immigrant-origin urban population has been forced to remain sharply socially, economically, and culturally distinct against its will. In addition, as a general rule valid up to the 1980s, when the range of actual and perceived cultural difference among immigrants increased over the years, so also did the class resources of typical immigrants. As a case in point, only 18 percent of recent adult immigrants claim to have less than ten years of schooling. Independent immigrants in particular today tend to be highly skilled and educated, regardless of where they came from.

Immigrants have also benefited from the establishment and validation of societal conventions that categorize ethnocultural discrimination as inappropriate. Many of those four of every ten Toronto residents who were born in another country came from places where ethnic intolerance is far more extensive and gets more public approval than in Canada. Inevitably, these prejudices are brought to Canada, but it is now difficult for a person to act publicly upon them without some risk of sanction. There is also considerable evidence that each new generation of Canadians is more accepting of diversity when they are young than the generation before them, and that tolerance instilled when young is generally maintained through life. Older Cana-

dians tend to be more intolerant, not because they have become more so as they age, but because they always were.

Comprehensive national data on Canadian attitudes toward specific ethnocultural and national populations have not been collected since 1991. At that time, a careful replication (Berry and Kalin 1995; Kalin and Berry 1996) of an earlier national study (Berry et al. 1977:106) found that at an aggregate level, Canadians continued to use perceived ethnicity and race to evaluate each other. In this, many maintained a perceptual hierarchy of groups that was not radically different than was prevalent fifty years previously (Table 19-3). What had changed significantly was the *range* of perceived differences between groups, which seems to have greatly decreased over time. Today's Canadians evidently do not see as large a cultural or racial difference between one ethnocultural population and another as did their parents. Moreover, assessments of certain established immigrant-origin populations such as Italians, Ukrainians, and Chinese had become far more positive than before.

Attitudinal indications of tolerance are given additional support by behavioral evidence. Incidents of extreme violence toward immigrant-origin visible minorities are rare, and are national news when they occur. Nothing approaching a race riot has occurred in the last fifty years. No immigrant-origin group is ghettoized or isolated from the mainstream except (like the Hutterites) through choice. Data collected in the census show no indication that immigrant-origin individuals from any group or population face profound economic obstacles when controlled for other variables.

These positive findings should not suggest that Canada lacks significant racial and ethnic problems. In terms of the number of people affected and the depth of the problem, various forms of discrimination toward First Nations people are clearly Canada's most serious and intractable ethnic and race relations challenge.

Table 19-3.   National Attitudinal Ranking of Ethnic and Racial Groups, 1977 and 1991

Group	Ranking in 1977	Score in 1977	Ranking in 1991	Score in 1991
English	1	.52	1	.46
Scottish	2	.49	–	–
French	3	.47	3	.30
Dutch	4	.46	–	–
Scandinavian	5	.39	–	–
Japanese	8	.13	–	–
Hungarian	9	.10	–	–
Polish	10	.08	–	–
Jewish	11	.04	7	.16
German	12	.02	5	.18
Ukrainian	18	–.13	4	.25
Italian	19	–.20	2	.32
Portuguese	20	–.25	6	.17
Chinese	21	–.26	8	.15
Greek	23	–.36	–	–
Negro, West Indian	25	–.52	9	–.15
Arab	–	–	10	–.38
East Indian	26	–.95	11	–.53
Sikh	–	–	12	–.68

Source: Buchignani and Indra, in Haines and Rosenblum, eds. *Illegal Immigration in America: A Reference Handbook* (Greenwood Press, CT, 1999). Copyright © 1999 by David Haynes and Karen Rosenblum. Reprinted with permission of Greenwood Publishing Group, Inc. All rights reserved.

Like Native Americans and African Americans, First Nations people once faced a severe regime of subordination that has had profound consequences long after the core elements of that regime were dismantled (see Brody 1975, 1988). In essence, historical ethnic, racial, and national disabilities were once so great and were in place so long that they have become enduring class disabilities.

Today, most of Canada's First Nations people face the daunting challenges, impediments, and disappointments that arise out of structural forces that continue to keep them very poor. First Nations incomes are dramatically lower than those of any other ethnocultural population. Unemployment rates reach 90 percent on some isolated rural reserves, and are probably not less than 50 percent anywhere in the country. Kept outside the mainstream for so long by forces that negated and destroyed their prior ways of life, many today face uncertainties of identity and feel profoundly deprived and powerless. These factors in turn affect diet, risk of accident, and patterns of substance abuse. The health of adults is, on average, so poor that researchers and health workers typically consider First Nations people old at age 50 (Buchignani and Armstrong-Esther 1999); life expectancy at birth on some reserves within ten minutes of towns and cities with world-class medical facilities is the same as in the Third World (Culhane Speck 1987). A far higher proportion of First Nations people is incarcerated than any other ethnocultural population. While most other Canadians now have very positive attitudes toward First Nations people, this is not necessarily true of those who interface with them on a daily basis. Both negative stereotypes of drunk, lazy Indians (Braroe 1975) and some historical patterns of everyday discrimination continue to persist in many of the places where First Nations people live (Henriksen 1978; Kennedy 1982; Plaice 1990; Waldram 1987). Those facing such prejudice and discrimination typically have few resources to combat them.

At the same time, the specifically ethnic and racial difficulties of First Nations people are not a high-profile public issue; they are almost never framed as such by First Nations leadership, who have other priorities, such as securing further services and advancing land claims. Health, economic, psychological, and other problems that clearly are at least partially dependent on historical and ongoing ethnic and race relations are often addressed by specific programs but almost never directly as race or ethnic issues.

There is also increasing evidence that Afro-Canadians—who share very little else with each other—face specifically *racial* disabilities that are not going away. Historically, "blacks" in the Maritimes, Ontario, and elsewhere who were longtime Canadians had full legal rights, in the narrowest sense of the term. However, they faced routine job, residential, and other forms of discrimination that were little different in character or intensity than in the northeastern United States. As in the United States, these forms of overt, specifically racial discrimination disappeared in the 1950s and 1960s. Less overt forms did not (Clairmont and Magill 1974; Henry 1973). The depth of specifically ethnic or racial prejudice and discrimination directed toward "African"-origin immigrants (who actually came chiefly from the Caribbean) during the same period is difficult to assess, as many also faced gender, class, and immigration-generated disabilities. Changes made in immigrant selection criteria in the late 1960s thereafter increased the range of nationalities and ethnicities among the Afro-Canadian population, although in the 1970s most continued to come from the Caribbean. These changes also affected the class backgrounds of "black" immigrants. By the 1980s, the skill and educational levels of the overall Afro-Canadian population was broadly comparable to those of other Canadians. In the 1980s and 1990s, the national range of Afro-Canadians was further expanded by the arrival of refugees, asylum seekers, and other immigrants directly from Africa—chiefly from the Horn of Africa.

Canadian reluctance to "talk race" notwithstanding, several types of evidence suggest that Afro-Canadians face racial disabilities (Breton 1998; Cannon 1995; Henry and Tator 1994). For one, it is clear that American popular culture images of African Americans have long had negative consequences across the border (Indra 1979a, 1982). No other people on earth receive as much exposure to American mass-distributed electronic and print materials as do Canadians, and one result is that other Canadians now sometimes associate Afro-Canadians with media stereotypes of African Americans. Even Canadian police evidently now believe that Afro-Canadians are prone to crime, even though it appears that neither their crime nor incarceration rates are different than those of the population at large. A number of studies show that Afro-Canadians are sensitive to the risk of racial discrimination (Dei et al. 1997; Ebanks 1996) and believe that it is prevalent. Several studies suggest that the racial climate of schools impedes the success of some Afro-Canadian children and disengages them from the educational process (Dei et al. 1997; Solomon 1992). A controlled study of hiring practices during the economic recession of the early 1980s showed that Afro-Canadian candidates in Toronto were being discriminated against (Henry and Ginzberg 1985), even if a restudy in more prosperous times did not (Henry 1989). West Indian male incomes in Toronto were then roughly $3,500 lower than would be predicted on the basis of their qualifications, chiefly as a result of their lower than expected job statuses (Breton et al. 1990:160).

Some other recent immigrant-origin populations are probably at some material risk. Immigrants from South Asia (India, Pakistan, etc.) were the focus of extensive stereotyping and occasional targets of serious, violent incidents in the late 1970s and 1980s. The frequency of attacks against South Asian individuals has decreased significantly since then (Buchignani 1993; Buchignani and Indra 1981, 1985, 1989). Even so, South Asians continue to be thought of as the most culturally different of all immigrant-origin populations, and ideas about South

Asians are still informed by negative media portrayal of those cultural differences and of India, Pakistan, and other South Asian source countries (Indra 1979b, 1982).

A positive stereotype of Chinese Canadians (T. Chan 1983; K. Chan 1987) has arisen over the last thirty years, one that characterizes them as "polite, economically self-sufficient, hardworking, and law abiding" (K. Chan 1987:126), strongly familial, apolitical, quickly integrating, and not socially disruptive. This has facilitated their almost seamless integration into Canada's urban fabric in most places. The partial exception has been in the Vancouver area. Hundreds of thousands of ethnic Chinese immigrated to Vancouver and the surrounding region during the economic boom affecting Asian Pacific Rim countries during the 1980s and early 1990s. A significant number were from Hong Kong, who established residence in Canada as insurance against what might occur when the British colony was transferred back to China. Both in numbers and economic power, these new Chinese residents transformed whole towns and neighborhoods without much local input. Large shopping malls were established to cater exclusively to Chinese. Thousands who were better off knocked down older houses in desirable areas and replaced them with what were locally termed "monster houses." A few others began to be associated in the media with gangs and the drug trade. This generated focused resentment toward local Chinese as the supposed cause of a wide range of societal changes and problems, from high real estate prices to the loss of established neighborhood ways of life (Cannon 1989). There are, however, no indications that this has translated into significant anti-Chinese discrimination.

Finally, to perhaps a smaller degree than in the United States, groups from the Middle East continue to contend with very negative media stereotypes of Arabs and Muslims (Kashmeri 1991).

GLOBAL CONNECTIONS, LOCAL STRUCTURES

There are three important additional ways in which the current Canadian situation is very similar to that in the United States. One is the persistent tendency of those who feel that they share a common ethnicity or nationality to associate with each other, and by doing so, to form local communities and institutions. Enduring identity and language-based community structures have been part and parcel of Canadian minority group life from the onset. This is not solely the case for immigrant-origin populations. Community structures have been critical to the lives of francophones, in and out of Québec, and to First Nations people everywhere. Today, such communities are a central source of support for identity, practical assistance, and access to goods and services. They are also often the result of, and an impetus to, further chain migration—of First Nations people moving between rural and urban contexts and of many immigrants. In many respects, informal community structure—the overlapping networks of personal relationships between one person and another among people who see themselves as "the same"—is at the very center of the set of phenomena called ethnicity.

As in the United States, the persistence of ethnic and national consciousness over time continues to vary dramatically from one group to another. Two key populations appear destined to persist indefinitely: francophones in Québec and First Nations people. Both are large, effectively instill group consciousness, are institutionally and legally distinguished by the state, face interactional barriers in associating with others, and maintain a wide range of parallel institutions. Racial identification by others continues to maintain a reactive form of consciousness among many Afro-Canadians, including those who neither affiliate with any immigrant source country nor maintain any significantly different cultural practices. Such consciousness remains strong in the Afro-Canadian populations of New Brunswick and Nova Scotia, which were founded over two hundred years ago.

Of all other groups and populations, only a few ethnoreligious groups–those in which religious and cultural distinctiveness have arisen together–otherwise appear to have the resources to maintain themselves successfully beyond the second generation without ongoing immigration. The most remarkable of these is undoubtedly the roughly 20,000 communal Hutterites living in the west, whose numbers are growing rapidly through natural increase and who lose fewer than 10 percent of their members in a generation. Over two generations, several Hassidic Jewish populations seem to have been equally effective in preserving a high degree of identity, and social and cultural separation from others in the challenging context of urban Montréal. Sikhs and Ismaili Muslims (Dossa 1985) appear to be able to maintain continuity of identity, religion, and some associated core cultural practices strongly into the second generation, particularly where they are members of large communities.

Immediate (often, extended) family, kinship, and informal community were vitally important to individuals from many immigrant-origin populations prior to immigration (particularly those from Asia), and almost always continue to be so afterwards. This, along with very high rates of chain migration, has led to the formation of large, deeply connected communities in almost every local Asian immigrant population across the country. Most of these communities are so new that it is still difficult to predict with certainty the degree to which the children of immigrants will significantly participate in them as adults. However, there are a number of indications that many children will either not participate in them beyond maintaining ties with relatives, or else will do so very selectively. This certainly has been so historically, even for large, institutionally complete communities like Italians in Toronto (Gabori 1993; Harney 1998; Jansen 1986). In such earlier cases, institutions created by and for immigrant adults proved unable to stem identity shift, acculturation, and assimilation among their children. Some measure of "British" (chiefly Scottish and Irish) ethnic identity persists from very early times in those parts of the country where recent levels of immigration have been low, and where notions of ethnicity and roots have become intertwined with local/regional culture, ethnic tourism, and images of local folk culture manufactured by folklorists and others (Macdonald 1988; Pocius 1991). In contrast, some immigrants like Americans do not form communities at all, and evidently do not even think of themselves in ethnic terms.

Second, most of Canada's institutions still have not extensively adapted themselves to meet the practical, everyday needs and aspirations of people whose language or core cultural values diverge from the mainstream. The barriers to a good life facing those whose knowledge of English or French is poor remains profound; and outside of major public institutions like hospitals in large cities (which now typically can access translators and cultural interpreters), the chief remedy to their plight continues to be access to ESL and FSL programs rather than institutional change. Language and cultural accommodation by the mainstream business community has been slight. Women or those who lack substantial class resources are at a particular disadvantage (Ng 1988; van Esterik 1991). Lack of facility with one of the two official languages continues to orient people toward those who share their birth language, strengthening interpersonal community relations and ethnic identity and building and maintaining group-specific parallel institutions (Indra 1986).

Finally, as in the United States, transportation and communication changes have dramatically altered ties between immigrants and their descendants and the rest of the world. Few of the countries from which today's immigrants come are much more than 24 hours' travel away. As a consequence, immigrant-origin populations and their source countries are often bound together by streams of visitors going in both directions (Patel 1999). Canadians are one of the most mobile populations in the world, and experience diversity both overseas and at home. Cheap international telephone and Internet service extend to what were once remote parts of the globe. Increased ease of communications has also facilitated access to world popular culture, augmenting the multilingual television and radio stations found in most cities. Like world music, literature is not so localized as before: "ethnic" Canadian authors such as Michael Ondaatje and Rohinton Mistry write of their source cultures, histories, and societies for an international audience.

All these factors mean that ethnic and race relations in Canada cannot now—if they ever could—be adequately addressed solely as localized "Canadian" phenomena. Neither people nor ideas are as fixed in place as before. Events in a small village in rural Punjab can have immediate implications for a Sikh family in Vancouver, and vice versa. Nationalist conflicts in the former Yugoslavia can polarize what were once amicable relations between Serbs and Croats in Toronto. World ecological ideologies can and are being used by First Nations people in Canada to re-engineer a more positive public image, at the same time that Inuit sealing practices challenge the hegemony of some of these same ecological dogmas overseas.

NOTES

1. Since the 1980s, "First Nations" has been the preferred term of reference for Canadians who claim an aboriginal (native) heritage.
2. Canada and the United States are each other's largest trading partners by far. Forty million to 50 million individual transits of the border are made each year.
3. Many First Nations people, however, are not covered by a specific treaty. This includes most of those in British

Columbia and most Inuit and Indians in the North. Neither Métis nor "nonstatus" Indians are covered by treaties. The Canadian Supreme Court declared that Inuit were "Indians" for purposes of the British North America Act in 1939.
4. The source of this and other otherwise unreferenced 1996 census data is the Web site of *Statistics Canada:* www.statcan.ca/english/.
5. See Aihwa Ong (1996) for a similar modern U.S. reaction to Lao immigrants.
6. Canada shares this distinction with South Africa, which also has two persisting charter groups: Dutch-origin Afrikaners and British.
7. The British connection was still so strong that Canada immediately joined the war on their side. Most Québec francophones could then trace their roots in North America back more than 250 years and had no commitment to any foreign power. Many actively resisted conscription.
8. Additional information on Canadian immigration is available at Citizenship and Immigration Canada's Web site, www.cic.gc.ca.
9. The number of francophones in Québec in 1996 (5,800,000) slightly exceeded the number of Québec residents who had French as a mother tongue (5,700,000).
10. See the *Canadian Ethnic Studies Journal* for the range of current research interests concerning Canadian ethnic and racial issues.
11. The following subsection (2) states that this provision "does not preclude any law, program or activity that has as its object the amelioration of conditions of disadvantaged individuals or groups including those that are disadvantaged because of race, national or ethnic origin, colour, religion, sex, age or mental or physical disability."

REFERENCES CITED

Asch, Michael. 1984. *Home and Native Land: Aboriginal Rights and the Canadian Constitution.* Toronto: Methuen.

Asch, Michael, ed. 1997. *Aboriginal Treaty Rights in Canada: Essays on Law, Equality, and Respect for Difference.* Vancouver: University of British Columbia Press.

Bauhn, Per, Christer Lindberg, and Svante Lundberg. 1995. *Multiculturalism and Nationhood in Canada: The Cases of First Nations and Québec.* Lund, Sweden: Lund University Press.

Bennett, John. 1967. *Hutterian Brethren: The Agricultural Economy of a Communal People.* Stanford: Stanford University Press.

Berry John W., and Rudolf Kalin. 1995. Multicultural and ethnic attitudes in Canada: An overview of the 1991 national survey. *Canadian Journal of Behavioural Science* 27(3):301–320.

Berry, John, Rudolf Kalin, and D. Taylor. 1977. *Multiculturalism and Ethnic Attitudes in Canada.* Ottawa: Information Canada.

Braroe, Niels. 1975. *Indian and White: Self Image and Interaction in a Canadian Plains Community.* Stanford: Stanford University Press.

BRETON, RAYMOND. 1964. Institutional completeness of ethnic communities and personal relations of immigrants. *American Journal of Sociology* 70(2):193–205.

___. 1998. Ethnicity and race in social organizations: Recent developments in Canadian society. In *The Vertical Mosaic Revisited.* R. Helmes-Hayes and J. Curtis, eds. Pp. 60–115. Toronto: University of Toronto Press.

BRETON, RAYMOND, WSEVOLOD ISAJIW, WARREN KALBACH, and JEFFREY REITZ. 1990. *Ethnic Identity and Equality: Varieties of Experience in a Canadian City.* Toronto: University of Toronto Press.

BRODY, HUGH. 1975. *The People's Land: Whites and the Western Arctic.* Harmondsworth, UK: Penguin.

___. 1988. *Maps and Dreams: Indians and the British Columbia Frontier.* Vancouver: Douglas & McIntyre.

BUCHIGNANI, NORMAN. 1983. Some comments on the elimination of racism in Canada. *Canadian Ethnic Studies* 15(2):118–124.

___. 1993. Refugees and ethnic relations in Canada. In *The International Refugee Crisis: British and Canadian Responses.* Vaughn Robinson, ed. Pp. 35–56. London: Macmillan.

BUCHIGNANI, NORMAN, and CHRISTOPHER ARMSTRONG-ESTHER. 1999. Informal care and older native Canadians. *Ageing and Society* 19:3–32.

BUCHIGNANI, NORMAN, and DOREEN INDRA. 1981. Intergroup conflict and community solidarity: Sikhs and South Asian Fijians in Vancouver. *Canadian Journal of Anthropology* 1(2):149–157.

___. 1985. *Continuous Journey: A Social History of South Asians in Canada.* Toronto: McClelland and Stewart.

___. 1989. Key issues in Canadian-Sikh ethnic and race relations, and their implications for the study of the Sikh diaspora. In *The Sikh Diaspora.* N. G. Barrier and V. Dusenbery, eds. Pp. 141–184. New Delhi: Manohar.

___. 1999. Vanishing acts: Illegal immigration in Canada as a sometime social issue. In *Illegal Immigration in America: A Reference Handbook.* David Haines and Karen Rosenblum, eds. Pp. 415–450. Westport, CT: Greenwood Press.

BUCHIGNANI, NORMAN, and PAUL LETKEMANN. 1993. Ethnographic research. In *Multiculturalism in Canada.* John Berry and Jean Laponce, eds. Pp. 203–237. Toronto: University of Toronto Press.

CANADA. Citizenship and Immigration Canada. 1999. Facts and Figures 1998: Immigration Overview. Ottawa: Minister of Public Works and Government Services Canada.

CANADA. Multiculturalism and Citizenship Canada. 1992. Multiculturalism Attitude Survey 1991. Ottawa: Multiculturalism and Citizenship Canada.

CANNON, MARGARET. 1995. *The Invisible Empire: Racism in Canada.* Mississauga, ON: Random House.

CHAN, KWOK. 1987. Perceived racial discrimination and response: An analysis of Indochinese experience in Montréal. *Canadian Ethnic Studies* 19(3):125–147.

CHAN, KWOK, LOUIS J. DORAIS, and DOREEN INDRA, eds. 1988. *Ten Years Later: Indochinese Communities in Canada.* Ottawa: Canadian Asian Studies Association.

CHAN, KWOK, and DOREEN INDRA, eds. 1986. *Uprooting, Loss and Adaptation: The Resettlement of Indochinese Refugees in Canada.* Ottawa: Canadian Public Health Association.

CHAN, TONY. 1983. *Gold Mountain: The Chinese in the New World.* Vancouver: New Star Books.

CLAIRMONT, D. H., and D. W. MAGILL. 1974. *Africville: The Life and Death of a Canadian Black Community.* Toronto: McClelland and Stewart.

CANNON, MARGARET. 1989. *China Tide: The Revealing Story of the Hong Kong Exodus to Canada.* Toronto: Harper & Collins.

CULHANE SPECK, D. 1987. *An Error in Judgment: The Politics of Medical Care in Indian/White Community.* Vancouver: Talon Books.

DEI, GEORGE J. S., JOSEPHINE MAZZUCA, ELIZABETH MCISAAC, and JASMIN ZINE. 1997. *Reconstructing Drop-Out: A Critical Ethnography of the Dynamics of Black Students' Disengagement from School.* Toronto: University of Toronto Press.

DIRKS, GERALD E. 1977. *Canada's Refugee Policy: Indifference or Opportunism?* Montreal: McGill-Queen's University Press.

DORAIS, LOUIS-JACQUES, L. PILON-LE, and N. HUY. 1987. *Exiles in a Cold Land: A Vietnamese Community in Canada.* Southeast Asia Studies. New Haven, CT: Yale University Press.

DOSSA, PARIN. 1985. Ritual and daily life: Transmission and interpretation of the Ismaili tradition in Vancouver. Ph.D. dissertation, University of British Columbia.

DRIBEN, PAUL. 1985. *Aroland Is Our Home: An Incomplete Victory in Applied Anthropology.* New York: AMS Press.

DYCK, NOEL. 1991. *What Is the Indian "Problem"? Tutelage and Resistance in the Canadian Indian Administration.* St. John's: Institute of Social and Economic Research.

___, ed. 1985. *Indigenous Peoples and the Nation State: "Fourth World" Politics in Canada, Australia and Norway.* St. John's: Institute of Social and Economic Research.

EBANKS, G. E. 1996. The Caribbean diaspora in Toronto: Learning to live with racism. *Canadian Ethnic Studies* 28(2):188–190.

ELLER, JACK D. 1998. *From Culture to Ethnicity to Conflict: An Anthropological Perspective on International Ethnic Conflict.* Ann Arbor: University of Michigan Press.

FOSTER, K. A. 1924. *Our Canadian Mosaic.* Toronto: Dominion Council of the YWCA.

GABORI, SUSAN. 1993. *In Search of Paradise: The Odyssey of an Italian Family.* Montreal: McGill-Queen's University Press.

GARIQUE, P. 1956. French Canadian kinship and urban life. *American Anthropologist* 58:1090–1101.

GILAD, LISA. 1990. *The Northern Route: An Ethnography of Refugee Experiences.* St. John's: Institute of Social and Economic Research.

GOLD, GERALD. 1975. *St. Pascal.* Toronto: Holt, Rinehart & Winston.

Grand Council of the Crees (of Québec). 1998. *Never without Consent: James Bay Crees' Stand Against Forcible Inclusion into an Independent Québec.* Toronto: ECW Press.

HANDLER, RICHARD. 1988. *Nationalism and the Politics of Culture in Québec.* Madison: University of Wisconsin Press.

HARNEY, NICHOLAS D. M. 1998. *Eh, Paesan! Being Italian in Toronto.* Toronto: University of Toronto Press.

HELMES-HAYES, R., and J. CURTIS, eds. 1998. *The Vertical Mosaic Revisited.* Toronto: University of Toronto Press.

HENRIKSEN, GEORG. 1978. *Hunters in the Barrens.* St. John's: Memorial University Press.

HENRY, FRANCIS. 1973. *Forgotten Canadians: The Blacks of Nova Scotia.* Don Mills, ON: Longmans Canada.

___. 1989. *Who Gets the Work in 1989?* Ottawa: Economic Council of Canada.

HENRY, FRANCIS, and E. GINZBERG. 1985. *Who Gets the Work: A Test of Racial Discrimination in Employment.* Toronto: Urban Alliance on Race Relations.

HENRY, FRANCES, and CAROL TATOR. 1994. The ideology of racism: "Democratic racism." *Canadian Ethnic Studies* 26(2):1–14.

HENRY, FRANCES, CAROL TATOR, WINSTON MATTIS, and TIM REES. 1995. *The Colour of Democracy: Racism in Canadian Society.* Toronto: Harcourt Brace.

HOSTETLER, J. A., and G. E. HUNTINGTON. 1996. *The Hutterites in North America.* Toronto: Holt, Rinehart & Winston.

INDRA, DOREEN. 1979a. Ethnicity, social stratification and opinion formation: An analysis of ethnic portrayal in the Vancouver newspaper press, 1905–1976. Ph.D. dissertation, Simon Fraser University.

___. 1979b. South Asian stereotypes in the Vancouver press. *Ethnic and Racial Studies* 2(2):166–189.

___. 1982. The production and legitimation of racial and ethnic stereotypes in the Vancouver press, 1905–82. In *Perspectives on Race, Education and Social Development: Emphasis on Canada.* Vincent D'Oyley, ed. Pp. 35–43. Vancouver: University of British Columbia.

___. 1986. Bureaucratic constraints, middlemen and community organization: Aspects of the political incorporation of Southeast Asians in Canada. In *Uprooting, Loss and Adaptation: The Resettlement of Indochinese Refugees in Canada.* Kwok Chan and Doreen M. Indra, eds. Pp. 147–170. Ottawa: Canadian Public Health Association.

JANSEN, C. 1986. *Italians in a Multicultural Canada.* Queenston, ON: Mellen.

KALIN, RUDOLF, and JOHN W. BERRY. 1995. Ethnic and civic self-identity in Canada: Analyses of 1974 and 1991 national surveys. *Canadian Ethnic Studies* 27(2):1–15.

___. 1996. Interethnic attitudes in Canada: Ethnocentrism, consensual hierarchy and reciprocity. *Canadian Journal of Behavioural Science* 28(4):253–261.

KASHMERI, ZUHAIR. 1991. *The Gulf Within: Canadian Arabs, Racism, and the Gulf War.* Toronto: J. Lorimer.

KENNEDY, J. 1982. *Holding the Line: Ethnic Boundaries in a Northern Labrador Community.* Memorial University, Institute of Social and Economic Research.

KNOWLES, VALERIE. 1997. *Strangers at Our Gates: Canadian Immigration and Immigration Policy, 1540–1997.* Rev. edition. Toronto: Dundurn Press.

KYMLICKA, WILL. 1998. *Finding Our Way: Rethinking Ethnocultural Relations in Canada.* Toronto: Oxford University Press.

LONEY, MARTIN. 1998. *The Pursuit of Division: Race, Gender, and Preferential Hiring in Canada.* Montreal: McGill-Queen's University Press.

MACDONALD, N. 1988. Putting on the kilt: The Scottish stereotype and ethnic community survival in Cape Breton. *Canadian Ethnic Studies* 20(3):132–146.

MATA, FERNANDO, and JENNA HENNEBRY. 1997. *Public Approval of the Federal Policy of Multiculturalism in the 90s.* Ottawa: Department of Canadian Heritage.

NG, R. 1988. *The Politics of Community Services: Immigrant Women, Class and State.* Toronto: Garamond Press.

ONG, AIHWA. 1996. Cultural citizenship as subject-making: Immigrants negotiate racial and cultural boundaries in the United States. *Current Anthropology* 37(5): 737–762.

PATEL, DHIRU. 1999. Technology, identity and cultural change in the South Asian diasporas. Paper presented at Citizens at the Crossroads: Whose Information Society? conference, University of Western Ontario, London, ON, October.

PLAICE, E. 1990. *The Native Game: Settler Perceptions of Indian/Settler Relations in Central Labrador.* St. John's: Institute of Social and Economic Research.

POCIUS, GERALD. 1991. *A Place to Belong: Community Order and Everyday Space in Calvert, Newfoundland.* Montreal: McGill-Queen's University Press.

PONTING, J. R. 1997. *First Nations in Canada: Perspectives on Opportunity, Empowerment, and Self-Determination.* Toronto: McGraw-Hill Ryerson.

PORTER, JOHN. 1965. *The Vertical Mosaic: An Analysis of Social Class and Power in Canada.* Toronto: University of Toronto Press.

PURICH, DONALD J. 1988. *The Métis.* Toronto: Lorimer.

REITZ, JEFFREY G., and RAYMOND BRETON. 1994. *The Illusion of Difference: Realities of Ethnicity in Canada & the United States.* Toronto: C. D. Howe Institute.

SALISBURY, RICHARD. 1986. *A Homeland for the Cree: Regional Development in James Bay, 1971–1981.* Montreal: McGill-Queen's University Press.

SCHEFFEL, DAVID. 1991. *In the Shadow of the Antichrist: The Old Believers of Alberta.* Peterborough: Broadview Press.

SOLOMON, ROVEL PATRICK. 1992. *Black Resistance in High School: Forging a Separatist Culture.* Albany: State University of New York Press.

VAN ESTERIK, JOHN. 1991. Communication claims in a refugee program: A case study of an anthropologist working with immigrant and refugee settlement agencies. In *Immigrants and Refugees in Canada: A National Perspective on Ethnicity, Multiculturalism, and Cross-Cultural Adjustment*. S. Sharma, A. Ervin, and D. Meintel, eds. Saskatoon: University of Saskatchewan and University of Montreal.

WALDRAM, JAMES B. 1987. Ethnostatus distinctions in the western Canadian subarctic: Implications for inter-ethnic and interpersonal relations. *Culture* 7(1):29–38.

20

CONCLUSION

Raymond Scupin

Lindenwood University

This textbook has emphasized the contribution of anthropology to an understanding of race and ethnicity issues. In the first section of the text we focus on the professionalization of the field of anthropology during the nineteenth century, and how the issues of race and ethnicity were at the center of the major research problems. Questions involving the evolution of different races and cultures throughout the world were investigated through research on fossils, artifacts, language, and cultural beliefs and practices. However, as we learned in Chapter 1, these early anthropological paradigms were based on both racist and ethnocentric beliefs that informed the theories and hypotheses that were developed in the nineteenth century. The pioneering European anthropologists reveled in the belief that their "race" and "civilizations" were superior to any others. They believed that the human species was divisible into a small, discrete number of racial categories. They assumed that these categories were fixed and immutable. These early European anthropologists also believed that an individual's behavior and a group's culture could be explained by "racial

characteristics," such as skin color and head size. They believed that there was a hierarchy of races, and that the European race was at the top of this hierarchy and Africans at the bottom. Early Greek ideas and the later Christian conception of the Great Chain of Being had paved the way for the early anthropological views of race.

It wasn't until the twentieth century that a more sophisticated understanding of the relationship between race and culture was developed through the scientific and empirical research efforts of anthropologists such as Franz Boas and others. As seen in Chapters 2 and 3, on the concept of race and the history of scientific racism, modern research in physical anthropology, based on both fossil and genetic evidence, demonstrates that the concept of "race" is fundamentally flawed as a scientific concept. Contemporary anthropological research has shown that there is no precise biological basis for the separation of human beings into races, and that the idea of race is a social and political construction that has been used to justify racism during various periods of human history. Despite the fact that some scholars and scientists assume the validity of racial categories, and ascribe to them the power to explain behavioral and cultural characteristics, genetic and other research efforts in physical anthropology in the twentieth and twentieth-first centuries have shown these assumptions to be erroneous. Race began to disappear within the scientific and anthropological vocabulary as an explanatory schematic. Yet, as the appearance of books such as *The Bell Curve* and of pop-sociobiological and racist views such as those of Phillipe Rushton demonstrate, scientific racism still surfaces within our society.

Though contemporary anthropologists have demonstrated that there are no valid biological criteria for separating humans precisely into different racial categories, and that the concept of race cannot be used as an analytic device in understanding human evolution and development or cultural behavior, there is still a proclivity to use "race" as a social construction to classify humans into different categories, and the utilization of these classifications as the basis of racism and ethnocentrism.

In Chapter 4 we focus on the characteristics of ethnicity, which emphasizes the cultural aspects of group and individual dynamics in defining human behavior and thought. With the debunking of the biological and racial explanations of human behavior and culture, modern anthropologists have focused on the analysis of ethnicity. Both primordialist and circumstantialist views of ethnicity are used as explanatory and interpretive techniques in assessing the role of culture and human behavior. However, as shown in examples of the construction of notions such as the "one drop rule" used to classify African Americans in U.S. society, biological notions are sometimes still conflated with cultural constructions of ethnicity. As indicated in later chapters on ethnic groups in the United States and throughout the world, these misconceptions of ethnicity are often used as the foundation of ethnonationalist movements, and become the foundation of defining one's own

group versus the "other." As seen in Chapter 5, some of the research within psychological anthropology and evolutionary psychology indicates that humans may be predisposed to distinguish in-groups and out-groups, which become the basis of an ethnocentric syndrome. These models need to be tested further with sophisticated empirical and ethnographic research techniques to confirm or refute these findings.

In the second section of the text we address the historical experience and contemporary conditions of various ethnic groups within the United States, based on broad historical and ethnographic research. In Chapter 6 we begin with an assessment of the Anglo-WASPs and the various "white ethnics" that immigrated into the United States. The WASPs, or English settlers, established the linguistic, economic, political, educational, and religious foundations for U.S. culture. Later, as discussed, various white ethnic immigrants from Germany, Ireland, Italy, Poland, and other European societies encountered the nineteenth- and early twentieth-century racial hierarchy that maintained that the WASPs were at the top of this hierarchy and other white ethnic groups occupied lower positions. Many of the leading scientists and politicians of the day worried that immigrants from Europe would debase America's exalted Anglo-Saxon racial stock. Despite this racism and ethnocentrism maintained by the WASPs, over time these ethnic groups from Europe have assimilated and eventually became accepted as "white" Europeans, who were categorized and treated differently than the nonwhite populations in the United States. These different ethnic groups have been experiencing their own "ethnogenesis," and have adopted "whiteness" as their ethnic category along with the WASPs.

Chapter 7 focuses on the prehistoric, historic, and contemporary conditions of the American Indians in U.S. society. Prior to European contact, these indigenous peoples made up linguistically and ethnically diverse groups throughout North America. When they encountered the

Euro-American settlers these Native American Indian groups were devastated by disease, slave labor, and warfare. After the U.S. government developed treaties, removal policies, and reservations, these native peoples faced ethnocide and were eventually treated as conquered people. American Indians have been positioned within systems of inequality and ideologies of racism that have affected their destiny in U.S. society. The struggle of the contemporary Native Americans with the U.S. government continues with political and legal battles, which has promoted an ongoing emergence of new forms of ethnic and religious identity.

Chapter 8 presents a historical and ethnographic overview of the African American community. Beginning with the debates that influenced anthropological portrayals of black Americans, and continuing with a survey of the periods of slavery, Jim Crow segregation, and the civil rights and black power movements, we gain a sense of the conditions and struggles of African Americans in U.S. society. African Americans faced the most blatant and persistent forms of racism and discrimination. Their continuing struggle for a pluralistic, multicultural society has been remarkable and inspirational for many peoples throughout the world.

As seen in Chapters 9 through 12, on Jewish Americans, Hispanic/Latino Americans, Asian Americans, and Arab Americans, anthropologists have been actively doing ethnographic work on the processes of ethnic change and persistence within these different communities. The portrait of U.S. society that has emerged from the 2000 census has demonstrated a trend that anthropologists have been aware of for some time: the United States has become ethnically much more diverse. The fact that the Hispanic population grew 58 percent, to 35.3 million people, since 1990, and has pulled into rough parity with the formerly largest minority, the African American population, reflects the new trends in immigration and globalization. In Florida, Hispanics now outnumber African Americans, and

in California they make up one-third of the population. Another fact from the 2000 census that anthropologists were cognizant of was that many more Americans identify themselves as belonging to more than one race. Nearly 7 million people described themselves as multiracial. In addition, the white European population is a shrinking share of the country's overall numbers, dropping to 69 percent from 76 percent in 1990. Descendants of white Europeans are now a minority in California and may soon be in Texas. Most demographers predict that before 2050 the non-European ethnic groups will outnumber the white European descendants. These new patterns and configurations of an ethnically more diverse population in the United States will require more ethnographic research in the future.

As seen in the third section, in the chapters on Latin America and the Caribbean, Africa, the Middle East, Asia, the Pacific Islands, Europe, and Canada, the entire world is becoming more ethnically diverse with resulting problems, conflict, and change. Traditional conceptions of race and ethnicity continue to plague many regions of the world. In some instances, these traditional notions of race and ethnicity become enshrined in important scholarly studies that have an impact on common understandings of these issues. For example, Samuel Huntington, a political scientist at Harvard University, wrote an influential book *The Clash of Civilizations and the Remaking of the World Order* (1996) that continues to resonate with many people in the West and other regions of the world. Huntington argues that a unitary "Western civilization and culture" is at odds with "Islamic civilization and culture," "Hindu civilization and culture," and "Confucian civilization and culture." He envisions these primordial ethnic and regional blocs as fragmenting the world order and resulting in more conflict and instability throughout the world. Huntington's perspective has perpetuated a new cold war type of mentality that draws on images of ancient ethnic bonds and animosities.

The anthropologists who have conducted research in the regions discussed by Huntington have produced a much different picture of ethnic relations and civilizations. Each of these regions contains tremendous internal ethnic diversity, and the voices of these many different groups are pursuing a wide range of economic-, political-, and religious-based goals and aspirations. These supposedly fixed "real" ethnic cultures and civilizations are in flux, producing plural, diverse, and continual dynamic change. Ethnic identities and civilizations are not static and stable. Processes of globalization and local-level political and economic processes are reproducing a constant tug of ethnic and national identity along with the weakening of those identities and commitments. Anthropologists continue to develop a more comprehensive understanding and explanation of these ethnic and global processes through intensive, in-depth research.

As globalization occurs with the rapid integration of nation-states, markets, and information technology, and the management of economic and political development goes to the World Bank, the International Monetary Fund, and the United Nations, many peoples at the local level feel threatened. These globalization processes often exacerbate ethnic tensions and conflicts. We have looked at ethnic tensions and conflicts in Latin America, the Caribbean, Africa, the Middle East, Asia, the Pacific Islands, Europe, and Canada. Undoubtedly, these ethnic conflicts are to some extent a result of earlier colonial policies and the new post–cold war trends in globalization. Many ethnic groups have expressed a desire to return to a more simple way of life and traditional culture and behavior. They distrust the new global managers in attending to their needs. New resurgent forms of ethnicity are reactions to these globalization tendencies. Restoring ethnic autonomy is sometimes seen as a strategy to rectify the globalization process. Anthropologists are studying the ethnic resurgence of the Scots, Welsh, and Irish and why they want more independence in the United Kingdom, and why Quebec wants to separate from the rest of Canada. These local ethnic movements for autonomy and separatism are a response to the weakening of older nation-state structures, induced by globalization. Globalization is fraught with anxieties and produces uncertainties in structures and institutions as it develops in anarchic, haphazard fashions, carried along by economic, technological, and cultural imperatives. Thus, the ethnic group becomes the refuge for people who feel they have no control over these new forces.

Though the ethnic trends discussed in this text are essentially global, they also obviously affect people on the local level. Cultural anthropologists are actively recording the various dislocations of global political and ethnic processes in these societies and the ways in which people have attempted to cope with these global changes. The continuing agony of separatist, ethnic, and religious conflicts in Bosnia, Kosovo, Sri Lanka, and elsewhere threatens people throughout the world. It appears that existing institutions such as the nation-state have not been able to manage this local conflict. Perhaps by understanding the specific aspirations of these different peoples, national governments and the international community will be more responsive to their diverse needs and interests.

As anthropologists identify the cultural and ethnic variations that can block international coordination, they may help to contribute to the reduction of ethnic tensions worldwide. Future anthropologists must continue to synthesize their local studies (the micro level) with studies of global conditions (the macro level) to identify trends that militate against international cooperation. A concerted effort must be made to understand the underlying historical and cultural motivations that contribute to ethnic conflicts. In doing so, these anthropologists may aid in humankind's understanding of its existence and the need for cooperation in the global village.

CONTRIBUTORS

Barbara Aswad is Professor Emeritus of Anthropology at Wayne State University. She is editor of *Arabic Speaking Communities in American Cities, Family and Gender among American Muslims,* and has published numerous articles on Arab and Turkish women in the Middle East and Arab American women. She is past president of the Middle East Studies Association of North America.

Pamela Ballinger is Assistant Professor in the Department of Sociology and Anthropology at Bowdoin College. She holds degrees in anthropology from Stanford University, Cambridge University, and Johns Hopkins University. She has published articles in the journals *History and Memory, the Journal of Genocide Studies,* and *Balkanologie.* Her book, *Submerged Politics, Exiled Histories: Memory and Identity at the Borders of the Balkans,* is forthcoming (Princeton University Press). Her research interests include nationalism and ethnicity, memory, Italian fascism, tourism, Italy, and the former Yugoslavia.

Janet Benson is Associate Professor of Anthropology in the Department of Sociology, Anthropology, and Social Work at Kansas State University. During 1988–90 she participated in the Ford Foundation Changing Relations Project in Garden City, Kansas, focusing on Southeast Asian refugees. Recent publications include "Undocumented Immigrants and the Meatpacking Industry in the Midwest" (2000) and "Vietnamese Refugees, Mexican Immigrants, and the Changing Character of a Community" (2001).

Ellen Bigler is Associate Professor at Rhode Island College where she holds a joint appointment in Anthropology and Educational Studies. She is the author of *American Conversations: Puerto Ricans, White Ethnics, and Multicultural Education.* She also served as a consultant to the New York State Department of Education on its K-12 Latino curriculum project, *Latinos in the Making of the USA: Yesterday, Today and Tomorrow.*

Rachel A. Bonney, Associate Professor of Anthropology at the University of North Carolina at Charlotte, earned her Ph.D. from the University of Arizona in 1975, with a specialization in American Indian culture. In addition to

American Indian studies, her interests include American ethnic groups, the anthropology of art, Native American art in miniature, and museum studies.

Karen Brison is Associate Professor of Anthropology at Union College, Schenectady, New York. She received her Ph.D from University of California, San Diego after conducting two years of field research among the Kwanga of the East Sepik Province of Papua New Guinea. This research resulted in a book *Just Talk: Gossip, Meetings, and Power in a Papua New Guinea Village* (University of California Press, 1992) as well as numerous articles about ethnic and national identity, village politics, bereavement, and gender identity. More recently, she has conducted research on personal and cultural identity in Rakiraki, Fiji (1997, 1999-2000). This research has resulted in an article on gender identity among Fijian children. She also currently has a manuscript entitled *Our Wealth Is Loving Each Other: Imagining Self and Community in Fiji,* under review.

Donald E. Brown is Emeritus Professor, Department of Anthropology, at the University of California, Santa Barbara. He has done field research in Brunei, Bali, Mexico, and the United States. His interests include Southeast Asia, social structure, history, and ethnicity. His principal publications are *Brunei: The Structure and History of a Bornean Malay Sultanate* (Brunei Museum, 1971); *Principles of Social Structure: Southeast Asia* (Duckworth, 1976); *Hierarchy, History, and Human Nature: The Social Origins of Historical Consciousness* (University of Arizona Press, 1988); and *Human Universals* (McGraw-Hill, 1991).

Susan Love Brown is Associate Professor of Anthropology at Florida Atlantic University in Boca Raton, where she has taught since 1993. She received her master's degree in anthropology from San Diego State University and her Ph.D. in anthropology from the University of California, San Diego. She is a political and psychological anthropologist whose areal interests

are the Caribbean and the United States. She is a co-author of *Meeting Anthropology* (Carolina Academic Press, 2000) and editor of a forthcoming volume, *Intentional Community: An Anthropological Perspective* (SUNY Press, 2002). She also teaches a course in African American anthropology.

Norman Buchignani is a Professor in the Department of Anthropology at the University of Lethbridge, Canada. He has been involved in studies of immigration, ethnic diversity, forced migration travel discourses, and community-based systems of meaning in Canada and elsewhere for twenty-five years.

Sheilah Clarke-Ekong is Associate Professor and Chair of Anthropology at the University of Missouri, St. Louis. She received her Ph.D. from UCLA. She has lived and taught in universities in Ghana and Nigeria, West Africa. Her research interests include the adaptation of traditional structures and the construction of indigenous identity. She currently teaches a number of Africa-focused courses and works closely with the Africa study abroad program at UMSL.

Jack Glazier is Professor and Chair of the Department of Anthropology at Oberlin College. His recent publications include *Ethnicity in Michigan: Issues and People*, with Arthur W. Helweg (Michigan State University Press, 2001) and *Dispersing the Ghetto: The Relocation of Jewish Immigrants across America* (Cornell University Press, 1998).

Ronald Kephart is Associate Professor in the Department of English and Foreign Languages at the University of North Florida, where he teaches courses in linguistics, Spanish, and anthropology. His interests include the structure of Caribbean Creole languages and their use in education, race and ethnicity issues, and human evolution. He is the author of *"Broken English": The Creole Language of Carriacou* (Peter Lang, 2000), and a co-author of *Meeting Anthropology Phase to Phase* (Carolina Academic Press, 2000). He has also published a number of articles on the use of Creole English in literacy education.

Laurie King-Irani, who holds a Ph.D. in Social Anthropology from Indiana University, Bloomington, has worked as a journalist and editor, serving as Editor of *Middle East Report* (Washington, DC) for two years, and Editor of *Al-Raida* ("The Pioneer"), the quarterly journal of the Institute for Women's Studies in the Arab World in Beirut, Lebanon. Her doctoral research comprised an ethnology of citizenship among Palestinian citizens of Israel in Nazareth. Currently living in British Columbia, she is interested in studying the cultural construction of the person and the social construction and political uses of collective stereotypes in multi-ethnic societies with histories of inequality.

Leonard Lieberman is Professor of Anthropology at Central Michigan University. Born in 1925, he received his B.A. and M.A. at the University of California, Berkeley and his Ph.D. at Michigan State University. He is co-editor with Larry T. Reynolds of *Race and Other Misadventures: Essays in Honor of Ashley Montagu* (Rowman, 1996). Among his articles are "The Debate over Race" (Phylon 39:127-41, 1968) and "How "Caucasoids" Got Such Big Crania and Why

They Shrank: From Morton to Rushton" (*Current Anthropology* 42:69-95, 2001).

Scott MacEachern is Associate Professor of Anthropology at Bowdoin College in Brunswick, Maine. His research interests include the prehistory of Central Africa, ethnoarchaeology, and the study of ethnicity and ethnic group formation processes. He has done archaeological research in Chad, Cameroon, Nigeria, Kenya, Ghana, and Canada. Recent publications include "Genes, Tribes and African History" (*Current Anthropology* 41(3):357-384) and "Setting the Boundaries: Linguistics, Ethnicity, Colonialism and Archaeology South of Lake Chad" (in *Language, Archaeology and Culture History: Essays on Language and Ethnicity in Prehistory*, edited by John Terrell, Greenwood Press).

Raymond Scupin is Professor of Anthropology and International Studies at Lindenwood University. His research interests include Asia, Islam, religion, race and ethnicity issues, and political economy. He has done ethnographic research in Thailand and among American Indians in California. Recent publications include *Cultural Anthropology: A Global Perspective* and *Religion and Culture: An Anthropological Focus*, both published by Prentice Hall.

CREDITS